NELSON EDUCATION SERIES
IN HUMAN RESOURCE MANAGEMENT

D0608356

FIFTH EDITION

Managing Performance through Training and Development

NELSON EDUCATION SERIES
IN HUMAN RESOURCE MANAGEMENT

FIFTH EDITION

Managing Performance through Training and Development

Alan M. Saks

CENTRE FOR INDUSTRIAL RELATIONS AND HUMAN RESOURCES
UNIVERSITY OF TORONTO

Robert R. Haccoun

UNIVERSITÉ DE MONTRÉAL

Series Editor:
Monica Belcourt

YORK UNIVERSITY

NELSON / E D U C A T I O N

NELSON EDUCATION

Managing Performance Through Training and Development, Fifth Edition
by Alan M. Saks and Robert R. Haccoun

Vice President, Editorial Director:
Evelyn Veitch

Editor-in-Chief, Higher Education:
Anne Williams

Executive Editor:
Jackie Wood

Marketing Manager:
Kathaleen McCormick

Developmental Editor:
Karina Hope

Permissions Coordinator:
Sheila Hall

Content Production Manager:
Christine Gilbert

Production Service:
Integra

Copy Editor:
Kelli Howey

Proofreader:
Integra

Indexer:
Integra

Manufacturing Manager-Higher Education:
Joanne McNeil

Design Director:
Ken Phipps

Managing Designer:
Franca Amore

Interior Design:
Katherine Strain

Interior Icon (chain link):
© Aliaksandr Stsiazhyn/ istockphoto

Cover Design:
Martyn Schmoll

Cover Image:
© René Mansi

Compositor:
Integra

Printer:
Edwards Brothers

Library and Archives Canada Cataloguing in Publication

Saks, Alan M. (Alan Michael)
   Managing performance through training and development / Alan M. Saks, Robert R. Haccoun ; series editor, Monica Belcourt.—5th ed.

(Nelson series in human resources management)
Earlier ed. by Monica Belcourt.
Includes bibliographical references and index.

1. Employees—Training of—Textbooks.   I. Haccoun, Robert R.   II. Title.   III. Series: Nelson series in human resources management

HF5549.5.T7S23 2009   658.3'124
C2009-902304-0

ISBN-13: 978-0-17-650176-1
ISBN-10: 0-17-650176-2

To Kelly, Justin, and Brooke, my best friends

Alan Saks

To four generations of exceptional women : Emma
Gamarra Haccoun, Lydia Abitbol, Jennifer Abramson
and most importantly, Orli Abramson

Robert Haccoun

Brief Contents

Contents

Chapter 2 Organizational Learning 33

Chapter 8   Technology-Based Training Methods   225

Chapter 9 Training Delivery 253

Chapter 10 Transfer of Training 285

About the Series

More than ever, human resource management (HRM) professionals need the knowledge and skills to design HRM policies and practices that not only meet legal requirements but also are effective in supporting organizational strategy. Increasingly, these professionals turn to published research and books on best practices for assistance in the development of effective HR strategies. The books in the *Nelson Education Series in Human Resources Management* are the best source in Canada for reliable, valid, and current knowledge about practices in HRM.

The texts in this series include

- *Managing Performance through Training and Development*
- *Management of Occupational Health and Safety*
- *Recruitment and Selection in Canada*
- *Strategic Compensation in Canada*
- *Strategic Human Resources Planning*
- *An Introduction to the Canadian Labour Market*
- *Research, Measurement and Evaluation of Human Resources*
- *Industrial Relations in Canada*
- *International Human Resource Management: A Canadian Perspective*

The *Nelson Education Series in Human Resources Management* represents a significant development in the field of HRM for many reasons. Each book in the series is the leading Canadian text in its area of specialization. Human resource (HR) professionals in Canada must work with Canadian laws, statistics, policies, and values, and this series serves their needs. It is the only opportunity that students and practitioners have to access a complete set of HRM books, standardized in presentation, which enables them to access information quickly across many HRM disciplines. The books are essential sources of information that meet the requirements for the CCHRA (Canadian Council of Human Resource Associations) National Knowledge exam for the academic portion of the HR certification process. This one-stop resource will prove useful to anyone looking for solutions for the effective management of people.

The publication of this series signals that the field of HRM has advanced to the stage where theory and applied research guide practice. The books in the series present the best and most current research in the functional areas of HRM. Research is supplemented with examples of the best practices used by Canadian companies that are leaders in HRM. Thus the books serve as an introduction to the functional area for the new student of HR and as a validation source for the more experienced HRM practitioner. Cases, exercises, and references provide opportunities for further discussion and analysis.

As you read and consult the books in this series, I hope you share my excitement in being involved in the development of a profession that has such a significant impact on the workplace.

Monica Belcourt, PhD, CHRP
Series Editor
March 2009

About the Authors

Alan M. Saks

Alan M. Saks, PhD, is a Professor of Organizational Behaviour and Human Resource Management at the University of Toronto, where he holds a joint appointment in the Department of Management—UTSC, the Centre for Industrial Relations and Human Resources, and the Joseph L. Rotman School of Management. Prior to joining the University of Toronto, Professor Saks was a member of the Department of Management in the Faculty of Commerce and Administration at Concordia University and in the School of Administrative Studies at York University.

Professor Saks earned his BA in Psychology from the University of Western Ontario, an MASc in Industrial-Organizational Psychology from the University of Waterloo, and a PhD in Organizational Behaviour and Human Resources from the University of Toronto. He conducts research in a number of areas in human resources and organizational behaviour including recruitment, job search, training, employee engagement, and the socialization and on-boarding of new employees. His research has been published in refereed journals such as the *Journal of Applied Psychology, Personnel Psychology, Academy of Management Journal, Journal of Organizational Behavior, Journal of Vocational Behavior, Human Resource Management, Human Resource Management Review,* and *Human Resource Development Quarterly* as well as in professional journals such as the *HR Professional Magazine, The Learning Journal,* and the *Canadian HR Reporter.* In addition to this text, he is also the author of *Research, Measurement and Evaluation of Human Resources,* and a co-author of *Organizational Behaviour: Understanding and Managing Life at Work.*

Professor Saks is currently on the editorial boards of the *Journal of Management, International Journal of Training and Development, Journal of Vocational Behavior, Journal of Business and Psychology,* and *Human Resource Development Review.*

Robert R. Haccoun

Educated at McGill University (BA 1969) and the Ohio State University (MA 1970, PhD 1973), Robert R. Haccoun is Professor of Psychology at the Université de Montréal. Prior to returning to academia in 1978, Professor Haccoun was a research scientist for Bell Canada in Montreal. He is a founding member and past president of the Industrial-Organizational Psychology section of the Canadian Psychological Association.

He has led a number of research studies, delivered papers at scientific conferences and published scholarly articles in French and in English mainly focused on training, absenteeism, and research methodology. He has contributed chapters to several books and published in journals such as *Personnel Psychology,* the *Journal of Applied Psychology, Canadian Psychologist, Applied Psychology: An International Review,* and *Canadian Journal of Administrative Studies.* His co-authored research book, *Comprendre l'organisation: Approches de recherches,* has been translated into Spanish, and the second edition of the statistics book he co-authored in 2007 is to be published in the fall of 2009. In addition to serving as a reviewer for many scientific journals and chairing committees of research funding agencies, such as SSHRC, he is Associate Editor of *Applied Psychology: An International Review*.

Active in the transfer of knowledge from academia to applied settings, he has lectured to practitioner audiences and written many professional articles. He has also provided consulting services to a number of leading organizations in Canada, the United States, and Europe.

Preface

In order to compete and survive in today's competitive and uncertain world, organizations must have the capacity for continuous learning, change, and improvement. Continuous learning, however, depends in large part on the effectiveness of an organization's training and development programs and systems—the focus of this textbook.

Since the last edition of this text was published, the science and practice of training and development has continued to advance. The increasing use of technology, blended approaches to training delivery, training on-demand and just-in-time learning, new models of training evaluation, and techniques to improve transfer of training are just some examples of the exciting developments in training and development. The fifth edition of *Managing Performance through Training and Development* reflects the many advances in both the science and practice of training and development.

As with the two previous editions, the fifth edition is co-authored by Alan Saks and Robert Haccoun. The two authors have been involved in training research for over 15 years and have collaborated on numerous research projects on training. With the fifth edition, they have continued to develop and improve this textbook in many ways.

First, almost every chapter in the fifth edition contains new sections, material, and content. Here are some examples to look for:

Chapter 1:   Quebec's training law.
Chapter 2:   Communities of practice.
Chapter 3:   Proximal and distal goals.
Chapter 4:   When training is the best solution.
Chapter 5:   Active learning and adaptive expertise.
Chapter 6:   Implementing behavioural modelling training.
Chapter 7:   Benefits of apprenticeship training.
Chapter 8:   Web 2.0 tools and mobile learning.
Chapter 9:   Guidelines for development of a lesson plan.
Chapter 10:   Post-training supplements.
Chapter 11:   Do organizations conduct training evaluations?
Chapter 12:   Training and the bottom line in Canadian organizations.
Chapter 13:   Essential skills.
Chapter 14:   Is management development effective?
Chapter 15:   Learning management systems (LMS).

In addition to new content, the fifth edition includes two new and exciting pedagogical features. *Make the Connection* alerts the reader to material in a chapter that has a connection to material that was presented in a previous chapter. For example, the reader is informed of the material on self-regulation and social cognitive theory in Chapter 3 (Learning and Motivation) when reading about a self-management transfer of training intervention in Chapter 10 (Transfer of Training). The purpose of this new feature is to help the reader integrate material across the chapters and to understand how material in one chapter is related to material that was presented in an earlier chapter.

MAKE THE CONNECTION

This feature appears in three ways: a chain link icon in the margin alerts the reader to a Make the Connection feature; the connection is explained to the reader in the text; and at the end of the chapter a Make the Connection section tells the reader the chapter and page number where they can find the relevant material. We hope this new feature helps readers to better understand how the material throughout the text is linked and interconnected.

The second new feature is an integrative case study that can be found at the end of Chapter 15. The purpose of this new feature is to provide students with an opportunity to work on a case that requires them to use and apply material from many chapters. The relevant chapter for the integrative questions is indicated so that instructors can use the integrative case throughout the term as each particular chapter is covered. Alternatively, the integrative case can be used at the end of a course as a review of all the chapters and material. Our hope is that this new feature will help students integrate and apply material throughout the text.

In addition to these new features, this text continues to provide both students and instructors a wide range of pedagogical features. Every chapter has a case study with questions on the main topics, principles, concepts, and theories covered in the chapter. In addition, every chapter has a case incident which consists of a short description of a training problem followed by several questions. They can be used to begin a discussion at the start of class or later in class when students can begin to apply the chapter material.

As with the previous edition, the fifth edition has two types of exercises in every chapter. In-Class exercises can be done during class time without any pre-class preparation. In-the-Field exercises require students to gather information in the field by talking to HR and training professionals. These exercises can also be used as projects and assignments.

Each chapter also has Discussion Questions, Using the Internet exercises, and the Great Training Debate. The Discussion Questions focus on the main issues, principles, and theories described in a chapter. The Using the Internet exercises require students to visit a website and gather information to answer questions or prepare a brief report on what they found. The Great Training Debate presents an issue for students to debate either early in a class to get students thinking about a topic or later in a class so students can begin to apply the chapter material to an important training issue. For example, The Great Training Debate in Chapter 1 asks students to debate whether all provinces should enact training legislation similar to the training law in Quebec.

In combination, the text offers a wide variety of pedagogical material at the end of every chapter. Our intent is to provide instructors and students with a wide selection of pedagogical material to choose from to best suit their learning needs and preferences.

Like the previous edition of the text, every chapter begins with a chapter-opening vignette. Each vignette tells the story of an actual training program in an organization that is of relevance to the material covered in the chapter. Many of the vignettes feature Canadian organizations, and the fifth edition includes 10 new ones that include service, manufacturing, profit, and non-profit organizations from across the country.

As with previous editions, you will also find in each chapter The Trainer's Notebook and Training Today features. The Trainer's Notebook presents practical, hands-on information for trainers and practitioners (e.g., Facilitating Informal Learning in Organizations, Chapter 2) and the Training Today feature describes the latest in training research and practice (e.g., CIBC Trains Newcomers for Work, Chapter 13). The fifth edition includes many new Training Today and The Trainer's Notebook features.

Also retained from the previous edition are Web links for students who want to learn more about an organization or association mentioned in the text. Web addresses can be found at the end of each chapter. This edition also includes RPC icons, which refer to "Required Professional Capabilities." RPCs represent the learning objectives in the area of Organizational Learning, Development and Training for the national Certified Human Resources Professional (CHRP) designation. Their appearance in the text alerts students to RPC-relevant content, and the actual RPC content is listed at the end of each chapter.

We have also retained other features that appeared in the fourth edition including: learning outcomes at the beginning of every chapter; key terms, which appear in the text in bold and in the margins and are also listed at the end of each chapter; and chapter-ending summaries which review the main content of each chapter.

Instructor and Student Resources

New to this edition is an Instructor's Resource CD containing an instructor's manual, PowerPoint slides, test bank, and ExamView computerized test bank. The ExamView Testing Software allows you to deliver and customize print and online tests in minutes with an easy-to-use Windows-based testing and assessment system. ExamView offers both a Quick Test Wizard and an Online Test Wizard that guide you step-by-step through the process of creating tests. With ExamView's complete word processing capabilities, you can enter your own new questions or edit existing questions. The instructor's manual and the PowerPoint slides can also be downloaded directly from **www.hrm.nelson. com**. For students, this edition is accompanied by Student Resources that are also available from **www.hrm.nelson.com**.

We hope that students and instructors find the fifth edition of the text as exciting as we do and that the pedagogical features help to facilitate and maximize learning.

Structure of the Book

Chapter 1 begins with examples of the importance and benefits of training and development for employees, organizations, and society. Training and development is defined and presented within the larger context of the environment, the organization, and the human resources management system. Chapter 1 also describes the instructional systems design (ISD) model of the training and development process, which sets the stage for the subsequent chapters in the text.

Chapters 2 and 3 focus on learning, which is first and foremost what training is all about. We feel that it is important that students first understand learning at both the organizational and individual levels before they begin to learn about the role of training and development in the learning process. Therefore, Chapter 2 describes organizational learning, the learning organization, types of knowledge and intellectual capital, informal learning, communities of practice, and knowledge management practices. The chapter concludes with a multilevel systems model of organizational learning which shows how learning at the organization, group, and individual levels are interrelated, as well as a model that shows how training is related to individual and organizational learning.

Chapter 3 focuses on how individuals learn and their training motivation. Learning outcomes, stages of learning, learning styles, learning theories, adult learning theory, and theories of motivation are described along with their implications for training and development. The chapter concludes with a model of training effectiveness which shows the variables that influence learning and retention, and how learning and retention are related to individual behaviour and performance and organizational effectiveness. The training effectiveness model is further developed in Chapters 5 and 10.

The training and development process begins with a needs analysis, the focus of Chapter 4. Chapter 4 describes the needs analysis process with particular emphasis on the three levels of needs analysis (organizational, task, and person) and how to determine solutions to performance problems. The chapter also describes the methods and sources of needs analysis and some of the obstacles to conducting a needs analysis.

Chapter 5 describes how to design training and development programs. The chapter begins with an overview of the importance of training objectives and how to write training objectives. The chapter then proceeds to cover the main steps involved in the design of training programs, including whether to purchase or design a training program; requests for proposals; the training content; training methods; active practice and conditions of practice; active learning and adaptive expertise; and error-management training.

One of the most important steps in the design of a training program is the choice of training methods. Given the vast array of training methods and instructional techniques available, Chapters 6, 7, and 8 are devoted to this topic. Chapter 6 describes the most frequently used off-the-job training methods, including lectures, discussions, audio-visual methods, case studies, case incidents, behavioural modelling, role plays, games, simulations, and action learning. Each training method is defined and described, along with tips for trainers. The chapter concludes with a discussion of the factors to consider when choosing training methods and the importance of a blended approach.

In Chapter 7, we turn to on-the-job training methods including job instruction training, performance aids, job rotation, apprenticeship programs, coaching, and mentoring. Like Chapter 6, we define and describe each instructional method and provide tips for trainers. The chapter concludes with a discussion of the advantages and disadvantages of off-the-job and on-the-job training methods.

Chapter 8 is devoted to technology-based training methods. The chapter begins with a definition of technology-based training followed by a description of computer-based training and e-learning. Distinctions are then made between instructor-led and self-directed learning and asynchronous and synchronous training. This is followed by a discussion of electronic performance support systems and video and Web conferencing. The chapter then describes how to design computer-based training programs and the advantages, disadvantages, and effectiveness of computer-based training methods. The chapter concludes with a discussion of the future of technology-based training with particular emphasis on Web 2.0 tools and mobile learning.

The focus of Chapter 9 is training delivery. The chapter begins with a description of a lesson plan and then describes the main components of a lesson plan including the characteristics of good trainers, the selection of trainees, training materials and equipment, the training site, and scheduling training programs. The chapter also describes how to create a climate for learning, Gagné's nine events of instruction, and common training delivery problems and solutions.

One of the biggest problems facing trainers and organizations is the transfer of training, the focus of Chapter 10. The chapter begins with a review of the transfer problem and barriers to transfer, followed by a description of Baldwin and Ford's (1988) model of the transfer process. The chapter then describes activities that can be undertaken by managers, trainers, and trainees for improving the transfer of training before, during, and after training. The chapter concludes with a description of transfer of training interventions, post-training supplements, and the transfer system.

Once a training program has been designed and delivered, it needs to be evaluated. Chapters 11 and 12 are devoted to training evaluation. In Chapter 11, we describe the purpose and barriers of training evaluation, and discuss three training evaluation models. The chapter also describes how to measure key variables for training evaluation and the different types of training evaluation designs.

The topic of training evaluation continues in Chapter 12 where the focus shifts to the costs and benefits of training. Chapter 12 describes how to calculate the costs of training programs as well as the benefits (e.g., net benefit, benefit-cost ratio, return on investment, and utility). The importance of the credibility of estimates is also discussed.

Chapters 13 and 14 describe the types of training programs that are provided in organizations. Chapter 13 describes the most common forms of training that employees receive including orientation training, essential skills training, technical skills training, information technology training, health and safety training, quality training, team training, sales training, customer-service training, sexual harassment training, ethics training, diversity training, and cross-cultural training.

Chapter 14 is devoted entirely to management development. This reflects both its importance to organizations and the large investments made by organizations in the development of management talent. The chapter begins with a definition of management and management development, and then describes the core functions, roles, and skills of management. Models of management development are also described as well as the content of management development programs. The chapter also provides an overview of management development programs including management education programs, management training programs, and on-the-job management development (job rotation and coaching). The chapter concludes with a discussion of research on the effectiveness of management development.

Finally, Chapter 15 concludes the text with a discussion of training trends and best practices. The chapter begins with a discussion of the changing role of training professionals, outsourcing training and development, and the ethics of training and development. We then discuss several trends in training and development including just-in-time learning, rapid e-learning, learning management systems, and lifelong learning. The chapter concludes with a review of training design features that facilitate learning and transfer and the main reasons why training programs fail.

Throughout the text we have tried to maintain a balance between theory and research on the one hand, and practice and application on the other. We have also tried to provide examples of the concepts and principles presented in the text by showcasing organizations, many of them Canadian, that have successfully designed and delivered effective training programs. Overall, we have tried to provide a thorough and comprehensive text on training and development that reflects both the science and practice of the field as well as our excitement and genuine love of the topic. We hope that the combination of text material as well as the pedagogical features will motivate students to learn about the science and practice of training and development.

Acknowledgments

Writing a textbook requires the support and assistance of many people who either directly or indirectly make important contributions to the process and outcome. We wish to thank all of those who have played important roles in our lives and in writing this text.

First, we thank all the reviewers who provided us with insightful and constructive feedback over the past few editions that led to many changes and improvements: Gordon Barnard of Durham College, Susan Fitzrandolph of Ryerson University, Morai Forer of SIAST, Stefan Groschl of the University of Guelph, Jamie Gruman of the University of Guelph, Jill Leedham of Mohawk College, Barbara Lipton of Seneca College, Jody Merritt of St. Clair College, Grace O'Farrell of the University of Winnipeg, Wiktor J. Tutlewski of Kwantlen Polytechnic University, Valerie Whyte of the University of New Brunswick, and Jeff Young of Saint Mary's University. Each one contributed to this text by lending us their expertise and by taking the time to share their teaching experiences. Their comments and feedback have helped us improve this text, including the creation of a separate chapter on training delivery as well as the addition of case incidents.

Second, we wish to express our appreciation to our many colleagues who have helped us formulate our ideas, who provided us with their own ideas and insights, or who were always available to lend a sympathetic ear. We are especially thankful to Tracey Starrett, who provided us with very detailed feedback and suggestions, many of which have been included in this edition of the text.

Third, we wish to express our gratitude to the team at Nelson Education that helped us develop and produce this text. First, we want to thank our Developmental Editor, Karina Hope, who has worked with us on previous editions of this text and has been instrumental in helping us improve and complete the fifth edition. In addition to her contributions and effort, Karina also makes our job and hard work much easier and enjoyable. We also wish to express our gratitude and appreciation to Executive Editor Jackie Wood, Acquisitions Editor Amie Plourde, Content Production Manager Christine Gilbert, and Copy Editor Kelli Howey. We are grateful for their support and all of their hard work and feel very lucky to be working with a team of professionals who care so much about what they do and their authors.

Finally, we also wish to thank our families, who have had to endure the burden of living with tired and overworked authors who sometimes don't have time to play or sleep! Alan Saks is grateful to Kelly, Justin, and Brooke for making it all worthwhile. Robert Haccoun is grateful to his family: thanks Jennifer, Bram, and Orli, et merci Lydia, Jonathan, Benjamin, and Gabrielle.

Alan M. Saks
University of Toronto

Robert R. Haccoun
Université de Montréal

The Training and Development Process

Chapter Learning Outcomes

After reading this chapter, you should be able to:

- understand the meaning of performance management, training, development, and human resource development
- describe the organization, employee, and societal benefits of training and development
- discuss training and development in Canada
- understand and explain the role of the environmental and organizational context of training and development
- understand the meaning of strategic human resource management (SHRM), strategic training and development, and high-performance work systems (HPWS)
- discuss the instructional systems design (ISD) model of training and development

STEDFAST INC.

Stedfast Inc. is a specialized manufacturer of high-tech barrier fabrics using multiple coating and laminating technologies (i.e., operating-room gowns, firefighting suits, and waterproof gloves) that employs approximately 100 workers in Granby, Quebec.

In recognition of the demands of a changing marketplace and the need for continued innovation, flexibility, and problem-solving skills among employees, Stedfast decided to implement a Skills and Learning facility to become the focal point of the company's on-the-job skills development initiatives.

Through a partnership with the Textiles Human Resources Council (THRC), Stedfast developed the fully equipped Skills and Learning Site, which is designed to provide workers with access to the industry's leading textile manufacturing skills, technical skills, essential skills, and business and personal development programs. The site will also support employees as they develop their communication skills through coaching and mentoring activities, workshops, and other collaborative learning opportunities.

A Training Needs Assessment tool is used to identify company-wide skills and knowledge gaps. By using this tool, Stedfast is better able to align and target its skills development resources. The assessment tool collects and reports three levels of data: individual, company-wide, and industry-wide. All three levels contribute to the design and implementation of appropriate and relevant training and skills development activities.

In addition to the Skills and Learning Site, Stedfast also offers its employees a range of training programs, including on-the-job training for new employees. Stedfast has also developed a Skills and Learning portal, which is a dedicated website designed to give employees access to a number of online skills development programs. The portal provides learners with a one-stop shop for skills development that includes a comprehensive workforce development system providing employees with learning and skills development programs that focus on textile manufacturing skills, technical and essential skills, and personal and business performance skills.

Stedfast is able to offer its current and future employees an industry-recognized and valued learning program. The Stedfast Skills and Learning Site is designed to give workers a place to share and transfer knowledge, ensuring continuity as the company faces a significant number of future retirements.

Some of the benefits include capturing the critical knowledge of retiring employees so that it can be passed on through training; a variety of programs including technical training programs, literacy programs, textile math programs, and other basic skills relevant to the workplace and other advanced learning initiatives; giving employees a consistent reference resource for learning about technical procedures and providing new employees with a starting point to gauge their technical skills development; and, with around-the-clock availability, allowing employees to learn and develop skills at their convenience and as their schedules permit.[1]

Stedfast Inc. is a good example of the role and importance of training and development in organizations today. The company's Skills and Learning Site ensures that employees will have the knowledge and skills the company requires to achieve its strategic business objectives and to be successful in an increasingly challenging and competitive environment. It is also an excellent example of how to design and implement effective training and development programs.

It is not hard to understand how investments in human capital and training can improve an organization's success and competitiveness. But have you ever considered how the training of employees can impact *your* life? Consider the emergency landing of an Air Transat Airbus on an island in the Atlantic Ocean on August 24, 2001. With both engines dead and the lives of 293 passengers and 13 crew members on Flight 236 at stake, the pilots successfully made an emergency landing after gliding for 19 minutes without power.

The loss of power was due to a fuel leak in the right engine that caused it to shut down. A chafing fuel line on the right engine, which had recently been replaced, leaked during the flight. Although there was a leak in the right engine causing a loss of fuel, the left engine should have been sufficient to keep the plane in the air. However, fuel from the undamaged left engine tanks was pumped to the leaking right side, where it was dumped overboard. This led to a loss of fuel in the left engine, which then caused it to lose power as well. The Airbus would have been able to fly safely with just the left engine operating had its fuel not been pumped to the leaking right side.

According to Airbus, the maker of the twin-engine A330, Air Transat improperly reconnected the main fuel line to the aircraft's right-side engine when it was changed four days before the near-disaster. The fuel line to the right-side engine chafed against a hydraulic pipe that eventually cracked and created the fuel leak. Air-safety investigators also blamed faulty mechanical work by Air Transat mechanics as the cause of the fuel leak that led to the near-catastrophic emergency landing.

Disaster was averted only by a skilled emergency landing by the pilots, who were hailed as heroes for safely landing the plane. However, one of the pilots, Captain Robert Piché, denied being a hero, stating that landing a plane with no engines is "what you train for."

Transport Canada fined Air Transat $250,000 and ordered the airline to provide pilots and flight crews with special training on fuel management and emergency landings. Senior Transport Canada officials and Air Transat top management agreed that the airline's pilots would take special training sessions. Air Transat also provided Transport Canada with a corrective-action plan to improve the performance of maintenance that included human-factors training for all technical personnel.[2]

In 2004, the official report into the incident concluded that the emergency landing could have been avoided if the pilots had followed established fuel-leak procedures. Accident investigators determined that a fuel leak was turned into a near-disaster because the pilots failed to determine the problem and then tried to correct it from memory rather than by following a computer checklist which would have warned them of the possibility of a fuel leak. The pilots believed the problem was a fuel imbalance so they pumped tonnes of fuel overboard. According to the report, the crew did not correctly evaluate the situation before taking action. At the time, there was no adequate training for the pilots in dealing with a catastrophic fuel leak, because it was considered a remote possibility.[3]

Although we cannot say that inadequate training was the cause of this near-disaster, we do know that training was required in order to prevent a similar incident from happening again. We also know that experience and training had a lot to do with the pilot's ability to safely land the plane. Air Transat has since reviewed its training programs and enhanced its maintenance and flight operations procedures. Its pilots are now required to attend a new training program on the procedures for overseas flights, which includes a review of fuel management.

In 2005, Air Transat agreed to a settlement of $7.65 million to a group of passengers who were aboard Flight 236 and had filed a class-action lawsuit against the airline.[4]

This is just one of many examples that illustrate how the training of employees affects our lives in ways that we are unaware of and seldom if ever think about. Another example is the worst subway accident in Canadian history, in which three people were killed and about 140 others injured when two trains collided in Toronto on August 11, 1995. The subway operator, who was only on his second shift, admitted he wasn't ready to operate the train. Although he had successfully completed the 12-day subway training course, he had wanted more instruction behind the controls and was not sure he was ready to operate the train. At an inquest into the accident, he said, "I really didn't understand a lot of this stuff, I really didn't understand the mechanics of the train."

Since then, the Toronto Transit Commission (TTC) has made many changes, including the way it trains its drivers. For example, the 12-day driver training program has been extended to six weeks and operators are now required to take three days of additional training every two years. Emergency training is also required for the recertification of all subway employees every two years. These changes, along with others, have made the TTC one of the safest transit systems in North America.[5]

The importance and adequacy of training has also become an issue for the country's RCMP officers following the killing of four young officers in Alberta in March 2005. A report by Canada's auditor general found that inadequate and incomplete training of the country's RCMP officers threatens to compromise public safety. Only 6.2 percent of the national police force's officers completed all of their mandatory training requirements in 2004, a dramatic drop from 57 percent in 2003. Furthermore, newly graduated RCMP cadets do not always spend the required first two months on the job paired with a senior officer or receive the six months of coaching they are supposed to receive once they begin active duty. The report concluded that, "Gaps in training, qualification, and certification may affect the health and safety of peace officers and the public."[6]

In August 2008, following a deadly propane explosion in Toronto, an inspection of propane facilities across Ontario found staff that appeared to lack proper training. The most serious infraction was employees who could not provide evidence they were properly certified in propane dispensing.[7] In November 2008, the Alberta government implemented mandatory safety training for all school bus drivers following two deadly school bus crashes. The specialized training will require all bus drivers to learn how to better deal with road hazards and rowdy students.[8]

As you can see, employees who are poorly trained can make mistakes and have accidents that threaten the public's safety and well-being as well as the employees' own safety. And while these examples are among the most extreme, it is important to recognize that poorly trained employees produce defective products and provide poor service. Thus, training is of vital concern not just to employees and their organizations, but to all of us who use public transportation and purchase goods and services every day of our lives.

For organizations, success and competitiveness are highly dependent on training and development. In fact, continuous learning and education has become a key factor for the success of individuals and organizations. Whether an organization is adopting new technology, improving quality, or simply trying to remain competitive, training and development is a critical and necessary part of the process.

A report by the Conference Board of Canada on learning and development in Canadian organizations states that continuous learning and the transfer of knowledge are key factors in fostering creativity and promoting organizational excellence.[9] Not surprisingly, training and education is one of the distinguishing characteristics of the best companies to work for in Canada.[10]

Therefore, it should not surprise you that organizations invest millions of dollars each year on training and development. This book will teach you about the exciting world of training and development and how to design, deliver, and evaluate training programs.

In this chapter, we introduce you to the topic of training and development and describe the training and development process. We begin with a discussion of performance management, since training and development is first and foremost all about managing performance in organizations.

Performance Management

As the title of the text indicates, training and development is all about managing performance. **Performance management** is the process of establishing performance expectations with employees, designing interventions and programs to improve performance, and monitoring the success of interventions

Performance management

The process of establishing performance expectations with employees, designing interventions and programs to improve performance, and monitoring the success of interventions and programs

Chapter 1: The Training and Development Process

and programs. This process signals to employees what is really important in the organization, ensures accountability for behaviour and results, and helps to improve performance.[11]

Performance management is not a single event, such as a performance appraisal or a training program; rather, it is a comprehensive process that involves various activities and programs designed to improve performance.

Training and Development

Training
The acquisition of knowledge, skills, and abilities to improve performance in one's current job

Training is one of the most important ways that performance can be improved. Training refers to the acquisition of knowledge, skills, and abilities to improve performance in one's current job. Training usually consists of a short-term focus on acquiring skills to perform one's job. You have probably experienced this type of training, such as when your company sends you to a workshop to learn a software package or to learn how to serve customers. The goal is to help you learn to do your current job better.

As indicated at the beginning of the chapter, Stedfast offers its employees a range of training programs including a website that gives employees access to a number of online skills development programs.

Development
The acquisition of knowledge, skills, and abilities required to perform future job responsibilities

Development refers to the acquisition of knowledge, skills, and abilities required to perform future job responsibilities and for the long-term achievement of individual career goals and organizational objectives. The goal is to prepare individuals for promotions and future jobs as well as additional job responsibilities. This process might consist of extensive programs such as leadership development, and might include seminars and workshops, job rotation, coaching, and other assignments. The goal is usually to prepare employees for managerial careers. You can read more about management development in Chapter 14.

Human resource development
Systematic and planned activities that are designed by an organization to provide employees with opportunities to learn necessary skills to meet current and future job demands

Training and development is part of a larger system that is known as human resource development (HRD). **Human resource development** involves systematic and planned activities that are designed by an organization to provide employees with opportunities to learn necessary skills to meet current and future job demands. The main functions of human resource development are training and development, organization development, and career development. The core of all three human resource development functions is learning.[12]

In summary, the creation of an organizational environment conducive to learning and optimum performance is a fundamental first step in the process of a performance management system. All systems are concerned with the goal of improving organizational effectiveness through the improvement of human resources. Key to the achievement of this goal is training and development, which, as described in the next section, has benefits for organizations, employees, and society at large.

The Benefits of Training and Development

Organizations that invest in the training and development of their employees reap many benefits. But so do employees and the society in which they live. In this section, we describe the benefits of training and development to organizations, employees, and society. As you will see, training and development play a critical role in the success of organizations, individuals, and Canadian society.

Benefits to Organizations

Organizations that invest in training and development benefit in many ways that ultimately help an organization obtain a sustained competitive advantage. Training and development can facilitate an organization's strategy, increase effectiveness, and improve employee recruitment and retention.

Strategy

The goal of all organizations is to survive and prosper. Training and development can help organizations achieve these goals. Organizations can be successful by training employees so they have the knowledge and skills necessary to help organizations achieve their goals and objectives. By linking training to an organization's strategy, training becomes a strategic activity that operates in concert with other programs and activities to achieve an organization's strategic business objectives.

As described at the beginning of the chapter, Stedfast's Skills and Learning Site addresses the company's strategic business needs as well as those of the Canadian textile industry. By providing employees with the latest manufacturing skills the company will be in a better position to achieve its business strategies. At Providence Health Care, a Vancouver-based health care organization with three hospitals and five long-term care facilities, training is an important component of its people strategy to ensure that the right people, with the right skills, are in the right roles.[13]

Effectiveness

There is a calculable benefit to training employees. Trained employees can do more and better work, make fewer errors, require less supervision, have more positive attitudes, and have lower rates of attrition. Trained employees also produce higher-quality products and services.[14] These benefits have a positive effect on an organization's competitiveness and effectiveness.

For example, a survey conducted by American Management Association found that companies that expanded their training programs showed gains in productivity and larger operating profits.[15] In another study, a 10 percent increase in training produced a 3 percent increase in productivity over two years.[16] Companies that invest more heavily in training are more successful and more profitable. These companies spend up to 6 percent of payroll on training, but they achieve 57 percent higher sales per employee, 37 percent higher gross profits per employee, and a 20 percent higher ratio in market-to-book values.

The link between training and an organization's effectiveness is strongly supported by research. Study after study has found that companies that invest more in training have higher revenues, profits, and productivity growth than firms that invest less in training.[17] A review of research on training and organizational effectiveness found that training is positively related to human resource outcomes (e.g., employee attitudes, motivation, behaviours), organizational performance outcomes (e.g., performance and productivity), and to a lesser extent financial outcomes (e.g., profit, financial indicators).[18]

Training has also been found to be more effective than other interventions. A recent study compared the impact of human resource practices to practices that place greater emphasis on operational initiatives, such as advanced manufacturing technology, on the productivity of 308 companies over 22 years. The results indicated that while none of the operational manufacturing practices related to productivity, the human resource practices were directly related to productivity. Both empowerment and extensive training were related to productivity and together they accounted for a 9 percent increase in value added per employee.[19]

But can training make the difference between business success and failure? To find out, see Training Today 1.1, "Training and Franchise Success."

Employee Recruitment and Retention

Training and development is considered an effective tool for attracting and retaining top talent, especially for those under the age of 30 who consider their career growth and professional development more important than salary.[20]

Thus, training can be used by organizations to increase their attractiveness to prospective employees and to retain their current employees. For many

Training Today 1.1

Training and Franchise Success

What makes a franchise a success? Why do some franchises prosper while others fail? To try to answer these questions, Steven Michael and James Combs examined 88 established restaurant franchisors in the United States.

Although the failure rate of restaurants is very high, the chances of success are greater if the restaurant is a franchise. As a rule, franchises generally do not fail. After all, they benefit from consumer brand recognition, support from the franchisor, buying power, national advertising, and many other factors. But the reality is that some franchisees do fail.

The reasons vary, so the authors considered a number of policy decisions made by franchisors that can influence the success of a franchisee such as franchisee industry experience, active owner-managers, the royalty rate, exclusive territories, brand name development, and the length of training (the number of weeks that franchisees underwent initial training).

The results indicated that all of these policy decisions were related to franchisee failure or survival. In particular, a franchisee was more likely to survive if the franchisee had prior industry experience, active ownership, a lower royalty rate, exclusive territory guarantees, a brand name, and a longer length of initial training. The more robust and lengthy the training program for the franchisee, the more likely the franchisee was to succeed. Franchises with the shortest franchisee training programs were the most likely to fail.

According to the authors, the results show that training can reduce the probability of failure and that improving business skills through training might reduce the failure of other businesses.

Sources: Michael, S. C., & Combs, J. G. (2008). Entrepreneurial failure: The case of franchisees. *Journal of Small Business Management, 46* (1), 73–90; Webb, W. (2008, October). Training = franchise success. *Training, 45* (8), 54.

Managing Performance Through Training and Development

organizations today, training is the number-one attraction and retention tool. An organization that fails to provide training opportunities to its employees will be at a disadvantage in attracting new employees and retaining current ones. In one study, 99 percent of the respondents said that there are job areas in which training would be useful to them, and in which training decreases their willingness to move to another company.[21]

Many organizations offer extensive training and development opportunities to retain employees. For example, at Delta Hotels and Resorts, employees are guaranteed ongoing training. If an employee does not receive proper training, he or she can claim an extra week's salary. About 30 employees a year receive an extra week's salary. Not surprisingly, Delta has an employee retention rate of 89 percent, which is considered one of the best in the hospitality industry. In addition, hotel-school graduates are attracted to Delta because of the training they will receive.[22]

Another company where training and development is an effective tool for recruitment and retention is Trojan Technologies. To learn more, see Training Today 1.2, "Ongoing Training at Trojan Technologies."

Benefits to Employees

Training and development also has benefits to employees. The benefits to employees can be categorized as those that are internal or intrinsic to an individual, such as knowledge and attitudes, and those that are external to an individual.

Training Today 1.2

Ongoing Training at Trojan Technologies

Trojan Technologies in London, Ontario, specializes in the design, manufacture, and sale of ultraviolet disinfection systems for wastewater, drinking water, and environmental contaminated treatment. It has offices and facilities in eight countries and more than 600 global employees.

Trojan Technologies needs to attract and retain employees with specialized skills who are willing to grow with an ever-expanding enterprise. What does this mean? First, Trojan has to find people who thrive in an environment that's constantly changing. Second, Trojan has to provide ongoing opportunities to learn. These include structured programs at colleges and universities, and on-the-job training in industry-specific technical skills.

Every engineering employee at Trojan has a development plan and meets with a career leader once a month.

An in-house leadership development program was created for all leaders and potential leaders. Leaders also work with associates in developing a plan that identifies elements for success, such as projects they should take on, study required, and the behaviours necessary to move into a leadership role. Many technical professionals have developed their leadership skills to take on a management position.

According to Gary Denomme, product engineering manager and mechanical engineering career leader at Trojan, "people feel more secure and satisfied about their jobs when they're developing their career."

Sources: Johnston, L. (2008, November 3). Employees put high price on learning, development. *Canadian HR Reporter, 21* (19), 29; www.trojanuv.com.

Intrinsic Benefits

Trained employees benefit by acquiring new knowledge and skills that enable them to perform their jobs better. Research has shown that training has a positive effect on employees' job behaviour and job performance.[23] In addition to improving their knowledge and skills, trained employees also develop greater confidence or self-efficacy (see Chapter 3 for a discussion of self-efficacy) in their ability to perform their job. They describe feelings of increased usefulness and belonging in the organization, and they seek out opportunities to fully exploit their new skills and abilities.[24] Trained employees also have more positive attitudes toward their job and organization.[25]

Extrinsic Benefits

Extrinsic benefits include things such as higher earnings as a result of increased knowledge and skills, improved marketability, greater security of employment, and enhanced opportunities for advancement and promotion. A number of studies have found that company-sponsored training programs increase workers' wages by 4 to 11 percent.[26] Many workers who have been laid off are attending training programs to acquire the skills they need for new careers.[27]

Benefits to Society

Training and development also has benefits for society that extend beyond the workplace. The training and development that organizations provide their employees helps to create an educated and skilled population that benefits the economy and our standard of living.

Educated and Skilled Population

The knowledge and skills that employees acquire through workplace training help to create an educated and skilled workforce. For example, some organizations offer literacy and numeracy training for employees who did not obtain them through regular educational channels but who require them to perform their jobs. This training also enables employees to function more effectively in their daily lives and therefore has a number of societal benefits.

Employees who have participated in organization-sponsored training programs report using their new skills to better manage their personal lives. They are more likely to be able to read instructions for assembling products and to be able to calculate bills and expenses. They are also more likely to be able to find employment if they are laid off or their employer closes a plant. Thus, many employees place a high value on learning and training.

Economy and Standard of Living

The key to a country's standard of living, incomes, and overall prosperity are its productivity and productivity growth. Canada currently lags behind the United States in its productivity performance. There are a number of ways to improve productivity, and one of them is by improving the education and skills of the workforce.[28] An improvement in Canada's productivity will have a positive effect on the economy and our standard of living, and a key factor for improving productivity is education.

The federal government spends billions of dollars annually on education and training because it sees a strong link between an educated workforce and a high-wage economy. Countries with higher education levels have more and better employment opportunities.[29] Training investments also lead to job creation and job opportunities.[30] In the 2009 federal budget, the government allocated $2 billion for job training including $1.5 billion for laid-off workers. The intent is for workers to develop new skills so that they will have more and better employment opportunities.

Of course, in order for organizations, employees, and society to reap the benefits of training, organizations must invest in training and development. In the next section, we focus on training and development in Canadian organizations.

Training and Development in Canada

In order to benefit from training and development, organizations must invest in it and provide their employees with training opportunities. Canadian organizations, however, have tended not to be leaders when it comes to training investments. According to one study, fewer than 30 percent of adult workers in Canada participate in job-related training.[31]

In 2006 Canadian employees received, on average, only 25 hours of training a year. The most training is received by professional and technical employees and supervisors (31 hours), while non-technical employees (22 hours) receive the fewest hours of training. Employees in services (32 hours) and not-for-profit (30 hours) receive the most training, while those in wholesale/retail (22 hours) receive the least. By comparison, organizations in the United States provide more than 34 hours of training per employee per year.[32]

According to the Conference Board of Canada, Canadian organizations underinvest in training and development.[33] For example, the total average investment in training and development across all industries in Canada was reported to be $4.9 million in 2004.[34] In the United States, organizations spend approximately $56.2 billion a year on formal training programs.[35]

Canadian organizations also lag when it comes to the amount spent on training per employee, which has remained relatively static over the past decade. In 2006, the total average direct investment in training per employee was $852 compared to $914 in 2004, $824 in 2003, $838 in 2002, $859 in 2000, $798 in 2001, $776 in 1998, and $842 in 1996. By comparison, organizational spending on training and development per employee in the United States increased from $1,003 (Cdn) in 2002 to $1,123 in 2004, and to $1,176 in 2005/06. In addition, the average investment in training as a percentage of payroll in Canada has remained constant at around 1.80 percent in 2006 compared to 2.25 percent in the United States. Thus, organizations in the United States currently spend about 40 percent more per employee on training and development than do Canadian organizations.[36]

These findings suggest a significant gap between Canadian and U.S. organizations in training investments and that a plateau in Canadian training investment might have been reached, as the amounts invested by Canadian organizations have remained relatively stable over the past decade. In other words, Canadian organizations may not be willing to invest much more in training and development. In fact, most organizations (63 percent) expect their training investments to remain the same in the next year and do not plan to increase their spending on training and development.[37]

Canadian organizations also spend less on training and development than organizations in other countries, including those in Europe, Asia, and the Pacific Rim. A recent international comparison of employee training ranked Canada 21st in 2006, down from 12th place in 2002. Ten countries pulled ahead of Canada between 2002 and 2006. According to the Conference Board of Canada, this underinvestment in training and development might lead to a gap in essential knowledge and skills. Further, if Canadian organizations are going to be able to compete effectively, they must increase their investments in training and development.[38]

Information about training and development in Canada is summarized in Table 1.1. This information will allow you to compare your organization and training experience against that of others. This information also highlights some differences in training across job categories and industries. In the next section, we consider why Canadian organizations do not spend more on training and development.

Is Training an Investment or an Expense?

Given the many benefits of training and development it is surprising that Canadian organizations do not invest more, and it begs the question, "Why don't organizations invest more in training and development?"

It may be that training is not considered a high priority. In fact, Canada currently ranks 20th out of 60 countries in its ranking of employee training as a high organizational priority, behind countries such as Finland (ranked number 1), Denmark, and Japan, but just ahead of the United States, which ranked 23rd.[39] Among Canadian organizations, half of the respondents in a study by the Conference Board of Canada indicated that training, learning, and development is either a top or a high priority.[40]

Another reason for the underinvestment in training and development is the perception that training, learning, and development expenditures represent a cost rather than an investment. The Conference Board of Canada found that most organizations in Canada view training and development as a necessary operating expense or cost that should be minimized.[41]

Organizations that view training as a cost tend to limit their training investments to only what is required by law or necessary to survive. As a result, training is often the first to go when there are cuts to discretionary spending. Organizations that view training as an investment expect direct benefits and a return on their investment. For these organizations, training is part of the organization's strategy and a key factor for its competitiveness and success.[42]

TABLE 1.1

Training and Development in Canada

- Percentage of Canadian full-time employees who took part in training in 2006: 69 percent.
- Total average training investment per employee in 2006: $852.
- Total average training investment per employee 1996–2004: $846.
- Small and medium-sized organizations spend more per employee on training, learning, and development than larger organizations.
- Percentage of payroll spent on training in 2006: 1.8.
- Sectors with the highest training investment per employee in 2006: not-for-profit, professional services, financial services, technology and communications, and government.
- Sectors with the lowest training investment per employee in 2006: personal services (e.g., accommodation, food), wholesale/retail, education and health care, primary and construction, and manufacturing.
- Average number of training hours received annually per employee in 2006: 25.
- Average number of training hours received annually by employee category in 2006: non-technical, 22; trades, 24; executive, 24; middle management, 29; professional/ technical, 31; supervisory, 31.
- Industries with highest average number of training hours per employee in 2006: Services, 32; not-for-profit, 30; government, 28; primary and construction, 27; technology and communications, 27.
- Industries with lowest average number of training hours per employee in 2006: wholesale/retail, 22; transportation and utilities, 24; professional services, 25; education and health care, 25.
- Anticipated changes in total training investment: increase, 32 percent; remain the same, 63 percent; decrease, 5 percent.

Sources: Parker, R. O., & Cooney, J. (2005). *Learning & development outlook 2005*. The Conference Board of Canada: Ottawa; Hughes, P. D., & Grant, M. (2007). *Learning & development outlook 2007*. The Conference Board of Canada: Ottawa. Reprinted by permission of The Conference Board of Canada.

All this is not to say that there are no Canadian organizations that invest heavily in training and development. In fact, there are large differences in the amount spent on training and development across organizations and industries. The Conference Board of Canada found that one in five organizations invests more than 3 percent of payroll in training.[43]

Scotiabank, for example, invests $47 million a year in training and education. Employees can receive tuition assistance, language training, and online programs for upgrading their skills. In addition, managers receive training on leadership skills and coaching techniques.[44] BMO invests an average of $1,800 a year in training per employee, which is more than double the national average, and provides a minimum of seven days of training a year.[45] Employees at Labatt Breweries of Canada attend beer school to learn how beer is made and to gain a greater knowledge of, and appreciation for, the company's products.[46]

However, the overall trend in training investments in Canada is cause for concern. According to the Conference Board of Canada, Canadian organizations are not investing enough resources in training, learning, and development at a time when skilled employees have become increasingly vital to an organization's success, and this threatens Canada's competitiveness. Perhaps not surprisingly, Canada's productivity growth lags behind its main competitors.[47]

What can be done to increase training investments in Canadian organizations? In the next section, we describe what one province has done to increase training investments.

Quebec's Training Law

In an attempt to increase training investments made by organizations in Quebec, in 1995 the government of Quebec passed the *Act to foster the development of manpower training* (often referred to by employers as the "1% or training law") making it the only payroll training tax in North America. The act was passed in part because at the time Quebec was substantially behind other provinces in its investment in adult learning and training. The law requires companies with payrolls of more than $1 million to invest a minimum of 1 percent of their payroll on government-sanctioned training, or pay that amount into a provincial fund. Companies with payrolls of less than $1 million are exempt. The funds acquired from companies that do not invest the 1 percent of payroll on training are placed in a government fund that supports training initiatives in the province.[48]

Although Quebec is the only jurisdiction in North America to have a training law, countries such as France, Denmark, Singapore, and Brazil have legislated levies to promote training. France introduced a training tax in 1971 and the rate of training has doubled to 1.5 percent of payroll.[49]

According to the Quebec government, the objective of the law is to ensure that training investment made by organizations develops employee competencies and skills that will result in improved organizational productivity and performance.[50]

In 2008 a report analyzed the landmark law, concluding that the law has had a significant effect on the way Quebec firms organize and deliver training, and has resulted in substantial growth in adult learning and training over the last decade. The main findings of the report are the following:

- The legislation has had a significant impact on the way firms in Quebec structure, organize, and deliver training.
- More companies are actively planning and implementing training programs for their employees.
- The participation rate in workplace training in Quebec increased from 21 percent to 33 percent between 1997 and 2002 (it increased from 29 percent to 35 percent in Canada), making it the fastest growth rate in Canada and closing the gap between Quebec and other provinces, although Quebec still slightly lags behind the national average in training participation rates.
- Employers, governments, unions, and community groups are working together to find ways to promote learning and training.[51]

Although the law has had a positive effect on adult learning and training in Quebec, some have expressed concerns about it. For example, many large organizations meet or exceed the 1 percent payroll requirement, so the law has no effect on them and there is no incentive for them to increase their training investments. Some Quebec-based multinational organizations spend between 8 and 10 percent of their payroll on training.

On the other hand, small companies with fewer than 50 employees are often the most affected by the law and have difficulty meeting the requirements. Some small companies just pay the 1 percent rather than spend time on the recordkeeping and reporting requirements. Thus, the effect of the legislation seems to have been greatest in medium-sized companies.[52]

To find out how the legislation works, see The Trainer's Notebook 1.1, "Quebec's Payroll Training Legislation."

The Context of Training and Development

Although we have been discussing training and development as an independent activity, the reality is that training and development are embedded within a larger environmental and organizational context as well as a human resource system. As shown in Figure 1.1, training and development is just one part of a system of human resource practices and functions.

The human resource system is influenced by environmental and organizational factors. Environmental factors such as legislation, the economic climate, competition, demographics, and social values have an impact on organizations. For example, if a competitor introduces a lower-priced product, the organization will have to decide whether to match the competitor's actions or compete in other ways, such as providing superior service. This strategic

The Trainer's Notebook 1.1

Quebec's Payroll Training Legislation

Companies in Quebec with payrolls over $1 million are required by law to spend 1 percent of their payroll on training, or pay a training tax. They must also carefully document their training activities and complete government forms every February. Some have complained that the process is too complicated and choose to pay the tax rather than complete the forms even if they are providing some training. The main aspects of the legislation are as follows:

1. Every February, companies must file paperwork in which they indicate how they spent 1 percent of their total payroll on training.

2. If they have not spent at least 1 percent of their total payroll on training, they must pay the difference to the government, and that money is then used to fund training programs in companies that have invested at least 1 percent in training.

3. Companies must use accredited training bodies, instructors, and services that follow a code of ethics. All types of training are eligible.

4. General information about the participation of employees in training exercises must be provided.

5. Companies that meet the 1 percent training investment can apply for provincial training grants.

Source: Harding, K. (2003, June 4). A taxing way to train staff. *The Globe and Mail*, C1, C6. Reprinted with permission from *The Globe and Mail.*

FIGURE 1.1

The Context of Training and Development

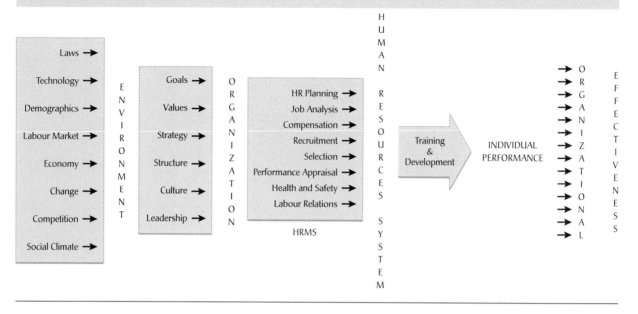

decision will in turn affect costs, the ability to pay employees, or the necessity to train and reward employees for effective performance. Events and concerns inside and outside an organization can lead to the need for new knowledge, skills, abilities, and training programs.

Sometimes sudden and unexpected changes in the environment can lead to changes in organizations and human resources policies and practices. For example, consider how concerns over terrorism have affected airport and flight security training. The Transportation Security Administration in the United States developed new guidelines for the training of baggage screeners and flight crews and made airport security fully federalized. The training of baggage screeners now includes technical training on metal detectors, X-ray scanners, bag searching, and how to deal with difficult passengers and manage stress. Training was increased to 40 hours of classroom training and 60 hours of on-the-job training. Pilots and flight attendants receive training on how to assess and react to dangerous situations.[53] Other changes in training as a result of the threat of terrorism include a shift to distance technologies and e-learning and an increase in training programs on diversity, security, stress management, and change management.[54]

Below, we discuss how changes in specific environmental and organizational factors can impact the human resource system and training and development.

The Environmental Context of Training and Development

Some of the key environmental factors that drive human resources and training and development are global competition, technology, the labour market, and change.

Global Competition

Increasing global competition has forced organizations to improve their productivity and the quality of their goods and services. Improvements in the production process and quality initiatives almost always require employees to learn new skills. And when Canadian organizations send workers on assignments in foreign countries, they need to provide them with cross-cultural training so they will be able to adapt and function in a different culture. Thus, global competition can require numerous changes to human resource practices and the need for training and development.

Technology

Technology has had a profound effect on the way organizations operate and compete. New technologies can provide organizations with improvements in productivity and a competitive advantage. However, such improvements depend on the training that employees receive. Technology will lead to productivity gains only when employees receive the necessary training to exploit the technology.[55] Thus, the adoption of new technologies will have a direct impact on the training needs of employees who will be required to use the technology.

The Labour Market

Changes in the labour market can have a major effect on training and development. For example, consider the impending shortage of skilled labour in Canada. It has been estimated that a critical shortage of skilled workers in Canada could reach 1 million by the year 2020. To deal with this looming crisis, the country will have to change its approach to education and training.[56] If organizations cannot hire people with the necessary knowledge and skills, they will have to provide more training if they are to compete and survive. As indicated earlier, the federal government included $2 billion in its 2009 budget for training. Changes in the labour market and the supply of labour require changes in the amount and type of training.

Change

The technological revolution, increasing globalization, and competition have resulted in a highly uncertain and constantly changing environment. In order to survive and remain competitive, organizations must adapt and change. As a result, managing change has become a normal part of organizational life, and training and development is almost always a key part of the process. This often involves training programs on the change process as well as training that is part of the change program. For example, if an organization implements a change program that involves a team-based work system, then employees will require team training (see Chapter 13 for a description of team training).

The Organizational Context of Training and Development

As indicated in Figure 1.1, training and development are also affected by internal events within the organization. Among the most important internal factors are strategy, structure, and culture.

Strategy

Strategy is one of the most important factors influencing training and development. As indicated earlier, training and development can help an organization achieve its strategic objectives and gain a competitive advantage when it is aligned with an organization's strategy. The alignment of human resources practices with an organization's business strategy is known as **strategic human resource management (SHRM).** Organizations that have greater alignment between their HR practices and their strategies tend to have superior performance.[57]

Training is strategic when it is aligned with business strategy and therefore enables an organization to achieve its strategic goals and objectives. Whether an organization has a strategy for quality, innovation, or customer service, training as well as other human resources practices must be designed to reinforce and support the strategy.

For example, if an organization decides to improve customer service or product quality, then employees will require training in order to learn how to provide better service or improve product quality. If an organization's strategy is to grow as rapidly as possible, then employees need to be trained in the management of mergers, acquisitions, joint ventures, and international ventures. All these growth components necessitate the building of new skills, and training is required to do this.

Recall that the Stedfast Skills and Learning Site initiative addresses the company's strategic business needs, as well as those of the Canadian textile industry as a whole. Thus, strategy is often a key factor driving the need for and type of training and development in organizations. By linking training to business strategy training becomes strategic rather than an isolated and independent activity, and as a result it is more likely to be effective. In fact, there is some evidence that training can lower an organization's market value when it is not strategically focused.[58]

Figure 1.2 depicts the role that strategy plays in the training and development process. The model shows how an organization's business strategy will have implications for its HRM strategy. The HRM strategy will then influence

Strategic human resource management (SHRM)
The alignment of human resources practices with an organization's business strategy

FIGURE 1.2

A Strategic Model of Training and Development

Managing Performance Through Training and Development

the organization's strategy for learning and training, which will determine the type of training and development activities and programs required.

Structure

The structure of an organization also affects training and development activities. Organizations are increasingly becoming flatter, with fewer levels of management. Employees are expected to perform tasks that were once considered managerial tasks and so they must be trained in traditional managerial activities such as problem solving, decision making, teamwork, and so on. Many organizations have experienced dramatic structural changes such as downsizing and reengineering in an effort to survive. These changes to an organization's structure often lead to changes in employees' tasks and responsibilities and necessitate the need for training.

Culture

Organizational culture refers to the shared beliefs, values, and assumptions that exist in an organization. An organization's culture is important because it determines the norms that exist in an organization and the expected behaviours. The culture of an organization, along with the norms and expected behaviours, are often communicated to employees through training programs.

Organizational culture
The shared beliefs, values, and assumptions that exist in an organization

For example, ethical practices are deeply ingrained in the culture of Molson Coors Brewing Company and they are communicated to employees through the company's ethics training programs. The company's training programs reflect a culture of integrity and the importance of acting in an honest and trustworthy manner based on business ethics and moral conviction.[59] Thus, the training programs are consistent with the company's core values and are a catalyst for achieving its business goals. In Chapter 4 you will learn about a learning culture and its effect on learning and training.

The Human Resources System

The human resources system and other human resource functions also influence training and development in organizations. In fact, in addition to being linked to business strategy, human resources practices should also be aligned and linked to each other. Thus, strategic human resource management involves two kinds of linkages. First, human resource practices should be linked to business strategy, as discussed earlier. Second, human resource practices should also be linked to each other so they work together to achieve an organization's strategy. Thus, what is most important is not individual human resource practices but rather the entire system of human resource practices.

The objective of human resources management is to attract, motivate, develop, and retain employees whose performance is necessary for the organization to achieve its strategic objectives. The human resources system accomplishes this through the provision of policies, guidelines, and practices such as human resource planning, recruitment, selection, orientation, training and development, performance appraisal, compensation and benefits, health and safety, and employment equity. In combination, these practices form an integrated and tightly linked human resources system that is known as a high-performance work system.

A **high-performance work system (HPWS)** consists of an interrelated system of human resource practices and policies that usually includes rigorous recruitment and selection procedures, performance-contingent incentive compensation, performance management, a commitment to employee involvement, and extensive training and development programs. High-performance work practices increase employees' knowledge, skills, abilities, and motivation. This leads to more positive attitudes, lower turnover, and higher productivity, which results in higher organizational performance. An increasing number of studies have found that organizations with high-performance work systems have superior productivity and financial performance.[60]

Each human resource function should be aligned with the others so they work in concert toward the organization's strategic objectives. For example, if an organization's strategy is to provide excellent customer service, then the organization will need to hire employees who have the skills required to interact with customers; they will need to train employees on how to provide excellent customer service; they will need to evaluate employees' customer-service behaviour and performance; and they will need to reward employees for providing excellent customer service.

In summary, external factors influence an organization's strategy, structure, and the way human resources are managed, and these factors in turn influence the design and delivery of training and development programs. Training and development should be tightly aligned with an organization's business strategy and the other human resource practices in the human resources system. In other words, there should be a good fit between strategy and training and development, and between training and development and other human resources practices. In this way, training and development is a strategic and important part of a high-performance work system that can improve individual performance and ultimately organizational effectiveness.

Thus, the model in Figure 1.1 not only explains the context of training and development, but also helps us to understand the link between training and development and organizational effectiveness.

The Instructional Systems Design (ISD) Model of Training and Development

In this section, we describe an approach to training and development that sets the stage for the remainder of the text. In particular, we describe a systems approach to training and development that is known as the instructional systems design model.

The **instructional systems design (ISD) model** of training and development depicts training as a rational and scientific process that consists of three major steps: needs analysis, design and delivery, and evaluation. The process

High-performance work system (HPWS)

An interrelated system of human resource practices and policies that usually includes rigorous recruitment and selection procedures, performance-contingent incentive compensation, performance management, a commitment to employee involvement, and extensive training and development programs

Instructional systems design (ISD) model

A rational and scientific model of the training and development process that consists of a needs analysis, training design and delivery, and training evaluation consists of an analysis of current performance and ends with improved performance.[61] The ISD model is a streamlined version of an earlier model of instructional design known as ADDIE (analysis, design, develop, instruct/implement, and evaluate).[62]

According to the ISD model of training and development, the training process begins with a performance gap or an *itch*. An *itch* is something in the organization that is not quite right or is of concern to someone. Perhaps customer complaints are too high, quality is low, market share is being lost, or employees are frustrated by management or technology. Or perhaps there is a performance problem that is making it difficult for employees or departments to achieve goals or meet standards. If some part of the organization itches, or is not satisfied with the performance of individual employees or departments, then the problem needs to be analyzed.

A critical first step in the instructional systems design model is a needs analysis to determine the nature of the problem and whether training is the best solution. A needs analysis is performed to determine the difference or gap between the way things are and the way things should be. Recall in the chapter opening vignette that Stedfast uses a Training Needs Assessment tool to identify company-wide skills and knowledge gaps to better align and target its skills development resources.

Needs analysis consists of three levels known as an organizational analysis, a task analysis, and a person analysis. Each level of needs analysis is conducted to gather important information about problems and the need for training. An organizational analysis gathers information on where training is needed in an organization; a task analysis indicates what training is required; and a person analysis identifies who in the organization needs to be trained.

Based on the data collected from managers, employees, customers, and/or corporate documents, strategies for closing the gap are considered. Before training is determined to be the best solution to the problem, alternatives must be assessed. The solution to the performance gap might be feedback, incentives, or other human resource interventions. If training is determined to be the best solution, then objectives—or measurable goals—are written to improve the situation and reduce the gap. The needs analysis, the consideration of alternative strategies, and the setting of objectives force trainers to focus on performance improvement, not the delivery of a training program. Training is only one solution and not necessarily the best one to performance problems.

If training is the solution to a performance problem, a number of factors must be considered in the design and delivery of a training program. The needs analysis information and training objectives are used to determine the content of a training program. Then the best training methods for achieving the objectives and for learning the training content must be identified. Other design and delivery factors, which are described in Chapters 5 and 9, must also be considered in the design and delivery of a training program in order to maximize trainees' learning.

After a training program has been designed and delivered, the next stage is training evaluation. The needs analysis and training objectives provide important information regarding what should be evaluated in order to determine if a training program has been effective. Some of the critical evaluation questions include: Did the training program achieve its objectives? What did employees learn? Did employees' job performance improve? Is the organization more effective? Was it worth the cost?

The purpose of all training and development efforts is ultimately to improve employee performance and organizational effectiveness. Thus, it is important to know if employee job performance has changed and if the organization has improved following a training program. In this stage, the trainer has to decide what to measure as part of the evaluation of a training program as well as how to design an evaluation study. On the basis of a training evaluation, decisions can be made about what aspects of a training program should be retained, modified, or discarded.

Figure 1.3 presents a simplified version of the instructional systems design model of training and development. As we have described, each stage leads into the subsequent stage, with needs analysis being the first critical step that sets the stage for the design and delivery and evaluation stages. Also notice that there are feedback loops from evaluation to needs analysis and training design and delivery. This indicates the process is a closed-loop system in which evaluation feeds back into needs analysis and training design and delivery. In this way, it is possible to know if performance gaps identified in the needs analysis stage have been closed, and if changes are required in the design and delivery of a training program in order to make the training program more effective. Thus, training programs are continuously modified and improved on the basis of training evaluation.

Although the ISD model is considered to be the best approach for managing the training and development process, in reality many organizations do not follow all of the steps of the ISD model. In other words, many organizations do not conduct a needs analysis, they implement training programs that are not well designed, and they do not evaluate their training programs. There has also been some criticism waged against the ISD model in recent

FIGURE 1.3

The Instructional Systems Design Model of Training and Development

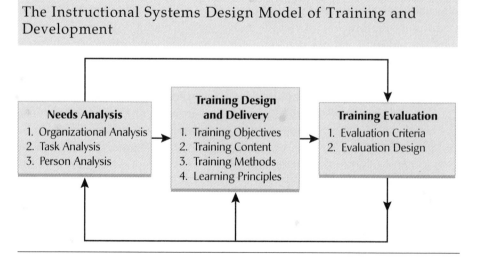

Managing Performance Through Training and Development

The Trainer's Notebook 1.2

The Application of the ISD Model

The instructional systems design model begins when somebody identifies a performance gap in the organization. According to the ISD model, the recognition of a performance gap should lead to the following sequence of activities:

1. Conduct an organizational analysis to investigate the performance gap and determine if training is a possible solution (when the cause of the problem is a lack of knowledge or skills).
2. If training is a possible solution, conduct a task analysis in order to determine how the job or jobs in question should be performed and the things that a skilled employee must know and be able to do.
3. Conduct a person analysis to determine how employees currently perform the job compared to how they should perform and how best to train them (e.g., training methods).

4. Design a training program using those methods and approaches that will be most effective to train employees who require training. Include specialists in various media and methods to assist in developing training material.
5. Develop and fine-tune the program. Pilot test it and revise as needed.
6. Deliver the program to its intended audience.
7. Monitor and evaluate the program and its results on an ongoing basis. The program is considered a success if the original performance gap is closed or reduced and if correcting the problem costs less than the cost of not correcting it.

Sources: Gordon, J., & Zemke, R. (2000, April). The attack on ISD. *Training*, 42–53; Zemke, R., & Rossett, A. (2002, February). A hard look at ISD. *Training*, 26–34.

years among professionals in the training industry who have seriously challenged its usefulness. However, if used correctly it remains the best approach for managing the training and development process.[63] Training programs often fail because they have ignored an important step in the process such as conducting a thorough needs analysis.

We will have more to say about each of the stages of the training and development process as they are covered in the remainder of the text. For now, you should understand the ISD model and the sequence of activities that are involved in the training and development process. To learn more about how to apply the ISD model, see The Trainer's Notebook 1.2, "The Application of the ISD Model."

Summary

This chapter introduced you to the training and development process and emphasized the important role that training and development plays in the effectiveness and competitiveness of organizations. The benefits of training and development for organizations, employees, and society were described as well as training investments made by organizations in Canada. We also described how training and development is embedded within the environmental and organizational context and is part of the human resources system. It was also noted that for training to be most effective, it should be strategic.

That is, it should be tied to an organization's business strategy and aligned with other human resource practices. Finally, we described the instructional systems design (ISD) model of training and development that sets the stage for the remainder of the text.

Key Terms

development   p. 6

high-performance work system (HPWS)   p. 20

human resource development   p. 6

instructional systems design (ISD) model
    p. 20

organizational culture   p. 19

performance management   p. 5

strategic human resource management (SHRM)
    p. 18

training   p. 6

Web Links

Delta Hotels and Resorts: www.deltahotels.com

Labatt Breweries of Canada: www.labatt.com

Scotiabank: www.scotiabank.com

Stedfast Inc.: www.stedfast.com

Trojan Technologies: www.trojanuv.com

Discussion Questions

1. According to the Conference Board of Canada, the investments made by Canadian organizations in training and development have remained relatively constant over the last decade and appear to have reached a plateau in terms of the amount organizations are willing to invest in training and development. Comment on the implications of this for organizations, employees, and the Canadian economy. Should governments get involved and enact laws that require organizations to invest a certain percentage of their payroll in training and development, as they have in Quebec?

2. Studies comparing the competitive performance of Canadian corporations indicate that among the countries in the G8 (Canada, the United States, Japan, Germany, France, Italy, Russia, and the United Kingdom), Canada ranks very low. Do you think that training and development in Canada has anything to do with this and, if so, what should governments and businesses do?

3. Discuss some of the reasons why organizations often fail to fully implement the instructional systems design (ISD) model of training and development. Why do you think the ISD model has come under attack in recent years and been seriously challenged and criticized?

4. Refer to the chapter opening vignette on Stedfast Inc. and discuss the extent to which the instructional systems design (ISD) model was used. In other words, describe the company's approach to training in terms of each stage of the ISD model.
5. Research on training and organizational effectiveness has found that training is positively related to human resource and performance outcomes but to a much lesser extent to financial outcomes. Explain why and how training is related to these outcomes. What are the implications of these findings for organizations? Why is training less strongly related to financial outcomes?
6. Why do many organizations view training, learning, and development as an expense rather than an investment? What are the implications of this? What can be done to change this perception so that organizations view training and development as an investment?
7. Discuss some of the reasons why Canadian organizations have not increased their investments in training and development over the last decade. Do you think they should increase their investments in training and development? Explain your answer.

The Great Training Debate

1. Debate the following: Training and development is the single most important factor for the competitiveness and success of an organization.
2. Debate the following: All provinces should enact training legislation similar to the law in Quebec.
3. Debate the following: Training is an operating cost that should be limited to only what is required by law and absolutely necessary.

Using the Internet

1. A number of associations and government departments provide useful information and services related to learning and training and development. To learn more about some of these associations, visit the following websites:

   www.cstd.ca (Canadian Society for Training and Development)

   www.astd.org (American Society for Training & Development)

   www.ccl-cca.ca/ccl (Canadian Council on Learning)

   www.hrsdc.gc.ca (Human Resources and Skills Development Canada)

   Write a brief report in which you describe the association and the information that can be obtained from each site about learning, education, and training and development.

2. Go to **www.cstd.ca/resources/tca.html** (Canadian Society for Training and Development) to find out about the Training Competency Architecture (TCA). What is the TCA and what are the five competency categories defined by the TCA?
3. To learn more about the benefits of training for Canadian organizations, go to Industry Canada at **www.collectionscanada.gc.ca/ webarchives/20060226114621/http://strategis.ic.gc.ca/epic/internet/ incts-scf.nsf/en/h_sl00003e.html** and answer the following questions:
   a. Why is training important?
   b. How is the workforce changing?
   c. What are companies doing to train employees?
   d. What are leading-edge learning organizations doing?
4. To learn about training and skills development in Canada, go to Industry Canada at **www.collectionscanada.gc.ca/ webarchives/20060205142510/http://strategis.ic.gc.ca/epic/internet/ incts-scf.nsf/en/sl00022e.html** and answer the following questions:
   a. Why is skills development important in Canada and what are the implications for organizations?
   b. What should organizations be doing and what are the implications for training and development?
   c. What are some initiatives to assist employee skill development?

Exercises

In-Class

1. Review the training and development facts in Table 1.1. Benchmark your experiences in a current or previous organization against the statistics in the table. Based on the statistics in the table, you might consider things such as: How does your organization compare to the Canadian averages in areas such as the amount of training hours employees receive a year and the amount spent per employee on training? Does your organization fare better or worse than the average Canadian organization? What do the results tell you about your organization? What are the implications of your findings for your learning and job performance and for your organization?
2. Consider how training and development is influenced by, and in turn can influence, other human resource functions. In particular, give an example of how training and development can influence and is influenced by activities within each of the following human resource areas: Recruitment; Selection; HR Planning; Performance Appraisals; Compensation; and Health and Safety.
3. Using the ISD model of training and development, examine the class your instructor has delivered to you today. In other words, what did your instructor have to do in terms of a needs analysis? How did he or she design and deliver the class? How was the class evaluated (or, How should the class be evaluated)?

4. Assume you are a director of training and development in a small organization. In order to reduce expenses, the company president has decided to cut the training budget in half and reduce the amount of training provided to employees. The president has asked to meet with you to discuss these plans. Your job is to prepare a short presentation to persuade the president to change his or her mind. What will you say and what can you do to convince the president of the importance and need for more, not less, training and development?

5. Recall the last time you attended an organization-sponsored training program. Describe the objectives and content of the training program and whether or not you think the program was strategic. In other words, was it an example of strategic training? Be specific in terms of why you think it was or was not a good example of strategic training. What would have made it more strategic?

6. Recall the last time you attended an organization-sponsored training program. Describe the objectives and content of the training program and whether or not you think the ISD model was used to develop the program. Be specific in terms of each stage of the model and the extent to which it was used in the development of the program. How effective was the training program in terms of your learning and in achieving the program's objectives? Based on your analysis, what could have been done to more fully make use of the ISD model, and what effect might this have had on the effectiveness of the program?

In-the-Field

1. Contact the human resource department of your own or another organization to discuss the organization's training programs. Try to learn about the extent to which the human resource staff use the ISD model of training and development. Find out about each stage of the model and the extent to which it is adhered to in the development of training programs. What aspects of the model are adequately carried out and which ones are not? If some of the stages are not adequately conducted, find out why this is the case and why the human resource department does or does not rigorously adhere to the ISD model. Based on the responses, what advice would you give the human resource department about its training and development programs?

Case Incident

Canadian American Transportation Systems

Canadian American Transportation Systems began running a new high-speed ferry between Toronto and New York State in 2004. The marine industry is highly regulated and most of the workers have no experience so a great deal of training was needed to meet the rigorous standards set by the U.S. Coast Guard and Transport Canada. There are two mandatory levels of training.

One is called SOLAS (safety of life at sea), which involves a very basic familiarization of the vessel, basic life saving procedures, and medical emergencies. There is also a more advanced program of survival training called STCW (seafarers' training certification and watch keeping). Employees were taken to Olympic-sized pools where they had to jump in the water, get people into safety rafts, and learn how to use equipment in cold water conditions. Good customer service is also important, so employees need to understand the customer experience.

Questions

1. To what extent has the instructional system design (ISD) model of training and development been used? Discuss how the ISD model is relevant for the training of the new staff and how it can be applied.
2. Discuss the benefits of the training described in the case for the organization, employees, and the public.

Source: Garcia, C. (2004, May 17). CloseUp: Training and development. *Canadian HR Reporter,* *17* (10), 7–10.

Case Study

Flotation Ltd.

"Great course, Sam!" said the trainees as they walked out the door and headed for the parking lot. Just like all the others. Sam Harris, a veteran trainer with Flotation Ltd., a manufacturer of life jackets and other flotation devices, smiled as he gathered his notes together.

He had just finished two hours of wisecracking and slightly off-colour storytelling as he worked his way through the third session of a human relations course for supervisors. "Keep 'em happy" was Sam's motto. Give the troops what they want, keep your enrolments up, and no one will complain.

Sam was good at it, too! For 20 years, he had earned an easy living, working the politics, producing good numbers (of trainees) for the top brass to brag about ("We give each employee up to 26 hours of training every year!"), and generally promoting his small training group as a beehive of activity.

Everybody knew Sam and everybody liked him. His courses were fun. He had no trouble convincing managers to send their people. He put out a little catalogue with his course list every year in January. He hadn't had a cancellation in more than 10 years. Some managers said that training was the best reward they had. Now, only three years from retirement, Sam intended to coast comfortably into pension-land. All his favourite courses had long been prepared. All he had to do was make adjustments here and there and create some trendy new titles.

But times were changing. The company president was thinking differently. "I need somebody to take a close look at our training function," he said. Sitting in the president's office, Jenny Stoppard, the newly hired Vice President of Human Resources, wondered what he meant. Flotation Ltd. had a reputation as a company with a well-trained workforce.

"We need to increase our productivity per person by 50 percent over the next three years," the president continued. "And you are going to spearhead that effort. We spend a lot on training and we cycle people through a lot of courses. But I'm not satisfied with the bottom line. I know that while Dad was president he swore by Sam and said he was the greatest. I don't know anymore. Maybe a whole new approach is needed. Anyway, I want you to take a close look at Sam's operation."

Later in the day, the president called Sam into his office. "Sam, I want you to meet Jenny Stoppard. I've just hired her as Vice President of Human Resources. She's your new boss. I think the next three years are going to be very exciting around here, and Jenny is going to be a key player in the drive to increase our competitiveness. I want you to do everything in your power to cooperate with her."

Questions

1. Comment on Sam's approach to training. Would you want him working for your company? What are the benefits of his training to employees and the organization?
2. To what extent is training at Flotation Ltd. strategic? What would make it more strategic?
3. To what extent has Sam used the instructional systems design (ISD) model of training and development? If he were to more fully use the ISD model, what should he do? Comment on each step of the ISD model.
4. How does Sam evaluate his training programs? Compare Sam's evaluation to the president's objectives. If Sam were to evaluate training based on the president's objectives, what would he have to do? What do you think the results might be?
5. The president has asked Jenny to "take a close look at Sam's operation." What should she do, and what should she report back to the president?

References

1. Excerpt from Watt, D. (2005, December). *Textiles Human Resources Council and Stedfast Inc.: Bringing Skills Development and Knowledge Management to the Workplace.* The Conference Board of Canada: Ottawa.
2. Norris, A. (2001, September 1). Transat work faulted. *The Gazette,* A1; Koring, P. (2001, August 31). Transat faces safety crackdown. *The Globe and Mail,* A1; Koring, P. (2002, August 30). Jet crew's handling of fuel leak questioned. *The Globe and Mail,* A1; Brazao, D. (2001, August 29). We had no second chance, pilot in jet emergency says. *The Toronto Star,* A1; Taylor, A., & Verma, S. (2002, August 31). Air Transat told to improve training on fuel handling. *The Toronto Star,* A1.
3. Koring, P. (2004, October 18). Transat report blames pilots; EXCLUSIVE: Emergency landing in Azores could have been avoided if crew followed fuel-management procedures, report says. *The Globe and Mail,* A1; Cernetig, M. (2004, October 19). Pilot's heroic flying tarnished in report; Mishandled fuel leak, probe finds Transat jet glided to safety in Azores. *The Toronto Star,* A7.

4. Koring, P. (2004, October 18); Cernetig, M. (2004, October 19); Koring, P. (2005, March 2). Air Transat agrees to settle lawsuit. *The Globe and Mail,* A6.
5. Campion-Smith, B. (1996, January 24). Rookie driver sorry for crash. *The Toronto Star,* A1, A22; Hall, J. (2005, August 6). Ten years after. *The Toronto Star,* B1, B4–B5.
6. Tandt, M. D. (2005, November 23). Poor training for RCMP imperils safety, auditor says. *The Globe and Mail,* A1, A7.
7. Girard, D. (2008, August 22). Audit halts 6 propane operations. *Toronto Star,* A7.
8. D'Aliesio, R., & Komarnicki, J. (2008, November 5). Required bus driver course in works. *Calgary Herald,* A6.
9. Parker, R. O., & Cooney, J. (2005). *Learning & development outlook 2005.* The Conference Board of Canada: Ottawa.
10. Gordon, A. (2000, February). 35 best companies to work for. *Report on Business Magazine,* 24–33.
11. Gosselin, A., Werner, J., & Hall, N. (1997). Ratee preferences concerning performance management and appraisal. *Human Resource Development Quarterly, 8* (4), 315–333.
12. Werner, J. M., & DeSimone, R. L. (2009). *Human resource development.* (5th edition). Mason, OH: South-Western.
13. Anonymous. (2008, May 19). CEOs talk: Training & development. *Canadian HR Reporter, 21* (10), 11–13.
14. Bowsher, J. (1990, May). Making the call on the CEO. *Training and Development Journal,* 65–66.
15. Adams, M. (1999). Training employees as partners. *HR Magazine, 44* (2), 64–70.
16. Bernstein, A., & Magnusson, P. (1993, February 22). How much good will training do? *BusinessWeek,* 76–77.
17. Betcherman, G., Leckie, N., & McMullen, K. (1997). *Developing skills in the Canadian workplace.* Ottawa: Canadian Policy Research Networks; Arthur, W. Jr., Bennett, W. Jr., Edens, P. S., & Bell, S. T. (2003). Effectiveness of training in organizations: A meta-analysis of design and evaluation features. *Journal of Applied Psychology, 88,* 234–245.
18. Tharenou, P., Saks, A. M., & Moore, C. (2007). A review and critique of research on training and organizational-level outcomes. *Human Resource Management Review, 17,* 251–273.
19. Birdi, K., Clegg, C., Pattersnon, M., Robinson, A., Stride, C. B., Wall, T. D., & Wood, S. J. (2008). The impact of human resource and operational management practices on company productivity: A longitudinal study. *Personnel Psychology, 61,* 467–501.
20. Hirsh, L. (2008, November 3). Non-monetary rewards gaining traction. *Canadian HR Reporter, 21* (19), 24; Harder, D. (2007, November 5). More than money. *Canadian HR Reporter, 20* (19), 21.
21. Schaaf, D. (1998). What workers really think about training. *Training, 35* (9), 59–66.
22. Roseman, E. (2001, August 29). Delta Hotels knows how to keep workers. *The Toronto Star,* E2.
23. Arthur, W. Jr., Bennett, W. Jr., Edens, P. S., & Bell, S. T. (2003).
24. Garavan, T. N., Costine, P., & Heraty, N. (1995). *Training and development in Ireland: Context policy and practice.* Dublin: Oak Tree Press.
25. Schaaf, D. (1998).
26. Bernstein, A., & Magnusson, P. (1993).
27. Howlett, K., & Church, E. (2009, January 13). Training for the new economy. *The Globe and Mail,* A4.
28. Crane, D. (2002, October 27). Innovation means productivity gains. *The Toronto Star,* C2.
29. Klie, S. (2007, December 3). Higher education leads to higher productivity. *Canadian HR Reporter, 20* (21), 7.
30. Bernstein, A., & Magnusson, P. (1993).
31. Saunders, R. (2007). *Moving forward on workplace learning.* Canadian Council on Learning: Ottawa.
32. Hughes, P. D., & Grant, M. (2007). *Learning & development outlook 2007.* The Conference Board of Canada: Ottawa.

33. Harris-Lalonde, S. (2001). *Training and development outlook*. The Conference Board of Canada: Ottawa.
34. Parker, R. O., & Cooney, J. (2005).
35. Anonymous. (2008, November/December). 2008 industry report: Gauges and drivers. *Training, 45* (9), 16–34.
36. Hughes, P. D., & Grant, M. (2007).
37. Parker, R. O., & Cooney, J. (2005); Hughes, P. D., & Grant, M. (2007).
38. Parker, R. O., & Cooney, J. (2005).
39. Parker, R. O., & Cooney, J. (2005).
40. Hughes, P. D., & Grant, M. (2007).
41. Hughes, P. D., & Grant, M. (2007).
42. Hughes, P. D., & Grant, M. (2007).
43. Parker, R. O., & Cooney, J. (2005).
44. Galt, V. (2002, June 5). Putting the human back into resources. *The Globe and Mail,* C1.
45. Galt, V. (2001, July 9). Training falls short: Study. *The Globe and Mail,* M1.
46. Galt, V. (2002, November 20). Training on tap. *The Globe and Mail,* C1.
47. Hughes, P. D., & Grant, M. (2007).
48. Bélanger, P., & Robitaille, M. (2008). A portrait of work-related learning in Quebec. Ottawa: Work and Learning Knowledge Centre.
49. Harding, K. (2003, June 4). A taxing way to train staff. *The Globe and Mail,* C1, C6.
50. Pangarkar, A., & Kirkwood, T. (2008, September 22). Jury still out on Quebec's training law. *Canadian HR Reporter, 21* (16), 16.
51. Bélanger, P., & Robitaille, M. (2008).
52. Pangarkar, A., & Kirkwood, T. (2008, September 22); Bélanger, P., & Robitaille, M. (2008).
53. (2002, April). Airport training ready to take off. *Training and Development,* 17–18.
54. (2002, February). ASTD survey results: The effect of terrorism on training. *Training and Development,* 28.
55. Crane, D. (1998, March 28). Time to take worker training seriously. *The Toronto Star,* B2.
56. McCarthy, S. (2001, February 27). Skilled-worker shortage could reach one million. *The Globe and Mail,* A1.
57. Becker, B. E., & Huselid, M. A. (1998). High performance work systems and firm performance: A synthesis of research and managerial implications. *Research in Personnel and Human Resources Management, 16,* 53–101.
58. Gibb-Clark, M. (2000, February 11). Employee training can backfire on firms: Survey. *The Globe and Mail,* B10.
59. Greengard, S. (2005, March). Golden values. *Workforce Management, 84* (3), 52–53.
60. Becker, B. E., & Huselid, M. A. (1998); Combs, J., Liu, Y., Hall, A., & Ketchen, D. (2006). How much do high-performance work practices matter? A meta-analysis of their effects on organizational performance. *Personnel Psychology, 59,* 501–528.
61. Dipboye, R. L. (1997). Organizational barriers to implementing a rational model of training. In M. A. Quinones and A. Ehrenstein (Eds.), *Training for a Rapidly Changing Workplace,* Washington, DC: American Psychological Association.
62. Gordon, J., & Zemke, R. (2000, April). The attack on ISD. *Training, 37* (4), 42–53; Zemke, R., & Rossett, A. (2002, February). A hard look at ISD. *Training, 39* (2), 26–34.
63. Gordon, J., & Zemke, R. (2000, April); Zemke, R., & Rossett, A. (2002, February).

Organizational Learning

Chapter Learning Outcomes

After reading this chapter, you should be able to:

- define organizational learning and describe a learning organization
- explain the five disciplines and the principles of a learning organization
- discuss the four key dimensions that are critical for creating and sustaining a learning organization
- define knowledge and give examples of explicit and tacit knowledge
- describe the meaning and types of intellectual capital
- define knowledge management and explain how knowledge is acquired, interpreted, disseminated, and retained in organizations
- define informal learning and describe what organizations can do to facilitate it
- define communities of practice and describe what organizations can do to create them
- describe the multilevel systems model of organizational learning
- explain how organizational learning and training and development are connected

TELUS

TELUS is a national telecommunications company in Canada with $9.5 billion in annual revenue. The company provides a wide range of communications products and services including data, Internet protocol (IP), voice, entertainment, and video.

TELUS is an organization with a strong commitment to learning and employee development. In 2007, the company's nearly 30,000 employees completed 216,000 online courses and 62,000 classroom courses.

TELUS learning consultants partner with business units to identify and implement strategic learning initiatives. As a result, organizational learning and performance plans are linked to corporate strategy. Only training that is directly linked to individual and organizational performance is provided.

Employees at TELUS have a customized career development plan that sets out personal objectives for performance and learning. The four-step process, called Growing for High Performance, helps team members grow their careers and develop to their highest potential and aligns individual performance objectives with corporate strategy.

The first step involves learning about the corporate strategy and business expectations and what the company expects of you personally. Employees have a range of opportunities for learning that include monthly or quarterly performance meetings with a team leader, a weekly online video, an online magazine, weekly e-letters from the CEO, company-wide emails and voicemail messages, and a portal providing information on business units, human resources, news developments, and share prices.

In the second step, employees assess themselves against the set expectations so that growth and developmental opportunities can be determined. This can be done using a TELUS self-assessment tool, a 360-degree survey tool, or through discussions with one's manager. In the third step, employees create a customized career development plan and set personal performance objectives. This involves a contract between employees and their manager as to what learning they will do in the next year, and what learning will be made available. The fourth step is to pursue learning options such as e-courses, instructor-led courses, job shadowing, mentoring, and individual coaching.

Sixty to 90 days after a learning program, employees meet with their manager to assess whether their learning has resulted in a change in on-the-job behaviour. Every learning event is expected to result in performance improvement or an action plan for more learning.

TELUS has received numerous rewards for its learning programs. For example, in 2004 TELUS was ranked sixth overall out of 24 recipients from five countries for using learning to drive corporate performance.

In 2005, TELUS was the only Canadian company to receive an international award in recognition of its commitment and excellence in enterprise learning. Josh Blair, Executive Vice President, Human Resources, was named the Learning Leader of the Year for making TELUS a learning organization. According to Judy Shuttleworth, TELUS Vice-Chair, Human Resources, "Under Josh's leadership, we have put strategies, programs, technologies and tools in place that enabled TELUS to become a true learning organization."

TELUS has also received the American Society of Training and Development's BEST awards four times. In 2007, the company was ranked third worldwide for implementing training programs that enable employees to better contribute to organizational performance.[1]

TELUS is a good example of how learning can be incorporated into the culture of an organization and how learning is a key component of corporate strategy and performance. It is also an example of how employee learning has a lot to do with the learning systems and infrastructure that exist in an organization.

In organizations like TELUS, learning is considered an important investment and receives a great deal of commitment and support from top management. As a result, employees have access to many opportunities for formal and informal learning.

In this chapter, we describe how organizations learn and how learning occurs at all levels of an organization. Training and development is an important part of the learning system in organizations, so you should understand how it fits into the larger picture of organizational learning.

What Is Organizational Learning?

Organizational learning refers to the process of creating, sharing, diffusing, and applying knowledge. However, organizational learning is not simply the sum of individual employee learning, nor is performance management limited to a training system that enables employees to learn and apply that learning. Organizational learning focuses on the systems used to create and distribute new knowledge on an organization-wide basis. Thus, organizational learning is a dynamic process of creating and sharing knowledge.

The traditional perspective of learning has always been strongly associated with training and development. The goals of training have been viewed from a traditional perspective that focuses on developing and improving employees' knowledge, skills, and abilities (KSAs). This is, of course, key for organizational learning because an organization can't learn unless individual employees learn. As noted by Peter Senge, the originator of the concept of the learning organization, "Organizations learn only through individuals who learn. Individual learning does not guarantee organizational learning. But without it, no organizational learning occurs" (p. 139).[2]

Organizational learning
The process of creating, sharing, diffusing, and applying knowledge in organizations

The training of employees usually focuses on current needs or deficiencies and is most effective when the future is relatively stable and predictable. However, in today's highly uncertain environment, organizations have realized the need to do more than just train employees for the current state of affairs. In a learning organization, employees learn through a variety of methods and processes, and they also learn how to continuously learn. This is of course the case at TELUS, where employees have a range of opportunities for learning that include meetings with a team leader, a weekly online video, an online magazine, weekly e-letters from the CEO, company-wide emails and voicemail messages, and a portal providing information on business units, human resources, news developments, and share prices.

To survive and develop, organizations must learn to manage by managing learning—the capacity to learn and change, consciously, continually, and quickly. A company's knowledge, including that contained in employees' minds, has always been a source of competitive advantage. The ability to learn faster than the competition is a source of sustainable competitive advantage.

For many organizations, creating learning systems and processes requires that they transform themselves into learning organizations. As you will learn in the next section, a learning organization does not represent the latest management fad. It represents a strategic shift and orientation in how organizations learn that can make an organization more competitive and effective.

The Learning Organization

In 1990, Peter Senge published a book called *The Fifth Discipline: The Art and Practice of the Learning Organization,* which set in motion a whole new approach to organizations that focuses on learning and, in particular, the "learning organization."

Learning organization

An organization that creates, acquires, organizes, shares, and retains information and knowledge, and uses new information and knowledge to change and modify its behaviour in order to achieve its objectives and improve its effectiveness

A **learning organization** is an organization that creates, acquires, organizes, shares, and retains information and knowledge, and uses new information and knowledge to change and modify its behaviour in order to achieve its objectives and improve its effectiveness. Learning organizations have established systems and structures to acquire, code, store, and distribute important information and knowledge so that it is available to those who need it, when they need it.

As a result, a learning organization is able to transform itself by acquiring and disseminating new knowledge and skills throughout the organization. Thus, it has an enhanced capacity to learn, adapt, and change its culture.[3]

Embedded in this concept is the ability to make sense of and respond to the surrounding environment. Organizational values, policies, systems, and structures support and accelerate learning for all employees. This learning results in continual improvements in work systems, products, services, teamwork, and management practices—a more successful organization. Organizational learning is learning that actually results in improvements.

In his groundbreaking book, Senge identified the following five "disciplines" to becoming a learning organization:[4]

1. *Personal mastery.* Individuals have to be open to others and willing to learn on a continual basis. People with personal mastery are always in a learning mode. This is fundamental for a learning organization because

Managing Performance Through Training and Development

organizations learn only if the individuals in them learn. If individuals do not learn, then organizational learning will not be possible.

2. *Building a shared vision.* This involves the development of a picture and vision of the future to which everyone can agree and be committed.

3. *Mental models.* Mental models refer to the images and assumptions that people have about themselves and the world. People need to be able to examine their mental models and be aware of how they influence their behaviour. Because such models can thwart or inhibit learning, people must understand them and hold them up to scrutiny.

4. *Team learning.* Learning takes place in teams through dialogue, discussion, and "thinking together." People need to be able to learn and act together.

5. *Systems thinking.* This discipline integrates the others and has to do with viewing the organization as a whole and being able to see and understand how its parts are interrelated.

In the next section, we discuss some important principles of learning organizations.

Principles of Learning Organizations

Learning organizations have a number of important principles. First, in a learning organization everybody is considered to be a learner. Employees recognize the need for learning and are actively involved in both formal and informal learning programs.

Second, in a learning organization, employees do not learn just by attending formal training programs. They also learn through informal means such as listening to and observing others. People learn from each other in a learning organization.

Third, learning is part of a change process and in fact enables change. When people are open to learning they are able to recognize the need for change, and learning is an important part of any change program. Thus, learning and change are closely related.

Fourth, continuous learning is considered to be a hallmark of learning organizations. Formal and informal learning are considered to be a regular part of every employee's job.

Fifth, learning organizations recognize that learning is an investment in the future of employees and the organization rather than an expense. Just as expenditures on plants and equipment are viewed as long-term capital investments, expenditures on learning are viewed as long-term investments in human capital.[5] Returning to the chapter-opening vignette, you will notice that all of these principles are characteristics of TELUS.

Learning Organizations in Canada

As described in the chapter-opening vignette, TELUS is a good example of a Canadian company that is a learning organization. But to what extent are other organizations in Canada learning organizations? The Conference Board of Canada has investigated this as part of a survey on learning and

TABLE 2.1

Key Dimensions of Learning Organizations

The Conference Board of Canada has identified the following four dimensions or pillars as critical in creating and sustaining a learning organization.

1. *Vision.* A clear vision of the organization's strategic direction and business goals and learning is part of the vision of the organization.
2. *Culture.* A learning organization has a culture that supports risk taking, experimentation, and learning. Knowledge, information sharing, and continuous learning are considered to be a regular part of organizational life and the responsibility of everybody in the organization. Informal learning is supported and encouraged.
3. *Learning dynamics and systems.* Employees are encouraged and expected to manage their own learning and development and are provided with formal and informal learning opportunities; they are coached and mentored by their managers.
4. *Knowledge management and infrastructure.* Learning organizations learn from their own experience and from competitors, customers, and experts. They have systems and structures to acquire, code, store, and distribute important information and knowledge so that it is available to those who need it and when they need it.

Sources: Parker, R. O., & Cooney, J. (2005). *Learning and development outlook 2005.* The Conference Board of Canada: Ottawa; Hughes, P. D., & Grant, M. (2007). *Learning and development outlook 2007.* The Conference Board of Canada: Ottawa.

development in Canadian organizations. First, they identified the following four dimensions or pillars of a learning organization/environment, which are described in Table 2.1:

1. Vision,
2. Culture,
3. Learning dynamics or systems, and
4. Knowledge management and infrastructure.

Second, they asked Canadian organizations to rate themselves on the four dimensions. They then formed a composite score based on scores for each of the dimensions and classified organizations as being a low, medium, or high learning organization/environment. What do you think they found? Are most Canadian organizations learning organizations?

As it turns out, not very many Canadian organizations are fully learning organizations. Only about half of Canadian organizations (56 percent) consider themselves to be a learning organization to some extent. In terms of the composite scores across the four dimensions, only 30 percent of the organizations were considered to be high learning organizations/environment; 50 percent were medium learning organizations/environment; and 20 percent were low learning organizations/environment.

However, there were differences across industries and regions. Organizations in the services industry scored higher than those in manufacturing and trade-based industries. Across regions, organizations in Quebec were the most likely to consider themselves a learning organization to some extent (78 percent), followed by organizations in Manitoba, Saskatchewan, and British Columbia.[6]

According to the Conference Board of Canada, Canadian organizations need to improve on a number of the key dimensions to become learning organizations. For example, senior management needs to be more explicit in terms of the type of knowledge that is important in their organization, and that they serve as learning role models to the rest of the organization (vision). Canadian organizations can also improve by creating a more positive learning culture and by encouraging and rewarding experimentation, risk taking, and challenging the status quo. As well, innovation, knowledge sharing, and productivity improvements should be a more frequent part of organizational life.

Canadian organizations can also improve by providing employees with more opportunities for formal and informal learning, and by supporting and developing managers in their roles as coaches, mentors, and facilitators of learning (learning dynamics and systems). Providing employees with opportunities to improve their learning skills is also necessary. They should be encouraged to participate in learning activities such as communities of practice, mentoring programs, job rotations, and cross training. Finally, Canadian organizations have to develop knowledge management systems and practices so that important information and knowledge that is essential to organizational success can be stored and made available to those who need it, whenever they need it.[7]

See Training Today 2.1, "Maintaining the Learning Culture at D&D Automation," for an example of a company with a learning culture.

Training Today 2.1

Maintaining the Learning Culture at D&D Automation

D&D Automation is a specialty engineering firm based in Stratford, Ontario, that designs and implements industrial automation control systems for industrial machinery, manufacturing lines, process environments, and other automated facilities. The company is a leading provider of discrete and process controls technology.

In the high-tech manufacturing industry, if employees are not up to date on all the latest technologies the company is doomed to fail. That's why training and development is part of the culture at D&D Automation and the firm's 40 employees are all responsible for maintaining this learning culture.

To stay on top, D&D introduced its Tech Leader program about five years ago. The company benchmarks all employees against the technologies they have to use and tracks their progress. The company highlights the technologies that are more important to the business and people can see where they should be learning.

To be at the minimum level in the Tech Leader program, an employee needs in-house or external training on

the technology. To move up, the employee needs to log a specific number of hours using the technology in different applications. And to achieve the level of guru, he needs formal, external training, which is paid for by the company.

To keep employees and the company as a whole up to date on new technologies, the company invites technology suppliers to weekly lunch-and-learn sessions. The supplier provides the lunch and 3 to 10 employees attend to learn about the new technology. Suppliers compete to get into the lunch-and-learn sessions, with the best coming back several times a year.

D&D Automation's culture of learning extends into the community as well. The company supports robotics and skills competitions at high schools and co-op education programs at post-secondary institutions.

Sources: Based on Anonymous. (May 19, 2008). CEOs talk: Training & development. *Canadian HR Reporter, 21* (10), 11–13; www.ddauto.com.

Learning Organizations and Organizational Effectiveness

While some people might find the notion of a learning organization to be a fad, there is evidence that learning organizations are highly effective. The Conference Board of Canada found that high learning organizations are almost 50 percent more likely to have higher overall levels of profitability than organizations not rated as learning organizations.[8]

High learning organizations also outperform other organizations in terms of employee retention, employee satisfaction, production of quality products and services, and overall organizational performance. High learning organizations believe they are more productive and profitable than their competition, and better able to satisfy their customers than low and medium learning organizations.[9] Research has also found a positive relationship between the practices of learning organizations and financial performance.[10]

Becoming a learning organization involves understanding the importance of knowledge and knowing how to manage it. In the next section, we focus on knowledge in organizations.

Knowledge in Organizations

Knowledge has become a critical resource for organizations in the information economy and is the main resource used to perform work in organizations. Employees require new knowledge to improve the products and services that their organizations provide, and organizations require knowledge to change and remain competitive in today's increasingly competitive and turbulent environment.[11]

Employee knowledge is a synthesis of information: all the facts, theories, and mental representations employees know about the world and, in the context of work, about their jobs and organization. **Knowledge** is the sum of what is known: a body of truths, information, and principles. Knowledge can be found in the minds of employees or transferred and stored in systems in organizations.

Knowledge

The sum of what is known; a body of truths, information, and principles

Knowledge is more than information, which we have in abundance, represented by dusty books filling shelves and facts floating across the Internet. Knowledge, on the other hand, is information that has been edited, put into context, and analyzed in a way that makes it meaningful and therefore valuable to an organization.[12] Knowledge can be grouped in two ways: explicit knowledge and tacit knowledge.

Explicit Knowledge

Explicit knowledge

Those things that you can buy or trade, such as patents or copyrights and other forms of intellectual property

Explicit knowledge refers to those things that you can buy or trade, such as patents or copyrights and other forms of intellectual property. The formula for making Coca-Cola and the brand name Coke are examples of intellectual properties that are extremely valuable. These tangible assets can normally be codified or formalized. Explicit knowledge can be written into procedures or coded into databases and is transferred fairly accurately. However, less than 20 percent of corporate knowledge is explicit. The other 80 percent of corporate knowledge is implicit and is difficult to quantify or even describe accurately.[13]

Tacit Knowledge

Implicit or **tacit knowledge** refers to the knowledge learned from experience and insight, and has been defined as intuition, know-how, little tricks, and judgment. Seasoned executives with tacit knowledge of a situation make million-dollar decisions.

Tacit knowledge is used by employees but is almost impossible to transfer. To grasp the concept of explicit knowledge and tacit knowledge, imagine describing the physical characteristics of your best friend; now try to describe the methods your friend would use to influence a supervisor. The former involves explicit knowledge, while the latter involves your tacit knowledge of your friend.

A well-known example of tacit knowledge is that of the decision-making behaviour of dealers in financial markets. That behaviour appears to be instinctual, but it is based on their past experience, what they read and hear, and the climate of the market. Extracting this knowledge from these dealers and then training others in this winning behaviour is extremely difficult.[14] The transfer of tacit knowledge requires personal contact. The personal contact must be extensive and built on trust and can include partnerships, apprenticeships, and mentoring.

Intellectual Capital

Intellectual capital is more than knowledge; intellectual capital is more like intelligence. Intelligence is the ability to create knowledge and includes the ability to learn, to reason, to imagine, to find new insights, to generate alternatives, and to make wise decisions.[15] By increasing the general level of intelligence of employees, organizations hope to create new knowledge that will result in new products, services, and processes.

Intellectual capital refers to an organization's knowledge, experience, relationships, process discoveries, innovations, market presence, and community influence. Intellectual capital is the source of innovation and wealth production—it is knowledge of value.[16] Intellectual capital has to be formalized, captured, and leveraged to produce a more highly valued asset.[17]

Intellectual capital is not like other assets; it grows with use. When an employee learns and uses that learning, he/she usually learns even more, and is motivated to learn again. He/she can share the learning and not deplete it or use it up, like other assets. Sharing learning results in the acquisition of even more knowledge, as you probably learned when you worked on projects with other people.

Intellectual capital is often divided into four types: human capital, renewal capital, structural capital, and relationship capital.

Tacit knowledge

Knowledge that is learned from experience and insight, and has been defined as intuition, know-how, little tricks, and judgment

Intellectual capital

An organization's knowledge, experience, relationships, process discoveries, innovations, market presence, and community influence

Human Capital

Human capital

The knowledge, skills, and abilities of employees

Human capital is the knowledge, skills, and abilities of employees. Included in this type of capital are some basic components of intelligence, such as the ability to learn, to reason, to analyze. Interpersonal skills, such as the ability to communicate with others and work in teams to generate better work methods, would also be part of an organization's human capital.

Renewal Capital

Renewal capital

Intellectual property, which consists of patents, licences, copyrights, and marketable innovations including products, services, and technologies

Renewal capital refers to what we have labelled intellectual property, which consists of patents, licences, copyrights, and marketable innovations including products, services, and technologies.

Structural Capital

Structural capital

Formal systems and informal relationships that allow employees to communicate, solve problems, and make decisions

Organizations are not amoebas; they need a skeleton or structure to function. Although the organizational chart captures some of the concept of **structural capital**, what we really mean are the formal systems and informal relationships that allow employees to communicate, solve problems, and make decisions. Structural capital is the set of structures, routines, and information systems that stay behind when employees go home. Sometimes these structures are represented by policies and procedures. For example, a company might require you to obtain the approval of the vice president of marketing before launching an innovative but costly advertising campaign. Another part of structural capital can be stored in databases and knowledge documents.

Relationship Capital

Relationship capital

An organization's relationships with suppliers, customers, and competitors that influence how they do business

Organizations, like individual employees, do not exist as islands. **Relationship capital** refers to an organization's relationship with suppliers, customers, and even competitors that influence how they do business. These relationships, particularly if they are based on trust and integrity, can be a source of competitive advantage.

Customer capital

The value of an organization's relationships with its customers

Customer capital is a subset of relationship capital. **Customer capital** is the value of an organization's relationships with its customers. For example, many small businesses enjoy high degrees of customer capital. Neighbours will shop at the local milk store even though the milk is more expensive because they know the owner and his/her family. In larger organizations, customer capital refers to all the efforts that a company makes to keep customers returning to buy its products or services.

Intellectual Capital Cycle

The four types of intellectual capital work in a cycle to increase intellectual capital. As more investments are made in human capital, employees are more capable and committed to increasing renewal and structural capital, leading to more productive relationship capital, resulting in better financial performance. The money can then be recycled to increase intellectual capital.

In this chapter, we focus on human capital: the sum and synergy of employee knowledge. Organizations want to develop their intellectual capital, and one way to do it is to create an environment in which learning is valued and actively managed.

The term *learning organization* refers to the programs and culture required to increase an organization's capacity to learn and to create intellectual capital. Creating and leveraging that knowledge has become a goal of many organizations. Training and performance specialists must understand that the creation and transfer of knowledge are strategic imperatives. Learning organizations have to actively manage this knowledge. TELUS is a good example of an organization that does this very well, as all employees at TELUS have a customized career development plan that sets out personal objectives for performance and learning, and organizational learning and performance plans are linked to corporate strategy.

In the next section, we discuss the different ways that organizations manage knowledge.

Knowledge Management

Knowledge management involves the creation, collection, storage, distribution, and application of compiled "know-what" and "know-how."[18] The value of knowledge occurs when it is available to those who need it, when they need it, and when it is put into action. Many companies today have realized the importance of knowledge management.

For example, at one automotive supplier, 30 percent of the design engineers' time was wasted solving problems that had already been solved in the company.[19] Companies know that knowledge isn't being shared when work is duplicated, or when expertise is available but hidden in the company and opportunities are lost, or when needless staffing takes place.

Recall from our earlier discussion of a learning organization that knowledge management/infrastructure is one of the four critical dimensions of a learning organization. Knowledge management/infrastructure refers to systems and structures that integrate people, processes, and technology so that important knowledge is coded, stored, and made available to members of an organization when they need it. Thus, in a learning organization, knowledge must be shared and distributed so that the organization can benefit from the cumulative knowledge of all employees.[20]

According to research conducted by the Conference Board of Canada, only 31 percent of respondents indicated that systems and structures exist within their organization to ensure that important knowledge is coded, stored, and made available to those who need it.[21] As noted earlier, Canadian organizations need to develop knowledge management systems and practices to ensure that important information is coded, stored, and made available for use throughout the organization.

In the remainder of this section, we describe four processes through which organizations manage knowledge—acquisition, interpretation, dissemination, and retention.[22] The ability to create and use knowledge is what characterizes a learning organization, and the practices used by organizations to manage knowledge are a critical part of knowledge management.

Knowledge management

The creation, collection, storage, distribution, and application of compiled "know-what" and "know-how"

Knowledge Acquisition

Companies acquire or create new knowledge in many ways. Some focus on well-respected creative processes such as brainstorming. Others may benchmark competitors or the best companies in the world. Some organizations engage in simulations or scenario planning to stimulate new ideas. Most scan the environment looking for new ideas or changing conditions and provide formal training to their employees.

Environmental Scanning

One of the most important ways for organizations to acquire information and knowledge is by scanning the environment. This involves tapping into both internal and external sources of information and establishing internal and external connections.

External sources of information include other organizations, customers, industry watchers, and the marketplace. These sources of information can provide an organization with information on how to improve their practices, services, and products. Internal sources of information include individuals, teams, and departments throughout an organization that might have information and knowledge that would be useful for others in the organization.

Learning organizations establish external connections through partnerships that involve the exchange of information. Internal connections might include the formation of cross-functional teams that meet to discuss changes in the industry and marketplace. Individual members form external connections through participation in professional associations, supplier forums, and through contacts with customers and others in the industry. The cross-functional team is therefore able to keep abreast of industry trends, tactics, and techniques. The key is for the organization to establish both internal and external connections and relationships in order to acquire and share information and knowledge.[23]

Formal Learning

One of the most traditional ways to increase the acquisition of new knowledge in an organization is through formal learning. Formal learning involves activities and events that are planned and designed by the organization with explicit goals and objectives. Training and development is an example of formal learning and an integral part of the knowledge-acquisition process in most organizations.

Informal Learning

In addition to formal learning, employees also learn through informal means. **Informal learning** refers to learning that occurs naturally as part of work and is not planned or designed by the organization. Informal learning is spontaneous, immediate, and task-specific. By comparison, formal learning has an expressed goal set by the organization and a defined process that is structured and sponsored by the organization.[24]

Informal learning

Learning that occurs naturally as part of work and is not planned or designed by the organization

TABLE 2.2

Formal and Informal Learning

FORMAL LEARNING

The organized transfer of work-related skills, knowledge and information. It includes activities such as classroom courses, structured on-the-job programs, workshops, seminars, instructional CDs and online courses.

INFORMAL LEARNING

The unstructured transfer of work-related skills, knowledge and information, usually during work. It includes ad hoc problem solving, incidental conversations, some types of coaching and mentoring, group problem-solving, lunch and learns, and communities of practice.

Source: Hughes, P. D., & Grant, M. (2007). *Learning and development outlook 2007*. The Conference Board of Canada: Ottawa.

Table 2.2 provides a more detailed definition of formal and informal learning, and Table 2.3 describes some of the differences between formal and informal learning.

It has been reported that as much as 70 percent of what employees learn and know about their jobs is learned through informal processes rather than through formal programs. This means that only 30 percent of what employees

TABLE 2.3

Differences between Formal and Informal Learning

FACTOR	FORMAL LEARNING	INFORMAL LEARNING
Control	The control of learning rests primarily in the hands of the organization	The control of learning rests primarily in the hands of the learner
Relevance	Variable relevance to participants because it is not tailored to the individual	Highly relevant and need-specific to the individual
Timing	There is usually a delay in that what is learned is not immediately used on the job	What is learned tends to be used immediately on the job
Structure	Highly structured and scheduled	Usually unstructured and occurs spontaneously
Outcomes	Tends to have specific outcomes	May not have specific outcomes

Sources: Day, N. (1998, June). Informal learning gets results. *Workforce Management, 77* (6), 31–35; Parker, R. O., & Cooney, J. (2005). *Learning and development outlook 2005*. The Conference Board of Canada: Ottawa. Reprinted by permission of The Conference Board of Canada.

learn is actually acquired through formal training and development programs sponsored by their organization.[25]

This is really not surprising. Employees have always learned without being formally trained. Many employees learn how to handle client problems by trial and error or from co-workers. For example, an employee might show co-workers a way to save time by combining two steps in handling customer complaints. Sometimes learning occurs when an employee returns from a formal training session and teaches others what he or she has learned. In fact, when a research team studied informal training at Motorola, they discovered that every hour of formal training yielded four hours of informal training. Thus, there is a strong connection between informal learning and formal training and there is evidence that informal learning has a significant effect on performance.[26]

Organizations are beginning to discover the importance and benefits of informal learning. For example, at Boeing Commercial Airplanes, researchers found that teams, personal documentation, supervisor–employee relationships, and shift changes provided rich examples of informal learning. At Motorola, during shift changes that overlap by half an hour or more assembly-line shift workers and their supervisors update the next shift on any problems that had occurred as well as the probable causes and possible solutions.

McDonald's has begun to focus on informal learning as a result of the large number of new employees who are hired and need to be trained every year. The company is looking for ways to foster episodes of informal learning between crew members. Given the increasing pace of work and the constant changes in technology, organizations are finding that informal learning is more important than ever as there often is not enough time for formal training.[27]

A recent study found that email was the most-used method for informal learning followed by accessing information from the organization's intranet. Other forms of informal learning include internet searches, communities of practice (see next section), voluntary mentoring, and coaching. Most of the best practices identified by the study involved the use of technology for information exchange (e.g., a social networking site for the company) and creating time for face-to-face interactions (e.g., team lunches and rearranging office layout to facilitate conversations).[28] To learn more about how to facilitate informal learning, see The Trainer's Notebook 2.1, "Facilitating Informal Learning in Organizations."

Communities of practice

Groups of people with common interests and concerns who meet regularly to share their experiences and knowledge, learn from each other, and identify new approaches for working and solving problems

Communities of Practice

Communities of practice refers to groups of people with common interests and concerns who meet regularly to share their experiences and knowledge, learn from each other, and identify new approaches for working and solving problems.[29] The core principles of communities of practice are that learning is social and that people learn from each other while working together on the job.[30] Thus, people in communities of practice share information and knowledge and in the process learn with and from each other.

The Trainer's Notebook 2.1

Facilitating Informal Learning in Organizations

Here are some strategies for facilitating informal learning in organizations:

- Encourage employees to actively foster informal learning opportunities on their own.
- Form casual discussion groups among employees with similar projects and tasks.
- Create meeting areas and spaces where employees can congregate and communicate with each other (e.g., water cooler, cafeteria).
- Remove physical barriers (e.g., office walls) that prevent employees from interacting and communicating.
- Create overlaps between shifts so shift workers on different shifts or from different departments can get to know each other and discuss work-related issues.
- Create small teams with a specialized focus on a product or problem.

- Allow groups to break from their routines for team discussions.
- Provide work teams with some autonomy to modify work processes when they have found a better way of doing things.
- Eliminate barriers to communication and give employees the authority to take training on themselves.
- Condense office spaces and make room for an open gathering area for coffee breaks and socializing.
- Match new hires with seasoned employees so they can learn from casual interaction and explicit teaching and mentoring.

Sources: Day, N. (1998, June). Informal learning gets results. *Workforce Management, 77* (6), 31–35; Dobbs, K. (2000, January). Simple moments of learning. *Training, 37* (1), 52–58; Stamps, D. (1998, January). Learning ecologies. *Training, 35* (1), 32–38.

Members ask each other for help, exchange best practices, and share information. Very often the information that is exchanged is implicit or tacit knowledge.[31]

According to Etienne Wenger, who along with Jean Lave coined the term communities of practice, three characteristics define a community of practice:[32]

- *Domain.* A community of practice must have a domain of interest that is shared among its members.
- *Community.* In a community of practice, there is interaction, discussion, sharing and exchanging information, and mutual assistance among members.
- *Practice.* Members in a community of practice are practitioners with resources, experiences, stories, and tools that they use to solve problems.

Communities of practice can exist within a department in an organization as well as across departments and regions and even include members from different organizations. Some communities of practice meet regularly face-to-face, while others use technology to communicate.[33]

Communities of practice have been found to be an effective method of learning that can improve organizational performance by driving strategy, generating new lines of business, solving problems, promoting the spread of best practices, developing skills, and aiding in the recruitment and retention of talent.[34] As a result, communities of practice are now being embraced by organizations all over the world.[35]

Chapter 2: Organizational Learning

Although communities of practice are informal, self-organizing groups that form naturally on their own, they can be created, fostered, and nurtured in organizations. To do so, managers need to focus on three things: [36]

- Identify potential communities of practice that will enhance an organization's strategic capabilities (identify potential members and bring them together).
- Develop an infrastructure to support communities of practice and enable members to share their expertise (they need to be integrated into the organization and supported).
- Assess the value of the organization's communities of practice (listen to stories from members about their experiences of how the community helped them solve a problem, save the company money, etc.).

For an example of an organization that has embraced communities of practice, see Training Today 2.2, "Communities of Practice at the Canada School of Public Service (CSPS)."

Knowledge Interpretation

Learning occurs when employees form their views of the organization and its environment. These views are often called mental models. Peter Senge describes **mental models** as "deeply ingrained assumptions, generalizations, or images that influence how we understand the world and how we take action" (p. 8).[37]

For example, if we have a mental model of managers as manipulators, then we will see all their actions as politically motivated and act accordingly. New knowledge will not be accepted because we cannot recognize and change our mental models. As one researcher noted, the acceptance of new

Mental models

Deeply ingrained assumptions, generalizations, or images that influence how we understand the world and how we take action

---

Training Today 2.2

Communities of Practice at the Canada School of Public Service (CSPS)

The Canada School of Public Service (CSPS) is the learning service provider for the Public Service of Canada. It helps to ensure that public service workers in Canada have the knowledge and skills they need to perform their jobs. The CSPS also plays a vital role in the delivery of the government's Learning, Training and Development Policy.

The CECP breaks the public service into six distinct learning communities. In 2006, the CSPS formed a Centre of Expertise in Communities of Practice (CECP) to provide expert guidance on the design of communities of practice for federal and public service employees. The CECP designs custom structures for each community and offers strategies, techniques, and tools. They also provide multiple methods for interaction such as face-to-face meetings, teleconferences, video conferences, and online functions such as listservs, email distribution lists, and threaded discussions.

So far the CECP has created more than 50 virtual communities of practice with more than 2,000 active participants across the country.

Sources: Salopek, J. (2008, July). Knowledge in numbers. T+D, 62 (7), 24–26; www.csps-efpc.gc.ca/index-eng.asp.

Managing Performance Through Training and Development

knowledge can be likened to an organ transplant—the possibility of rejection is highly probable.[38] Even when employees are aware of best practices in other companies or units, it might take more than two years for the information to be understood in a way that can be acted upon.

An effective way to develop shared mental models is to establish teams. The most valuable and innovative work-related learning occurs in work teams, solving real problems.[39] At Chevron Corporation, based in San Francisco, best-practice teams save the company millions of dollars annually by improving processes.[40]

Knowledge cannot be valued unless there is a shared understanding of its importance. Learning is social, and as teams work together they not only learn but also develop a common way of thinking about things, and a common identity emerges. These common perspectives are termed mental maps and are vitally important to the interpretation of the work environment and any lessons it contains. New learning is difficult to accept and apply without this shared perspective.

Knowledge Dissemination

Moving products, services, and money through and between organizations is a standard process for most organizations. Moving ideas requires a different set of skills and even different norms.

Companies must design systems or ways of sharing knowledge so that others can improve their work practices. You might say that information has always been shared between employees, and knowledge management is just a new way of describing communication. Although employees have always passed on new ideas by talking with each other, the difference is that these informal systems can be replaced by formal mechanisms grounded in technology.

Information and communication technologies (ICTs) allow for increased codification of knowledge; that is, its transformation into information that can easily be transmitted. Today, most organizations have electronic bulletin boards, libraries, virtual conference rooms, or connected knowledge bases. Through technology, employees can exchange proposals, presentations, spreadsheets, specifications, and so on.

An intranet is a critical component for managing knowledge. An employee who posts a question or seeks advice can receive that information in hours, not weeks. Just as we use the little help wizards in our software, we could use a company expert or subject-matter specialist who would pop up on the monitor while we are working on a new project—an instant coach!

Knowledge Retention

As noted earlier, knowledge resides in the minds of employees or in systems created to store that knowledge. To capitalize on these sources of knowledge, organizations must build tools to quickly compile, store, and retrieve this knowledge, a kind of intellectual inventory. These are called knowledge repositories.

Chapter 2: Organizational Learning

Knowledge repositories should not be seen as sacred libraries in which great books are stored and never read. The system has to be designed to encourage its use, to facilitate interaction. One reason for the growth of interest in this area is that the cost of managing it has been significantly lowered through technology.

There are ways to capture and store knowledge in information systems for later use. Some of these are highly structured databases. Digitalized knowledge can be more easily and cheaply processed, indexed, searched, converted, and transmitted.

Some knowledge repositories are more informal lists of lessons learned, white papers, presentations, and so on. Others are more actively stored in discussion groups. Most have links to the originators of the documents or at least to those who tend to access the repositories, thus signalling who is actively interested in that area. These collaborative filters monitor databases and intranet sites, and can tell you which sites others with interests similar to yours have found useful.

Not all knowledge repositories are based on computer technology. Some knowledge is tacit and not easily codified. Some more traditional means of storing knowledge might include transcripts or audiocassettes from strategic planning sessions, consultants' reports in text or multimedia formats, video-taped presentations, market-trend analyses, and any number of information-rich resources.

Oral histories are another way to capture knowledge, particularly when organizations suffer the memory loss associated with departures and downsizing. For example, in the United Kingdom, Rothschild PLC used an exit interview to capture the vast amount of knowledge that its departing head of public relations held. A professional with HR and PR experience interviewed the executive for an entire afternoon, and the conversation was recorded. Information that would not normally be transmitted to the successor was uncovered, edited, and indexed.[41] Other companies record oral histories from retiring managers.

At Kraft General Foods, the brand manager of Cracker Barrel Cheese was facing declining sales. She consulted the archives, where the interview transcripts with the manager who had launched the brand were recorded. Based on these insights into the original goals for the cheese, the current brand manager was able to reinvigorate the brand.

A Multilevel Systems Approach to Organizational Learning

Although the emphasis of this chapter has been on organizational learning and knowledge management, it is important to understand that learning in organizations involves a multilevel and integrated systems approach. This means that we have to understand the linkages between different organizational levels (i.e., organization, groups, and individuals) within the organizational system.

Figure 2.1 presents a multilevel systems approach to organizational learning. The model shows that there are three levels of learning in organizations: the organizational level, the group level, and the individual

FIGURE 2.1

A Multilevel Systems Model of Organizational Learning

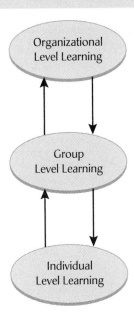

An environment for learning and the acquisition and exchange of knowledge and information.

Organizational Level Learning

The opportunity for groups to interact, communicate, and share information.

Group Level Learning

Individuals must have formal and informal opportunities for learning. Learning and the transfer of knowledge and information must be rewarded.

Individual Level Learning

level. Each level is connected to the levels above and below it which means that learning at each level is influenced by the other levels.

Organizational Level

The organizational level consists of the organization's leadership, culture, vision, strategy, and structure. Leadership is extremely important because top management needs to articulate a vision for learning and must support it and devote resources and time to the development of a learning organization. The organization must also develop and implement strategies for knowledge management and learning.

Organizational systems are necessary for the organization to acquire information and to distribute it throughout the organization. Thus, an organization must create processes, practices, policies, and structures that enable the acquisition, exchange, and distribution of information and knowledge throughout the organization. As well, the organization's culture for learning will influence the extent to which teams and individuals seek out new information and learning opportunities, and transfer new knowledge and skills on the job. There must be a culture that supports and encourages continuous learning.

Group Level

Important factors at the group level include group climate, culture, norms, group dynamics, and processes, as well as the nature of the group task in terms of its complexity and task interdependence. Learning at the group level will be influenced by these factors.

For example, the extent to which informal learning occurs will be influenced by the group's culture and norms for learning, and the extent to which it is rewarded will be influenced by the group's climate. The nature of the group's tasks will also influence learning. Groups that perform more complex tasks are more likely to realize the benefits of training and learning. When the tasks that group members perform are interdependent, there will be a greater need for the group to interact and share information. Thus, these group-level factors will influence the extent to which learning occurs at the group level.

Individual Level

At the individual level, employees must have formal and informal opportunities to learn. This means that the organization needs to provide structured and formal training and development programs in order for employees to acquire new knowledge and skills, as well as opportunities to share and exchange information. In addition, employees must also be rewarded for learning and applying what they learn on the job.

Multilevel Linkages

The multilevel systems model of organizational learning also shows how each level is connected to the other levels. For example, the systems and processes that exist at the organizational level influence the extent to which learning occurs at the group level, and group-level factors influence learning at the individual level. In addition, individual learning will influence group learning, and group learning will influence organizational learning.[42]

In summary, the multilevel systems approach to organizational learning demonstrates the importance of each level of the organization for learning. In order for organizations to learn, systems and processes must be in place at each level. After all, organizations cannot learn if individuals and groups do not learn, and individuals and groups cannot learn if organizations do not provide opportunities for learning and the sharing and exchange of knowledge and information.

Organizational Learning and Training

In this chapter, we have focused on learning in organizations, the learning organization, and knowledge management. The emphasis has been on the organization, although the focus of this text is on the training and development of individuals.

At this point, you might be asking yourself, "What is the connection between organizational learning and training?" Based on the previous section, you know that training and development is an important element of organizational learning and a key element of organizational learning is individual learning. In fact, research conducted by the Conference Board of Canada found a positive relationship between a learning organization and an organization's expenditures on formal training programs.

TABLE 2.4

Training and Development in Learning Organizations

Research conducted by the Conference Board of Canada found that high-learning organizations invest more in training and development than low-learning organizations in the following ways:

1. Average total training expenditure per employee.
2. Average percentage of payroll spent on training.
3. Average total hours per employee.
4. Average percentage of training delivered by technology.
5. Training, learning, and development is part of employees' formal goals.
6. Leadership development is believed to be more effective.

Sources: Parker, O., & Cooney, J. (2005). *Learning and development outlook 2005.* The Conference Board of Canada: Ottawa; Hughes, P. D., & Grant, M. (2007). *Learning and development outlook 2007.* The Conference Board of Canada: Ottawa.

High learning organizations invest more in training and development and have more effective training systems than low and medium learning organizations. For example, high learning organizations spend over $1,000 per employee, while low learning organizations spend $615 per employee. They also spend more as a proportion of their payroll (2.0 versus 1.5 for low learning organizations), and more full-time employees receive training in high learning organizations (81 percent) compared to low learning organizations (56 percent). Table 2.4 provides more information about training and development in high learning organizations.[43]

These findings indicate that there is a connection between training and development and organizational learning. Learning organizations exceed other organizations in terms of both training practices and expenditures.

In summary, it should now be clear to you that formal training and development is important and necessary for organizational learning. While we have focused on learning at the organizational level, the fact is that organizational learning occurs only if individuals learn, and one of the major ways that individuals learn is through training and development.

In the next chapter, we shift our focus to individual learning. For now, we leave you with a model (Figure 2.2) that shows the linkages from training and

FIGURE 2.2

Training and Development and Organizational Learning

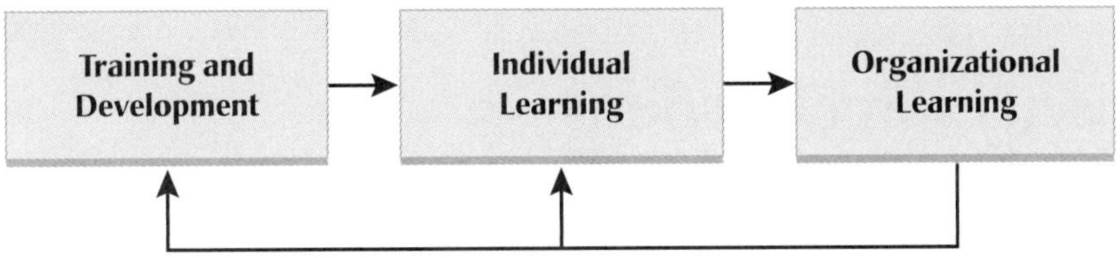

development to individual learning and organizational learning. The model shows how the design and delivery of training programs influence individual learning, and how individual learning leads to organizational learning. The feedback loops show that organizational learning also influences training and development as well as individual learning.

Summary

In this chapter, we described the meaning and importance of learning in organizations and the management of knowledge. The five disciplines and the principles of a learning organization were described as well as four dimensions that are critical for creating and sustaining a learning organization. We also discussed different types of knowledge in organizations and intellectual capital. The knowledge management practices that organizations use to acquire, interpret, disseminate, and retain knowledge were also described. The chapter concluded with a multilevel systems model of organizational learning and a discussion of how training and development is connected to individual and organizational learning. In the next chapter, we focus on individual learning.

Key Terms

communities of practice   p. 46

customer capital   p. 42

explicit knowledge   p. 40

human capital   p. 42

informal learning   p. 44

intellectual capital   p. 41

knowledge   p. 40

knowledge management   p. 43

learning organization   p. 36

mental models   p. 48

organizational learning   p. 35

relationship capital   p. 42

renewal capital   p. 42

structural capital   p. 42

tacit knowledge   p. 41

Web Links

Canada School of Public Service (CSPS): www.csps-efpc.gc.ca

D&D Automation: www.ddauto.com

Kraft General Foods: www.kraftfoods.com

TELUS: www.telus.com

Discussion Questions

1. Discuss the role of teams and leaders in a learning organization. How do teams and leaders contribute to a learning organization, and what are some of the tasks and activities that they should perform?

Managing Performance Through Training and Development

2. Discuss the importance and relevance of technology for a learning organization and knowledge management. How important is technology and how should it be used in a learning organization and for knowledge management?
3. Discuss the role of the training function and the role of the trainer in a learning organization. How do these roles change in a learning organization? What knowledge and skills does a trainer require in a learning organization?
4. Discuss the multilevel systems model of organizational learning. How are the three levels related and what should organizations do to facilitate learning at each level?
5. Why are there not more learning organizations in Canada? What should Canadian organizations do to become learning organizations?
6. What is the difference between formal and informal learning and what can organizations do to facilitate informal learning? What are the advantages and disadvantages of formal and informal learning?
7. What are communities of practice and how do they contribute to learning and knowledge management in organizations? What can organizations do to create communities of practice?

The Great Training Debate

1. Debate the following: Informal learning is more important than formal learning (e.g., training programs) and organizations should focus more on informal learning and less on formal training programs.

Using the Internet

1. The Conference Board of Canada has developed the Learning Performance Index. To find out about the Learning Performance Index, go to: **www.conferenceboard.ca/topics/humanresource/lpi/default.aspx**. Answer the following questions:

   a. What is the Learning Performance Index (LPI) and what are its advantages and benefits?
   b. How does the LPI work?
   c. What are the LPI deliverables?
   d. Download the LPI (click Free Assessment Tool) and complete the LPI for an organization you are currently working in or the most recent organization where you were employed. Calculate the total score for each section (vision, infrastructure, culture, learning dynamics, training and investment evaluation) and the overall total score. Refer to Section 4 to interpret your results. Based on your results, what can you say about the organization you evaluated? What does the

organization need to improve to become a high-performing learning organization?

2. To learn more about organizational learning and the learning organization, go to: **www.brint.com/papers/orglrng.htm** and find answers to the following questions:

   a. What is organizational learning?
   b. What is a learning organization?
   c. What is the difference between organizational learning and a learning organization?
   d. What is adaptive learning versus generative learning?
   e. What is the manager's role in the learning organization?
   f. What is the relationship between strategy and organizational learning?
   g. What is the role of information systems in the learning organization?
   h. Does IT impose any constraints on organizational learning?

3. To find out more about learning organizations in Canada, go to Industry Canada at **www.collectionscanada.gc.ca/ webarchives/20060205045403/http://strategis.ic.gc.ca/epic/internet/ incts-scf.nsf/en/sl00019e.html** and answer the following questions:

   a. What is a leading-edge learning organization?
   b. What are the performance characteristics of a leading-edge learning organization?

Exercises

In-Class

1. Develop a checklist to determine if the organization in which you work (or have worked) is a learning organization. How many of the four critical elements and principles of a learning organization are characteristic of your organization? What does your organization have to do to become a learning organization?

2. Think about a previous or current job you have held in terms of what you learned and how you learned it. Make a list of the three or five most important things you learned on your job. Once you have made your learning list, indicate how each item on your list was learned. Was it through formal or informal means? Be specific in terms of the formal or informal activity that contributed to your learning. What does your list tell you about learning in organizations? What should you do if you want to improve your learning?

3. Imagine that you are a director of training in an organization and the company president wants to meet with you to discuss becoming a learning organization. What will you tell him or her about learning organizations and what the organization must do to become a learning organization? Prepare a short presentation in which you present your main ideas and suggestions for becoming a learning organization. When complete, pair up with another member of the class and take

turns presenting and evaluating each other's presentation. If time permits, presentations to the class can also be made.

4. Imagine that you are a director of training and development in an organization and the company president wants to meet with you to discuss how the organization can improve its management of knowledge. What will you tell him or her about knowledge management and what the organization must do to improve its management of knowledge? Prepare a short presentation in which you present your main ideas and suggestions for knowledge management. When complete, pair up with another member of the class and take turns presenting and evaluating each other's presentation. If time permits, presentations to the class can also be made.

5. As a student, you spend a great deal of time learning. But how exactly do you learn? Make a list of the formal and informal ways you learn. Do you learn more from formal or informal methods? If you want to improve your learning, what are some of the things you might do? Be specific in terms of both formal and informal ways to improve your learning.

6. If you were asked to help an organization learn about and create communities of practice, what would you tell them and how would you proceed? Prepare an outline for your presentation that describes the following: What is a community of practice? Who should be in a community of practice? What will the community of practice do and how will it do it? What are the potential benefits of a community of practice? When complete, pair up with another member of the class and take turns presenting and evaluating each other's presentation. If time permits, presentations to the class can also be made.

In-the-Field

1. Contact the human resources department of an organization and ask them if you can talk about their attempts to become a learning organization. Ask them if they are a learning organization and what they have done in order to become a learning organization. How do they rate on the four key dimensions of a learning organization (see Table 2.1)? Do you think they are a learning organization? What do they still need to do to become a learning organization?

2. Contact the human resources department of an organization and ask them if you can talk about how they manage knowledge. Ask them about their knowledge management practices and what they do to acquire, interpret, disseminate, and retain knowledge. How can the organization improve its management of knowledge?

3. Conduct an interview with several people you know who are currently employed. Interview them about how they learn in their organization. Ask questions about how and what they have learned through formal

and informal learning opportunities. Based on their responses, answer the following questions:

a. Did they learn more or less from formal or informal learning?
b. Did they have more or fewer formal or informal opportunities for learning?
c. Which type of learning was most effective for them: formal or informal learning?
d. What did they learn from formal and informal learning? Did they learn similar or different things from each?
e. What kinds of practices were used in their organization for formal and informal learning?

4. Contact the human resources department of an organization and ask if you can talk to them about communities of practice. Once you have found an organization that has communities of practice, ask the following questions:

a. How many communities of practice does the organization have and why were they implemented?
b. Who are the members of the communities of practice and how were they chosen?
c. How were the communities of practice created and how are they structured?
d. What are the methods used to interact and exchange information?
e. How effective are the communities of practice and how are they evaluated?

Based on the answers to these questions, prepare a brief report or presentation on how to create and structure communities of practice and how to make them effective.

Case Incident

NASA's Knowledge Management Crisis

In the 1990s, NASA's lunar program lost critical knowledge as a result of downsizing when Saturn 5 engineers were encouraged to take early retirement. Commenting on the early retirements, one NASA manager said, "If we want to go to the moon again, we'll be starting from scratch . . . all of that knowledge has disappeared. It would take at least as long and cost at least as much to go back." Now NASA wants to ensure that the expertise of other senior engineers isn't lost when they retire.

Questions

1. What kind of knowledge and intellectual capital is NASA losing and what effect does this have on the organization?
2. What should NASA do to prevent the loss of knowledge when senior engineers retire?

Sources: Foord Kirk, J. (2005, December 3). The cost of disappearing knowledge. *The Toronto Star*, D10; Weinstein, M. (2005, December). NASA training program blasts off. *Training, 42* (12), 8–9.

Case Study

Knowledge Management at the Ontario Ministry of Education

Kathryn Everest, knowledge management consultant for IBM Canada Ltd. Business Consulting Services, was preparing for a meeting with Ontario's Deputy Minister of Education. The purpose of the meeting was to secure top-level support for an early-stage knowledge management program at the ministry.

The interest in knowledge management began in early 2000 as a few managers from EDU realized that something had to be done to correct some of the inefficiencies. For example, the rate at which electronic data was generated was increasing and electronic data was significantly different from paper-based documents in the way it was used and handled. For every document created, there were often up to 20 different versions.

On a broader scope, there was increasing difficulty finding out what knowledge was available and who to approach for that expertise. For example, new policy development required a thorough review of the old policy, a review of the internal discussion concerning the direction in which the new policy should take, the results of external consultation (if conducted and if available), and the location of resident experts with the ministry who could guide the new policy's development. Gathering data and experts together was not an easy task. And loss of knowledge due to turnover could be better managed.

For the past few weeks, Everest had conducted an initial study of ministry needs and believed that the organization could benefit from one or more knowledge management solutions.

The first project involved assessing the current state of knowledge management at EDU and drafting proposals to improve upon it. The IBM team included Everest and another full-time IBM consultant, Jill Goodridge. They relied on a series of meetings, 15 interviews, workshops, and one social capital survey. IBM's social capital survey evaluates an organization's social capital. According to IBM, social capital, the critical "bandwidth" for knowledge transfer in an organization, consisted of the following: Trust, informal networks, culture and common context, and vocabulary.

Both Everest and Goodridge worked with members of EDU's steering committee to schedule meetings with busy directors and staff members. Rooms were booked for the workshops and interviews. The social capital survey covered topics such as the perceived degree of sharing and trust within the organization and the degree to which requests for information were met and credit was received. Prior to administering the social capital survey, the questions were distributed to key officials to ensure that the questions were appropriate and meaningful.

After three months, the IBM consultants presented their findings. Focus groups revealed that the ministry had strong informal networks used by policy professionals and issue coordinators, and well-defined roles for issue management. There were pockets of specialized tacit knowledge and strong research skills within the organization.

For example, at EDU, there were two different experts in child psychology with specialized knowledge relevant to a particular education policy formation

Chapter 2: Organizational Learning

project. But neither expert had ever met the other because each was located in different offices. The ministries were already engaged in knowledge sharing opportunities such as "Lunch and Learn," integrated planning forums, and regular staff meetings; there was informal mentoring for new hires; and there was verbal support to improve the performance measurement capability of managers.

Managers were keen on learning how to measure and manage partners such as school boards. Although EDU set up education policies and frameworks, it was up to the school boards to execute the plans as they were the service providers – hence the requirement for EDU managers to monitor and measure school board progress towards goals.

The consultants found that much of the ministries' knowledge was tacit. For example, when asked what information sources they relied on, participants invariably stated that they referred to other people. Particular Web sites or documents were never relied on for information.

Document knowledge was difficult to locate and share. Participants displayed less confidence in documented knowledge versus key personnel contacts. They typically wondered whether documented knowledge was complete, up-to-date and available for public consumption (just in case the document was meant only for internal use).

There were significant cultural issues that inhibited knowledge sharing; confidentiality issues inhibited and restricted collaboration and knowledge sharing. Participants were extremely careful with data, information and knowledge that came their way, preferring to err on the side of limited disclosure versus full disclosure. They believed that being conservative with regard to how much information was released would be a good safeguard against unwittingly releasing sensitive information both internally or externally.

EDU had a weak knowledge-sharing infrastructure, and limited knowledge and information-sharing resulted in duplication of efforts. There were instances where two different parties proceeded to conduct similar research on the same topic because each was unaware of the other's intentions (and even existence).

Miscellaneous findings included the following: managers could not readily identify experts in relevant fields; employee attrition resulted in lost knowledge; there was a general sense of "information overload"; much of the information was thought to be obsolete; and efforts to research topics were inefficient.

Kathryn Everest wondered how she should approach her meeting with the Deputy Minister of Education, given that there seemed to be internal ministry concerns about knowledge sharing. As she reviewed her notes, Everest wanted to know which solution or combination of solutions she should recommend and what implementation challenges she could expect to face.

Source: Excerpt from a case prepared by Ken Mark under the supervision of Professor Darren Meister. (2004). IBM's knowledge management proposal for the Ontario Ministry of Education. Richard Ivey School of Business, The University of Western Ontario. 9B05E007. Ken Mark prepared this case under the supervision of Professor Darren Meister solely to provide material for class discussion. The authors do not intend to illustrate either effective or ineffective handling of a managerial situation. The authors may have disguised certain names and other identifying information to protect confidentiality. Ivey Management Services prohibits any form of reproduction, storage or transmittal without its written permission. This material is not covered under authorization from any reproduction rights organization. Copyright © 2004, Ivey Management Service. One-time permission to reproduce Ivey cases granted by Ivey Management Services on February 27, 2009.

Questions

1. To what extent do you think the Ontario Ministry of Education (EDU) is a learning organization? Refer to Table 2.1 on the key dimensions of learning organizations and evaluate the EDU on each dimension. What does the EDU have to improve to become a learning organization?

2. Comment on the extent to which knowledge at the EDU is explicit and tacit. What are the implications for knowledge management?

3. How well does the EDU manage knowledge? Evaluate the EDU's knowledge-management practices with respect to the acquisition, interpretation, dissemination, and retention of knowledge. What do they need to improve and why?

4. Do you think Everest should recommend communities of practice as a solution? What are some implementation challenges of communities of practice for the EDU?

5. What solutions would you recommend to the EDU to improve their management of knowledge? What are some potential problems that might arise in implementing your solutions?

6. What does this case tell you about the role of knowledge in organizations and knowledge management?

References

1. Anonymous. (2007, October). TELUS Communications. *T+D, 61* (10), 79; Anonymous. (2004, March 8). TELUS awarded for development system. *Canadian HR Reporter, 17* (5), 16; Anonymous. (2003, November). Canada calling. *T+D, 57* (11), 34, 46, 47; (2005, March 29). Executive honoured for making TELUS a learning organization, www.telus.ca (obtained July 4, 2006).

2. Senge, P. M. (1990). *The fifth discipline: The art and practice of the learning organization.* New York: Doubleday.

3. Bennet, J. K., & O'Brien, M. J. (1994, June). The building blocks of the learning organization. *Training, 31* (6), 41–49.

4. Senge, P. M. (1990).

5. Sigler, J. (1999). Best practices and guiding principles: A training guide to successful development of a learning organization. *Futurics, 23* (1&2), 67–73.

6. Parker, R. O., & Cooney, J. (2005); Hughes, P. D., & Grant, M. (2007). *Learning and development outlook 2007.* The Conference Board of Canada: Ottawa.

7. Harris-Lalonde, S. (2001); Cooney, J., & Cowan, A. (2003). *Training and development outlook 2003.* The Conference Board of Canada: Ottawa.

8. Harris-Lalonde, S. (2001). *Training and development outlook.* The Conference Board of Canada: Ottawa.

9. Parker, R. O., & Cooney, J. (2005). *Learning & development outlook 2005.* The Conference Board of Canada: Ottawa.

10. Ellinger, A. D., Ellinger, A. E., Baiyin, Y., & Howton, S. W. (2002). The relationship between the learning organization concept and firms' financial performance: An empirical assessment. *Human Resource Development Quarterly, 13,* 5–21.

11. Sigler, J. (1999).

12. Tapscott, D. (1998). Make knowledge an asset for the whole company. *Computerworld, 32* (51), 32.

13. Stamps, D. (1999, March). Is knowledge management a fad? *Training, 36* (3), 36–42.

14. Baets, W. R. J. (1998). *Organizational learning and knowledge technologies in a dynamic environment*. Boston: Kluwer Academic Publishers.
15. Miller, W. (1999, January). Building the ultimate resource. *Management Review*, 42–45.
16. Miller, W. (1999, January).
17. Stewart, T. (1994, October 3). Intellectual capital. *Fortune*, 68–74.
18. Miller, W. (1999, January).
19. Kransdorff, A. (1997, September). Fight organizational memory loss. *Workforce Management*, 34–39.
20. Sigler, J. (1999).
21. Cooney, J., & Cowan, A. (2003).
22. Garvin, D. A. (1998). The processes of organization and management. *Sloan Management Review, 39* (4), 33–50.
23. Jeppesen, J. C. (2002). Creating and maintaining the learning organization. In K. Kraiger (Ed.), *Creating, implementing, and managing effective training and development: State-of-the-art lessons for practice* (pp. 302–330). San Francisco, CA: Jossey-Bass.
24. Stamps, D. (1998, January). Learning ecologies. *Training, 35* (1), 32–38; Roseman, E. (2001, August 29). Delta Hotels knows how to keep workers. *The Toronto Star*, E2.
25. Day, N. (1998, June). Informal learning gets results. *Workforce Management, 77* (6), 31–35; Dobbs, K. (2000, January). Simple moments of learning. *Training, 37* (1), 52–58.
26. Day, N. (1998, June).
27. Stamps, D. (1998); Dobbs, K. (2000, January).
28. Paradise, A. (2008, July). Informal learning: Overlooked or overhyped? *T+D, 62* (7), 52–53.
29. Wenger, E. C., & Snyder, W. M. (2000). Communities of practice: The organizational frontier. *Harvard Business Review, 78* (1), 139–145.
30. Stamps, D. (1997). Communities of practice. *Training, 34* (2), 34–42.
31. Stamps, D. (1997); Salopek, J. (2008, July). Knowledge in numbers. *T+D, 62* (7), 24–26.
32. Salopek, J. (2008, July).
33. Wenger, E. C., & Snyder, W. M. (2000).
34. Wenger, E. C., & Snyder, W. M. (2000).
35. Salopek, J. (2008, July).
36. Wenger, E. C., & Snyder, W. M. (2000).
37. Senge, P. M. (1990).
38. Stamps, D. (1999).
39. Stamps, D. (1997). Communities of practice: Learning is social, training is irrelevant? *Training, 3* (2), 34–42.
40. Neely Martinez, M. (1998, February). The collective power. *HRM Magazine*, 88–94.
41. Kransdorff, A. (1997, September).
42. Kozlowski, S. W. J., & Salas, E. (1997). A multilevel organizational systems approach for the implementation and transfer of training. In J. K. Ford, S. W. J. Kozlowski, K. Kraiger, E. Salas, and M. S. Teachout (Eds.), *Improving training effectiveness in work organizations*. Mahwah, NJ: Lawrence Erlbaum Associates.
43. Parker, R. O., & Cooney, J. (2005); Hughes, P. D., & Grant, M. (2007).

Learning and Motivation

Chapter Learning Outcomes

After reading this chapter, you should be able to:

- define learning and describe learning outcomes
- describe the three stages of learning and Kolb's learning styles
- describe conditioning theory and social cognitive theory and their implications for training and development
- describe adult learning theory and its implications for training and development
- define motivation and describe need and process theories of motivation and their implications for training and development
- describe the differences between mastery and performance goals and between distal and proximal goals and their implications for training and development
- define training motivation and discuss its predictors and consequences
- describe the variables in the model of training effectiveness and how they relate to learning and retention

The Ontario Division of the Canadian Cancer Society recently decided to take a more strategic approach to its on-boarding program. The division has hundreds of employees and thousands of volunteers across Ontario.

Senior staff at the society consulted with key groups including the executive team, regional employees, and recent hires so that they could customize an approach that resonates with new hires. One of the objectives of the new program was to reduce voluntary turnover by equipping new hires with a greater understanding of and connection to the work of the society as a whole.

The on-boarding program contains many elements. One part focuses on "foundation knowledge" to provide every new hire, regardless of position or level, a consistent understanding of the society including things such as key people, portfolios, and programs. Another important element is experience. A new hire needs to engage in certain activities to develop the partnerships and personal insights critical to early visibility, credibility, and success.

Thought was also given to the timing of different on-boarding activities so the process unfolds in a logical and integrated way throughout the first year of employment. The activities are incorporated into detailed checklists to promote a consistent experience and ensure all elements are covered.

To help guide new employees through the organization's massive intranet, a typical volunteer named Ray was selected as a guide. Through his story as both a volunteer and cancer survivor, Ray helps the new hire absorb information—mission, cancer research and statistics, organization structure, and fundraising activities—in a more logical, dynamic, and memorable way.

For example, Ray talks about his community work and his family's participation in the Canadian Cancer Society Relay for Life, a national fundraising event. He then invites the new hire to click on appropriate links to drill deeper into fundraising information. Ray's story reinforces the importance of volunteers and provides the perspectives of both a client and volunteer.

Because of the importance of developing quality relationships early in a new employee's tenure, the society also developed a series of discussion guides to help new employees, their managers, and their internal and external clients talk about mutual expectations. In one guide, a new hire and her manager ask each other a set of questions to help define the "soft" side of the working relationship. Another guide helps the new employee interview key clients to understand their priorities and expectations. This helps the employee take action and establish credibility early on.

Another part of the experience is learning how the society's work touches the lives of Canadians. Whether it is a visit to a regional cancer centre, participating in one of many fundraising activities, or sitting in on a call from a cancer patient in the call centre, new employees gain a personal understanding of how the society operates. The end result is that every employee and volunteer feels empowered to be an ambassador in their community by being able to talk from the heart based on their own experiences.[1]

The Canadian Cancer Society's new employee on-boarding program focuses on not only *what* new employees must learn but also *how* they learn, two topics that are the focus of this chapter.

In Chapter 2, we discussed organizational learning and the learning organization. However, in order for organizations to learn and become learning organizations, the people in them must learn. In this chapter, we focus on how people learn and their motivation to learn. First, we define what we mean by learning and describe learning outcomes. We then discuss the stages of learning followed by a review of learning and motivation theories and their implications for training. We conclude the chapter with a model that links training and personal factors to learning, behaviour, and organizational effectiveness.

What Is Learning?

Although training is the focus of this book, it is important to keep in mind that what we are really trying to accomplish through training and development is learning. In other words, training is simply the means for accomplishing the goal, and the goal is learning.

Learning is the process of acquiring knowledge and skills. It involves a change of state that makes possible a corresponding change in one's behaviour. Learning is the result of experiences that enable one to exhibit newly acquired behaviours.[2] Learning occurs "when one experiences a new way of acting, thinking, or feeling, finds the new pattern gratifying or useful, and incorporates it into the repertoire of behaviours" (p. 833).[3] When a behaviour has been learned, it can be thought of as a skill.

New hires and volunteers at the Ontario division of the Canadian Cancer Society acquire knowledge and understanding of the society, fundraising, developing quality relationships, interviewing clients, and how the society operates. The intent is for them to develop an understanding of and connection to the work of the society as a whole and to be an ambassador in their community.

In the realm of training, the most fundamental issue is whether trainees have learned what was covered in a training program.[4] But what exactly do trainees learn in training? In the next section, we describe two schemes for categorizing learning outcomes.

Learning
The process of acquiring knowledge and skills, and a change in individual behaviour as a result of some experience

Learning Outcomes

Learning can be described in terms of domains or outcomes of learning. Table 3.1 shows the learning outcomes of two categorization schemes. The first one is by Robert Gagné, who developed the best known classification of learning outcomes. According to Gagné, learning outcomes can be classified according to five general categories:[5]

1. *Verbal information.* Facts, knowledge, principles, and packages of information or what is known as *declarative knowledge*.
2. *Intellectual skills.* Concepts, rules, and procedures that are known as *procedural knowledge*. Procedural rules govern many activities in our daily lives such as driving an automobile or shopping in a supermarket.
3. *Cognitive strategies.* The application of information and techniques, and understanding how and when to use knowledge and information.
4. *Motor skills.* The coordination and execution of physical movements that involve the use of muscles; for instance, learning to swim.
5. *Attitudes.* Preferences and internal states associated with one's beliefs and feelings. Attitudes are learned and can be changed. However, they are considered to be the most difficult domain to influence through training.[6]

TABLE 3.1

Learning Outcomes Classification Schemes

Gagné's Classification Scheme
Verbal information (declarative knowledge)

Intellectual skills (procedural knowledge)

Cognitive strategies (how and when to use information and knowledge)

Motor skills (physical movements)

Attitudes (internal states)

Kraiger, Ford, & Salas Classification Scheme
Cognitive (quantity and type of knowledge)
- Verbal knowledge
- Knowledge organization
- Cognitive strategies

Skill-Based (technical and motor skills)
- Compilation (proceduralization and composition)
- Automaticity

Affective (attitudinal and motivational)
- Attitudinal
- Motivational (goal orientation, self-efficacy, goals)

Sources: Gagné, R. M. (1984). Learning outcomes and their effects: Useful categories of human performance. *American Psychologist, 39,* 377–385; Kraiger, K., Ford, J. K., & Salas, E. (1993). Application of cognitive, skill-based, and affective theories of learning outcomes to new methods of training evaluation. *Journal of Applied Psychology, 78,* 311–328.

Drawing on Gagné's classification scheme, Kurt Kraiger and colleagues developed a multidimensional classification scheme of learning outcomes that includes some additional indicators of learning. Their classification scheme consists of three broad categories of learning outcomes. Each category has several more specific indicators of learning:[7]

1. *Cognitive outcomes.* The quantity and type of knowledge and the relationships among knowledge elements. This includes *verbal knowledge* (declarative knowledge), *knowledge organization* (procedural knowledge and structures for organizing knowledge or mental models), and *cognitive strategies* (mental activities that facilitate knowledge acquisition and application, or what is known as metacognition).
2. *Skill-based outcomes.* This involves the development of technical or motor skills and includes *compilation* (fast and fluid performance of a task as a result of proceduralization and composition) and *automaticity* (ability to perform a task without conscious monitoring).
3. *Affective outcomes.* These are outcomes that are neither cognitively based nor skills-based and include *attitudinal* (affective internal state that affects behaviour) and *motivational* outcomes (goal orientation, self-efficacy, goals).

A training program can focus on one or more of the learning outcomes and, as you will see in the next section, some of the outcomes are associated with certain stages of the learning process. It is also important to realize that the extent to which a training program has an effect on any of these outcomes depends in large part on the objectives of a training program. In addition, different training methods will be more or less effective depending on the learning outcome a training program was designed to influence.

According to Gagné, different instructional events and conditions of learning are required for each of the learning outcomes. Further, the learning outcomes are often interrelated, which means that changes in one might imply changes in another.[8]

However, regardless of the learning outcome, learning generally occurs over a period of time and progresses through a series of stages as described in the next section.

Stages of Learning

In the chapter-opening vignette you were told that the new on-boarding program at the Canadian Cancer Society was designed to unfold in a logical and integrated way throughout the first year of employment. This highlights the fact that learning and the acquisition of new knowledge and skills occur over a period of time and in a meaningful sequence.

A theory developed by John Anderson called the Adaptive Character of Thought theory, or ACT theory, describes the learning process as it unfolds across three stages.[9] According to ACT theory, learning takes place in three stages that are known as declarative knowledge, knowledge compilation, and procedural knowledge or proceduralization.

Declarative knowledge

Learning knowledge, facts, and information

The first stage of learning involves learning knowledge, facts, and information, or what is known as **declarative knowledge**. For example, think of what it was like when you learned how to drive a car. At first, you acquired a great deal of information such as what to do when you get into the car, how to start the car and put it in gear, how to change gears if it is a standard shift, and so on. These pieces of information or units are called chunks.

During this first stage of learning one must devote all of one's attention and cognitive resources to the task of learning. In other words, it is not likely that you could make a phone call, listen to the radio, or carry on a conversation during this period of learning to drive a car. This is because all of your attention and cognitive resources are required to learn the task of driving. Furthermore, your driving performance at this stage is slow and prone to errors.

In the declarative stage of learning, performance is resource-dependent because all of one's attention and cognitive resources are required to learn the task. Any diversion of attention is likely to affect your learning and lower your performance. Just think of what it is like when you are in class and somebody starts talking to you. Your learning is seriously affected because you need all of your attention and cognitive resources for the task of learning. Listening or talking to somebody during class will require your attention and your learning will suffer.

Knowledge compilation

Integrating tasks into sequences to simplify and streamline the task

The second stage of learning is called **knowledge compilation**. Knowledge compilation involves integrating tasks into sequences to simplify and streamline the task. The learner acquires the ability to translate the declarative knowledge acquired in the first stage into action. During this stage, performance becomes faster and more accurate. For example, when learning how to drive a car, you are able to get into the car and begin to drive without having to think about every single thing you must do. In other words, what was once many single tasks or units and chunks during the declarative stage (e.g., put on your seatbelt, lock the car, adjust the seat, adjust the mirror, start the car, etc.) is now one smooth sequence of tasks. You get into the car and do all of the tasks as part of an integrated sequence.

Although the attention requirements during the knowledge compilation stage are lower than the declarative stage, performance is still somewhat fragmented and piecemeal. So when you are learning to drive a car, this might mean popping the clutch from time to time and occasionally rolling backwards when on an incline, stalling the car, and so on.

Procedural knowledge

The learner has mastered the task and performance is automatic and habitual

The final stage of learning is called **procedural knowledge**, or proceduralization. During this stage, the learner has mastered the task and performance is automatic and habitual. In other words, the task can now be performed without much thought. The transition from knowledge acquisition to application is complete. This is what most of us experience when we drive. We simply get into a car and drive without giving much thought to what we are doing. The task of driving becomes habitual and automatic.

Because tasks at this stage can be performed with relatively little attention, it is possible to divert one's attention and cognitive resources to other tasks such as conversing with passengers or talking on the phone. Performance at this stage is fast and accurate and the task can be performed with little impairment even when attention is devoted to another task. At this stage,

TABLE 3.2

The Stages of Learning

Stage 1
Declarative Knowledge
Learning: Knowledge, facts, and information
Performance: Resource-dependent

Stage 2
Knowledge Compilation
Learning: Integrating tasks into sequences
Performance: Fragmented and piecemeal

Stage 3
Procedural Knowledge
Learning: Task mastery
Performance: Automatic and habitual; resource-insensitive

performance is said to be resource-insensitive because changes in attention will not have much of an impact on performance. See Table 3.2 for a summary of the stages of learning.

IMPLICATIONS FOR TRAINING   ACT theory has some important implications for learning and training. First, it recognizes the fact that learning is a stage-like process that involves three important stages. Second, it indicates that different types of learning take place at different stages. And third, motivational interventions might be more or less effective depending on the stage of learning. As you will learn later in the chapter, goal setting is a motivational theory with implications for training and development. However, research has shown that goal setting can be harmful to learning during the early stages of learning when all of one's attention and cognitive resources must be devoted to learning the task. During the early stages of learning, cognitive ability is more important than motivational strategies.

However, when goals are set during the later stages of learning (e.g., procedural knowledge) they can have a positive effect on learning and performance. Cognitive ability becomes less important than it was during the declarative stage of learning. Thus, the effects of both cognitive ability and motivational interventions on learning and performance depend on the stage of learning.[10]

Learning Styles

An important aspect of learning is the way in which people learn. According to David Kolb, individuals differ in terms of how they prefer to learn or what are known as learning styles. A **learning style** is the way in which an individual gathers information and processes and acts on it during the learning process.[11]

An individual's learning style is a function of the way he/she gathers information (concrete experience, or CE, and abstract conceptualization,

Learning style

The way in which an individual gathers information and processes and evaluates it during the learning process

Chapter 3: Learning and Motivation

or AC) and the way he/she processes or evaluates information (active experimentation, or AE, and reflective observation, or RO). It is the combination of these "learning modes" that results in a learning style.

People who prefer to learn through direct experience and involvement are CE types (feeling). Those who prefer to learn by thinking about issues, ideas, and concepts are AC types (thinking). If you prefer to process information by observing and reflecting on information and different points of view you are an RO type (watching). If you prefer to process information by acting on it and actually doing something to see its practical value you are an AE type (doing).[12]

An individual's learning style is a function of how they gather information and how they process information. For example, a *converging* learning style combines abstract conceptualization and active experimentation (thinking and doing). People with this learning style focus on problem solving and the practical application of ideas and theories. A *diverging* learning style combines concrete experience and reflective observation (feeling and watching). People with this orientation view concrete situations from different points of view and generate alternative courses of action. An *assimilating* style combines abstract conceptualization and reflective observation (thinking and watching). These people like to process and integrate information and ideas into logical forms and theoretical models. Finally, an *accommodating* learning style combines concrete experience and active experimentation (feeling and doing). People with this learning style prefer hands-on experience and like to learn by being involved in new and challenging experiences.[13] Table 3.3 shows Kolb's learning styles and the associated learning modes.

Although people might prefer a particular learning style, ideally people can learn best by using all four styles. In fact, Kolb notes the importance of a learning cycle in which people use each of the four modes of learning in a sequence. The learning cycle begins with concrete experience (learning by experience), followed by reflective observation (learning by reflecting), then abstract conceptualization (learning by thinking), and finally active experimentation (learning by doing). This kind of learning cycle has been shown

TABLE 3.3

Learning Styles

LEARNING STYLE	LEARNING MODES	MEANING
Converging	Abstract conceptualization and active experimentation	Thinking and doing
Diverging	Concrete experience and reflective observation	Feeling and watching
Assimilating	Abstract conceptualization and reflective observation	Thinking and watching
Accommodating	Concrete experience and active experimentation	Feeling and doing

to improve learning and retention as well as the development of behavioural skills. Learning is most effective when all four steps in the learning cycle are part of the learning experience.[14]

IMPLICATIONS FOR TRAINING Kolb's theory has several implications for learning. First, it recognizes that people differ in how they prefer to learn. This means that a person's comfort and success in training will depend on how well the training approach matches their learning style. Thus, trainers need to be aware of these differences and design training programs to appeal to people's different learning styles. At AmeriCredit, an auto finance company in Fort Worth, Texas, course facilitators receive a report prior to a training session that allows them to adjust course delivery, content, and design based on the learning styles of the trainees.[15] The use of technology in training makes it much easier to tailor learning and training to a trainee's learning style. To learn more, see Training Today 3.1, "The Personalization of Learning."

Second, training programs should be designed with each learning mode as part of a sequence of learning experiences. At Capital One Financial Corp., after employees are taught a new set of skills they are given work projects to implement the skills and then they must report on the experience. The approach closely mirrors Kolb's learning cycle.[16]

Training Today 3.1

The Personalization of Learning

Personalization makes theory, concepts, and content more relevant for the learner. Learning personalization includes parsing of information that is most relevant to the user based on his role, language, culture, learning style, and personal preferences.

Some e-learning requires the learner to take a pre-assessment. With personalization, that pre-assessment can be presented in a specific learning style that is conducive to the individual. If the learner is more comfortable with auditory formats, the online content often will be sound-enabled or have a narrator speaking throughout the lesson.

If the individual is a visual learner, then the bulk of the content may be offered with compelling visuals. Learners who speak English as a second language can take courses that contain captioning in their native language to facilitate learning.

The more personalized the learning content and experiences, the more they will resonate with the learner and the greater chance that the learner will be able to recall the key lessons learned.

Personalization is critical in the information age because a typical worker gets hundreds of emails, dozens of instant messages, multiple phone calls, and several texts messages daily, which makes it more difficult to focus on basic tasks. In addition, the amount of time the learner has to focus on learning activities is often compromised by increased expectations, decreased staff, and increased responsibility and accountability.

Thus, spending additional time in the analysis and design phases of training to identify personalization strategies could prove to be an invaluable exercise, especially if the contact time available for the learner and the learning solution is minimized. The key to successful personalization is inclusion of the target audience in the development and delivery of the content.

Source: Hartley, D., & West, K. (2007, November). Taking it personally: Tailoring training for more relevance. *T+D, 61* (11), 21–23. Copyright © 2007. Reprinted with permission of American Society for Training & Development.

Learning Theories

Researchers have studied learning and developed a body of knowledge and theories about the learning process. Theories are important because they help us understand how people learn and how to better design training programs. In this section, we describe two theories of learning that have important implications for training: conditioning theory and social cognitive theory.

Conditioning Theory

The famous psychologist B. F. Skinner defined learning as a relatively permanent change in behaviour in response to a particular stimulus or set of stimuli.[17] Skinner and the behaviourist school of psychology believe that learning is a result of reward and punishment contingencies that follow a response to a stimulus.

The basic idea is that a stimulus or cue is followed by a response, which is then followed by a positive or negative consequence. If the response is positively reinforced, it strengthens the likelihood that the response will occur again and that learning will result.

For example, behaviourists argue that similar principles are at work when an adult submits an innovative proposal and is praised, and when a pigeon pecks a red dot and is given a pellet of food. When a response is reinforced through food, money, attention, or anything pleasurable, then the response is more likely to be repeated. If there is no reinforcement, then over time the response will cease. If the response is punished, then it will not be repeated. The conditioning process is illustrated in Figure 3.1.

Negative reinforcement is the removal of a stimulus after an act. To illustrate this concept, think of an alarm clock ringing. When you turn it off, the noise stops (the stimulus is removed). Similarly, think of your course instructor chewing out the class for not participating and threatening to start picking students at random to answer questions. When students participate, the instructor stops chewing them out and threatening to choose students at random. Thus, the response of increased class participation results in the removal of a negative stimulus.

It is important to realize that negative reinforcement is not the same as punishment, in which one receives a negative consequence for doing something undesirable. In the example above, a desirable behaviour is being

FIGURE 3.1

The Conditioning Process

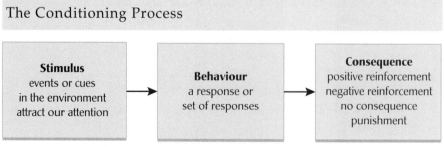

| **Stimulus** events or cues in the environment attract our attention | **Behaviour** a response or set of responses | **Consequence** positive reinforcement negative reinforcement no consequence punishment |

learned and increased (e.g., class participation) by a negative reinforcer that is removed when the desirable behaviour occurs.

Managers and trainers use conditioning theory principles when they attempt to influence employee behaviour. For example, at Capital One, a financial services company in the United States, new hires attend monthly reinforcement sessions in which they discuss what they did on the job that directly relates to the skills being developed. Once the skills are mastered they are taught new skills and the reinforcement cycle continues.[18]

Linking desired behaviour to pleasurable consequences is based on three connected concepts: *shaping, chaining,* and *generalization*. **Shaping** refers to the reinforcement of each step in the process until it is mastered, and then withdrawing the reinforcer until the next step is mastered. Shaping is extremely important for learning complex behaviour. Behaviour modelling is a training method (see Chapter 6) that makes extensive use of this concept by rewarding trainees for the acquisition of separate skills performed sequentially.

Shaping
The reinforcement of each step in a process until it is mastered

Chaining is the second important concept and involves the reinforcement of entire sequences of a task. During shaping, an individual learns each separate step of a task and is reinforced for each successive step. The goal, however, is to learn to combine each step and perform the entire response. This combination is what chaining involves, and it is accomplished by reinforcing entire sequences of the task and eventually reinforcing only the complete task after each of the steps have been learned.

Chaining
The reinforcement of entire sequences of a task

The third important concept is **generalization**, which means that the conditioned response occurs in circumstances different from those during learning.[19] Thus, while a trainee might have learned a task through shaping and chaining, he or she might not be able to perform the task in a different situation or outside of the classroom. To achieve generalization, the trainer must provide trainees with opportunities to perform the task in a variety of situations.

Generalization
The conditioned response occurs in circumstances different from those during learning

For example, the trainer can change a role-play script from negotiating with one's supervisor on the deadline of a project to negotiating the starting salary with a new employer. As a result, the trainee learns to generalize the skill from a simple, controlled environment to a different, more difficult one. This is a goal of training—that learning acquired during training will be generalized to, and used in, different situations and contexts.

IMPLICATIONS FOR TRAINING   When applied to training, conditioning theory suggests that trainees should be encouraged and reinforced throughout the training process. In other words, they should be reinforced for attending training, learning the training material, and applying it on the job. Based on conditioning theory, training should be more effective to the extent that trainees are reinforced for learning and the successful performance of training tasks.

Social Cognitive Theory

According to social cognitive theory, people learn by observing the behaviour of others, making choices about different courses of action to pursue, and by managing their own behaviour in the process of learning.[20] Thus, learning does not just occur as a result of reward and punishment contingencies. Learning also occurs through cognitive processes such as imitation and modelling. We observe the actions of others and make note of the reinforcing or punishing outcomes of their behaviour. We then imitate observed behaviour and expect certain consequences to follow. Considerable research has shown that people observe and reproduce the actions and attitudes of others.[21]

Social cognitive theory involves three key components: observation, self-efficacy, and self-regulation.

Observation

Observation

Learning by observing the actions of others and their consequences

As already indicated, people learn by **observation**. They observe the actions of others and the consequences of those actions. If the person being observed (the role model) is credible and knowledgeable, their behaviour is more likely to be imitated. The imitation will occur particularly if the role model is reinforced for the behaviour. New recruits watch the intense work hours of the senior staff. They then work the same long hours, in the expectation that they, too, will be rewarded with promotions.

Four key elements are critical for observational learning to take place: attention, retention, reproduction, and reinforcement. Learners must first attend to the behaviour (i.e., be aware of the skills that are observable). Second, they must remember what they observed and encode it in their own repertoire so that they can recall the skills. Third, they must then try out the skill (i.e., try to reproduce it) through practice and rehearsal. Fourth, if the reproduction results in positive outcomes (i.e., it is reinforced), then the learner is likely to continue to reproduce the behaviour and retain the new skills.

Many training programs use social cognitive theory concepts to model desired behaviour that is then followed by opportunities for practice and reinforcement. Some organizations assign new recruits to mentors or senior co-workers so that they can learn by observing them. The financial services firm Edward Jones has a mentoring program in which new investment representatives are paired with more established ones. New employees shadow their mentor for three weeks to learn about the company and how things are done.[22]

Self-Efficacy

While observation may provide the observer with information necessary to imitate the modelled behaviour, we know that people do not always attempt to do things they observe other people doing. For example, a novice skier might watch his friends skillfully make their way down a steep hill but refuse to follow suit. This is because he or she might not have the confidence or the belief that he or she will be able to do it. Such beliefs are known as self-efficacy beliefs.

Self-efficacy

Judgments that people have about their ability to successfully perform a specific task

Self-efficacy refers to judgments that people have about their ability to successfully perform a specific task. Self-efficacy is a cognitive belief that is task-specific, as in the example of the skier's confidence that he or she can ski down a steep hill. The novice skier might have low self-efficacy to ski down the hill but very high self-efficacy that he or she can get an "A" in a training course!

Self-efficacy is influenced by four sources of information. In order of importance they are: task performance outcomes, observation, verbal persuasion and social influence, and one's physiological or emotional state.[23] The self-efficacy of the skier can be strengthened not only by observing his/her friends' behaviour, but also by their encouragement that he/she can make it down the hill, his/her feelings of comfort and relaxation rather than fear and anxiety, and, most importantly, his/her own successful attempts at skiing down the hill.

Self-efficacy has been shown to have a strong effect on people's attitudes, emotions, and behaviour in many areas of human behaviour. Self-efficacy influences the activities people choose to perform, the amount of effort and persistence they devote to a task, affective and stress reactions, and performance outcomes.[24]

Self-efficacy is also a key factor in training. Research has shown that the effectiveness of many training programs is partly due to the strengthening of trainees' self-efficacy to perform the training task. In other words, training increases trainees' self-efficacy to perform a task, and self-efficacy is related to improved task performance.[25]

Self-Regulation

The third component of social cognitive theory is self-regulation. **Self-regulation** involves managing one's own behaviour through a series of internal processes.

Conditioning theory takes the position that an individual's behaviour is regulated by external factors such as rewards and punishments. However, self-regulation suggests that people can control and manage their own behaviour through a series of internal processes that enables them to structure and motivate their behaviour. These internal processes involve observing or monitoring one's own behaviour as well as the behaviour of others, setting performance goals, practising new and desired behaviours, keeping track of one's progress, and rewarding oneself for goal achievement.[26]

Self-regulation has been found to be related to cognitive, affective, and behavioural outcomes and to be an important method of training. For example, one study found that self-regulation training increased the job attendance of employees with above-average absenteeism. The results indicated that, compared to a group that did not receive the training, employees who received self-regulation training had higher self-efficacy for attending work and increased job attendance. In a follow-up study, these benefits were shown to continue up to nine months after training.[27] Several other studies have also found that self-regulation training leads to improvements in skill acquisition, maintenance, and performance.[28]

IMPLICATIONS FOR TRAINING   Social cognitive theory has important implications for the design of training programs. In particular, learning can be improved by providing trainees with models who demonstrate how to perform a training task; by strengthening trainee self-efficacy for successfully learning and performing the task; and by teaching trainees how to regulate their behaviour and performance while learning and on the job.

Self-regulation

Managing one's own behaviour through a series of internal processes

Adult Learning Theory

Consider the learning environment most people have experienced throughout their lives. As children, we are told what, when, and how to learn. Learning is supposed to pay off in some unknown way in the distant future. The question is whether this is an appropriate way to educate and train adults given that adults differ from children in a number of important ways.

First, unlike children, adults have acquired a great deal of knowledge and work-related experience that they bring with them to a training program. Adults also like to know why they are learning something, the practical implications of what they are learning, and its relevance to their problems and needs. Adults are also problem-centred in their approach to learning and prefer to be self-directed. They like to learn independently and they are motivated to learn by both extrinsic and intrinsic factors. Other contrasts between the learning needs of children and adults are highlighted in Table 3.4.

These differences have led to the development of an adult learning theory known as andragogy. **Andragogy** is a term coined by adult learning theorist Malcolm Knowles and refers to an adult-oriented approach to learning that takes into account the differences between adult and child learners. Andragogy involves making the learning experience of adults self-directed and problem-centred, and takes into account the learner's existing knowledge and experience. By contrast, the term **pedagogy** refers to the more traditional approach of learning used to educate children and youth.[29]

IMPLICATIONS FOR TRAINING Adult learning theory has important implications for training at every stage of the training process. The design and instruction of training programs should be the joint responsibility of the trainer and trainees. That is, adult learners should have some input about the training they will receive as well as how it is designed. You might recall from the

Andragogy

An adult-oriented approach to learning that takes into account the differences between adult and child learners

Pedagogy

The traditional approach to learning used to educate children and youth

TABLE 3.4

Teaching Children versus Adults

FACTOR	CHILDREN	ADULTS
Personality	Dependent	Independent
Motivation	Extrinsic	Intrinsic
Roles	Student	Employee
	Child	Parent, volunteer, spouse, citizen
Openness to change	Keen	Ingrained habits and attitudes
Barriers to change	Few	Negative self-concept
	Limited opportunities	
	Time	
	Inappropriate teaching methods	
Experience	Limited	Vast
Orientation to learning	Subject-centred	Problem-centred

The Trainer's Notebook 3.1

Implications of Adult Learning Theory for Training

- Adults need to know why they are learning.
- Adults should have some input into the planning and instruction of training programs.
- Adults should be involved in the needs analysis and have input into things such as training content and methods.
- The designers of training programs should consider the needs and interests of trainees.
- The training content should be meaningful and relevant to trainees' work-related needs and problems.

- Trainers should be aware of trainees' experiences and use them as examples.
- Adults can learn independently, and may prefer to do so.
- Adults are motivated by both intrinsic and extrinsic rewards.
- Adults should be given safe practice opportunities.

chapter-opening vignette that senior staff at the Ontario division of the Canadian Cancer Society consulted with key groups including the executive team, regional employees, and recent hires to customize the new on-boarding program so that it resonates with new hires.

The Trainer's Notebook 3.1, "Implications of Adult Learning Theory for Training," describes the implications of adult learning theory for training.

Theories of Motivation

Learning and the effectiveness of a training program are also a function of people's motivation. Motivation is an important predictor of performance and, as you will learn shortly, it is also a key factor for learning. First, it is important to understand what motivation is, the major theories of motivation, and the implications of motivational theories for training and development.

Motivation refers to the degree of persistent effort that one directs toward a goal. Motivation has to do with effort, or how hard one works; persistence, or the extent to which one keeps at a task; and direction, or the extent to which one applies effort and persistence toward a meaningful goal. In organizations, this usually means that one directs one's effort and persistence toward organization goals or in a manner that benefits the organization, such as high productivity or excellent customer service.

There are two forms of motivation: extrinsic and intrinsic motivation. **Extrinsic motivation** is associated with factors in the external environment such as pay, fringe benefits, and company policies. These are motivators that are applied by somebody in the work environment such as a supervisor. **Intrinsic motivation** is the result of a direct relationship between a worker and the task. Unlike extrinsic motivation, it is self-applied and includes feelings of achievement, accomplishment, challenge, and competence that are the result of performing a task or one's job.

Motivation

The degree of persistent effort that one directs toward a goal

Extrinsic motivation

Motivation that stems from factors in the external environment such as pay, fringe benefits, and company policies

Intrinsic motivation

Motivation that stems from a direct relationship between a worker and the task

Theories of motivation can be described as need theories or process theories. Need theories have to do with the things that motivate people and the conditions in which they will be motivated to satisfy them. Process theories of motivation address the process of motivation and how motivation occurs. In the remainder of this section, we will describe need theories of motivation as well as two process theories of motivation (expectancy theory and goal-setting theory).

Need Theories

Need theories of motivation are concerned with the needs people have and the conditions in which they will be motivated to satisfy them. Needs refer to physiological and psychological desires. In organizations, individuals can satisfy their needs by obtaining incentives such as money to satisfy physiological needs, or by challenging work that allows them to fulfill higher-level psychological needs. Therefore, needs are motivational to the extent that people are motivated to obtain things that will satisfy their needs.

Maslow's Need Hierarchy

The best-known theory of motivation is Abraham Maslow's need hierarchy. According to Maslow, humans have five sets of needs that are arranged in a hierarchy, with the most basic needs at the bottom of the hierarchy and higher-order needs at the upper levels of the hierarchy. The five needs from lowest to highest are physiological, safety, belongingness, esteem, and self-actualization needs.[30]

Physiological needs are needs that people must satisfy to survive and include things such as food, water, and shelter. Physiological needs can usually be satisfied with pay. Safety needs refer to needs for security, stability, and freedom from anxiety. Safe working conditions and job security can satisfy safety needs. Belongingness needs have to do with the need for social interaction, companionship, and friendship. The opportunity to interact with others at work and friendly and supportive co-workers and supervision can satisfy belongingness needs. Esteem needs have to do with feelings of competence and appreciation and recognition by others. The opportunity to learn new things and challenging work can satisfy esteem needs.

The highest need in Maslow's hierarchy is self-actualization. Self-actualization involves developing one's true potential as an individual and experiencing personal fulfillment. This can be fulfilled by work experiences that involve opportunities for creativity, growth, and self-development.

According to Maslow, people are motivated to satisfy their lowest-level unsatisfied need. If one's physiological need is unsatisfied, then one will be motivated to satisfy it. The basic premise is that the lowest-level unsatisfied need has the greatest motivating potential, which means that motivation depends on one's position in the need hierarchy. Once a need has been satisfied it will no longer be motivational, and the next highest need in the hierarchy will become motivational. The one exception to this is the self-actualization need, which becomes stronger.[31]

Alderfer's ERG Theory

Another need theory of motivation was developed by Clayton Alderfer. Alderfer's ERG theory consists of three needs. Existence needs are similar to Maslow's physiological and safety needs. Relatedness needs are similar to Maslow's belongingness need. And growth needs are similar to Maslow's esteem and self-actualization needs.[32]

Alderfer's ERG theory differs from Maslow's need theory in a number of ways. To begin with, ERG theory is not a rigid hierarchy of needs in which one must move up the hierarchy in a lock-step fashion. Although both theories argue that once a lower-level need is satisfied the desire for higher-level needs will increase, ERG theory does not state that a lower-level need must be gratified before a higher-level need becomes motivational. Thus, one can be motivated to fulfill relatedness or growth needs even if they have not fulfilled their existence needs. Maslow, however, would argue that a lower need must first be satisfied before a higher-level need will become motivational.

Another difference is that ERG theory states that if individuals are unable to satisfy a higher-level need, the desire to satisfy a lower-level need will increase. Maslow of course would say that this is not possible because once a need has been satisfied it is no longer motivational.

IMPLICATIONS FOR TRAINING   Need theories have important implications for training and development. They highlight the fact that employees' needs must be considered in the design of a training program. For example, if trainees' needs are not being fulfilled on the job then their behaviour and performance are not likely to change as a result of a training program unless the training program leads to need fulfillment. Improving employees' knowledge and skill through training and development will be most effective when employees are motivated on the job.

Another implication of need theories has to do with employees' motivation to attend a training program, to learn the training material, and to apply it on the job. Employees are not likely to be motivated to attend training or to learn and apply the training material if doing so does not fulfill their needs. Therefore, trainers and managers should be aware of trainees' needs and ensure that training programs are designed in part to fulfill them.

Expectancy Theory

Expectancy theory is a process theory of motivation. According to expectancy theory, the energy or force that a person directs toward an activity is a direct result of a number of factors. These factors are known as expectancy, instrumentality, and valence:[33]

1. Expectancy refers to an individual's subjective probability that they can achieve a particular level of performance on a task. For example, what is the probability that you can get an "A" in this course? What is the probability that you can get a "C" in this course? These outcomes are referred to as first-level outcomes since they are a direct result of one's effort or motivational force.

2. Instrumentality refers to the subjective likelihood that attainment of a first-level outcome such as an "A" or "C" in this course will lead to attractive consequences that are known as second-level outcomes. The consequences can be either intrinsic or extrinsic outcomes. For example, what is the probability that an "A" in this course will result in a job offer or a sense of accomplishment? What is the probability that a "C" will result in a job offer or a sense of accomplishment?

3. Valence refers to the attractiveness of the first- and second-level outcomes. The attractiveness of a second-level outcome such as a job offer or a sense of accomplishment is simply one's subjective ratings. For example, on a scale of 1 to 10 with 10 being the most attractive, how attractive would you rate receiving a job offer? The valence or attractiveness of a first-level outcome (an "A" or "C" grade in this course) is a result of the instrumentalities multiplied by the valence of each second-level outcome ($I \times V$). For example, the attractiveness of receiving an "A" in this course would be a function of:

$$(I \times V \text{ of receiving a job offer}) + (I \times V \text{ of experiencing a sense of accomplishment})$$

This calculation will determine the valence or attractiveness of the first-level outcome (receiving an "A" in this course). The same calculation would also be done to determine the valence of receiving a grade of "C" in the course.

To determine one's motivation or effort, the expectancy or probability of receiving an "A" or "C" grade must be multiplied by the valence of the first-level outcomes. This would result in a force or motivational value for pursuing an "A" and a "C" grade. In other words, it will indicate what grade you are most motivated to attain. If you feel that you can put in the effort and time required to obtain an "A" (i.e., your expectancy), and you believe that obtaining an "A" will result in a high probability of getting a job offer and experiencing a sense of accomplishment (instrumentality), then chances are you will be motivated to get an "A" in the course.

The expectancy theory linkages can be written as the following equation:

$$\text{Effort} = \text{Expectancy} \times (\text{Instrumentality} \times \text{Valence})$$

In effect, what all this means is that people's effort or motivation is a function of their beliefs that they can achieve a particular level of performance (first-level outcome), and that this will lead to consequences that are attractive to them (the valence of the first-level outcome). The attractiveness of a first-level outcome is simply the probability that it will lead to attractive consequences (e.g., the probability that getting an "A" in the course will result in a job offer and a sense of fulfillment). Thus, you are likely to be motivated to obtain an "A" in this course if you believe that there is a high probability that you can get an "A" and if you believe that getting an "A" will lead to consequences that are attractive to you.

IMPLICATIONS FOR TRAINING   There are a number of implications of expectancy theory for training and development. First, trainees must believe that there is a high probability they will be able to learn the training material and fulfill the training objective(s) (high expectancy). Second, learning the training material and using it on the job must result in consequences (high instrumentality) that are attractive to trainees (high valence of second-level outcomes). Simply put, you are more likely to learn something and apply it on the job if you believe that you can in fact learn it and that you will be rewarded with something that is attractive to you once it has been learned and used on the job.

The major implication of expectancy theory for training revolves around trainees' motivation to attend a training program, to learn, and to apply what is learned on the job. Along these lines, trainees must believe that there is a high probability they will be able to learn and apply the training material, and that doing so will result in attractive consequences for them.

Goal-Setting Theory

Goal-setting theory is based on the idea that people's intentions are a good predictor of their behaviour. According to the theory, goals are motivational because they direct people's efforts and energies and lead to the development of strategies to help them reach their goals. For goals to be motivational, however, they must have a number of characteristics.

First, goals must be *specific* in terms of their level and time frame. General goals that lack specificity tend not to be motivational. Second, goals must be *challenging* to be motivational. Goals should not be so easy that they require little effort to achieve, and they should not be so difficult that they are impossible to reach. Third, goals must be accompanied by *feedback* so that it is possible to know how well one is doing and how close one is to goal accomplishment. Finally, for goals to be motivational, people must accept them and be *committed* to them.[34]

Research on goal-setting theory has provided strong support for the motivational effects of goals. Studies across a wide variety of settings have consistently shown that challenging and specific goals that are accompanied with performance feedback result in higher levels of individual and group performance.[35]

However, in some instances high performance goals are not always the most effective. For example, recall from the discussion on the stages of learning that goal setting can be harmful for learning during the declarative stage when trainees' attention and cognitive resources are required to learn the task. Setting high performance goals can interfere with learning because they force trainees to focus on the outcomes of their effort rather than learning. This is especially a concern for learning complex tasks where trainees lack the knowledge and skill to perform the task and require all of their cognitive resources for learning. Setting a high performance goal will be more effective for tasks that are less complex and straightforward.

Another factor that needs to be considered is whether the goal is a distal or proximal goal. A **distal goal** is a long-term or end-goal, such as achieving a certain level of sales performance. A **proximal goal** is a short-term goal or sub-goal that is instrumental for achieving a distal goal. Proximal goals involve breaking down a distal goal into smaller more attainable sub-goals. Proximal goals provide clear markers of progress toward a distal goal because

Distal goal
A long-term or end goal

Proximal goal
A short-term goal or sub-goals

they result in more frequent feedback. As a result, individuals can evaluate their ongoing performance and identify appropriate strategies for the attainment of a distal goal. Distal goals are too far removed to provide markers of one's progress, making it difficult for individuals to know how they are doing and adjust their strategies.[36]

Proximal goals are especially important for complex tasks. Research has found that distal goals can have a negative effect on the performance of a complex task. However, when distal goals are accompanied with proximal goals they have a significant positive effect on the discovery and use of task-relevant strategies, self-efficacy, and performance.[37]

A study of provincial and federal government managers who attended a self-awareness training program found that trainees who set distal and proximal outcome goals at the end of the training program were more likely to apply what they learned in training on the job six weeks after training than those who only set a distal outcome goal. Thus, distal goals are effective for learning a new task only when they are accompanied by proximal goals.[38]

IMPLICATIONS FOR TRAINING   Goal-setting theory has a number of implications for training. For example, prior to a training program trainees should have specific and challenging goals for learning, and they should be provided with feedback during and after the training program so that they know if they have accomplished their goals. Setting specific and challenging goals should improve trainees' motivation to learn as well as their performance on the training task.

However, setting high performance goals during the declarative stage of learning can be detrimental for learning, especially for complex tasks. Therefore, special attention needs to be given to the stage at which goals are set and the complexity of the task. In addition, attention must also be given to the type of goal. For tasks that are novel and complex, a distal goal should be accompanied with proximal goals. Proximal goals should be set for knowledge and skill acquisition during training. It is also important to distinguish between a mastery goal and a performance goal, a topic we now turn to.

Goal Orientation

An important characteristic of goals is goal orientation. There are two general types of goal orientations—a mastery or learning goal and a performance goal orientation.

Mastery goals are process-oriented and focus on the learning process. They enhance understanding of the task and the use of task strategies. **Performance goals** are outcome-oriented goals that focus attention on the achievement of specific performance outcomes.

Goal orientation is important because it can influence task performance as well as cognitive, affective, and motivational processes. The type of goal set (i.e., mastery versus performance) also affects skill acquisition and learning. Trainees who have mastery goals have been found to have higher intrinsic motivation, self-efficacy, and metacognitive activity, and these factors are all related to learning and performance.[39]

Mastery goals

Process-oriented goals that focus on the learning process

Performance goals

Outcome-oriented goals that focus attention on the achievement of specific performance outcomes

Managing Performance Through Training and Development

Evidence also exists that individuals differ with respect to their goal orientation. Goal orientation has been found to be a stable individual difference such that some individuals have a preference for mastery goals while others have a preference for performance goals. Individuals with a mastery goal orientation are most concerned about developing competence by acquiring new skills and mastering new situations. Individuals with a performance goal orientation are more concerned about demonstrating their competence by seeking favourable judgments and avoiding negative judgments.

Mastery goals are especially important for learning because individuals need to acquire knowledge and learn strategies required to perform a task. When learning is required rather than motivation, setting a difficult performance outcome goal has been found to be detrimental for performance. This is because performance goals can distract attention from learning. Thus, during the learning process a specific, difficult mastery goal should be set as it has been shown to result in higher self-efficacy and performance. Once an individual has acquired the knowledge and skills necessary to perform a new task, he/she can focus on performance goals.[40]

IMPLICATIONS FOR TRAINING Research on goal orientation suggests that trainers should consider the goal orientation of trainees and the type of goals that are set for training. Mastery goals that focus on skill development appear to be particularly important for learning, especially for individuals who have a performance goal orientation and need to be assigned learning goals. Thus, trainers should emphasize the importance of learning and the need to focus on mastery goals during training. High mastery goals appear to be especially important for challenging tasks and when new skills must be learned. Setting high performance goals for a task that is still being learned can be detrimental for learning. Therefore, mastery goals should be set for learning and performance goals for motivation once learning has been achieved.[41]

Training Motivation

In the previous section, we described motivation theories and their implications for training and development. In this section, we focus more specifically on the role of motivation in training. In particular, we introduce the concept of *training motivation* and describe both the predictors and consequences of trainees' motivation to learn.

Training motivation (also known as motivation to learn) refers to the direction, intensity, and persistence of learning-directed behaviour in training contexts. Research has found that training motivation predicts learning and training outcomes and is influenced by individual and situational factors.[42]

Among the individual factors that predict training motivation, personality variables as well as factors associated with one's job and career are important. Personality variables that predict training motivation include locus of control, achievement motivation, anxiety, and conscientiousness.

Locus of control refers to people's beliefs about whether their behaviour is controlled mainly by internal or external forces. Persons with an internal locus of control believe that the opportunity to control their own behaviour

Training motivation
The direction, intensity, and persistence of learning-directed behaviour in training contexts

Locus of control
People's beliefs about whether their behaviour is controlled mainly by internal or external forces

Chapter 3: Learning and Motivation

resides within themselves. Persons with an external locus of control believe that external forces determine their behaviour. Thus, internals perceive stronger links between the effort they put into something and the outcome or performance level they achieve. Persons with an internal locus of control tend to have higher levels of training motivation.

In addition, persons who are high in achievement motivation or the desire to perform challenging tasks and are high on conscientiousness also tend to have high training motivation. Persons with higher anxiety, however, tend to have lower training motivation. Self-efficacy is also positively related to training motivation.

Several job and career variables are also related to training motivation. For example, employees with higher job involvement or the degree to which an individual identifies psychologically with work and the importance of work to their self-image have higher training motivation. Organizational commitment and career planning and exploration are also associated with higher training motivation. Organizational factors such as supervisor support, peer support, and a positive climate predict training motivation.

Training motivation is important because it is related to a number of training outcomes. For example, training motivation is positively related to declarative knowledge and skill acquisition as well as trainees' reactions to training and the likelihood that trainees apply on the job what they learn in training.

IMPLICATIONS FOR TRAINING   A trainer can do at least two things to ensure that trainees' training motivation is high. First, they can assess trainee motivation prior to a training program and ensure that trainees are motivated to learn. In fact, this is what the U.S. auto finance company AmeriCredit does. Employees complete a motivation questionnaire that is used to predict their likelihood of success in learning from a training program.[43] Second, managers can try to influence the factors that predict training motivation. They might lower trainees' anxiety, increase self-efficacy, improve attitudes, and provide support for learning and training.

In summary, training motivation is an important factor in the training process. Training is more likely to be effective and result in learning, skill acquisition, and improved job performance when trainees are motivated to learn.[44]

A Model of Training Effectiveness

In this final section of the chapter, we present a model of training effectiveness that highlights the linkages between training and learning as well as between learning and individual performance and organizational effectiveness.

Figure 3.2 presents a model of training effectiveness. Recall from Chapter 1 that training involves the acquisition of knowledge, skills, and abilities to improve performance on one's current job, and development refers to the acquisition of knowledge, skills, and abilities required to perform future job responsibilities. Thus, the first important link in the model is a path from training to learning and retention. In other words, training leads to declara-

FIGURE 3.2

Model of Training Effectiveness

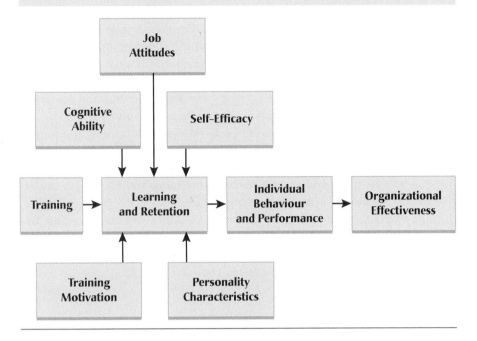

tive knowledge and the acquisition of skills and abilities and the retention of them over time.

In addition to training, we also know that there are personal factors that influence learning. Among the most important is **cognitive ability**, which is one of the most often examined individual characteristics in training research. Cognitive or mental ability is similar to intelligence. It reflects an individual's basic information-processing capacities and cognitive resources. It generally refers to the knowledge and skills an individual possesses and may include cognitive skills and psychomotor skills. Examples of cognitive skills include basic numeracy and literacy, the intelligence to learn complex rules and procedures, and so on. Cognitive ability (verbal comprehension, quantitative ability, and reasoning ability) is related to the ability to learn and to succeed on the job.

Recall the earlier discussion of ACT theory in which it was noted that cognitive ability is particularly important during the early stages of learning. In fact, research has consistently shown that general cognitive ability is a strong predictor of learning, training success, and job performance. It is an especially good predictor of job performance on complex jobs. In training research, cognitive ability has been found to predict declarative knowledge, skill acquisition, and the application of trained skills on the job.[45]

Training motivation is also a strong predictor of learning and training outcomes. Like cognitive ability, training motivation predicts declarative knowledge, skill acquisition, and the application of trained skills on the job. Self-efficacy and personality characteristics also have an effect on learning. Trainees with higher self-efficacy are more likely to learn during training.

Cognitive ability

An individual's basic information processing capacities and cognitive resources

In addition, trainees with an internal locus of control and a high need for achievement also learn more during training.

An additional factor that can influence learning is trainees' attitudes. Three attitudinal variables that are important for learning are job involvement, job satisfaction, and organizational commitment. Employees with higher job attitudes are more likely to learn and apply what they learn on the job.[46]

The model also shows a path from learning to individual behaviour and performance. This is called transfer of training and refers to the application of learning on the job. Employees must first learn and retain training content in order to change their behaviour and improve their job performance.

The final path in the model is between individual behaviour and performance and organizational effectiveness. This path indicates that employees' behaviour and job performance have an effect on organizational effectiveness. In other words, more effective employee behaviours and higher job performance will result in a more effective organization.

In summary, the training effectiveness model shows how training and personal factors influence learning and retention. We will further develop the model in Chapter 5 when we discuss training design and again in Chapter 10 when we discuss transfer of training.

Summary

We began this chapter by stating that a major goal of training and development is learning. We also described two classification schemes for learning outcomes. The learning process was described in terms of three stages (declarative, knowledge compilation, and procedural knowledge), and Kolb's learning styles were also discussed. Two major theories of learning (conditioning theory and social cognitive theory) as well as adult learning theory were described along with their implications for training and development. This chapter also described need theories and process theories of motivation and their implications for training. Training motivation was also discussed along with its predictors and consequences. The chapter concluded with a model of training effectiveness that shows the linkages between training, personal factors, and attitudes with learning and retention, individual behaviour and performance, and organizational effectiveness.

Key Terms

andragogy   p. 76

chaining   p. 73

cognitive ability   p. 85

declarative knowledge   p. 68

distal goal   p. 81

extrinsic motivation   p. 77

generalization   p. 73

intrinsic motivation   p. 77

knowledge compilation   p. 68

learning   p. 65

learning style   p. 69

locus of control   p. 83

mastery goals   p. 82

motivation   p. 77

observation   p. 74

pedagogy   p. 76

performance goals   p. 82

procedural knowledge   p. 68

proximal goal   p. 81
self-efficacy   p. 74
self-regulation   p. 75

shaping   p. 73
training motivation   p. 83

Make the Connection

p. 84: the meaning of training and development is discussed in Chapter 1 on page 6

Web Links

Canadian Cancer Society: www.cancer.ca

Capital One: www.capitalone.com

Edward Jones: www.edwardjones.com

RPC Icons

RPC 3.1 Ensures the application of appropriate development methods and techniques based upon generally accepted principles of adult learning.

Discussion Questions

1. Given the importance of motivation for learning and other training outcomes, what should trainers do to ensure that trainees are motivated to learn? What should managers do? Discuss the pros and cons of different approaches.
2. What are the differences between pedagogy and andragogy and what are the implications of adult learning theory for the design of training programs?
3. Discuss Kolb's four learning styles and the implications of them for the design of training programs. How should training programs be designed if people differ in their learning styles?
4. What are the sources of information that influence self-efficacy? How can trainers improve trainees' self-efficacy? How can supervisors improve trainees' self-efficacy? What can trainees do to improve their own self-efficacy?
5. What are the three stages of learning according to ACT theory? Give an example of how a training program might be designed according to ACT theory.
6. If an instructor of one of your courses wanted to maximize student learning, what should he/she do according to conditioning theory,

social cognitive theory, and adult learning theory? If he/she wanted to motivate students to attend class and learn, what should he/she do according to need theories, expectancy theory, and goal-setting theory?

7. Discuss how goal-setting theory can be used to improve trainee learning in a training program. What kind of goal should be set for trainees? Discuss the relevance of task complexity, goal orientation, and type of goal (proximal and distal).

8. Compare and contrast the two learning outcomes classification schemes in Table 3.1. How are they are similar and how do they differ?

9. Based on the description at the beginning of the chapter of the Ontario Division of the Canadian Cancer Society's new employee on-boarding program, what are some of the learning outcomes that the program is designed to achieve? What activities are being used to achieve each learning outcome? Use both classification schemes in Figure 3.1 to answer this question.

The Great Training Debate

1. Debate the following: Given that cognitive ability (or training motivation) is a strong predictor of learning, only trainees with high cognitive ability (or high training motivation) should be allowed to attend training programs, since those with low cognitive ability (or low training motivation) are not likely to learn and benefit from costly training programs.

Using the Internet

1. Learn about your learning style and motivation style by visiting the Learnativity website at **www.learnativity.com**. To find out your preferred learning style, click on "Learning Styles Assessment" in the Resources column and complete the assessment. To find out about your motivation style, click on "Motivation Styles Assessment" and complete the assessment. Write a brief report in which you indicate your primary and secondary learning style and motivation style. What do the results say about your learning and motivation preferences, and what are the implications of this for your learning? What can you do with this information to improve your learning?

2. How do you like to learn and how do you learn best? Do you have a visual, doing, or hearing learning style? To find out, go to **www.jobsetc.gc.ca/eng/toolbox/quizzes/quizzes_home.do** and take the Seeing, Hearing, and Doing Quiz (in the section Learning Style Quizzes). Answer the following questions:

   a. What are the results for your visual, hearing, and doing learning style?
   b. What do the results tell you about yourself?

c. What are the implications of the results for your ability to learn?

d. How can the information from this quiz be used by trainers and trainees?

Exercises

In-Class

1. If you had a friend who was about to attend a training program on how to use computers and she had very low self-efficacy about her ability to learn and to use a computer, what would you do to increase her self-efficacy? Describe some of the things you might do prior to the training program to increase your friend's self-efficacy.

2. Consider Kolb's four learning modes and how they might apply to your course on training and development or another course you are taking. How should the course be structured so that students' learning occurs in the following sequence of experiences: concrete experience, reflective observation, abstract conceptualization, and active experimentation? Be specific in terms of what the instructor will have students do at each stage of the learning cycle.

3. Using the material on goal-setting theory, set a goal for your training and development course. That is, set a specific and challenging goal that you will be committed to. In addition, determine how and when you will be able to obtain feedback. Be sure to also set a mastery goal and a performance goal as well as a proximal and distal goal. Once you have set your goals, meet with another member of the class and review and evaluate each other's goals for the course.

4. Consider a course you are currently taking and examine it in terms of adult learning theory. To what extent does your course incorporate the principles of adult learning theory? What aspects of the course incorporate adult learning theory and what aspects do not? If you were to redesign the course to make it more consistent with adult learning theory, what are some of the things you would change and do?

5. Training motivation is an important predictor of training outcomes, so it is important that trainers ensure trainees' training motivation is high. You might have noticed how your own training motivation influences your learning and performance in a course or training program. Using each of the theories of motivation (Maslow, Alderfer, expectancy, and goal setting), describe what a course instructor or trainer might do to increase students' or trainees' training motivation. Be specific in describing the techniques that follow from each theory.

6. Review the model of training effectiveness in Figure 3.2. Assess your potential learning and retention of a course you are currently taking by evaluating yourself as best you can on each of the predictors in the model (i.e., cognitive ability, attitudes, self-efficacy, personality

characteristics, and training motivation). Based on your assessment, how successful will your learning and retention of the course material be? What predictors can you try to change in order to enhance your learning and retention of the course material?

7. Review the material on self-regulation in the chapter and then design a self-regulation training program to help you learn and improve a skill or behaviour that you want to improve (i.e., making presentations, time management, exercising, quitting smoking, etc.). Once you have chosen a skill or behaviour, prepare a self-regulation program. Be specific in terms of what exactly you are going to do at each step in the process (i.e., how and when you will observe and keep track of your behaviour and observe the behaviour of others; set specific goals; when you will practise and rehearse the desired behaviours; how you will keep track of your progress; and how you will reward yourself for goal achievement). Once you have prepared your program, meet with another member of the class to review and evaluate each other's self-regulation program.

8. Technocell Canada (TCC) is a subsidiary of the German group Felix Schoeller Holding, the world's largest producer of photographic and décor paper (see Chapter 4). After implementing a training program, the benefits listed below were realized. Use Gagné's learning outcomes classification scheme to classify each of the benefits:

- improved literacy and numeracy skills
- enhanced understanding by machine operators, managers, and supervisors of the importance of basic skills in the workplace;
- improved attitudes and behaviour and a stronger sense of community within the workplace;
- enhanced teamwork
- improved employee motivation to do better and take pride in their work
- improved ability of employees to troubleshoot
- improved workplace safety record
- increase self-confidence, self-esteem, and activity in the workplace and community

In-the-Field

1. Contact the human resource department of your own or another organization to discuss the organization's training programs. Find out the extent to which aspects of some of the following learning theories are used to improve trainees' learning: conditioning theory, social cognitive theory, and adult learning theory. Then find out the extent to which aspects of some of the motivation theories (need theory, expectancy theory, and goal-setting theory) are used to motivate trainees to attend training programs and learn. What aspects of these theories are being used for training and what can the HR department do to improve trainee learning and training motivation?

Case Incident

Management Training at IKEA

IKEA is a Sweden-based home furnishings chain with stores in Canada and the United States. A single store can have 40 managers, making the task of training enough new managers quickly and well a challenge. To get managers trained for new store openings, IKEA has established certain stores as centres of excellence. These centres of excellence become learning sites for one or more management competencies that managers must master.

Manager trainees have a carefully developed, objectives-based curriculum and access to a 17-module online learning program that covers the basics of each of nine management competencies. Once a trainee has mastered the learning material as well as a series of practicum assignments, he or she is eligible to be certified as successful by the competence centre store manager. Trainees can be at a competence centre for two to six weeks depending on the competency to be mastered and number of competencies to be mastered at each centre. Part of the process involves shadowing successful managers. This is followed by two weeks of classroom training at IKEA Business College where managers are introduced to the philosophies and theories behind IKEA store operations. They get exposed to the "big picture," the theory of how the company operates, and what the IKEA vision is all about. Six months after a location opens, managers begin rotating back to Business College for advanced store operations training.

Questions

1. What learning outcomes are the focus of the IKEA manager training program? What do managers learn and how do they learn it?
2. Discuss the stages of learning as well as Kolb's learning styles, modes, and cycle with respect to the manager training program. To what extent does the program reflect the stages of learning and Kolb's learning styles and cycle?

Source: Zemke, R. (2004, March). Training Top 100: Editor's Choice: IKEA U.S.A., *Training, 41* (3), 70. V N U Business Publications. This work is protected by copyright and it is being used with the permission of Access Copyright. Any alteration of its content or further copying in any form whatsoever is strictly prohibited.

Case Study

The Performance Appraisal Training Program

Although the performance appraisal process is an important part of employee evaluation and development, many organizations do not conduct performance appraisals and managers tend to not like doing them. This was the case at a large hospital where nurse supervisors seldom met with nurses to review and discuss their performance.

Many of the supervisors seldom conducted performance appraisal interviews and some had never done one. They complained that there was no time to meet with every nurse and that it was a difficult and unpleasant process that was a waste of time. Some were uncomfortable with the process and found it to be very stressful for everybody concerned. They said that it caused a lot of anxiety for them and the nurses.

However, the administration was in the process of introducing a new model of nursing that required the nurses to perform certain critical behaviours when interacting with and counselling patients and their families. It was therefore imperative that performance appraisals be conducted to ensure that nurses were implementing the new model of nursing. The nurse supervisors would be required to evaluate their nurses' performance every six months and then conduct a performance appraisal interview with each nurse in which the previous six months' performance would be discussed. An action plan would then be developed with specific goals for improvement.

The administration decided to hire a performance management consultant to provide a one-day workshop on how to conduct performance appraisals for all nurse supervisors. The training program was mandatory and all nurse supervisors had to attend. Many of them reluctantly did so complaining that it would be a waste of time and that it would not make any difference in how things were done in the hospital.

The training program began with a lecture about how to conduct performance appraisal interviews. The consultant first explained that the purpose of a performance appraisal interview is to give feedback to employees on how well they are performing their jobs and then plan for future growth and development. He then discussed different types of performance appraisal interviews such as the "tell-and-sell interview," the "tell-and-listen interview," and the "problem-solving interview." This was followed by a list of guidelines on how to conduct effective interviews such as asking the employee to do a self-assessment, focusing on behaviour not the person, minimizing criticism, focusing on problem-solving, and being supportive. The trainees were then instructed on how to set goals and develop an action plan for improvement.

After the lecture, the trainees were asked to participate in a role play in which they took turns playing the part of a supervisor and employee. They were provided with information about a nurse's job performance to discuss in the role play and then develop an action plan. However, some of the trainees left the session, refusing to participate. Others did not take it seriously and made a joke out it. There was a lot of laughing and joking throughout this part of the program.

After the role play there was a group discussion about the role-play experience followed by a review of the key points to remember when conducting performance appraisal interviews.

Although the supervisors were supposed to begin performance reviews and interviews shortly after the training program, very few actually did. Some said they tried to do them but could not find time to interview all of their nurses. Others said that they followed the consultant's guidelines but they did not see any improvement in how they conducted interviews or in how nurses reacted to them. Some said it continued to be a stressful experience that was uncomfortable for them and the nurses and so they decided to stop doing them.

One year later, performance appraisals were still a rare occurrence at the hospital. Furthermore, many of the nurses were not practising the new nursing model and as a result nursing care was inconsistent throughout the hospital and often unsatisfactory.

Questions

1. Consider Gagné's learning outcomes for the performance appraisal interview training program. What were the expected learning outcomes of the training program and what did trainees learn? What learning outcomes were not learned?

2. Explain the success of the training program using conditioning theory and social cognitive theory. How do these theories explain why the training program was not more effective? How could the program be improved by using some of the concepts from each theory?

3. Discuss the extent to which adult learning principles were incorporated into the training program. What principles were included and which ones were absent? What could the consultant have done differently to make better use of adult learning theory?

4. Describe the training program in terms of Kolb's learning styles and the learning cycle. What aspects of the program relate to each of the modes of learning? What learning style or styles are most likely to benefit from the program and which ones are not? How could the program be changed to make better use of Kolb's learning cycle?

5. Comment on the supervisors' training motivation. What effect did their training motivation have on the success of the training program? Apply the theories of motivation to explain how the hospital administration and the consultant might have increased supervisors' training motivation.

References

1. Nador, S. (2008, March 10). "Canadian Cancer Society launches new onboarding program." *Canadian HR Reporter, 21* (5), 12. Reprinted by permission of Carswell, a division of Thomson Canada Ltd.

2. Hinrichs, J. R. (1976). Personnel training. In M. D. Dunnette (Ed.), *Handbook of industrial and organizational psychology* (pp. 829–860). Skokie, IL: Rand McNally; Gagné, R. M. (1984). Learning outcomes and their effects: Useful categories of human performance. *American Psychologist, 39,* 377–385.

3. Hinrichs, J. R. (1976).

4. Kraiger, K., Ford, J. K., & Salas, E. (1993). Application of cognitive, skill-based, and affective theories of learning outcomes to new methods of training evaluation. *Journal of Applied Psychology, 78,* 311–328.

5. Gagné, R. M. (1984).

6. Zemke, R. (1999). Toward a science of training. *Training, 36* (7), 32–36.

7. Kraiger, K., Ford, J. K., & Salas, E. (1993).

8. Kraiger, K., Ford, J. K., & Salas, E. (1993).
9. Kanfer, R., & Ackerman, P. L. (1989). Motivation and cognitive abilities: An integrative/aptitude-treatment interaction approach to skill acquisition. *Journal of Applied Psychology, 74*, 657–690.
10. Kanfer, R., & Ackerman, P. L. (1989).
11. Kolb, D. A. (1984). *Experiential learning*. Englewood Cliffs, NJ: Prentice-Hall.
12. Kolb, D. A. (1984).
13. Kolb, D. A. (1984).
14. Whetten, D. A., & Cameron, K. S. (2002). *Developing management skills* (5th ed.). Upper Saddle River, NJ: Prentice Hall.
15. Barbian, J. (2002, March). Training top 100: AmeriCredit. *Training, 39* (3), 46–47.
16. Delahoussaye, M. (2001, March). Training top 50: Capital One. *Training, 38* (3), 70–71.
17. Skinner, B. F. (1953). *Science and human behaviour*. New York: McMillan.
18. Delahoussaye, M. (2001, March).
19. Pearce, J. M. (1987). A model of stimulus generalization in Pavlovian conditioning. *Psychological Review, 94*, 61–73.
20. Bandura, A. (1986). *Social foundations of thought and action: A social cognitive theory*. Englewood Cliffs, NJ: Prentice-Hall.
21. Luthans, F., & Davis, T. (1983). Beyond modelling: Managing social learning processes in human resource training and development. In C. Baird, E. Schneier, & D. Laird (Eds.), *The training and development sourcebook*. Amherst, MA: Human Resource Development Press.
22. McLaughlin, K. (2001, March). Training top 50: Edward Jones. *Training, 38* (3), 78–79.
23. Bandura, A. (1997). *Self-efficacy: The exercise of control*. New York: W. H. Freeman & Co.
24. Bandura, A. (1997).
25. Haccoun, R. R., & Saks, A. M. (1998). Training in the twenty-first century: Some lessons from the last one. *Canadian Psychology, 39*, 33–51.
26. Bandura, A. (1986).
27. Frayne, C. A., & Latham, G. P. (1987). Application of social learning theory to employee self-management of attendance. *Journal of Applied Psychology, 72*, 387–392. Latham, G. P., & Frayne, C. A. (1989). Self-management training for increasing job attendance: A follow-up and a replication. *Journal of Applied Psychology, 74*, 411–416.
28. Gist, M. E., Stevens, C. K., & Bavetta, A. G. (1991). Effects of self-efficacy and post-training intervention on the acquisition and maintenance of complex interpersonal skills. *Personnel Psychology, 44*, 837–861.
29. Knowles, M. (1990). *The adult learner*. Gulf Publishing: Houston, TX.
30. Maslow. A. H. (1970). *Motivation and personality* (2nd ed.). New York: Harper & Row.
31. Maslow. A. H. (1970).
32. Alderfer, C. P. (1969). An empirical test of a new theory of human needs. *Organizational Behavior and Human Performance, 4*, 142–175.
33. Vroom. V. H. (1964). *Work and motivation*. New York: Wiley.
34. Locke, E. A., & Latham, G. P. (1990). *A theory of goal setting and task performance*. Englewood Cliffs, NJ: Prentice-Hall.
35. Locke, E. A., & Latham, G. P. (1990).
36. Seijts, G. H., & Latham, G. P. (2001). The effect of distal learning, outcome, and proximal goals on a moderately complex task. *Journal of Organizational Behavior, 22*, 291–307; Latham, G. P., & Seijts, G. H. (1999). The effects of proximal and distal goals on performance on a moderately complex task. *Journal of Organizational Behavior, 20*, 421–429.
37. Seijts, G. H., & Latham, G. P. (2001).
38. Brown, T. C. (2005). Effectiveness of distal and proximal goals as transfer-of-training interventions: A field experiment. *Human Resource Development Quarterly, 16*, 369–387.
39. Bell, B. S., & Kozlowski, S. W. J. (2008). Active learning: Effects of core training design elements on self-regulatory processes, learning, and adaptability. *Journal of Applied Psychology, 93*,

296–316; Cannon-Bowers, J. A., Rhodenizer, L., Salas, E., & Bowers, C. A. (1998). A framework for understanding pre-practice conditions and their impact on learning. *Personnel Psychology, 51,* 291–320.

40. Seijts, G. H., & Latham, G. P. (2001); VandeWalle, D., Cron, W. L., & Slocum, J. W. Jr. (2001). The role of goal orientation following performance feedback. *Journal of Applied Psychology, 86,* 629–640; VandeWalle, D., Brown, S. P., Cron, W. L., & Slocum, J. W. Jr. (1999). The influence of goal orientation and self-regulation tactics on sales performance: A longitudinal field test. *Journal of Applied Psychology, 84,* 249–259.

41. Colquitt, J. A., Lepine, A., & Noe, R. A. (2000). Toward an integrative theory of training motivation: A meta-analytic path analysis of 20 years of research. *Journal of Applied Psychology, 85,* 678–707.

42. Colquitt, J. A., Lepine, A., & Noe, R. A. (2000).

43. Barbian, J. (2002, March). Training top 100: AmeriCredit. *Training, 39* (3), 46–47.

44. Colquitt, J. A., Lepine, A., & Noe, R. A. (2000).

45. Colquitt, J. A., Lepine, A., & Noe, R. A. (2000).

46. Burke, L. A. (2001). Training transfer: Ensuring training gets used on the job. In L. A. Burke (Ed.), *High-impact training solutions: Top issues troubling trainers.* Quorum Books: Westport, CT; Colquitt, J. A., Lepine, A., & Noe, R. A. (2000).

The Needs-Analysis Process

Chapter Learning Outcomes

After reading this chapter, you should be able to:

- define needs analysis and describe the needs-analysis process
- define and explain how to conduct an organizational, task, and person analysis
- define and describe the purpose of a cognitive task analysis and a team task analysis
- describe the process of determining if training is the best solution to performance problems
- describe the different methods and sources for conducting a needs analysis
- describe the obstacles to conducting a needs analysis and how to overcome them

TECHNOCELL CANADA (TCC)

Technocell Canada (TCC) is a subsidiary of the German group Felix Schoeller Holding, the world's largest producer of photographic and décor paper. In 2001, Technocell Canada purchased a paper plant in Drummondville, Quebec, as it was the only plant in Canada with the capability of fabricating the specialized paper product needed. The Drummondville plant employs 150 people and exports approximately 80 percent of its production to the United States.

However, most of Technocell's newly acquired workforce was not familiar with the materials or the technology required to produce the quality standard required by Technocell. In addition, the employees had not received any training for the various positions associated with the paper machine production line and they were also lacking in basic skills.

With the introduction of new products, higher quality standards, and significant increases in production volume and speed, staff had difficulty adapting to the new work methods. Furthermore, market requirements demanded a much more in-depth knowledge of the production processes than what was typically required in traditional paper factories.

The reality of an untrained workforce had a direct negative impact on the organization and, in particular, on product quality, efficiency, and productivity. It was clear to both local and German managers that the skill deficiencies were taking their toll on the company and its bottom line. Immediate action was required to stabilize and improve the productivity of the Drummondville plant.

The company's goal of developing a highly skilled workforce was further complicated by difficulties in finding and recruiting specialized and qualified staff. The only solution to overcoming the shortage was to improve the quality of training provided to current employees to ultimately increase both productivity and staff retention.

Before training could take place, a full analysis of the skill set and training needs of each employee was required. To ensure impartiality, an external firm was hired to survey the employees, evaluate and measure their essential skills, analyze the results, and prepare a structured training plan. The audit consisted of preparing, distributing, and analyzing employee surveys and results. The external company then tested the technical and generic competencies of employees at all levels.

In addition to a lack of important skills, the survey results also indicated a need for improvement in employees' attitudes and behaviours as the results indicated that employees were not sensitive to the urgency of completing a task; employees did not take responsibility for product quality; workplace safety was not exercised; management were not necessarily well qualified for their job responsibilities; and employees were not concerned by the consequences of their actions on the company's fragile bottom line.

After analyzing the results, a matrix of training needs was prepared. Training schedules and activities were then put into place. To maintain employee support, the external assessors met with all employees individually to discuss the results of their evaluations, review their training needs, and discuss next steps.

All job descriptions were reviewed and revised and a skill set was identified for each job, including the attitudes and behaviours required to be successful in that position. A proficiency assessment was implemented for each position, identifying a set of competencies which had to be met in order to be proficient in the job. The criteria were based on academic skills, work skills, technical skills, and generic skills. Once all employees had been tested and their skill sets evaluated and identified, the company was then in a better position to match jobs to each employee's qualification.

As a result of this process, Technocell Canada was able to tailor the training program to meet the specific needs of individual learners. At the same time, the program ensures that the workforce will acquire the essential job skills specific to the décor paper industry and that workplace safety and productivity goals are met. The company counts on the training program to improve the quality of its products and services as well as productivity.[1]

The Technocell Canada vignette highlights an important aspect of the training and development process. It shows how a new business strategy has important implications for training and development, and how a needs analysis is required to determine who needs training and what type of training they need. It also shows how training is often necessary to improve productivity and a company's success. As you can tell from this case, needs analysis is a critical first step in the training and development process.

In Chapter 1 you were introduced to the instructional systems design (ISD) model of training and development, which depicts training and development as a rational and scientific process that consists of three major steps: needs analysis, design and delivery, and evaluation. The process involves an analysis of current performance and ends with improved performance. The critical first step in the ISD model is a needs analysis to determine the nature of the problem and if training is the best solution. A needs analysis is performed to determine the difference or gap between the way things are and the way things should be. In this chapter, you will learn all about the needs-analysis process and how to determine if training is the best solution to performance problems.

What Is a Needs Analysis?

Needs analysis (also known as needs assessment) is the cornerstone and foundation of training and development. In fact, it is often referred to as the most important step in the training and development process.[2] **Needs analysis** is a process designed to identify gaps or deficiencies in employee and organizational performance. Needs analysis is concerned with the gaps between actual performance and desired performance. It is a "formal process of identifying needs as gaps between current and desired results, placing those needs in priority order based on the cost to meet each need versus the cost for ignoring it, and selecting the most important needs (problems or opportunities) for reduction or elimination."[3]

Needs analysis helps to identify gaps or deficiencies in individual, group, or organizational performance. The way to identify performance gaps is to solicit information from those who are affected by the performance problem. A needs analyst gathers information from key people in an organization about the organization, jobs, and employees to determine the nature of performance problems. This information identifies the problem, which is simply the difference between the way the work is being done and the most cost-effective way of doing it. In the simplest terms, needs = required results – current results.[4]

The goal of needs analysis is to identify the differences between what is and what is desired or required in terms of results, and to compare the magnitude of gaps against the cost of reducing them or ignoring them. Obviously, performance gaps could be the result of many factors, and the solutions might include training as well as other interventions. A thorough needs analysis can help an organization prioritize its needs and make informed decisions as to what problems need to be resolved. Thus, needs analysis identifies, prioritizes, and selects needs that will have an impact on internal and external stakeholders.[5] Needs analysis helps to identify the causes and solutions to performance problems.

RPC 4.1

The Needs-Analysis Process

Needs analysis is a process that consists of a series of interrelated steps. Figure 4.1 outlines the needs-analysis process that we will be discussing in this chapter. As described in Chapter 1, the process starts with an *itch* or a problem. If the performance problem is important, stakeholders are consulted and a needs analysis is conducted. There are three levels of needs analysis: an organizational analysis, a task analysis, and a person analysis. The collection of information and the needs-analysis process concludes with a number of important outcomes.

FIGURE 4.1

The Needs-Analysis Process

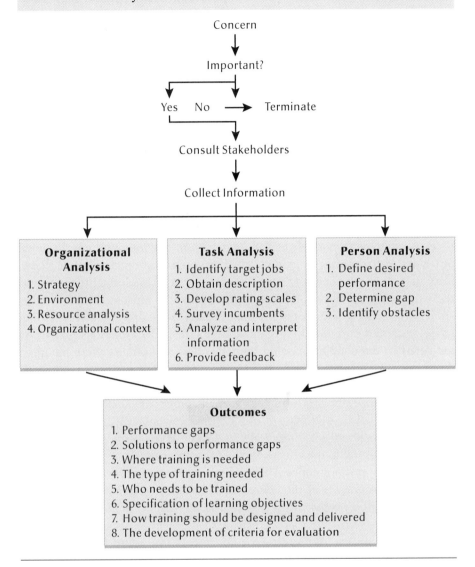

Concern

↓

Important?

Yes No ⟶ Terminate

↓

Consult Stakeholders

↓

Collect Information

Organizational Analysis
1. Strategy
2. Environment
3. Resource analysis
4. Organizational context

Task Analysis
1. Identify target jobs
2. Obtain description
3. Develop rating scales
4. Survey incumbents
5. Analyze and interpret information
6. Provide feedback

Person Analysis
1. Define desired performance
2. Determine gap
3. Identify obstacles

Outcomes
1. Performance gaps
2. Solutions to performance gaps
3. Where training is needed
4. The type of training needed
5. Who needs to be trained
6. Specification of learning objectives
7. How training should be designed and delivered
8. The development of criteria for evaluation

Step One: A Concern

The process of identifying training needs originates slowly and informally with a concern. This concern is sometimes referred to as an *itch* or a *pressure point*, something that causes managers to notice it. This concern might be as subtle as noticing that employees are treating customers in an abrupt manner, or observing that employees are spending a lot of time asking one another for help with a new system. Other concerns might be recognizing a shift in regular activities, such as an increase in defective parts, accidents, or complaints.[6] At Technocell Canada, there were concerns about product quality, efficiency, and productivity as a result of an unskilled workforce.

At Boston Pizza, the top casual dining chain in Canada, a growing skills gap among the company's store managers was noticed. Although managers are familiar with the Boston Pizza concept and have the necessary hard skills, they are lacking in soft skills because most of them have come up through the ranks and have not had any formal management education. In order to remedy the soft-skills concern, the company launched Boston Pizza College, a classroom-based management training program.[7]

Sometimes the pressure comes from the external environment, such as when legislation regarding employee relations is changed, or the competition introduces a highly competitive service feature. At IBM, one needs-identification program began with the CEO's comment that about 10 percent of all complaints addressed to him involved client dissatisfaction with IBM's handling of telephone calls.[8]

Step Two: Importance

After a concern has been raised, the next step is to determine if the concern is central to the effectiveness of the organization. The training manager must be aware of the strategic orientation of the organization. The goals, plans, introduction of products and services, changes in technology, practices, and regulations should be clear. Human resource policies must be linked with the strategic directions of the company as discussed in Chapter 1, and the training strategy should support the organization's efforts to achieve its goals.[9] As indicated in the chapter-opening vignette, skill deficiencies were having a direct negative effect on Technocell Canada. Immediate action was required to stabilize and improve the productivity of the plant.

In IBM's case one strategic goal was customer satisfaction, and further analysis revealed that 70 percent of all customer contact was by telephone. The complaints about telephone calls had to be taken seriously because the concern was central to the effectiveness of the organization.[10]

Another important concern is the cost implications of a problem. Does current performance cost the company in lost productivity or dissatisfied customers? If the performance problem is important, then there must be some way to demonstrate that correcting the problem will result in increased productivity or client satisfaction. A concern is important (i.e., worthy of further exploration and analysis) if it has an impact on outcomes that are important to the organization and its effectiveness. Clearly, the concern at Technocell Canada was very important as it was affecting the company's bottom line.

Step Three: Consult Stakeholders

The next step in the needs-analysis process is to involve the stakeholders who have a vested interest in the process and outcomes. Support from key players in the organization is necessary from the beginning of the needs-analysis process. At Technocell Canada, both local and German managers believed that the skill deficiencies of the workforce was a serious problem and that immediate action was required to achieve the company's goal of developing a highly skilled workforce.

At a minimum, top management should understand the rationale for the needs analysis. Training analysts must obtain agreement on why the needs analysis is being done and who will be involved. Managerial expectations must be clarified.[11] Likewise, other stakeholders, such as employees or their collective representatives, should be consulted. At Technocell Canada, the external assessors met with all employees individually to discuss the results of their evaluations, review their training needs, and discuss next steps.

At IBM, interviews with employees revealed that they believed they treated customers courteously and that the managers were antagonistic about learning telephone skills. The attitude was, "just train the secretaries and switchboard operators," even though managers and even financial analysts were receiving calls from customers. The trainers at IBM worked hard to obtain agreement and support from employees on the need for a full analysis. Management sent out a strongly worded message to employees that there was a problem and that together they were going to fix it. Indeed, the manager of U.S. operations made telephone effectiveness one of five key measures of effectiveness. (The others included profit and revenue measures.)[12]

All stakeholders must buy into the needs-analysis process to ensure that the data collection will result in accurate information and that they have a vested interest in the success of the program. The linking of the training plans to business strategy and the involvement of key stakeholders resulted in dramatic improvements in customer satisfaction at IBM.

Step Four: Data Collection

The next stage in the needs-analysis process is the most extensive and involves the documentation of the concern through the collection of information from three levels of analysis. Recall from the chapter-opening vignette that before training could take place at Technocell Canada, a full analysis of the skill set and training needs of each employee was required.

The three levels of needs analysis are the *organizational*, the *task*, and the *person* or *employee*. Although overlaps among the three areas of analysis occur, each plays a distinctive role. The analysis of the organization provides information about its strategies and context and answers the question, "Where is training needed in the organization?" The task analysis provides information about the tasks and the relevant knowledge, skills, and abilities needed to perform selected jobs and answers the question, "What knowledge, skills, and abilities are required to perform the job effectively?" And a person analysis provides information about an employee's level of performance and answers the question, "Who needs to be trained?"

Needs-Analysis Outcomes

At the beginning of this chapter we referred to needs analysis as the cornerstone of the training and development process and noted that it is one of the most important steps. This is due in large part to the outcomes of needs analysis as shown in Figure 4.1.

Once a needs analysis has been completed, the information has to be examined and interpreted. The focus then shifts to an understanding of the performance problem and the search for the most effective solution.

The needs analysis results in a number of outcomes that set the stage for the rest of the training and development process. Besides clarifying the nature of performance gaps, a needs analysis helps to determine if training and development is a good solution to performance problems or if some other intervention might be more effective. If training and development is part of the solution, needs analysis information is used to determine where training is needed in the organization, what type of training is required, and who in the organization should receive training.

For example, Technocell Canada was able to tailor its training program to meet the specific needs of individuals, to ensure that the workforce acquires the essential job skills specific to the décor paper industry, and to ensure that workplace safety and productivity goals are met as a result of the needs-analysis process.

Needs-analysis information is also used to write training objectives and to design training programs (e.g., what training content should be included in the training program, what training methods would be most effective, etc.). Finally, the information from a needs analysis is also used in the development of measures for training evaluation.

Most of the outcomes of the needs-analysis process revolve around determining the best solution to performance problems and how to proceed if training is to be part of the solution. Later in the chapter we discuss a process for determining if training is the best solution to performance problems. In the following sections, we describe how to conduct an organizational, task, and person needs analysis.

Organizational Analysis

RPC 4.2

Organizational analysis
The study of the entire organization including its strategy, environment, resources, and context

Organizational analysis involves the study of the entire organization: its strategy, environment, resources, and context. An understanding of each of these components will provide information not only for the identification of training needs, but also for the probability of the success of a training program. Key to an organizational analysis is finding out if a training program is congruent with an organization's strategy, and the existence of any constraints as well as support for the delivery and success of a training program. An organizational analysis can help identify potential constraints and problems that can derail a training program so that they can be dealt with prior to the design and delivery of a costly program.

Strategy

Most organizations have a strategy that consists of an organization's mission, goals, and objectives such as a dedication to quality or innovation. These broad statements trickle down to specific goals and objectives for each department or unit, and reflect an organization's plan for growth, adaptation, profitability, and survival.

In the past, an organization's strategy was set and implemented independently of the training function and human resources. During the last decade, however, it became increasingly apparent that human resource functions such as training and development are essential for the accomplishment of an organization's strategy and objectives. As a result, vice presidents and directors of human resources are now often involved in the setting of an organization's strategy, and as a result the human resource function has become more strategic.

In Chapter 1, we defined strategic human resource management (SHRM) as the alignment of human resource practices with an organization's business strategy. Although SHRM refers in general to the human resource system, in actuality it involves aligning specific HRM functions and activities with an organization's business strategy. In this regard, we can describe particular HR functions such as training and development as being strategic.

Thus, **strategic training** can be defined as the alignment of an organization's training needs and programs with an organization's strategy and objectives. You might recall from Chapter 1 that one of the organizational benefits of training and development is facilitating and supporting an organization's strategy.

Strategic training

The alignment of an organization's training needs and programs with the organization's strategy and objectives

An organization's strategy should indicate the type and amount of training required. Training is more likely to be effective and contribute to an organization's success when it is congruent with its business strategy. When training and development programs are designed and implemented in isolation of an organization's strategy, they are not likely to be effective in helping an organization achieve its goals.

As indicated in Chapter 1, there is some evidence that training can actually detract from an organization's bottom line and negatively impact shareholder value if it is not aligned with an organization's strategy. Training that is not linked to an organization's strategy can lower a company's market value by as much as 1.9 percent.[13] In the chapter-opening vignette, the training program was designed to support Technocell's strategy, which included the introduction of new products, higher quality standards, and significant increases in production volume and speed.

Environment

In Chapter 1, we described how training and development is embedded within the external environment and how factors in the environment can impact the organization, human resource practices, and training and development. The environment is dynamic and uncertain. New technologies, competitors, recessions, and trade agreements can profoundly affect not only the need for and content of training, but also employees' receptivity to being trained.

Training programs are often a direct result of government regulations (e.g., safety regulations). In the United States, several recent laws require organizations to provide certain kinds of training. For example, a new sexual harassment prevention training law in California requires organizations with 50 or more employees to provide at least two hours of sexual harassment training to all supervisory employees.[14] The Sarbanes-Oxley Act of 2002, which was passed in the United States to protect investors from fraudulent accounting activities by corporations in the wake of high-profile scandals such as Enron and WorldCom, requires organizations to provide compliance training which must be documented. The implications for training are especially being felt by accounting firms, where the Act has forced auditors and accountants to do their jobs differently. As a result, some firms have had to double the time their staff spend in training and substantially increase their investment in training.[15]

Besides this regulatory influence, organizations are conscious of the strategies of their competitors. The nature of a training program can be a direct result of an organization's attempt to establish a new market niche. For example, Technocell's need for training is a result of its purchase of the only plant in Canada with the capability of fabricating specialized paper.

Resource Analysis

An important component of an organizational analysis is determining an organization's ability to design and deliver a training program. Does the organization have the resources (money, time, and expertise) to design and deliver a training program if one is needed?

A **resource analysis** involves identifying the resources available in the organization that might be required to design and implement training and development programs. Training programs are costly and require considerable resources. In addition to the financial costs, the design and implementation of a training program requires considerable time and expertise. Not all organizations have the expertise required to design and deliver training programs. In addition, the human resource staff might not have the time required to design new training programs. Furthermore, training programs also require materials, equipment, and facilities, and these too can be expensive.

A resource analysis enables an organization to determine if it has the resources required for a training and development solution or if another less costly solution will be better. Ultimately, one has to answer the question of whether or not the organization has the resources required for training if in fact it is needed. Training was of course needed at Technocell Canada and the company invested approximately $2 million in the development of employee skills and expertise, which translated into an average of $30,000 per employee.[16]

Organizational Context

Organizations consist of more than buildings, equipment, and paper. They are social entities made up of people. The people within the buildings have feelings, attitudes, and values that make up the climate of an organization. The climate of an organization refers to the collective attitudes of its employees toward work, supervision, and company goals, policies, and procedures. One aspect of climate that is particularly important for training is the training transfer climate.

Training transfer climate refers to characteristics in the work environment that can either facilitate or inhibit the application of training on the job. A strong training transfer climate is one in which there exist cues that remind employees to apply training material on the job, positive consequences such as feedback and rewards for applying training on the job, and supervisor and peer support for the use of newly acquired skills and abilities. The training transfer climate has been found to be a strong predictor of training effectiveness and whether or not trainees apply newly trained skills on the job.[17]

Another important component of an organization's context is its culture. Recall from Chapter 1 that an organization's culture refers to the shared beliefs and assumptions about how things are done in an organization. Organizations can be differentiated from each other on the basis of their culture. For example, some organizations have innovative cultures, while others have risk-taking cultures. One type of culture that is particularly important for training and development is a learning culture.

A **learning culture** refers to a culture in which members of an organization believe that knowledge and skill acquisition are part of their job responsibilities and that learning is an important part of work life in the organization.[18]

Information about an organization's training transfer climate and learning culture is important because it can help to determine if a training program is likely to be effective in an organization as well as whether a pre-training intervention might be required to improve the climate and/or culture prior to the design and delivery of a training program. It might also indicate that an alternative solution to a performance problem would be more effective than a training program. This is an important part of an organizational analysis because training is not likely to be effective in organizations where the climate for training transfer and/or the culture for learning are not strong.

The influence of the training transfer climate and learning culture on training effectiveness demonstrates how important the role of the organizational context is for a training program's success and the need to conduct an organizational analysis. Whether or not employees apply what they learn in training on the job has a lot to do with an organization's transfer climate and learning culture, because they can either facilitate or hinder the implementation and success of a training program. The Trainer's Notebook 4.1, "Learning Culture Diagnosis," describes how to determine if an organization has a learning culture. In Chapter 10 we discuss the role of climate and culture in the transfer of training in more detail.

Once the strategy, environment, resources, and context of an organization have been assessed, the information gathered can be used to determine if a training program is required to help an organization achieve its goals and objectives and if it will be successful. However, additional information is required about the tasks that employees perform, as well as employees' knowledge, skills, and abilities and current level of job performance and task mastery. This additional information can be obtained by conducting a task analysis and a person analysis.

Training transfer climate
Characteristics in the work environment that can either facilitate or inhibit the application of training on the job

Learning culture
A culture in which members of an organization believe that knowledge and skill acquisition are part of their job responsibilities and that learning is an important part of work life in the organization

Task Analysis

Before we discuss task analysis, it is useful to first review the terms used to describe jobs. A job consists of a number of related activities, duties, and tasks. A task is the smallest unit of behaviour studied by the analyst and describes the specific sequence of events necessary to complete a unit of work.

A **task analysis** consists of a description of the activities or work operations performed on a job and the conditions under which these activities are performed. A task analysis reveals the tasks required for a person to perform a job and the knowledge, skills, and abilities that are required to perform the tasks successfully.

There are six steps involved in a task analysis:

1. Identify the target jobs.
2. Obtain a job description.
3. Develop rating scales to rate the importance of each task and the frequency with which it is performed.
4. Survey a sample of job incumbents.
5. Analyze and interpret the information.
6. Provide feedback on the results.

Task analysis

The process of obtaining information about a job by determining the duties, tasks, and activities involved and the knowledge, skills, and abilities required to perform the tasks

IDENTIFY THE TARGET JOBS   After a problem or performance discrepancy has been identified in an organization, the focus shifts to the job level in order to determine which jobs are contributing to the performance problem and have a performance gap. More than a job title is required here. For example, the title *associate* often describes quite different types of jobs, depending upon the department or level within any organization. These target jobs may be identified by managers. At Technocell, targeted jobs were from all levels including supervisors, mill operators, laboratory technicians, maintenance and shipping and receiving workers, mill management and support staff, office personnel, and senior management.

OBTAIN A JOB DESCRIPTION A **job description** lists the specific duties carried out through the completion of several tasks. In large organizations, most positions have a description of the tasks and minimum qualifications required to do the job. If this description has not been updated within the last year, consult with both the manager and several employees in the position (subject-matter experts) to obtain a current listing of tasks and qualifications. The job description should contain a summary of the major duties of the job, a listing of these duties, the knowledge, skills, and abilities required to perform the tasks, and the conditions under which they are performed. All tools and specialized knowledge should be listed.

Job description
A statement of the tasks, duties, and responsibilities of a job

After preparing a job description, the list of duties should be reviewed with subject-matter experts, managers, job incumbents in interviews, or focus groups. The analyst will then develop a list of tasks to be performed; the knowledge, skills, and abilities needed to perform the tasks; a list of necessary tools, software, or equipment; and an understanding of the conditions under which the tasks are performed. You can see that the result looks very much like a job description with job specifications (a job specification is a statement of the knowledge, skills, and abilities required to perform a job).

Creating job descriptions and making lists of tasks and duties does have its downside. Critics argue that jobs change too rapidly and these lists are quickly out of date. Therefore, some job analysts have begun to develop a list of job competencies. A **competency** is a cluster of related knowledge, skills, and abilities that forms a major part of a job and that enables the job holder to perform effectively.[19] Competencies are behaviours that distinguish effective performers from ineffective performers. Competencies can be knowledge, skills, behaviour, or personality traits. However, most analysts prefer not to use personality traits, such as "charisma," and instead prefer to describe the behaviour underlying the trait.

Competency
A cluster of related knowledge, skills, and abilities that enables the job holder to perform effectively

Examples of competencies for managers include setting goals and standards, coaching, making decisions, and organizing. As you can see, competencies are very similar to skills. Skills, however, can be very specific, such as "negotiate a collective agreement," whereas competencies are generic and universal such as "win agreement on goals, standards, expectations, and time frames." The Banff Centre for Management has developed competency profiles for senior leaders so that they can assess needs and then train.[20] An example taken from their profile is listed in Table 4.1.

The goal is to develop competencies that are teachable (i.e., we can observe them and describe them). If these competencies are then associated with effective performance, we can use them as a base to increase the effectiveness of an employee's on-the-job work behaviour. Competencies can then be used instead of job descriptions.

TABLE 4.1

A Competency Profile for Senior Leaders

Core Competency Ability to obtain buy-in of key stakeholders to new directions

Level 1: Communicates new directions so that everyone affected knows the new directions

Level 2: Leads team through discussions and research to identify key new themes and goals that everyone can accept and use

Level 3: Key stakeholders are consulted and have input into direction-setting

Level 4: All stakeholders are engaged in a process to rewrite the new directions in terms that relate specifically to their roles

Source: MacNamara, D. (1998, November 16). Learning contracts, competency profiles the new wave in executive development. *Canadian HR Reporter*, pp. G8–G10. Reprinted by permission of Carswell, a division of Thomson Canada Ltd.

At Technocell Canada, all job descriptions were reviewed and revised and a skill set was identified for each job that indicated the attitudes and behaviours required to be successful in that position. A set of competencies which had to be met for each position to be proficient was also identified.

DEVELOP RATING SCALES TO RATE THE IMPORTANCE OF EACH TASK AND THE FREQUENCY WITH WHICH IT IS PERFORMED Rating scales must be developed in order to rate the importance of each task as well as how often a task is performed. Tasks that are more important for the effective performance of a job as well as those that are frequently performed need to be identified. These ratings are important for determining the content of a training program and for identifying what employees must do in order to perform a job effectively.

SURVEY A SAMPLE OF JOB INCUMBENTS Job incumbents as well as supervisors and subject-matter experts who are familiar with the job must then provide task importance and frequency ratings. A questionnaire and a structured interview as well as observation of employees performing their jobs can be used to rate the importance of tasks and the frequency with which they are performed. An example of a survey is shown in Table 4.2.

ANALYZE AND INTERPRET THE INFORMATION Once the tasks have been identified and the importance and frequency ratings have been made, the information must be analyzed and interpreted. This usually involves some elementary statistical analyses to identify those tasks that are the most important and most frequently performed. Statistical software packages can assist in this task and can be used for more complex analyses. Comparisons between groups may reveal additional important information. Job incumbents may rate their own performance highly, while their managers may feel that employees are not working up to standard. New employees may feel that there are no barriers to optimum performance, while those with several years of service might perceive problems.

TABLE 4.2

Sample Task Analysis Survey

For each of the following areas of skill, knowledge, and ability, please make two ratings. Looking at your own job, assess the importance of the task by circling a number from 1 (not important) to 5 (very important). Then, consider your own level of competence in that task and rate it from 1 (not at all competent) to 5 (extremely competent).

TASK	IMPORTANCE	COMPETENCE
Knowledge: Ability to explain technical information to co-workers	1 2 3 4 5	1 2 3 4 5
Control: Ability to develop procedures to monitor and evaluate activities	1 2 3 4 5	1 2 3 4 5
Planning: Ability to schedule time, tasks, and activities efficiently	1 2 3 4 5	1 2 3 4 5
Coaching: Ability to provide verbal feedback to assist in the development of more effective ways of handling situations	1 2 3 4 5	1 2 3 4 5

One study found that experienced police officers spent less time in traffic activities and more in non–crime-related tasks than recent recruits, validating the need to collect background information on respondents.[21] Conducting a training course without understanding the participants and the environment may result in less-effective learning and transfer of skills to the workplace.

PROVIDE FEEDBACK ON THE RESULTS   Because employees and managers might not be aware of the need for training, it is important to provide small groups of managers and employees with feedback about the responses to task analysis. This feedback encourages employees to talk about areas of strengths and weaknesses and to propose solutions to problems. By owning the problem and generating the solution, employees may be more willing to change their behaviours and managers will be more likely to support a training program. To maintain employee support at Technocell Canada, the external assessors met with all employees individually to discuss the results of their evaluations, review their training needs, and discuss next steps.

The result of a task analysis should be information on the key task requirements for certain job categories and the associated job specifications (knowledge, skills, and abilities). This sets the stage for the design of training programs because it specifies the tasks that employees must be trained to perform as well as the knowledge and skills that they need to learn. At Technocell Canada, the result was a matrix of training needs along with training schedules and activities.

A limitation of a task analysis, however, is that it emphasizes observable behaviours rather than mental processes, and it assumes that the tasks are performed by individuals rather than groups. Many jobs today, however, involve mental processes and teamwork. In the following sections, we briefly describe two new approaches to task analysis that focus on mental processes and teamwork: cognitive task analysis and team task analysis.

Chapter 4: The Needs-Analysis Process

Cognitive Task Analysis

The traditional approach to a task analysis focuses on behaviours rather than mental processes such as decision making. However, many jobs today involve complex mental tasks. How then does one conduct a task analysis for jobs that involve mental tasks that are not easy to observe? The answer is a cognitive task analysis.

Cognitive task analysis

A set of procedures that focuses on understanding the mental processes and requirements for performing a job

A **cognitive task analysis** refers to a set of procedures that focuses on understanding the mental processes and requirements for performing a job.[22] It differs from the more conventional task analysis in that the focus is on the mental and cognitive aspects of a job rather than observable behaviours like typing or driving that are the focus of a traditional task analysis.

Cognitive task analysis describes mental and cognitive activities that are not directly observable, such as decision making, problem solving, pattern recognition, and situational assessment. A traditional task analysis focuses on what gets done, while a cognitive task analysis focuses more on the details of how tasks get done.

Although cognitive task analysis is useful for any job that has cognitive elements, it is especially useful in jobs that are complex, dynamic, and have high-stakes outcomes. It can identify important elements of job performance such as decisions, cues, judgments, and perceptions that are important for effective job performance and are usually not identified by a traditional task analysis. As a result, important cognitive elements can then be incorporated into training and development programs. Although cognitive task analysis has begun to receive a great deal of attention in recent years, it is a relatively new technique that is still being developed.[23]

Team Task Analysis

As indicated earlier, the traditional task analysis is not suited to the analysis of jobs that involve group work. However, many jobs today involve groups. Thus, a task analysis must be able to identify the knowledge and skills required to work in a group. In recent years, there has been an attempt to find ways to conduct a team task analysis.

Team task analysis

An analysis of tasks as well as the team-based competencies (knowledge, skills, and attitudes) associated with the tasks

A **team task analysis** is similar to a task analysis in that the tasks of the job must be identified. However, an assessment of team-based competencies (knowledge, skills, and attitudes) associated with the tasks is also required.

Teamwork competencies include things such as how to communicate, interact, and coordinate tasks effectively with team members. The main objective is to identity the key team competencies required for the tasks of the job, which will be used to write training objectives and to design a training program.[24]

There are a number of important differences between a traditional task analysis and a team task analysis. The main difference is that a team task analysis must identify the interdependencies of the job as well as the skills required for task coordination. Another difference is that a team task analysis must also identify the cognitive skills that are required for interacting in a team.

In general, a team task analysis should focus on the knowledge of task-specific goals; knowledge of task procedures, strategies, and timing; knowledge of team members' roles and responsibilities; interpositional knowledge; and knowledge of teamwork. A team task analysis can be conducted through the use of individual and group interviews, a review of existing documents, observation, questionnaires, and by examining past important events.[25]

Like task analysis, team task analysis and cognitive task analysis identify the tasks an employee must be able to perform and the knowledge, skills, and abilities required. However, they do not indicate how well employees are able to perform the tasks or whether they have the necessary knowledge, skills, and abilities. This information must be obtained from a person analysis, the topic to which we now turn.

Person Analysis

The third level of a needs analysis focuses on the person performing a job. **Person analysis** is the process of studying employee behaviour to determine if performance meets the work standards. A standard is the desired level of performance—ideally the quantifiable output of a specific job.

A person analysis examines how well an employee performs the critical tasks and their knowledge, skills, and abilities. The objective is to provide answers to these kinds of questions: How well does the employee perform the tasks? Who, within the organization, needs training? And what kind of training do they need? A three-step process should help answer these questions:

1. Define the desired performance.
2. Determine the gap between desired and actual performance.
3. Identify the obstacles to effective performance.

Person analysis

The process of studying employee behaviour to determine whether performance meets standards

DEFINE THE DESIRED PERFORMANCE The first step is to establish standards for performance. These norms will be important in the needs analysis, during training, and in evaluating the effectiveness of training. The idea is to determine the standard or the acceptable level of task performance. This enables a comparison of each employee's performance level against the standard in order to identify discrepancies and the need for training.

As indicated earlier, at Technocell Canada all job descriptions were revised and a skill set was identified for each job, including the attitudes and behaviours required to be successful in that position. In addition, a proficiency assessment was implemented for each position which identified a set of competencies that had to be met in order to be proficient in the job.

DETERMINE THE GAP BETWEEN DESIRED AND ACTUAL PERFORMANCE In this step, a comparison is made between the standard level of performance and each employee's performance. Employee performance data can be obtained from performance appraisals, work samples, observations, self-assessments of competencies, and formal tests. CIBC uses formal tests to determine competencies of financial advisers.[26] Results from the "Financial Advisor Skills and Capabilities Assessment" are used by employees to gain self-awareness and to prepare a developmental plan. More objective sources might be found in records of output, complaints, accidents, rejects, lost time, maintenance hours, and equipment efficiency. The employee's performance can be compared with industry norms or with that of other workers.

Chapter 4: The Needs–Analysis Process

At Technocell Canada, the external firm surveyed, evaluated, and measured employees' essential skills as well as their attitudes and behaviours. They also tested the technical and generic competencies of employees at all levels.

IDENTIFY THE OBSTACLES TO EFFECTIVE PERFORMANCE When a gap exists between the standard and an employee's performance, it is necessary to determine the cause or source of the gap. Performance problems can be the result of deficiencies in execution as well as deficiencies in knowledge, skills, or abilities. Sometimes, the gap is the result of the worker not knowing the standard, not receiving adequate feedback about performance relative to the standard, and not being rewarded for meeting the standard. A lack of goals and feedback is often the reason for substandard performance. At Technocell Canada, the main obstacle to effective performance was the lack of essential job skills specific to the décor paper industry.

Once the obstacles to performance have been identified, the next step in the needs-analysis process is to determine solutions to performance problems and if training is a possible solution to a performance problem. In the next section, we present a framework for determining solutions to performance problems.

RPC 4.3 Determining Solutions to Performance Problems

Table 4.3 lists a variety of potential barriers to effective performance. If you consider all the barriers to performance listed in Table 4.3, only the first two (lack of knowledge and skills) suggest a training solution. Clearly, the solution to performance problems is not always going to be training. Saying "I've got a training problem" is like going to the doctor and saying you have an Aspirin problem.[27] Training, like Aspirin, is a solution, not a problem. How then do we determine if training is the best solution to performance problems?

Figure 4.2 presents a flowchart developed by Mager and Pipe to assist in analyzing performance problems and determining solutions to performance problems. Let's review the steps in the flowchart.

TABLE 4.3

Barriers to Effective Performance

HUMAN	TECHNICAL	INFORMATION	STRUCTURAL
Lack of knowledge	Poor job design	Ill-defined goals/objectives	Overlapping roles and responsibilities
Lack of skills	Lack of tools/equipment	Lack of performance measurements	Lack of flexibility
Lack of motivation	Lack of standardized procedures	Raw data, not normative or comparative data	Lack of control systems
Counterproductive reward systems	Rapid change in technology	Resources sub-optimized	Organizational political climate
Group norms	Ineffective feedback	Informal leaders	

Source: Adapted from Chevalier, R. D. (1990). Analyzing performance discrepancies with line managers. *Performance and Instruction, 29* (10). www.ispi.org. Reprinted by permission of International Society for Performance Improvement. Copyright 1990.

FIGURE 4.2

Mager and Pipe's Performance Analysis Flowchart for Determining Solutions to Performance Problems

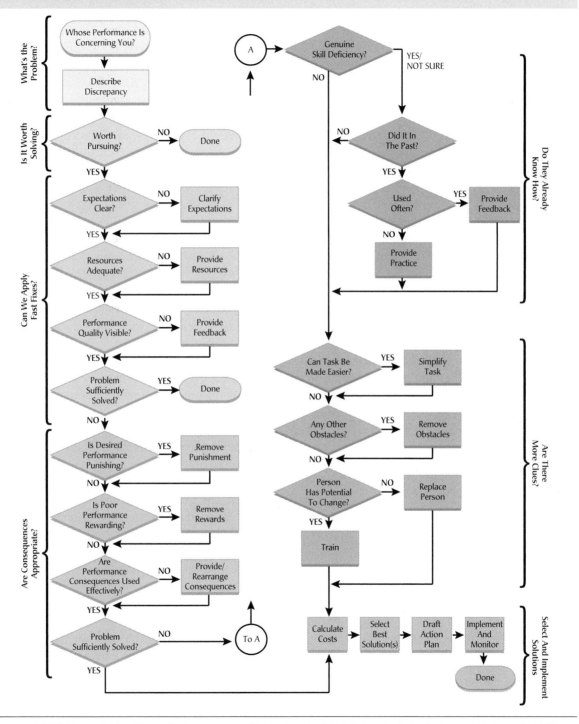

Source: © 1997, The Center for Effective Performance, Inc., Atlanta, Georgia. Adapted from *Analyzing Performance Problems*, 3rd Edition by Robert F. Mager & Peter Pipe. www.cepworldwide.com, 800-558-4237.

When there is a performance problem, the manager must first describe the problem and decide if it is worth spending either time or money to correct. Is it worth pursuing? For example, a manager might be irritated by employees who wear their hair shoulder-length, but having short hair will make absolutely no difference to productivity or other measures of performance. The exception might be in a manufacturing environment, where long hair would pose a safety hazard (solved easily by wearing a head covering). If the performance problem is important and worth pursuing, then the true analysis begins.

First, we consider some basic solutions or quick fixes. For example, are the work expectations, standards, and goals clear? Does the employee have adequate resources? Is the outcome of the employee's performance visible and known to the employee? If the answer to any of these questions is *No,* then the solution might involve clarifying expectations, standards, and setting goals; providing necessary resources; and/or providing performance feedback.

If the problem cannot be solved by these quick fixes, the analyst must then attempt to determine the cause of poor performance by asking a number of additional questions about the environment. For example: Is the person punished for desired performance? While this question seems odd, organizational life is full of examples of punishment for good performance. The assistant who works twice as hard as co-workers is punished by being given more work. The manager who stays within his/her budget is punished by having it slashed the following year. In these and other cases, behaviour that should be rewarded is actually punished. Such penalties and punishments for what is in effect good performance should be eliminated.

Sometimes undesirable performance is rewarded, such as when employees get paid for each unit produced. Under these circumstances you might find that employees are very good at producing lots of defective units. Of course, if they get paid for each unit produced they will continue to produce as many as they can regardless of quality. Thus, it is also important to ensure that undesirable behaviour is not rewarded. High volume should not be rewarded if quality is desired.

The next issue is whether or not rewards are linked to effective performance. Are there positive consequences for performing as desired? Sometimes when an employee does something good, the manager says nothing, on the assumption that the employee is being paid to do the work. Good performance that is not rewarded will eventually disappear. Sometimes, employees assume that their performance does not matter to anyone. When managers sit in their offices and fume over sloppy work but give no feedback to employees, or arrange no consequences for poor performance, the sloppy work will continue.

MAKE THE CONNECTION

Contingency management

Practices based on the belief that every act has a consequence and if the consequence is a reward then the act will be repeated

Working with the human resource staff, managers need to develop contingency management programs that reward employees for good performance. **Contingency management** is grounded in the belief that every act has a consequence and if the consequence is a reward then the act will be repeated. If there is no consequence or the consequence is something negative or punishing, the action will not be repeated. If this sounds familiar to you it is because it has its basis in conditioning theory, which was described in Chapter 3. Recall that according to conditioning theory, learning is the result of reward and punishment contingencies that follow a response to a stimulus. Thus, contingency management represents an application of conditioning theory.

Imagine a classroom where the instructor never acknowledges students whose hands are raised to ask questions. Eventually, the students will learn to keep their hands down. Ensuring that no students ask questions can be done even faster by punishing those who ask questions with sarcastic or humiliating replies. Thus, the behaviour of hand raising or asking questions is eliminated, even when the instructor insists that he/she values classroom participation and discussion.

By analyzing rewards and punishments, managers might realize that they are asking for safe procedures but punishing those who slow down production. Quality might be the all-important word on the sign in the factory, but employees might be praised for quantity. The determination of what constitutes effective performance, and the management of reinforcement for achieving it, is a far more powerful instrument of change than a training program.

If contingency management does not solve the problem, the next step is to consider whether or not there is a genuine skill deficiency. The key to getting at this issue is to ask a critical question: *Could the employee perform the task if his or her life depended on it?* Could your employees produce six units per hour if their lives depended on it? If the answer is *Yes*, then the solution is not to teach them something they already know how to do. Rather, the solution is to provide an environment that allows and encourages them to do it.

Following the right side of Figure 4.2, consider if the employee has ever performed the task and perhaps does not do it often and just needs some practice. Or perhaps the task is done frequently and the employee needs feedback. Thus, if an employee knows how to perform a task, it is important to consider practice and feedback before training.

To restate the critical question asked earlier: *Could the employee perform the task if his or her life depended on it?* If the answer is *Yes*, they could perform the task if their life depended on it, then say *No* to training. If the employee cannot do the task if his/her life depended on it, then consider a number of other changes before training.

Other solutions might be to lower expectations, simplify the task, or perhaps transfer the employee to a job that better fits his or her knowledge and skills. It is also important to remove any other obstacles in the environment. Training will not be a good solution when the environment is the cause of poor performance.

Environmental obstacles to effective performance might involve a lack of authority, inadequate tools or technology, conflicting responsibilities, work overload, and so on. Removing these obstacles in the work environment and replacing them with a more supportive environment might be the best solution to a performance problem.

Finally, if there exists a genuine skill deficiency and the person does not have the potential to change, then replacing the person might be the only solution. If, however, the person does have the potential to change, then consider training as a potential solution.

When Is Training the Best Solution?

As you can see, training is just one solution for managing performance problems. Other solutions might be more effective. Furthermore, even the best-designed training programs are not always effective because the environment does not support the change in behaviour and performance. Thus, one has to consider how practical and feasible each solution will be as well as its overall potential to solve the problem.

If the needs analysis reveals that the tasks are not frequently performed, that they are not critical, and that perfection is not required, then performance-improvement solutions such as job aids and on-the-job training might be more appropriate. Sometimes more radical solutions might be necessary, such as changing employees through firing and hiring, re-designing the job, changing the equipment, or changing the organizational structure.

Even if training is determined to be the best solution, the costs and benefits of training must first be estimated. Trainers must ask questions such as "What is the cost of the training?" and "What are the benefits to training?" Chapter 12 addresses these questions.

In summary, the best way to determine if training is an appropriate solution to performance problems is to first conduct a thorough needs analysis, identify performance obstacles, and then consider various solutions to a performance problem as shown in Figure 4.2. A checklist of the questions to ask to determine if training is the best solution to performance problems is provided in The Trainer's Notebook 4.2, "The Training Solution Checklist."

The Trainer's Notebook 4.2

The Training Solution Checklist

Trainers are often asked to provide training to correct a performance problem. Training is not always the best solution, and trainers should ask the following questions to determine if training is an appropriate solution:

1. What are the performance (or operating) problems? Don't ask, "What is the training need?"
2. Describe the current performance and desired performance.
3. Can employees perform as desired if they had to? Did they ever perform as expected in the past?
4. If employees have performed as expected in the past, do they need practice, feedback, or specific and challenging goals?
5. If employees perform as you want them to, what are the consequences for them? Are they rewarded for good performance and goal accomplishment?
6. Are there any other reasons why employees might not be performing as desired?
7. If we find a solution to the performance problem, how will we know that the problem has been solved? What behaviours, skills, or results will change?
8. Is training the solution?

TABLE 4.4

Performance Problems and Training

Training is often the best solution to performance problems under the following conditions:

- The task is performed frequently
- The task is difficult
- Correct performance is critical
- The employee does not know how to perform as required (cannot do it)
- Performance expectations and goals are clear, and employees receive feedback on their performance
- There are (or will be) positive consequences for correct work behaviour; there are not negative consequences for performing as required
- Other solutions (such as coaching) are ineffective or too expensive (e.g. terminating employees and rehiring those with required skills)

Table 4.4 provides a list of the conditions when training is most likely to be the best solution to performance problems.

Needs-Analysis Methods

We have been discussing the needs-analysis process and the collection of information about the organization, task, and employees. By this point, you might be wondering where the information for a needs analysis comes from and how it is collected. In this section we review the methods of needs analysis; the following section discusses the sources of needs-analysis information.

There are many methods and techniques for conducting a needs analysis. The methods tend to differ in terms of the quality and type of information obtained, as well as the time and cost of collecting it. This section describes some of the most common methods of needs analysis.

Steadham has developed a useful summary of nine basic needs analysis methods that are described in Table 4.5 along with their advantages and disadvantages. The nine methods are: observation, questionnaires, key consultation, print media, interviews, group discussion, tests, records and reports, and work samples.

Some methods of needs analysis are better than others in terms of response rate, quality, usefulness of the data, and cost. One study tested three techniques: closed-ended survey, open-ended survey, and focus groups. A combination of the closed-ended survey and focus-group interviews provided the most practical, useful, and cost-effective information.[28] The best method, however, depends on the time and money available, the experience of the analyst, and the nature of the responses.

TABLE 4.5

Advantages and Disadvantages of Nine Basic Needs-Analysis Methods

Methods	Advantages	Disadvantages
Observation		
• Can be as technical as time–motion studies or as functionally or behaviourally specific as observing a new board or staff member interacting during a meeting.	• Minimizes interruption of routine work flow or group activity.	• Requires a highly skilled observer with both process and content knowledge (unlike an interviewer who needs, for the most part, only process skills).
• May be as unstructured as walking through an agency's offices on the lookout for evidence of communication barriers.	• Generates in situ data, highly relevant to the situation where response to identified training needs/interests will impact.	• Carries limitations that derive from being able to collect data only within the work setting (the other side of the first advantage listed in the preceding column).
• Can be used normatively to distinguish between effective and ineffective behaviours, organizational structures, and/or process.	• (When combined with a feedback step) provides for important comparison checks between inferences of the observer and the respondent.	• Holds potential for respondents to perceive the observation activity as "spying."
Questionnaires		
• May be in the form of surveys or polls of a random or stratified sample of respondents, or an enumeration of an entire "population."	• Can reach a large number of people in a short time.	• Make little provision for free expression of unanticipated responses.
• Can use a variety of question formats: open-ended, projective, forced-choice, priority-ranking.	• Are relatively inexpensive.	• Require substantial time (and technical skills, especially in survey model) for development of effective instruments.
• Can take alternative forms such as Q-sorts, or slip-sorts, rating scales, either predesigned or self-generated by respondent(s).	• Give opportunity of expression without fear of embarrassment.	• Are of limited utility in getting at causes of problems or possible solutions.
• May be self-administered (by mail) under controlled or uncontrolled conditions, or may require the presence of an interpreter or assistant.	• Yield data easily summarized and reported.	• Suffer low return rates (mailed), grudging responses, or unintended and/or inappropriate respondents.
Key Consultation		
• Secures information from those persons who, by virtue of their formal or informal standing, are in a good position to know what the training needs of a particular group are: a. board chairman b. related service providers c. members of professional associations d. individuals from the service population	• Is relatively simple and inexpensive to conduct.	• Carries a built-in bias, since it is based on views of those who tend to see training needs from their own individual or organizational perspective.
	• Permits input and interaction of a number of individuals, each with his or her own perspectives of the needs of the area, discipline, group, etc.	• May result in only a partial picture of training needs due to the typically nonrepresentative nature (in a statistical sense) of a key informant group.
	• Establishes and strengthens lines of communication between participants in the process.	

Print Media

- Can include professional journals, legislative news/notes, industry "rags," trade magazines, in-house publications.
- Is an excellent source of information for uncovering and clarifying normative needs.
- Provides information that is current, if not forward-looking.
- Is readily available and is apt to have already been reviewed by the client group.

- Can be a problem when it comes to the data analysis and synthesis into a useable form (use of clipping service or key consultants can make this type of data more useable).

Interviews

- Can be formal or casual, structured or unstructured, or somewhere in between.
- May be used with a sample of a particular group (board, staff, committee) or conducted with everyone concerned.
- Can be done in person, by phone, at the work site, or away from it.
- Are adept at revealing feelings, causes of, and possible solutions to problems that the client is facing (or anticipates); provide maximum opportunity for the client to represent himself spontaneously on his own terms (especially when conducted in an open-ended, nondirective manner).

- Are usually time-consuming.
- Can be difficult to analyze and quantify results (especially from unstructured formats).
- Unless the interviewer is skilled, the client(s) can easily be made to feel self-conscious.

Group Discussion

- Resembles face-to-face interview technique, e.g., structured or unstructured, formal or informal, or somewhere in between.
- Can be focused on job (role) analysis, group problem analysis, group goal setting, or any number of group tasks or themes, e.g., "leadership training needs of the board."
- Uses one or several of the familiar group facilitating techniques: brainstorming, nominal group process, force-fields, consensus rankings, organizational mirroring, simulation, and sculpting.
- Permits on-the-spot synthesis of different viewpoints.
- Builds support for the particular service response that is ultimately decided on.
- Decreases client's "dependence response" toward the service provided since data analysis is (or can be) a shared function.
- Helps participants to become better problem analysts, better listeners, etc.

- Relies for success on a skilful interviewer who can generate data without making client(s) feel self-conscious, suspicious, etc.
- Is time-consuming (therefore initially expensive) both for the consultant and the agency.
- Can produce data that are difficult to synthesize and quantify (more a problem with the less structured techniques).

Tests

- Are a hybridized form of questionnaire.
- Can be very functionally oriented (like observations) to test a board, staff, or committee member's proficiency.
- May be used to sample learned ideas and facts.
- Can be administered with or without the presence of an assistant.
- Can be especially helpful in determining whether the cause of a recognized problem is a deficiency in knowledge or skill, or by elimination, attitude.
- Results are easily quantifiable and comparable.

- The availability of a relatively small number of tests that are validated for a specific situation.
- Do not indicate if measured knowledge and skills are actually being used in the on-the-job or "back home group" situation.

TABLE 4.5 (CONTINUED)

Advantages and Disadvantages of Nine Basic Needs-Analysis Methods

METHODS	ADVANTAGES	DISADVANTAGES
Records, Reports		
• Can consist of organizational charts, planning documents, policy manuals, audits, and budget reports.	• Provide excellent clues to trouble spots.	• Causes of problems or possible solutions often do not show up.
• Employee records (grievance, turnover, accidents, etc.)	• Provide objective evidence of the results of problems within the agency or group.	• Carry perspective that generally reflects the past situation rather than the current one (or recent changes).
• Include minutes of meetings, weekly, monthly program reports, memoranda, agency service records, program evaluation studies.	• Can be collected with a minimum of effort and interruption of work flow since they already exist at the work site.	• Need a skilled data analyst if clear patterns and trends are to emerge from such technical and diffuse raw data.
Work Samples		
• Are similar to observation but in written form.	• Carry most of the advantage of records and reports data.	• Case study method will take time away from actual work of the organization.
• Can be products generated in the course of the organization's work, e.g., ad layouts, program proposals, market analyses, letters, training designs.	• Are the organization's data (its own output).	• Need specialized content analysts.
• Written responses to a hypothetical but relevant case study provided by the consultant.		• Analyst's assessment of strengths/weaknesses disclosed by samples can be challenged as "too subjective."

Source: From Steadham, S. V. (1980, January). Learning to select a needs assessment strategy. *Training & Development, 30,* 56–61. Copyright January 1980. Adapted from *Training and Development* magazine, American Society for Training and Development. Reprinted with permission. All rights reserved.

Surveys are one of the most often used methods of needs analysis due to their low cost and the ability to collect information from large numbers of respondents. Some software firms have developed surveys that can be customized to include questions from broad-climate issues to specific job standards. Many firms have designed needs-analysis software, some of which can be tailored to clients' needs. This technology allows HR staff to develop customized surveys quickly, and to analyze results by region, unit, and so on. One HR system contained 200,000 pieces of information on 500 employees. This system tapped every skill of every employee ranging from forklift and fuel-tank exchange procedures to probing abilities.[29]

Needs-Analysis Sources

There are many sources of needs-analysis information. Among the most important and often used are employees and managers as well as subject-matter experts who are familiar with a job. Some retail stores assess the competence of their sales staff through the use of professional shoppers who rate sales performance against established standards. A bank tests employee knowledge using a computer-based analysis, and then compares the results with supervisory rankings.[30]

In many cases, data on employees' performance and training needs is obtained from employees who rate their own performance and indicate their training needs. This is usually referred to as self-assessment. Self-assessment has its benefits and its limitations. Employees might be more motivated to be trained if they have some input in deciding on their needs. However, expressions of needs include feelings or desires and may have no relation to performance.[31]

Several studies have found weak relationships between employees' self-assessment of performance and managerial assessments.[32] A review of 55 studies failed to find a strong relationship between self-evaluation of ability and other measures of performance.[33] However, a study at IBM demonstrated that employees can be trained in self-assessment by learning to break down a job into its component parts and to analyze skills.[34] This method has the added benefit of the employees accepting ownership of their development plans.

In summary, there are many methods and sources for conducting a needs analysis. Because of the differences in information provided by the various methods and sources, the best approach is usually one that includes multiple methods and sources. Surveying only job incumbents about their perceptions of their own abilities might not result in the most objective information about performance gaps. Employees may have wish lists for training that do not meet the needs of their units or that do not address their own weaknesses. Managers, too, should be asked for their performance evaluations. Those who have frequent interaction with job incumbents, such as customers and employees in other departments, should also be surveyed. These different perspectives will result in more accurate and complete information. It also enables analysts to distinguish between perceived needs (what training employees feel they need), demand needs (what managers request), and normative needs (training needed to meet industry, unit, or job comparative standards).

Obstacles to Needs Analysis

Now that you know all about the needs-analysis process, you might be surprised to learn that many organizations do not conduct a thorough needs analysis, at least not to the extent that it is described in training and development textbooks.[35] Given the importance of needs analysis in the training process, you might wonder why this is the case.

As it turns out, there are a number of obstacles to conducting a formal needs analysis. Understanding what these obstacles are is important because if you are aware of them then you can also learn how to overcome them.

To begin with, trainers often claim that they are not rewarded for taking the time (and money) to conduct a needs analysis. Managers prefer action over analysis and they want to see training resources used to train employees. They may also feel that they can accurately identify training needs and that more analysis is a waste of time and money. Managers may even have their own agendas, such as rewarding employees by sending them to exotic locations for training, and therefore resist any attempt to redefine training needs.

Time can also be a constraint. New equipment might be arriving and it is easier to train all employees on all procedures instead of determining who needs training on which aspects of the new equipment. In fact, time is increasingly becoming a concern: a thorough needs analysis can take months to complete, and yet employees need to be trained and back on the job in a matter of weeks or even days.

Ultimately, what everyone is most concerned about is getting people trained as soon as possible. Because needs analysis is costly and time consuming, it is often seen as an unnecessary constraint on resources, staff, and time. The identification of training needs can turn into a comprehensive research study that takes months to complete.

The cost, time, and rigour necessary for doing a thorough needs analysis means that many organizations will simply not do one. However, conducting some data collection and analysis, rather than having no information, will almost always result in a better training program. It is therefore important for trainers to persuade management of the importance of conducting a needs analysis, and to ensure that it is included in the training budget. Furthermore, trainers need to be creative in finding ways to conduct a needs analysis within the constraints that exist in their organizations. To learn more about some creative techniques that training experts use to overcome needs analysis obstacles, see Training Today 4.1, "Just-in-Time Needs Analysis."

Summary

This chapter described the needs-analysis process. Three levels of needs analysis were discussed: organizational, task, and person analysis as well as cognitive task analysis and team task analysis. We also described the process of how to determine solutions to performance problems and if training and development is the best solution to performance problems. Data-collection methods and sources of information were also described as well as the

Just-in-Time Needs Analysis

Needs analysis can be a time-consuming process that is hard to sell to managers who want just-in-time solutions to urgent problems. When an organization is introducing new equipment, or an employee has to learn to perform an important task, the last thing that managers want to hear is "Wait, we have to do a needs analysis."

Very few trainers have the time and resources to follow the complete needs-analysis process described in a textbook. However, most trainers would use some means of detecting the underlying cause of a performance problem and training needs. Here are some ways experienced trainers conduct a needs analysis in a timely and less cumbersome manner.

- *Ask a series of questions.* When a manager demands a training course for employees, the trainer should start by asking questions related to the nature of the problem and its impact on the business. (The questions of the needs-analysis decision tree could be used.) Some trainers even agree to conduct a training course, as per the manager's demand, and then renegotiate the assignment as information emerges from interviews with employees before the course. Managers may be receptive to the emerging data,

recognizing the need to design solutions that solve the problem.

- *Use existing information.* Surveys, interviews, and observations are expensive data-collection methods. But most organizations keep customer complaint letters, grievance files, exit interviews, and sales data, which can be re-assessed for needs-assessment purposes.
- *Speed up data collection.* Use the intranet to survey employees. Start discussion groups around issues, concerns, and problems.
- *Link assessment and delivery.* Rather than conduct a lengthy needs analysis and then design a training program, some trainers attempt to join the two together, in small steps. For example, if there are star performers, bring them together in a forum with poorer performers to discuss effective techniques. The poorer performers not only are able to compare performance, but they learn how to improve at the same time.

Source: Adapted from Zemke, R. (1998). How to do a needs assessment when you think you don't have time. *Training, 35 (3), 38–44. Training: The Human Side of Business* by Zemke, R. ©1998–2006 VNU Business Media, Inc. Used with permission from *Training.*

obstacles to needs analysis. It should now be clear to you that a needs analysis is critical for determining the nature of performance problems and whether or not training and development is the best solution to a performance problem. The importance of a needs analysis, however, does not end here. As you will see in the next chapter, a needs analysis is also necessary for writing training objectives and the design of a training program.

Key Terms

cognitive task analysis   p. 112
competency   p. 109
contingency management   p. 116
job description   p. 109
learning culture   p. 107
needs analysis   p. 100
organizational analysis   p. 104

person analysis   p. 113
resource analysis   p. 106
strategic training   p. 105
task analysis   p. 108
team task analysis   p. 112
training transfer climate   p. 107

Make the Connection

p. 99: the instructional systems design model is discussed in Chapter 1 on page 20

p. 105: strategic human resource management is discussed in Chapter 1 on page 18

p. 105: the external environment and training is discussed in Chapter 1 on page 16

p. 107: organizational culture is discussed in Chapter 1 on page 19

p. 116: conditioning theory is discussed in Chapter 3 on page 72

Web Links

The Banff Centre: www.banffcentre.ca/departments/leadership/

Boston Pizza: www.bostonpizza.com

CIBC: www.cibc.com

IBM: www.ibm.com/ca

Technocell Canada: www.technocell.com

RPC Icons

RPC 4.1 Establishes priority of responses to needs-assessment results.

RPC 4.2 Conducts training needs assessments by identifying individual and corporate learning requirements.

RPC 4.3 Recommends the most appropriate way to meet identified learning needs (e.g., courses, secondments, and on-the-job activities).

Discussion Questions

1. Organizations often have data on file that can be used for the purposes of a needs analysis. Discuss the kinds of information that might exist in an organization and how it might be useful for an organizational, task, and/or person analysis.
2. If needs-analysis information has not been used as the basis for the design and delivery of a training program, what are some of the reasons why organizations decide to design and deliver training programs? Are these good reasons for investing in training and development programs?
3. Discuss the reasons why organizations do not always conduct a needs analysis and what a trainer might do to overcome needs-analysis obstacles. What are the implications of designing and implementing a training program without conducting a needs analysis?

4. Discuss the advantages and disadvantages of the different sources of needs-analysis information. What sources are best for a person, task, and organizational needs analysis?
5. Discuss the process involved in determining solutions to performance problems. When is training likely to be a good solution? When is training not likely to be a good solution?
6. What is the difference between a training transfer climate and a learning culture? Why should an organization obtain information about the transfer climate and learning culture before designing and implementing a training program?
7. What is the difference between a task analysis, a cognitive task analysis, and a team task analysis? Discuss when and how each type of needs analysis should be conducted.
8. Review the chapter-opening vignette on Technocell Canada and discuss the methods and sources used to conduct the needs analysis. Why do you think they used certain sources and methods, and how useful were they for determining training needs and solutions?

The Great Training Debate

1. Debate the following: Needs analysis is a waste of time. What is most important is getting people trained as soon as possible rather than wasting precious time to find out who needs training.

Using the Internet

1. To find out how some organizations conduct needs analysis to determine their training needs, go to Industry Canada at **www.collectionscanada. gc.ca/webarchives/20060205142404/http://strategis.ic.gc.ca/epic/internet/ incts-scf.nsf/en/sl00032e.html** and answer the following questions:

   a. What are organizations doing to assess their training needs?
   b. Read the case studies and briefly summarize the approaches that each organization used for needs analysis and the diagnostic tools they used. How does the use of diagnostic tools assist organizations and employees?

Exercises

In-Class

1. Think of a problem you had or were aware of at an organization that you worked for. Describe the problem and then use Mager and Pipe's flow diagram for determining solutions to performance problems (Figure 4.2) to determine the best solution. Also consider each solution

in the figure and explain why it would or would not be a good solution to the problem. Finally, if you know what the organization did about the problem, describe what it did and if it was an effective solution.

2. Consider your job and performance as a student and conduct each of the following types of needs analysis: a) task analysis, b) cognitive task analysis, c) team task analysis, and d) person analysis. Based on your results, indicate the critical tasks of a student as well as how well you perform each task, and on which tasks you need to improve your performance. What do you need to do to become a better student?

3. Find a partner in the class and take turns conducting a task-analysis interview. Before beginning your interview, prepare a task-analysis interview guide with questions that will help you identify tasks; rate their importance and frequency; and determine the task specifications (knowledge, skills, and abilities). The interviewee can refer to a current or previous job when answering the interviewer's questions. Also consider the relevance of a cognitive task analysis and a team task analysis.

4. Table 4.5 describes nine different methods of needs analysis. Review each method and then explain what methods you think would be most appropriate for each of the following kinds of needs analysis: a) organizational analysis, b) task analysis, c) cognitive task analysis, d) team task analysis, and e) person analysis. Be sure to explain your reasoning as to why a particular method would be best for each type of needs analysis.

5. Recall a training program that you have attended as part of a current or previous job. To what extent do you think the program was based on an organizational, task, and person analysis? Try to relate specific aspects of the training program to each level of needs analysis. What performance problem was the training designed to address, and how effective was the program as a solution to the performance problem?

6. Imagine that you are a trainer in an organization that prides itself on providing employees with frequent opportunities for training. The president of the company has asked you to design and deliver a training program on team skills so that employees will be able to work in groups. He or she wants you to start training employees as soon as possible and does not want you to spend time and money conducting a needs analysis. He or she wants you to develop an action plan for the design and delivery of the program and present it in one week. How will you handle the needs analysis issue and what will you recommend? Prepare your presentation and present it to the class.

In-the-Field

1. To find out about the extent to which organizations conduct needs analyses, contact the human resources staff of an organization and request an interview about needs analysis. In particular, find out if

the staff conduct an organizational, task, and person analysis; the kinds of information they gather when they conduct each level of needs analysis; what methods and sources they use to gather the information; and what they do with the information and how it is used as part of the training and development process. If they do not conduct needs analyses, find out why and how they determine training needs. Students should come to class prepared to present the results of their interviews.

Case Incident

Beer School

As part of Labatt's training and development strategy, all non-unionized employees attend beer school to learn about the art of brewing and serving. In fact, the company plans to send 4000 of its employees through the program, either at the employee pub at the company's head office in Toronto or at satellite locations across the country. Labatt employees who have completed beer school can talk knowledgeably about the fine points of beer with clients, friends, and family.

Questions

1. What information from a needs analysis (organizational, task, and person) might have suggested the need for employees to attend beer school?
2. Beer school is part of the company's training and development strategy. Do you think it is an example of strategic training? Explain your answer.

Source: Humber, T. (2003, November 17). Serving up training. *Canadian HR Reporter, 16* (20), G1, G4. Reprinted with permission—Torstar Syndication Services.

Case Study

U-Haul's Performance Problem

In Ontario, the Highway Traffic Act has in place tough sanctions and fines that apply to commercial vehicles. However, there is an exemption in the Act that some refer to as a loophole, which indicates that trucks rented for short-term personal use are not commercial vehicles and are therefore exempt from some of the sanctions and tough penalties. The exemption includes do-it-yourself movers who are the target market for U-Haul. In fact, U-Haul is the market leader among do-it-yourself truck rental companies.

If police feel that the general maintenance on a commercial truck is poor, they can issue a $20,000 fine against the trucking company. However, a company falling under the exemption such as a U-Haul truck is immune from fines and also from having its safety violations recorded against the company's provincial Commercial Vehicle Operating Record (CVOR).

In July 2005, the *Toronto Star* conducted an investigation of the safety of U-Haul vehicles. One of their conclusions was that if you rent a U-Haul, you have a 50-50 chance of getting a truck that will not pass a road safety check. The *Star* based its investigation on three sources: Ontario Provincial Police data that show police failed 109 of 220 U-Haul vehicles during road-side safety checks between 2002 and 2004; an independent test conducted by the Ontario Safety League of four U-Haul vehicles rented at random, in which all four failed a standard North American provincial and state commercial vehicle safety inspection that every truck must pass yearly to continue operating; and U-Haul's driving record, accessed through the Ontario Ministry of Transportation, which showed that 17 of 35 U-Haul vehicles failed safety inspections over a two-year period.

Some of the violations found by the Ontario Safety League included holes on the floor on the driver's side, axle sealant leaking onto brake pads, one flat tire, one bulging tire, one tire with a nail in it, power-steering fluid leaks, coolant leaks, oil leaks, and a loose king pin on the front axle. In all the trucks there were problems with the lights and signals.

Upon hearing of the Ontario Safety League investigation, U-Haul pulled the four vehicles in question out of service and hired independent mechanics to look at them. U-Haul agreed that three of the four trucks had "unacceptable" flaws and should not have been rented. The vice president of U-Haul Ontario said the company was dealing with the four locations that rented the four vehicles and stated that "employees and dealers are responsible for seeing that our equipment is in safe operating condition, scheduling repairs throughout the life of the vehicle."

U-Haul says it runs preventative maintenance inspections at 8000 kilometres, 24 000 kilometres, and 48 000 kilometres that "meet or exceed the federal specifications." Prior to the rental of a vehicle, the employee or dealer is required to check for fuel leaks, engine-oil leaks and levels, power steering leaks and levels, transmission-oil levels, broken seals, anti-freeze levels, tires for treads and air pressure, and to make sure all lights and signals are working and that the windshield is clean. And after every rental, an employee is required to ask the renter if there are any problems that need to be fixed "before the next customer rents this truck" including braking problems, engine overheating, and electrical problems.

U-Haul operates 1800 vehicles in Ontario. According to U-Haul's provincial operating record for the past two years, 35 trucks have had safety inspections and 17 failed. If not for the exemption, every OPP citation against U-Haul would be on record. During one weekend safety blitz, U-Haul vehicles failed six of eight inspections and were pulled off the road until they are repaired.

At the time, Harinder Takhar, Ontario's Minister of Transportation, said he will investigate closing the loophole in the Highway Traffic Act. "If we are having some evidence that there are safety concerns out there . . . I will get a full report. I'm asking the Ministry, what kind of problems did we find and if those problems are serious. I want to make sure the consumers are protected and safety is maintained on our highways." Police and the Ontario Safety League are calling for the loophole to be closed.

Following the *Toronto Star* investigation, the Ontario transportation ministry launched a province-wide investigation of the truck rental industry including surprise spot checks of U-Haul vehicles and other major truck rental companies and determined that U-Haul had the poorest safety record. This resulted in high-level meetings among MTO, OPP, and U-Haul executives. U-Haul subsequently promised that it would clean up its act and begin removing older vehicles from service, and more thoroughly check vehicles before they are rented.

However, in December of 2005 a 43-year-old Peterborough man died after being thrown from a U-Haul truck when it flipped over. And in September of 2006, the Ontario government told U-Haul that its licence will be suspended if it does not meet stringent safety benchmarks.

Sources: Dale, D. (2007, August 30). U-Haul lags behind in safety. *Toronto Star*, A4; McGran, K. (2005, July 4). Traffic act loophole puts drivers at risk. *Toronto Star*, A1; McGran, K. (2005, July 5). ABCs of do-it-yourself rentals. *Toronto Star*, A10; McGran, K. (2005, July 5). U-Haul rentals to get spot checks. *Toronto Star*, A1; McGran, K. (2005, July 5). U-Haul trails after trucks. *Toronto Star*, A10; McGran, K. (2005, July 6). Province to probe truck rental industry. *Toronto Star*, A1; McGran, K. (2005, December 5). Driver faults U-Haul in death. *Toronto Star*, A4. Reprinted with permission—Torstar Syndication Services.

Questions

1. Assume that you have been hired by U-Haul to conduct a needs analysis. How can the needs-analysis process (refer to Figure 4.1) and each level of needs analysis help you understand the safety problem and whether or not training should be part of the solution to solve it? Explain what you will learn from an organizational, task, and person analysis.

2. If you were to conduct a needs analysis at U-Haul, what methods and sources would you use? Be specific about why you would or would not use a particular method and source.

3. Using the Mager and Pipe flowchart in Figure 4.2, determine some possible solutions to the safety problem at U-Haul. Do you think that training is part of the solution? If so, who should be trained and what kind of training should they receive? What other solutions might be necessary to solve the safety problem?

4. What effect do you think the government's surprise spot checks and threat to suspended U-Haul's licence will have on U-Haul, its employees, and its training? Do you think these actions by the government are a good idea or should it be doing something else?

5. If the Ontario Government closes the loophole in the Highway Traffic Act, what effect do you think this will have on U-Haul? Will it have an effect on training? Explain your answer.

References

1. Based on Scott, L. (2005, December). Awards for Excellence in Workplace Literacy, Medium Business Winner, 2005. *Upgrading employee skills to meet corporate standards—Technocell Canada, A Felix Schoeller Group Company.* Case Study December 2005 E/F. The Conference Board of Canada: Ottawa.

2. Salas, E., & Cannon-Bowers, J. A. (2001). The science of training: A decade of progress. *Annual Review of Psychology, 52,* 471–499.

3. Leigh, D., Watkins, R., Platt, W. A., & Kaufman, R. (2000). Alternate models of needs assessment: Selecting the right one for your organization. *Human Resource Development Quarterly, 11,* 87–93.

4. Kaufman, R. (1991). *Strategic planning plus: An organizational guide.* Glenview, IL: Scott Foreman Professional Books.

5. Leigh, D., Watkins, R., Platt, W. A., & Kaufman, R. (2000).

6. Mills, G. R., Pace, W., & Peterson, B. (1989). *Analysis in human resource training and organization development.* Reading, MA: Addison-Wesley.

7. Hall, B. (2003, February). The top training priorities for 2003. *Training, 40* (2), 38–42.

8. Estabrooke, M., & Foy, N. F. (1992). Answering the call of tailored training. *Training, 29* (10), 84–88.

9. Carr, C. (1992, June). The three Rs of training. *Training, 29* (6), 60–61.

10. Estabrooke, M., & Foy, N. F. (1992).

11. Goldstein, I. L. (1993). *Training in organizations* (3rd ed.). Pacific Grove, CA: Brooks/Cole.

12. Estabrooke, M., & Foy, N. F. (1992).

13. Gibb-Clark, M. (2000, February 11). Employee training can backfire on firms: Survey. *The Globe and Mail,* B10.

14. Heller, M. (2005, March). State's measure could undercut damage awards. *Workforce Management, 84* (3), 21–22.

15. Johnson, G. (2004, October). The perfect storm. *Training, 41* (10), 38–49.

16. Scott, L. (2005, December).

17. Rouiller, J. Z., & Goldstein, I. L. (1993). The relationship between organizational transfer climate and positive transfer of training. *Human Resource Development Quarterly, 4,* 377–390.

18. Tracey, J. B, Tannenbaum, S. I., Kavanagh, M. J. (1995). Applying trained skills on the job: The importance of the work environment. *Journal of Applied Psychology, 80,* 239–252.

19. Parry, S. B. (1998). Just what is a competency? *Training, 35* (6), 58–64.

20. MacNamara, D. (1998, November 16). Learning contracts, competency profiles the new wave in executive development. *Canadian HR Reporter,* G8–G10.

21. Landey, F. J., & Vasey, J. (1991). Job analysis: The composition of SME samples. *Personnel Psychology, 44,* 27–50.

22. Salas, E., & Cannon-Bowers, J. A. (2001).

23. DuBois, D. A. (2002). Leveraging hidden expertise: Why, when, and how to use cognitive task analysis. In K. Kraiger (Ed.), *Creating, implementing, and managing effective training and development: State-of-the-art lessons for practice* (pp. 80–114). San Francisco, CA: Jossey-Bass.

24. Salas, E., Burke, C. S., & Cannon-Bowers, J. A. (2002). What we know about designing and delivering team training: Tips and guidelines. In K. Kraiger (Ed.), *Creating, implementing, and managing effective training and development: State-of-the-art lessons for practice* (pp. 234–259). San Francisco, CA: Jossey-Bass.

25. Salas, E., Burke, C. S., & Cannon-Bowers, J. A. (2002).

26. Trainor, N. L. (1998, November 16). Using measurement to predict performance. *Canadian HR Reporter,* 7–8.

27. Mager, R. F., & Pipe, P. (1970). *Analyzing performance problems or you really oughta wanna.* Belmont, CA: Lear Siegler, Inc./Fearon.

28. Preskill, H. (1991). A comparison of data collection methods for assessing training needs. *Human Resource Development Quarterly, 2* (2), 143–156.

29. Rockburn, J. (1991, October 15). Streamlining human resources. *The Globe and Mail,* B15.

30. Tritsch, C. (1991, May). Assessing your training. *Human Resource Executive.*

31. Latham, G. P. (1988). Human resource training and development. *Annual Review of Psychology, 39,* 545–582.

32. McEnery, J., & McEnery, J. M. (1987). Self-rating in management training needs assessment: A neglected opportunity. *Journal of Occupational Psychology, 60,* 49–60. Staley, C. C., & Shockley-Zalaback, P. (1986). Communication proficiency and future training needs of the female professional: Self-assessment versus supervisors' evaluations. *Human Relations, 39,* 891–902.

33. Mabe, P. A., & West, S. G. (1982). Validity of self-evaluation of ability: A review and a meta-analysis. *Journal of Applied Psychology, 67,* 280–296.

34. Bardsely, C. A. (1987, April). Improving employee awareness of opportunity at IBM. *Personnel, 64* (4), 58–63.

35. Saari, L. M., Johnson, T. R., McLaughlin, S. D., & Zimmerle, D. M. (1988). A survey of management training and education practices in U.S. companies. *Personnel Psychology, 41* (4), 731–744.

CHAPTER 5

Training Design

Chapter Learning Outcomes

After reading this chapter, you should be able to:

- define and write training objectives and describe their five elements and three components
- discuss the factors to consider when deciding to purchase or design a training program
- discuss the purpose of a request for proposal (RFP) and how to create an effective one
- describe the ways to determine the content of a training program
- describe the types of training methods and define blended training
- define practice and active practice and describe conditions of practice before and during training
- discuss the difference between routine expertise and adaptive expertise and the implications of each for training design
- define active learning and describe training design elements to develop it
- define error-management training and describe when it is most likely to result in positive training outcomes

BMO FINANCIAL GROUP

For the BMO Financial Group, employee training and development is a top priority. Over the past 10 years, BMO has invested more than $500 million in employee training and development. As a result, more than 8,000 employees annually receive training at the company's Institute for Learning.

Built in 1994 at a cost of $50 million, the Institute for Learning is a 13-acre complex with 14 high-tech classrooms, 150 bedrooms to accommodate out-of-town students, and a presentation hall that seats 400, as well as dining facilities and a gymnasium.

The Institute for Learning offers more than 700 courses to more than 34,000 employees who receive about six and a half days of training a year. Because BMO courses are custom-made, they are able to connect learning to the organization's strategies. Further, sending employees to the institute for training helps to reinforce BMO's corporate culture and engenders a sense of community among co-workers.

BMO offers a wide variety of courses and programs including internal accreditations across many disciplines. One of its primary programs is a four-year MBA program in financial services operated in conjunction with Dalhousie School of Management and the Institute for Canadian Bankers. Managerial leadership training is designed to prepare new managers by enhancing their strategic capabilities. Risk management training, offered in partnership with York University's Schulich School of Business, is available for seasoned risk managers. Project management programs are aimed at instilling change-management expertise.

The company also designed a Corporate Audit Professional Upgrading of Skills program to improve the internal audit division's value to the company. Auditors complete an online, role-specific competency assessment that is used to create a customized learning plan. The program has resulted in a 100-percent increase in the audit division's service score, which is provided by clients based on the quality of auditors' work. A series of selling training sessions to personal banker sales teams resulted in a 35 percent increase in personal deposits and sales points.

Whatever the program, training and development programs at BMO deal with real-world issues the company faces. Trainees often are asked to draft solutions and strategies for existing BMO concerns rather than tackle hypothetical scenarios. And because almost 30 percent of BMO's annual revenue comes from the United States, the company goes to great lengths to incorporate U.S.-specific rules and legislative matters into its training programs. In order to ensure the quality and relevance of its programs, the company conducts employee surveys to gather feedback from employees.

In the last several years BMO Financial Group has been on Training magazine's list of the Top 125 best companies for training and development.[1]

BMO Financial Group is a good example of a company that invests a great deal of resources in the design of training and development programs. In order to stay competitive and ensure that employees have the knowledge and skills to perform their jobs, companies regularly need to design new training programs. In the case of BMO Financial Group, it recently designed the Corporate Audit Professional Upgrading of Skills program, which was recognized by *Training* magazine as an outstanding initiative.[2]

The design of training and development programs involves many important decisions, such as whether to purchase a training program from a vendor or design it in-house; what content to include and what training methods to use; and how to design a program so that trainees have opportunities for practice that maximize their learning and retention.

In the previous chapter, we described the process of identifying training needs and determining solutions to performance problems. When it has been determined that training is part of the solution to performance problems, the needs-analysis information must then be translated into training objectives and a training program. Training design involves many activities; these are shown in Table 5.1 and are the focus of this chapter.

Training Objectives

A **training objective** is a statement of what trainees are expected to be able to do after a training program. Training objectives answer the question, "What should trainees be able to do at the end of a training program?" Put another way, an objective is the expected outcome of training. Training objectives also describe the knowledge and skills to be acquired.

The emphasis of training is usually learning, on-the-job behaviour, and job performance. Learning involves the process of acquiring new knowledge,

Training objective

A statement of what trainees are expected to be able to do after a training program

TABLE 5.1

Training Design Activities

1. Write training objectives.
2. Decide to purchase or design a training program.
3. Create a request for proposal (RFP) to purchase training services and programs.
4. Determine the training content.
5. Decide on the training methods.
6. Incorporate active practice and conditions of practice into the training program.
7. Consider design elements for active learning if adaptive expertise is required.

skills, and attitudes, while performance involves the use of these new skills, knowledge, and attitudes on the job. Training objectives usually refer to the acquisition of knowledge and/or skills as well as behaviour on the job.

Training objectives are an important link between the needs-analysis stage and the other stages of the training and development process. In addition to stating what employees will learn and be able to do following a training program, training objectives serve a number of purposes for trainees, trainers, and managers which are described in Table 5.2.

RPC 5.1 Writing Training Objectives

Writing training objectives involves more than making lists of behaviour verbs such as "recognize" and "evaluate." The real skill is the ability to rework needs-analysis information into performance outcomes. A training objective should contain five key elements of the desired outcome as follows:

1. *Who is to perform the desired behaviour?* Employees and managers are the easiest to identify. In a training situation more accurate

TABLE 5.2

Purposes of Training Objectives

Training objectives serve a number of purposes for trainers, trainees, and managers.

TRAINERS

1. Trainees can be assessed prior to training to determine if they have mastered any of the objectives. Depending on the results, trainees can either omit certain sections of a training program or undertake additional training to master the prerequisites.
2. The selection of training content and methods is simplified by objectives. The choice of content and methods will be guided by the need to achieve certain objectives.
3. Learning objectives enable trainers to develop measures for evaluation and to determine how to evaluate a training program and how to calculate the benefits of a program.

TRAINEES

4. Objectives inform trainees of the goals of a training program and what they will be expected to learn and do at the end of a training program.
5. Objectives allow trainees to focus their energies on achieving specific goals, rather than waste energy on irrelevant tasks or on trying to figure out what is required of them.
6. Objectives communicate to employees that training is important and that they will be accountable for what they learn in training.

MANAGERS

7. Objectives communicate to managers, professional groups, and others what the trainee is expected to have learned by the end of a training program and what the trainee should be able to do.
8. Management and supervisors know exactly what is expected of trainees and can reinforce and support newly trained knowledge and skills on the job.

descriptors might be "all first-level supervisors," "anyone conducting selection interviews," or "all employees with more than one month of experience." The trainer is not the "who," although it is tempting for some trainees to write, for example, that the trainer will present five hours of information on communication. The goal of the instructor is to maximize the efficiency with which all trainees achieve the specified objectives, not just present the information.[3]

2. *What is the actual behaviour to be employed to demonstrate mastery of the training content or objective?* Actions described by words like "type," "run," and "calculate" can be measured easily. Other mental activities such as comprehension and analysis can also be described in measurable ways.

3. *Where and, 4., When is the behaviour to be demonstrated and evaluated (i.e., under what conditions)?* These could include "during a 60-minute typing test," "on a ski hill with icy conditions," "when presented with a diagram," or "when asked to design a training session." The tools, equipment, information, and other source materials for training should be specified. Included in this list may be things the trainee may not use, such as calculators.

5. *What is the standard by which the behaviour will be judged?* Is the trainee expected to type 60 words per minute with fewer than three errors? Can the trainee list five out of six purposes for training objectives?

An example of a training objective that includes the five elements is as follows:

> The sales representative (*who*) will be able to make 10 calls a day to new customers in the territory assigned (*what, where, when*), and will be able to generate three (30 percent) sales worth at least $500 from these calls (*how, or the criterion*).

Training objectives should closely resemble the task analysis. For example, one task of the job of a receptionist could be: *The receptionist* (who) *sorts 100 pieces of incoming mail by categories of complaints, requests for information, and invoices* (what) *within 60 minutes, with less than one percent processing errors* (how). This could easily become a training objective. A training objective that reads like an actual job behaviour is more likely to be approved, learned, and used on the job.

When the five elements are included in a training objective, the final written objective should contain three key components:

1. *Performance:* What the trainee will be able to do after the training. In other words, what work behaviour the trainee will be able to display.
2. *Condition:* The tools, time, and situation under which the trainee is expected to perform the behaviour. In other words, where and when the behaviour will occur.
3. *Criterion:* The level of acceptable performance or the standard or criteria against which performance will be judged.

Representative workers should be involved in the development of the training objectives. A team consisting of the trainer, trainees, and their supervisors would be ideal.[4] At some point, the objectives should be reviewed with, and approved by, the management and the supervisors of the trainees.

In summary, a training objective contains an observable action with a measurable criterion outlining the conditions of performance. Once training objectives have been developed, the next step is to design a training program. However, at this point one has to first decide if a training program should be designed in-house by the organization and its training staff or by an external consultant or vendor. This is known as the purchase-or-design decision and is described in the next section.

The Purchase-or-Design Decision

Once the training objectives have been developed, the organization faces a make-or-purchase decision. Many private training companies and consultants in Canada offer an extensive array of courses on general topics such as computer training and customer service (see the Using the Internet exercise at the end of this chapter).

In many cases, it is more economical for an organization to purchase these materials, packaged in a professional format, than to develop the materials themselves, which in many cases will be used only once or twice.

For example, most organizations do not design training courses in basic skills; they form alliances with educational institutions, community colleges, or private organizations that specialize in developing and delivering basic skills training programs.[5] Recall from the chapter-opening vignette that BMO forms alliances with several universities that provide specialized training programs in areas such as the MBA program, in financial services, and in risk management training.

Organizations are particularly likely to purchase training programs that do not require organization-specific content and are of a more generic nature. For example, organizations prefer to use outside consultants for sexual harassment training.[6]

The advantages of packaged programs are high quality, immediate delivery, ancillary services (tests, videos), the potential to customize the package to the organization, benefits from others' implementation experience, extensive testing, and often less expense than internally developed programs.[7]

Training programs developed internally by an organization also have some advantages including security and confidentiality, use of the organization's language, incorporation of the organization's values, use of internal content expertise, understanding of the specific target audience and organization, and the pride and credibility of having a customized program.[8]

Because many of BMO's programs are custom-made they are able to connect learning to the organization's strategy and the training reinforces the company's corporate culture.

Purchase Decision Factors

Given the pros and cons of purchasing and designing a training program, what factors should be considered when making a decision? Obviously, one of the most important factors to consider is the cost of each alternative. A cost–benefit analysis would be necessary to determine the best option. Some types of training programs will be much more costly to design than to purchase. However, other factors should also be considered in addition to cost.

For example, does the human resource department have the time and expertise to design a training program? Designing a training program requires expertise in many areas such as training methods and principles and theories of learning. If the human resource department does not have this expertise in-house then it will need to purchase all or part of a training program. As well, developing a training program is time-consuming. Unless a human resource department has a training function and training staff or is otherwise well staffed, it may not have the time to design training programs.

Time is also a factor in terms of how soon the organization wants to begin training. Given the amount of time required to design a new training program, if there is a need or desire to begin training as soon as possible then the organization will need to purchase a training program. In effect, the sooner the organization wants to begin training, the less likely there will be sufficient time to design a new training program.

Another important consideration is the number of employees who need to be trained and the extent to which future employees will also require training. If a relatively small number of employees require training, then it is probably not worthwhile to design a new training program. However, if a large number of employees need to receive training now and in the future then designing a new training program in-house makes more sense. Thus, to the extent that the training program will be used for many employees in both the short and the long term, a decision to design the program is more likely.

Although we have been referring to the purchase of an entire training program, it is important to realize that purchasing can involve buying particular training materials such as a video package or buying an entire training program that is specially designed for the organization. Organizations can also purchase off-the-shelf training programs which are already designed and that contain all the materials required to deliver a training program. As well, a consultant could be hired to design and deliver a training program or it can be delivered by people within the organization once it has been designed by a consultant. For a good example, see Training Today 5.1, "Personal Development and Literacy Training at Vecima Networks."

When an organization decides to purchase a training program, it needs to begin the process of finding a vendor or consultant who will be able to design and/or deliver the program. This requires a request for proposal and is described in the next section.

Personal Development and Literacy Training at Vecima Networks

Vecima Networks is a manufacturer of computer hardware and software that connects cable, wireless, and telephone networks to the computer for cable and telecom operators to optimize network efficiency. The company is a world-class designer and manufacturer of advanced broadband products.

Based in Victoria, Vecima employs approximately 600 people in western Canada. The industry is small, and there is not a large pool of trained people working in electronics manufacturing. As a result, Vecima has had to design its own training programs to train its 400 manufacturing workers. A few years ago the company partnered with the Saskatchewan Institute of Applied Science and Technology (SIAST) to create a journeyperson curriculum for electronic assembly.

Six full-time trainers provide new hires with 40 hours of training that covers a range of topics, from how to hold a soldering iron to how to inspect a circuit board. Once the base training is complete, new hires go on the line and are trained in a buddy system that brings their training to 60 hours.

However, based on supervisor feedback, the company realized that many issues employees have to deal with are not technical, and a non-technical training program on personal development and literacy was required. Rather than design the program in-house, Vecima went to the community for the expertise. It teamed up with READ Saskatoon and Radium Communication Centre, two not-for-profit agencies that have been offering similar training for years.

Vecima received a $50,000 grant from Saskatchewan-Canada Career and Employment Services. The funding was used to develop a 16.5-hour course that included employability skills such as communication, time management, business etiquette, decision making, and team building. Employees have a personal portfolio to keep a record of their training and their career goals.

The funding also covers the cost of the classroom training to be delivered by the community agencies. When the funding runs out, Vecima training staff will take over and give the course in-house.

Sources: Based on Anonymous. (May 19, 2008). CEOs talk: Training & development. *Canadian HR Reporter, 21* (10), 11–13; www.vecima.com/careers.php.

RPC 5.2

Request for proposal (RFP)

A document that outlines to potential vendors and consultants an organization's training and project needs

Request for Proposal (RFP)

The process of identifying and hiring a vendor or consultant begins with a **request for proposal (RFP),** which is a document that outlines to potential vendors and consultants the organization's training and project needs. Vendors and consultants can then review the RFP and determine if they are able to provide the products and services required by the organization and if they should prepare a proposal and bid on the job. The organization must then evaluate the proposals it receives and choose a vendor that can provide the best solution and is also a good match for the organization.

A request for proposal should provide detailed information about the organization's training needs and the nature of the project and will often include the following sections:[9]

- Pre-qualification checklist.
- Detailed description of the opportunity.
- Description of the company and its culture.
- Scope of the project.
- Detailed statement of work.
- Detailed instructions on how to respond to the RFP.

- Schedule for the entire RFP and selection process with milestones.
- Basis of the award.
- Definition of the level of service required.
- Request for additional information.
- Confidentiality agreements.

Creating an RFP is an important step in searching for a vendor because it requires the organization to describe its most critical training needs and the nature of the training solution required. This will help to ensure that the organization purchases what it really needs and also communicates the training needs and required project to stakeholders and potential vendors.

Failure to prepare a detailed RFP can result in an organization purchasing a program that it really does not need and at a much higher cost than necessary. There are many stories of companies that failed to create a good RFP and then purchased programs and systems that went well beyond what they really needed.[10] Thus, it is also important that an organization determine the extent to which a vendor's products and services match its needs for training services and products. To learn more about how to write an effective RFP, see The Trainer's Notebook 5.1, "An Effective Request for Proposal (RFP)."

The Trainer's Notebook 5.1

An Effective Request for Proposal (RFP)

Creating an effective RFP is a difficult and time-consuming task. However, a good RFP will ensure that an organization gets the training program and systems it needs from the right vendor at an appropriate cost. Here are eight things to consider when creating an RFP.

- *Have a clear vision of your overall learning strategy.* There must be a master strategy that is based on the primary needs of the various departments involved.
- *Create proper scope for the project.* Set a budget and align the most critical needs with project requirements.
- *Develop a vendor pre-qualification checklist.* Write a pre-qualification checklist before writing the RFP so that vendors can quickly decide if they can provide the required products and services. The checklist should have between 10 and 20 items and indicate the qualifications for the most critical needs.
- *Create a vendor scorecard.* Create a scorecard to grade vendors before writing the RFP to ensure that you request the necessary information in the RFP. The evaluators should rate each item on the scorecard on a scale of zero to five.

- *Use a template.* Use a template to create the RFP if one exists in the organization. Even one used for non-training purchases can be helpful in creating an RFP.
- *Don't overstate the positive or understate the negative.* Be candid about the project so vendors can adequately determine their suitability for it.
- *Design a request-for-information questionnaire.* The questionnaire should be designed to obtain additional information about a vendor's products, services, experience, and background. Most of the questions should be directly related to the needs of the project and the vendor's ability to provide a solution that meets the organization's needs.
- *Allow sufficient time for responses.* Provide at least two to three weeks for most standard projects so that vendors can carefully analyze the requirements and prepare a detailed response.

Source: Based on Chapman, B. (2004, January). How to create the ideal RFP. *Training, 41* (1), 40–43.

Training Content

Once a decision has been made to design a training program, decisions must be made about the training content. This is a crucial stage as the training content must be based on the training needs and objectives. As noted by Campbell, "By far the highest-priority question for designers, users, and investigators of training is, 'What is to be learned?' That is, what (specifically) should a training program try to accomplish, and what should the training content be?" (p. 188).[11]

To understand the importance of this, consider an organization that sells dental equipment and supplies. Although the company regularly offers new products, they do not sell very well. The reason for this is because the sales force concentrates on repeat sales of more common supplies and materials. There are a number of reasons why this might be the case. For example, the sales force might not be sufficiently informed about the new products or they might not have the skills required to sell them. Other reasons could be a lack of motivation or an attitude problem. Obviously, designing a training program to inform the sales force about the new products will not be very effective if what they are lacking are sales skills. Getting the content right is one of the most important stages in training design.

A trainer will have a good idea about the required training content from the needs analysis and training objectives. This is another reason why it is important to conduct a thorough needs analysis prior to designing a training program. As well, employees' current levels of knowledge and skills can be compared to the organization's desired levels as indicated by the performance goals or objectives. The gap between the two represents the organization's training needs and the required content of a training program.

 **5.3**

According to Donald Kirkpatrick, trainers should ask themselves, "What topics should be presented to meet the needs and accomplish the objectives?" (p. 11).[12] In some cases, the required training is legislated, such as the Workplace Hazardous Materials Information System (WHMIS), which requires that workers in certain occupations receive training on the potential hazards of chemicals in the workplace and emergency procedures for the clean-up and disposal of a spill (see Chapter 13). In such cases, the content of training is specified in the legislation as well as in the requirements for employee certification.

Subject-matter expert (SME)

A person who is familiar with the knowledge, skills, and abilities required to perform a task or job

In other cases, it might be necessary to consult a **subject-matter expert (SME)** who is familiar with the knowledge, skills, and abilities required to perform a task or job and can specify the training content.[13] For example, to determine the content of a training program on sales techniques, one might consult with experienced salespersons, consultants, or managers. At BMO, they survey the highest-ranking commercial account managers in order to identify their best work habits and key drivers of success. Their responses are then incorporated into a guide that is given to all employees within the account management sales force.[14]

Training Methods

 **5.4**

Once the training content has been determined, the next step is to decide what training methods will be used.[15] The topic of training methods is extensive, and as a result the next three chapters are devoted to it. For now we will present a brief introduction to this important part of training design.

Training methods can be arranged into a number of different categories such as active versus passive methods, one-way versus two-way communication, or informational versus experiential. For our purposes, we distinguish training methods in terms of where they take place, since this is a fairly tangible distinction. That is, some training methods occur on the job, such as coaching and performance aids, while others take place off the job and usually in a classroom with an instructor. A third category of training methods includes those that use technology to deliver training such as computer-based training and e-learning.

A variety of off-the-job and on-the-job training methods are described in Chapters 6 and 7, and technology-based training methods are described in Chapter 8. These methods differ in terms of their effectiveness for teaching different types of training content and learning outcomes. There are many training methods from which to choose and the choice will also be influenced by time, money, and tradition.

Research shows that learning and retention are best achieved through the use of training methods that promote productive responses from trainees.[16] **Productive responses** are those in which the trainee actively uses the training content rather than passively watches, listens, or imitates the trainer. In addition, it is believed that training methods that encourage active participation during training also enhance learning.[17] Recall in the chapter-opening vignette that BMO requires trainees to draft solutions and strategies for existing concerns facing the company. Thus, trainees are required to solve real-world problems facing the company. In the next section, we discuss the importance of active practice in the design of training programs.

Ultimately, the objectives of a training program and the training content should determine the most appropriate training methods. For many organizations today, however, the best approach is a **blended training** approach to learning that consists of a combination of classroom training, on-the-job training, and computer technology.

Active Practice

One of the most important ways that people learn and acquire new skills is through practice.[18] It is therefore important to incorporate practice into the design of a training program. But what exactly is practice?

Practice refers to physical or mental rehearsal of a task, skill, or knowledge in order to achieve some level of proficiency in performing the task or skill or demonstrating the knowledge.[19] There is a certain degree of truth to the adage "practice makes perfect." A student who practises answering exam questions learns more than a student who just reads the textbook. A manager will probably learn more about interviewing by actually conducting a mock interview than by listening to a lecture on interviewing. In general, both adults and children learn through practice.

In training, we often refer to **active practice**, which means that trainees are provided with opportunities to practise the task or use the knowledge being learned during training. Thus, training programs should include opportunities for active practice. The effectiveness of active practice, however, depends on a number of conditions that occur before and during training.

Productive responses
The trainee actively uses the training content rather than passively watches, listens, or imitates the trainer

Blended training
The use of a combination of approaches to training such as classroom training, on-the-job training, and computer technology.

Practice
Physical or mental rehearsal of a task, skill, or knowledge in order to achieve some level of proficiency in performing the task or skill or demonstrating the knowledge

Active practice
Providing trainees with opportunities to practice performing a training task or using knowledge during training

Conditions of practice

Practice conditions that are implemented before and during training to enhance the effectiveness of active practice and maximize learning and retention

In the following sections, we describe **conditions of practice** that can be implemented before (prepractice) and during training to enhance the effectiveness of active practice and maximize trainee learning and retention. Table 5.3 summarizes the conditions of practice.

Prepractice Conditions

Conditions of practice that can be implemented prior to a training program to prepare trainees for practice include: 1. Attentional advice, 2. Metacognitive strategies, 3. Advance organizers, 4. Goal orientation, 5. Preparatory information, and 6. Prepractice briefs.[20]

Attentional Advice

Attentional advice

Providing trainees with information about the task process and general task strategies that can help them learn and perform a task

Attentional advice involves providing trainees with information about the task process and general task strategies that can help them learn and perform

TABLE 5.3

The Conditions of Practice

The following conditions of practice can be used before and during training to enhance the effectiveness of practice and maximize trainee learning and retention.

PREPRACTICE CONDITIONS

1. *Attentional advice.* Providing trainees with information about the task process and general task strategies that can help them learn and perform a task.
2. *Metacognitive strategies.* Refers to ways in which trainees can be instructed to self-regulate their learning of a task.
3. *Advance organizers.* Activities that provide trainees with a structure or framework to help them assimilate and integrate information acquired during practice.
4. *Goal orientation.* The type of goal that is set during training (mastery or performance).
5. *Preparatory information.* Providing trainees with information about what they can expect to occur during practice sessions.
6. *Prepractice briefs.* Sessions in which team members establish their roles and responsibilities and establish performance expectations prior to a team practice session.

CONDITIONS DURING TRAINING

1. *Massed or distributed practice.* Refers to how the segments of a training program are divided and whether the training is conducted in a single session or is divided into several sessions with breaks or rest periods between them.
2. *Whole or part learning.* Refers to whether the training material is learned and practised at one time or one part at a time.
3. *Overlearning.* Continued practice even after trainees have mastered a task so that the behaviour becomes automatic.
4. *Task sequencing.* Refers to dividing training material into an organized and logical sequence of sub-tasks.
5. *Feedback and knowledge of results.* Providing trainees with information and knowledge about their performance on a training task.

a task. This helps focus trainees' attention on task strategies that can aid learning and performing a task as well as generalizing what is learned in practice to other situations in which the strategies can be applied.

Metacognition

Trainees can also benefit more from practice if they know how to regulate their learning through a process known as metacognition. **Metacognition** refers to a self-regulatory process that helps people guide their learning and performance. In this way, people can assess and adjust their progress and strategies while learning to perform a task. You might recall the discussion of learning outcomes in Chapter 3, where metacognition was described as a cognitive learning outcome.

Metacognition consists of two primary functions: monitoring and control. *Monitoring* involves identifying the task, checking and evaluating one's progress, and predicting the outcomes of that progress. *Control* involves decisions about where to allocate one's resources, the specific steps to complete a task, the speed and intensity to work on a task, and the prioritization of activities.[21]

Metacognition involves the use of metacognitive activities or strategies. **Metacognitive strategies** (e.g., thinking out loud, self-diagnosing weaknesses, posing questions to yourself during practice, answering the question, "Why am I doing this?") refer to ways in which trainees can be instructed to self-regulate their learning of a task. Metacognitive strategies can be taught to trainees prior to training so they can self-regulate and guide their own learning and performance during practice sessions. The use of metacognitive strategies during training has been found to be positively related to declarative knowledge, self-efficacy, and training performance.[22] To find out if you use metacognitive strategies when learning, answer the questions in Table 5.4.

Advance Organizers

Advance organizers refer to structures or a framework to help trainees assimilate and integrate training content. In other words, they help trainees structure and organize information. Examples of advance organizers include outlines, text, diagrams, and graphic organizers. Advance organizers have been found to be particularly useful for learning highly complex and factual material and for low-ability trainees.

Goal Orientation

Goal orientation refers to the type of goal that is set during training. You might recall the discussion in Chapter 3 about the two types of goal orientations: a mastery goal orientation and a performance goal orientation. *Mastery goals* focus trainees' attention on the learning process while *performance goals* focus attention on the achievement of specific performance outcomes.

Because mastery goals focus trainees' attention on the process of learning and skill acquisition, they tend to be more effective. In fact, mastery goals have been found to be related to more metacognitive activity and to result

Metacognition
A self-regulatory process that helps people guide their learning and performance

Metacognitive strategies
Refers to ways in which trainees can be instructed to self-regulate their learning of a task

Advance organizers
Activities that provide trainees with a structure or framework to help them assimilate and integrate information acquired during practice

Goal orientation
The type of goal that is set during training (mastery goal or performance goal)

TABLE 5.4

Rate Your Metacognitive Activity

Metacognitive activity involves the use of strategies to monitor and control one's learning. More broadly, it has been described as "thinking about your thinking." In a study by Arron Schmidt and J. Kevin Ford, trainees who scored higher on this scale of metacognitive activity acquired more declarative knowledge, had higher levels of self-efficacy, and demonstrated superior training performance. To find out the extent to which you engage in metacognitive activities when learning, answer the following questions the next time you attend a training program or after your next class!

Answer each question using the following scale:

1 = Almost never

2 = Not very often

3 = Sometimes

4 = Often

5 = Almost always

1. During this class or training program, I made up questions to help focus on my learning.
2. During this class or training program, I asked myself questions to make sure I understood the things I had been trying to learn.
3. During this class or training program, I tried to change the way I learned in order to fit the demands of the situation or topic.
4. During this class or training program, I tried to think through each topic and decide what I am supposed to learn from it, rather than just jumping in without thinking.
5. During this class or training program, I tried to determine which things I didn't understand well and adjusted my learning strategies accordingly.
6. During this class or training program, I set goals for myself in order to direct my activities.
7. If I got confused during this class or training program, I made sure I sorted it out as soon as I could before moving on.
8. During this class or training program, I thought about how well my tactics for learning were working.
9. During this class or training program, I thought carefully about how well I had learned material I had previously studied.
10. During this class or training program, I thought about what skills needed the most practice.
11. During this class or training program, I tried to monitor closely the areas where I needed the most improvement.
12. During this class or training program, I thought about what things I needed to do to learn.
13. During this class or training program, I carefully selected what to focus on to improve on weaknesses I identified.
14. During this class or training program, I noticed where I made mistakes and focused on improving those areas.
15. When I practised a new skill in this class or training program, I monitored how well I was learning its requirements.

Source: Schmidt, A. M., & Ford, J. K. (2003). Learning within a learner control training environment: The interactive effects of goal orientation and metacognitive instruction on learning outcomes. *Personnel Psychology, 56*, 405–429; Blackwell Publishing, 2003.

in faster skill acquisition. Thus, mastery goals appear to be most effective for practice because they focus trainees' attention on learning the task rather than on their performance. Research has found a mastery goal orientation to be positively related to training outcomes including knowledge, self-efficacy, and performance.[23]

Preparatory Information

Preparatory information involves providing trainees with information about what they can expect to occur during practice sessions (e.g., events and consequences) so that they can develop strategies to overcome performance obstacles. Trainees provided with preparatory information prior to practice are better prepared to learn and perform a task. They know what to expect and how to overcome performance obstacles. Preparatory information is particularly useful for learning to perform stressful tasks where the ability to cope and overcome obstacles is critical for task performance.

Prepractice Briefs

The final example of a prepractice condition is specific to team training. **Prepractice briefs** involve sessions in which team members establish their roles and responsibilities and performance expectations prior to a team practice session. Prepractice briefs can improve team practice sessions especially for tasks that are fast-paced and stressful.

Conditions of Practice during Training

Practice conditions that can be implemented during training include: 1. Massed or distributed practice, 2. Whole or part learning, 3. Overlearning, 4. Task sequencing, and 5. Feedback and knowledge of results.

Massed versus Distributed Practice

Massed versus distributed practice has to do with how segments of a training program are divided. Massed practice, or cramming, is practice with virtually no rest periods, such as when the training is conducted in one single session instead of being divided into several sessions with breaks or rest periods between them. Distributed or spaced practice conditions include rest intervals during the practice session.

Students might argue that they can succeed on an exam for which they have crammed, but research shows that memory loss after cramming is greater than if a student had studied over several weeks. Furthermore, organizations would prefer that trainees retain material over many months, rather than just knowing it for the course, test, or simulation.

Research has shown that material that was learned under distributed practice is retained longer.[24] Furthermore, a review of research on practice conditions found that distributed practice sessions resulted in higher performance than massed practice conditions.[25] Thus, practice is more effective when practice periods are spread over time, rather than massed together. Trainers teaching a new skill, such as negotiation, could increase learning by

Preparatory information
Providing trainees with information about what they can expect to occur during practice sessions so that they can develop strategies to overcome performance obstacles

Prepractice briefs
Sessions in which team members establish their roles and responsibilities and performance expectations prior to a team practice session

Massed versus distributed practice
Refers to how the segments of a training program are divided and whether the training is conducted in a single session (massed) or is divided into several sessions with breaks or rest periods between them (distributed)

spacing the training and practices over a week of two-hour sessions, rather than cramming it into an eight-hour day. Distributed practice is most effective for trainees with little or no experience, when the rest periods are shorter early on but longer later in training, and for learning motor skills.[26]

Whole versus Part Learning

Whole versus part learning

Refers to whether the training material is learned and practiced at one time or one part at a time

Whole versus part learning has to do with whether all of the training material is learned and practised at one time or one part at a time.[27] For example, piano students often learn complex pieces one hand at a time. Research has found that the best strategy depends on the trainee and the nature of the task. Whole learning is more effective when the trainee has high intelligence, practice is distributed, the task organization of the training material is high, and task complexity is low. Generally speaking, when the task itself is composed of relatively clear and different parts or sub-tasks, it is best for trainees to learn and practise each part at a time and then perform all parts in one whole sequence. However, if the task itself is relatively simple and consists of a number of closely inter-related tasks, then a strategy of whole learning makes more sense.[28]

Overlearning

Overlearning

Continued practice even after trainees have mastered a task so that the behaviour becomes automatic

Overlearning refers to learning something until the behaviour becomes automatic. In other words, trainees are provided with continued opportunities for practice even after they have mastered the task.[29] It is an effective way to train people for emergency responses or for complex skills in which there is little time to think in a job situation. It is also important for skills that employees might not need to use very often on the job.

Automaticity

The performance of a skill to the point at which little attention from the brain is required to respond correctly

Overlearning helps ensure that task performance will become habitual or automatic. **Automaticity** refers to the performance of a skill to the point at which little attention from the brain is required to respond correctly.[30] You might recall the discussion of learning outcomes in Chapter 3 where automaticity was described as a skill-based learning outcome.

Overlearning has been found to be an effective method for improving retention for both cognitive and physical tasks. The greater the overlearning the longer the resulting retention of the training material. However, the benefits of overlearning for retention are reduced by half after 19 days and to zero after 5 to 6 weeks. Thus, additional training is required after about three weeks to maintain the benefits of overlearning.[31]

Task Sequencing

Task sequencing

Dividing training material into an organized and logical sequence of sub-tasks

Task sequencing has to do with the manner in which the learning tasks are organized and arranged. The basic idea is that learning can be improved by dividing the training material into an organized sequence of sub-tasks. The idea behind task sequencing was proposed by Robert Gagné, who argued that practice is not enough for learning to occur.[32] Rather, what is most important is that the distinct sub-tasks are identified and arranged in a logical sequence. In this manner, a trainee will learn each successive sub-task before the total task is performed. The trainee learns to perform each step or task in the proper order or sequence.

According to Gagné, what is most important in the design of a training program is the identification of the component tasks or sub-tasks and the arrangement of them into a meaningful and suitable sequence.[33]

Feedback or Knowledge of Results

Feedback or knowledge of results involves providing trainees with feedback and information about their performance on a training task. Research indicates that feedback is critical for learning for at least four reasons.[34] First, feedback lets trainees know if they are effectively performing the training task. This enables them to correct mistakes and improve their performance. Second, positive feedback can help build confidence and strengthen trainees' self-efficacy. Third, positive feedback can be reinforcing and stimulate continued efforts and learning. And fourth, feedback is necessary for trainees to know if they have attained their goals and if they need to revise them or set new ones.

During training, feedback can be provided to guide trainees as they attempt new behaviours. This feedback should be designed to correct performance. When incorrect responses are given, the feedback should include the correct response. Negative feedback ("You failed to acknowledge the client's problem") will not be perceived as punishing if the source is knowledgeable, friendly, trustworthy, and powerful enough to affect outcomes like promotions.[35]

To be most effective, feedback should be accurate, specific, credible, timely, and positive.[36] In a study of the effect of feedback on the performance of hourly workers, Miller concluded that the relevance, specificity, timing, and accuracy of the feedback are the critical factors in mastery of learning.[37] Trainees receiving this type of feedback are more likely to adjust their responses toward the correct behaviour, more likely to be motivated to change, and more likely to set goals for improving or maintaining performance.[38] Some training methods such as computer-assisted instruction and behaviour modelling have feedback as an integral component. For more on giving feedback, see The Trainer's Notebook 5.2, "How to Give Training Feedback."

Feedback or knowledge of results

Providing trainees with feedback and information about their performance on a training task

---

The Trainer's Notebook 5.2

How to Give Training Feedback

Feedback during training can be very effective for learning and changing behaviour if the feedback is perceived as being constructive rather than critical. Here are some tips on how to give effective training feedback.

- *Timing.* Try to provide the feedback immediately after the behaviour or performance is observed.
- *Be specific.* Feedback works best when it is specific. Don't say, "You moved the arm wrong," but, "You have the arm tilted at 30 degrees."

- *Correct performance.* After discussing what was incorrectly done, provide guidance and demonstrate the correct performance ("You had the arm tilted at a 30-degree angle; you will find it easier or quicker to tilt it 90 degrees.")
- *Reinforce correct performance.* Provide positive feedback and reinforcement following correct performance: "Good, you have the right 90-degree angle."

Summary

In summary, training programs can be designed to facilitate and maximize trainees' learning and retention by providing trainees with opportunities for active practice. In addition, a number of conditions of practice before and during training can be used to improve the benefits of active practice for learning and retention. In Chapter 10, we describe learning principles that can also be incorporated into the design of a training program (identical elements, general principles, stimulus variability) to facilitate the transfer of training.

Active Learning and Adaptive Expertise

The traditional approach to learning is to train individuals to reproduce specific behaviours in similar settings and situations. This is known as **routine expertise** and many training programs are designed with this in mind. However, routine expertise is not always sufficient or effective for more complex jobs that often involve novel, unstructured, ill-defined, and changing task demands and work environments.

For more complex jobs and tasks employees have to be able to adapt their knowledge and skills to different problems and situations. This requires much more than routine expertise; it requires **adaptive expertise**, which is the ability to use knowledge and skills across a range of tasks, settings, and situations. Adaptive expertise requires a much deeper understanding of a task because the learner has to understand how to use his/her knowledge and skills in new and novel situations. This has important implications for the design of training programs.[39]

Although research on training design and adaptive expertise is relatively new, a key factor in training design for adaptive expertise is active learning. **Active learning** is an approach to training that gives trainees control over their own learning so that they become active participants in the learning experience. For example, the learner has responsibility for choosing learning activities and monitoring and judging progress. In contrast, traditional approaches to training give the trainer primary responsibility for learning decisions and limits trainees' control. In addition, active learning promotes an *inductive* learning process in which the learner discovers rules, principles, and strategies for performing a task on their own through exploration and experimentation. Traditional approaches to learning are *deductive* because they transmit knowledge to the learner and provide more guidance and structure on how and what to learn.[40]

But how do you design a training program for active learning? Several design elements have been identified including exploratory or discovery learning, error framing, and emotion control. **Exploratory/discovery learning** provides trainees with the opportunity to explore and experiment with training tasks to infer and learn the rules, principles, and strategies for effective task performance. By contrast, **proceduralized instruction** provides trainees with step-by-step instructions on how to perform a task and the rules, principles, and strategies for effective performance.[41]

Error framing involves encouraging trainees to make errors and to view errors as instrumental for learning. Thus, trainees are encouraged to make

Routine expertise

The ability to reproduce specific behaviours in similar settings and situations

Adaptive expertise

The ability to use knowledge and skills across a range of tasks, settings, and situations

Active learning

An approach to training that gives trainees control over their own learning.

Exploratory/discovery learning

Trainees are given the opportunity to explore and experiment with the training tasks to infer and learn the rules, principles, and strategies for effective task performance

Proceduralized instruction

Trainees are provided with step-by-step instructions on how to perform a task and the rules, principles, and strategies for effective performance.

Managing Performance Through Training and Development

and learn from errors during practice. We discuss this in more detail in the next section on error-management training, which has become an important topic on its own.

Emotion control is a strategy to help trainees control their emotions during training, which is important given that active learning can provoke stress and anxiety that can hinder learning and performance. For example, trainees might be instructed to manage negative emotions by increasing positive thoughts and self-statements and to avoid negative ones.[42]

Research on active learning has found that it is effective for developing adaptive expertise. A key reason for the effects of active learning is the development and use of metacognitive strategies. Recall that metacognitive strategies refer to ways in which trainees self-regulate their learning. Research has found that active learning stimulates metacognitive activities to a greater extent than proceduralized instruction and helps to explain the effects of active learning strategies on adaptive learning and performance.[43]

Error-Management Training (EMT)

In the previous section, we described training design elements that can be used to promote active learning. One of the design elements encourages trainees to make errors and to view errors as instrumental for learning. At first, this might seem like a ridiculous idea. After all, we usually try to avoid errors because they can be frustrating and lead to anger and despair. But think again. Isn't it the case that errors and mistakes happen quite frequently during the learning process? If so, then, why not design training programs so that trainees make errors and learn from them?

First, it is helpful to understand why errors might be important for learning. According to Michael Frese and his colleagues, errors are a source of negative feedback which can have a positive and informative function in training. In fact, they argue that negative feedback is a necessary prerequisite for learning. Thus, rather than being avoided, errors should be incorporated into the training process, a training method that is known as error-management training.[44]

Error-management training (EMT) involves explicitly encouraging trainees to make errors during training and to learn from them. This can be done by providing trainees with only basic information or minimal instructions about how to perform a task they are learning. As a result, trainees need to try out different approaches when practising a task, which means that they will make a number of errors along the way. In contrast, when the training is **error-avoidant**, trainees are given detailed step-by-step instructions on how to perform a task so they are less likely to make errors, and if they do the trainer intervenes and corrects them.[45]

There are two key characteristics of EMT. First, trainees are provided with only basic training relevant information and introduced to various problems which they are invited to explore and solve on their own (active exploration). Thus, trainees are provided with little guidance and active exploration is encouraged. Because they have insufficient information they are very likely to make errors.

Emotion control

A strategy to help trainees control their emotions during active learning

Error-management training

Training that explicitly encourages trainees to make errors during training and to learn from them

Error-avoidant training

Trainees are given detailed step-by-step instructions on how to perform a task so they are less likely to make errors

Error-management instructions

Statements that emphasize the positive function of errors

Second, because making errors can be frustrating, trainees are told to expect errors and to frame them positively. Thus, making errors is encouraged during training. This is known as **error-management instructions** and it involves instructions that errors are a necessary and natural part of learning. Trainees are told that they should make errors and learn from them. Error-management instructions reduce the negative effects of errors and enable trainees to be open to learning from error feedback.[46] For example, when learning a new task, instructors might repeat statements such as "The more errors you make, the more you learn" and "You have made an error? Great! Because now you can learn something new!"[47]

Error training can improve learning and performance for a number of reasons. First, errors inform trainees of knowledge and skills that need improvement and what they should focus on. Second, errors force trainees to develop thoughtful strategies and a deeper processing of information, which leads to mental models of how to perform a task. Third, errors can lead to greater practice because trainees tend to practise those things they have not yet mastered. Fourth, errors force trainees to learn "error-recovery strategies," which means they are better able to respond to and correct errors which can lead to improved performance. And fifth, errors lead to greater exploration because people often want to find out why an error has occurred. Thus, errors are likely to result in greater learning and therefore better performance on the learned task.[48]

Several studies have found that EMT is more effective than error-avoidant training for learning and performance. However, some studies have found that EMT is not more effective than error-avoidant training and in some cases it is less effective. To better understand this discrepancy in results, Nina Keith and Michael Frese reviewed of all of the studies that have compared EMT to error-avoidant training. They found that overall EMT results in more positive training outcomes than training that does not encourage errors. However, they also found that EMT is especially effective in certain circumstances.[49]

Adaptive tasks

Tasks that differ from those worked on during training and require different solutions

First, EMT is effective for post-training performance but not for performance during training. This should not be surprising, because it is only after training that the benefits of EMT are realized: during training, trainees are involved in active exploration and are making errors along the way. Second, EMT was found to be particularly effective on the performance of tasks that require adaptive expertise or what are known as **adaptive tasks** (tasks that differ from those worked on during training and require different solutions) than for tasks that require routine expertise or **analogical tasks** (tasks that are similar to those worked on during training). This follows from the previous discussion of active learning. Recall that EMT is an element of active learning and so it follows that it is more effective for tasks that require adaptive expertise.[50]

Analogical tasks

Tasks that are similar to those worked on during training

Finally, EMT was most effective when it was accompanied with error-management instructions. In other words, it is the combination of active exploration and error-management instructions that results in more positive training outcomes of EMT.[51]

In summary, EMT is an effective design element for facilitating active learning. It is especially effective for post-training performance on adaptive tasks in which trainees must work on problems and find solutions that are novel and different from those that they worked on during training.

FIGURE 5.1

Model of Training Effectiveness

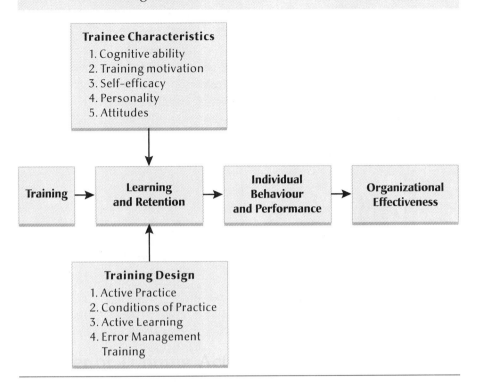

Model of Training Effectiveness—Training Design

Before concluding this chapter, let's return to the model of training effectiveness that was presented in Chapter 3. Recall that the model showed that, in addition to training, trainees' cognitive ability, training motivation, self-efficacy, personality, and attitudes influence trainee learning and retention; learning and retention then lead to individual behaviour and performance; and individual behaviour and performance influences organizational effectiveness.

Based on what you have learned in this chapter, we can add training design to the model. Recall that active practice and practice conditions before training (prepractice) and during training influence learning and retention. As well, design elements that promote active learning (exploratory/discovery learning, emotion control, and EMT) are necessary to develop adaptive expertise.

Figure 5.1 shows a revised model of training effectiveness in which training, trainee characteristics, and training design influence learning and retention.

Summary

This chapter described the main activities involved in the design of a training program. First, we described the elements, components, and writing of training objectives. Next we discussed the decision to purchase or design a training program and the factors to consider when making a purchase-or-design decision. The importance of a request for proposal (RFP) was also discussed when a decision has been made to purchase a training program. We then described the factors involved in the design of a training program including training content, methods, active practice, and the conditions of practice. This was followed by a discussion of active learning and design elements that promote adaptive expertise. The chapter concluded with a discussion of error-management training.

One of the most important design factors discussed in this chapter was training methods. As you will see in the next three chapters, there are many types of off- and on-the-job training methods as well as many forms of technology-based training.

Key Terms

active learning   p. 152
active practice   p. 145
adaptive expertise   p. 152
adaptive tasks   p. 154
advance organizers   p. 147
analogical tasks   p. 154
attentional advice   p. 146
automaticity   p. 150
blended training   p. 145
conditions of practice   p. 146
emotion control   p. 153
error-avoidant training   p. 153
error-management instructions   p. 154
error-management training (EMT)   p. 153
exploratory/discovery learning   p. 152
feedback or knowledge of results   p. 151

goal orientation   p. 147
massed versus distributed practice   p. 149
metacognition   p. 147
metacognitive strategies   p. 147
overlearning   p. 150
practice   p. 145
preparatory information   p. 149
prepractice briefs   p. 149
proceduralized instruction   p. 152
productive responses   p. 145
request for proposal (RFP)   p. 142
routine expertise   p. 152
subject-matter expert (SME)   p. 144
task sequencing   p. 150
training objective   p. 137
whole versus part learning   p. 150

Make the Connection

p. 147: metacognition is discussed in Chapter 3 on page 67
p. 147: goal orientation is discussed in Chapter 3 on page 82
p. 150: automaticity is discussed in Chapter 3 on page 67

Web Links

BMO Financial: www.bmo.com

Vecima Networks: www.vecima.com

RPC Icons

RPC 5.1 Recommends the most appropriate way to meet identified learning needs (e.g., courses, secondments, and on-the-job activities).

RPC 5.2 Develops requests for proposals (RFP) and reviews submissions by third parties.

RPC 5.3 Ensures legislated training obligations are met within the organization.

RPC 5.4 Participates in course design and selection/delivery of learning materials via various media.

Discussion Questions

1. Discuss the purpose of training objectives for trainees, trainers, and managers.
2. What factors should an organization consider when deciding to purchase or design a training program?
3. What are the advantages and disadvantages of purchasing a training program and designing a training program in-house?
4. Why is it important to include active practice in a training program? Give an example of how active practice was used in a training program you have attended.
5. Discuss the conditions of practice before and during training and how they can improve learning and retention.
6. Explain how error-management training works and the circumstances in which it is most likely to be effective. When should error-management training be used?
7. Explain what a request for proposal (RFP) is and why an organization should carefully write one before purchasing a training program.
8. What are the main sections of a request for proposal (RFP) and what are the steps involved in creating an effective one?
9. What is the difference between active practice and active learning and what are the implications of each for the design of training programs?

The Great Training Debate

1. Debate the following: Practice makes perfect and enough practice will always lead to learning and retention.
2. Debate the following: Errors are frustrating and upsetting to trainees and should be avoided in training.

Using the Internet

1. To find out about the kinds of training programs that can be purchased, go to Industry Canada at **www.collectionscanada.gc.ca/ webarchives/20060226034454/http://strategis.ic.gc.ca/epic/internet/ incts-scf.nsf/en/h_sl00010e.html.** What can you find out on this site about training suppliers? What are the different areas of training and types of training providers? Does your college or university provide training and, if so, what kind of training?

2. To find out about how to choose a training supplier in Canada, go to Industry Canada at **www.collectionscanada.gc.ca/ webarchives/20060201093624/http://strategis.ic.gc.ca/epic/internet/ incts-scf.nsf/en/h_sl00011e.html.** When choosing a training supplier, what questions should be asked and what issues should you consider? What does this site tell you about choosing a training provider?

Exercises

In-Class

1. Think of the best and worst training experience you have ever had. For each one, indicate the purpose of the training, the objectives, content, and methods. Then, using the material presented in this chapter, make a list of all the reasons why you feel that it was the best or worst training experience you have ever had. Based on your lists, what are some of the things that make a training program effective?

2. If you have a driver's licence then you probably remember what it was like to learn to drive. Chances are you stepped into a car with a friend or family member who told you what to do. And if you have ever taught someone how to drive, you probably did the same thing. Did you remember to tell them everything they needed to know? What did you tell them to do first? Could you have done a better job teaching them to drive? Refer to the section of this chapter on task sequencing. Recall that task sequencing involves dividing a task into its component parts or sub-tasks, and then ordering them into a meaningful or logical sequence. Now try to design a driver training program based on task sequencing. In other words, make a list of all of the sub-tasks involved in driving a car and then organize them into a logical sequence for the purpose of teaching somebody how to drive.

3. Have you ever wondered what your instructor does to prepare for a class? To find out, choose one of your classes and try to describe each of the following:

   - the objectives of the class
   - the content of the class
   - the training methods used
   - opportunities for active practice

- conditions of practice
- active learning

Based on your description, how effective was the class? How can it be improved?

4. Recall a training program that you attended in a previous or current job. Describe the objectives and content of the program and any opportunities for active practice. What did you practice and how helpful was it for your learning and retention? Describe the extent to which any of the conditions of practice were used either before or during the training program and how they affected your learning and retention. What changes would you recommend to improve learning and retention?

5. Identify a skill that you would like to acquire. Some examples might be to use a particular software package or perhaps to improve your written or oral presentation skills. Now develop training objectives for a training program on the skill that you have chosen, using the five elements and three components of training objectives described in the chapter. Exchange your objectives with another student and assess each other's objectives in terms of the criteria outlined in the chapter for writing training objectives.

6. Read the following training objectives and identify what is wrong with them. Then rewrite them so that they conform to the elements and components of training objectives described in the chapter.

   - The trainer will spend 30 minutes discussing time-management tips.
   - The trainees will be able to manage their time more effectively.
   - The purpose of the seminar is to teach time-management techniques.
   - After attending the course, employees will be able to make lists and put letters beside the items on the list, enabling them to manage time more effectively.

7. Recall a training program that you attended in a previous or current job. Describe the objectives and content of the program and the extent to which errors were part of the program. Did you make any errors while learning and what effect did it have on your learning and the training experience? If you were to redesign this training program, how would you change it so that it included error-management training?

In-the-Field

1. Contact the human resources department of an organization and request a meeting with a department member whom you can interview about the organization's training programs. Develop some questions so that you can learn about each of the following design

factors in terms of a particular training program that the organization has implemented:

- Was the training program designed by the organization or purchased? What were the reasons for designing or purchasing the program?
- If the training program was purchased, was a request for proposal (RFP) used and what was included in it?
- What is the content of the training program and how was it developed?
- What training methods were used and why?
- Was active practice designed into the training program and what kind of practice opportunities did trainees have?
- To what extent were the conditions of practice listed in Table 5.3 incorporated into the training program?

Based on the information you have acquired, conduct an evaluation with respect to how effectively you think the training program was designed and list some recommendations for improvement.

Case Incident

Play to Win at Dofasco

Hamilton-based steel manufacturer Dofasco has a training program that it calls "play to win." Nearly every new hire participates in the program as an initiation to the company which takes place at a resort. Employees go to the resort in groups of between 50 and 70 and there are about four trips a year to the resort.

Over 7000 employees have taken part in the program since it was launched in 1993. The intent is to get a better understanding of the organization and the things it is trying to accomplish. The program focuses on issues facing the company, what the company does, and who the company's customers are. The program is placed within the context that nobody can do it alone and that they need to look out for each other. Employees also take part in a variety of unique exercises such a rope course and climbing up a pole. In addition, new hires get a chance to sit down with senior management and participate in a question-and-answer session. The context is that when you are back at the company you can help out. The program teaches respect and concern for others, that strength is our people, and what those things mean.

Questions

1. What are the training objectives of Dofasco's play-to-win training program and what purpose do they serve for employees and managers?
2. Discuss the training content and methods used in the training program. What is the nature of the content and what type of methods are used and why?

Source: Humber, T. (2003, November 17). Serving up training. *Canadian HR Reporter, 16* (20), G1, G4.

Case Study

Training the Sales Force

Sales at a large telecommunications company were down for the third quarter. Management reviewed several strategies to improve sales and concluded that one solution would be to improve training for the large, dispersed sales force.

For the sake of expediency, the training department began using a needs analysis it had conducted several years before as a basis to develop enhanced training. Their plan was first to update the original needs analysis, and then to develop new training strategies on the basis of what they found. They also began investigating new training technologies as a possible means to reducing training delivery costs. However, management was so intent on doing something quickly that the training department was ultimately pressured into purchasing a generic, off-the-shelf training package from a local vendor.

One of the features of the package that appealed to management was that the course could be delivered over the Web, saving the time and expense of having the sales force travel to the main office to receive the training. Hence, even though the package was costly to purchase, the company believed that it was a bargain compared to the expense of developing a new package in-house and delivering it in person to the sales force.

Six months after the training had been delivered, sales were still declining. Management turned to the training department for answers. Because no measures of training performance had been collected, the training department had little information upon which to base its diagnosis. For lack of a better idea, members of the training department began questioning the sales force to see if they could determine why the training was not working.

Among other things, the sales people reported that the training was slow and boring, and that it did not teach them any new sales techniques. They also complained that, without an instructor, it was impossible to get clarification on things they did not understand. Moreover, they reported that they believed that sales were off not because they needed training in basic sales techniques, but because so many new products were being introduced they could not keep up. In fact, several of the sales people requested meetings with design engineers just so they could get updated product information.

The training department took these findings back to management and requested that they be allowed to design a new training package, beginning with an updated needs analysis to determine the real training deficiencies.

Source: Excerpt taken from Salas, E., & Cannon-Bowers, J. A. (2000). Design training systematically. In E. A. Locke (Ed.), *Handbook of principles of organizational behavior*. Oxford, UK. Blackwell Publishers Ltd. Case questions prepared by Alan Saks.

Questions

1. Comment on the company's decision to purchase a generic, off-the-shelf training package by a local vendor. What were the advantages and disadvantages of this and do you think that it was a good idea for

the company to purchase the training rather than to have it designed in-house? Explain your answer.

2. Explain how the use of a request for proposal (RFP) might have changed the company's decision to purchase the training program. Do you think that the company would have purchased the same training program from the same vendor if they had created a detailed RFP? Explain your answer.

3. What effect did the use of the original needs analysis have on the content of the training program and the decision to have it delivered over the Web? Do you think that a new needs analysis should have been conducted and what effect might it have had on the design of the training program?

4. Comment on the use of the Web as the main method of training. What are the advantages and disadvantages of this method of training? What other methods might have been more effective?

5. Discuss the role that practice played in the training program and its effectiveness. What does the case say about the role of active practice in training?

6. If you were to design the training program, describe what you would do in terms of: a) training objectives, b) training content, c) training methods, d) active practice and conditions of practice, and e) active learning. How would your training program be different from the one described in the case and would it be more effective?

References

1. Waxer, C. (2005, October 24). Bank of Montreal opens its checkbook in the name of employee development. *Workforce Management, 84* (11), 46–48; Anonymous. (2006, March). Top 100 ranking. *Training, 43* (3), 42; Anonymous (2007, March). Top 125 ranking. *Training, 44* (2), 58–83; Lee, C., Dolezalek, H., & Johnson, G. (2005, March). Training top 100: Top 10, 30.
2. Lee, C., Dolezalek, H., & Johnson, G. (2005, March). *Training, 42* (3), 26–47.
3. Kibler, R. J., Barker, L. L., & Miles, D. T. (1970). *Behavioral objectives and instruction.* Boston: Allyn and Bacon, Inc.
4. Laird, D. (1985). *Approaches to training and development* (2nd ed.). Reading, MA: Addison-Wesley.
5. Hays, S. (1999, April). Basic skills training 101. *Workforce Management, 78* (4), 76–78.
6. Ganzel, R. (1998, October). What sexual harassment training really prevents. *Training, 35* (10), 86–94.
7. Nadler, L., & Nadler, Z. (1990). *The handbook of human resource development* (2nd ed.). New York: John Wiley and Sons.
8. Nadler, L., & Nadler, Z. (1990).
9. Chapman, B. (2004, January). How to create the ideal RFP. *Training, 41* (1), 40–43.
10. Chapman, B. (2004, January).
11. Campbell, J. P. (1988). Training design for performance improvement. In Campbell, J. P. & Campbell, R. J. (Eds.), *Productivity in organizations: Frontiers of industrial and organizational psychology* (pp. 177–216). San Francisco, CA: Jossey-Bass.
12. Kirkpatrick, D. L. (1994). *Evaluating training programs: The four levels.* San Francisco, CA: Berrett-Koehler Publishers.

13. Campbell, J. P. (1988).

14. Waxer, C. (2005, October 24).

15. Campbell, J. P. (1988).

16. Campbell, J. P. (1988).

17. Thoms, P., & Klein, H. J. (1994). Participation and evaluative outcomes in management training. *Human Resource Development Quarterly, 5,* 27–39.

18. Hinrichs, J. R. (1976). Personnel training. In Dunnette, M. D. (Ed.), *Handbook of industrial and organizational psychology* (pp. 829–860). Skokie, IL: Rand McNally.

19. Cannon-Bowers, J. A., Rhodenizer, L., Salas, E., & Bowers, C. A. (1998). A framework for understanding pre-practice conditions and their impact on learning. *Personnel Psychology, 51,* 291–320.

20. Cannon-Bowers, J. A., Rhodenizer, L., Salas, E., & Bowers, C. A. (1998).

21. Schmidt, A. M., & Ford, J. K. (2003). Learning within a learner control training environment: The interactive effects of goal orientation and metacognitive instruction on learning outcomes. *Personnel Psychology, 56,* 405–429.

22. Schmidt, A. M., & Ford, J. K. (2003).

23. Schmidt, A. M., & Ford, J. K. (2003).

24. Baldwin, T. T., & Ford, J. K. (1988). Transfer of training: A review and directions for future research. *Personnel Psychology, 41,* 63–105.

25. Donovan, J. J., & Radosevich, D. J. (1999). A meta-analytic review of the distribution of practice effect: Now you see it, now you don't. *Journal of Applied Psychology, 84,* 795–805.

26. Bass, B. M., & Vaughn, J. A. (1969). *Training in industry: The management of learning.* Belmont, CA: Wadsworth; Donovan, J. J., & Radosevich, D. J. (1999).

27. Baldwin, T. T., & Ford, J. K. (1988).

28. Baldwin, T. T., & Ford, J. K. (1988).

29. Baldwin, T. T., & Ford, J. K. (1988).

30. Yelon, S., & Berge, Z. (1992, September). Practice-centred training. *Performance and instruction,* 8–12.

31. Driskell, J. E., Willis, R. P., & Copper, C. (1992). Effects of overlearning on retention. *Journal of Applied Psychology, 77,* 615–622.

32. Gagné, R. M. (1962). Military training and principles of learning. *American Psychologist, 17,* 83–91.

33. Gagné, R. M. (1962).

34. Baldwin, T. T., & Ford, J. K. (1988).

35. Ilgen, D. R., Fisher, C. D., & Taylor, M. S. (1979). Consequences of individual feedback on behaviour in organizations. *Journal of Applied Psychology, 64,* 349–371.

36. Campbell, J. P. (1988).

37. Miller, L. (1965). *The use of knowledge of results in improving the performance of hourly operators.* General Electric Company, Behavioral Research Service: Detroit.

38. Locke, E. A., & Latham, G. P. (1990). *A theory of goal setting and task performance.* Englewood Cliffs, NJ: Prentice-Hall.

39. Machin, M. A. (2002). Planning, managing, and optimizing transfer of training. In Kurt Kraiger (Ed.), *Creating, implementing, and managing effective training and development* (pp. 263–301). San Francisco, CA: Jossey-Bass; Smith, E. M., Ford, J. K., & Kozlowski, S. W. J. (1997). Building adaptive expertise: Implications for training design strategies. In M. A. Quinones and A. Ehrenstein (Eds.), *Training for a Rapidly Changing Workplace,* Washington, DC: American Psychological Association.

40. Bell, B. S., & Kozlowski, S. W. J. (2008). Active learning: Effects of core training design elements on self-regulatory processes, learning, and adaptability. *Journal of Applied Psychology, 93,* 296–316.

41. Bell, B. S., & Kozlowski, S. W. J. (2008).

42. Bell, B. S., & Kozlowski, S. W. J. (2008).

43. Bell, B. S., & Kozlowski, S. W. J. (2008).

44. Heimbeck, D., Frese, M., Sonnentag, S., & Keith, N. (2003). Integrating errors into the training process: The function of error management instructions and the role of goal orientation. *Personnel Psychology, 56,* 333–361.

45. Heimbeck, D., Frese, M., Sonnentag, S., & Keith, N. (2003).

46. Keith, N., & Frese, M. (2008). Effectiveness of error management training: A meta-analysis. *Journal of Applied Psychology, 93,* 59–69.

47. Keith, N., & Frese, M. (2008).

48. Heimbeck, D., Frese, M., Sonnentag, S., & Keith, N. (2003).

49. Keith, N., & Frese, M. (2008).

50. Keith, N., & Frese, M. (2008).

51. Keith, N., & Frese, M. (2008).

CHAPTER 6

Off-the-Job Training Methods

Chapter Learning Outcomes

After reading this chapter, you should be able to:

- describe the following off-the-job instructional methods: lecture, discussion, audio-visual, case study, case incidents, behavioural modelling, role plays, games, simulations, and action learning
- list the advantages and disadvantages of each instructional method
- describe how and when to use each instructional method
- define physical and psychological fidelity
- describe the factors to consider when choosing an instructional method
- define aptitude-treatment interaction and discuss its implications for training
- discuss a blended delivery approach to training

L'ORÉAL CANADA

L'Oréal Canada, headquartered in Montreal, Quebec, is the leader of the cosmetics industry in Canada. Its operations include the manufacture, marketing, sales, and distribution of its colour cosmetics, skin care, sun protection, hair care, and hair colour products.

Training and development is an integral part of life at L'Oréal Canada. Every year about 100 of its 1,200 employees attend industry-specific and leadership development training and conferences at L'Oréal's management development centres in Tokyo, New York, and Paris.

After three months on the job, product managers at L'Oréal Canada are given their own company and required to market their products to consumers around the world. The company is virtual, the consumers are computer-based, and the product managers' success or failure is simply a simulation. But the learning is real, says the company's director of learning and development.

Employees work in pairs and play the "game" for four hours a week over six weeks. Each week, there's an e-learning component where employees have to study a new topic such as market segmentation, brand positioning, and working with media. This is done online with a trainer and participants from L'Oréal offices around the world.

The next day the pairs go online and use the skills they learned from the e-learning module to make business decisions. Two days later, all participants go back online and, along with the trainer, look at the market share of their companies. This allows them to immediately see the impact of their marketing decisions on the company.

After employees see how they've done, they have a face-to-face meeting with their manager to talk about how they can apply what they learned to their specific job at L'Oréal Canada.

Along with other online simulations and business games, L'Oréal incorporates in-person simulations and role plays to train all employees. L'Oréal uses role plays extensively to train its sales force. Junior sales representatives and key account managers are given information on a product line and the potential clients, such as Shoppers Drug Mart or Wal-Mart. The vice president of sales and sales directors play the role of customers.

L'Oréal Canada recently celebrated its 50th anniversary, and in 2008 the company was named one of Canada's Top 100 Employers for the fifth consecutive year.[1]

In this chapter, we introduce you to instructional methods that take place off-the-job. **Instructional methods** refer to the techniques used to convey the training content within a training program, such as lectures, discussions, or role plays.[2] In effect, these are training methods that usually take place in a classroom or formal setting for the purpose of learning. L'Oréal Canada's use of simulations, games, and role plays is a good example of a company that uses a number of instructional training methods.

Although the instructional methods presented in this chapter usually take place in a classroom setting, some methods such as games and simulations can also take place outside of a classroom and even incorporated into computer-based training like L'Oréal Canada's simulation for product managers.

In both Canada and the United States, classroom delivery is the primary and most popular method of providing training. In Canada, 75 percent of all training is delivered via the classroom while in the United States 67 percent of all formal training hours occur in the classroom with a live instructor. According to the Conference Board of Canada, most Canadian organizations offer some formal in-class training to their employees.[3]

This chapter describes the most common instructional training methods. The instructional methods are presented in order of degree of trainee involvement, from passive to active. We start with lectures, because there is relatively little trainee input, and end with action learning, where trainees manage the learning process. Table 6.1 lists the 10 off-the-job instructional training methods described in this chapter.

Lecture Method

Few people have not experienced a lecture, given the method's widespread use. A **lecture** transmits information orally with little trainee involvement. The trainer organizes the content to be learned and then presents it to trainees. Thus, it involves a unidirectional flow of information from the instructor to the trainee. Although lectures have a reputation as a boring training method, the research evidence indicates that lectures are effective for training several types of skills and tasks.[4]

The lecture offers a number of advantages. Large amounts of information can be transferred to large groups of trainees in a relatively short period of time, at a minimal expense. Key points can be emphasized and repeated. Trainers can be assured that trainees are all hearing the same message, which is useful when the message is extremely important, such as instructions or changes in procedures. A lecture is also useful as a method to explain to trainees what is to follow in the rest of a training session. For example, a lecture could be used to highlight the key learning points of a video or role play. Many employees are comfortable with the lecture method because they are familiar with it and it requires little participation.

However, a lecture, as some of us have experienced, has some drawbacks as a training method. While useful for the acquisition of declarative knowledge and immediate recall, it is not as effective for the development of skills or for changing

Instructional methods
The techniques used to convey the training content within a training program such as lectures, discussions, or role plays

RPC RPC 6.1

Lecture
A training method in which the trainer organizes the content to be learned and presents it orally with little trainee involvement

TABLE 6.1

Off-the-Job Instructional Training Methods

1. *Lecture.* A training method in which the trainer organizes the content to be learned and presents it orally with little trainee involvement.
2. *Discussion.* Two-way communication between the trainer and trainees as well as among trainees.
3. *Audio-visual methods.* Various forms of media that are used to illustrate key points or demonstrate certain actions or behaviours.
4. *Case study.* A training method in which trainees discuss, analyze, and solve problems based on a real situation.
5. *Case incident.* A training method in which one problem or issue is presented for analysis.
6. *Behaviour modelling.* A training method in which trainees observe a model performing a task and then attempt to imitate the observed behaviour.
7. *Role play.* A training method in which trainees practise new behaviours in a safe environment.
8. *Games.* Activities characterized by structured competition that allow employees to learn specific skills.
9. *Simulations.* Operating models of physical or social events designed to represent reality.
10. *Action learning.* A training method in which trainees accept the challenge of studying and solving real-world problems and accept responsibility for the solution.

attitudes. The lecture does not accommodate differences in trainee ability, and all trainees are forced to absorb information at the same rate. Trainees are also forced to be passive learners with little opportunity to connect the content to their own work environment, or to receive feedback on their understanding of the material. To overcome these disadvantages, trainers often include time for discussion, questions and answers, and other opportunities for trainee involvement.

Tips for Trainers

Trainers can use the lecture method effectively by following a number of guidelines. For example, "Where do I begin?" is a question asked by most first-time trainers. The answer is: "First you have to know what you want to do (the objective) and how much information you need to impart." Training objectives were described in Chapter 5, but on a pragmatic level the trainer should begin a lecture with an introduction to the topic and inform trainees about what they will know and/or be able to do or accomplish by the end of the lecture.

The trainer must then present the content or body of the lecture. Either through previously gained knowledge or the ability to research a topic, the trainer will gather and arrange information in a logical manner. Logic could dictate a progression from the general to the specific or from the specific to the general, depending upon the subject matter. This information can be transcribed onto cards or sheets of paper. An effective technique is to rule off a wide (5 cm to 8 cm) margin down the right-hand side of each page. Detailed information can then be placed in the body of the page, while headings are written in the margins.

It has been suggested that no more than six major points should be presented during each half hour of a lecture.[5] It takes practice to get the timing of a lecture right. Only through experience can one judge the amount of material needed for any given amount of time. It is helpful to break the lecture into 10- to 15-minute segments with a short stretch of time in between and to summarize the material at both the beginning and the end, stopping occasionally to allow trainees to catch up and to write their own summaries.

A trainer who drones on for an entire hour is rarely effective. Depending on audience needs and motivation level, the delivery should be punctuated with a variety of supplementary material or exercises. Stories, case incidents, graphics, humour, trainee presentations, videos, and question-and-answer sessions are some of the techniques a trainer can use to maintain interest and, perhaps even more important, to instill in the trainee the love of—or at the least respect for—the subject matter. The trainer should conclude the lecture with a summary of the key learning points followed by some time for questions and answers.

Discussion Method

The **discussion method** is one of the primary ways to increase trainee involvement in the learning process by allowing two-way communication between the trainer and trainees as well as among trainees. Group discussion serves at least five purposes:

Discussion method

Allows two-way communication between the trainer and trainees as well as among trainees

1. It helps trainees recognize what they do not know but should know.
2. It is an opportunity for trainees to get answers to questions.
3. It allows trainees to get advice on matters that are of concern to them.
4. It allows trainees to share ideas and derive a common wisdom.
5. It is a way for trainees to learn about one another as people.[6]

Group discussions facilitate the exchange of ideas and are good ways to develop critical thinking skills. Social and interpersonal skills are also enhanced. However, group discussions are not effective with large numbers of participants because many remain silent or unable to participate. Some group members will dominate while the contributions of others will not be useful. Still others may become dogmatic in their positions on issues. Group discussions take a lot of training time and must be carefully facilitated to manage the outcomes.

Tips for Trainers

The discussion method is most effective when the trainer can convince group members that a collective approach has some advantage over individual approaches to a problem.[7] Thus, the trainer should create a participative culture at the beginning of a training program. The trainer's task, then, is to get trainees to buy into the process as an activity that is both interesting and useful.

The major difficulty with the discussion method is that comments tend to be addressed to the trainer. When faced with this situation, it is best to reflect the questions or comments back to the trainees. Positive reinforcement is critical. Reluctant participants are drawn out, while the trainer utilizes the energy of more assertive individuals. When the group strays off topic, the trainer gently refocuses the discussion, supporting the participation while changing the substance.[8]

The key to successful discussions is to ensure that one trainee does not dominate the discussion. The trainer does not have to be obvious (e.g., by putting all the dominant personalities together). More subtle techniques can be used. For example, trainees can be given roles that change with each discussion—scribe, presenter, and discussion leader. If groups are kept small—four to six seems to work best—then most trainees have something to do, increasing participation and decreasing chances for some individuals to dominate the process. It is harder to be aggressive when taking notes or trying to summarize the thoughts of others.

Trainers dealing with groups of mixed educational backgrounds must also be aware of reading speed and literacy problems. Often group discussions require trainees to read a passage, case incident, or problem. Reluctance or hostility to do so might point to illiteracy. Be gentle, work the informal group process by finding a place in a hallway for someone to quietly read the material, or if this process is too obvious, summarize the main points before you assign the work. People who don't read well often have excellent memories; with care, they'll get by.[9]

Groups should be assigned a well-defined, easily understood task, one that is doable within the allotted time frame. Trainees should be given every opportunity to look good in front of their peers, especially if they have to report back to the group. Since many training facilities are less than ideal, seating arrangements will vary. Any configuration that puts trainees in close proximity to one another will do, but a circle arrangement with no obvious leader's position or place is probably best. Size of the group is also important. More than 10 would be hard to handle if everyone is to participate.

Audio-visual methods

Various forms of media that are used to illustrate key points or demonstrate certain actions or behaviours

Audio-Visual Methods

Audio-visual methods refer to various forms of media that trainers can use in the classroom to illustrate key points or demonstrate certain actions or behaviours. Videos, DVDs, and slides are often used by trainers to supplement lectures and discussions. A video is often used to illustrate how to behave in a certain situation or to demonstrate effective and ineffective behaviours. For example, at pharmaceutical company Nycomed Canada, a performance management training program for managers uses videos of performance management scenarios to guide managers through the process and to show them how to handle different issues.[10] Many managers have learned correct interviewing techniques through videos. Slides highlight important parts of a lecture or discussion, allowing trainees to remember key points. The use of videos during training has been made easier with the internet as trainers can now find relevant video clips online that can be shown during training.

One advantage of audio-visual methods is the ability to control the pace of training. A slide or a video clip can be used to clarify a concept. Trainees receive consistent information from these methods no matter where or how often the training is given. Most important, a video can show a situation that is difficult for a trainer to describe, such as a hostile customer or a dangerous malfunction in equipment. Video allows a trainer to show complex and dynamic situations in a realistic manner. Not surprisingly, videos remain one of the most popular methods of training.

Tips for Trainers

Before a video is shown, the trainer should discuss the learning objectives and the key points, and instruct trainees to pay particular attention to certain key parts. Trainees should understand how the video fits into the rest of the training program and be given sufficient guidance so that they know what to look for and what they should focus on. Slides should not overwhelm trainees with information and they should be easy to read and follow. Too much information or print that is too small and difficult to read can undermine their usefulness.

Case Study Method

A **case study** is a training method in which trainees discuss, analyze, and solve problems usually based on a real situation. The primary use of the case study method is to encourage open discussion and analysis of problems and events. Trainees apply business-management concepts to relevant real-life situations. Most cases present situations in which the problems are correctable.

Case study

A training method in which trainees discuss, analyze, and solve problems based on a real situation

The objectives of a case study are to:

1. Introduce realism into trainees' learning.
2. Deal with a variety of problems, goals, facts, conditions, and conflicts that often occur in the real world.
3. Teach trainees how to make decisions.
4. Teach trainees to be creative and think independently.[11]

The case study method teaches trainees to think for themselves and develop problem-solving skills while the trainer functions as a catalyst for learning. Case studies develop analytical ability, sharpen problem-solving skills, encourage creativity, and improve the organization of thoughts and ideas.[12]

The case study method is often used in business schools to teach students how to analyze and solve realistic organizational problems. In fact, more than 70 percent of business schools use the case study method. Several studies have found that using cases improves communication skills and problem solving, and enables students to better understand management situations.[13]

Cases vary depending on the intended purpose of the writer and according to the issue being examined. Some case studies disclose what management decisions were made when attempting to solve an organization's problems, while others require one to develop solutions and recommend courses of action.

For the case method to be effective, however, certain requirements must be met. For example, the qualifications of both the trainees and the trainer affect the ability to analyze cases and to draw conclusions. As well, space and time dimensions are important. Trainees need time to analyze cases properly. Finally, case studies and discussions work best in an open and informal atmosphere.[14]

Cases may be written in various styles, presenting either single problems or a number of complex, interdependent situations. They may be concerned with corporate strategy, organizational change, management, or any problem relating to a company's financial situation, marketing, human resources, or a combination of these activities. Some case reports describe the organization's difficulties in vague terms, while others may state the major problems explicitly.

In addition to the various styles of case writing, methods of presentation also differ. Cases do not always have to be in written form. Sometimes it is more effective to present cases using audio-visual techniques. This approach has advantages for both the trainees and the trainers in that trainers do not have to do as much research and writing, and trainees are able to identify better with the characters.[15]

A second alternative to a written case presentation is the live case method. Businesses may contact schools to report certain problems. Students then analyze the situation and report back to the company. This approach has been called operational consulting.[16]

Tips for Trainers

Certain requirements should be met when writing a case study. The case should be a product of a real organizational situation. A fictitious case could be regarded with boredom and distrust as the setting might seem too unrealistic.[17] Ideally, cases should be written by more than one person. Collaboration on the presentation of facts ensures a more realistic situation and helps to reduce biases. Although it is difficult, the case writer must not make assumptions and only facts should be included. The author of a case, then, must relate core issues to the reader, not personal bias.

Because a case study is a description of a typical management situation, it is often difficult to know what to include and what to omit. Most cases give an overall description of the company and the industry situation although the length of a case report varies. A typical case, however, will be up to 20 typewritten pages. The key issues and the relevant details should be included to give the reader enough information to make a qualified decision.

A teaching note provides communication between the case writer and those who teach the case. In its strictest sense, a teaching note would include information on approaches to teaching a specific case. Some teaching notes, however, are more detailed, containing samples of analyses and computations. In addition, teaching notes may state the objectives of the case and contain additional company information not available to trainees.[18]

Case Incident Method

Unlike the typical case study, a **case incident** is usually no more than one page in length and is designed to illustrate or to probe one specific problem, concept, or issue. Most management textbooks include a case incident at the end of each chapter. The case incident has become one of the most accessible ways of injecting an experiential or real-world component into a lecture.

Case incidents are useful when the trainer wants to focus on one topic or concept. Because they are short, trainees can read them during a training session and valuable time will not be taken up by differences in trainees' reading speeds. When larger, more traditional cases are used, advance preparation is necessary to read and review the case material. The brevity of a case incident reduces the need for preparation and reading skills so all trainees can participate without a lot of advance reading and preparation.

Another advantage of a case incident is that trainees are able to use their own experiences. If the material is written well, the problem presented in each incident will encourage the application of current knowledge, leading to increased confidence and trainee input and participation.

The main disadvantage of case incidents is that some trainees are bothered by the lack of background material. Indeed, at times it is necessary for trainees to make assumptions and trainers may be asked by some trainees to sketch in the background. They can be especially problematic for trainees who have limited knowledge and work experience. A lack of work or life experiences tends to elicit shallow answers based on speculation and ill-informed opinion.

Case incidents have been used successfully in higher education and organizations. Supervisors seem to like the hands-on aspects of solving a specific management problem. Similarly, students have found the case incident method to be a welcome relief from the traditional lecture method.

Tips for Trainers

Case incidents can be used in several ways. Trainees can be divided into groups with one member assigned the task of making notes while another can be designated the group spokesperson. The groups discuss the case incident and answer questions. The trainer then has each group spokesperson present their answers. This process can then lead into a general group discussion.

Another approach is to have the trainees read the case incident and then discuss it as one group. This method is especially useful when an example is needed to illustrate a specific point. The trainer would ask the trainees to read the incident, and then lead the group in a short discussion. As soon as the point has been made, the trainer should continue quickly, so as not to lose

Case incident

A training method in which one problem or issue is presented for analysis the trainees' interest. Alternatively, a case incident can be used to illustrate a point at the start of a training program or used as an exercise at the end of a training program.

Behaviour Modelling

Behaviour modelling

A training method in which trainees observe a model performing a task and then attempt to imitate the observed behaviour

MAKE THE
CONNECTION

People learn by observing the behaviour of others, and so it should not surprise you that observation is a popular and effective method of training. **Behaviour modelling** is a training method in which trainees observe a model performing a task and then attempt to imitate the observed behaviour.

Behaviour modelling is based on social cognitive theory and observational learning as described in Chapter 3. You might recall that four key elements are critical for observational learning to take place: attention, retention, reproduction, and reinforcement. These are also important for behavioural modelling training, which is an extremely effective method for learning skills and behaviours.

Behavioural modelling is one of the most widely used and researched training methods.[19] It has been used to teach interpersonal skills such as supervision, negotiation, communication, and sales as well as motor skills and it is the most popular method for teaching interpersonal and supervisory skills. In recent years it has been extended to other areas such as cross-cultural skills and technical skills.[20]

Behaviour modelling is based on four general principles of learning:[21]

1. Observation (modelling).
2. Rehearsal (practice).
3. Reinforcement (reward).
4. Transfer.

The process is fairly straightforward. Trainees observe a model performing a specific task such as handling a customer complaint or operating a machine and then practise performing the task. The performance of a task can be observed on video or it can be performed live.

The training task should be broken down into key learning points or behaviours to be learned as a series of critical steps that can be modelled independently. After viewing the model, the participants practise the behaviour, one step at a time. When one step is mastered and reinforced, the trainer moves to the next critical skill. Specific feedback must follow the performance of each step. This step-by-step process results in the development of skills and self-efficacy needed to use them. The final step involves specific actions to maximize the transfer of learning on the job.[22]

A review of research on behaviour modelling training found that it has a particularly strong effect on learning but also has a positive effect on skills development and job behaviour. The effect on skills development was greatest when learning points were used and presented as rules to be followed and when training time was longest. Transfer of learning on the job was greatest when models displaying both positive and negative behaviours were used, when trainees were instructed to set goals, when trainees' superiors were trained, and when rewards and sanctions were provided for using or failing to use newly learned skills on the job.[23]

Tips for Trainers

The model used in behavioural modelling training should be someone with whom the trainee can identify and who is perceived as credible. Under these conditions, the trainee is more likely to want to imitate the model's behaviour. In addition, trainers have to carefully plan behaviour modelling training and ensure that trainees are provided with opportunities to practise the observed behaviour, receive feedback on their performance of the task, and are motivated to use the new behaviour on the job. Trainees will resist behaviour modelling if the behaviours are incongruent with common work practices.

To be effective, trainees must have sufficient trust in the trainer to experiment (i.e., to try new behaviour in front of a group). Sometimes, a traditional and ineffective scenario is demonstrated first to increase motivation to try the new positive behaviour (John Cleese of Monty Python fame used this technique very effectively in his humorous video series on interviewing.) In fact, one study found that exposing trainees to a negative and a positive model was more effective for behavioural generalization (using the trained skills on a task that was different from the training task) than exposing trainees to only a positive model. However, exposure to only a positive model was most effective for behavioural reproduction of the training task.[24]

Transfer of the new skill and behaviours to the workplace is the weakest link in the process. Old patterns are comfortable and familiar, especially when there is some resistance in the work environment to new ways of doing things. However, by overlearning the skill, as discussed in Chapter 5, its use can become automatic. In addition, the reinforcement of newly acquired skills on the job ensures their repetition and continued application. When these reinforcers are in place, behaviour modelling can have long-lasting and positive outcomes.[25]

MAKE THE
CONNECTION

For guidelines to implement behaviour modelling, see The Trainer's Notebook 6.1, "Implementing Behavioural Modelling Training."

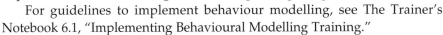

The Trainer's Notebook 6.1

Implementing Behavioural Modelling Training

1. Describe to trainees a set of well-defined behaviours (skills) to be learned.
2. Provide a model or models displaying the effective use of those behaviours.
3. Provide opportunities for trainees to practise using those behaviours.
4. Provide feedback and social reinforcement to trainees following practice.

5. Take steps to maximize the transfer of those behaviours to the job.

Source: Taylor, P. J., Russ-Eft, D. F., & Chan, D. W. L. (2005). A meta-analytic review of behavior modeling training. *Journal of Applied Psychology, 90,* 692–709.

Role Play

Role play

A training method in which trainees practise new behaviours in a safe environment

A **role play** is a method of training in which employees are given the opportunity to practise new behaviours in a safe environment. The emphasis is on doing and experiencing. This training method is most useful for acquiring interpersonal and human relations skills and for changing attitudes. You might recall that L'Oréal uses role plays to train its sales force.

A role play consists of three phases: 1. Development, 2. Enactment, and 3. Debriefing. First, a role play must be carefully *developed* to achieve its objectives. A role play usually consists of a scenario in which there are two actors. For example, if sales clerks are learning how to interact with customers, a role play might involve a customer returning an item and asking for a refund. The scenario provides information on the time, place, roles, encounter, and instructions on what each role player should do.

During the *enactment* phase, trainees are provided with the role-play information and scenarios and are assigned roles. Usually there are two role players and sometimes a third trainee who is an observer. Trainees are given some time to become familiar with the scenario and their roles, and then act out the role play. Usually the trainees will rotate so that each one spends some time in each role.

By playing a role, trainees can develop empathy for others and learn what it feels like to be in a particular role. For example, when a customer-service representative is given instructions to play the part of a disgruntled customer with a major problem, he or she can experience the frustrations of responses like, "That's not my department," and, "Just fill in that form over there, no, not that one."

After the enactment phase is the *debriefing* phase, which is considered to be the most important phase of a role play, and should last two to three times longer than the enactment phase. In this phase, participants discuss their experiences and the outcomes of their role play. Correct behaviours are reinforced and connections with key learning points and trainees' jobs are made. This is done by establishing the facts (what happened, what was experienced), analyzing the causes and effects of behaviours, and planning for skill or attitude changes on the job.

Role playing can take on various forms and does not always have to involve just two actors. A role play can involve groups of trainees acting out various roles in what is known as multiple role playing. They can also vary in terms of how much detail and structure the actors are provided. In some role plays the actors are provided a great deal of detail about what they are supposed to do and how they should feel, while less structured role plays might just indicate the actors' roles without any detail about them. A role play can also involve one trainee playing him/herself (e.g., manager) while the other trainee acts out a role (e.g., employee who is being coached). Recall that at L'Oréal Canada junior sales representatives participate in role plays in which the vice president of sales and sales directors play the role of customers.

Another variation is to have a single role play performed that is observed by the rest of the trainees. In other cases, it might be preferable to have all of the trainees participate in a role play. The type of role play will depend on the training content and objectives.

Tips for Trainers

While role playing allows trainees to practise and learn new skills, trainees sometimes resist it. As a result, the role of the trainer is crucial. Trust has to be established and an open and participative climate is necessary. Trainees should be warmed up by involving them in minor role situations. The trainer can reinforce risk taking and use mistakes as learning opportunities. Trainers could ask people to show all the incorrect ways to handle an angry customer. When a critical mistake is made, the trainer can start again or rewind the case. In one role play, a police officer was testing methods of talking to a potential suicide victim on a bridge. The officer made the fatal mistake of saying, "Go ahead, I dare you," and the role-play partner jumped. The trainer immediately stated, "Well, that approach didn't work, would you like to try another?" He rewound the case and demonstrated the true value of role playing—the opportunity to practise behaviours in a safe environment.

One of the limitations of a role play is that unlike behaviour modelling, trainees are not shown exactly what to do and how to behave prior to participating in a role play. As a result, some trainees might not be successful in a role play and might even display incorrect behaviours. Furthermore, much of what happens during a role play is left in the hands of the role players. This means that it is extremely important for the trainer to draw out the incorrect and correct behaviours during the debriefing phase. Otherwise, trainees might not learn the appropriate behaviours following a role play.

Games

Games involve structured competition that allows trainees to learn specific skills. Games tend to have rules, principles, and a system for scoring. For example, an employment law game called *Winning through Prevention* teaches human resource managers about lawful termination, discrimination, and workplace safety. Players who answer correctly get promoted and those who answer incorrectly are faced with a lawsuit.[26]

Business games often require teams of players to compete against each other to gain a strategic advantage, to gain market share, or to maximize profits. They can involve all areas of management practice and often require the players to gather and analyze information, and to make business management decisions. As a result, business games tend to focus on the development of problem-solving, interpersonal, and decision-making skills.

Some business games are relatively simple and focus on a particular functional area such as marketing, human resources, or finance. Other games are much more complex and try to model an entire organization. Participants might have to operate a company and make all kinds of decisions and solve business problems. They then receive feedback and have the opportunity to practise particular skills.

Games incorporate many principles of learning such as learning from experience, active practice, and direct application to real problems. They are used to enhance the learning process by injecting fun and competition, generating energy, and providing opportunities for people to work together.

Games

Activities characterized by structured competition that allow trainees to learn specific skills

A disadvantage of the use of games is the possibility of learning the wrong things, a weak relation to training objectives, and an emphasis on winning.[27] In addition, trainees sometimes get so caught up in the game that they lose sight of the importance of learning. Although trainees seem to enjoy games and respond enthusiastically to them, there is not very much evidence on how effective they are for improving skills and on-the-job performance.

Tips for Trainers

The design of a game begins with a critical question: "What is the key task to be learned?" At the beginning of the exercise, the trainer should state the learning objective so that trainees don't just focus on winning the game but understand what they will learn. In addition, the roles of the players must be clearly defined.

Games should be as realistic as possible and be a meaningful representation of the kind of work that participants do. If they are not realistic, participants might not take them seriously. This will undermine learning and the application of new skills on the job. To be most effective, games should be well planned and prepared, linked to training objectives, and include a debriefing session so that trainees understand the purpose of the game and the critical skills and behaviours to be learned.[28] As well, because many kinds of games are available, trainers need to be familiar with them and to carefully choose one that best meets an organization's needs and objectives.

Simulations

Simulations are a form of training that involves the use of operating models of physical or social events that are designed to represent reality. They attempt to recreate situations by simplifying them to a manageable size and structure. They are models or active representations of work situations that are designed to increase trainee motivation, involvement, and learning. They are also used when training in the real world might involve danger or extreme costs.

Simulations are a popular method of training and are widely used in business, education, and the military. For example, simulations are typically used in medicine, maintenance, law enforcement, and emergency management settings. The military and the commercial aviation industry are purported to be the biggest users of simulation-based training.[29]

Equipment simulators are mechanical devices that are similar to those that employees use on the job. They are designed to simulate the kinds of procedures, movements, and/or decisions required in the work environment.

A good example of an equipment simulator is a flight simulator used to train pilots. Flight simulators mimic flights exactly but pose no risk to humans or equipment. Equipment simulators are also used to train astronauts, air traffic controllers, and maintenance workers. Trucking companies have also begun to use simulations to train new drivers. For a good example of this, see Training Today 6.1, "Truck Driving School."

Simulations can also be used to develop managerial and interpersonal skills. For example, organizational simulations like the one used for product

Simulations

Operating models of physical or social events designed to represent reality

Equipment simulators

Mechanical devices that are similar to those that employees use on the job managers at L'Oréal Canada require participants to solve problems, make decisions, and interact with various stakeholders. Trainees learn how organizations operate and acquire important managerial and business skills.

Simulations are also used to train employees involved in emergency response work, such as firefighters and police officers. For example, in December 2005 a series of truck bombs in Toronto knocked out the city's power, destroyed a terminal at Pearson airport, an office tower on Bay Street, and much of the St. Michael's Hospital. Fortunately, it was just an imaginary scenario that was part of a training simulation for riot police to practise their emergency response strategy. The simulation included army reservists as well as Toronto police, firefighters, and paramedics. The objective of the program was to look for areas that can be improved, to coordinate with other agencies, and to be prepared in case such a scenario ever happens.[30]

Training Today 6.1

Truck Driving School

Dennis Colwell stared hard at the side-view mirror and gripped the steering wheel before attempting to manoeuvre around a pickup parked between his 18-wheeler and the loading dock. "If I make it, it's going to be paper thin," Colwell said to his instructor, Jay Gamble. But the implicit request for guidance was denied. "If I wasn't here," Gamble reminded Colwell, "what would you do?" Colwell took a deep breath, put the truck into gear and inched forward.

In many ways, this scenario could be found at truck driving schools across the country. But Colwell's experience at Schneider National's training program was very different from the industry norm in one respect. He wasn't driving, or even sitting in, a real truck. Instead, he was in a classroom, buckled into the seat of what looked and sounded very much like a high quality video game but was actually a state-of-the art training simulator.

The virtual parking lot Colwell navigated was created with animation software, though the experience was quite realistic. Three wide-screen monitors gave a 180-degree field of vision, and images appeared in reverse through the side-view mirrors. The simulator was equipped with a steering wheel and clutch that put up life-like resistance, an electronic dashboard that tracked the truck's vital statistics and a horn, which Colwell honked before backing up.

Up until the moment Colwell had to squeeze his rig past a blue pickup truck, he moved around the simulated parking lot with ease. But he found himself in a tight spot and, rather than back up to give himself more wiggle room, he went for it. In an instant, there was the sound of a crash and the word "COLLISION" flashed in red across his windshield.

Schneider is one of only a small handful of U.S. trucking companies using simulators for driver training. Simulation now accounts for about one-third of the time every new Schneider recruit spends behind the wheel during a two-week training program. They will also be used in refresher courses for veteran drivers. The simulators provide a safe environment in which to practise driving hazardous road conditions. And because scenarios from a parking lot or mountain road can be instantly replayed, it is easy for students to concentrate on their weaknesses.

Since Schneider began incorporating simulators into the training at its headquarters, the company said the number of new drivers who have accidents during their first 90 days on the job has fallen by 25 percent. There has been an equivalent decline in the number of people dropping out of the training program or quitting their jobs within the first 90 days.

Source: Excerpt from Foss, B. (2006, February 4). Simulators help teach truckers safety; Danger-free way to practise driving 'It takes white knuckles off wheel.' *Toronto Star*, G32. Reprinted with permission - Torstar Syndication Services.

A major disadvantage of simulations is that they are expensive to develop and, in the case of emergency response simulations, very expensive to stage. On the positive side, simulations are an excellent method for adding some realism into a training program. They are especially useful in situations where it would be too costly or dangerous to train employees on the actual equipment used on the job. To learn about how simulations and games are being used for training, see Training Today 6.2, "Training Games and Simulations."

Tips for Trainers

Physical fidelity

The similarity of the physical aspects of a simulation (e.g., equipment, tasks, and surroundings) to the actual job

In order to be most effective, simulations should have physical and psychological fidelity. **Physical fidelity** has to do with the similarity of the physical aspects of a simulation (e.g., equipment, tasks, and surroundings) to the actual job. Simulators should be designed to physically replicate and resemble the work environment. That is, the simulation should have the appearance of the actual work site. For example, a flight simulator should look like the cockpit of an actual airplane with respect to the various controls, lights, and instruments.

Psychological fidelity

The similarity of the psychological conditions of the simulation to the actual work environment

Psychological fidelity has to do with the similarity of the psychological conditions of the simulation to the actual work environment. Simulations should be designed so that the experience is as similar as possible to what trainees experience on the job. In other words, the simulation should include on-the-job psychological conditions such as time pressures, problems, conflicts, and so on.

Training Today 6.2

Training Games and Simulations

Games and simulations can take many different forms. For example, "Drill and repeat" games can be used for rote learning and for reinforcing concepts.

Cisco Systems found that its certified network engineers around the world would be more effective if they were able to master binary math—converting between base 10 numbers and binary ones and zeros. As a solution, Cisco developed a binary game and made it available for free on its website and for use on mobile devices. This simple but effective drill and repeat game not only solved a key training challenge, but it also turned out to be an effective corporate marketing tool used at various events, with prizes awarded to top scorers. This same type of approach can be used to improve learning about investment concepts, accounting terms, and management techniques.

Budding entrepreneurs can learn what life might be like by playing a business simulation that recreates the day-to-day experiences of being an entrepreneur. Customer service agents can participate in simulated role playing exercises. Employees can learn to complete an expense form in a tutorial that simulates the task.

IBM recently launched INNOV8, a business process management simulation program that it donates to educational institutions to better prepare students for the workforce. IBM's game puts students in a 3-D world inside a virtual company, interacting with other characters to accomplish specific on-the-job objectives.

Source: Excerpt from Georghiou, M. (2008, May 5). Games, simulations open world of learning. *Canadian HR Reporter, 21* (9), 24. Reprinted by permission of Carswell, a division of Thomson Canada Ltd.

The Trainer's Notebook 6.2

Getting the Most Out of Experiential Training Methods

Experiential training methods such as role playing, games, and simulations encourage trainee participation. However, sometimes they put trainees on the spot—literally in the spotlight, forced to act in situations in which they feel very uncomfortable. Here are some tips for trainers to make effective use of experiential training methods:

- Don't use games and role plays just to play and have fun. There must be a purpose, a learning outcome that you should share with the trainees.
- Try the exercise you have designed or chosen. If you are uncomfortable doing it, don't use it.
- Don't think that unlearning previous habits means going through extremely difficult events, like boot camp. People don't learn to swim by being thrown into the deep end of the swimming pool.
- Not everyone has to participate in a participative workshop. Some people can play different roles

(such as observing or note taking) rather than the high-profile "let us show them how they are doing it wrong" simulations.

- Warm-up exercises and limiting the size of the group might also create a supportive environment in which to risk behaviour by role playing or asking questions.
- If an individual does lose face, trainers can make favourable comments by focusing on the correct actions, inviting observers to empathize with the person facing the difficulties of the task in the exercise, and asking the others to appreciate the risks taken by those who did play the game.

Sources: Becker, R. (1998). Taking the misery out of experiential training. *Training, 35* (2), 79–88; *Training: The human side of business* by Becker, R.

Simulations allow a great deal of flexibility as complicating factors or unexpected events can be built into the program. For example, in a pilot-training simulation, a blizzard can be introduced. However, trainers should ensure that simulations have both physical and psychological fidelity.

To learn more about how to make experiential training methods effective, see The Trainer's Notebook 6.2, "Getting the Most Out of Experiential Training Methods."

Action Learning

In Chapter 5, active practice was described as an important component of a training program for trainee learning and retention. A good example of a training method that provides active practice is action learning.

Action learning provides trainees with opportunities to test theories in the real world. Reginald Revans, the originator of action learning principles, emphasizes that the learner develops skills through responsible involvement in some real, complex, and stressful problem.[31] Action learning requires trainees to identify problems; develop possible solutions; test these solutions in a real-world, real-time situation; and evaluate the consequences. The aim is to solve an actual business problem.

The goals of action learning are to involve and to challenge the trainee and move employees from passive observation to identification with the

MAKE THE CONNECTION

Action learning

A training method in which trainees accept the challenge of studying and solving real-world problems and accept responsibility for the solution people and the vision of the organization. This method moves trainees from information receivers to problem solvers. Action learning incorporates more of the adult learning principles than any other method of training.

The majority of the time spent in action learning is dedicated to the diagnosis of problems in the field. The problems and the inherent value systems supporting the problems are assessed and challenged. This work is always done in groups, and learning by-products include group and interpersonal skills, risk taking, responsibility, and accountability.[32]

Professions use action learning to train and socialize their students. For example, students in social work are often sent to work with the homeless or welfare recipients. These students are encouraged to apply their theoretical knowledge in the field. Industry is using the precepts of action learning when employees take responsibility for quality-improvement projects.

Action learning requires a commitment of energy and time from participants and their managers. Solving real organizational problems can be stressful for trainees. The difficulties of working in teams on real problems can lead to conflict and increased anxiety and stress.

Although action learning is more popular in Europe than in North America, a number of Canadian companies have recently developed action learning programs. For example, TD Bank Financial Group has a leadership development program in which action learning plays an integral part. The bank's senior managers attend a three-day course to learn about the competencies that comprise a new leadership profile. Then they must use the learning to solve an action learning opportunity that they identified before attending the courses. TELUS also has an action learning program for its director-level managers. The company partnered with several universities to deliver courses in several key areas. After taking the courses, participants are expected to use the learning to solve work-related problems and they are held accountable for applying the learning and making changes.[33]

Tips for Trainers

Action learning projects must be challenging and deal with real organizational concerns. Trainees should buy into the importance of the project and the organizational problem and receive some release time to work on the project. In addition, some training in group skills to enable collaboration might also be necessary. The group working on the project should be small enough (four to seven members) to develop trust but contain a diverse set of skills to enable creative solutions. The learning process should be monitored and the trainees held accountable for their proposed solutions.

RPC **RPC 6.2**

What Training Method Is Best?

In this chapter, we have described some of the most common off-the-job instructional training methods. In Chapter 7, you will learn about on-the-job training methods and in Chapter 8 you will find out about technology-based training methods. With so many training methods available, it is natural to ask, "What training method is best?" and "How does a trainer choose a

Managing Performance Through Training and Development

training method?" There is of course no easy or straightforward answer to this question. However, we will try to provide some guidelines for choosing training methods.

In terms of the effectiveness of the various methods, a survey completed by 150 experienced professional trainers (members of the Canadian Society of Training and Development) revealed a hierarchy of effectiveness. As a general principle, the more highly involved the trainee in the learning process and the more the training situation resembles the job, the more likely that transfer to the job will occur. These methods include on-the-job and one-on-one training, simulations, role plays, behaviour modelling, self-study, case studies, and multimedia. A combination of these methods results in even greater transfer. Other methods, such as lectures, discussions, video conferencing, and lunch and learn programs, were not as effective for transfer to the job, perhaps because these techniques allow (and indeed require) trainees be passive absorbers of information.[34]

Two large surveys of training directors found that nine different training methods were effective in achieving different types of training goals.[35] For example, the case study method was rated most effective for problem-solving skills, and computer-based instruction was rated best for knowledge retention. The role-play method was evaluated best for changing attitudes and developing interpersonal skills. However, these are only individual perceptions and do not provide information on actual trainee achievements.

It is important to realize that the effectiveness of a training method depends on the training objectives and learning outcomes. Thus, the choice of what training method to use for a particular training program should start with the program's objectives. For example, if the objective is declarative knowledge, you might choose the lecture method. However, if the objective is the acquisition of interpersonal skills, you might want to use the role-play method.

In general, the lecture method will be most effective when you want to impart large amounts of information quickly and at low cost to large groups of trainees. To teach interpersonal skills such as interviewing or negotiations, the most effective methods are behaviour modelling and role playing.

In addition to training objectives, other factors that should be considered when choosing a training method include cost and resource availability, on-the-job application, trainer skill and preferences, and trainee preferences and characteristics. We will now briefly discuss each of these factors.

Cost and Resource Availability

A training method might be extremely effective for achieving a program's objectives, but it might be too costly to develop and implement. For example, a simulation might be appropriate for a training objective but very expensive. Thus, trainers must consider the cost and resources available for developing and implementing training methods.

On-the-Job Application

Another important factor to consider is on-the-job applications. Trainers will choose some methods over others if trainees are expected to apply the newly acquired skills on the job. For example, a lecture is not a good choice if the objective is on-the-job applications. If trainees are expected to apply new knowledge and skills on the job then a role play or behavioural modelling will be more effective.

Trainer Skill and Preferences

A trainer might be more skilled at using some methods than others and might have a personal preference for using some methods. For example, if a trainer is not experienced or comfortable conducting role plays or simulations then these methods might not be considered. Thus, the choice of a training method will also depend on the skills and preferences of trainers.

Trainee Preferences and Characteristics

When choosing a training method the trainer must consider what is best for trainees given their preferences and characteristics. For starters, you might recall the discussion of Kolb's learning styles in Chapter 3. Learning style refers to the way individuals gather information and process it during the learning process. Trainees with different learning styles are likely to prefer different training methods (e.g., lecture versus role playing) and will differ in terms of what training methods will maximize their learning.

Also important is a trainee's ability to benefit from a particular method of instruction. There is some evidence that training methods have differential effects on trainees as a result of differences in aptitudes (e.g., abilities, skills, knowledge). This is known as an aptitude-treatment interaction.

An **aptitude-treatment interaction** occurs when a training method is more effective for some trainees than others. In other words, the training method has differential effects on trainees with different aptitudes. An aptitude is broadly defined as any characteristic of trainees that affects their ability to learn from the training method. For example, there is some evidence that high-ability students benefit more from programs with less structure and greater complexity while low-ability students benefit more from explicit and structured programs.[36] Thus, it is important that the training methods are suitable for trainees' aptitudes.

Table 6.2 summarizes 10 on-the-job and off-the-job training methods against three of the criteria (objectives, costs, and on-the-job transfer).

Blended Training

Although we have been discussing training methods as if only one can be used in a training program, in reality trainers mix and combine them (e.g., case studies with lecturing). In fact, you might recall in Chapter 5 the reference to **blended training** as an approach that combines classroom training, on-the-job training, and computer technology.

Blended training programs are becoming more common and increasingly the norm. A blended delivery approach has a number of benefits. It allows

Aptitude-treatment interaction

When a training method has differential effects on trainees with different aptitudes

Blended training

The use of a combination of approaches to training such as classroom training, on-the-job training, and computer technology.

TABLE 6.2

Choosing a Training Method

Method	TRAINING OBJECTIVES[1]			COSTS[2]		USE ON THE JOB[3]
	Knowledge	Skills	Attitudes	Dev$	Admin$	Transfer
Lecture	yes	no	no	low	low	low
Video	yes	no	yes	high	low	med
Discussion	no	no	yes	low	low	low
Behaviour modelling	no	yes	no	high	high	high
Role play	no	yes	yes	med	med	high
Case study	yes	med	yes	med	low	med
Case incident	med	med	med	med	med	med
Games	no	med	no	med	med	low
Simulations	yes	yes	no	high	high	high
Tech-based training	yes	yes	no	high	low	high

[1] Determine the training objective and match the training methods to that objective

[2] Consider the costs of the method (development and administration) and its potential benefits

[3] Determine suitability for transfer to the job

participants to learn in ways that work for them, allows multiple learning outcomes to be achieved, and increases the possibility that the training will be applied on the job. Trainers must therefore be skilled in a variety of training methods. According to a survey in the United States, 15 to 30 percent of responding organizations reported that they use both traditional training methods and e-learning.[37]

In conclusion, when it comes to training methods, each method has its place. There are many factors to consider when deciding on training methods. Ultimately, mixing, adapting, and blending training methods will usually be the best approach for maximizing trainee learning and a training program's effectiveness.

Summary

This chapter described 10 of the most common off-the-job instructional training methods. The advantages and disadvantages of each method were described as well as suggestions for their use. The chapter concluded with a discussion of how to choose training methods and the main factors to consider. The importance of combining methods and using a blended delivery approach was also discussed.

Key Terms

Make the Connection

p. 174: social cognitive theory is discussed in Chapter 3 on page 74

p. 175: overlearning is discussed in Chapter 5 on page 150

p. 181: active practice is discussed in Chapter 5 on page 145

p. 184: learning style is discussed in Chapter 3 on page 69

Web Links

L'Oréal Canada: www.loreal.ca

Nycomed Canada: www.nycomed.ca

RPC Icons

RPC 6.1 Using a variety of methods facilitates the delivery of development programs to groups and individual learners.

RPC 6.2 Recommends the most appropriate way to meet identified learning needs (e.g., courses, secondments, and on-the-job activities).

Discussion Questions

1. What is the difference between a role play and behavioural modelling and what are the advantages and disadvantages of each method?
2. Review the instructional training methods listed in Table 6.1 and discuss the advantages and disadvantages of using each method to train airport passenger-and-baggage screeners. What methods do you think will be most effective and why?
3. What are the advantages and disadvantages of each of the instructional training methods listed in Table 6.1, and when would it be best to use each method? What method do you prefer when you are being trained and why?

4. What are the main factors a trainer should consider when choosing a training method? Explain how each factor will suggest some training methods over others.
5. What is the difference between physical fidelity and psychological fidelity and how would you design a training program to have both?
6. What is an aptitude-treatment interaction and how is it relevant for the use of training methods?
7. What is a blended training program and what are the implications of blended programs for trainers and trainees?
8. What is the difference between games and simulations and what are the advantages and disadvantages of each method?
9. Explain how the four key elements of observational learning (attention, retention, reproduction, and reinforcement) are relevant for behavioural modelling training.

The Great Training Debate

1. Debate the following: Lectures are not a very effective method of training and should not be used as often as they have in the past.
2. Debate the following: No single training method is the best and all training programs should use a blended approach to training.

Using the Internet

1. To find out about the kinds of games and simulations that are used in training, visit the following websites:

   www.survivalinthebushinc.com

   www.paradigmlearning.com

   Answer the following questions:

   a. What kinds of games and simulations does each company offer for corporate and business training?
   b. What are the objectives of the games and simulations and what do trainees do?
   c. What knowledge and skills do employees learn from the games and simulations and how effective do you think they are?
   d. Using the factors described in the chapter for choosing a training method, evaluate the use and effectiveness of the games and simulations for the training objectives.

2. To learn more about action learning, visit the World Institute for Action Learning at **www.wial.org** and answer the following questions:

   a. Provide an overview of action learning and discuss what companies are using it for.

b. What are the six components of action learning?

c. What are the benefits of action learning?

d. Describe some action learning success stories.

Exercises

In-Class

1. Prepare a five-minute lecture on a topic of your choice using the information on lectures described in the text. Find a partner in your class and review each other's lecture. If time permits, give your lecture to the class or a small group and discuss its effectiveness. What would make your lecture more effective?

2. Choose a training program you have taken that you really liked and one that you did not like. For each one, indicate the instructional training methods that were used (see Table 6.1) and how they were used. What effect did the methods have on your satisfaction of the program and your learning? What methods might have improved your satisfaction and learning?

3. Think of a work situation you have either experienced or observed that would lend itself to a role play (e.g., a customer complaining to an employee). Design a role play in which you describe a scenario and the role of two role players. Be clear about the purpose of the role play in terms of its objectives and what the role players are expected to learn. Be sure to include instructions to participants about the scenario and the relationship between the characters. The instructor can have you describe your role play to the class and/or have class members enact it. If role plays are enacted, be sure to also include a debriefing session afterwards.

4. Describe the major tasks involved in performing a previous or current job and how employees are trained. Then review each of the instructional training methods in Table 6.1 and describe how they might be used to train employees for the job. What training methods do you think would be most effective? What methods would you recommend and why?

5. For this exercise, your task is to design a short game that can be played in class to learn an interpersonal skill such as communication, team skills, leadership, negotiations, etc. In groups of two or three, choose a skill to focus on, and then design a game to learn the skill. Your game must be designed so that other members of the class can play it during class time. Write a brief description of your game indicating the objectives, the players, the rules, and what team members have to do to get points or win. The instructor can either have you describe your game to the class and/or have class members actually play it. After playing the game, be sure to discuss how effective it was for learning the skill and the participants' reaction to it.

6. You have been asked to develop a course to teach senior executives how to use e-mail. What instructional training method would you use and why (see Table 6.1)?

7. Consider the potential of action learning as a training method for your course on training and development. Do you think that action learning would be an effective method? Design an action learning project for your training and development course. Be specific in terms of the objectives, the skills to be developed, and the problems to be worked on and solved.

8. For this exercise you are to design a training program for a task you currently perform or have performed on a job. Once you have decided on a task, prepare an outline of a lecture that you could use to train other employees to perform the task. Be sure to indicate the main content and points you will include in your lecture. When your lecture outline is complete, review the instructional training methods in Table 6.1 and consider adding some of them to your training program. What other instructional methods will you include and why? At what point in your lecture will you include them? Be specific when describing how the other training methods will be incorporated into your training program and what they will involve.

9. Many organizations today are using structured employment interviews as part of the selection process. However, not all interviewers or managers know how to conduct a structured employment interview. If your task was to design a training program on how to conduct a structured employment interview, what instructional training method(s) would you use? For each of the methods in Table 6.1, indicate whether you would use it for your training program. Be sure to explain your reasoning. Once you have decided which method(s) you will use, briefly describe how you will use them and for what purpose.

In-the-Field

1. Contact the human resources department of an organization to learn about the instructional training methods they use to train employees. In particular, you should inquire about:

   - What instructional training methods they use, what they use them for, and why they use them. (Refer to Table 6.1.)
   - Do they use a blended approach to training? Why or why not?
   - Do they use certain methods for particular training programs?
   - Do they prefer to use certain methods more than others?
   - What methods do they believe to be the most effective for training employees in their organization?
   - What factors do they consider when choosing instructional training methods?

Case Incident

In-Flight Crew Training at JetBlue

JetBlue Airways was launched in 2000. In 2005, the company had just over 20 000 applicants for in-flight crew (flight attendants) positions with only 600 selected for training. After a rigorous recruitment and selection process, new hires must attend in-flight crew training and learn how to serve customers miles in the air and how to respond to emergencies. JetBlue trainees must also learn how to open cabin doors and shout the appropriate commands to evacuate the aircraft in 90 seconds.

Questions

1. How should JetBlue train new flight attendants? What are the advantages and disadvantages of each instructional method of off-the-job training?
2. Which instructional training methods do you think are most effective for training new flight attendants and why?

Source: Weinstein, M. (2006, April). JetBlue: Training in the air. *Training, 43* (4), 26–27.

Case Study

The Customer-Service Training Program

Intense competition among retailers has made customer service a top priority. At stores such as the Gap and Wal-Mart, employees welcome customers into the store with cheery greetings. Thus, sales staff must have good communication and interpersonal skills to provide customers with excellent service. They also need to be courteous, polite, friendly, and helpful.

A large retail clothing store decided that it needed to improve customer service to be more competitive. It wanted employees to be more active and involved with customers to provide excellent service and improve customer satisfaction ratings.

The company designed a new customer-service training program to train employees how to greet customers, offer assistance, help them find what they are looking for, solve customer complaints and problems, and provide courteous, helpful, and friendly service. An important objective of the program was to provide employees with better interpersonal and communication skills so that they would be able to spend more time interacting with customers and ensure that every customer leaves the store satisfied with his/her shopping experience.

The training program, which was designed in-house and delivered by the company's training staff, began with a lecture in which the trainer described the importance of customer service and the objectives of the training program. Trainees were instructed on the importance of good customer service and how they should behave when they are interacting with customers.

Following the lecture, a video was shown that consisted of different scenarios in which employees were shown interacting with customers. In one scenario, a customer could not find what he was looking for and asked the employee for assistance. The employee was not friendly and told the customer to try looking in another aisle. In another incident, a customer complained to an employee about something she had purchased that was less expensive at another store. She demanded a price reduction or her money back. The customer began raising her voice and the employee yelled at the customer and told her to leave the store. Similar incidents of poor customer service were also shown in the video.

After the video, the trainer asked trainees what was wrong with each scenario and how the employee should have behaved to provide better customer service. At the end of the discussion, the trainer provided a brief lecture outlining the key points shown in the video. This was followed by a video that showed scenarios of employees providing good customer service. A brief discussion and lecture followed in which the trainees were asked to describe what the employee did in each situation to provide good service. The trainer concluded the session by highlighting the key customer-service behaviours.

Trainees then had to take a test on their knowledge of customer service. The test consisted of multiple choice questions that asked trainees to choose the most appropriate behaviour in different situations with customers. Most of the trainees did very well on the test and upon completing the training program they received a customer-service qualification certificate. Trainees reacted positively to the training program, which was considered to be a success.

However, back on the job some employees still had difficulty interacting and communicating with customers. For example, in one incident a customer demanded his money back for a pair of pants that had shrunk after cleaning. He blamed the employee for the store's poor quality and called the employee an idiot. The employee didn't know what to do and just walked away in tears.

In another incident, a customer came into the store to pick up a shirt that he had asked an employee to hold for him. The item had been sold and it was the last one in the store. The employee apologized saying that it was sold to somebody else by accident. However, the customer insisted that the employee call the customer who bought the shirt and have him return it. The employee said she could not do that and told the customer how sorry she was. The customer refused to leave the store unless the employee called the customer who bought the shirt. The employee threatened to call security if the customer did not leave the store. He finally left but not before causing a big scene in the store in front of many other customers. Later that day the employee quit.

One month after the training program there was no improvement in customer satisfaction ratings and four of the sales staff who had attended the training program had quit. Management began to wonder if the training program was effective. They were not sure if more time was needed for the effects of the training program to show up in customer satisfaction scores or if the training program was a failure.

Questions

1. How effective was the training program? What are its strengths and weaknesses?
2. Describe the instructional training methods used in the customer-service training program. Do you think these were appropriate methods to use and were they used appropriately?
3. What other instructional training methods could have been used to make the training program more effective? Review the methods in Table 6.1 and indicate how effective each one would be using the criteria in the chapter to select training methods.
4. If you were to redesign the customer-service training program, what instructional training methods would you use and why?
5. What does this case say about training methods and the effectiveness of a training program? What does it say about choosing training methods?

References

1. Based on Klie, S. (2008, October 6). L'Oréal plays games with training. *Canadian HR Reporter, 21* (17), 26; Klie, S. (2007, October 22). L'Oréal a pretty picture of diversity, training. *Canadian HR Reporter, 20* (18), 11; www.loreal.ca.
2. Sitzman, T., Kraiger, K., Stewart, D., & Wisher, R. (2006). The comparative effectiveness of web-based and classroom instruction: A meta-analysis. *Personnel Psychology, 59,* 623–664.
3. Hughes, P. D., & Grant, M. (2007). *Learning & development outlook 2007.* The Conference Board of Canada: Ottawa; (2007, November/December). 2008 Industry report: Gauges & drivers. *Training, 45* (9), 1–34.
4. Arthur, W. Jr., Bennett, W. Jr., Edens, P. S., & Bell, S. T. (2003). Effectiveness of training in organizations: A meta-analysis of design and evaluation features. *Journal of Applied Psychology, 88,* 234–245.
5. Renner, P. (1988). *The quick instructional planner.* Vancouver: Training Associates Ltd.
6. Zander, A. (1982). *Making groups effective.* San Francisco: Jossey-Bass Publishers.
7. Gabris, G. (1989). Educating elected officials in strategic goal setting. *Public Productivity and Management Review, 13* (2), 161–175.
8. Conlin, J. (1989). Conflict at meetings: Come out fighting. *Successful Meetings, 38* (6), 30–36; Renner, P. (1988); Wein, G. (1990). Experts as trainers. *Training and Development Journal, 44* (7), 29–30.
9. Keller, S., & Chuvala, J. (1992). Training: Tricks of the trade. *Security Management, 36* (7).
10. Anonymous. (2008, May 19). CEOs talk: Training & development. *Canadian HR Reporter, 21*(10), 11–13.
11. Yin, R. K. (1985). *Case study research: Design and methods.* Beverly Hills: Sage Publications.
12. Pearce, J. A., Robinson, R. B., Jr., & Zahra Shaker, A. (1989). *An industry approach to cases in strategic management.* Boston: Irwin Publishing.
13. Wright, P. (1992). The CEO and the business school: Is there potential for increased cooperation? *Association of Management Proceedings: Education, 10* (1), 41–45.
14. Craig, R. L. (1987). *Training and development handbook: A guide to human resource development* (pp. 414–429). New York: McGraw-Hill Inc.

15. Craig, R. L. (1987).

16. Schnelle, K. (1967). *Case analysis and business problem solving.* New York: McGraw-Hill.

17. Craig, R. L. (1987).

18. Leenders, M. R., & Erskine, J. A. (1973). *Case research: The case writing process.* London: University of Western Ontario Press.

19. Taylor, P. J., Russ-Eft, D. F., & Chan, D. W. L. (2005). A meta-analytic review of behavior modeling training. *Journal of Applied Psychology, 90,* 692–709.

20. Baldwin, T. T. (1992). Effects of alternative modeling strategies on outcomes of interpersonal-skills training. *Journal of Applied Psychology, 77,* 147–154; Taylor, P. J., Russ-Eft, D. F., & Chan, D. W. L. (2005).

21. Robinson, J. C. (1982). *Developing managers through behaviour modelling.* Austin: Texas.

22. Georges, J. C. (1988). Why soft-skills training doesn't take. *Training, 25* (4), 44–45.

23. Taylor, P. J., Russ-Eft, D. F., & Chan, D. W. L. (2005).

24. Buller, M., & McEvoy, G. (1990). Exploring the long-term effects of behaviour modelling training. *Journal of Organizational Change Management, 3* (1).

25. Atkins, E. (1999, March) Winning through prevention. *Workplace News,* p. 9.

26. Greenlaw, B., Herron, M., & Ramdon, L. (1962). *Business simulation in industrial and university education.* Englewood Cliffs, NJ: Prentice-Hall.

27. Baldwin, T. T. (1992).

28. Tannenbaum, S. I., & Yukl, G. (1992). Training and development in work organizations. *Annual Review of Psychology, 43,* 399–441.

29. Salas, E., & Cannon-Bowers, J. A. (2001). The science of training: A decade of progress. *Annual Review of Psychology, 52,* 471–99.

30. Powell, B. (2005, December 5). Troops rehearse for disaster. *Toronto Star,* B1.

31. Revans, R. W. (1982). *The origins and growth of action learning.* Gock, Sweden: Bratt–Institute for Neues Lernen.

32. Revans, R. W. (1984). Action learning: Are we getting there? *Management Decision Journal, 22* (1), 45–52.

33. Vu, U. (2005, April 25). Action learning popular in Europe, not yet caught on in Canada. *Canadian HR Reporter, 18* (8), 1, 17.

34. Belcourt, M., & Saks, A. M. (1998, February). Training methods and the transfer of training. *Canadian Learning Journal, 3.*

35. Newstrom, J. W. (1980). Evaluating the effectiveness of training methods. *Personnel Administrator, 25* (1), 55–60; Carrol, S. J., Paine, F. T., & Ivancevich, J. J. (1972). The relative effectiveness of training methods—expert opinion and research. *Personnel Psychology, 25,* 495–510.

36. Tannenbaum, S. I., & Yukl, G. (1992). Training and development in work organizations. *Annual Review of Psychology, 43,* 399–441.

37. Dolezalek, H. (2005, December). 2005 industry report. *Training, 42* (12), 14–28.

CHAPTER 7

On-the-Job Training Methods

Chapter Learning Outcomes

After reading this chapter you should be able to:

- describe the following on-the-job training methods: job instruction training, performance aids, job rotation, apprenticeships, coaching, and mentoring
- list the advantages and disadvantages of each training method
- describe how and when to use each training method
- describe the coaching process and how to design a coaching program
- define mentoring and describe how to develop a formal mentoring program
- describe the advantages and disadvantages of on-the-job and off-the-job training methods

WHITE SPOT

White Spot restaurant was founded in Vancouver in 1928 by Nat Bailey. It started as a small log cabin drive-in with a white spot painted on its roof. White Spot now has 63 locations throughout British Columbia and Alberta and employs more than 4,000 people.

As part of its commitment to quality and culinary excellence, White Spot offers its chefs an in-house skills upgrading program. Chefs can learn the skills they need to become a Red Seal certified chef from James Kennedy, the chain's Corporate Training Chef. The Red Seal certification is the standardized certification for Canadian chefs and is a recognized symbol of quality.

In an effort to increase the training and skill of its chefs and the number of nationally certified chefs in its restaurants, White Spot implemented a Red Seal Chef Certification program in 2008. Chefs with the Red Seal certification are in high demand, and finding certified chefs is difficult. The traditional certification process for new chefs takes three years and includes an annual month-long classroom component, which can interfere with an individual's career and leave a restaurant without a chef.

According to White Spot president Warren Erhart, "Unlike the traditional model, where they would have to leave their employer and go to college to get their skill-level training, we can provide that through the White Spot environment. We think it's a more pragmatic way for people to both work in our restaurant and get paid to get their papers. We can customize our learning and training times around the business needs."

White Spot is the first restaurant to offer all the components of a full indentured apprenticeship program in-house, something that has been available only at post-secondary institutions. The program is conducted by White Spot's Corporate Training Chef at its corporate training kitchen and with key industry partners at their facilities. White Spot's Red Seal chefs who complete the skills upgrading program supervise the apprentices while they work in the kitchens. The Corporate Training Chef oversees the classroom component in the chain's corporate kitchen for one day every three weeks.

According to Erhart, the restaurant hopes the program will help the chain retain more of its cooking staff. Before the skills upgrading program was available, White Spot lost several cooks who took jobs at other establishments in order to get their certification. White Spot is now keeping people longer because they can get their chef papers while working.

The Red Seal Certification program is an opportunity for White Spot's chefs to develop their skills and pursue certification on the job without disrupting their regular work schedule and earnings. Today, White Spot is one of British Columbia's most popular restaurants and in 2008 celebrated its 80th anniversary.[1]

White Spot is a good example of an organization that uses on-the-job training to train its employees. In this chapter, we focus on some of the most common methods of on-the-job training. According to the Conference Board of Canada, most Canadian organizations report using on-the-job training to train employees.[2]

Table 7.1 lists six types of on-the-job training methods described in this chapter. We begin with the most basic form of on-the-job training—when one person trains another person on how to do something—and conclude with some of the more expensive and time-consuming methods.

On-the-Job Training (OJT) Methods

The most common method of training is **on-the-job training**, in which a trainee receives instruction at his/her workstation from a supervisor or an experienced co-worker. Most of us can probably remember a time when a co-worker was assigned the job of training us to perform a task such as operating a cash register or learning how to make a request for supplies. Although on-the-job training has been practised since at least the Middle Ages, the United States army formalized the concept during World War II.

There are a number of different approaches for on-the-job training. Table 7.2 provides a description of the various ways in which on-the-job

R P C 7.1

On-the-job training

A training method in which a trainee receives instruction and training at his or her workstation from a supervisor or an experienced co-worker

TABLE 7.1

On-the-Job Training Methods

1. *Job instruction training*. A formalized, structured, and systematic approach to on-the-job training that consists of four steps: preparation, instruction, performance, and follow-up.
2. *Performance aid*. A device that helps an employee perform his/her job.
3. *Job rotation*. A training method in which trainees are exposed to many functions and areas within an organization.
4. *Apprenticeship*. Training for skill trades workers that combines on-the-job training with classroom instruction.
5. *Coaching*. A training method in which a more experienced and knowledgeable person is formally called upon to help another person develop the insights and techniques pertinent to the accomplishment of their job.
6. *Mentoring*. A method in which a senior member of an organization takes a personal interest in the career of a junior employee.

TABLE 7.2

Approaches to On-the-Job Training

On-the-spot lecture Gather trainees into groups and tell them how to do the job.

Viewed performance/Feedback Watch the person at work and give constructive feedback, such as when the sales manager makes a call with a new salesperson.

Following Nellie The supervisor trains a senior employee, who in turn trains new employees (showing the ropes).

Job-aid approach A job aid (step-by-step instructions or video) is followed while the trainer monitors performance.

The training step The trainer systematically introduces the task.

Sequence Following a planned sequence. On-the-spot lecture, gather trainees into groups, and tell them how to do the job.

training can be accomplished, such as training a group of employees on the spot, observing performance and providing feedback, and so on.

On-the-job training is an important part of training at McDonald's Canada. As one of Canada's largest employers of youth, the company needs to train thousands of new crew members every year. Although the company once used videos and classroom training, it now uses a buddy system combined with hands-on training and visual aids. A more experienced employee or "buddy" works with a new member individually on the job. In addition, laminated visual aids are used to show the steps in a task at each station and as a form of visual reinforcement. New crew members can refer to it during training and on the job. The combination of hands-on training and visual reinforcement is believed to result in higher levels of trainee self-efficacy and performance.[3]

OJT is especially useful for small businesses because of the limited investment needed to conduct the training. In fact, a survey found that 43 percent of small- and medium-sized enterprises use informal training methods such as on-the-job training, tutoring, and mentoring, while just 2 percent use only formal training such as the classroom, seminars, and workshops. Forty-three percent said that they use both informal (on-the-job) and formal training methods.[4]

Although on-the-job training is the most common approach to training, it has also been described as the most misused.[5] This is because on-the-job training is often not well planned or structured. Another problem is that most people assigned the task of training others on the job have not received training on how to be a trainer. As a result, managers and employees do not have the knowledge and skills required to be effective trainers and are not familiar with important learning principles such as practice, feedback, and reinforcement.

Another problem is that poor employees teach undesirable work habits and attitudes to new employees. In addition, the traditional ways of doing things will be passed on to new employees, which means that existing problems as well as poor attitudes and behaviours will persist.

Other problems occur when those doing the training are worried that newly trained employees will one day take over their jobs. Some trainers might abuse their position by making the trainee do all the dirty work and the trainee might not learn important skills. In addition, OJT can be time consuming and some employees feel penalized when they can't earn as much money or meet their goals because of the time they have to spend training others. Thus, for all these reasons OJT is not always effective and has been referred to as the most used and misused training method.[6]

The main problem with the traditional unstructured approach to on-the-job training is that it results in training that is inconsistent, inefficient, and ineffective. However, when the process is carefully planned and structured, it can be a highly effective and efficient method of training.[7]

In fact, in one of the few studies to test the effectiveness of on-the-job training, structure was shown to be very important. In the study, a group of newly hired workers received training on how to operate a manufacturing process. One group received traditional on-the-job training in which one worker was trained by the supervisor, and then each person trained another one (similar to the Following Nellie approach described in Table 7.2). A second group was trained by a supervisor who used a structured approach to on-the-job training.

The results showed that the structured approach was considerably more effective. Trainees who received structured on-the-job training reached a pre-determined level of skill and productivity in one-quarter of the time it took to train the other group. They also produced 76 percent fewer rejects, and their troubleshooting ability increased by 130 percent. This study highlights the importance of building structure into on-the-job training and the positive effect it can have on trainee learning and performance.[8]

In the next section, we describe an approach for planning and structuring on-the-job training that is known as job instruction training.

Job Instruction Training

While the traditional unstructured approach to on-the-job training is ineffective, more structured approaches can be highly effective. The best known structured approach to on-the-job training is job instruction training.

Job instruction training is a formalized, structured, and systematic approach to on-the-job training that consists of four steps: preparation, instruction, performance, and follow up. To some extent, job instruction training incorporates the principles of behaviour modelling. You might recall from Chapter 6 that behavioural modelling is a training method in which trainees observe a model performing a task and then attempt to imitate the observed behaviour. With job instruction training, the trainer demonstrates task performance on the job and then provides the trainee with opportunities to practise while the trainer provides feedback and reinforcement. The trainer then monitors the trainees' performance on the job. Thus, like behaviour modelling, job instruction training involves observation, rehearsal, reinforcement, and transfer. Let's now consider each of the steps of job instruction training.

Job instruction training

A formalized, structured, and systematic approach to on-the-job training that consists of four steps: preparation, instruction, performance, and follow up

Preparation Step

During the preparation step, the trainer breaks down the job into small tasks, prepares all the equipment and supplies necessary to do the task, and allocates a time frame to learn each task. A key activity during the preparation step is to develop a communication strategy that fits the trainee and to find out what the trainee already knows. The trainer needs to understand the background, capabilities, and attitudes of trainees as well as the nature of the tasks to be performed before choosing a technique or combination of techniques. If the training is too easy or difficult for a trainee, the trainer can make adjustments to suit his or her needs.

The second part of preparation concerns the trainee. There are three stages: putting the trainee at ease, guaranteeing the learning, and building interest and showing personal advantage.[9]

Putting the Trainee at Ease

The trainer must remember that the trainee might be apprehensive. It is unwise to begin too abruptly. Some small talk might be appropriate to relax the trainee and to set the tone for the training session. Most individuals learn more readily when they are relaxed. A short conversation concerning any matter of interest—the weather, sports, a work-related item—should be effective. Obviously, the topic chosen must be suitable for the situation.

Guaranteeing the Learning

When the conversation does turn to the training, the trainer needs to guarantee to the trainee that learning is possible. Again, use a simple statement, "Don't worry about this machine, Sally. In about three hours you will be operating it almost as well as everyone else. I've trained at least 10 people in this procedure." The trainee now knows that it is possible to learn (i.e., learning will take place) and that the trainer has the ability to teach the process, adding to her self-efficacy.

Building Interest and Showing Personal Advantage

Although the trainer might be interested, the trainee might be apprehensive or might not understand the effect that training will have on the quality of his or her work. Developing trainee enthusiasm is sometimes difficult, but pointing out some personal gain helps to create interest. The idea that the training will lead to something positive creates the opportunity to design rewards: more self-esteem, easier work, higher-level work, less routine, more control over work, greater opportunity or security. Once the appropriate reward is found (provided it can be obtained), most employees will respond positively.

Some people will resist, as training is change and individuals accept change at different rates. The trainee preparation step will identify those who are not responding. As the trainer is responsible for meeting measurable objectives, it is important to evaluate the likelihood of cooperation among trainees so that individual remedial action can be taken. One way to defuse resistance is to train employees in order of their perceived enthusiasm. When the resisters see others reaping the rewards of training, they usually agree to be trained.

Instruction Step

The instruction step involves telling, showing, explaining, and demonstrating the task to the trainee. If the trainee is to perform a task or an operation, he or she should be positioned slightly behind or beside the trainer so that the job is viewed from a realistic angle. The trainer can then proceed as follows:

Show the Trainee How to Perform the Job
- Be sure to break the job into manageable tasks and present only as much as can be absorbed at one time. Remember that individuals learn at different speeds, so while some trainees might be able to learn six or seven sequences at once, others can absorb only four or five.
- Repeat Step 1 as necessary and be patient.
- Don't forget to tell why as well as how.
- Point out possible difficulties as well as safety procedures.
- Encourage questions.

Repeat and Explain Key Points in More Detail
- Safety is especially important.
- Take the time to show how the job fits into any larger systems.
- Show why the job is important.
- Show why key points are more important than others.
- Repeat Step 2 as necessary and be patient.
- Encourage questions.

Allow the Trainee to See the Whole Job Again
- Ask questions to determine the level of comprehension.
- Repeat Step 3 as necessary and be patient.
- Encourage questions.

Performance Step

During the performance step, the trainee performs the task under the trainer's guidance and the trainer provides feedback and reinforcement. Each task is learned in a similar way until the whole job can be completed without error. This can be done in the following manner:

Ask the Trainee to Perform Less Difficult Parts of the Job
- Try to ensure initial success.
- Don't tell how. If possible, ask questions, but try to keep trainee's frustration level low.
- Ask the trainee to explain the steps.

Allow the Trainee to Perform the Entire Job

- Gently suggest improvements where necessary.
- Provide feedback on performance.
- Reinforce correct behaviour.

Follow-up Step

Once the performance step is complete, the trainee will be left on his/her own to perform the task. This does, not, however mean that the training is over. In the follow-up step, the trainer monitors the trainee's performance. It is important that the trainer keep track of the trainee's performance and provide support and feedback. The trainer should leave the trainee to work alone, indicate when and where to find help if necessary, supervise closely and check performance periodically, and then gradually taper off instruction as the employee gains confidence and skill.

Tips for Trainers

Sloman developed a set of rules for effective on-the-job training based on a study of three British National Training Award winners.[10] First, job instruction training should not be managed differently from other types of training. Second, it should be integrated with other training methods. Third, ownership must be maintained even when consultants are used. And fourth, trainers must be chosen with care and trained properly. In addition to being experts in the skill area, they must want to be trainers and have good communication skills. Patience and respect for differences in the ability to learn are also important as the trainer sets the initial mood or climate of the learning experience.[11]

Once suitable individuals are found they should be trained (train-the-trainer) and then recognized and rewarded for training others. It is of little use to give training responsibilities to an already busy employee without restructuring his or her job to include a training element. Nor is increased pay always the most sought-after reward (although it doesn't hurt). Recognition, the chance to add variety to the work day, respect from new employees, training certificates, and the prospect of either promotion or cross training help to make the experience worthwhile for the individual.

While the steps of job instruction training might seem elaborate, they must be applied with the complexity and possible safety hazards of the job in mind. Very simple tasks might require only one demonstration. As well, employees bring different skills and backgrounds to the workplace. Competent preparation will eliminate overtraining and the resultant boredom and inattention.

Performance Aids

Performance aid

A device that helps an employee perform his/her job

A **performance aid** is a device that helps an employee perform his/her job. Performance aids can be signs or prompts ("Have you turned off the computer?"); trouble-shooting aids ("If the red light goes on, the machine needs oil"); instructions in sequence ("To empty the machine, follow the next five steps"); a special tool or gauge (a long stick to measure how much gas is in an inaccessible tank); flash cards to help counsel clients; pictures (of a perfectly set table, for example); or posters and checklists.[12]

For example, employees learning about hazardous-waste management might be provided with a checklist that summarizes the major steps for handling radioactive material. This checklist, if prepared as a colourful poster, will increase the chances of employee application. As indicated earlier, McDonald's uses laminated visual aids to remind trainees of the steps in a task and as a form of visual reinforcement that they can refer to during training and on the job.

The reasoning behind the use of performance aids is that requiring the memorization of sequences and tasks can take too much training time, especially if the task is not repeated daily. They are also useful when performance is difficult, is executed infrequently, can be done slowly, and when the consequences of poor performance are serious.[13] As well, new employees can be on the job more quickly if armed with a series of temporary performance aids. Finally, routine (and not-so-routine) trouble-shooting and repair responses can be performed much more quickly and with less frustration.

Employees who are placed in positions where they must react very quickly might not be able to rely on memory. A panel operator in a nuclear power plant, for example, may have 15 seconds (or less) to perform a series of safety sequences. In the less hectic world of insurance sales, one manager found that a potentially sound sales trainee constantly neglected to complete the entire sales sequence and paperwork. Both these employees, despite their vastly different work environments, were helped by performance aids.

In the first instance, an indexed manual containing various operating sequences was developed and placed on a wheeled trolley within easy reach of all the operators' positions. The sales problem was solved by creating a checklist containing all the steps or tasks to be completed each time the salesperson visited a prospective client. The employee completed and checked off each step and the sheet was signed and dated. The manager then reviewed each call with the trainee. In this case, the checklist was discarded after about three weeks as the sales trainee was performing to the standards set by management.[14]

For an example of a performance aid that can save lives, see Training Today 7.1, "Operating Room Checklist Saves Lives," and Table 7.3.

Tips for Trainers

When designing visual performance aids that help employees remember key information, all the skills of the graphic artist's craft should be utilized. Ease in reading, space between letters, colour, boldness, symbols, and graphic language ("Pull Here!") are all used to communicate more effectively.[15] Audio aids also must clearly communicate intent. A taped warning ("Connect your safety harness!") may be useless, but a buzzer alarm is hard to ignore.

When designing a training program, it is important to consider how performance aids might save time and money. With ingenuity, the trainee's work-life not only can be made easier, but significant improvements in performance, downtime, and safety records can result. Performance aids work even better with the use of technology. Performance aids that use technology are called electronic performance-support systems and are described in Chapter 8.

Training Today 7.1

Operating Room Checklist Saves Lives

Surgical complications are a common yet often preventable problem that causes the death and disability of patients all around the world. In an effort to reduce the rate of major surgical complications, The World Health Organization (WHO) has developed a surgical safety checklist to be used during major operations. The Surgical Safety Checklist (see Table 7.3) requires surgeons to perform safety checks at three times during surgical procedures: before induction of anaesthesia (Sign In); before skin incision (Time Out); and before the patient leaves the operating room (Sign Out).

The checklist includes a total of 19 checks and is designed to ensure that the correct surgery site is marked, that prophylactic antibiotics are given, that blood loss is closely monitored, that sponge and needle counts are correct, and effective teamwork by the operating room staff. A check in which the surgical team introduce themselves to each other by name is crucial because it increases the chance that a member of the team will speak up when something is going wrong. A checklist coordinator is required to confirm that the team has completed each task on the checklist before it proceeds with the operation.

Eight hospitals in eight cities (Toronto, New Delhi, Amman, Auckland, Manila, Ifakara, London, and Seattle) participated in the World Health Organization's Safe Surgery Saves Lives program. Data were collected from 3,733 patients who underwent surgery without the use of the Surgical Safety Checklist and from 3,955 patients who had surgery after the introduction of the checklist.

A comparison of the two groups of patients indicated that the use of the checklist resulted in one-third fewer surgery-related deaths and complications. The rate of major complications following surgery fell from 11 percent to 7 percent after introduction of the checklist. Inpatient deaths following major operations fell by more than 40 percent (from 1.5 percent to 0.8 percent).

The Toronto General Hospital was the only Canadian hospital that took part in the study. The results were so impressive that the checklist has also been adopted by the Toronto Western Hospital and the Princess Margaret Hospital.

The chief executive officer of the Canadian Patient Safety Institute is requesting that health ministers in every province and territory have the checklist implemented in all acute-care hospitals. Countries such as England, Ireland, Jordan, and the Philippines have already established nationwide programs to implement the checklist in operating rooms.

The checklist is considered to be a no-cost innovation and one of the most significant safeguards in the past three decades. The use of the checklist in Canada could prevent an estimated 40,000 complications a year and result in enormous savings to the health-care system.

Sources: Haynes, A. B. et al. (2009). A surgical safety checklist to reduce morbidity and mortality in a global population. *The New England Journal of Medicine, 360* (5), 491–499; Priest, L. (2009, January 15). Simple checklist saves lives in the operating room, study finds. *The Globe and Mail*, A4; Checklist helps reduce surgical complications, deaths. *World Health Organization, News Release.* www.who.int/en/.

Job Rotation

Job rotation

A training method in which trainees are exposed to different jobs, functions, and areas within an organization

Job rotation is a training method in which trainees are exposed to different jobs, functions, and areas within an organization. It broadens an individual's knowledge and skills by providing him/her with multiple perspectives and areas of expertise.

Job rotation is often used as part of an ongoing career-development program, especially for employees who are destined to management positions. The objective is for an employee to learn a variety of skills from

TABLE 7.3

World Health Organization's Surgical Safety Checklist

Surgical Safety Checklist (First Edition)

Before induction of anaesthesia ▶▶▶▶▶▶▶▶▶▶ Before skin incision ▶▶▶▶▶▶▶▶▶▶▶▶ Before patient leaves operating room

Sign in	Time out	Sign out
☐ Patient has confirmed • Identity • Site • Procedure • Consent	☐ Confirm all team members have introduced themselves by name and role	Nurse verbally confirms with the team: ☐ The Name of the procedure recorded
☐ Site marked/not applicable	☐ Surgeon, anaesthesia professional and nurse verbally confirm • Patient • Site • procedure	☐ That instrument, sponge and needle counts are correct (or not applicable)
☐ Anaesthesia safety check completed	Anticipated critical events	☐ How the specimen is labelled (including patient name)
☐ Pulse oximeter on patient and functioning	☐ Surgeon reviews: What are the critical or unexpected steps, operative duration, anticipated blood loss?	☐ Whether there are any equipment problems to be addressed
Does patient have a: Known Allergy? ☐ No ☐ Yes	☐ Anaesthesia team reviews: Are there any patient-specific concerns?	☐ Surgeon, anaesthesia professional and nurse review the key concerns for recovery and management of this patient
Difficult airway/aspiration risk? ☐ No ☐ Yes, and equipment/assistance available	☐ Nursing team reviews: Has sterility (including indicators results) been confirmed? are there equipment issues or any concerns?	
Risk of >500Ml blood loss (7Ml/Kg in children)? ☐ No ☐ Yes, and adequate intravenous access and fluids planned	Has antibiotic prophylaxis been given within the last 60 minutes? ☐ Yes ☐ Not applicable Is essential imaging displayed? ☐ Yes ☐ Not applicable	

This checklist is not intended to be comprehensive. Additions and modifications to fit local practice are encouraged.

Source: Reprinted with permission from the World Health Organization, http://www.who.int/patientsafety/safesurgery/tools_resources/SSSL_Checklist_finalJun08.pdf

both doing a variety of tasks and by observing the performance of others. Typically the individual will be supervised by a supervisor who is responsible for the individual's training. Through this process a trainee can acquire a number of skills required to perform different tasks and also learn about the organization.

Job rotation is also an effective means of cross training employees. **Cross training** involves training employees to perform each other's jobs so that anyone can step in and perform any member's job if necessary. Cross training is particularly popular with cross-functional teams. By rotating team members to the various positions on a team, each team member learns the skills required to perform all of the team's tasks and jobs. Cross training not only provides greater flexibility for organizations, but also enables employees to learn and use more skills. Toronto Hydro uses cross training for its supervisors so that they can work across specializations.[16]

Job rotation is an effective method of training employees who need to learn a variety of skills. By providing employees with a series of on-the-job experiences in which they work on a variety of tasks, jobs, and assignments, they will acquire the skills required to perform their current job as well as future job responsibilities.

Research on job rotation has generally been supportive. It not only results in an improvement in knowledge and skills but also has a number of career benefits such as higher job satisfaction, more opportunities for career advancement, and a higher salary.[17]

Cross training
Training employees to perform each other's jobs

Tips for Trainers

A disadvantage of job rotation is that if an employee does not spend enough time in a department or working on an assignment, he or she might not have sufficient time to get up to speed and complete an assignment. Thus, a trainee might acquire only a superficial understanding of a job or department and this might result in some frustration. Therefore, it is important that job rotation be carefully planned and structured so that trainees receive sufficient exposure and experience on each assignment to make it a worthwhile learning experience. In addition, the assignments should be tailored to each individual's training.

It is also important that job rotation be part of a larger training program and integrated with other training methods. That is, job rotation should be only one component of a training program and learning process and supplemented with classroom instruction and coaching or mentoring. Coaching and mentoring are important because trainees need some guidance and supervision throughout the job rotation process.

Apprenticeships

Apprenticeship

A training method for skilled trades workers that combines on-the-job training and classroom instruction

An **apprenticeship** is a training method that combines on-the-job training and classroom instruction. It is the primary method of training skilled trades workers in Canada. The practical on-the-job training component makes up 80 percent of the training and is used to teach the requisite skills of a particular trade or occupation. Classroom instruction, which usually takes place in community colleges, focuses on technical training and comprises a relatively minor portion of apprenticeship programs (20 percent, or 180 hours).[18]

As described at the beginning of the chapter, White Spot apprentices are now able to complete their on-the-job training and classroom instruction in-house. Toronto Hydro developed its own trade school and since 2003 it has hired eight overhead power-line apprentices with plans to hire many more of its overhead and underground apprentices.[19]

In Canada, the apprenticeship system covers more than 65 regulated occupations in four occupational sectors: construction (e.g., stone mason, electrician, carpenter, plumber), motive power (motor-vehicle mechanic, machinist), industrial (industrial mechanic, millwright), and service (baker, cook, hairstylist).

The regulation and administration of apprenticeship programs as well as the certification of tradespersons is the responsibility of the provinces and territories. The federal government works with the provinces and territories through the Canadian Council of Directors of Apprenticeship (CCDA) to support the development of a skilled workforce and to facilitate interprovincial mobility of the skilled trades.[20]

In the 1950s the federal, provincial, and territorial governments established the Interprovincial Standards Red Seal Program (also known as the Red Seal Program) to facilitate the interprovincial mobility of skilled workers throughout Canada. The CCDA is responsible for the management of the program, which ensures the standardization of training requirements and certification of 49 skilled trades that are covered under the Red Seal program.[21] Recall from the chapter-opening vignette that White Spot's in-house apprenticeship program provides Red Seal certification for its chefs.

Apprentices must be trained and supervised by at least one qualified tradesperson known as a journeyperson and pass a provincial government examination to earn a certificate of qualification. Apprentices who pass an interprovincial examination with a minimum grade of 70 percent are awarded a Red Seal certification and achieve the status of journeyperson.

Apprenticeship training differs from other training methods in that it is regulated through a partnership among government, labour, and industry. In Canada, the federal government pays for in-school training and income support. Provincial governments administer the programs and pay for classroom facilities and instructors. Employers absorb the costs of workplace training and apprentices initiate the process by finding employers to sponsor them.

Unlike corporate-sponsored training programs that address the specific needs of an organization, apprenticeships are focused on the collective training needs of specific occupations within broad industrial categories.[22] Thus, the skills learned through apprenticeship training are transferable within an occupation across Canada. This flexibility provides advantages to the worker and the industry when regional fluctuations occur in the supply and demand of skilled labour.

However, the system is highly dependent on employers as they must be willing to sponsor apprentices and provide the on-the-job training component, something that many Canadian organizations are not willing to do.[23]

Many employers are reluctant to provide apprentice training because they do not see the benefits. However, there is evidence that the returns on apprenticeship training investments are realized much sooner than many employers believe. A recent study by the Canadian Apprenticeship Forum (CAF) found that employers receive a return of $1.38 for every dollar invested in an apprentice and that an apprentice's productive value exceeds the training costs by the end of the second year or earlier. They also found that "homegrown" journeypersons are more productive than externally trained journeypersons.[24]

Tips for Trainers

There has been an increasing demand for skilled tradespersons in Canada and the registration in apprenticeship programs has increased in recent years to record levels. However, the number of people completing apprenticeship programs each year has changed very little over the last several decades.[25]

In addition, Canada's aging population means that many workers in the skilled trades are approaching retirement. As a result, there is a growing skills shortage facing many industrial sectors and it has been predicted that the shortage of skilled workers in Canada could reach one million by the year 2020.[26]

An increased emphasis on apprenticeship training remains the most effective and practical method of teaching skilled trades occupations and dealing with the skills shortage. However, youth interest and entry in apprenticeships has been on the decline and many employers are reluctant to take on apprentices. Recent reports indicate that only 18 percent of Canadian employers sponsor and train apprentices.[27]

Over the years, the federal government has organized a series of round table meetings with government, business, and labour to find ways to address the skills shortage problem and improve apprenticeship training.[28]A number of programs have been implemented to encourage students to enter and remain in the skilled trades and for organizations to sponsor apprentices.

For example, the Apprenticeship Incentive Grant (AIG) is a taxable cash grant of $1,000 that is available to registered apprentices once they have successfully completed their first or second year/level of an apprenticeship program in one of the Red Seal trades. In 2009, the federal government introduced the Apprenticeship Completion Grant (ACG), which is a $2,000 taxable cash grant for apprentices who complete their apprenticeship training in a designated Red Seal trade. Apprenticeship tax credits are also provided by the federal and provincial governments to employers that train apprentices.[29]

The Ontario government is spending $7 million for 700 spaces in pre-apprenticeship training in 38 programs with the aim of increasing the number of people entering full apprenticeships by 7,000 per year. Pre-apprenticeship training provides academic upgrading, technical training, and job placements to prepare potential apprentices in a variety of skilled trades that are facing serious labour shortages.[30]

Another concern is that not all Canadians participate fully in apprenticeship programs. Thus, efforts need to be made to encourage Aboriginal peoples, women, visible minorities, and foreign-trained skilled workers to pursue apprenticeship programs and employment in the skilled trades. Several provinces have implemented programs that introduce women to skilled trades and provide them with hands-on experience.[31]

Finally, human resource and training professionals have a key role to play in promoting and championing apprenticeship training in their organizations and educating their employers on the benefits of apprenticeships. Apprenticeship training can be an effective recruitment and retention strategy that provides organizations with many benefits and can improve their bottom line.[32]

Table 7.4 provides an overview of the benefits of apprenticeship training for organizations. To learn how to increase employer participation in apprenticeship training, see The Trainer's Notebook 7.1, "Increasing Employer Participation in Apprenticeship Training."

Coaching

Coaching is a training method in which a more experienced and knowledgeable person is formally called upon to help another person develop the insights and techniques pertinent to the accomplishment of their job. The coach also guides the employee in learning by helping to find experts and resources for learning and development.

Coaching has become very popular in many organizations today. Coaching programs have been effective in enhancing skills and improving performance in

Coaching
One-on-one individualized learning experience in which a more experienced and knowledgeable person is formally called upon to help another person develop the insights and techniques pertinent to the accomplishment of their job

TABLE 7.4

Benefits of Apprenticeship Training

Effective recruitment strategy. Leads to higher retention rates and lower turnover and provides a competitive advantage over non-participating organizations.

Two-way skills development. Mentoring apprentices renews and revitalizes journeypersons' skills leading to greater productivity.

Higher-quality work. Helps to maintain high standards and quality on the job and develops skills and competencies that meet industry standards and build quality products.

Increased productivity. Productivity is increased because apprentices are trained in the company's systems and work processes.

Improved safety. Makes journeypersons more aware of safe work practices as they teach apprentices; makes employees more familiar with the organization's safety practices leading to fewer accidents which results in reduced compensation costs; and leads to reduced insurance costs for some employers because insurance companies recognize the lower risk of a skilled workforce.

Improve company reputation. Demonstrates an organization's professionalism because it shows it is dedicated to delivering high-quality products through employing highly trained and skilled workers.

Source: (2008, July). Strategies to increase employer participation in apprenticeship training in Canada. Ottawa: Canadian Apprenticeship Forum.

The Trainer's Notebook 7.1

Increasing Employer Participation in Apprenticeship Training

A forum held by the Canadian Apprenticeship Forum made the following recommendations to increase employer participation in apprenticeship training:

- *Educate employers about mentoring*. The process of taking on an apprentice needs to be demystified. Employers may not understand what is involved in mentoring and therefore may be reluctant to take on an apprentice.
- *Inform employers that apprenticeship training is industry driven*. Industry designs the method of delivery in apprenticeship training and a variety of training delivery options are available.
- *Provide incentives to employers*. Incentives are an important way to maintain and enhance participation in apprenticeship training, and some employers might need clarification on the federal/provincial/territorial incentives available.
- *Ensure apprentices understand their value*. Apprentices need to understand their value to an organization and be informed about wage subsidies and tax credits so they can show what they have to offer to an employer when trying to find a sponsor.
- *Encourage employers to participate in talking to their peers*. Participating employers should inform their colleagues of the benefits of apprenticeship training and encourage non-participating employers to go to schools to discuss with youth a career in the trades; bring non-participating employers to networking events; and give presentations to non-participating employers on the business case for apprenticeship.
- *Build appreciation for skilled labour*. Employers will participate in apprenticeship training if customers and consumers start demanding that they have a skilled labour force and their employees have trade certification.

Source: (2008, July). Strategies to increase employer participation in apprenticeship training in Canada. Ottawa: Canadian Apprenticeship Forum.

a wide range of areas including interpersonal skills, communication skills, leadership skills, cognitive skills, and self-management skills. It is especially effective for helping people apply what they have learned in the classroom on the job.[33]

The coaching process involves the planned use of opportunities in the work environment to improve or to enhance employee strengths and potential. Weaknesses are considered only if they prevent the employee from functioning, or if they are below the manager's tolerance level.[34]

The key elements in the coaching process are "planned," "opportunities in the work environment," and "strengths." First, the process revolves around an agreed-upon plan or set of objectives developed mutually by employee and coach. Development does not occur haphazardly or by chance. The process proceeds in a logical agreed-upon fashion. Second, the work environment is the training laboratory (sometimes expanded to include the community). Transfers, special assignments, vacation replacements, and conference speaking engagements are all potential coaching opportunities. The necessary formal infrastructure, perhaps attached to the firm's appraisal or evaluation system, must be in place for the system to work.[35]

The coaching process begins with a dialogue between coach and employee, during which a set of objectives is defined. Then, coaching opportunities are identified by a mutual examination of the environment. A long-term plan is struck, along with an evaluation or measurement procedure. As well, the process is fitted into the employee's career-development goals and made part of the organization's long-term strategies.

The employee performs the agreed-upon task and then reports to the coach both informally and formally during the annual or semi-annual evaluation. They discuss the results of the current program and then plan the next round of activity.[36] With practice, this approach develops into a continual transfer of skills and an ongoing process.[37]

Research has found coaching to be highly effective for both individuals and organizations. In general, the results of a number of studies indicate that individuals who participated in coaching showed dramatic improvements in specific skills and overall performance. Coaching has also been found to improve working relationships and job attitudes, and to increase the rate of advancement and salary increases.

Benefits to organizations have been found in productivity, quality, customer service, reduced customer complaints, retention, cost reductions, and bottom-line productivity. Thus, coaching is not only popular, it is also effective.[38]

Tips for Trainers

For coaching to work, the employee and the coach must trust each other. Otherwise the employee will see development as extra work. Indeed, perhaps the most important aspect of the coaching process is ongoing dialogue and feedback. It is only under these conditions that employees participate willingly in a two-way process that often requires extra effort and risk taking.[39]

Thus, it is important that the coach build trust and understanding so that employees will want to work with him/her. It is also important that a coach is able to relate to the person he/she is coaching. To be most effective,

Coaching at SaskEnergy

SaskEnergy is a Regina-based provincial Crown corporation that distributes natural gas in Saskatchewan and employs nearly 1,000 people. Based on the results of employee engagement surveys, the company realized that to achieve its strategic vision it would need to make improvements on managing performance and recognizing employees for achievements.

A long-term coaching program to develop successful leadership behaviours and provide skills that managers can apply to their teams was recommended by a consultant. The program was designed to include integrated assessments, workshops, long-term peer-to-peer coaching triangles involving groups of three people with varying levels of experience, and follow-up evaluations.

Managers from all levels participated in the program including senior-level executives who launched the program with talks in support of the company's mission. The program began with evaluations using coaching assessments that incorporated information from supervisors and reports. Participants then devised an action plan during a workshop.

The broad focus on leadership development has paid off throughout the ranks of the company. A recent employee survey resulted in the highest level of participation in the history of the company. Areas tied to employee engagement, including leadership, direction, recognition and opportunity, showed marked improvement over earlier surveys and compared to other companies that were surveyed.

The success of the program can be attributed to a number of factors. Coaching goals were tied to the organizational strategy and to succession planning. The support of the senior executive team was vital and the number of managers enrolled in the program (more than 200) meant that what was learned cascaded throughout the organization. And by organizing coaching triangles into teams that functioned over the course of several months, SaskEnergy ensured long-term support for the development of new behaviours. A workshop that included follow-up evaluations helped to drive the learning home.

Source: Based on Finkelstein, L. (2008, December 1). Coaching SaskEnergy to higher performance. *Canadian HR Reporter, 21* (21), 23. Reprinted by permission of Carswell, a division of Thomson Canada Ltd.

coaching should be used as part of a broader process of learning rather than a standalone program.[40]

Finally, like any training program, the effectiveness of coaching should be evaluated. Coaching programs are expensive and time-consuming so it is important to determine if they are accomplishing what they are supposed to.

To learn how one company implemented a successful coaching program, see Training Today 7.2, "Coaching at SaskEnergy."

Mentoring

Mentoring is a method in which a senior member of an organization takes a personal interest in the career of a junior employee. A mentor is an experienced individual, usually a senior manager, who provides coaching and counselling to a junior employee.

Mentors play two major roles: career support and psychosocial support. **Career support** activities include coaching, sponsorship, exposure, visibility, protection, and the provision of challenging assignments. **Psychosocial support** includes being a friend who listens and counsels, who accepts and provides feedback, and who offers a role model for success.[41]

Mentoring
A method in which a senior member of an organization takes a personal interest in the career of a junior employee

Career support
Mentoring activities that include coaching, sponsorship, exposure, visibility, protection, and the provision of challenging assignments

Psychosocial support
Mentoring activities that include being a friend who listens and counsels, who accepts and provides feedback, and a role model for success

The mentor–protégé relationship was once an informal one with a senior person recognizing the talent of a junior employee and wishing to help. However, organizations now recognize mentoring as a valuable employee development tool and have begun to formalize mentor relationships by implementing formal mentoring programs.

Like coaching, mentoring is popular in organizations today and is also an expensive investment.[42] However, mentoring has a more narrow focus than coaching in that its focus is on the career development of junior employees.

According to David Peterson, mentoring can serve a number of purposes for organizations. It can help to accelerate the career progress of underrepresented groups; transmit the culture and values to newer managers; and pass on the accumulated wisdom of seasoned leaders.[43] Mentoring involves exposure to senior management activities that are valuable and beneficial for one's growth and development.

Research has found that mentoring is highly effective for those who are mentored and their organizations. Both professional and academic research consistently has indicated that mentored individuals have greater career prospects and higher incomes than those who have not been mentored. A recent review of mentoring research found that compared to non-mentored individuals, mentored individuals had more promotions, higher compensation, as well as greater career commitment and higher career and job satisfaction. Furthermore, career mentoring was more strongly related to objective career success such as compensation and promotion while psychosocial mentoring was more strongly related to satisfaction with the mentor.[44]

Tips for Trainers

Mentoring can be an effective method of training that benefits both the mentor and the person being mentored. However, to be effective it is important that the roles and expectations of the mentor and protégés are clear and well understood. It is also important that they agree on how often they will meet, what types of topics they will discuss, and what career activities will be part of the protégé's development.

Both the mentor and protégé should have some guidelines on how the process will work. Researchers have highlighted several areas of concern to managers wishing to implement formal mentoring programs:[45]

- *Choice of mentors.* Mentors must be motivated to participate in the program and to make sufficient time available to their protégé. They also need to be knowledgeable about how the organization really works. Participation should be voluntary. Inevitably, some assigned relationships will not work out. A procedure needs to be in place to allow either party to cancel the arrangement without too much loss of face, and employees should feel free to end the relationship without fear of retaliation.
- *Matching mentors and protégé(s).* Matching is an important process that needs to be handled with care. Should males be matched with males; females with females? There may not be enough senior women to

mentor all the junior women. Hostility from men when women network with one another make some women reluctant to take on the mentoring role.[46] Those mentors close to retirement perform better in both the career and psychosocial functions.[47] It is important that the relationship remain confidential and for the protégé to know that it will be confidential. The protégé is unlikely to feel comfortable, for example, if the mentor is his or her boss. Research has also found that having input into the matching process is important. Both mentor and protégé input into the matching process has been found to be related to perceived program effectiveness.[48]

- *Training.* Mentors and protégés both need training. This process should entail more than giving mentors a book to read about mentoring. It should, for example, involve the opportunity to share experiences about mentoring. The training of protégés, usually as part of the induction process, is partly concerned with demonstrating the organization's commitment to mentoring, but also involves setting appropriate expectations for the mentoring relationship. Mentors could be chosen for this training based on their previous track record in developing employees. Research has found that both the receipt of training and the quality of training is related to perceived program effectiveness for mentors and protégés.[49]

- *Structuring the mentoring relationship.* Some programs set out time limits on the relationship and specify minimum levels of contact. Goals, projects, activities, and resources are spelled out. The program is evaluated and those areas in which either mentors or protégés report dissatisfaction are redesigned. While commitment must be made at all levels, it is at the individual level that the process can most easily break down. Signals sent by derailed mentoring schemes include delay between assignment and first meeting with protégé, poor meeting locations (e.g., the cafeteria), and infrequent contacts.

Finally, to be effective, mentoring programs must receive continued support from management. And because most mentors are volunteers, there should be some benefits and incentives to those who participate as mentors in mentoring programs. To learn more about how to design a formal mentoring program, see The Trainer's Notebook 7.2, "Developing a Formal Mentoring Program."

Off-the-Job versus On-the-Job Training Methods

You have now learned a great deal about on-the-job and off-the-job training methods. In Chapter 6, we discussed some of the factors to consider when choosing a training method. A related issue is whether to use on-the-job or off-the-job training methods. In the final section of this chapter, we review some of the advantages and disadvantages of on-the-job and off-the-job training methods.

The Trainer's Notebook 7.2

Developing a Formal Mentoring Program

A well-designed formal mentoring program should consider the following issues:

- *Business objectives.* Determine the business objectives of establishing a mentoring program in order to tie it back to business success.
- *Selection criteria.* Determine key criteria for the recruitment and selection of mentors and mentees (job descriptions, expectations, capabilities).
- *Mentee assessment.* Mentees should be assessed on their appetite for risk, handling mistakes, and their mindset.
- *Training.* Determine the type of training participants should receive.
- *Matching process.* Make sure there is an effective process for optimum matching between participants.

- *Criteria for success.* Determine what the success factors will be. How will you be able to measure success?
- *Rewards.* Decide what the rewards of being involved in the mentoring program should be.
- *Timeline.* Establish a concrete timeline for the mentoring relationship. Most mentoring relationships average one or two years.
- *Feedback.* Build a feedback loop for continuous improvements to ensure a viable and dynamic mentoring program.

Source: Based on Butyn, S. (2003, July 27). Mentoring your way to improved retention. *Canadian HR Reporter, 16* (2), 13 & 15. Reprinted by permission of Carswell, a division of Thomson Canada Ltd.

Off-the-Job Training Methods

Advantages

Off-the-job training methods have a number of advantages. First, a trainer can use a wide variety of instructional training methods when training is off-the-job. For example, a trainer can combine a lecture with discussion and audio-visual methods such as a video and slides, a case study or case incident, as well as games and simulations. Thus, a trainer has many options when training is off-the-job and can tailor a training program to the needs and preferences of trainees. The trainer is also able to choose a combination of methods that will be most effective given the objectives and content of a training program.

Another advantage of off-the-job training is that the trainer is able to control the training environment. In other words, the trainer can choose a training site that is comfortable, free of distractions, and conducive to learning. A trainer does not have as much control of the learning environment when training is on-the-job.

A third advantage is that a large number of trainees can be trained at one time. This is especially the case when the lecture method is used. Thus, off-the-job training is generally more efficient given that so many more trainees can be trained at one time.

Disadvantages

There are of course some disadvantages of off-the-job training methods. First, off-the-job training can be much more costly than on-the-job training. This is because of the costs associated with the use of training facilities, travel, accommodation, food, and so on. However, as you will see in the next chapter, such costs can be almost completely eliminated with the use of technology.

A second disadvantage of off-the-job training is that because the training takes place in an environment that is different from the work environment where trainees will be required to apply what they learn in training, trainees might have difficulty in the transfer of training. For example, while a trainee might be able to perform a training task in a role play during training, he or she might have difficulty performing the task on the job. Thus, the application of training on the job, or what is known as the transfer of training (see Chapter 10), can be more difficult with off-the-job training.

On-the-Job Training Methods

Advantages

There are also advantages and disadvantages of on-the-job training. A major advantage of on-the-job training is that the cost is much lower given that the need for training facilities, travel, accommodation, and so on is eliminated. Thus, on-the-job training tends to be much less costly than off-the-job training.

A second advantage is the greater likelihood of the application of training on the job. That is, because training takes place in trainees' actual work area, the application is much more direct and in some cases immediate. Thus, there is less difficulty in the transfer of training since the training site and work site are the same.

Disadvantages

There are a number of disadvantages of on-the-job training. First, the work environment is full of distractions that can interfere with learning and interrupt training. Noise might make it difficult for trainees to hear and understand the trainer, and at times the trainer might be interrupted and called to solve a problem or work on something else.

Second, when trainees are being trained on an actual machine or equipment on the job, there is always the potential for damage to expensive equipment. This could also shut down production for a period of time, adding to the cost of damaged equipment that needs to be repaired or replaced.

A third problem is the disruption of service or slowdown in production that occurs during training. You have probably had the experience of being served by an employee who is being trained. The result is usually slower service and the potential for errors. Thus, on-the-job training can result in a reduction in productivity, quality, and service.

Finally, when safety issues are associated with the use of equipment or dangerous chemicals, on-the-job training can compromise safety. A trainee learning on the job can make a mistake and harm him/herself, other employees, or customers. Therefore, extra precaution and care need to be taken whenever on-the-job training involves working with equipment or dangerous chemicals.

Combining On- and Off-the-Job Training Methods

As you can see, there are advantages and disadvantages associated with on-the-job and off-the-job training methods. Being aware of and understanding them can be helpful when choosing a training method. For example, when there is a need to train a large number of employees, off-the-job training would be more practical. When the cost of training is an issue, on-the-job training might be more feasible. Thus, issues of practicality and feasibility are important considerations when choosing a training method.

Finally, it should be apparent to you that the choice of a training method is not really about whether training should be on-the-job or off-the-job. In fact, effective training programs often combine on-the-job and off-the-job training methods.

Ultimately, what is most important is mixing and combining methods to best suit a particular training need and objective. In fact, a government study found that a combination of on-the-job and off-the-job training methods is the best approach for getting employees up to speed. The report found that on average Canadian organizations provide off-the-job or classroom training to 63 percent of their workforce, and on-the-job training to 66 percent of the workforce. However, it also found that larger organizations are more likely to use only off-the-job training while smaller organizations can't afford off-the-job training and therefore tend to rely on on-the-job training.[50]

Thus, once again the best approach appears to be a blended approach that combines different methods of training. This is the case not only with respect to on-the-job and off-the-job training methods, but also for technology-based training methods, which are discussed in Chapter 8.

Summary

This chapter described some of the most common methods of on-the-job training and serves as a complement to the off-the-job instructional training methods described in Chapter 6. We noted that on-the-job training is the most common method of training as well as the most misused. However, job instruction training that is carefully planned and structured can have a positive effect on employee learning and performance. On-the-job training can also involve the use of performance aids and job rotation. Apprenticeship programs combine on-the-job training and classroom instruction and are the primary method of training skilled trades workers. Coaching and mentoring are also popular methods of on-the-job training.

Although each method described in this chapter takes place on the job, the methods differ in terms of what they are best suited for and when they should be used. Therefore, it is important to match each method with the objectives of a training program and the needs of trainees. Finally, we noted that there are advantages and disadvantages of on-the-job and off-the-job training methods. Effective training programs mix and combine both methods along with technology-based methods, which are described in the next chapter.

Key Terms

apprenticeships p. 206

career support p. 211

coaching p. 208

cross training p. 205

job instruction training p. 199

job rotation p. 204

mentoring p. 211

on-the-job training p. 197

performance aid p. 202

psychosocial support p. 211

Make the Connection

p. 199: behaviour modelling is discussed in Chapter 6 on page 174

Web Links

McDonald's Canada: www.mcdonalds.ca

Toronto Hydro: www.torontohydro.com

White Spot: www.whitespot.com

World Health Organization: www.who.int

RPC Icons

RPC 7.1 Using a variety of methods facilitates the delivery of development programs to groups and individual learners.

RPC 7.2 Recommends the most appropriate way to meet identified learning needs (e.g., courses, secondments, and on-the-job activities).

Discussion Questions

1. Describe the similarities and differences between coaching and mentoring. When would you use coaching and when would you use mentoring?
2. What are the main issues to consider when developing a mentoring program?
3. How should an organization decide if it should use on-the-job training? What are the advantages and disadvantages?
4. Why do you think on-the-job training is the most common method of training? Why is it also the most misused method of training? What can organizations do to avoid the problems of on-the-job training?
5. Describe the objectives of apprenticeships and how they are different from other on-the-job training methods. What should be done to increase the number of people who pursue apprenticeship training and why is this important? What should be done to increase the number of employers that are willing to provide apprenticeship training?

6. Describe the four steps of job instruction training and what you would do in each step if you were training someone on the job. Explain how you would train somebody to drive a car or fix a flat tire if you were using job instruction training.
7. Discuss the advantages and disadvantages of on-the-job and off-the-job training methods.

The Great Training Debate

1. Debate the following: On-the-job training can result in employees who are poorly trained and it should be avoided whenever possible.
2. Debate the following: The apprenticeship system in Canada is no longer effective and organizations would be better off if they implemented their own in-house apprenticeship programs.

Using the Internet

1. Do you have what it takes to be a good mentor? To find out, go to **www.mentors.ca** and click on "All about Mentoring" and then click on "Take" to take the mentor test. After you have found out your score, see if you can find a mentor. Click on "Profile" and then "Tips to find and gain a Mentor." What are some of the ways you can find a mentor on your own?
2. To find out about job rotation and cross training, go to **www.jobquality.ca/indicators/job_design/des1.shtml** and answer the following questions:
   a. To what extent do organizations of different sizes use job rotation?
   b. To what extent is job rotation and cross training used in different provinces? Where is it most and least frequent?
   c. Comment on the use of job rotation and cross training across industries. Where is it most and least common?
   d. What are the benefits of job rotation and cross training?
3. To find out about implementing a job rotation system, go to **www.danmacleod.com/Articles/Job_Rotation.htm** and answer the following questions:
   a. What are the roadblocks in setting up a job rotation system?
   b. What are the limitations of job rotation?
   c. What are the steps involved in implementing a job rotation system?
4. To learn more about apprenticeships in Canada, visit the Canadian Apprenticeship Forum (CAF) at **www.caf-fca.org** and answer the following questions:
   a. What is the CAF and what do they do?
   b. What are some of the resources available on the CAF website for employers, educators, and youth?

c. What are some current activities being undertaken by the CAF? Choose one and write a brief summary of the objectives and project status.

Exercises

In-Class

1. Recall the most recent job you had and how you were trained. Were you trained on-the-job? If you were trained on-the-job, describe your experience. What exactly did the trainer do and how did it influence your learning? Was your on-the-job training experience effective? Why or why not? What could have been done differently to make it more effective? If you have not been trained on-the-job, describe how on-the-job training might be used to train employees doing your job.

2. As a student, you have probably experienced some problems studying, writing assignments, or perhaps writing exams. If you were to act as a tutor to train another student with some of these problems, what method of training would you use and why? Consider each of the on-the-job training methods in Table 7.1 and indicate how you would use them and how effective they would be for training a student to become a "better" student.

3. Assume that you have just been hired as a trainer in an organization that hires recent college and university graduates every year. The company does not have a formal mentoring program and your job is to try to get one started. Prepare a proposal to convince management of the importance and need for a formal mentoring program. You should also describe how the program will work and what will be required to get it started. You can then either have another member of the class review your proposal and provide feedback or you can present your proposal to the class.

4. Using the job instruction training method, design a training program to perform a task you are familiar with. It could be a task you have had to perform in a current or previous job, or it could be something that is not work-related such as how to fix a flat tire, how to drive a car, how to ride a bike, etc. Design your training program following the steps outlined in the chapter. Then have another member of the class review your training program and provide feedback. Alternatively, you can provide a demonstration in front of the class and have the class critique your training program and provide feedback.

5. Very often, experienced employees are called upon to train a new employee on the job. In most cases, the employee has not received any training on how to train others. Chances are that some day you will be asked to train a new employee, or perhaps you have already had to. To prepare yourself for this task, consider how well prepared and qualified you are. What are your strengths and weaknesses? Prepare an action plan to develop areas that need improvement. If you have

already had to train somebody on the job, how effective were you and what do you need to work on to improve?

6. On-the-job training can be very effective if the trainer is knowledgeable about learning principles and theories. Make a list of all the principles, concepts, and theories described in the text that can be used to make on-the-job training more effective. Explain the relevance of each principle, concept, or theory on your list for on-the-job training.

In-the-Field

1. Ask your friends if they would accept a paid training experience that consisted of the following benefits:

   - They would be given structured classroom training and on-the-job assignments.
   - They would be coached and supervised throughout the learning experience.
   - They would be paid to learn.
   - They would be certified at the end of learning the job.
   - They would be guaranteed employment at high wages.

   If they answer "Yes!" then tell them about becoming an apprentice electrician, carpenter, plumber, or chef. What is their reaction? Do students resist the certification programs in the traditional vocations and embrace certification in human resources or technology? Why? What can be done to increase the likelihood that students will choose a skilled trade and enter an apprenticeship program?

2. Contact the human resource department of an organization to find out about their use of on-the-job training. In particular, you should inquire about the following:

   - Do they use on-the-job training, and if so what do they use it for (what employees, what kinds of job)? Why do they use it? How effective is it?
   - How formal and systematic is their on-the-job training? Is it carefully planned, do trainers receive training and instruction, are the trainers carefully selected, are they rewarded for their efforts? Are they evaluated?
   - Do they follow the steps of the job instruction training method? How well is each of the steps performed?
   - Based on what you have learned in this chapter, is the organization doing a good job in providing on-the-job training? What is it doing right and wrong?
   - What advice would you give the organization to improve its on-the-job training?

Case Incident

Davco Machine Ltd.

Davco Machine Ltd. is located in Grande Prairie in northern Alberta, where it designs and builds equipment for the forestry, construction, and oil and gas industries. The company has 66 employees, most of whom are machinists, welders, mechanics, or millwrights. Davco formed a partnership with technical schools in Edmonton and was able to generate interest among students to apprentice at the company. However, the facility didn't have enough journeypersons to meet the requirement of one journeyperson for every apprentice.

The company representatives travelled to Germany to take part in a job fair hosted by the provincial government. When a worker in Germany is unemployed the government requires him/her to go back to school. As a result, Germany has a low unemployment rate and a highly educated labour pool. Once in Germany, Davco had no problem recruiting four journeyperson machinists.

Questions

1. What does this case tell you about the importance and need for apprenticeship training in Canada and its future as a method of on-the-job training?
2. What should governments and companies like Davco do to increase the number of apprentices and journeypersons in Canada?

Source: Franceschini, T. (2005, December). CloseUp: CEOs talk workforce development. *Canadian HR Reporter, 18* (21), 7–10.

Case Study

TPK Appliances

When TPK, a manufacturer of small appliances—electric kettles, toasters, and irons—automated its warehouse, the warehouse crew was reduced from 14 to 4. Every one of the displaced employees was assigned to another department, as TPK had a history of providing stable employment.

Jacob Peters, an employee with more than 15 years of service, was transferred to the toaster assembly line to be retrained as a small-parts assembler. When he arrived to begin his new job, the supervisor said, "This may be only temporary, Jacob. I have a full staff right now, so I have nothing for you to do, but come on, I'll find you a locker." As there really was no job for him, Jacob did nothing for the first week but odd jobs such as filling bins. At the beginning of week two, Jacob was informed that a vacancy would be occurring the next day, so he reported for work eager to learn his new job.

The operation was very simple. All Jacob had to do was pick up two pieces of metal, one in each hand, place them into a jig so that they were held together in a cross position, and press a button. The riveting machine then put a rivet through both pieces and an air jet automatically ejected the joined pieces into a bin.

"This job is so simple a monkey could do it," the supervisor told Jacob. "Let me show you how it's done," and he quickly demonstrated the three steps involved. "Now you do it," the supervisor said. Of course, Jacob did it right the first time. After watching him rivet two or three, the supervisor left Jacob to his work.

About three hours later, the riveter started to put the rivets in a little crooked, but Jacob kept on working. Finally, a fellow worker stopped by and said, "You're new here, aren't you?" Jacob nodded. "Listen, I'll give you a word of advice. If the supervisor sees you letting the rivets go in crooked like that, he'll give you hell. So hide these in the scrap over there." The co-worker then showed Jacob how to adjust the machine.

Jacob's next problem began when the air ejection system started jamming. Four times he managed to clear it, but on the fifth try, he slipped and his elbow hit the rivet button. The machine put a rivet through the fleshy part of his hand, just below the thumb.

It was in the first-aid station that the supervisor finally had the opportunity to see Jacob once again.

Questions

1. Comment on the strengths and weaknesses of the on-the-job training that Jacob received. What did the supervisor do that was consistent with job instruction training? What did he fail to do?
2. What does this case tell you about the traditional approach to on-the-job training? What does it tell you about job instruction training?
3. If you were the supervisor, how would you have trained Jacob? What would you do differently?
4. If the job instruction training method was used, how would Jacob's training have been conducted? Explain how each step would proceed.
5. Describe any other on-the-job and off-the-job training methods that might be used to train Jacob. What do you think would be the most effective, practical, and feasible methods? What methods would you use and why?
6. Describe how some of the principles, concepts, and theories described in previous chapters might be relevant for training Jacob.

References

1. Based on Klie, S. (2008, June 2). Restaurant's training a recipe for success. *Canadian HR Reporter, 21* (11), 8, 9; www.whitespot.com (At 80 years young, white spot celebrates milestone anniversary; White Spot introduces a ground-breaking Red Seal chef certification program).
2. Hughes, P. D., & Grant, M. (2007). *Learning & development outlook 2007.* The Conference Board of Canada: Ottawa.
3. (1999, May/June). McDonald's stresses hands-on training. *The Training Report,* p. 10.
4. Dulipovici, A. (2003, May). Skilled in training: Results of CFIB surveys on training.
5. Sisson, G. R. (2001). *Hands-on training.* Berrett-Koehler Publishers, Inc. San Francisco: CA.
6. Sisson, G. R. (2001).
7. Sisson, G. R. (2001).
8. Sisson, G. R. (2001).
9. Broadwell, M. (1969). *The supervisor and on-the-job training.* Reading, MA: Addison-Wesley.
10. Sloman, M. (1989). On-the-job training: A costly poor relation. *Personnel Management 21* (2), 38–42.
11. Renner, P. F. (1989). *The instructor's survival kit.* Vancouver: Training Associates Ltd; Tench, A. (1992). Following Joe around: Should this be our approach to on-the-job training? *Plant Engineering, 46* (17), 88–92.

12. Meyers, D. (1991). Restaurant service: Making memorable presentations. *Cornell Hotel and Restaurant Administration Quarterly, 32* (1), 69–73; Ukens, C. (1993). Cards help pharmacists counsel patients in a flash. *Drug Topics, 137* (1), 24–27.

13. Ruyle, K. (1991, February/March). Developing intelligent job aids. *Technical and Skills Training,* 9–14.

14. Arajis, B. (1991). Getting your sales staff in shape. *Graphic Arts Monthly, 63* (5), 125–127.

15. Arajis, B. (1991); Cowen, W. (1992). Visual control boards are a key management tool. *Office Systems, 9* (10), 70–72; King, W. (1994). Training by design. *Training and Development, 48* (1), 52–54.

16. Young, L. (2008, March 24). All in the family at Toronto Hydro. *Canadian HR Reporter, 21* (6), 16.

17. Campion, M. A., Cheraskin, L., & Stevens, M. J. (1994). Career-related antecedents and outcomes of job rotation. *Academy of Management Journal, 37,* 1518–1542.

18. Ménard, M., Menezes, F., Chan, C. K. Y., & Walker, M. (2007). *National apprenticeship survey: Canada overview report 2007.* Ottawa: Statistics Canada.

19. Young, L. (2008, March 24).

20. Ménard, M., Menezes, F., Chan, C. K. Y., & Walker, M. (2007).

21. Ménard, M., Menezes, F., Chan, C. K. Y., & Walker, M. (2007).

22. Moskal, B. (1991). Apprenticeship: Old cure for new labor shortage? *Industry Week, 240* (9), 30–35.

23. Galt, V. (2006, March 22). Few employers taking on apprentices: New survey. *The Globe and Mail,* C2.

24. (2008, July). Strategies to increase employer participation in apprenticeship training in Canada. Ottawa: Canadian Apprenticeship Forum.

25. Ménard, M., Menezes, F., Chan, C. K. Y., & Walker, M. (2007).

26. McCarthy, S. (2001, February 27). Skilled-worker shortage could reach one million. *The Globe and Mail,* A1.

27. Galt, V. (2006, March 22).

28. McCarthy, S. (2001, February 27).

29. Apprenticeship training in Canada. (2006, July 25). www.ccl-cca.ca/CCL/Reports/LessonsInLearning/apprenticeship-LinL.htm

30. Funston, M. (2007, March 29). Free training targets labour shortages. *The Toronto Star,* K2.

31. Apprenticeship training in Canada. (2006, July 25).

32. Starrett, T. (2004, February/March). The eager apprentice: Has HR forgotten about a valuable resource? *HR Professional, 21* (2), 32.

33. Peterson, D. B. (2002). Management development: Coaching and mentoring programs. In K. Kraiger (Ed.), *Creating, implementing, and managing effective training and development: State-of-the-art lessons for practice* (pp. 160–191). San Francisco, CA: Jossey-Bass.

34. Lovin, B., & Casstevens, E. (1971). *Coaching, learning, and action.* New York: American Management Association; Frankel, L., & Otazo, K. (1992). Employee coaching: The way to gain commitment. *Employment Relations Today, 19* (3), 311–320.

35. Blakesley, S. (1992). Your agency . . . leave it better than you found it. *Managers Magazine, 67* (4), 20–22.

36. Kroeger, L. (1991). Your team can't win the game without solid coaching. *Corporate Controller, 3* (5), 62–64.

37. Azar, B. (1993). Striking a balance. *Sales and Marketing Management, 145* (2), 34–35; Whittaker, B. (1993). Shaping the competitive organization. *CMA Magazine, 67* (3), 5.

38. Peterson, D. B. (2002).

39. Kruse, A. (1993). Getting top value for your payroll dollar. *Low Practice Management, 19* (3), 52–57.

40. Peterson, D. B. (2002).

41. Noe, R. A. (1999). *Employee training and development.* Boston: Irwin McGraw-Hill.

42. Peterson, D. B. (2002).

43. Peterson, D. B. (2002).

44. Allen, T. D., Eby, L. T., Poteet, M. L., Lentz, E., & Lima, L. (2004). Career benefits associated with mentoring for protégés: A meta-analysis. *Journal of Applied Psychology, 89*, 127–136.

45. Jackson, C. (1993). Mentoring: Choices for individuals and organizations. *The International Journal of Career Management, 5* (1), 10–16; Noe, R. A. (1999).

46. Gallege, L. (1993). Do women make poor mentors? *Across the Board, 30* (6), 23–26.

47. Mullen, E. J. (1998). Vocational and psychosocial mentoring functions: Identifying mentors who serve both. *Human Resource Development Quarterly, 9* (4), 319–331.

48. Allen, T. D., Eby, L. T., & Lentz, E. (2006). The relationship between formal mentoring program characteristics and perceived program effectiveness. *Personnel Psychology, 59*, 125–153.

49. Allen, T. D., Eby, L. T., & Lentz, E. (2006).

50. Harding, K. (2003, May 9). Combined training works best, study says. *The Globe and Mail*, C1.

CHAPTER 8

Technology-Based Training Methods

Chapter Learning Outcomes

After reading this chapter you should be able to:

- define technology-based training and traditional training
- describe different methods of technology-based training
- compare and contrast instructor-led and self-directed learning
- define and give examples of asynchronous and synchronous training
- define and discuss computer-based training and e-learning, electronic performance support systems, and video and Web conferencing
- describe how to design computer-based training programs
- discuss the advantages and disadvantages of computer-based training
- discuss the effectiveness of computer-based training
- discuss the future of technology-based training and describe Web 2.0 tools and mobile learning

UNITED WAY OAKVILLE

The United Way of Canada raises more than $480 million each year, making it the largest fundraiser of the voluntary sector and social services in Canada. Most of the funds are reinvested in local communities to support programs and services for improving the social conditions of Canadians.

Across Canada, 120 United Way organizations employ approximately 900 staff and involve the assistance of thousands of volunteers. Each United Way—or Centraides, as they are called—is an autonomous organization that is operated by a voluntary Board of Directors chosen from the community it serves.

One of Canada's 120 Centraides is United Way Oakville (UWO), which has been in operation for more than 50 years. UWO is the largest funder of social services in Oakville outside of government and currently provides funding to more than 30 local health and social service agencies and 60 different programs. UWO-funded programs and services assist approximately 30,000 residents and impact more than one in five people each year.

UWO also provides professional development workshops to its staff and volunteers in the non-profit sector. A survey conducted by UWO in 2006 indicated that the training and consulting process could be improved with an e-learning program. In November 2008, the UWO launched a new e-learning program for staff and volunteers of the non-profit industry—the first of its kind for United Way of Canada. One of the UWO's priorities was to provide staff and volunteers in the non-profit sector access to high-quality and affordable training programs.

The Roadmap to Success e-learning program has more than 80 e-learning modules covering a wide array of professional and personal development topics such as business fundamentals, leadership development, communications and presentation, computer skills, conflict management, personal and workplace skills, and human resources management.

The programs are simple to use, cost-effective, and flexible. At a cost of $50 per subscriber per year, employees and volunteers gain unlimited access to the 80 modules. The program is open to all non-profit agencies.

While the new programs will not take the place of face-to-face training, they will be an appealing alternative. Besides being accessible from the comfort of one's own home at any time, the audio component means that users will not have to read excessive amounts of text and can work through the material at their own pace. And of course unlike traditional training programs, there are no scheduling problems.

The modules include quizzes and assessments so that trainees can see how they are progressing. At the end of every module there is a test, and when trainees have successfully completed a module they receive a certificate.

The availability of high-quality and affordable training programs for staff and volunteers in the non-profit sector will enable non-profit agencies to develop the knowledge and skills they require to become more effective change agents in their communities. It will also help non-profit agencies attract and retain high-calibre staff.[1]

Like many organizations today, the United Way of Oakville has begun to invest in technology for training. Besides being able to offer a wide assortment of training programs, technology-based training can be provided to large numbers of employees at any time with many benefits to employees and organizations.

In Chapters 6 and 7, we described traditional methods of off-the-job and on-the-job training. In this chapter, we focus on technology-based training methods. You will learn about how technology is being used for training, how to design computer-based training programs, their advantages and disadvantages, and the effectiveness of computer-based training. But first, let's be clear about what technology-based training is and how it differs from traditional training methods.

What Is Technology-Based Training?

RPC 8.1

Industry, government, and educational organizations are using technology to deliver training.[2] In Canada, the use of learning technology represents 16 percent of all formal training time.[3] In the United States, 16 percent of all formal training hours were online in 2008.[4] Thus, although training technology is becoming more popular, it is doing so at a relatively slow pace.

Technology-based training refers to training that involves the use of technology to deliver it, such as Web-based training; computerized self-study (including CD-ROMs, DVDs, and diskettes); satellite or broadcast TV; and video-, audio-, or teleconferencing. Any technology that delivers education or training, or supports the delivery of these subjects, would be included in the definition.[5]

By contrast, **traditional training** refers to training that does not involve the use of technology to deliver it, such as classroom training with a live instructor (regardless of the instructor's or learners' use of technology during the class); non-computerized self-study, such as textbooks or workbooks; non-computerized games; seminars; lectures; or outdoor programs.[6]

While most people understand that computers are being used for training, one of the most confusing things about technology-based training is the many different terms used to refer to the various forms of technology-based training. Although there are technical distinctions between some of the methods, the

Technology-based training
Training that involves the use of technology to deliver courses

Traditional training
Training that does not involve using technology to deliver courses

distinctions are generally not apparent to trainees and often have to do with where the programs and data are located and the ease with which they can be updated.[7]

Nonetheless, it is important to understand the terms used to describe the different types of technology-based training. Table 8.1 provides a list and definitions of the major types of technology-based training.

The use of technology for training in Canada has increased over the last decade, and some companies have made major advances.[8] For example, at Cisco Systems Canada Co. most sales training is now done online, compared to just a few years ago when 90 percent was done in the classroom. Employees now access the company's website to find out about new Cisco networking products and how to install products. Because the courses are up and running much faster than traditional classroom programs, employees can learn about new products in one week compared to three months.[9]

As part of an initiative to better meet changing customer requirements that involved replacing existing business processes as well as 200 different business systems, Hydro-Québec now delivers training online for close to 3,000 employees.[10] SaskTel has an advanced e-learning system and recently implemented a training program for its sales force. To learn more, see Training Today 8.1, "Sales Training at SaskTel."

TABLE 8.1

Major Types of Technology-Based Training

Internet: A loose confederation of computer networks around the world that is connected through several primary networks

Intranet: A general term describing any network contained within an organization. It refers primarily to networks that use Internet technology

Extranet: A collaborative network that uses Internet technology to link organizations with their suppliers, customers, or other organizations that share common goals or information

CD-ROM: A format and system for recording, storing, and retrieving electronic information on a compact disc that is read using an optical drive

Electronic performance support system (EPSS): An integrated computer application that uses any combination of expert systems, hypertext, embedded animation, and/or hypermedia to help a user perform a task in real time quickly and with a minimum of support by other people

Electronic simulation: A device or system that replicates or imitates a real device or system

Multimedia: A computer application that uses any combination of text, graphics, audio, animation, and/or full-motion video

Teleconference: The instantaneous exchange of audio, video or text between two or more individuals or groups at two or more locations

Television (cable, satellite): The transmission of television signals via cable or satellite technology

Source: Cooney, J., & Cowan, A. (2003). *Training and development outlook 2003.* Reprinted by permission of The Conference Board of Canada. Ottawa. Reprinted by permission of The Conference Board of Canada.

Sales Training at SaskTel

SaskTel is the leading full-service communications company in Saskatchewan. The provincial Crown corporation and its wholly-owned subsidiaries has a workforce of approximately 5,200 employees that serves more than 425,000 business and residential customers.

SaskTel noticed that its sales department was having difficulty keeping pace with advancing technology and customer needs. Past training efforts were ineffective in increasing focus on IP (Internet protocol) sales initiatives. Workers were not consistently applying the new information to their jobs, and the company was concerned about maintaining and growing market share and customer loyalty.

To address the problem, the company's learning professionals designed an IP certification program. The blended program delivers a curriculum based on strategic IP communications, products and services, solution selling, and return on communications.

Skill gaps are identified by an online assessment, and employees and their managers prescribe personalized development plans based on the results. Participants learn through a combination of courses, mentoring relationships, and self-study resources such as white papers and technical guides. Because it is the company's first in-house certification program, a knowledge and skills library on the learning management system was created to supplement on-the-job reference resources.

The results so far suggest the program is a success. Employee credibility with customers has increased, the sales force feels more confident about its knowledge of products and services, and IP sales are up by 14 percent.

Sources: Anonymous (2007, October). Better than the rest (Saskatchewan Telecommunications). *T+D, 61* (10), 76–77; www.sasktel.com.

Computer-Based Training

Over the last decade, the use of computers to deliver training has been referred to as computer-based training and e-learning. Although these terms are often used synonymously, there are differences. **Computer-based training** refers to training that is delivered via the computer for the purpose of teaching job-relevant skills. It can include text, graphics, and/or animation and be delivered via CD-ROMs, intranets, or the internet.[11] Among the various forms of computer-based training, Web-delivered and CD-ROM formats have received the most attention.

A related and increasingly popular term for technology-based training is e-learning. **E-learning** (also known as Web-based instruction or WBI) refers to the use of computer network technology such as the intranet or internet to deliver information or instruction to individuals.[12] Thus, e-learning is a specific type of computer-based learning and refers to the use of computer network technology. It would not include the use of CD-ROMs. In the remainder of this chapter, we will use the broader term, computer-based training, which includes e-learning.

One of the ways that computer-based training methods differ is in terms of whether the training is instructor-led or self-directed, the focus of the next section.

Computer-based training

Training that is delivered via the computer for the purpose of teaching job-relevant knowledge and skills

E-learning

The use of computer network technology such as the intranet or Internet to deliver information or instruction to individuals

Self-Directed Learning

Instructor-led training (ILT)

Training methods that involve an instructor or facilitator who leads, facilitates, or trains online

Like traditional training methods, computer-based training can involve an instructor or facilitator who leads, facilitates, or trains online. Computer-based training that is instructor-led is known as **instructor-led training** or **ILT**. Some examples of ILT are online discussions and video conferencing.

In some cases, the instructor is highly involved in the training and leads the process. In other cases, a course or program involves self-study and the instructor is available for answering questions and providing assistance.[13]

However, one of the main advantages of computer-based training is that it can be initiated and controlled by the trainee. This is known as self-directed learning.

Self-directed learning (SDL) is a process that occurs when individuals or groups take the initiative and responsibility for learning and manage their own learning experiences. They seek out the necessary resources to engage in learning that will enhance their careers and personal growth. Employees assess their own needs, use a variety of organizational resources to meet those needs, and are helped with evaluating the effectiveness of meeting their needs. SDL can be as simple as a booklet that describes a new procedure or a multimedia program.

Self-directed learning (SDL)

A process in which individuals or groups take the initiative and responsibility for learning and manage their own learning experiences

Self-directed learning has become increasingly popular because traditional methods of training lack the flexibility to respond quickly to dramatic and constant organizational change and trainees' needs. Self-directed learning allows trainees to access training materials and programs when they want to, at their own pace, and sometimes in the sequence they prefer.

See Table 8.2 for some of the benefits and limitations of self-directed learning.

Asynchronous and Synchronous Training

Computer-based training can be asynchronous or synchronous. When training is **asynchronous**, it is available to employees at any time and from any location. For example, an asynchronous program might simply involve the posting of text, information, or instructions on a website. More sophisticated programs can include graphics, animation, audio, and video, thereby providing a multimedia program. This combined with simulations, interactive exercises, tests, and feedback can result in a much more engaging and active learning experience. While the use of multimedia involves greater involvement on the part of the trainee, it is much more expensive to design and develop. The United Way of Oakville's Roadmap to Success e-learning program is an example of asynchronous training.

Asynchronous training

Training that is pre-recorded and available to employees at any time and from any location

When training is **synchronous**, it is live and in real-time so trainees must be at their computer at a specific time. A basic synchronous program might simply involve "chat" sessions in which trainees log on at the same time and participate in a discussion of some topic. More sophisticated programs might have trainees from various locations log in to the training at a set time and receive instruction from a trainer who facilitates a discussion, shows slides, and answers trainees' questions and provides feedback.[14]

Synchronous training

Training that is live and requires trainees to be at their computer at a specific time

In the following sections, we describe some of the most common types of asynchronous and synchronous training.

TABLE 8.2

The Benefits and Limitations of Self-Directed Learning

BENEFITS

Trainees can learn at their own pace and determine their desired level of expertise

Trainees build on their knowledge bases and training time may be reduced; trainees learn what is relevant to their needs

Trainees become independent and acquire skills enabling them to learn more efficiently and effectively, reducing dependence on formal training

People can learn according to their own styles of learning

LIMITATIONS

Trainees may learn the wrong things or may not learn all there is to know; one suggestion to remedy this problem is to negotiate a learning contract with specific learning objectives and performance measures

Trainees may waste time accessing resources and finding helpful material; the trainer could become a facilitator, directing employees toward useful resources

SDL takes time—the employee has to learn active knowledge-seeking skills, has to acquire knowledge-gathering skills, must learn to tolerate inefficiencies and mistakes; the trainer, too, must learn to give up a power base and move from expert to helper

Electronic Performance Support Systems

A common method of asynchronous training is an electronic performance support system. An **electronic performance support system (EPSS)** is a computer-based system that provides access to integrated information, advice, and learning experiences.[15] EPSS provide several types of support including assisting, warning, advising, teaching, and evaluating. Employees can obtain information to help solve work-related problems.

The goal of an EPSS is to provide whatever is necessary to aid performance and learning at the time it is needed. When the accounting firm KPMG needed to train all its employees on a new tax planning service, it chose EPSS over classroom training. The EPSS saved in delivery time (consultants did not need to spend three weeks in classrooms) and reduced costs in updates.[16]

Alberta Pacific Forest Industries at its Sarnia plant extols the advantages of EPSS for safety, maintenance, and laboratory training: learning occurs when workers need it most, on-site; it allows for continual upgrading; it allows for individual differences in the pace of learning; and it allows links to suppliers' training and tracks learning accomplishments.[17]

With an EPSS, information is accessed only when it is needed. Only the information that is needed is given; there is no information overload. EPSS is particularly useful for training in high-turnover jobs, like hotel staff, and tasks that are difficult, performed infrequently, and must be performed perfectly.[18]

A recent development of EPPS is online reference tools that are available to employees to refresh their memories about work-related tasks or to

Electronic performance support system (EPSS)

A computer-based system that provides information, advice, and learning experiences to improve performance provide them with instant help on how to perform a task. Employees access an intranet page where content can be downloaded to a mobile device or a computer. The site might include a short video on topics such as the main features of a product that a retailer sells or the steps involved in performing a task. Thus, not only can employees go online to get what they need when they need it, but they can also get it from wherever they are using a mobile device, which means they don't have to be at their computer.[19]

Video and Web Conferencing

A common method of synchronous training is video conferencing. **Video conferencing** involves linking a subject-matter expert or trainer to employees by means of two-way television and satellite technology. This can involve the transmission of television signals via cable or through satellite technology. Whatever the actual means of transmission, the basic idea is that people at two or more locations are able to see, hear, and speak with one another, thus permitting simultaneous meetings in different locations.

Video conferencing is used to bring in an expert from another location, to hold meetings with staff working in various locations, and to communicate corporate information that needs to be rapidly disseminated.

Scotiabank uses interactive training sessions that are broadcast to employees across the country by satellite television. As a result, the bank is able to train employees in branches across Canada. For example, a program on RRSPs trained 2,000 employees at 25 locations across the country. Trainees had to first use the internet to review course materials online prior to attending the training. To keep employees engaged, they completed quizzes and participated in opinion polls throughout the session by pushing buttons on their phone sets. During breaks, group discussions and case study analyses were led by previously trained managers at each meeting site. During the broadcast, trainees asked questions by telephone.

With some 28,000 employees spread all over the country, Scotiabank is able to train thousands of employees at one time without having to bring them together in one location or to send trainers all over the country. It also ensures that a consistent message is sent to all employees and everyone "hits the ground running" at the same time. In fact, employees return to their branches the day after training and begin to apply their new product knowledge.

An added benefit to employees is the opportunity to learn about what their fellow employees around the country are doing and to share ideas and best practices. This also helps to create a sense of cohesion, which is difficult in such a large and geographically diverse organization.[20]

The disadvantage of video conferencing is that less personal attention is given to trainees. However, this problem can be remedied by having a facilitator on-site or by allowing for interactive questioning while training takes place.

The use of computer technology provides additional ways to hold training conferences and seminars. For example, Web conferencing is similar to a video conference except that the trainees are connected to the trainer

Video conferencing

Linking an expert or trainer to employees via two-way television and satellite technology and each other via the internet and participate from their own computer. Thus, **Web conferencing** is a live meeting or conference that takes place on the internet. Similar to Web conferencing is a **webinar**, which is a seminar or workshop that takes place live over the Web (a Web-based seminar). It can be a presentation, lecture, or workshop and can be interactive by allowing participants to ask and answer questions. Many organizations prefer a webinar over a seminar because it reduces the costs associated with renting a room, travel, and catering.[21]

Finally, a **webcast** is a live or recorded video or audio broadcast over the internet. Webcasts are used primarily for presentations, while Web conferencing and webinars are used for live meetings and seminars, respectively. Webcasts are usually one-way communications that do not have an interactive component.[22]

Now that we have described how technology is being used for training, let's consider how to design computer-based training programs.

The Design of Computer-Based Training Programs

When designing computer-based training programs, it is important to keep in mind that the technology is just the medium for delivering the training. Whether or not a training program is effective depends on how it is designed rather than the sophistication of the technology used to deliver it.

As described in Chapter 5, to maximize learning and retention, training programs should include active practice and conditions of practice (e.g., feedback). In addition, many of the instructional methods described in Chapter 6 can be used, such as games, simulations, and role plays. Other important design factors include stories, customizing and personalizing the training, human interaction, and feedback.

GAMES Games are useful for engaging trainees with realistic and entertaining experiences. Learning games such as crossword puzzle games have been used in the presentation and practice of training material. Games can improve trainee learning and performance by increasing the appeal of e-learning; encourage trainees to practise; and facilitate the discovery of patterns and relationships in the training material.[23]

Some games involve multimedia simulations that are designed to entertain and motivate trainees to learn. For example, in a leadership training program called Executive Challenge, teams of executives are given a virtual company with information and scenarios tailored to different positions in the company. Using computers, team players work on tasks presented as stories with colourful images and are tested on leadership skills, teamwork, and the ability to make their virtual companies successful.[24]

COMPUTER SIMULATIONS Computer simulations provide trainees with hands-on training for a particular task. They are designed to replicate on-the-job experiences by providing trainees with opportunities to practise and master knowledge and skills in an interactive environment.

Web conferencing

A live meeting or conference that takes place on the internet

Webinar

A seminar that takes place live over the Web

Webcast

A live or recorded video or audio broadcast over the internet

 8.2

Mr. Lube uses an online simulation for new technicians to learn how to perform an oil change. The simulation takes trainees through all the checks and assessments and times them on the tasks. The simulation provides new technicians with a safe learning environment to learn and master their job before they actually work on a vehicle. As a result, on-the-job training time and errors are reduced. The program also ensures that the same process will be used by all technicians across the country. Computer simulations are also being used for soft skills training for various skills such as leadership, sales, customer service, and financial services.[25]

ROLE PLAYS Role plays can be used with computer-based training programs. For example, Rogers Wireless Communications Inc. has an interactive customer-service training program for sales representatives that includes online role playing. Trainees interact with animated characters that present different customer-service challenges and learn different approaches for interacting with them. An animated coach provides guidance and feedback.

Rogers noticed improvements in service and employee satisfaction not long after the program was implemented. The role-playing makes the program engaging and the lessons—which are based on real-life scenarios—are having an effect on employees' performance.[26]

STORIES Stories and narratives have also been used in e-learning in order to engage trainees. Abstract concepts as well as dry material can be livened up with stories that involve dialogue and characters. The characters can be created to be similar to the trainees and learning can occur as the characters solve problems in the story.

Sprint and Volvo have used stories to train employees on how to deliver the company's brand image when interacting with customers. Trainees also practise communicating the brand image in simulated customer interactions.[27]

Customization

Tailoring instructional elements to meet trainee preferences and needs

CUSTOMIZATION **Customization** involves tailoring instructional elements to meet trainee preferences and needs. This can increase trainee satisfaction with the training and improve learning. Hewlett-Packard is an example of one company that has been very successful at customization. The company has found that preferences for e-learning and other training media differ around the world. For example, it found that employees in Asia prefer instructor-presented or blended learning, while in the United States and Europe employees prefer self-paced and instructor-presented learning approaches, respectively. Differences in e-learning preferences indicate that one type of e-learning program is not likely to meet the needs and preferences of all employees.[28]

Personalization

Structuring the program so that trainees feel that they are engaged in a conversation with the program

PERSONALIZATION **Personalization** refers to structuring the program so that trainees feel they are engaged in a conversation with the program. This can be achieved by using conversational rather than formal language in the on-screen text and audio recording.[29]

HUMAN INTERACTION A potential problem of computer-based training for some trainees is the lack of face-to-face interaction with an instructor and other trainees. This can result in trainees feeling isolated and less motivated to learn. One way to overcome this is to include human interaction in the design of computer-based training programs.

Human interaction refers to the extent that trainees are able to interact with the instructor and each other during a training program. This can be built into computer-based programs using a number of formats including e-mail exchanges, chat rooms, discussion boards, and group projects. There is some evidence that more interaction with the instructor and between trainees is associated with higher motivation, more positive attitudes toward learning, and improved learning outcomes.[30]

FEEDBACK Regardless of the nature of the training experience, it is important that feedback be provided to trainees. In fact, students who received feedback in computer-based training have been found to learn more than students who were not given feedback.[31]

Feedback can be incorporated into computer-based training in many ways. It can range from a simple prompt indicating that an answer to a question or a quiz is right or wrong to the execution of another program segment in which trainees are routed through a complex maze of reviews and reinforcements based on their responses and answers. Trainees who take the modules in the UWO Roadmap to Success e-learning program receive feedback by completing quizzes and assessments during the program, and then take a test at the end of the module.

Feedback can also be incorporated into simulations and role plays. For example, in a role play in which trainees must choose from a number of options how to respond to different customers, immediate feedback can be provided following each response chosen by a trainee. In addition, an on-screen virtual coach can be used to provide trainees with feedback about the correctness of their choices, what they did wrong, and hints on how to proceed and improve. Trainees can then take the program again until their performance improves.

To learn about some additional design principles for computer-based training, see The Trainer's Notebook 8.1, "Design Principles for Computer-Based Training."

Computer-Based Training: Advantages and Disadvantages

Like on-the-job and off-the-job training methods, computer-based training has advantages and disadvantages for trainees and organizations.

Advantages

Trainees

A major advantage for trainees is greater flexibility. For example, trainees do not have to coordinate and arrange their schedule and workload to accommodate training schedules. Trainees do not have to take courses when they

Human interaction

The extent that trainees are able to interact with the instructor and each other during a training program

The Trainer's Notebook 8.1

Design Principles for Computer-Based Training

The following principles cover many different aspects of computer-based training design and are well grounded in both theory and research.

- *The multimedia principle.* Graphics and text should be used rather than simply text alone. Trainees will engage in a deeper and more active processing of the learning material.
- *The contiguity principle.* When text is used to explain a graphic or vice versa, the text and graphics should be placed near each other on the screen. This permits trainees to focus on the instructional material rather than on trying to match a miscellaneous set of pictures to text.
- *The modality principle.* Audio technology should be used to present information instead of on-screen text. Trainees are likely to become overwhelmed with visual information when only presented with text, graphics, illustrations, and figures during learning.
- *The personalization principle.* Text should be written in first and second person and trainees should have access to on-screen virtual coaches that provide guidance and direction. This will help trainees to see the computer as a conversational partner rather than as an information delivery agent.

Source: DeRouin, R. E., Fritzsche, B. A., & Salas, E. (2005). E-Learning in organizations. *Journal of Management*, 31, 920–940. Based on Clark, R. C., & Mayer, R. E. (2003). *E-learning and the science of instruction: Proven guidelines for consumers and designers of multimedia learning.* San Francisco: Jossey-Bass.

---

are scheduled or wait until a group of trainees are ready to take a course. They can learn when they want to or "just in time." Trainees also do not have to leave work to attend training, and can even learn while they are at home or away from work.

Another advantage for trainees is greater control over their learning, or what is known as learner control. **Learner control** refers to trainee control over the content, sequence, and pace of training.[32] In other words, trainees can enter and leave training as they choose and also can progress at their own pace. **Self-pacing** means that trainees can work on training tasks as quickly or as slowly as they want. In some cases, trainees even have control over various instructional elements of a program such as the sequence of instructional material, the content of instruction, and the amount of instruction during training.

There is also some evidence that trainees are not as shy online as they are in a classroom. Trainees who encounter difficulties during training are less likely to feel embarrassed about their pace or performance, and they don't have to admit to not knowing something. As a result, they are more likely to be comfortable online than in a classroom and this can improve their satisfaction with the training as well as their learning.[33]

Perhaps most beneficial for trainees is the convenience of being able to learn whenever they want to or need to, and to do so from any location where they have access to a computer. This, of course, is the ultimate example of "just-in-time" training. Employees do not have to sign up and wait for a course to be available; it is available whenever they need it. And during training, employees can pause and continue at a later time without missing a beat.

Learner control

Trainee control over the content, sequence, and pace of training

Self-pacing

Trainees can work on training tasks as quickly or as slowly as they want

Furthermore, because of the ability to learn at work or at home, employees do not have to spend time travelling to distant training locations. Geographic flexibility is a major advantage.

Organizations

A major advantage for organizations is that they can ensure that all trainees receive the same training regardless of where they are situated. Thus, organizations can deliver standardized and consistent training to large numbers of employees across the organization and even worldwide. This is especially important when employees in many locations require training. Leaving the training to each location could result in differences in content, delivery, and effectiveness.

Another advantage is that large numbers of employees can be trained within a short period of time. There is no limit to the number of employees who can be trained, as one is not constrained by the number of instructors available or the need for classroom space.

Computer-based training also makes it possible to track employees' performance on learning exercises and tests. This kind of tracking is especially important for training programs that are mandatory and completion, certification, or attaining a certain level of performance is legally mandated. The technology can generate tests that can provide legal documentation for proof of competency levels. When an accident or safety incident results in a lawsuit, the employer can prove that a training program was completed and that a desired level of competence was achieved. Such training statistics can reduce corporate liability. Technology also allows trainees to track their own progress and test themselves.

Perhaps the greatest advantage for organizations is the reduction in the cost of training as a result of the elimination of the cost of travel, training facilities, hotel rooms, meals, trainers, and employee time off from work while travelling and attending training.[34] In addition, the high overhead costs of traditional training make computer-based training especially advantageous to companies with national or international employees.

The savings reported by some companies are quite significant. For example, Dow Chemical estimates that the implementation of a Web-based training system saved the company $30 million in one year. It saved $20 million as a result of a reduction in the time employees spend in training, and $10 million due to a reduction in administrative time, classroom facilities, trainers, and the cost of printed material.[35]

Disadvantages

Trainees

There are also some disadvantages of computer-based training. For trainees, there is less interpersonal contact and interaction with other trainees. Furthermore, individuals have learning preferences and styles, and if a trainee prefers to receive training in a classroom with a trainer and other trainees then computer-based training would disadvantage that employee.

Trainers who are not computer literate might also resist and fear the change to technology. A low-threat opportunity to allow trainers to test the technology is to place the learning stations in the classroom.[36] However, industry analysts perceive these barriers as temporary problems. Computer-based training will become a standard way of providing training, particularly for the current generation which is comfortable with computers and technology.

Organizations

For organizations, a disadvantage is that some employees will be uncomfortable with computers and might resist training. This is especially likely for older workers who have less experience using computers. There is also the potential for problems to arise if employees do not have access to computers.

However, the major disadvantage for organizations is the cost of development, especially for sophisticated multimedia programs. Estimates are that it takes 200 to 300 hours of design and development time to produce one hour of instruction.[37] Full-motion colour-and-sound courseware would likely cost $200,000 for 30 hours of instruction. This requires a considerable upfront investment in information technology and staff. At Motorola, where about 30 percent of employee training is computer-based, it was estimated that $20 million to $27 million will be spent in one year on e-learning.[38]

Although the cost to design and develop computer-based training is considerably higher than traditional classroom training, once a program has been developed there is the potential for considerable cost savings given the elimination of variable costs such as travel, lodging, meals, materials, and in many cases an instructor's salary. Thus, computer-based training has the potential to be less costly than classroom training once the program has been developed. This is most likely to be the case when there are large numbers of employees to be trained, they are geographically dispersed, and the training will be frequently repeated.[39]

How Effective Is Computer-Based Training?

While computer-based training provides many advantages for trainees and organizations, ultimately what really matters is how effective it is for learning. Many have claimed, for various reasons, that computer-based training is more effective than classroom instruction. One reason is that it provides a greater variety of instructional methods (e.g., text, audio, graphics) that are tailored to individual needs and preferences for learning. Other explanations include greater learner ease, control, flexibility, and immediate feedback. Still some argue that it is a more cost-effective method of training than face-to-face instruction.[40]

Research that has compared computer-based training to classroom instruction has produced conflicting results. Some studies have found that computer-based training is more effective, some found classroom instruction is more effective, and still others found no differences. However, because there are many differences across studies (e.g., course content, type of trainee, instructional methods used, etc.) it is difficult to reach a conclusion from a single study. Much more can be learned by examining the results of many studies that take into account these differences.

One study recently summarized the results of 96 studies that compared the effectiveness of computer-based training to classroom instruction. The results indicated that, on average, computer-based training was 6 percent more effective than classroom instruction for declarative knowledge. However, both methods were equally effective for teaching procedural knowledge. In addition, trainees were equally satisfied with both training methods.

The authors also compared the effectiveness of blended training, in which computer-based training was used to supplement classroom instruction. Blended training was 13 percent more effective than classroom instruction for teaching declarative knowledge, and 20 percent more effective for teaching procedural knowledge. However, trainees reacted 6 percent more favourably toward classroom instruction than blended training.

Perhaps most importantly, the effectiveness of computer-based training for declarative knowledge was found to depend on a number of factors. First, computer-based training was more effective than classroom instruction for older trainees, while classroom instruction was more effective for younger trainees. Computer-based training was not any more effective for employees or college students.

Second, computer-based training was more effective than classroom instruction when the instructional methods (i.e., the techniques used to deliver the training content such as lecture, video, textbooks, etc.) were different. However, computer-based training and classroom instruction were equally effective when the instructional methods were the same.

This is an important finding because it suggests that one reason why computer-based training has at times been found to be more effective than classroom instruction is because the instructional methods differ, such as when classroom instruction involves a lecture and computer-based training involves a variety of instructional techniques. In fact, the authors found that computer-based training was 11 percent more effective than classroom instruction for teaching declarative knowledge when different instructional methods were used. This suggests that instructional methods are more important for learning than the media used to deliver the training (computer versus face-to-face).

Third, computer-based training was more effective than classroom instruction only when trainees were able to choose the training method. Furthermore, when trainees were not able to choose a training method (i.e., they were randomly assigned to computer-based training or classroom instruction), classroom instruction was 10 percent more effective. This suggests that there might be preexisting differences between trainees who choose a computer-based program compared to those who choose classroom instruction (e.g., motivation, cognitive ability, computer experience, skills, and self-efficacy) and these differences might be the reason why computer-based training is more effective than classroom instruction. For example, the authors found that trainees with more computer experience learned more from computer-based training.

Computer-based training was also more effective than classroom instruction when trainees had greater learner control and the training included practice and feedback, especially when classroom instruction did not include practice and feedback. However, it should be noted that both training methods were more effective when they included opportunities for practice and feedback. Finally, computer-based training was more effective than classroom instruction when the length of the training program (i.e., number of days) was greater.[41]

There is also some evidence that computer-based training can result in a reduction in the time to completion. However, this appears to be most likely only when trainees have some prior experience using technology. In some cases, such as when trainees do not have experience or when trainees experience technology problems and interruptions, the time to completion might actually be greater for computer-based training compared to classroom training.[42]

A final issue is trainees' ability to use computers and their attitudes and motivation toward computer-based training. For example, individuals with greater computer literacy and higher computer self-efficacy tend to be more willing and able to learn. Thus, some trainees will learn more in a traditional classroom setting and should not be forced into computer-based training programs. At the very least, they might require some basic computer training to improve their computer skills and computer self-efficacy before participating in a computer-based training program.

There is also some evidence that employees are not likely to take or complete training courses that are optional or have little impact on them. That is, unless a course is required or when there is a strong reason for employees to complete it, they are not likely to do so. Employees have been found to be more likely to complete a computer-based training program when there is an incentive for doing so, some form of accountability, or when the program content is job-relevant and useful.

Finally, unless trainees experience technical problems, they tend to respond positively to computer-based training programs. A number of studies have reported that after taking a computer-based training program, trainees report satisfaction with their learning experience, more positive attitudes toward technology-based training, and a willingness to try it again.[43]

Effectiveness of Computer-Based Training: Summary

In summary, research has found that computer-based training can be more effective than classroom instruction; however, it depends on a number of factors (e.g., type of learning outcome, age of trainee, instructional methods, learner control, trainee choice of training method, opportunities for practice, feedback provided, and length of program). Thus, while the research does not indicate that computer-based training is superior to classroom instruction, there is evidence that it can be effective for learning declarative and procedural knowledge, and trainees are just as satisfied with it as they are with classroom instruction.

On the other hand, it might not be as effective for learning complex skills, soft skills, psychomotor skills, or team skills. Furthermore, the effectiveness of computer-based training is likely to depend on many other factors such as the content of the program, the trainees, and the type of technology used.[44] Thus, one has to be cautious when making assertions that computer-based training is better or more effective than traditional classroom instruction; *it depends*. Particularly important is how the training is designed and the use of important design principles such as active practice and feedback.

The Future of Technology-Based Training

In a recent article on learning, Kurt Kraiger argued that we are on the cusp of a new model of learning called social constructivism, which places greater emphasis on the learner and learning through social interaction. According to **social constructivism**, "the goal of instruction should be to create interactive learning environments in which training participants learn from instructors, participants learn from each other, and the instructor learns from participants" (p. 461). Kraiger also argues that Web-based instruction is especially well suited for fostering interactive learning environments.[45]

In fact, in the last several years we have seen the emergence of new learning technology that can facilitate social constructivism. These new tools are known as Web 2.0 and involve social networks and Web-based communities for sharing and exchanging information. Thus, **Web 2.0** refers to internet tools that enable the sharing and creation of knowledge. With this technology, anybody can create and distribute knowledge and collaborate with others in the process.[46] In many respects, Web 2.0 facilitates communities of practice and informal learning, which were described in Chapter 2.

Some of the most popular Web 2.0 tools are blogs, wikis, and podcasts. A **blog** is a website that contains commentary and information on a subject. It is like a journal in which an individual posts information about a topic or subject. Blogs can include text, video, and audio as well as links to other individuals' blogs. Thus, they provide a network of conversations and the exchange of information on a particular topic, subject, or issue.[47]

A **wiki** is a webpage or collection of webpages in which users share, contribute, and modify information on a topic. Although there are many public wikis (Wikipedia, for example, is the best known), some companies have internal wikis that focus on particular topics such as company products. The content can be created and shared among the users of the website on an ongoing basis. Wikis enable relevant information to be obtained on-demand and training material to be constantly revised and updated. Many large organizations now use wikis on team projects.[48]

A **podcast** is a short audio or video recording that can be downloaded and played on a mobile device such as an iPod or cell phone. Employees can access information on-demand from any location at their convenience. For example, a sales team can learn about new products directly from the designers, and truck drivers can learn how to drive in a storm while driving.[49]

Social constructivism

An approach to learning that emphasizes interactive learning environments

Web 2.0

Internet tools that enable the sharing and creation of knowledge

Blog

A website that contains commentary and information on a subject

Wiki

A webpage or collection of webpages in which users share, contribute, and modify information on a topic

Podcast

A short audio or video recording that can be downloaded and played on a mobile device such as an iPod or cell phones

Mobile learning

The use of mobile or portable technologies across locations.

Another interesting trend is mobile learning, which involves the use of mobile or portable technologies such as iPods, MP3 players, and smart phones across locations. **Mobile learning** enables employees to obtain information and training not only whenever they need it, but also wherever they are when they need it. Mobile devices can be used to deliver short videos or small amounts of information. For example, if an employee is away from the workplace and needs to learn a specific procedure, he/she can access a short video or information on the company's intranet using a mobile device. As a result, mobile employees can stay current and up to date with the latest knowledge and information.[50]

For example, Black & Decker has replaced paper-based training materials with mobile learning content to train its 300 field reps. The field reps are responsible for setting up store displays for retailers. In the past, they were provided with manuals, photographs, and other paper materials. Now they receive short two- to three-minute learning modules directly to their PDA (personal digital assistant). In addition to learning about the products and displays, the modules also include task lists, images, quizzes, and short videos about the products. The use of mobile learning costs less, takes less time, and also provides better quality control over training.[51]

Thus, as these new trends suggest, the use of technology for training continues to advance. The advantages and benefits far outweigh the disadvantages. At this point, the main issues have to do with how best to use and design technology-based training and how to blend technology with more traditional training methods to make it most effective for trainee learning, retention, and transfer.

However, it should be recognized that although many have predicted the demise of traditional classroom methods of training, the reality is that classroom instruction will continue to be used and combined with technology-based methods. In fact, most training in organizations today in both Canada and the United States is in the classroom.[52] Furthermore, a blended approach to learning is likely to be the most effective, especially for certain types of training and for trainees with different learning styles and preferences.

For trainers, the important issues revolve around when to use technology-based training and when it is most likely to be effective. This means that trainers need to consider training objectives, the desired learning outcomes, training content, design factors, and trainee characteristics. For some types of skills such as soft skills, psychomotor skills, and team skills, more traditional methods of training will still be necessary and perhaps even more effective than technology-based training methods. Thus, not surprisingly, most experts agree that technology-based training will never completely replace traditional classroom or face-to-face training methods.[53]

Summary

This chapter described technology-based training methods and serves as a complement to the on-the-job and off-the-job training methods described in Chapters 6 and 7. Different types of technology-based training methods were described and distinctions were made between instructor-led and self-directed training, and between asynchronous and synchronous training. The advantages, disadvantages, and effectiveness of computer-based training were discussed as well as how to design computer-based training programs. The chapter concluded with a discussion of Web 2.0 tools for training and mobile learning.

Key Terms

asynchronous training   p. 230

blog   p. 241

computer-based training   p. 229

customization   p. 234

e-learning   p. 229

electronic performance support system
     (EPSS)   p. 231

human interaction   p. 235

instructor-led training (ILT)   p. 230

learner control   p. 236

mobile learning   p. 242

personalization   p. 234

podcast   p. 241

self-directed learning (SDL)   p. 230

self-pacing   p. 236

social constructivism   p. 241

synchronous training   p. 230

technology-based training   p. 227

traditional training   p. 227

video conferencing   p. 232

Web 2.0   p. 241

Web conferencing   p. 233

webcast   p. 233

webinar   p. 233

wiki   p. 241

Make the Connection

p. 233: active practice and conditions of practice are discussed in Chapter 5 on page 145 and instructional methods are discussed in Chapter 6 on page 167

p. 241: communities of practice and informal learning are discussed in Chapter 2 on pages 44–48

Web Links

Cisco Systems Canada Co.: www.cisco.com

Dow Chemical: www.dow.com

Hydro-Québec: www.hydroquebec.com

Motorola Inc.: www.motorola.com

SaskTel: www.sasktel.com

Scotiabank: www.scotiabank.com

United Way Oakville: www.uwoakville.org

RPC Icons

RPC 8.1 Using a variety of methods facilitates the delivery of development programs to groups and individual learners.

RPC 8.2 Participates in course design and selection/delivery of learning materials via various media.

Discussion Questions

1. In both Canada and the United States, the actual use of training technologies has fallen below projections and, in fact, the adoption of training technologies has been relatively slow. What are some of the reasons for this and what are the potential barriers to the adoption of training technologies?
2. Compare and contrast technology-based training methods to traditional training methods. Why would an organization choose to use some forms of technology-based training rather than traditional training methods? Are there some types of industries, organizations, or jobs in which technology-based training or traditional training would be more appropriate and effective?
3. What are the advantages and disadvantages of technology-based training for trainees, trainers, and organizations?
4. If you had the choice, would you choose a computer-based training program or a traditional classroom program? Which would you prefer and why? Do you think your satisfaction, learning, and performance would differ in a computer-based program versus a traditional classroom program? Explain your reasoning.
5. Discuss how computer-based training programs can be designed to engage trainees and improve their motivation and learning.
6. Discuss how games, simulations, and role plays can be used in computer-based training programs.
7. Some have argued that there is nothing uniquely advantageous about technology-based training methods and that any effect they have on learning is not due to the use of any particular technological device. Do you agree or disagree with this position? Explain your reasoning and why you think it might be true or false.
8. Research on the effects of computer-based training has found that it is more effective than classroom instruction when trainees can choose the program (computer-based or classroom) and when the instructional methods used to deliver the programs are different. What are the implications of these two findings for understanding the effects of computer-based training and for the design and delivery of computer-based training programs?
9. What is social constructivism and how can it be facilitated by technology?

The Great Training Debate

1. Debate the following: Given the many benefits of computer-based training, organizations should convert all of their traditional training programs to computer-based programs and make formal classroom training a thing of the past.
2. Debate the following: There is nothing inherently superior about technology-based training. The effectiveness of a training method depends on how it is designed rather than how it is delivered.

Using the Internet

1. To learn more about e-learning in Canada, read the report by the Conference Board of Canada, "E-Learning in Canada: Findings from 2003 E-Survey," at **www.conferenceboard.ca/Libraries/EDUC_ PUBLIC/TopLine_report.sflb**.
    Review the report and summarize the main findings and concerns facing Canadian organizations. Some of the things to consider include:

    a. What are the challenges to implementing e-learning?
    b. What are the benefits of e-learning?
    c. How should e-learning programs be evaluated?
    d. What is the future use of e-learning by Canadian organizations?

2. To find out about technology-based training in Canada, visit Industry Canada at **www.collectionscanada.gc.ca/ webarchives/20060201093632/http://strategis.ic.gc.ca/epic/internet/ incts-scf.nsf/en/h_sl00009e.html.**
    Read the following sections and summarize the main findings:

    a. What is the impact of learning technologies?
    b. Does e-learning help companies save money and improve productivity?
    c. How can you find out which learning technology is right for you?
    d. How can you assess the quality of e-learning products and services?
    e. Read the case studies and briefly summarize how each organization has used technology-based learning and the benefits and outcomes that resulted from it.

3. Industry Canada has created a website to help small- and medium-sized businesses learn about e-learning. To find out what information is available, go to: **www.ic.gc.ca/eic/site/direct.nsf/eng/h_uw00264.html.**
    Answer the following questions:

    a. What are some of the objectives of e-learning?
    b. What are the types of e-learning?
    c. What are the costs and benefits of e-learning?
    d. What are the main kinds of e-learning technologies?
    e. Describe the step-by-step approach to organize a successful e-learning program.
    f. Describe the criteria for selecting a course delivery format.
    g. What are some public and private e-learning product suppliers?

Exercises

In-Class

1. Describe the most recent classroom training program you attended in terms of the objectives, content, methods, and conditions of practice. Now think about how the program might be converted to a

computer-based training program. Describe what the program would be like and how you would design it. Do you think it would be more or less effective than the classroom training program?

2. Choose a class from a course you are currently taking and describe it in terms of the following design factors from Chapter 5:

   - What are the objectives?
   - What is the content?
   - What training methods are used?
   - What practice conditions are used?

   Now consider how the class might be designed and delivered as a computer-based course. Review your answers to each of the above design factors, and then convert them into a computer-based program. In other words, what would be the objectives, content, methods, and practice conditions?
   How effective do you think the course will be as a computer-based course? Compare and contrast it to the classroom course. What are the advantages and disadvantages for students, instructors, and the university or college? Which course would you prefer and why?

3. One of the concerns about technology-based training is the tendency to focus too much on the technology and not enough on learning and the conditions of practice. Refer back to Chapter 5 and the conditions of practice in Table 5.3. Describe how each of the conditions of practice can be included in the design of a computer-based training program.

4. After learning about computer-based training, you realize that your organization can benefit by converting some of its traditional classroom training programs to computer-based programs. Describe how you would proceed if you were to convert a particular training program (e.g., customer service, sales, negotiations, etc.) to a computer-based program. What would you have to do to convert the program, and how would you proceed?

5. You have just been hired by an organization to help convert some of its classroom training programs to computer-based programs. However, the company does not have a tradition of using computers in the workplace and there is likely to be a great deal of resistance from managers and employees. You have to meet with employees and managers to help them understand why computer-based training will be better for them and the organization than classroom training. Prepare a brief presentation of what you will tell the employees and managers and then present it to another student or the class.

In-the-Field

1. Contact the human resource department of an organization and ask them if you can conduct a brief interview with the training staff about their use of computer-based training. Some of the things you might consider include:

a. Do they use computers for training, and if so, what forms of computer-based training are they using and what are they using them for?

b. Why did they decide to use computers for training?

c. How effective has the use of computers been for training? How have they evaluated its effectiveness and what has the impact been on employees and the organization?

d. Do they plan to use computer-based training in the future, and if so, in what way, for what purposes, and for what reasons?

2. Contact the human resource department of an organization to find out if they have computer-based training programs. Once you have found an organization that has developed a computer-based program, find out how they designed the program and how effective it is. Some of the things to consider include:

a. What are the training objectives?

b. What is the training content?

c. Who are the trainees?

d. How has the program been designed and does it include interactive elements?

e. Does the program include active practice and conditions of practice, and if so, how have they been incorporated into the program?

f. How effective has the program been and how does it compare to traditional classroom training? How have trainees reacted to it?

3. Contact the human resource department of an organization to find out if they are using any Web 2.0 tools for learning. Once you have found an organization that is using Web 2.0 tools, find out what tools they are using and what they are using them for. Some of the things to consider include:

a. What Web 2.0 tools are being used?

b. What are the tools being used for and who is using them?

c. How have employees reacted to the use of Web 2.0?

d. How effective has Web 2.0 been for learning?

e. What are some of the benefits and limitations of using Web 2.0 for learning?

Case Incident

SKU at Nike

One of the biggest problems facing retailers is turnover where retention is very low in certain retail businesses and turnover is 100 percent. This makes training a real challenge. At Nike, for example, every few months an employee leaves and another starts and so does the training process. As a result, training new staff in a classroom setting is not cost-effective. So Nike decided to design an online training program that the company could offer to employees in its own stores as well as at other retailers that sell its products. The program would have to convey a lot of information quickly but also be easy to digest.

The solution was a program called Sports Knowledge Underground or SKU. The layout for the program resembles a subway map with different stations representing different training themes. For example, Apparel Union Station branches off into the apparel technologies line, the running products line, and the Nike Pro products line. The Cleated Footwear Station offers paths to football, whereas the Central Station offers broad lines like customer skills. Each segment is three to seven minutes long and gives the employee the basic knowledge he/she needs about various products.

Questions

1. How effective do you think Nike's SKU e-learning program will be for employee learning? Do you think it will reduce turnover?
2. How should the SKU program be designed to be most effective for learning and retention? Should other retailers design similar e-learning programs?

Source: Marquez, J. (2005, August). Faced with high turnover, retailers boot up e-learning for quick training. *Workforce Management, 84 (8)*, 74–75.

Case Study

E-learning at Flotation Ltd.

Jenny Stoppard was excited about her new position as Vice President of Human Resources at Flotation Ltd., a manufacturer of life jackets and other flotation devices. However, she knew she had her work cut out for her.

The president of the company had clearly stated that one of her first tasks was to take a close look at the training function. Although Flotation Ltd. had a reputation as a company with a well-trained workforce, the president now wanted to see some hard evidence to back up the company's training investment. The president wanted to increase productivity per person by 50 percent over the next three years, and Jenny was expected to spearhead the effort.

Sam was the company's veteran trainer, who was liked by everybody in the organization. For 20 years he had been training employees at Flotation Ltd. He was only three years away from retirement and was not likely to respond favourably to Jenny and her new mandate.

The president introduced Jenny to Sam as his new boss and the key player in the drive to increase the company's competitiveness. He also asked Sam to do everything in his power to cooperate with her.

Jenny not only had to revamp the training function, but she also had to deal with Sam, who was pretty much set in his ways. How was she going to achieve the president's goals and at the same time get Sam on board?

After thinking about her situation for several days, Jenny came across an article on e-learning and how it has saved some companies millions of dollars a year in training costs. Suddenly, she had an idea.

"Why not convert some of Sam's training courses to e-learning programs on the company's website?" she thought to herself. "This would certainly be a whole new approach and I could save the company money and get Sam involved since he would be responsible for preparing his course material for the program. Surely Sam would be excited to know that his training courses would continue even after he has retired."

Both the president and Sam were very excited about the potential of e-learning at Flotation Ltd. Jenny was given the go-ahead to begin designing the first course. Jenny and Sam decided that the first course would be Sam's sales training program, which was one of his best. It would also be useful for the company's sales staff, who would be able to do the program while they were on the road selling.

The first thing that Jenny did was to arrange for Sam to be videotaped delivering the course. Then she had Sam prepare some text material and additional information about some of the key learning points. With the help of the IT people, the video and text were placed on the company's website. The program was designed so that employees would watch the video of Sam and at certain points during the video they could click on an icon for more information. The video would then stop and the additional information would appear on the screen. After reading the material they could then return to the video.

When the program was set up and ready to go, the sales staff received a memo telling them about the company's first e-learning program and how to access it on the company's website. The memo was titled "Learn how to improve your sales skills on the road" and "Attend Sam's best training program any time and anywhere." Everybody was very excited about this new approach to training, and Sam was thrilled to know that he was the main attraction.

However, although the program was launched with much fanfare, the results were less than glowing. In fact, after the first six months very few of the sales staff had taken the course. Many said that they did not have time to take it. And of those who did, fewer than half actually completed it.

When asked about it, some of the sales staff said that it was not very interesting. Some said they would rather attend a live version of the course in the classroom and others said they didn't see what the advantage was of taking an e-learning course. Some thought it was just a big waste of the company's time and money.

The president asked to see Jenny to find out how things were going and if they were on track for achieving the company's productivity goals. Jenny did not know what she would tell him. Sam tried to console her by telling her that it had only been six months and the sales staff just needed a little more time to get used to e-learning. Jenny wasn't so sure. She began to wonder if the e-learning strategy was a big mistake.

Questions

1. Do you think that e-learning was a good idea for Flotation Ltd.? Could e-learning help the company realize the president's productivity goals?

2. Comment on the e-learning program that Jenny and Sam designed. What are the indicators that suggest it has not been a success? Is it possible there are other indicators that might suggest it is more effective than it appears?

3. Comment on how the program was designed and the use of learning principles and the conditions of practice. Do you think the program could be redesigned to make it more effective, and if so how would you proceed?

4. If you were Jenny, what would you tell the president and what would you do about e-learning at Flotation Ltd.? Should Jenny give up on e-learning, or wait another six months before making a decision?

5. What do you think are the main reasons for the negative reaction to the e-learning program? What are the most important things that need to be changed to improve the program?

References

1. Lea, D. (2007, October 26). United Way gives non-profit groups an e-learning boost. *The Oakville Beaver*, 11; Anonymous (2008, November 7). E-learning on the map. *The Oakville Beaver*, www.oakvillebeaver.com/printarticle/218045; Ferenc, L. (2008, November 12). United Way helps itself with training program; Staff receive affordable new online education. *Toronto Star*, A19; Anonymous (2007, October 12). United Way agencies serve one in five people in Oakville. *The Oakville Beaver*, www.oakvillebeaver.com/printarticle/128149; Blackburn, A. (2008, September 10). United Way aims high for its hometown. *The Oakville Beaver*, www.oakvillebeaver.com/printarticle/204239; Anonymous (2008, October 3). United Way helps with more than just funding. *The Oakville Beaver*, www.oakvillebeaver.com/printarticle/210038; www.unitedway.ca; www.uwoakville.org.

2. Tomlinson, A. (2002, March 25). T & D spending up in U.S. as Canada lags behind. *Canadian HR Reporter, 15* (6), 1; Sitzmann, T., Kraiger, K., Stewart, D., & Wisher, R. (2006). The comparative effectiveness of web-based and classroom instruction: A meta-analysis. *Personnel Psychology, 59*, 623–664.

3. Hughes, P. D., & Grant, M. (2007). *Learning & development outlook 2007.* The Conference Board of Canada: Ottawa.

4. Anonymous. (2008, November/December). 2008 industry report: Gauges & drivers. *Training, 45* (9), 16–34.

5. Dolezalek, H. (2005, December). 2005 industry report. *Training, 42* (12), 14–28.

6. Dolezalek, H. (2005, December).

7. Brown, K. G., & Ford, J. K. (2002). Using computer technology in training: Building an infrastructure for active learning. In K. Kraiger (Ed.), *Creating, implementing, and managing effective training and development: State-of-the-art lessons for practice* (pp. 160–191). San Francisco, CA: Jossey-Bass.

8. Harris-Lalonde, S. (2001). *Training and development outlook.* The Conference Board of Canada: Ottawa.

9. Ray, R. (2001, May 25). Employers, employees embrace e-learning. *The Globe and Mail*, E2.

10. Anonymous. (2007, December 3). Hydro-Quebec takes training online. *Canadian HR Reporter, 20* (21), 28.

11. Brown, K. G., & Ford, J. K. (2002).

12. Welsh, L. T., Wanberg, C. R., Brown, K. G., & Simmering, M. J. (2003). E-learning: Emerging uses, empirical results and future directions. *International Journal of Training and Development, 7*, 245–258.

13. Welsh, L. T., Wanberg, C. R., Brown, K. G., & Simmering, M. J. (2003).

14. Welsh, L. T., Wanberg, C. R., Brown, K. G., & Simmering, M. J. (2003).

15. Raybould, B. (1990, November–December). Solving human performance problems with computers—A case study: Building an electronic performance support system. *Performance and Instruction*, 4–14.

16. Smith, K. (1996, April). EPSS helps accounting firm reduce training time, improve productivity during transition to new service emphasis. *Lakewood Report on Technology for Learning*, 8.

17. Kulig, P. (1998, March 23). When training meets performance support. *Canadian HR Reporter, 11* (6), 17–18.

18. Gebber, B. (1991). Help! The rise of performance support systems. *Training, 28* (12), 23–29; Ruyle, K. (1991, February/March). Developing intelligent job aids. *Technical and Skills Training*, 9–14.

19. Weinstein, M. (2006, October). On demand is in demand. *Training, 43* (10), 31–35.

20. Galt, V. (2003, January 22). Bank tunes in to TV training. *The Globe and Mail*, C1, C5.

21. Shankar, C. (2006, September 25). Rise in webinars among e-learning trends. *Canadian HR Reporter, 19* (16), 19, 21.

22. Anonymous (2008, September). What does it cost to host web conferences and webcasts? *T+D, 62* (9), 88.

23. DeRouin, R. E., Fritzsche, B. A., & Salas, E. (2005). E-learning in organizations. *Journal of Management, 31*, 920–940.

24. Anonymous. (2005, December 12). Simulation games score with trainees. *Workforce Management, 84* (15), 70.

25. Bowness, A. (2004, September 27). Hands-on learning through computer simulations. *Canadian HR Reporter, 17* (16), 15.

26. Galt, V. (2004, June 12). Employers jumping on e-learning bandwagon. *The Globe and Mail*, B10.

27. DeRouin, R. E., Fritzsche, B. A., & Salas, E. (2005).

28. DeRouin, R. E., Fritzsche, B. A., & Salas, E. (2005).

29. DeRouin, R. E., Fritzsche, B. A., & Salas, E. (2005).

30. Sitzmann, T., Kraiger, K., Stewart, D., & Wisher, R. (2006).

31. Sitzmann, T., Kraiger, K., Stewart, D., & Wisher, R. (2006).

32. Sitzmann, T., Kraiger, K., Stewart, D., & Wisher, R. (2006).

33. Galt, V. (2004, June 12).

34. Brown, K. G., & Ford, J. K. (2002).

35. Welsh, L. T., Wanberg, C. R., Brown, K. G., & Simmering, M. J. (2003).

36. O'Keefe, B. (1991, September/October). Adopting multimedia on a global scale. *Instruction Delivery Systems*, 6–11.

37. Miles, K. W., & Griffith, E. R. (1993, April/May). Developing an hour of CBT: The quick and dirty method. *CBT Directions*, 28–33.

38. Eure, R. (2001, March 21). Companies embrace e-training. *The Globe and Mail*, B16.

39. Welsh, L. T., Wanberg, C. R., Brown, K. G., & Simmering, M. J. (2003).

40. Sitzmann, T., Kraiger, K., Stewart, D., & Wisher, R. (2006).

41. Sitzmann, T., Kraiger, K., Stewart, D., & Wisher, R. (2006).

42. Welsh, L. T., Wanberg, C. R., Brown, K. G., & Simmering, M. J. (2003).

43. Welsh, L. T., Wanberg, C. R., Brown, K. G., & Simmering, M. J. (2003).

44. Welsh, L. T., Wanberg, C. R., Brown, K. G., & Simmering, M. J. (2003).

45. Kraiger, K. (2008). Transforming our models of learning and development: Web-based instruction as enabler of third-generation instruction. *Industrial and Organizational Psychology, 1*, 454–467.

46. Jarche, H. (2008, April). Skills 2.0. *T+D, 62* (4), 22–24.

47. Jarche, H. (2008, April).

48. Shankar, C. (2006, September 25).

49. Shankar, C. (2006, September 25); Anonymous (2006, April). Podcast popularity grows. *Training, 43* (4), 14.

50. Ally, M. (2008, February 11). Learn anywhere, anytime. *Canadian HR Reporter, 21* (3), 18.

51. Fister Gale, S. (2008, May). Dial M for mobile learning. *Workforce Management Online* (www.workforce.com).

52. Hughes, P. D., & Grant, M. (2007); Anonymous (2008, November/December).

53. Eure, R. (2001, March 21).

CHAPTER 9

Training Delivery

Chapter Learning Outcomes

After reading this chapter, you should be able to:

- describe a lesson plan and the information to include in one
- describe the characteristics of an effective trainer
- describe how to decide who should attend a training program
- describe what makes an effective training site
- describe the elements of a positive learning climate
- discuss Gagné's nine events of instruction
- discuss some of the problems and solutions of training delivery

STARBUCKS

Starbucks takes coffee very seriously. In fact, they have a boot camp for store development partners called Store Development Boot Camp. Since 1997, store development partners have been attending the training program, which is a required one-week course on the process and participants involved in developing a new Starbucks store.

Each session takes place at the company's headquarters in Seattle and is attended by 15 to 20 participants, most of whom are store development partners along with some others from operation areas. They listen to subject-matter experts make presentations from various departments on how IT systems support development, how the real estate team selects store sites, how construction budgets are created, how to make purchasing decisions about materials, equipment, and furniture, and how designers lay out a new store. Participants also learn how the store development finance team contributes, and how store development fits in with recycling and other corporate social responsibility issues.

In addition to presentations, the program also involves games and learning activities to help participants review what they have learned such as coffee tasting, a tour of downtown Seattle stores, and a social evening at the end of the program with presenters and other operations partners.

It has been estimated that between 750 and 1100 participants have gone through the program, which usually takes place quarterly but due to demand may eventually become a monthly event. The program has also changed over the years and has been adjusted and modified to reflect new aspects of the business.

Store development partners usually attend boot camp between three and six months after their start date, although this might be changed to about 90 days after starting based on participants' feedback that it is harder for them to get away the longer they are in the position.[1]

In the previous four chapters, we described how to design training programs and the different methods of training. However, as you can tell from the Starbucks Boot Camp training program there are other important aspects of a training program, such as deciding on the trainer and trainees, scheduling the training program, and choosing the location of the training. In this chapter, we focus on issues that have to do with the delivery of training programs.

Table 9.1 lists the main activities associated with training delivery that are described in this chapter.

The Lesson Plan

Once a training program has been designed, the trainer needs to prepare a lesson plan. The **lesson plan** is the blueprint that outlines the training program in terms of the sequence of activities that will take place. As such, it is a guide for the trainer that provides a step-by-step breakdown for conducting a training program. A lesson plan should be prepared for each lesson in a program. A **lesson** is a cohesive unit of instruction with a specific learning objective.[2]

A good lesson plan should be prepared in advance of a training program and be detailed enough that any trainer could use it to guide him/herself through the program. Most of what will be required to deliver a training program will be indicated in the lesson plan. Although there is no one best format for lesson plans, a good rule of thumb is to focus on what the trainee will be doing.[3] A lesson plan should reflect the interaction of content, sequence, trainer, trainee, and the norms of the organization.[4]

Some of the things that should be listed on the first page or cover of a lesson plan are the training objectives, the trainees, trainer, time allocation, location, classroom requirements and seating, training materials and equipment, and supplies and handouts.[5] The detailed lesson plan for each lesson should indicate the activities that will occur during the lesson as well as what the trainer and trainees will be doing and when they will be doing it.

An important consideration in the development of a lesson plan is the sequencing or ordering of the content for a training program. Clearly, there is no one best way to order the training content as it will depend on the nature of the content and the trainees. However, there are a number of general

Lesson plan

The blueprint that outlines the training program in terms of the sequence of activities that will take place

Lesson

A cohesive unit of instruction with a specific learning objective

TABLE 9.1

Training Delivery Activities

1. Develop a lesson plan.
2. Choose the trainer.
3. Decide on the trainees who should attend a training program.
4. Determine the training materials and equipment required.
5. Prepare the training site.
6. Schedule the training program.
7. Administer the training.
8. Implement the training program.

approaches for content sequencing that reflect the ease of learning, such as general to specific, easy to difficult, concrete to abstract, old to new, simple to complex, familiar to unknown, practical to theoretical, and present to future.[6] Beginning with simple and familiar is generally recommended because it builds trainee self-efficacy and allows trainees to see how their current level of knowledge and experience is relevant for the training. This also provides some comfort to trainees and lowers their anxiety about learning.

Table 9.2 presents the cover page of a lesson plan for a one-day training program on structured employment interviews. Table 9.3 presents the detailed

TABLE 9.2

Lesson Plan Cover Page

Organization:	Vandalais Department Stores
Department:	Human Resources
Program Title:	Structured Employment Interviews
Instructor(s):	Interview Training Consultant
Time Allocation:	1 day
Trainees:	All employees in the Human Resource Department
Where:	Vandalais Learning Centre

TRAINING OBJECTIVES

Employees will be able to conduct a structured behaviour description interview and correctly perform the seven key behaviours.

CLASSROOM REQUIREMENTS

Seating for 50 people that allows for high involvement.

TRAINING MATERIALS AND EQUIPMENT

DVD player and TV monitor; DVD: *How to Conduct a Structured Employment Interview*; computer and projector with screen; flipchart; paper; markers.

TRAINEE SUPPLIES

Pen and paper.

TRAINEE HANDOUTS

1. Course objectives and outline.
2. Article on structured employment interviews.
3. Article on behaviour description interviews.
4. List of the seven key behaviours for conducting a structured employment interview.
5. Copy of the behaviour description interview for the sales associate position with interview questions and scoring guide and instructions.
6. Role-play exercise.

TABLE 9.3

Structured Employment Interview Detailed Lesson Plan

OBJECTIVE

Employees will be able to conduct structured behaviour description employment interview and correctly perform the seven key behaviours.

Trainees: Members of the Human Resource Department.

Time: 9 a.m.–5 p.m.

COURSE OUTLINE

9:00–10:00	Introduction lecture on the problem of poor employee performance and high turnover and the use of structured and unstructured employment interviews for selection.
10:00–10:30	Show DVD of an unstructured employment interview followed by a discussion.
10:30–10:45	Break
10:45–11:15	Show DVD of a structured employment interview followed by a discussion.
11:15–12:00	Review the seven key behaviours of conducting a structured employment interview.
12:00–1:00	Lunch
1:00–2:00	Lecture on behaviour description interview questions and review of the interview questions and guide developed for sales associates.
2:00–2:30	Review of the seven key behaviours in conducting a structured employment interview.
2:30–2:45	Break
2:45–3:30	Role-play practice exercise: In groups of three, assign participants the roles of interviewer, interviewee, and observer. Review script for roles and instruct trainees to demonstrate the seven key behaviours of a structured interview using the sales associate behaviour description interview questions. Have observer provide feedback using feedback guidelines contained in the role-play exercise booklet and evaluate the interviewer's performance on the seven key behaviours using the evaluation form provided. Switch roles until each group member plays the role of the interviewer.
3:30–4:30	Regroup for discussion of role-play exercise. Discuss how it felt to be the interviewer and the interviewee, and get the observer's feedback and evaluation.
4:30–4:45	Review the seven key behaviours of the structured employment interview and the importance of using structured interviews and the behaviour description interview for hiring sales associates.
4:45–5:00	Closing. Review objectives and give pep talk about conducting structured employment interviews and using the behaviour description interview. Thank participants and hand out training certificates.

lesson plan for this program. As shown in Table 9.2, a detailed lesson plan should indicate what will happen and when as well as what the trainees and trainer will be doing. Note that if this training program lasted for more than one day there would be a detailed lesson plan for each day of the program.[7]

The development of a lesson plan is a critical phase in the design of a training program. It allows for the approval and the smooth operation of training activities. It also enables expenditures to be budgeted for and monitored. The development of a lesson plan sets the stage for the implementation of the training program and it is a signal to other members of the organization that training is to be conducted in a professional manner. In the following pages, we describe the main elements in the lesson plan in more detail. For some guidance on what to include in a lesson plan, see The Trainer's Notebook 9.1, "Guidelines for Developing a Lesson Plan."

The Trainer

The lesson plan cover sheet in Table 9.2 indicates that the trainer will be a consultant. But how do you decide who the trainer will be? At first, this might seem like a trivial question. After all, isn't this the job of the human resources department or the training staff? In some cases the answer is yes, but in many training situations the answer to this question depends on a number of factors.

First, it is important to realize the role of a good trainer. Regardless of how well a training program is designed, the success of a program rests in large part on the trainer. In other words, no matter how good the training program, if the trainer is ineffective the program will suffer.

The Trainer's Notebook 9.1

Guidelines for Developing a Lesson Plan

Use the following guidelines to develop a lesson plan.

1. Write the lesson objective (what the trainee will be able to do at the end of the lesson).
2. Determine the knowledge and skills the trainee must learn to accomplish the objective. This enables the developer to determine the subtopics of the lesson.
3. Put the subtopics of the lesson in a preliminary sequence in a way that is most meaningful to the trainee and enables the trainee to master the knowledge and skills.
4. Identify the content of the various subtopics of the lesson. Answer the question: What must the trainee know or be able to do for satisfactory performance of each lesson subtopic?
5. Select the instructional procedures appropriate to the learning of each lesson subtopic. Identify materials and equipment needed.
6. Review the instructional sequence. Adjust as necessary to provide variety and movement for the trainees.
7. Provide a means of monitoring and trainee feedback.
8. Prepare a test to evaluate the degree to which trainees have achieved the learning objective of the lesson.

Source: Carnevale, A. P., Gainer, L. J., & Meltzer, A. S. (1990). *Workplace basics training manual.* San Francisco, CA: Jossey-Bass Publishers.

What are the qualities of a good trainer? This question should be easy for students to answer if they consider the courses they have enjoyed and those that they found less memorable. One of the first things that might come to mind is the extent to which the instructor was knowledgeable about the course material, or what is known as a subject-matter expert.

A **subject-matter expert (SME)** is someone who is familiar with the knowledge, skills, and abilities required to perform a task or job and has subject-matter expertise. In Chapter 5 we noted the importance of subject-matter experts in determining the content of a training program. A trainer should also be an expert on the topic or content area being taught. Not only will trainees learn more, but the trainer will be perceived as more credible.

Very often persons who conduct training in an organization do so because they have expertise in a particular area. At Starbucks' Store Development Boot Camp, subject-matter experts from various departments give presentations. However, it can be difficult to find subject-matter experts in an organization who are willing to become trainers. To find out how one organization does this, see Training Today 9.1, "Finding Subject-Matter Experts (SMEs)."

An effective trainer must also have the ability to make the material interesting. Students probably have had instructors who knew the material and were able to deliver it, but all the same, they did not make it very interesting. A good trainer should be enthusiastic and excited about the training material and capable of motivating and arousing the interest of trainees.

Subject-matter expert (SME)

A person who is familiar with the knowledge, skills, and abilities required to perform a task or job

---

Training Today 9.1

Finding Subject-Matter Experts (SMEs)

Export Development Canada (EDC) is a Crown corporation wholly owned by the Government of Canada with headquarters in Ottawa. They specialize in global financing, insurance, and bonding and are a recognized leader in financial reporting and economic analysis. EDC has been named as one of Canada's Top 100 Employers for eight consecutive years.

Because the industry in which it operates is heavily regulated, the learning and development team has the good fortune of knowing, at the beginning of each year, which courses it needs to update, develop, and deliver.

Armed with this information, the team meets with the director or vice president of each business unit and provides each leader with a detailed accounting of the company's course development, delivery, and SME needs. Each business unit director, in turn, is responsible for identifying those within his or her group that are either extremely knowledgeable SMEs or would benefit from delivering

or developing training as a professional developmental assignment.

There are many advantages of this approach. The fact that managers themselves handpick SMEs goes a long way toward demonstrating to SMEs that training is important to the organization, has management's buy-in, and deserves their time and attention. In addition, the fact that SME's managers enlist SMEs to help with training sends a strong message to SMEs that their managers support and encourage their SME efforts, and won't penalize them for performing training-related work that isn't directly associated with their regular day job.

Of course, the greatest advantage is that EDC has 120-plus internal SMEs that it utilizes each year to develop and deliver courses.

Sources: Boehle, S. (2007, April). Subject matter expert trouble? *Training, 44* (4), 28–30; www.edc.ca.

One way for trainers to generate interest and increase trainee motivation is by being expressive during the delivery of a training program. Expressive trainers are more physically animated (e.g., posture, gesturing, eye contact) and use linguistic devices such as an enthusiastic voice as opposed to a monotone voice, and vocal fluency rather than speaking with hesitancies (e.g., "ums"). Research has found that trainees recall a greater amount of the training content when a trainer is more expressive. There is also evidence that a trainer's expressiveness enhances trainees' training motivation and self-efficacy.[8]

In addition to being expressive, a good trainer is also engaging. In other words, a good trainer is able to draw trainees into the training program and keep them interested, focused, and involved in learning. No doubt, you can think of course instructors you have had who either put you to sleep or kept you on the edge of your seat as you were absorbed in what was being taught. When a trainer is engaging, trainees are more likely to be motivated to learn, attentive, and absorbed in the learning process.

Train-the-Trainer

One of the difficulties of finding a good trainer is that individuals who are skilled trainers often do not have the subject-matter expertise to deliver a training program in their organization. On the other hand, individuals who have subject-matter expertise often are not experienced trainers.

Students know, perhaps all too well, that no matter how well informed or knowledgeable an instructor might be, a course can still be poor if the instructor is not effective in delivering the material. In addition to subject-matter expertise, good trainers must also have good verbal and communication skills, interpersonal skills, and organizing and planning skills. The trainer must be able to deliver the training material in a manner that is understandable to trainees. Trainees are more likely to learn and recall training content when the trainer is well organized and easy to follow.[9]

Train-the-trainer

Training programs that teach subject-matter experts how to design and deliver training programs

One solution to this problem is to teach subject-matter experts how to be effective trainers. These programs are known as train-the-trainer and focus on the skills that are required to be an effective trainer. **Train-the-trainer** refers to training programs that teach subject-matter experts how to design and deliver training programs. With the increasing use of technology in the workplace, more subject-matter experts are being asked to become trainers and attend train-the-trainer programs. To learn more about train-the-trainer programs, see The Trainer's Notebook 9.2, "Train-the-Trainer Fundamentals."

The Trainees

The lesson plan cover page indicates that the trainees will be members of the human resources department. This raises another question. Who should attend a training program? This is an important question because money and time can be wasted if the wrong people attend training. Performance problems are likely to continue if those who need training do not attend.

The Trainer's Notebook 9.2

Train-the-Trainer Fundamentals

Subject-matter experts (SMEs) often are asked to design and/or deliver a training program because of their unique knowledge, the needs of a particular group of training participants, or the requirements of a specific project. However, they may not have experience as a trainer and will require some training on how to be an effective trainer. Here are some things to consider when you need to train-the-trainer:

1. Explain the specific reasons for why the SME was selected for the role.
2. Review the training materials with the SME and make sure they are well scripted and marked up with plenty of visual cues for the trainer.
3. Coach the SME on facilitation skills and provide detailed information about the participants.
4. Give the SME permission to delegate tasks during the training (e.g., a volunteer for clicking through the slides).
5. Prepare the SME by providing a checklist of the basics of engaging facilitation, including setting up the room to meet the participants' needs, and establishing rapport with the participants by presenting a friendly demeanour and sharing stories. Incorporate tips such as using interactive activities. Review the checklist with the SME and explain the reasons behind each tip.
6. Discuss adult learners' needs and learning styles so that the SME understands how and why to vary the training activities to maximize learning. Help the SME think about charts, illustrations, and other visuals that would help participants understand the content. Make sure the SME understands the need to design interactive activities that appeal to visual, kinesthetic, and auditory learning styles.
7. Teach the SME how to facilitate a workshop accurately without reading from the leader's guide. Offer tips for remembering content such as creating note cards with key points.
8. Watch the SME conduct a practice session and provide feedback beginning with all the positive behaviours demonstrated and include one or two constructive comments that the SME can work on before the actual training program.
9. Offer assistance during the training with flipcharts or distributing materials.
10. Provide SMEs who must design their programs with PowerPoint templates, sample training materials, and examples they can build on.
11. Provide access to experienced instructional designers who can assist the SME when he/she has questions.
12. Provide the SME with access to a content reviewer to make sure everything is covered clearly and effectively for participants who are not experts.

Source: Adams, Trinée, Kennedy, A., & Marquart, M. (2008, March). The reluctant trainer. *T+D, 62* (3), 24–27. Copyright © March 2008. Reprinted with permission of American Society for Training & Development.

According to Donald Kirkpatrick, the following four decisions need to be made when selecting participants for a training program:[10]

1. Who can benefit from the training?
2. What programs are required by law or by government edict?
3. Should the training be voluntary or compulsory?
4. Should the participants be segregated by level in the organization, or should two or more levels be included in the same class?

Some employees stand to benefit from a training program given the tasks they perform and the extent to which the training will provide them with knowledge and skills that will help them improve their performance. Some training programs are required by law, such as health and safety programs for employees who work with hazardous materials. Other training programs, like the Starbucks Store Development Boot Camp, are compulsory for all employees in a particular job category or position.

According to Kirkpatrick, some programs should be compulsory. If a training program is voluntary then there will be some employees who need the training but will not attend. When the training is required for a group of employees the program should be compulsory, as is the case for store development partners at Starbucks.[11] However, what if an employee refuses to attend a compulsory training program? To learn more, see Training Today 9.2, "The Right to Train."

As for segregating participants by organizational level or including them in the same training session, this really depends on the culture of the organization and the rapport that exists between different levels in the organization. The main issue is whether employees will feel comfortable enough to speak and participate if their supervisors are present. If this is the case then it is often a good idea for different levels to attend a training program together.

Training Today 9.2

The Right to Train

If an employer orders an employee to attend a training program and the order is lawful and reasonable, the employer has a right to expect the order to be followed. But what if the employee refuses?

An employee's refusal to obey a reasonable order would constitute insubordination. However, it is important that the directive to train is unambiguous. Condoning the refusal to train, such as allowing an employee to work despite the refusal, could eliminate any consideration of insubordination.

An unreasonable training order would include one that endangers the health and safety of an employee or that is not within the reasonable scope of an employee's work. If an employee argues that he has sufficient work already and training on something new is not needed, it is important that the employer ensure the training is, in fact, necessary.

As well, an employee should be paid for training and not be penalized for the inability to complete existing assignments while undergoing training. To reduce the risk of a constructive dismissal claim, an employer should also avoid saddling an employee with an unreasonable amount of extra work as a result of introducing a new system.

When an employee refuses a lawful and reasonable order to train, discipline may be warranted. Progressive discipline for an employee who continues to refuse training could include warning letters, suspensions, and dismissal.

Although employers generally have a right to order training, unionized and non-unionized employers alike must ensure any order is lawful and reasonable. Employers must act reasonably when employees resist or refuse training. If an employee has a reasonable explanation to refuse training, an employer may be required to accommodate. Moreover, if an employee has a disability that would limit training or his use of a new system, an employer is required to accommodate to the point of undue hardship.

Source: Based on Na, G. (2008, October 6). An employer's right to train. *Canadian HR Reporter, 21* (17), 25, 32. Reprinted by permission of Carswell, a division of Thomson Canada Ltd.

Trainability Test

One way to determine if an employee is ready to attend a training program is to have him/her take a trainability test. A **trainability test** is a test that measures an individual's ability to learn and perform training tasks in order to predict whether an individual will successfully complete a training program.[12]

This is typically done by having individuals take a mini-course or learn a sample of the training that is representative of the content of a training program. They then take a test that measures their learning and performance of the tasks.

Trainability tests have been shown to be effective in predicting training success and job performance in many jobs such as carpentry, welding, dentistry, and forklift operating. Although they have most often been used for psychomotor skills, they are just as applicable for other types of skills and knowledge tests. These kinds of training pre-tests can also be used to determine what kind of remedial training an individual might require in order to prepare him/her for a training program or to tailor a training program to his/her needs. Thus, managers can maximize trainee learning by assessing employees' readiness to learn and trainability prior to training.[13]

Information on who requires training can be incorporated into a training plan. A **training plan** indicates who in an organization needs training (e.g., human resource staff), the type of training needed (e.g., structured employment interviewing), and how the training will be delivered (e.g., in a formal classroom).[14]

Training Materials and Equipment

All training programs require the use of training materials, supplies, and equipment, and this should be indicated on the lesson plan cover page. The content of a training program as well as the methods and exercises determine the materials, supplies, and equipment that will be required.

Materials refers to expendable items such as note pads, pens, markers, tape, and so on. Common supplies include computer equipment, a projector, and workbooks or manuals. Handouts such as course outlines that indicate the course objectives, the material to be covered, and a schedule of training activities, as well as articles and copies of the trainer's slides, are often required and will have to be prepared in advance. Equipment refers to things that have a life beyond a single use, such as projectors, computers, DVD player, and so on. The trainer must identify the materials and equipment that will be required for a training program.[15]

As shown in Table 9.2, the materials and equipment required for the structured employment interview training program include a TV monitor and DVD player, a DVD on how to conduct a structured employment interview, a computer and projector with screen, a flipchart, pen, paper, and markers. Handouts for trainees include a course outline, readings, a list of the key learning behaviours, and a role-play exercise.

Trainability test

A test that measures an individual's ability to learn and perform training tasks

Training plan

Indicates who in an organization needs training, the type of training that is needed, and how the training will be delivered

 9.1

With the determination of the materials and equipment necessary for training the cost of training and the budget is more easily determined, and the actual training session is more likely to run smoothly.

The Training Site

The training site is the facility or room where the training will take place. Off-the-job training can take place at the organization if rooms are available; at an organization's headquarters, such as Starbucks' Store Development Boot Camp; or at a rented facility such as a hotel or conference centre. As indicated in Table 9.2, the structured employment interview training program takes place at the company's learning centre.

Some organizations, like the Bank of Montreal, have their own learning centre for training and development. However, for organizations that do not have training facilities, space must be found and rented. In this case, an important concern will be the amount of travel time required for trainees to get to the training site and ensuring that trainees have transportation. If trainees have to stay overnight, plans for transportation, accommodation, and meals will have to be made and included in the training budget.

Whether the training takes place in an organization's facilities or in one that needs to be rented, a number of factors need to be considered to ensure the training program runs smoothly. First, the training site should be conducive to learning. This means that the training environment should be comfortable in terms of things like space, lighting, and temperature. This might seem like a trivial point, but have you ever attended a class and the room temperature was on the cold side? Or how about a classroom that was too crowded and you had to stand or sit on the floor because there was not enough seating? Chances are it caused you some discomfort and interfered with your learning.

Second, the training site should be free of noise or distractions that might interfere with or disrupt learning. How often have you been in a class where you had to strain to hear the instructor over the chatter coming from outside the classroom? Obviously, noise can interfere with learning. Distractions can also be a problem. This is one reason why it is sometimes preferable to conduct a training program away from the organization. Otherwise, trainees might be tempted to step out of the training session to check for messages or take care of business. This, of course, is not likely if they are far from their desk and the workplace.

Third, the training site should be set up in a manner that is appropriate for the training program. For example, if trainees will be viewing a DVD, will they be able to see the screen and hear the sound? If trainees will be required to work in groups, will there be sufficient room for them to move around the room and interact with group members? Are break-out rooms necessary for group work? Are the seats arranged in a way that will allow trainees to interact and work with each other, and will the trainer be able to interact with trainees? Are the chairs movable or fixed? These are important considerations that the trainer needs to determine before the training.

Given the importance of the training room for trainee motivation and learning, trainers should inspect and prepare the room in advance of a training program to ensure that it will be conducive for learning. The trainer should also arrive early on the day of the training to make sure that the room is properly set up and that the required equipment has arrived and is functioning. As discussed in the next section, one of the most important things that the trainer needs to prepare is the seating arrangement.

Seating Arrangement

The seating arrangement is especially important because it can facilitate or limit trainee involvement and participation; it can energize or inhibit trainees; and it also communicates the trainer's style.[16]

Figure 9.1 shows examples of different seating arrangements for low, moderate, and high levels of trainee involvement. The low involvement seating represents a traditional classroom arrangement in which the instructor is in control and stands or sits at the front of the room behind a desk or table. With this seating arrangement, communication is one-way and flows from the instructor to trainees. Communication among the trainees is not possible. This arrangement is most common for the lecture method.

When a moderate amount of involvement is desired, the instructor is still at the front of the room. However, trainees are seated around a table, thereby allowing them to interact and exchange ideas with each other. Although the instructor remains in control and one-way communication still dominates, participants can also communicate with and learn from each other.

Finally, with a high involvement seating arrangement, small groups of trainees are seated together in groups around small tables. As a result, group members can interact and work together on projects. The instructor's role is more of a resource person or facilitator. This allows the instructor to present

FIGURE 9.1

Seating Arrangements

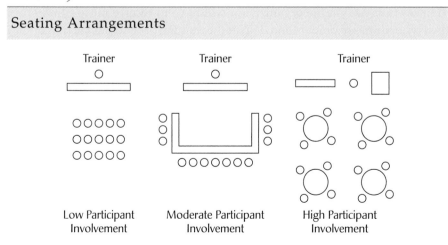

Low Participant Involvement | Moderate Participant Involvement | High Participant Involvement

Source: Eitington, J. E. (1989). *The Winning Trainer: Winning Ways to Involve People in Learning.* Houston, TX: Gulf Publishing Company. Reprinted with permission from Elsevier.

material to the class (the work table and flipchart are at the front of the room), engage the class in discussions, move around the room and listen in on groups, provide help and assistance, and spend time with each group while they work on projects and solve problems.[17]

The seating arrangement has important implications for the trainer and trainees and should be arranged in accordance with the objectives of a training program and the desired level of trainee involvement.

Scheduling the Training Program

As indicated in Table 9.2, the structured employment interview training program is scheduled as a one-day program. Scheduling a training program must take into consideration a number of factors. In effect, one has to arrange the training schedule to accommodate all of the participants.

For example, when is the best time for employees to attend a training program in terms of the day of the week, the time of day, and the time of year? When will the participants be available to attend training? This will probably depend on the organization and the nature of its business. Most businesses have periods or seasons when they are especially busy and scheduling a training program during these times is likely to result in some resistance and low attendance.

It is also important to be sensitive to the needs and desires of employees and their supervisors. Would it be preferable to hold the training during office hours or after hours, such as in the evenings or on the weekend? Employees and their supervisors should be consulted to determine the best time for them to attend a training program.[18] Recall that the store development partners at Starbucks attend Store Development Boot Camp between three and six months after their start date but this might need to be changed to 90 days because it is harder for them to get away the longer they have been on the job.

Another factor to consider is the availability of the trainer. Whether the trainers are from the human resource department or elsewhere in the organization, they will likely have responsibilities that will restrict their availability. Trainers from within the organization will have to receive release time from their other duties to prepare and deliver the training program. If the trainers are from outside the organization, they will also have some restrictions regarding their availability and will have to be contracted for a particular date.

A third consideration in scheduling a training program is the availability of the training site, equipment, materials, and so on. If the training site and facilities are frequently used a training program will have to be scheduled well in advance. In addition, if materials need to be designed or purchased, they must be prepared and available in time for the training program.

MAKE THE
CONNECTION

Finally, when scheduling a training program one must also consider whether it would be best to offer it all at one time, such as one day versus four two-hour sessions in the case of an eight-hour program, or all in one week versus one day each week for five weeks (or once a month for five months) in the case of a five-day program. Recall from Chapter 5 that this distinction refers to massed versus distributed practice. As indicated in Chapter 5, massed practice is practice with no rest periods, while distributed practice includes rest intervals. There are also issues of resources and logistics. Sometimes it is just not feasible to conduct a training program over a longer period of time.

Kirkpatrick recommends that it is best to spread the training out as an ongoing program, such as a three-hour session once a month.[19] The Store Development Boot Camp program at Starbucks takes place over the course of one week.

Training Administration

Once the lesson plan has been completed, a number of activities must be undertaken to effectively manage and administer a training program. **Training administration** involves the coordination of all the people and materials involved in a training program. The maintenance of trainee records, training histories, customized learning opportunities, schedules, and course and material inventories is a routine, but necessary, activity. In addition to tracking registrations for programs, it is also useful to track individual career development and learning plans. Software is available that can do all these things.

Employees and their supervisors have to be informed of training programs with respect to the objectives and content as well as where and when the training will take place. In addition, employees who are required to attend a training program must be notified and enrolled in the program. Trainers must also be informed as they need to know how many trainees will be attending a training program.

If trainees are to receive training materials prior to a program, then arrangements have to be made for this. In addition, all of the materials and equipment must be ordered and prepared in time for the training program. The training site must be booked and equipment must be made available. In some cases, this might involve renting equipment. As well, supplies such as pens and paper must be ordered.

Finally, the training administrator has to prepare a budget that includes the costs of all of the expenses incurred in the design and delivery of a training program. The calculation of the costs and benefits of training programs is discussed in Chapter 12.

Implementing the Training Program

Once the lesson plan has been prepared and the administrative activities have been completed, the training program is ready to be implemented. For many trainers and especially novices, this is actually the most difficult part of the training process. There are, however, a number of important steps to follow when implementing a training program. In this section, we describe how to create a climate for learning and Gagné's nine events of instruction.

Learning Climate

When implementing a training program, the trainer has to ensure that the training climate is conducive for learning. This means that trainees should feel relaxed, comfortable, and safe in the training environment. Creating a climate

RPC 9.2

Training administration
The coordination of all the people and materials involved in the training program

that is conducive for learning is a key factor for facilitating learning and it involves four elements: pre-arrival factors, greeting participants, the learning facility/environment, and the trainer's style and behaviour.[20]

Pre-Arrival Factors

Although trainees form perceptions of the learning climate during training, there are some things a trainer can do before their arrival that can create a positive learning climate. For example, contacting trainees before the training begins can help set a positive tone. This might just be a welcome message that describes the program and its objectives. However, it can also include information about the location, when the program starts and ends, meals, clothes to wear, what to bring, and so on. Pre-arrival activities might include pre-work readings or assignments, a pre-session get-together (to hand out materials or perhaps for a cocktail party or dinner), or an attempt to find out about trainees' needs, ideas, and input for the program.

Greeting Participants

While the tone of the climate can be set before participants arrive, even more important are the perceptions trainees form once they arrive for training. Trainees might be anxious about the training and some will be skeptical about its value. Others will be upset that they are spending time away from work. Therefore, the trainer should meet and greet participants and make them feel welcome when they arrive for training. A nice touch is to have a welcome message posted on the board or a flipchart in the room. Some trainers like to have trainees write their name on a name card to get them doing something simple when they arrive rather than sitting alone and waiting for the program to start. An early-morning welcome session with coffee and refreshments can facilitate interactions among trainees and create a relaxed and comfortable atmosphere.

Learning Facility/Environment

A major factor in trainees' climate perceptions is the training site itself. In this regard, the trainer should ensure that the physical set-up of the training room is attractive, comfortable, bright, relaxing, and clean. Some of the things that the trainer needs to pay attention to include lighting, noise, space, and room temperature, as discussed earlier. Making sure that drinks, refreshments, and lunch arrive on time is also important for creating a positive training climate.

Trainer's Style and Behaviour

Trainees' perceptions of the learning climate will also be based on how the trainer interacts with trainees and conducts the training. If the trainees do not know the trainer, then one of the first things trainers should do is to provide a brief personal introduction about themselves and their involvement in the training program. The trainer should let trainees know how they can address him/her (e.g., first name is fine) and should address trainees by their first name. The trainer should circulate throughout the room during training and at times be seated rather than standing at the front of the room throughout the session. It is also a good idea to take advantage of opportunities to interact with trainees. This can be achieved by mingling with trainees during breaks and joining them at lunch and other meals.

Finally, key to creating a positive learning climate is the style of the trainer. A trainer can create a positive climate by listening with empathy, accepting different ideas, showing sensitivity to the communication process, supporting people who take risks, providing a fun-type atmosphere, stressing opportunities for discovery, making learning gradual, asking for feedback, and making him/herself accessible for questioning.[21]

In summary, creating a positive climate that is conducive for learning is a critical factor in the successful implementation of a training program. Also important is how the trainer actually conducts the training, our next topic.

Gagné's Nine Events of Instruction

Once a positive learning climate has been created, the trainer can begin to conduct the training. According to Robert Gagné, a training program should have nine events of instruction. Following is a brief description of his nine events of instruction. Something you might notice is that some of the design principles discussed in previous chapters are incorporated in the events of instruction.

Table 9.4 lists Gagné's nine events of instruction along with the relevant training design principles.[22]

Gain Attention

The first thing a trainer needs to do is to draw trainees into the learning process. In other words, get the attention of trainees (recall the earlier discussion of trainee engagement). This can be achieved in a number of ways. For example, the trainer might present a thought-provoking problem. For the structured employment interview training program, the trainer might ask trainees, "What should we do to ensure that we hire great employees?" Other questions might focus trainees on the problem at hand and the need for training, such as, "How do you conduct a valid employment interview?" Or the trainer might point out that bad hiring is costing the organization thousands of dollars. Having the CEO make an impassioned plea on the importance of the training program can also get the attention of trainees. Getting trainees interested and motivated is an important way to begin a training program. Trainees should know why the training program is important for them and the organization.

Describe the Objectives

In Chapter 5, we discussed the purpose of objectives for trainees, trainers, and managers (refer to Table 5.2). However, objectives are important for trainees only if they have been informed of them. Therefore, the trainer must communicate to trainees what they will learn in a training program, what to expect,

MAKE THE
CONNECTION

TABLE 9.4

Gagné's Nine Events of Instruction and Training Design Principles

Gagné's nine events of instruction reflect important principles of training design discussed in previous chapters.

1. *Gain attention.* Reflects adult learners' need to know why they are learning something and their training motivation.
2. *Describe the objectives.* Reflects adult learners' need to know how the learning relates to their job and the importance of goals as indicated in goal-setting theory.
3. *Stimulate recall of prior knowledge.* Reflects adult learners' existing knowledge and experience and how that can be linked to the training material. Providing a framework for learning is similar to an advance organizer.
4. *Present the material to be learned.* Reflects task sequencing as well as incorporating adult learners' job-relevant experiences into the training content.
5. *Provide guidance for learning.* Reflects the use of metacognitive strategies, attentional advice, and advance organizers.
6. *Elicit performance practice.* Reflects the importance of active practice and experiential training methods (e.g., role plays, games, simulations).
7. *Provide informative feedback.* Reflects the importance of feedback and knowledge of results during training.
8. *Assess performance.* Reflects the importance of linking training objectives to trainee learning and ensuring that the objectives are being met as well as the stages of learning.
9. *Enhance retention and transfer.* Reflects generalization from conditioning theory and self-regulation and self-efficacy from social cognitive theory.

and what they will be able to accomplish at the end of the program. Trainees should understand what they will learn and how they will be able to use it on the job. The trainer might even provide a demonstration of the desired performance to help trainees form a mental picture of the skill to be performed. This will help trainees begin to focus on what they will need to learn and do after training and think about goals for learning.

Stimulate Recall of Prior Knowledge

MAKE THE
CONNECTION

The trainer should discuss what trainees already know that is relevant to the training material (facts, rules, procedures, or skills). It is important to show trainees that they know some things that are related to what they will learn in training. This enables trainees to think about what they know and can do that is related to what they will learn in the training program. You might recall from the discussion of andragogy and adult learning theory in Chapter 3 that adults have a great deal of knowledge and work-related experience that the trainer should ask about and incorporate into the training.

The trainer might also provide a framework to help trainees learn and retain the training material. By providing a solid grounding, trainees will feel more confident about their ability to learn. For example, trainees in the structured employment interview training program might begin to think about what they have already learned about hiring and interviewing and how they currently conduct employment interviews.

Present the Material to Be Learned

The organization and presentation of the training material should be done in a logical and consistent manner. As discussed in Chapter 5, this involves teaching the material in a logical sequence or one sub-task at a time (i.e., task sequencing). The trainer can ensure learning and understanding by asking questions at various points or junctures during the training and by asking trainees to provide examples from their own work experience. For the structured employment interview training, the trainer might present each of the seven key behaviours in a logical order and ask trainees how they perform the behaviours when conducting employment interviews (e.g., how have you decided what questions to ask job candidates?).

Provide Guidance for Learning

The trainer should provide trainees with guidance and direction on how best to learn the material. This can be done by providing trainees with relevant examples that demonstrate what they need to learn and ask questions to help them generate ideas and solutions. The combination of examples, questions, and discussion should help to guide trainees toward the main learning points.

Elicit Performance Practice

Trainees should be given the opportunity to practise and apply the training material. You might recall from Chapter 5 that providing trainees with opportunities to practise performing a training task or using knowledge during training is called active practice. Trainers should provide sufficient time for trainees to do something with the information they have received during training. In a training program on the employment interview, trainees would have the opportunity to practise conducting an interview. If they have been taught seven key learning points, they would practise them in a mock interview during training.

Provide Informative Feedback

Trainees should receive feedback on their performance during training. Recall the discussion of feedback and knowledge of results in Chapter 5, where we described the importance of feedback as a condition of practice during training. It is essential that trainees know and understand what they did correct, what they did wrong, and how to correct what they did wrong to improve their performance. Trainees should leave training with an understanding of what they can do well and what they need to improve.

Assess Performance

It is important to test trainees on their learning during and after a training program. Ideally, learning should be assessed after each topic is completed. The assessment of learning can be either declarative (recall the discussion in Chapter 3 on the stages of learning), in which case trainees are simply asked to recall information, or it can involve knowledge compilation or procedural knowledge, in which case trainees have to explain how they would do something or to display the learned behaviour in a role play or behavioural demonstration. The assessment of performance can involve a formal test or it might simply involve an informal question-and-answer session. The main issue is to ensure that trainees have learned the material before moving on to new topics.

Enhance Retention and Transfer

Trainees need to know how their learning can be used and applied on the job. Therefore, it is important that trainers discuss how the training material can be applied on the job and in actual work situations. The trainer might show trainees how the material they are learning applies to actual situations that they will encounter at work. Asking trainees to describe situations in which they will be able use the training content in their job can also enhance retention and transfer. More detail about transfer of training and what a trainer can do to facilitate it is described in Chapter 10.

Closing a Training Program

Once a training program has ended, the trainer must close the program. Like the rest of the program, the closing should be well planned and include a closing activity that signals the successful completion of the program. Some kind of event or form of recognition is common such as a ceremony in which certificates are awarded to trainees who have completed the program. Recall that the Starbucks Store Development Boot Camp program ended with a social evening with presenters and other operations partners. The lasting impression following the closing should be that the next step is a change in behaviour and performance.[23]

Training Delivery Problems

Although Gagné's nine events of instruction might seem straightforward, there are many potential problems that trainers might experience during a training program. One of the most common problems is the uncooperative and difficult trainee. While most trainees are cooperative, some can make it difficult for a trainer to deliver a training program by talking too much, putting others down, complaining, displaying negative or hostile behaviour, or just being plain irritating.

Table 9.5 lists some of the types of problem participants. Dealing with problem participants requires patience and avoiding arguments and put downs. In most cases, it is best to deal with them in a polite fashion and, if possible, let the group decide how to manage them.[24]

TABLE 9.5

Types of Problem Participants

Some of the most common types of problem participants in training include the following:

1. *The hesitant one.* Shy, reluctant, and silent most of the time.
2. *The monopolizer.* The "big talker" who will use up all of the available air time if permitted.
3. *The voice of experience.* Has a strong need to be heard and to bring in incidents and anecdotes that are tedious and unnecessary.
4. *The arguer.* Constantly looks for opportunities to disagree, to show up the other participants and the trainer.
5. *The non-listener.* Tends to interrupt, cuts others off, leaps in before others have had their say, and does not listen to others.
6. *The idea zapper.* Puts down other participants' ideas and anything new or different.
7. *The complainer.* A problem magnifier who finds the world unfair and is a specialist in blaming and fault-finding.
8. *The rigid one.* Staunchly takes a position on an issue and will rarely, if at all, move from it.
9. *The hostile one.* Presents highly hostile questions that are designed to embarrass or inflame the trainer.
10. *The angry one.* Will find loopholes in your ideas and present impossible "what-if" scenarios.
11. *The negative one.* Finds the gloomy side of things and will dredge up gripes, past grievances, and cantankerous complaints.
12. *The clown.* Has an abundance of ill-fitting and sometimes irritating and annoying humour.
13. *The show-off.* Likes to parade his/her knowledge before everyone.
14. *The tangent-taker.* Has interesting inputs but they do not relate to the topic.

Source: Based on Eitington, J. E. (1989). *The Winning Trainer: Winning Ways to Involve People in Learning.* Houston, TX: Gulf Publishing Company. Reprinted with permission from Elsevier.

To learn about the various types of problems that a trainer might encounter, Richard Swanson and Sandra Falkman conducted a study in which they asked novice trainers about the problems they have had when delivering a training program. After content-analyzing the responses, the authors identified the following 12 common training delivery problems:[25]

1. *Fear.* Fear that is due to a lack of confidence and a feeling of anxiousness while delivering the training program.
2. *Credibility.* The perception that they lack credibility in the eyes of the trainees as subject-matter experts.
3. *Personal experiences.* A lack of stories about personal experiences that can be used to relate to the training content.
4. *Difficult learners.* Don't know how to handle problem trainees who may be angry, passive, or dominating.
5. *Participation.* Difficulty getting trainees to participate.
6. *Timing.* Trouble with the timing and pacing of the training material and worries about having too much or too little material.

7. *Adjusting instruction.* Difficulty adjusting the training material to the needs of trainees or being able to redesign the presentation of material during delivery.
8. *Questions.* Difficulty using questions effectively and responding to difficult questions.
9. *Feedback.* Unable to read trainees and to use feedback and evaluations effectively.
10. *Media, materials, facilities.* Concerns about how to use media and training materials.
11. *Opening, closing techniques.* The need for techniques to use as ice-breakers, introductions, and effective summaries and closings.
12. *Dependence on notes.* Feeling too dependent on notes and having trouble presenting the material without them.

These 12 common delivery problems of novice trainers have three basic themes: 1. Problems pertaining to the trainer, 2. Problems pertaining to how the trainer relates to the trainees, and 3. Problems pertaining to presentation techniques. The authors also asked expert trainers for strategies and solutions for dealing with the 12 delivery problems. For example, to deal with the problem of fear, a trainer should be well prepared, use ice-breakers, begin with an activity that relaxes the trainees and gets them talking and involved, and acknowledge his/her own fear, understanding that it is normal.[26] See The Trainer's Notebook 9.3, "Solutions to Training Delivery Problems," for solutions to all 12 delivery problems.

The Trainer's Notebook 9.3

Solutions to Training Delivery Problems

1. Fear.

A. Be well prepared and have a detailed lesson plan.
B. Use ice-breakers and begin with an activity that relaxes trainees.
C. Acknowledge the fear and use self-talk and relaxation exercises prior to the training.

2. Credibility.

A. Don't apologize. Be honest about your knowledge of the subject.
B. Have the attitude of an expert and be well prepared and organized.
C. Share personal background and talk about your area of expertise and experiences.

3. Personal experiences.

A. Relate personal experiences.
B. Report experiences of others and have trainees share their experiences.
C. Use analogies, refer to movies or famous people who relate to the subject.

4. Difficult learners.

A. Confront the problem learner and talk to them to determine the problem.
B. Circumvent dominating behaviour by using nonverbal behaviour such as breaking eye contact or standing with your back to the person.
C. Use small groups to overcome timid behaviour and structure exercises where a wide range of participation is encouraged.

(Continued)

5. Participation.

A. Ask open-ended questions and provide positive feedback when trainees participate.
B. Plan small-group activities such as dyads, case studies, and role plays to increase participation.
C. Invite participation by structuring activities to allow trainees to share early in the program.

6. Timing.

A. Plan for too much material and prioritize activities so that some can be omitted if necessary.
B. Practise presenting the material many times so that you know where you should be at 15-minute intervals.

7. Adjusting instruction.

A. Determine the needs of the group early in the training and structure activities based on them.
B. Request feedback by asking trainees how they feel about the training during breaks or periodically during the training.
C. Redesign the program during breaks and have a contingency plan in place.

8. Questions.

Answering questions

A. Anticipate questions by writing out key questions that trainees might have.
B. Paraphrase and repeat a question so everyone hears the question and understands it.
C. Redirect questions you can't answer back to the trainees and try to find answers during the break.

Asking questions

A. Ask concise and simple questions and provide enough time for trainees to answer.

9. Feedback.

A. Solicit informal feedback during training or breaks on whether the training is meeting their needs and expectations and watch for nonverbal cues.
B. Do summative evaluations at the conclusion of the training to determine if the objectives and needs of trainees have been met.

10. Media, materials, facilities.

Media

A. Know how to operate every piece of equipment you will use.
B. Have back-ups such as extra bulbs, extension cords, markers, tape, and so on, as well as bringing the material in another medium in case one has problems.
C. Enlist assistance from trainees if you have a problem and need help.

Materials

A. Be prepared and have all the material placed at trainees' workplace or ready for distribution.

Facilities

A. Visit facility beforehand to see the layout of the room and where things are located and how to set up.
B. Arrive at least one hour early to set up and handle any problems.

11. Opening, closing techniques.

Openings

A. Develop a file of ideas based on experimentation and observation.
B. Develop and memorize a great opening.
C. Relax trainees by greeting them when they enter, taking time for introductions, and creating a relaxed atmosphere.

Closings

A. Provide a simple and concise summary of the course contents using objectives or the initial model.
B. Thank participants for their time and contribution to the course.

12. Dependence on notes.

A. Notes are necessary.
B. Use cards with an outline or key words as prompts.
C. Use visuals such as notes on the frames of transparencies or your copy of the handouts.
D. Practise and learn the script so you can deliver it from the key words on your note cards.

Source: Swanson, R. A., & Falkman, S. K. (1997). Training delivery problems and solutions: Identification of novice trainer problems and expert trainer solutions. *Human Resource Development Quarterly, 8*, 305–314. © 1997 by Jossey-Bass Inc. Reprinted with permission of John Wiley & Sons, Inc.

Summary

This chapter described the steps involved in delivering a training program. We began with a discussion of the lesson plan, which should describe how a training program will be implemented. This was followed by a description of the characteristics of effective trainers and how to determine who should attend a training program. We also described the training equipment and material, the training site and seating arrangement, scheduling a program, and training administration. We then described how to create a positive climate for learning and Gagné's nine events of instruction. The chapter concluded with a discussion of common delivery problems and solutions.

Key Terms

lesson   p. 255
lesson plan   p. 255
subject-matter expert (SME)   p. 259
train-the-trainer   p. 260

trainability test   p. 263
training administration   p. 267
training plan   p. 263

Make the Connection

p. 259: subject-matter experts (SME) are discussed in Chapter 5 on page 144
p. 266: massed versus distributed practice is discussed in Chapter 5 on page 149
p. 269: training objectives are discussed in Chapter 5 on page 137
p. 270: andragogy and adult learning theory are discussed in Chapter 3 on page 76
p. 271: task sequencing is discussed in Chapter 5 on page 150
p. 271: active practice is discussed in Chapter 5 on page 145
p. 271: feedback and knowledge of results is discussed in Chapter 5 on page 151
p. 272: the stages of learning and learning outcomes are discussed in Chapter 3 on pages 66–69

Web Links

Bank of Montreal: www4.bmo.com

Export Development Canada (EDC) www.edc.ca

Starbucks: www.starbucks.com

RPC Icons

RPC 9.1 Participates in course design and selection/delivery of learning materials via various media.

RPC 9.2 Ensures arrangements are made for training schedules, facilities, trainers, participants, and equipment and course materials.

Discussion Questions

1. Discuss Gagné's nine events of instruction and how they relate to training design principles.
2. What are some of the common problems and solutions encountered in training delivery?
3. What are the characteristics of a good trainer and what effect do these characteristics have on learning? Do you think that you can learn to be a good trainer, or is it something you are born with?
4. How can you decide if an employee should attend a training program?
5. Describe the different types of problem trainees and how a trainer might manage them during training.
6. What factors need to be considered when deciding on a training site?
7. Why is it important for subject-matter experts to design and/or deliver training programs? What can organizations do to find and encourage SMEs to get involved in training?
8. What is a train-the-trainer program and how would you proceed if you had to develop and deliver one?

The Great Training Debate

1. Debate the following: Great trainers are born, not made.
2. Debate the following: All training programs should be compulsory.

Using the Internet

1. To find out what it means to be a Certified Training Practitioner (CTP) and a Certified Training and Development Professional (CTDP) in Canada, visit the Canadian Society of Training and Development (CSTD) at **www.cstd.ca/ProfessionalDevelopment/Certification/tabid/231/Default.aspx** and answer the following questions:

   a. What does it mean to be a CTP and a CTDP?
   b. What are the objectives and requirements?
   c. Describe the CTP and CTDP process.

Exercises

In-Class

1. Think about the last time you attended a course or training program. How effective was the instructor/trainer and what effect did it have on your training motivation and learning? What was it about

the instructor/trainer that had a positive or negative effect on your motivation and learning? What could the instructor/trainer have done differently to improve your motivation and learning?

2. How expressive are you as a trainer? To find out and improve your expressiveness, prepare a short lecture (5–10 minutes) on a topic of interest to you or perhaps something on training from the text. Then give your lecture to the class. The class can then evaluate your verbal and nonverbal expressiveness. Make a list of the things you can do to improve your expressiveness.

3. Choose a class you are taking and evaluate your instructor's use of Gagné's nine events of instruction. Evaluate the instructor on each of the following events of instruction:

   - Gain attention
   - Describe the objectives
   - Stimulate recall of prior knowledge
   - Present the material to be learned
   - Provide guidance for learning
   - Elicit performance practice
   - Provide informative feedback
   - Assess performance
   - Enhance retention and transfer

   Based on your evaluation, how effective was your instructor? How can he/she improve?

4. Recall a training program that you attended in a previous or current job. Describe the extent to which the trainer used Gagné's nine events of instruction. Provide specific examples of how each of the events was applied. How effective was the training program and what might the trainer have done differently to make it more effective?

5. Consider some of the factors that make a training site conducive for learning. Now consider the room of one of your courses. Is the room adequate for learning? What aspects, if any, are affecting your ability to learn and what needs to be improved?

6. Think about the last time you attended a training program, or one of the courses you are currently taking. Describe the climate for learning and its effect on your motivation, learning, and satisfaction with the program or course. What can the trainer or instructor do to improve the climate?

In-the-Field

1. Contact the human resources department of an organization and request a meeting with somebody in the department whom you can interview about the organization's training programs. Develop some questions to learn about each of the following issues in terms of a particular training program that the organization has implemented:

   - Was a lesson plan prepared for the program? If not, why? If so, what things were included in it?

- Who is the trainer of the program and how was he or she chosen?
- Who were the trainees and how and why were they chosen to attend the program?
- What training materials and equipment were used?
- Describe the training site and why it was chosen.
- Describe the scheduling of the training program and how it was determined.
- Who administered and coordinated the training program and what did this involve?
- How was the training program implemented (refer to Gagné's nine events of instruction)?
- What are some problems that have occurred in the delivery of the training program and what strategies are used to deal with them?

Based on the information you have acquired, how effectively do you think each of the above were performed? List some recommendations for improvement.

Case Incident

Training the Trainer at the Running Room

The Running Room has more than 60 stores and 600 employees across Canada and plans for expansion into the United States. The company does not have an HR department and relies heavily on a train-the-trainer approach to training. The store managers are in effect the human resource managers and training takes place at the store level. Each year, all store managers are brought together to talk about training issues, initiatives, and challenges. The focus is usually floor sales training because customer service on the floor is the essence of the business. Training is dynamic and interactive and does not rely on lectures. Role playing is used to teach such things as how to greet customers, how to do merchandising, how to handle security, and how to sell. The goal is make it fun and enjoyable.

Questions

1. What do you think about the train-the-trainer approach to training used at the Running Room? What are the advantages and disadvantages?
2. As the company grows and expands into the United States, do you think it will have to change its approach to training and development? If so, how should it change and why?

Source: Garcia, C. (2004, May 17). CloseUp: Training and development. *Canadian HR Reporter*, 17 (10), 7–10.

Case Study

The Houghton Refrigeration Company

Houghton Refrigeration Company builds refrigerators for large appliance companies. It employs about 300 people, mostly assembly line workers, and is located in a small rural town in Ohio. The company typically builds, on a contract basis, chest-type freezers and small bar-type refrigerators. On occasion, however, it also builds standard size refrigerators. The president of the company is a former engineer, as are most of the other executives. These individuals are very knowledgeable about engineering, but have received little training in the basic principles of management.

During the summer months, volume at the factory increases significantly, and the company needs to hire about 40 new employees to handle the heavy workload. Most of these new employees are college students who attend a small private college located about 15 minutes from the plant. Some high school students are hired as well.

When a new employee is hired, the company asks him or her to complete an application blank and then to show up at the plant gate ready for work. Employees receive no orientation. The worker is shown to a work station and, after a minimum amount of on-the-job training, the new employee is expected to start performing a job. Most of the jobs are quite simple and the training is typically completed within 10 minutes. The first-line supervisor usually shows the employee how to do a job once, then watches while the employee does the job once, leaves, and comes back about 20 minutes later to see how the employee is progressing. Typical jobs at the plant include screwing 14 screws into the sides of a freezer, placing a piece of insulation into the freezer lid, and handing out supplies from the tool room.

The company has had excellent experience with college students over the years. Much of the success can be attributed to the older workers coming to the aid of the new employees when difficulties arise. Most new employees are able to perform their jobs reasonably well after their on-the-job training is completed. However, when unexpected difficulties arise, they are usually not prepared for them and therefore need assistance from others.

The older workers have been especially helpful to students working in the "press room." However, Joe Gleason, the first-line supervisor there, finds it amusing to belittle the college students whenever they make any mistakes. He relishes showing a student once how to use a press to bend a small piece of metal, then exclaims, "You're a hot-shot college student; now let's see you do it." He then watches impatiently while the student invariably makes a mistake and then jokingly announces for all to hear, "That's wrong! How did you ever get into college anyway? Try it again, dummy."

One summer, the company experienced a rash of injuries to its employees. Although most of the injuries were minor, the company felt it imperative to conduct a series of short training programs on safe material-handling techniques. The company president was at a loss as to who should conduct the training. The Human Resource Director was a 64-year-old former engineer who was about to retire and was a poor speaker. The only other employee in the Human Resource Department was a new 19-year-old secretary who knew nothing about proper handling techniques. Out of desperation, the president finally decided to ask Bill Young, the first-line supervisor of the "lid-line," to conduct the training.

Bill had recently attended a training program himself on safety and was active in the Red Cross. Bill reluctantly agreed to conduct the training. It was to be done on a departmental basis with small groups of 10 to 15 employees attending each session.

At the first of these training sessions Bill Young nervously stood up in front of 14 employees, many of whom were college students, and read his presentation in a monotone voice. His entire speech lasted about one minute and consisted of the following text:

> Statistics show that an average of 30 persons injure their backs on the job each day in this state. None of us wants to become a "statistic."
>
> The first thing that should be done before lifting an object is to look it over and decide whether you can handle it alone or if help is needed. Get help if there's any doubt as to whether the load is safely within your capacity.
>
> Next, look over the area where you're going to be carrying the object. Make sure it's clear of obstacles. You may have to do a little housekeeping before moving your load. After you have checked out the load and route you're going to travel, the following steps should be taken for your safety in lifting:
>
> 1. Get a good footing close to the load.
> 2. Place your feet 8 to 12 inches apart.
> 3. Bend your knees to grasp the load.
> 4. Bend your knees outward, straddling the load.
> 5. Get a firm grip.
> 6. Keep the load close to your body.
> 7. Lift gradually.
>
> Once you've lifted the load, you'll eventually have to set it down—so bend your legs again—and follow the lifting procedures in reverse. Make sure that your fingers clear the pinch points. And, finally, it's a good idea to set one corner down first.

After Bill's speech ended, the employees immediately returned to work. By the end of the day, however, everyone in the plant had heard about the training fiasco, and all, except the president, were laughing about it.

Source: From *Applications in Human Resource Management, Cases, Exercises, and Skill Builders,* 5th Edition, by Nkomo/Fottler/McAfee © 2005. Reprinted with permission of South-Western, a division of Thomson Learning: www.thomsonrights.com. Fax 800 730-2215. Case questions prepared by Alan Saks.

Questions

1. Comment on the president's choice to conduct the training. Was it a good idea for Bill Young to be the trainer? How else might the president have chosen a trainer?
2. How effective was Bill Young as a trainer? What characteristics of an effective trainer did he display and which ones were lacking?
3. Discuss how the company determined who should attend the training program. How else might they have decided who should attend the training program?
4. Describe the climate for learning. How positive was the climate? What might Bill Young have done to create a more positive climate?
5. Evaluate Bill Young's delivery of the training program in terms of Gagné's nine events of instruction. Which of the events were included in his delivery and which ones were absent? Describe what he might have done if he had followed Gagné's nine events of instruction.
6. What are the most serious problems in the delivery of the training program and how could they have been avoided?

References

1. Dolezalek, H. (2004, July). Boot camp brew-ha-ha. *Training, 41* (7), 17, V N U Business Publications. This work is protected by copyright and it is being used with the permission of Access Copyright. Any alteration of its content or further copying in any form whatsoever is strictly prohibited.
2. Carnevale, A. P., Gainer, L. J., & Meltzer, A. S. (1990). *Workplace basics training manual.* San Francisco, CA: Jossey-Bass Publishers.
3. Carnevale, A. P., Gainer, L. J., & Meltzer, A. S. (1990).
4. Nadler, L. (1982). *Designing training programs: The critical events model.* Reading, MA: Addison-Wesley.
5. Donaldson, L., & Scannell, E. E. (1986). *Human resource development: The new trainer's guide* (2nd ed.). Reading, MA: Addison-Wesley.
6. Nadler, L. (1982).
7. Nadler, L. (1982).
8. Towler, A. J., & Dipboye, R. L. (2001). Effects of trainer expressiveness, organization, and trainee goal orientation on training outcomes. *Journal of Applied Psychology, 86,* 664–673.
9. Towler, A. J., & Dipboye, R. L. (2001).
10. Kirkpatrick, D. L. (1994). *Evaluating training programs: The four levels.* San Francisco, CA: Berrett-Koehler Publishers.
11. Kirkpatrick, D. L. (1994).
12. Tannenbaum, S. I., & Yukl, G. (1992). Training and development in work organizations. *Annual Review of Psychology, 43,* 399–441.
13. Goldstein, I. L., & Ford, J. K. (2002). *Training in organizations.* Belmont, CA: Wadsworth.
14. Ford, J. K., Major, D. A., Seaton, F. W., & Felber, H. K. (1993). Effects of organizational, training system, and individual characteristics on training director scanning practices. *Human Resource Development Quarterly, 4,* 333–351.
15. Nadler, L., & Nadler, Z. (1994). *Designing training programs.* Houston, TX: Gulf Publishing Company.

16. Eitington, J. E. (1989). *The winning trainer*. Houston, TX: Gulf Publishing Company.

17. Eitington, J. E. (1989).

18. Kirkpatrick, D. L. (1994).

19. Kirkpatrick, D. L. (1994).

20. Eitington, J. E. (1989).

21. Eitington, J. E. (1989).

22. Zemke, R. (1999). Toward a science of training. *Training, 36* (7), 32–36.

23. Nadler, L., & Nadler, Z. (1994).

24. Eitington, J. E. (1989).

25. Swanson, R. A., & Falkman, S. K. (1997). Training delivery problems and solutions: Identification of novice trainer problems and expert trainer solutions. *Human Resource Development Quarterly, 8,* 305–314.

26. Swanson, R. A., & Falkman, S. K. (1997).

CHAPTER 10

Transfer of Training

Chapter Learning Outcomes

After reading this chapter, you should be able to:

- define transfer of training and positive, negative, zero, far, near, horizontal, and vertical transfer
- describe the major barriers to transfer of training
- describe Baldwin and Ford's model of the transfer of training process
- describe the activities that managers, trainers, and trainees can do before, during, and after training to improve the transfer of training
- define identical elements, general principles, and stimulus variability and explain how they can improve the transfer of training
- explain what a transfer of training intervention is and describe relapse prevention, self-management, and goal-setting interventions
- explain what a post-training supplement is and describe booster sessions, self-coaching, and upward feedback interventions
- define transfer system and describe the transfer system factors

ONTARIO LOTTERY AND GAMING CORPORATION (OLG)

Ontario Lottery and Gaming Corporation (OLG) is one of the largest gaming organizations in the world and the top lottery business in Canada. The organization has over 8,300 direct staff across Ontario and over 22,000 employees including outsourced operations with staff at commercial casinos.

Recognizing that strong leadership is one of the keys to a successful future, OLG's Corporate Learning Development created a leadership model to address key leadership competencies demanded by the corporation's strategy. The Leadership Excellence Model is a four-pronged approach to develop the corporation's managers through a combination of an orientation program, a core leadership development program called Launch Pad to Success, follow-up Booster Modules, and In Flight sessions consisting of ongoing application workshops.

The OLG partnered with the Rotman School of Management at the University of Toronto to design the Launch Pad to Success program, which includes customized content to support the key competencies and values that OLG leaders are expected to demonstrate. Key content areas include team building, change management, coaching, communications, conflict management, and decision making. The three-day program includes interactive training sessions as well as simulations, self-study, job aids, case studies, and team learning activities.

At the conclusion of each session, participants are asked to write down the key things they learned and one or two skills that they will apply on the job. During the final session of the program, participants prepare an action plan for how they will apply three key learning objectives that they will focus on after completing the program.

Five Booster Modules that cover advanced coaching, problem solving, managing paradoxes, strategic thinking, and negotiation were created to reinforce key learning objectives. In addition, a number of follow-up activities to support participants' application of what they learned in the program on the job are being tested including pre- and post-tests of learning, individual goal setting, action planning, a buddy system of coaching, as well as follow-up coaching. A manager's guide and toolkit is also being developed to ensure long-term positive impact on behaviour and improved productivity.

The effectiveness of these activities is monitored with measures that are consistent with the OLG's Leadership Model. To date, there has been a 12 percent increase in participants' use of the desired behaviours and a 24 percent increase in skill and confidence level among those who participated in the follow-ups. Initial follow-up with some participants has shown that individuals have surpassed some of their financial and non-financial goals by using their action plans.

As the OLG continues to develop the program, ongoing follow-up activities such as participant forums to share success stories and best practices are being explored. Participants have indicated that they would like ongoing support after completing the core program to assist them in implementing their action plans. As a result, a new phase of the program has been introduced. In Flight sessions were designed to help managers and supervisors in their ongoing application of skills learned through the Launch Pad to Success Program and the Booster Modules.[1]

Research has found that many trainees do not use and apply what they learn in training on the job. As a result, organizations like the OLG have designed training programs that include activities to facilitate trainees' application of training on the job. This is what is known as the transfer of training, and in this chapter we describe the transfer of training process and how to facilitate and improve the transfer of training in organizations.

What Is Transfer of Training?

Organizations concerned about their training investments are interested in knowing how much of what is learned in training translates into changes on the job and improved performance. A training program is just the acquisition phase for knowledge, skills, and/or attitudes. Trainers can often demonstrate that trainees leave training programs with new knowledge and skills. But if trainees do not apply their newly acquired knowledge and skills on the job, then most of the investment in training is wasted.

Organizations are increasingly concerned about the value-added of human resource programs. When it comes to training, they are concerned about the transfer of training. **Transfer of training** refers to the application of the knowledge and skills acquired in a training program on the job and the maintenance of acquired knowledge and skills over time.[2]

There are two conditions of transfer of training. **Generalization** refers to the use or application of learned material to the job. **Maintenance** refers to the use or application of learned material on the job over a period of time. Transfer of training occurs when learned material is generalized to the job context and maintained over a period of time on the job.

The extent to which a training program transfers to the job can be described as zero, positive, or negative transfer. When transfer is positive, trainees effectively apply their new knowledge, skills, and attitudes acquired in training on the job. If transfer is zero, then trainees are not using new knowledge and skills on the job. When transfer is negative, training has had a negative

Transfer of training

The generalization of knowledge and skills learned in training on the job and the maintenance of acquired knowledge and skills over time

Generalization

The use or application of learned material to the job

Maintenance

The use or application of learned material on the job over a period of time effect and trainees are performing worse as a result of a training program. The purpose of this chapter is to find out why transfer is sometimes zero or negative and what can be done to make it positive.

Transfer of training can also be considered in terms of the type of situations in which trainees can apply what was learned in training on the job. For example, **near transfer** refers to the extent to which trainees can apply what was learned in training to situations that are very similar to those in which they were trained. On the other hand, **far transfer** refers to the extent to which trainees can apply what was learned in training to novel or different situations from those in which they were trained.[3]

A final distinction about the transfer of training is the difference between horizontal and vertical transfer. **Horizontal transfer** involves the transfer of knowledge and skills across different settings or contexts at the same level. This is in fact the focus of this chapter and is consistent with how we have defined transfer of training. That is, we are concerned about the extent to which trainees transfer what they learn in training from the training setting to the job setting.

Vertical transfer refers to transfer from the individual or trainee level to the organizational level. In other words, it is concerned with the extent to which changes in trainee behaviour or performance transfer to organizational-level outcomes. For example, will a change in trainees' customer service result in an improvement in the organization's service and customer satisfaction? Vertical transfer represents the link between employee behaviour and organizational effectiveness.

This is an important distinction to understand because transfer to the job (i.e., horizontal transfer) might not lead to changes in organizational outcomes (i.e., vertical transfer). Furthermore, there are differences in terms of how to improve each type of transfer. The focus of this chapter is on horizontal transfer, which is a necessary condition for vertical transfer.[4]

The Transfer Problem

Transfer of training is a major problem for trainers and organizations. For decades it has been reported that there exists a transfer of training problem in organizations. Although the estimates of transfer have varied over the years, they have for the most part been quite low, with studies reporting that between 60 and 90 percent of what is learned in training is not applied on the job.[5]

In the only Canadian study—conducted by one of the authors of this text—it was found that although trainees apply 62 percent of what they learn in training on the job immediately after attending a training program, it declines to 44 percent after six months, and to 34 percent one year after attending training. The respondents, who were experienced training professionals, also indicated that an average of 51 percent of training investments results in a positive change or improvement in employees' performance, and an average of 47 percent results in an improvement in organizational performance.[6]

There are many reasons why training does not transfer. Table 10.1 provides a list of some of the major barriers to the transfer of training. One of the

TABLE 10.1

Barriers to the Transfer of Training

- Immediate manager does not support the training.
- The culture in the work group does not support the training.
- No opportunity exists to use the skills.
- No time is provided to use the skills.
- Skills could not be applied to the job.
- The systems and processes did not support the skills.
- The resources are not available to use the skills.
- Skills no longer apply because of changed job responsibilities.
- Skills are not appropriate in our work unit.
- Did not see a need to apply what was learned.
- Old habits could not be changed.
- Reward systems don't support new skills.

Source: Phillips, J. J., & Phillips, P. P. (2002). 11 reasons why training and development fail ... and what you can do about it. *Training, 39* (9), 78–85. © ROI Institute, www.roiinstitute.net. Used with permission.

things you will notice is that many of the barriers have to do with factors in the work environment and can be traced to trainees, managers, and the organization. Furthermore, many of the barriers have to do with a lack of support from supervisors and the organization. Supervisor support has to do with the extent to which supervisors reinforce and support the use of learning on the job.[7]

As you can see in Table 10.1, the number one barrier to transfer of training is the immediate manager's lack of support for training. Supervisor support has been found to be one of the most important factors for transfer along with the social support system in an organization.[8]

In the next section we describe the transfer of training process, which sets the stage for understanding how to improve and facilitate the transfer of training.

The Transfer of Training Process

RPC 10.1

One way to understand how to improve the transfer of training is to identify the factors that contribute to positive transfer of training. A good place to start is a well-known model of the transfer of training process by Tim Baldwin and Kevin Ford.[9]

As shown in Figure 10.1, Baldwin and Ford's model of the transfer of training process can be understood in terms of three main factors: training inputs, training outputs, and the conditions of transfer. The training inputs include trainee characteristics, training design, and the work environment. The training outputs include learning and retention. The conditions of transfer refer to transfer generalization and maintenance.

According to the model, trainee characteristics, training design, and the work environment have a direct effect on learning and retention. Trainee characteristics, the work environment, and learning and retention have a direct effect on transfer generalization and maintenance.

FIGURE 10.1

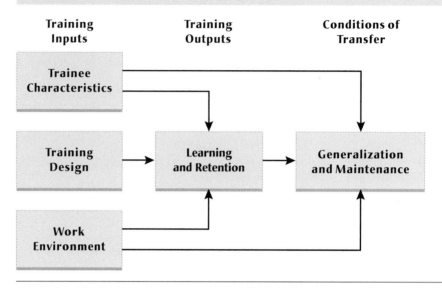

Baldwin and Ford's Model of the Transfer of Training Process

Source: From Baldwin, T. T., and Ford, J. K., Transfer of Training: A Review and Directions for Future Research. *Personnel Psychology, 41,* 63–105; Blackwell Publishing, 1988.

An important implication of the model is that learning and retention are a necessary but not sufficient condition for transfer. This is because trainee characteristics and the work environment also play a critical role in whether or not trainees apply what they learn in training on the job. To better understand the role of training inputs, we will now describe them in more detail.

Trainee Characteristics

In Chapter 3, you learned that trainee characteristics are important predictors of trainee learning and retention. Thus, it should not surprise you that trainee characteristics are also important for the transfer of training. In fact, the same trainee characteristics that influence learning and retention are also important for transfer. Trainee differences in these characteristics can help us understand why some trainees are more likely to transfer than others.

In Chapter 3, the importance of cognitive ability, training motivation, self-efficacy, job attitudes, and personality traits were discussed in relation to learning and retention. Recall that these factors were included in the training effectiveness model and they have a direct effect on learning and retention. They also have a direct effect on the conditions of transfer. In other words, trainees with higher cognitive ability, training motivation, and self-efficacy are more likely to transfer. In addition, trainees with an internal locus of control and a high need for achievement are more likely to apply what they learn in training on the job, and employees with higher job involvement, job satisfaction, and organizational commitment are more likely to learn and transfer.[10]

Another trainee characteristic that is particularly relevant to transfer is motivation to transfer. Recall from Chapter 3 that training motivation refers to the direction, intensity, and persistence of learning-directed behaviour in training contexts. So what then is motivation to transfer? **Motivation to transfer** is a trainee's intended efforts to utilize skills and knowledge learned in training on the job. Motivation to transfer has been found to be a significant predictor of positive transfer.[11]

Motivation to transfer
A trainee's intended effort to utilize skills and knowledge learned in training on the job

Training Design

 10.2

Another important training input is the design of a training program. Recall the discussion in Chapter 5 on active practice and the conditions of practice. We noted that the benefits of active practice for learning and retention can be maximized by incorporating practice conditions before and during training in the design of a training program. At that time the focus was training design factors to improve learning and retention.

A number of learning principles can be incorporated into the design of a training program to improve the transfer of training. These learning principles include identical elements, general principles, and stimulus variability, and they complement the practice conditions described in Chapter 5.

Identical Elements

Trainers should ensure that the training situation reflects the work environment, or what is known as identical elements. **Identical elements** involve providing trainees with training experiences and conditions that closely resemble those in the actual work environment. Identical elements theory states that transfer will occur only if identical elements are present in both the old (training course) and new situations.[12] Identical elements are especially important for near transfer and have been shown to increase trainees' retention of motor and verbal behaviours.[13]

Identical elements
Providing trainees with training experiences and conditions that closely resemble those in the actual work environment

But what exactly is identical? We discussed this in Chapter 6 with respect to simulations. At that time it was noted that to be most effective, simulations should have physical and psychological fidelity. Physical fidelity involves making the conditions of a training program such as the surroundings, tasks, and equipment similar to the work environment. Psychological fidelity has to do with the extent that trainees attach similar meanings to the training experience and the job context.

General Principles

A second principle is known as general principles. **General principles** involve teaching trainees the general rules and theoretical principles that underlie the use and application of trained knowledge and skills. In other words, the training program provides trainees with an explanation of the theory and principles behind a skill or task that they are learning how to perform. On-the-job application is more likely when trainees are taught the general rules and theoretical principles that underlie training content.[14]

General principles
Teaching trainees the general rules and theoretical principles that underlie the use and application of particular skills

Stimulus Variability

Stimulus variability involves providing trainees with a variety of training stimuli and experiences such as multiple examples of a concept or practice experience in a variety of situations. The idea is that trainees' understanding of training material can be strengthened by providing numerous examples of a concept because they will see how the concept can be applied in a variety of situations. This will enable greater generalization of the new skills and prevents the potential problem that learning will be limited to a narrow range of situations.[15] Thus, stimulus variability is especially important for far transfer.

Stimulus variability can be incorporated into a training program in a number of ways, such as by using different models that vary in terms of their characteristics (e.g., gender or age), by modelling different situations (e.g., different types of negotiation scenarios for a training program on negotiation skills), and by using models with different levels of competence in performing the training task (successful and unsuccessful). As well, trainers can increase stimulus variability simply by describing a variety of examples and experiences related to the training content, and by asking trainees to discuss their own work experiences in relation to the training material. Using several examples during the course of a training program has been found to be more effective than simply repeating the same example.[16]

The Work Environment

The third input factor in Baldwin and Ford's model is the work environment. Characteristics of the work environment can influence transfer of training before training (the pre-training environment) as well as after training (the post-training environment). Let's first consider the pre-training environment.

Pre-training Environment

Management actions prior to a training program send signals and messages to employees about the importance of training and the extent to which the organization supports training. These messages can influence employees' training motivation. For example, if management actions convey messages that training is not important, employees will not be motivated to attend training and less likely to learn. In addition, if employees face constraints in their job such as a lack of time, equipment, and/or resources, they will not be highly motivated to learn given that the work environment would prevent them from using new skills.[17]

Post-training Environment

Events that occur after a training program in the post-training environment can also influence the transfer of training. Factors in the post-training environment can encourage, discourage, or prevent employees from applying new knowledge and skills on the job. As indicated earlier, one of the most important characteristics of the post-training environment is the amount of support provided by trainees' supervisors. Supervisor support for training is a key factor that affects the transfer process. Trainees who have supervisors who are more supportive of training are more likely to be motivated to attend training, to learn and retain training content, and to transfer what they learn in training on the job. A number of important activities that supportive supervisors can do before and after training are described later in this chapter.[18]

Training Transfer Climate

At this point, it would be helpful to recall the discussion from Chapter 4 on the organizational context. At that time, two important aspects of the work environment were described: the training transfer climate and a learning culture. As described in Chapter 4, a **training transfer climate** refers to characteristics in the work environment that can either facilitate or inhibit the application of training on the job. A strong transfer climate is one in which there exist cues that remind employees to apply training material on the job, positive consequences such as feedback and rewards for applying training on the job, and supervisor and peer support for the use of newly acquired skills and abilities. A positive and supportive transfer climate has been shown to result in greater learning, retention, and transfer of training.[19]

Training transfer climate

Characteristics in the work environment that can either facilitate or inhibit the application of training on the job

Learning Culture

A **learning culture** refers to a culture in which members of an organization believe that knowledge and skill acquisition are part of their job responsibilities and that learning is an important part of work life in the organization. Research has shown that the transfer of training is greater in organizations that have a learning culture.[20]

Learning culture

A culture in which members of an organization believe that knowledge and skill acquisition are part of their job responsibilities and that learning is an important part of work life in the organization

Summary

In summary, Baldwin and Ford's model of the transfer of training process indicates that transfer generalization and maintenance is a function of trainee characteristics, the work environment, and learning and retention. Learning and retention are a function of trainee characteristics, training design, and the work environment.

Now that you know what factors are important for the transfer of training, what do you think training professionals know about transfer of training? To find out, see Training Today 10.1, "What Do Training Professionals Know About Transfer of Training?"

Facilitating and Improving Transfer of Training

In the previous section, we described how transfer of training is influenced by factors before a training program (i.e., the pre-training environment), during training (training design), and after training (the post-training environment). In this section, we describe practices and activities before, during, and after training to improve the transfer of training. We will also show that positive transfer of training requires the involvement of three key role players (management, trainers, and trainees) and describe transfer activities for each role player at each of the three time periods.

What Do Training Professionals Know About Transfer of Training?

Research on the transfer of training has provided some important information about the factors that can hinder or facilitate transfer. However, given the low rates of transfer reported in several studies, one has to wonder if training professionals are aware of the research findings from transfer of training research.

To find out, Holly Hutchins and Lisa Burke conducted a study to assess the extent to which there is a gap in transfer knowledge among training professionals. They sent a survey to training professionals who had on average 15 years of professional experience in training or workplace learning. The survey included items about the training inputs in Baldwin and Ford's model of the transfer of training process as shown in Figure 10.1.

The results indicated that the average participant correctly answered 78 percent of the survey items. However, the participants differed on the extent to which they agreed on specific items and specific categories which suggests that there are some areas where knowledge gaps exist.

In terms of the three main input factors, knowledge differences were greatest for trainee characteristics (i.e.,

cognitive ability, personality, and motivation). In other words, training professionals' knowledge of how trainee characteristics influence transfer varies widely and/or is limited. Most of the participants were in agreement on the importance of training design factors for the transfer of training, especially the use of specific design elements (i.e., identical elements, stimulus generalization, modelling, practice, and feedback). Training professionals were also in agreement on the importance of the work environment for transfer of training, especially manager support and peer support.

Some training professionals were more knowledgeable about transfer research than others. In particular, those with more education, training certification, and higher job levels were more knowledgeable of transfer of training research findings. The results of this study suggest that there exists a research-to-practice gap among training professionals in some areas of transfer of training knowledge.

Source: Hutchins, H. M., & Burke, L. A. (2007). Identifying trainers' knowledge of training transfer research findings—Closing the gap between research and practice. *International Journal of Training and Development, 11,* 236–264.

Table 10.2 presents a transfer of training framework that guides this section of the chapter. It shows the activities that can be performed by each of the role players before, during, and after training to facilitate and improve the transfer of training.

TABLE 10.2

Transfer of Training Framework

TRANSFER OF TRAINING ACTIVITIES BEFORE TRAINING

Management
- Decide who should attend training.
- Meet with employees prior to training to discuss training programs (e.g., WIIFM).
- Get employee input and involvement in the training process.
- Provide employees with support for learning and training (e.g., release time to prepare for training).

Trainer
- Ensure application of the ISD model.
- Make sure that trainees and supervisors meet and discuss the training.

- Find out supervisor and trainee needs and expectations.
- Make sure that trainees are prepared for the training.

Trainees
- Find out about training programs prior to attendance.
- Meet with supervisor to discuss the training program and develop an action plan.
- Prepare for the training program.

TRANSFER OF TRAINING ACTIVITIES DURING TRAINING

Management
- Participate in training programs.
- Attend training programs before trainees.
- Reassign employees' work while they are attending training.

Trainer
- Incorporate conditions of practice, adult learning principles, and other learning principles (e.g., identical elements) in the design of training programs.
- Include content and examples that are relevant and meaningful to trainees.
- Provide transfer of training interventions at the end of the content portion of a training program (e.g., relapse prevention, self-management, goal setting).
- Have trainees prepare and commit to a performance contract for the transfer of trained skills on the job.

Trainees
- Enter a training program with a positive attitude and the motivation to learn.
- Engage yourself in the training program by getting involved and actively participating.
- Develop an action plan for the application of training on the job.

TRANSFER OF TRAINING ACTIVITIES AFTER TRAINING

Management
- Ensure that trainees have immediate and frequent opportunities to practise and apply what they learn in training on the job.
- Encourage and reinforce trainees' application of new skills on the job.
- Develop an action plan with trainees for transfer and show support by reducing job pressures and workload, arrange practice sessions, publicize transfer successes, give promotional preference to employees who have received training and transfer, and evaluate employees' use of trained skills on the job.

Trainer
- Stay involved in the training and transfer process by conducting field visits to observe trainees' use of trained skills, provide and solicit feedback, and continue to provide support and assistance to trainees.

Trainees
- Begin using new knowledge and skills on the job as soon and as often as possible.
- Meet with supervisor to discuss opportunities for transfer.
- Form a "buddy system" or a network of peers who also attended the training program.
- Consider high-risk situations that might cause a relapse and develop strategies for overcoming them and avoiding a relapse.
- Set goals for transfer and use self-management.

Transfer of Training Activities before Training

Strategies for positive transfer of training should begin before a training program is delivered. Many activities are relatively easy to implement before a training program to facilitate the transfer of training. This is in part due to the fact that the pre-training work environment has a direct effect on trainees' training motivation, learning, and transfer.

The work environment sends messages to employees about the importance of training and should therefore be carefully constructed and managed. This means that management has an especially important role to play before training.

Management

One of the first things that a manager or supervisor should do prior to training is to decide who should attend training. This involves more than just the identification of employees' needs for training. Recall from our earlier discussion that trainee characteristics are an important determinant of learning and retention as well as transfer. Therefore, it is important that trainees selected to attend training programs will learn to perform training tasks and transfer what they learn on the job.

The extent to which a trainee is likely to learn and benefit from a training program is known as readiness to learn or trainability. **Readiness to learn/trainability** refers to the extent to which an individual has the knowledge, skills, and abilities and the motivation to learn the training content. An equation for readiness to learn and trainability combines ability, motivation, as well as perceptions of the work environment as follows:[21]

Readiness to Learn and Trainability = (Ability × Motivation × Perceptions of the Work Environment)

According to this equation, trainees are more likely to learn and are more trainable when they have the ability to learn the training content, when they are motivated to learn, and when they perceive the work environment as supportive of their learning and use of new knowledge and skills on the job. All three of these components are important, and they are not additive. In other words, being high on one factor will not make up for a low rating on another factor. For example, a trainee might have the ability to learn and be motivated to learn, but if he/she does not believe that the work environment will support learning, then he/she will score low on readiness to learn and trainability. Therefore, it is important that all three components are high before sending trainees to a training program.

One way to determine if an employee has the ability to learn the training content is to have him/her take a trainability test as described in Chapter 9. Recall that a trainability test is a test that measures an individual's ability to learn and perform training tasks.

If employees lack the motivation to attend training, there are several ways for managers to increase training motivation. First, they can meet with employees to discuss their training needs and decide on a training plan to

Readiness to learn and trainability

The extent to which an individual has the knowledge, skills and abilities and the motivation to learn the training content meet those needs. Prior to actually attending a training program, managers can discuss the content and the benefits of a training program with their employees and set goals for learning and how they will apply what they learn on the job. They should also discuss the objectives of a training program so that employees know what is expected and what they will be accountable for in terms of learning and the use of new knowledge and skills on the job. Trainees who know that they will be required to participate in follow-up activities or will be evaluated have stronger intentions to transfer what they learn in training.[22]

Employees also need to know why they are attending a training program and the potential benefits. It is up to management to inform trainees about the importance and relevance of a training program and the benefits of learning and transfer. Trainees need to know what's in it for them, or what is sometimes referred to as **WIIFM** (what's in it for me?).

Some evidence exists that trainees will be more motivated and will achieve greater learning when they have some choice in attending a training program than when attendance is mandatory. In one study, managers who could choose whether to attend a performance-appraisal workshop achieved more from attending the workshop than those who were forced to attend. Providing detailed information about the workshop, which was designed to facilitate the managers' attendance decision, rather than just providing the typical positive overview, also resulted in greater achievement.[23]

Some, however, argue that it is better to make attendance mandatory. The idea behind this argument is that by making attendance mandatory, managers communicate the importance of training and ensure that all employees are using the same skills.[24] One study did find that a mandatory course resulted in higher intentions to transfer.[25] However, this appears to be the case when training is highly valued in an organization, which is the case with OLG's Launch Pad to Success program. When training is not so highly valued, however, providing employees with some choice is beneficial. The main point is that trainee involvement and input in the training process, whether it is discussing training needs, allowing trainees to decide what training programs to attend, and/or providing input regarding training content and methods, can enhance training motivation, learning, and transfer.

Finally, managers also need to show their support for training before an employee is sent to a training program. One way of doing this is to have them complete a questionnaire and respond to questions about the need for and potential application of training material. For example, managers who have requested training might be required to answer questions such as: What is the training need? What are the employees doing now and what should they be doing? Why do you feel that training will solve the problem? What would you want employees to be able to do after the training? Having managers complete a contract can also commit them to a training program and ensure their support for it (an example of a contract is shown in Table 10.3). Supervisors can also demonstrate their support for training by providing employees release time to prepare for training and by providing encouragement.[26]

TABLE 10.3

Training Support Contract—Supervisor

I, _____ , agree to

- provide time for the employee to complete pre-course assignments.
- provide release time for attendance, and ensure that the employee's workload is undertaken by others to eliminate interruptions.
- review the course outline with the employee, and discuss situations in which the newly acquired knowledge and skills can be used.
- provide timely opportunities to implement the skills, and reinforce new behaviours upon the return of the trainee.

Signature _____

Title _____

Trainer

MAKE THE
CONNECTION

Trainers can do a number of things before training to facilitate the transfer of training. First, trainers should ensure that the training system is operating according to the instructional systems design (ISD) model presented in Chapter 1. That is, a trainer should ensure that a needs analysis has been conducted, that appropriate training objectives have been developed, and that important learning and design principles have been incorporated into the design of the training program. The Launch Pad to Success program was customized to meet the needs of the OLG Leadership Excellence Model and the program was designed based on behavioural and measurable learning objectives.

Second, the trainer should ensure that supervisors and trainees are prepared for the training program. For example, the trainer should see that supervisors have taken appropriate actions with respect to trainees' readiness to learn/trainability. The trainer should also make sure that supervisors and trainees have met to discuss the objectives, content, and benefits of the training program, and that trainees know what they are expected to learn and do after training.

Third, the trainer should know what supervisors and trainees expect from the trainer and the training program. Thus, to some extent a trainer might have to tailor a training program to the particular needs and expectations of supervisors and trainees. The trainer should also be aware of the needs of trainees in terms of relevant content, examples, and methods. In other words, the trainer must ensure that the training program is relevant and meaningful for trainees.

Finally, the trainer should ensure that trainees have taken any required prerequisite courses and have the necessary readings, assignments, and/or pre-training exercises. Preparation might also include asking trainees to think about work-related problems and issues that they are currently dealing with and how the training program might help solve them. Thus, when trainees show up for a training program they should be ready and motivated to learn.

Trainees

Trainees often show up for training with little knowledge of what they are going to learn or what is expected of them. This is obviously not going to lead to a high level of motivation, learning, or transfer. Trainees must be involved in their training and the training process. Trainees can do a number of things before training to increase their involvement and the likelihood that they will learn and transfer.

First, trainees should find out why they are being asked to attend a training program, what the training objectives are, and what is expected of them in terms of learning and on-the-job behaviour. Second, trainees should meet with their supervisors to discuss the training program and develop a plan of action for learning and transfer. Trainees should also ask their supervisor about the support they can expect while they are away from work and attending a training program, and the support they will receive when they return to work.

Finally, trainees should prepare for the training program to ensure that they are ready to learn and that they will benefit from the training. This might involve preparatory reading, pre-training exercises or assignments, or simply thinking about work-related problems that they can bring with them to the training program. These activities will help ensure that trainees are knowledgeable about the training program and its objectives and they are prepared and motivated to learn.

Transfer of Training Activities during Training

Although it is the responsibility of the trainer to implement and deliver a training program, there are also important activities that trainees and managers can perform during training to improve learning and transfer.

Management

Managers can facilitate the transfer of training during training by showing their support for training. One way of doing this is to attend a training program. If managers cannot attend a training program, then they should consider speaking about the importance and relevance of the training at the start of a program or participating as a trainer if possible. At the very least, they should visit the session at some time to show their support.[27] In the case of the OLG's Launch Pad to Success program, senior executives were actively involved in the design of the program and as speakers during the program.[28]

It also helps if managers have already taken a training program. Managers are more likely to support training if they have been trained or have participated as trainers in a training program. In this way, managers can model the behaviour and observe its occurrence. Senior executives at Vancouver-based Finning Ltd., the world's largest Caterpillar dealer, are the first to attend training and help deliver the training.[29] This cascading effect tells employees that management is serious about learning and the application of new skills on the job. In addition, when managers are required to teach the new skills, they learn them very well. They are also aware that their employees are watching them to see if they practise what they preach.

Management can do a number of things to assist employees while they are away from work and attending a training program. For example, they can reassign some of their workload so that they don't worry about falling behind while they are being trained. They can also ensure that trainees will not be interrupted during training. This not only puts trainees at ease while they are being trained, but also signals to employees that management supports training and considers it a high priority.

Trainer

As described earlier, there are several ways to design training programs to improve and facilitate transfer of training. In particular, training programs should include active practice and the conditions of practice (e.g., task sequencing, feedback, and knowledge of results), adult learning principles (e.g., problem-centred focus, use of work-related experience), as well as principles of learning (i.e., identical elements, general principles, and stimulus variability). The Launch Pad to Success program was built on adult learning principles.[30]

Trainers can also increase trainees' training motivation during training. This can be done by explaining the value of a skill and by using training content and examples that are familiar and meaningful to trainees.[31] Trainees learn and remember meaningful material more easily than material unrelated to their work.[32] Trainers can use information, problems, and anecdotes collected from the needs analysis to provide the link between training material and work situations. New material should be introduced using terms and examples familiar to trainees. The customization of the Launch Pad to Success program resulted in the use of tools and examples that the trainees could relate to.[33]

Before a training program ends, trainers should also provide some instruction on the difficulty of transfer and ways to facilitate it. One way of doing this is to provide an intervention at the end of the content portion of a training program that is designed specifically for the purpose of improving the transfer of training. These transfer interventions include relapse prevention, self-management, and goal-setting and are discussed in more detail later in the chapter.

Performance contract

An agreement outlining how the newly learned skills will be applied on the job

Trainers can also have trainees prepare a performance contract. A **performance contract** is a statement, mutually drafted by the trainee and the trainer near the end of a training program, that outlines which of the newly acquired skills are beneficial and how they will be applied to the job. A copy can then be given to the trainer, a peer, or the supervisor, who will monitor progress toward these goals. Trainees submit progress reports to human resources and their supervisor. A variation on the timing (i.e., signing the contract jointly before a training program) alerts the trainee to the critical elements of the program and commits the supervisor to monitoring progress.[34]

Trainees

Trainees should begin a training program with a positive attitude and a willingness and motivation to learn. During the actual training program, trainees should actively engage themselves by taking notes, participating in discussions and exercises, asking and answering questions, and interacting with the trainer and the other trainees.

Before leaving a training program, trainees should develop an action plan for the application of training on the job and be prepared to discuss their learning and action plan with their supervisor and co-workers. These activities should help maximize trainee learning and facilitate the transfer of training. Recall from the chapter-opening vignette that trainees in the Launch Pad to Success program develop an action plan in which they describe how they will apply three key learning objectives on the job.

Transfer of Training Activities after Training

After a training program has ended and trainees return to work, they often are motivated to try to use their new skills on the job. However, only some are able to do so successfully. Some will stop trying after a few attempts because they receive no support or reinforcement for the use of their new knowledge and skills on the job. Others will give up because they encounter barriers and obstacles that make it difficult if not impossible for them to apply their new knowledge and skills on the job. Still others will give up just because the old ways of doing things are easier and faster. Therefore, it is extremely important that managers, trainers, and trainees participate in activities after training that facilitate the transfer of training.

Management

Transfer of training can be inhibited by the "bubble" syndrome, in which the trainee is expected to use the new skills without support from the environment.[35] Management can burst the bubble by ensuring that the time between training and on-the-job application is minimal, and by providing trainees with support and reinforcement for the use and application of new knowledge and skills on the job.

One of the most important things that managers can do following a training program is to ensure that employees have immediate and frequent opportunities to practise and apply what they learned in training on the job. Assignments and opportunities to try new skills should be given as soon as trainees return from a training program. Managers can also help by allowing trainees time to try or experiment using new behaviours without adverse consequences.

Managers should also encourage and reinforce the application of new skills on the job. In fact, one of the major reasons for a lack of transfer is that reinforcement is usually infrequent or nonexistent. Behaviour that is not reinforced is not repeated. If the sales representative dutifully submits the reports as learned in training but no one even notices they are filed, then the representative will waste no further energy doing this task.

A Xerox study showed that only 13 percent of trainees were using their new skills six months after training when management did not coach and support their use.[36] Therefore, managers must reward and reinforce employees for using new skills and behaviours acquired in training on the job. Trainees who use new skills on the job should be provided with praise, recognition, positive feedback, more challenging assignments, additional opportunities for training, and other extrinsic rewards. This not only directly reinforces employees for their transfer behaviour, but also sends a signal to other employees that training is important and learning and transfer will be rewarded. In effect, it helps to create a positive transfer climate and learning culture.

Managers can do many other things to facilitate transfer, such as developing an action plan for transfer, reducing job pressures and workload, arranging for co-workers to be briefed by trainees about a training program, arranging practice sessions, publicizing successes, giving promotional preference to employees who have received training, and evaluating employees' use of trained skills on the job.[37] Calgary-based Western Gas Marketing Ltd., a subsidiary of TransCanada PipeLines Ltd., rates its managers on the application of new skills on their performance-appraisal forms.[38] At the Bank of Montreal, managers conduct performance assessments to gauge the transfer of learning to the job.[39]

Trainer

Once a training program has ended, it is important for trainers to remain involved in trainees' learning and transfer. Trainers should maintain their involvement in the training and transfer process by conducting field visits to observe trainees' use of trained skills, provide and solicit feedback, and provide continued support and assistance to trainees.[40]

Trainees

After attending a training program, trainees should begin to use their new knowledge and skills on the job as soon as possible. Failure to use the training material when one returns to work is likely to result in a low likelihood of transfer. To ensure adequate opportunities for skill application and support, trainees should meet with their supervisor and discuss opportunities for transfer. Trainees might also benefit by establishing a "buddy system," or a network of peers who have attended a training program and can provide assistance and support and reinforce each other for using their trained skills on the job.[41] One of the follow-up activities being tested by the OLG is a buddy system of coaching.

Trainees should think about high-risk situations that might make it difficult for them to apply the training material on the job. They should anticipate potential obstacles and develop strategies for overcoming them. It is also helpful for trainees to set goals for practising their newly acquired skills on the job.

Now that we have described strategies for facilitating and improving transfer of training, you might be wondering which ones are most effective. For more, see The Trainer's Notebook 10.1, "Best Practice Strategies for Transfer of Training."

Best Practice Strategies for Transfer of Training

According to a sample of training professionals, the best practice strategies for transfer of training are the following:

1. *Supervisory support and reinforcement.* Recognize and reinforce the use of new knowledge and skills on the job.
2. *Coaching and opportunities to practise.* Provide time to practise skills immediately when returning from training.
3. *Use of interactive activities to encourage participation.* Collaborative activities, role plays, small group exercises.

4. *Post-training evaluation of skills.* Tracking and measuring transfer of training.
5. *Making the content relevant to actual job duties.* Activities that resemble work behaviours, challenges, and scenarios.

Source: Burke, L. A., & Hutchins, H. M. (2008). A study of best practices in training transfer and proposed model of transfer. *Human Resource Development Quarterly, 19,* 107–128.

Transfer of Training Interventions

As indicated earlier, one of the things a trainer can do at the end of a training program is discuss the transfer problem with trainees and instruct them on how to transfer newly acquired knowledge and skills on the job. In the last decade, many studies have found that a number of interventions provided at the end of a training program can be effective for improving the transfer of training. In this section, we discuss three types of transfer of training interventions that can be implemented at the end of a training program: relapse prevention, self-management, and goal-setting. We then describe interventions that can be implemented on the job following training (post-training supplements).

Relapse Prevention

Relapse prevention (RP) is an intervention that instructs trainees to anticipate transfer obstacles and high-risk situations in the work environment and to develop coping skills and strategies to overcome them. A relapse occurs when trainees revert back to using the old skills or their pre-training behaviour. Relapse prevention sensitizes trainees to the possibilities of a relapse and "immunizes" them against obstacles in the environment that might cause one.[42] RP sensitizes trainees to barriers in the workplace that might inhibit or prevent successful transfer.

Relapse prevention interventions make trainees aware that relapse can occur and that temporary slips are normal. Trainees are asked to identify obstacles and barriers to transfer and high-risk situations in which a relapse is likely to occur. Some high-risk situations that might lead to a relapse are time pressure and deadlines, work overload, lack of necessary tools, equipment, and resources, and the lack of opportunities to apply trained skills on the job.[43]

For each barrier or high-risk situation, trainees develop a coping strategy. For example, if workers think they will abandon their new skills when there is too much work, time-management techniques could be discussed and used to prevent a relapse. Thus, RP prepares trainees to anticipate, prevent, and

Relapse prevention

An intervention that instructs trainees to anticipate transfer obstacles and high-risk situations in the work environment and to develop coping skills and strategies to overcome them

TABLE 10.4

Relapse Prevention Intervention

Step 1. State the trained skill you wish to apply and maintain from this training.

Step 2. Set your skill maintenance goal, based upon this training. Set a specific, measurable, short-range goal. Then, specifically define a slip and a relapse.

Skill Maintenance Goal: _____

Slip: _____

Relapse: _____

Step 3. Understand positive and negative consequences of using the skill at work.

Positive consequences of using your new skills: _____

Negative consequences of not using your new skills: _____

Positive consequences of not using your new skills: _____

Negative consequences of using your new skills: _____

Step 4. Apply the relapse prevention strategies to maintain trained skills.

RP Strategy   Trainee Notes/Comments

1. Understand the relapse process (i.e., slip, then relapse).
2. Understand the difference between the training environment and job contexts.
3. Create a support network.
4. Be aware of subordinate skepticism of new skills.
5. Identify high-risk situations.
6. Apply skills in the appropriate setting.
7. Understand seemingly unimportant behaviours that may lead to a relapse.
8. Reduce interfering and unproductive emotions.
9. Retain your self-confidence, despite slips.
10. Diagnose support skills needed to maintain training.
11. Review disruptive lifestyle patterns.
12. Mix enjoyable and tedious work tasks.
13. Diagnose support back at work for skill application.
14. Create meaningful self-rewards for skill retention.

Step 5. Describe the nature of circumstances that will likely surround a first slip.

Step 6. Generate ideas for how you will deal with such difficult situations.

Step 7. Monitor your behaviour at work using a self-monitoring record.

Sources: Burke, L. A. (2001). Training transfer: Ensuring training gets used on the job. In L. A. Burke (Ed.), *High-impact training solutions: Top issues troubling trainers.* Wesport, CT: Quorum Books; Hutchins, H. M. & Burke, L. (2006). Has relapse prevention received a fair shake? A review and implications for future transfer research. *Human Resource Development Review, 5* (1), 8–24.

recover from temporary lapses. Table 10.4 provides an outline of a relapse prevention intervention.

Relapse prevention programs have been found to be effective. Trainees who receive RP interventions have higher levels of course knowledge and use the knowledge on the job more than trainees who do not receive it. Relapse prevention has also been found to improve trainees' ability and desire to transfer. There is also evidence that relapse prevention interventions are especially effective when the transfer climate is not very supportive of training.[44]

Self-Management

In Chapter 3, we discussed self-regulation as one of the components of social cognitive theory. We also noted that employees can be trained to learn how to regulate their behaviour. **Self-management** interventions focus on behavioural change and have their basis in self-regulation and social cognitive theory. Self-management interventions involve teaching trainees to perform a series of steps to manage their transfer behaviour.

The steps of self-management interventions include anticipating performance obstacles, planning to overcome obstacles, setting goals to overcome obstacles, monitoring one's progress, and rewarding oneself for goal attainment. Research has found self-management interventions to result in greater skill generalization and higher performance on a transfer task.[45]

Self-management

A post-training transfer intervention that teaches trainees to manage their transfer behaviour

Goal-Setting

In Chapter 3, we described goal-setting theory and its relevance for the design and effectiveness of training programs. Many studies have shown that individuals who set specific, difficult, and challenging goals achieve higher levels of performance.[46]

The importance of goal-setting for training has been the focus of many studies in recent years. From these studies, we know that learning and transfer is more likely when trainees set specific and challenging goals. Therefore, it makes sense to use goal-setting as a transfer intervention.

Goal-setting interventions teach trainees about the goal-setting process and how to set specific goals for the use of trained skills on the job. This usually involves a discussion of why goal-setting is important and a definition of goals; a description of the goal-setting process; characteristics of effective goals (specific and challenging); an explanation for the effectiveness of goals; examples of how goal-setting has been used in organizations; and a discussion of how goal-setting can be effective in one's own organization.

Following a discussion of how to set specific and challenging goals, trainees develop their own goal-setting plan that indicates the steps they will take to achieve their goals and the date that each step will be achieved.[47] In the chapter-opening vignette it was noted that individual goal setting is being tested as a way to support participants' application of learning on the job.

Goal-setting interventions have been shown to improve learning and the extent to which trainees apply their newly learned skills on the job. In addition, one study found that goal-setting was particularly effective for enhancing transfer for trainees who work in a supportive work environment.[48]

Goal-setting intervention

An intervention that instructs trainees about the goal-setting process and how to set specific goals for the use of trained skills on the job

Post-Training Supplements

Transfer of training interventions take place in the classroom at the end of a training program, before trainees return to work. **Post-training supplements** are transfer interventions that take place on the job following a training program and include booster sessions, self-coaching, and upward feedback.

Post-training supplements

Transfer interventions that take place on the job following a training program

Booster Sessions

Booster sessions

Extensions of training programs that involve a review of the training material

A common example of a post-training supplement is a booster session or a refresher course following a training program. **Booster sessions** are extensions of training programs that involve a review of the training material. A booster session can also involve a discussion of problems that trainees are having using their trained skills on the job as well as success stories. Recall that the Launch Pad to Success program includes five booster modules, and the In Flight sessions are designed to help managers apply the skills learned in the program. In addition, follow-up activities such as participant forums to share success stories and best practices are being considered.

Self-Coaching and Upward Feedback

Self-coaching

Trainees examine the extent to which they have engaged in trained behaviours and establish performance maintenance and improvement goals

Upward feedback

Trainees receive data on the frequency with which they engaged in trained behaviours and written comments from subordinates on their performance

Self-coaching involves reflecting on one's performance and setting transfer goals for several weeks following completion of a training program. Trainees complete an assessment in which they examine the extent to which they have engaged in trained behaviours and then establish performance maintenance and improvement goals. An **upward feedback** supplement involves providing trainees with data on the frequency with which they engaged in the trained behaviours along with written comments from subordinates on their performance. Trainees then establish performance maintenance and improvement goals.[49]

A study of newly hired managers of a large restaurant chain found that both self-coaching and the upward feedback supplements resulted in greater post-training performance following a training program on interpersonal skills development. Thus, both supplements proved to be effective extensions of formal classroom training for improving transfer of training.[50]

The Transfer System

Transfer system

All factors in the person, training, and organization that influence transfer of learning to job performance

In this chapter, we have described many activities that contribute to the transfer of training. These activities can occur throughout the training process and have to do with the training program itself as well as trainees, trainers, management, and the organization. One way of thinking about all of the variables that can influence transfer is in terms of a transfer system. According to Elwood Holton and colleagues, the **transfer system** refers to all factors in the person, training, and organization that influence transfer of learning to job performance.[51]

Sixteen factors make up the transfer system. The 16 factors represent important predictors of transfer of training that we have already discussed in the chapter, including trainee ability, motivation, and the work environment. Learning as well as the transfer system factors influence transfer performance, which in turn influence organizational performance.[52]

Holton and his colleagues have developed a diagnostic instrument called the Learning Transfer System Inventory (LTSI) to assess the transfer system in organizations. The instrument consists of 16 factors that have been found to be the most important in transfer research. Some of the factors are used to assess a specific training program while others are general factors that are important for all training programs. Table 10.5 lists the 16 factors and their definitions.

Transfer System Factors

The Learning Transfer System Inventory (LTSI) consists of sixteen factors that assess the transfer system in organizations. Eleven factors are for specific training programs (Factors 1 to 11) and the remaining five (Factors 12 to 16) are more general and apply to all training programs.

SPECIFIC FACTORS

1. **Learner readiness.** The extent to which individuals are prepared to enter and participate in training.
2. **Motivation to transfer.** The direction, intensity, and persistence of effort toward utilizing in a work setting skills and knowledge learned.
3. **Positive personal outcomes.** The degree to which applying training on the job leads to outcomes that are positive for the individual.
4. **Negative personal outcomes.** The extent to which individuals believe that not applying skills and knowledge learned in training will lead to outcomes that are negative.
5. **Personal capacity for transfer.** The extent to which individuals have the time, energy, and mental space in their work lives to make changes required to transfer learning to the job.
6. **Peer support.** The extent to which peers reinforce and support use of learning on the job.
7. **Supervisor support.** The extent to which supervisors-managers support and reinforce use of training on the job.
8. **Supervisor sanctions.** The extent to which individuals perceive negative responses from supervisors-managers when applying skills learned in training.
9. **Perceived content validity.** The extent to which trainees judge training content to reflect job requirements accurately.
10. **Transfer design.** The degree to which (1) training has been designed and delivered to give trainees the ability to transfer learning to the job, and (2) training instructions match job requirements.
11. **Opportunities to use.** The extent to which trainees are provided with or obtain resources and tasks on the job enabling them to use training on the job.

GENERAL FACTORS

1. **Transfer effort–performance expectations**. The expectation that effort devoted to transferring learning will lead to changes in job performance.
2. **Performance–outcomes expectations**. The expectation that changes in job performance will lead to valued outcomes.
3. **Resistance or openness to change**. The extent to which prevailing group norms are perceived by individuals to resist or discourage the use of skills and knowledge acquired in training.
4. **Performance self**-efficacy. An individual's general belief in the ability to change performance at will.
5. **Performance coaching**. Formal and informal indicators from an organization about an individual's job performance.

Source: Holton, E. F., III, Bates, R. A., & Ruona, W. E. A. (2000). Development of a generalized learning transfer system inventory. *Human Resource Development Quarterly, 11*, 333–360. © 2000 Jossey-Bass Inc. Reprinted with permission of John Wiley & Sons, Inc.

NEL   Chapter 10: Transfer of Training   307

The LTSI can be used by organizations to diagnose their transfer system. It is usually administered to trainees after a training program in order to identify potential barriers in an organization's transfer system and to determine the type of intervention to overcome barriers and facilitate transfer. Factors with particularly low scores can be identified and made the focus of interventions.[53]

One of the benefits of this approach to transfer is that it recognizes the importance of a systematic approach to the transfer of training. Organizations are able to diagnosis their transfer system, identify barriers, and implement programs to eliminate the barriers. This is important because transfer systems differ across organizations, which means that the barriers and the most effective intervention to eliminate them will also differ across organizations.[54]

To learn more about how to diagnose and change a transfer system, see The Trainer's Notebook 10.2, "Learning Transfer System Change Process."

The Trainer's Notebook 10.2

Learning Transfer System Change Process

Assessing and improving the transfer system is a change process that involves the following steps:

1. *Plan system assessment.* An effective diagnosis begins with good planning and involves logistical issues and political issues with managers. Substeps include:

   - Determine employee groups to be assessed.
   - Build partnerships with managers.
   - Address confidentiality issues.
   - Obtain management support.
   - Decide logistical issues.

2. *Diagnose system.* Use the Learning Transfer System Inventory (LTSI) to collect diagnostic data as a pulse-check to identify areas for further inquiry. Substeps include:

   - Collect initial diagnostic data.
   - Conduct focus groups to understand meaning behind data.
   - Identify key transfer system gaps.

3. *Provide feedback to system members.* It is recommended that the diagnostic findings be reported to system members who should be involved if diagnosis is to become action and solution oriented. Substeps include:

   - Arrange feedback meeting (or meetings, if needed).
   - Report diagnostic data.

   - Avoid blame and criticism.
   - Overcome objections to identified gaps.

4. *Plan system changes.* Attempts should be made to involve system members in joint change planning as they are frequently best equipped to recommend specific improvements. Substeps include:

   - Build support from management and transfer agents for change.
   - Engage transfer agents in collaborative decision making.
   - Make realistic decisions.

5. *Implement system improvements.* System improvements are most likely to endure if ownership is shared with system members. Substeps include:

   - Share ownership of system improvements.
   - Overcome resistance of system members.
   - Monitor change progress.
   - Plan for reassessment.

Source: Holton, E. F. III. (2003). What's really wrong: Diagnosis for learning transfer system change. In E. F. Holton III & T. T. Baldwin (Eds.), *Improving learning transfer in organizations.* San Francisco, CA: John Wiley & Sons, Inc.

Model of Training Effectiveness—Transfer of Training

Before concluding this chapter, let's return to the model of training effectiveness that was presented in Chapters 3 and 5. Recall that the model shows that: 1. Trainee characteristics (i.e., cognitive ability, training motivation, personality, self-efficacy, and attitudes) and training design (i.e., active practice, conditions of practice, active learning, error-management training) have a direct effect on trainee learning and retention; 2. Learning and retention have a direct effect on individual behaviour and performance; and 3. Individual behaviour and performance has a direct effect on organizational effectiveness.

As shown in Figure 10.2, we can now add a number of other factors and links to the model based on the material presented in this chapter. First, we can add the work environment to the model which includes the training transfer climate, a learning culture, and the transfer system. Second, we can add the learning principles (i.e., identical elements, stimulus variability, and general principles) to training design.

In terms of the paths, we can add a direct link from trainee characteristics and the work environment to individual behaviour and performance. This follows from Baldwin and Ford's model of the transfer process. We can also add a direct link from training design to individual behaviour and performance given that the learning principles are important for transfer. The model

FIGURE 10.2

Model of Training Effectiveness

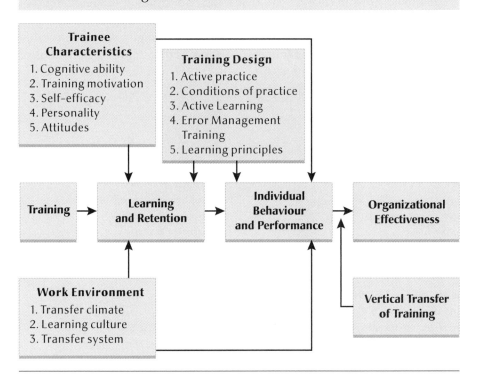

now shows that individual behaviour and performance (i.e., transfer) is influenced by trainee characteristics, training design, the work environment, and learning and retention.

The final linkage in the model is from transfer behaviour and performance to organizational effectiveness. Recall that this linkage is known as vertical transfer. Vertical transfer refers to the link between individual-level training outcomes and organizational outcomes. While a change and improvement in employees' behaviour and performance (i.e., horizontal transfer) is necessary for vertical transfer, it is important to realize that the relationship is not one-to-one. In other words, positive horizontal transfer does not guarantee vertical transfer because many other factors also contribute to organizational effectiveness.

Summary

This chapter has described the transfer of training process and the reasons why transfer is a serious problem for organizations. Baldwin and Ford's model of the transfer of training process was presented as a framework for understanding how to facilitate and improve transfer of training. Activities for improving the transfer of training were described in terms of when they should be implemented during the training process (before, during, and after training) and who should implement them (management, trainers, and trainees). The chapter concluded with a discussion of transfer of training interventions (relapse prevention, self-management, and goal-setting), post-training supplements (booster sessions, self-coaching, and upward feedback), and the transfer system.

It should now be clear to you that transfer of training is something that must be addressed throughout the training process—before, during, and after training. Furthermore, positive transfer of training is the responsibility of management, trainers, and trainees. This means that improving the transfer of training requires a systematic approach and the involvement of all the key players throughout the training process.

Key Terms

booster sessions   p. 306
far transfer   p. 288
general principles   p. 291
generalization   p. 287
goal-setting intervention   p. 305
horizontal transfer   p. 288
identical elements   p. 291
learning culture   p. 293
maintenance   p. 287
motivation to transfer   p. 291
near transfer   p. 288
performance contract   p. 300

post-training supplements   p. 305
readiness to learn/trainability   p. 296
relapse prevention   p. 303
self-coaching   p. 306
self-management   p. 305
stimulus variability   p. 292
training transfer climate   p. 293
transfer of training   p. 287
transfer system   p. 306
upward feedback   p. 306
vertical transfer   p. 288
WIIFM   p. 297

Make the Connection

p. 290: trainee characteristics that predict trainee learning and retention are discussed in Chapter 3 on pages 85–86

p. 291: training motivation is discussed in Chapter 3 on page 83

p. 291: conditions of practice before and during training are discussed in Chapter 5 on pages 146–152

p. 291: physical and psychological fidelity are discussed in Chapter 6 on page 180

p. 293: training transfer climate and learning culture are discussed in Chapter 4 on page 107

p. 296: a trainability test is discussed in Chapter 9 on page 263

p. 298: the instructional systems design (ISD) model is discussed in Chapter 1 on pages 20–23

p. 305: self-regulation is discussed in Chapter 3 on page 75

p. 305: goal setting is discussed in Chapter 3 on page 81

Web Links

Finning Ltd.: www.finning.com

Ontario Lottery and Gaming Corporation: www.olg.ca

Western Gas Marketing Ltd.: www.transcanada.com

Xerox: www.xerox.com

RPC Icons

RPC 10.1 Facilitates coaching and post-training support activities to ensure transfer of learning to the workplace.

RPC 10.2 Participates in course design and selection/delivery of learning materials via various media.

Discussion Questions

1. Refer to Table 10.1, "Barriers to the Transfer of Training." For each of the barriers, indicate who is responsible for the barrier (trainer, trainee, management) and when the barrier is most likely to occur (before, during, and/or after).
2. Refer to Table 10.1, "Barriers to the Transfer of Training." For each of the barriers, describe what can be done to remove the barrier and facilitate the transfer of training. Be sure to indicate at what stage in the training process you would do something to remove the barrier

(i.e., before, during, and/or after), and who would be involved (i.e., manager, trainer, and/or trainee).

3. Refer to the OLG vignette at the beginning of the chapter and describe the activities that were used to facilitate the transfer of training. At what point during the training process were these activities implemented and how effective were they?

4. What is the difference between horizontal and vertical transfer and how are they related? What is the difference between near transfer and far transfer and what should a trainer do to maximize each of them?

5. Describe the main factors in Baldwin and Ford's model of the transfer of training process and how they are related. What are the practical implications of the model for improving transfer of training?

6. What is the transfer system and what are the specific and general factors associated with it? Review each of the factors in Table 10.5 and discuss who is responsible for each factor (i.e., trainee, trainer, supervisor) and what can be done to improve them.

7. Discuss how technology can be used to facilitate the transfer of training in organizations.

The Great Training Debate

1. Debate the following: Low rates of transfer of training are inevitable and will always be a problem for trainers and organizations.

2. Debate the following: Trainers should be responsible only for trainee learning and retention because what happens when trainees return to the work environment and the transfer of training is beyond their control.

Using the Internet

1. To find out more about the Learning Transfer System Inventory (LTSI), go to **www.trainingtransfersolutions.com/LTSI.html.** Read about the LTSI and view the video where Dr. Ed Holton discusses each factor in the LTSI. Answer the following questions:

   a. What is the LTSI?
   b. What can a practitioner use it for?
   c. How do you administer the LTSI?
   d. Describe the learning transfer system change process.
   e. What is the conceptual structure of the LTSI?

2. Find out why transfer of training is the number one problem in the training business today at **www.trainingtransfersolutions.com** and answer the following questions:

   a. Why does Dr. Ed Holton believe that transfer of training is the number one problem in the training business today?
   b. What does he think should be done about it?

Exercises

In-Class

1. After the final exam, many students claim to forget most of what they learn in their courses. How could you design an educational experience for students so that they will remember and use most of the material learned in the classroom?

2. Think about the most recent training experience you had in a current or previous job. What did you learn and to what extent did you apply what you learned on-the-job? Did you transfer immediately after training? Six months after training? One year after training? What factors explain why you did or did not transfer what you learned in training on-the-job? Is there anything that the trainer or your supervisor could have done to increase your transfer? Is there anything you could have done yourself to improve your transfer? (*Note:* This exercise can also be done by interviewing somebody about their training experiences, e.g., another member of the class, a friend, or family member.)

3. Students acquire a great deal of knowledge and information from their courses, but does it transfer to their work experiences? Describe any courses you have taken that resulted in transfer from school-to-work. What factors do you think contributed to your transfer and could they be used in the design of other courses?

4. Describe how you would use identical elements, general principles, and stimulus variability to improve the learning and transfer of your courses. In other words, what can an instructor do to incorporate these learning principles into his/her classes?

5. Assume the role of a training consultant who has been hired by an organization with a transfer of training problem. Your task is to conduct a diagnosis of the transfer system to find out why there is a transfer problem. Therefore, you need to develop a diagnostic tool to find out what barriers exist. Using the material in this chapter, develop some questions that take into account the different time periods of the training process (i.e., before, during, and after) and the main role players (management, trainer, and trainees) to assess the transfer problem in the organization. What questions will you ask and whom will you interview and/or survey?

6. Review the transfer of training interventions described in the chapter and think about how they might be used to help students learn their course material and apply it on-the-job. You could consider your course on training and development or perhaps a course on managerial skills. Your task is to design one of the following interventions: relapse prevention, self-management, or goal-setting. You can then have another member of the class review your intervention and provide feedback, or if time permits present your intervention to the class.

In-the-Field

1. To find out about transfer of training in an organization, contact the human resource department of an organization and ask the following questions:

   - To what extent do trainees apply what they learn in training on the job immediately after training, six months after training, and one year after training?
   - What are the main barriers or obstacles to transfer of training in your organization?
   - What kinds of things do you do to try to improve the transfer of training?
   - Are there things you do before, during, and after training to improve transfer?
   - What are the responsibilities of managers, trainers, and trainees for the transfer of training?
   - What have you found to be most effective for ensuring that trainees apply what they learn in training on the job?

   Based on your interview, how well do you think the organization is managing the transfer of training process? What recommendations do you suggest for the organization to improve its transfer system and the transfer of training?

Case Incident

Standard Life Canada

Standard Life Canada has a total customer satisfaction philosophy based on seven core competencies: customer focus, teamwork, action orientation, leadership, business acumen, strategic thinking, and professional development. Several years ago, the company decided it was time to repeat its total customer satisfaction training and brought all of its employees from Canada to Montreal for one day of training on customer service. The focus was on what sorts of things are essential for the customer, what adds value to the customer, and looking at things from the customer's perspective.

Questions

1. What should employees be able to do on-the-job after attending this training program? In other words, what should transfer?
2. What factors might limit the extent to which employees transfer what they learn in this training program on-the-job? What can be done to facilitate their transfer of training?

Source: Garcia, C. (2004, May 17). CloseUp: Training and development. *Canadian HR Reporter, 17* (10), 7–10.

Case Study

The School Board

For years, parents, students, and teachers had been complaining that nobody listened, that decisions were made without participation, and that good ideas went unacknowledged. A needs analysis that involved a survey of teachers and students confirmed that these problems were widespread.

As a recently appointed trainer with a strong background in teaching, Carlos DaSilva tackled the communications problem as his first assignment. He designed what he considered to be the finest three-day communications program in any school board. He spent months on the design: finding videos, exercises, and games that taught active listening, upward communication, brainstorming, and other areas identified in the survey.

Carlos was excited to deliver his new training program and was sure that the participants would like it. On the first day, Carlos began with a brief introduction on the importance of communication, followed by a lecture on communication channels. Afterwards, he showed a video about manager–employee communication problems and how to improve communication. This was followed by a discussion of the key points in the video and what the trainees might do to improve their communication skills.

On day two of the training program, Carlos began with a lecture on brainstorming. He then had trainees participate in a group brainstorming exercise. Each group had to brainstorm as many ideas as possible for improving communication in the school board. Afterwards, the groups presented their ideas followed by a discussion of the most creative ways to improve communication with teachers, students, and parents.

On the third day of the training program, Carlos began with a lecture on active listening. Trainees then participated in an exercise in which they had to develop a message and then communicate it to the other trainees. At the end of the exercise, each trainee had to recall the message sent by the other trainees. This was then followed by a discussion of how to be a more effective listener and with tips on active listening.

Carlos ended the training program by having trainees participate in a communication game. First, he had trainees complete a self-assessment of how they send messages and the channels they use for communication. Then groups of trainees had to develop a message that they would communicate to the other groups. Each group had to determine the best way for their message to reach the other groups as accurately and timely as possible. At the end of the game, each group read out the message they received from the other groups. Carlos then scored each group in terms of the accuracy of the message received by the other groups as well as how long it took for each group to receive the message.

The game was a lot of fun for the participants, who left the training program on a high. Carlos thanked them for attending the training program and encouraged them to apply what they learned in training when they return to work. The trainees applauded Carlos and thanked him for providing such an enjoyable training experience.

Two months after the training program, Carlos was sitting at his desk, thinking about his meeting scheduled for 2 p.m. with the school board superintendent. He was looking forward to the meeting with the superintendent, knowing that he would be praised for the successful interactive communications program he had designed and delivered.

However, the meeting with the superintendent went poorly. Although some participants loved the exercises and games in the communications course, most did not change their work behaviour. Furthermore, a review of the situation showed that the old problems persisted and communication remained a serious problem at the school board. Carlos did not know what to say or what he should do.

Several days later, Carlos approached several of the participants who attended the training program and asked them how things were going. One participant laughed at him and said, "Well that was a lot of fun, but training is training and work is work. Besides, nothing ever changes around here." Carlos asked her what she meant and she explained to him that supervisors don't get it and continue to call the shots. "The only thing they know about communication is downward," she said. "Maybe they should have attended your training program!"

Questions

1. What are some reasons why Carlos's training program did not transfer?
2. Discuss some of the barriers to transfer that might be operating at the school board. Who is responsible for these barriers?
3. Describe some of the things that Carlos might have done before, during, and after the training program to improve the transfer of training.
4. Discuss the role of the training transfer climate and the transfer system. How might they have contributed to the transfer problem at the school board?
5. What should Carlos do about the transfer problem at the school board?

References

1. Jones, E., & Arnold, H. (2006, Spring). Hitting the jackpot in leadership development: A case study. *The Canadian Learning Journal, 10* (1), 9–11. Reprinted with permission from CSTD.
2. Baldwin, T. T., & Ford, J. K. (1988). Transfer of training: A review and directions for future research. *Personnel Psychology, 41,* 63–105.
3. Broad, M. L., & Newstrom, J. W. (1992). *Transfer of training.* Reading, MA: Addison-Wesley.
4. Kozlowski, S. W. J., Brown, K. G., Weissbein, D. A., Cannon-Bowers, J. A., & Salas, E. (2000). A multilevel approach to training effectiveness: Enhancing horizontal and vertical transfer. In K. J. Klein & S. W. J. Kozlowski (Eds.), *Multilevel theory, research, and methods in organizations* (pp. 157–210). San Francisco: Jossey-Bass.
5. Phillips. J. J., & Phillips, P. P. (2002, September). 11 reasons why training and development fails . . . and what you can do about it. *Training, 39* (9), 78–85.

6. Saks, A. M. (2002). So what is a good transfer of training estimate? *The Industrial-Organizational Psychologist*, 29–30.
7. Cromwell, S. E., & Kolb, J. A. (2004). An examination of work-environment support factors affecting transfer of supervisory skills training to the workplace. *Human Resource Development Quarterly, 15,* 449–471.
8. Cromwell, S. E., & Kolb, J. A. (2004); Tracey, J. B, Scott, I. T., & Kavanagh, M. J. (1995). Applying training on the job: The importance of the work environment. *Journal of Applied Psychology, 80* (2), 239–252.
9. Baldwin, T. T., & Ford, J. K. (1988).
10. Colquitt, J. A., Lepine, A., & Noe, R. A. (2000). Toward an integrative theory of training motivation: A meta-analytic path analysis of 20 years of research. *Journal of Applied Psychology, 85,* 678–707.
11. Burke, L. A., & Hutchins, H. M. (2007). Training transfer: An integrative literature review. *Human Resource Development Review, 6,* 263–296.
12. Bass, B. M., & Vaughn, J. A. (1969). *Training in industry: The management of learning.* Belmont, CA: Wadsworth.
13. Baldwin, T. T., & Ford, J. K. (1988).
14. Baldwin, T. T., & Ford, J. K. (1988).
15. Baldwin, T. T., & Ford, J. K. (1988).
16. Baldwin, T. T., & Ford, J. K. (1988).
17. Tannenbaum, S. I., & Yukl, G. (1992). Training and development in work organizations. *Annual Review of Psychology, 43,* 399–441.
18. Baldwin, T. T., & Ford, J. K. (1988); Tannenbaum, S. I., & Yukl, G. (1992).
19. Rouiller, J. Z., & Goldstein, I. L. (1993). The relationship between organizational transfer climate and positive transfer of training. *Human Resource Development Quarterly, 4,* 377–390.
20. Tracey, J. B., Scott, I. T., & Kavanagh, M. J. (1995).
21. DeSimone, R. L., Werner, J. M., & Harris, D. M. (2002). *Human resource development.* Orlando, FL: Harcourt.
22. Baldwin, T. T., & Magjuka, R. J. (1991). Organizational training and signals of importance: Linking pretraining perceptions to intentions to transfer. *Human Resource Development Quarterly, 2,* 25–36.
23. Hicks, W. D., & Klimoski, R. J. (1987). Entry into training programs and its effects on training outcomes: A field experiment. *Academy of Management Journal, 30,* 542–552.
24. Broad, M. L., & Newstrom, J. W. (1992).
25. Baldwin, T. T., & Magjuka, R. J. (1991).
26. Tannenbaum, S. I., & Yukl, G. (1992).
27. Burke, L. A. (2001). Training transfer: Ensuring training gets used on the job. In L. A. Burke (Ed.), *High-impact training solutions: Top issues troubling trainers.* Westport, CT: Quorum Books.
28. Jones, E., & Arnold, H. (2006, Spring).
29. Clemmer, J. (1992, September 15). Why most training fails. *The Globe and Mail,* B26.
30. Jones, E., & Arnold, H. (2006, Spring).
31. Bass, B. M., & Vaughn, J. A. (1969).
32. McGehee, W., & Thayer, P. W. (1961). *Training in business and industry.* New York: Wiley.
33. Jones, E., & Arnold, H. (2006, Spring).
34. Leifer, M. S., & Newstrom, J. W. (1980, August). Solving the transfer of training problems. *Training and Development Journal,* 34–46.
35. Hatcher, T., & Schriver, R. (1991, November–December). Bursting the bubble that blocks training transfer. *Technical and Skills,* 12–15.
36. Zucker, L. (1987). Institutional theories of organization. *Annual Review of Sociology, 13,* 443–464.
37. Broad, M. L., & Newstrom, J. W. (1992).
38. Clemmer, J. (1992, September 15).

39. Waxer, C. (2005, October 24). Bank of Montreal opens its checkbook in the name of employee development. *Workforce Management, 84* (11), 46–48;
40. Burke, L. A. (2001).
41. Baldwin, T. T., & Ford, J. K. (1988); Burke, L. A. (2001).
42. Tziner, A., & Haccoun, R. R. (1991). Personal and situational characteristics influencing the effectiveness of transfer of training improvement strategies. *Journal of Occupational Psychology, 64* (2), 167–177.
43. Burke, L. A. (2001).
44. Burke, L. A. (2001).
45. Gist, M., Bavetta, A., & Stevens, C. (1990). Transfer training method: Its influence on skill generalization, skill repetition, and performance level. *Personnel Psychology, 43,* 501–523; Gist, M., Stevens, C., & Bavetta, A. (1991). Effects of self-efficacy and post-training intervention on the acquisition and maintenance of complex interpersonal skills. *Personnel Psychology, 44,* 837–861.
46. Locke, E. A., & Latham, G. P. (1990). *A theory of goal setting and task performance.* Englewood Cliffs, NJ: Prentice-Hall.
47. Richman-Hirsch, W. L. (2001). Posttraining interventions to enhance transfer: The moderating effects of work environments. *Human Resource Development Quarterly, 12,* 105–120; Wexley, K. N., & Nemeroff, W. F. (1975). Effectiveness of positive reinforcement and goal setting as methods of management development. *Journal of Applied Psychology, 60,* 446–450.
48. Richman-Hirsch, W. L. (2001).
49. Tews, M. J., & Tracey, J. B. (2008). An empirical examination of posttraining on-the-job supplements for enhancing the effectiveness of interpersonal skills training. *Personnel Psychology, 61,* 375–401.
50. Tews, M. J., & Tracey, J. B. (2008).
51. Holton, E. F. III. (2003). What's really wrong: Diagnosis for learning transfer system change. In E. F. Holton III & T. T. Baldwin (Eds.), *Improving learning transfer in organizations.* San Francisco, CA: John Wiley & Sons, Inc.
52. Holton, E. F. III. (2003).
53. Holton, E. F. III. (2003).
54. Holton, E. F. III., Chen, H., & Naquin, S. S. (2003). An examination of learning transfer system characteristics across organizational settings. *Human Resource Development Quarterly, 14,* 459–482.

CHAPTER 11

Training Evaluation

Chapter Learning Outcomes

After reading this chapter, you should be able to:

- define training evaluation and the main reasons for conducting evaluations
- discuss the barriers to evaluation and the factors that affect whether or not an evaluation is conducted
- describe the different types of evaluations
- describe the models of training evaluation and the relationships among them
- describe the main variables to measure in a training evaluation and how they are measured
- discuss the different types of designs for training evaluation as well as their requirements, limits, and when they should be used

Years ago, when Bell Canada installed a new telephone system for its business clients, it also sent out service advisers whose task it was to train the employees to use the new system. These training sessions consisted of "show-and-tell" activities in which the instructors demonstrated the use of the telephone. Simple as the training was, it was expensive, costing millions of dollars annually. With the introduction of electronic equipment, the functionality of the telephone systems—and complexity for the users—increased exponentially.

Initially, the company attempted to use its traditional training approach with purchasers of the electronic systems. However, a training evaluation was conducted and it showed that following the training experience, customer knowledge of the operation of the electronic telephones was quite low. Training was not effective.

A number of attempts were then made to improve the situation. Different types of training, presented by either Bell Canada or user personnel, were tried and evaluated. None made any significant difference in terms of training effectiveness.

However, these training evaluation studies did detect an important fact. No matter how training was conducted, the users' knowledge of a limited number of functions—those they used a lot—increased after training, indicating that practice seemed to have a significant effect on learning.

This suggested that providing end users with an instructional aid might help them gain greater benefit from the electronic system. To that end, a special instruction booklet was carefully prepared and trainees were provided with a brief instructional session teaching the users how to use the instruction booklet. The evaluation of this approach showed, empirically, that the use of the instruction booklet resulted in greater user mastery than the formal training course.

Thus, the training evaluations conducted throughout this process demonstrated a) that the traditional training method was ineffective, b) that changing the instructors had no effect, but c) that the use of a well-developed instruction booklet had greater effect.

This demonstrates the two main objectives of training evaluation: to assess the effectiveness of training and, equally important, to identify ways of enhancing that effectiveness. At Bell, the traditional program was discontinued and replaced with an inexpensive booklet that was both more effective and considerably cheaper.

Training programs are designed to have an effect on learning and behaviour. However, as the Bell Canada story demonstrates, this is not always the case. Fortunately, in that case, the organization launched an evaluation program that involved several studies, the results of which served not only to assess the effectiveness of the existing training but also to identify and test different strategies for improving the situation.

In this chapter, you will learn about the evaluation of training and development programs. In particular, you will learn about the training evaluation models, the different types of evaluation, the variables to measure and how to measure them, as well as the different data collection designs for conducting a training evaluation.

What Is Training Evaluation?

Organizations invest in improving employee competencies, attitudes, and behaviours because such improvements are expected to lead to positive results for organizations (e.g., improved productivity). Training programs may be launched for a number of reasons: they may be used to improve competencies (e.g., learning new software), to modify attitudes (e.g., preparing a manager posted to an international assignment), and/or to modify behaviours (e.g., leadership training).

Training evaluation is concerned with whether or not these expected outcomes materialize as a result of training. They are designed to assist decision making about training programs: Should the organization cancel or continue a training program? Should an existing training program be modified? How should it be modified?

Training evaluation is a process designed to assess the value—the worthiness—of training programs to employees and to organizations. Training evaluation assesses this value by analyzing data collected from trainees, supervisors, or others familiar with the trainees and with the job context. Using a variety of techniques, objective and subjective information is gathered before, during, and after training to provide the data required to estimate the value of a training program.

Training evaluation is not a single procedure. Rather, it is a continuum of techniques, methods, and measures that informs management about the value of training programs. At one end of the continuum lie simple procedures that are easy to implement and that can provide some potentially useful information about the value of a training program. Asking participants how much they enjoyed a training program is one example of a simple evaluation procedure.

At the other end of the training evaluation continuum lie more elaborate procedures that provide managers with more information of a richer quality about the value of a training program. More involved training evaluations might assess how much of the trained skills trainees apply on the job (i.e., transfer of training) and how much performance improvement has resulted from the training effort. More extensive training evaluations might be used to diagnose the training program's success in enhancing key psychological

RPC 11.1

Training evaluation
A process to assess the value–the worthiness–of training programs to employees and to organizations

factors, such as trainee motivation and self-efficacy. Some evaluation designs can even estimate the specific contribution of training to any changes observed in the organization, sometimes in dollar terms. The more sophisticated the design, the more complete the information, the better the conclusions, and the greater the confidence with which they can be stated.

However, more sophisticated evaluation procedures are more costly and more complex and difficult to implement. Hence, the quality and completeness of the information gathered involves a trade-off with the costs, complexity, and practicality of the techniques chosen. In some cases, less sophisticated evaluation procedures may be quite suitable, while in other cases the same procedures will not yield useful information.[1] Conversely, very sophisticated procedures required in one situation might be overkill in another. The key is that the specific training evaluation procedures required depend on the specifics of the training situation and on the decisions that need to be made as a result of that evaluation.

Why Conduct Training Evaluations?

Organizations have many reasons for conducting evaluations of training programs and systems. In the contemporary business environment understaffing is chronic, constraining the amount of time available for training. With the 2009 financial crisis characterized by layoffs and the urgent need for efficiency, this tendency is likely to increase. It is critical that employees and organizations not waste time and resources on unprofitable training programs. Guided by evaluation results, it is a managerial responsibility to improve training. Training evaluation is therefore of value to:

- Assist managers in identifying the training programs most applicable to employees and to assist management in the determination of who should be trained.
- Determine the cost benefits of a program and to help ascertain which program or training technique is most cost-effective (see Chapter 12).
- Determine if the training program has achieved the expected results or solved the problem for which training was the anticipated solution.
- Diagnose the strengths and weaknesses of a program and pinpoint needed improvements.
- Use the evaluation information to justify and reinforce the value and credibility of the training function to the organization.

Do Organizations Conduct Training Evaluations?

Currently, most organizations evaluate their training programs; this has been a consistent finding over the last decade.[2] A survey of practices conducted on behalf of the American Society for Training and Development (ASTD) has repeatedly shown that most organizations conduct some sort of evaluation of most of the training programs they offer to their employees.[3] It remains, however, that the overwhelming majority of training evaluations are simple and limited to trainee reactions.

Managing Performance Through Training and Development

FIGURE 11.1

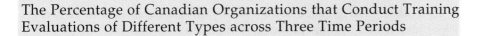

The Percentage of Canadian Organizations that Conduct Training Evaluations of Different Types across Three Time Periods

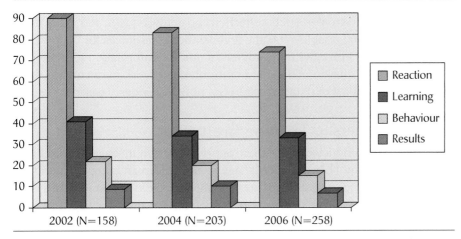

Source: The Conference Board of Canada figure: "The Percentage of Organizations that Conduct Training Evaluations of Different Types Across Three Time Periods." Adapted from Hughes, P.D. & Grant, M (2007) Learning and development outlook 2007. E/F (Ottawa: The Conference Board of Canada, (chart 29).

Data compiled by the Conference Board of Canada show a highly similar situation for Canadian organizations. Figure 11.1 graphs these results: In Canada, most organizations (about three-quarters) evaluate trainee reactions; one-third evaluate learning; fewer (about 15 percent) evaluate behaviour; and only a minority assess the impact of training on organizational results.[4] As you will note from Figure 11.1, there has been a slight drop in evaluation activities in the last decade. One reason for this may be the barriers to training evaluation.

Barriers to Training Evaluation

Studies of training professionals showed that some employers do not conduct training evaluations because they are perceived to be too complicated to implement, too time consuming, and/or too expensive.[5] Some training managers do not conduct evaluations because top management does not demand them and because it is difficult to isolate the effects of training among many other variables that might also be having an effect on employees and the organization. Thus, barriers to training evaluation fall into two categories: pragmatic and political.

Pragmatic Barriers to Training Evaluation

As you will learn in this chapter, evaluating training programs requires knowledge about research design, measurement, and data analysis. Understandably, some training managers feel insecure about taking on such a task. However, the training evaluation process has been unduly mystified. The principles, techniques, and procedures involved in training evaluation are logical and straightforward, and most can be easily implemented. Moreover, training evaluations require that information (objective and/or perceptual measures) about trainees be gathered from the trainees, their supervisors, and/or co-workers, and in some cases even by subordinates and/or customers. These measures are sometimes collected before and after training as well as after trainees return to the job. Valuable training and job time as well as money needs to be diverted to these data collection and analysis tasks, and many managers hesitate or are unable to tax the organizational resources for the purpose of evaluation. However, with the advent of modern information technologies (e.g., Web-based questionnaires and computerized work-performance data) the disruptive impact of data collection can now be seriously eased.

Political Barriers to Training Evaluation

Evaluations are conducted when there is pressure from management to do so (see Training Today 11.1, "Upper Management's Role in Training Evaluation"). In the absence of such pressures, many training managers would rather forgo the exercise. One risk associated with training evaluation is that they might demonstrate that part of a training program—or even an entire training program—is not effective. While this should be considered a valuable finding (as in the Bell Canada case), some trainers fear that negative evaluation results might reflect poorly on them, the training function, and the training choices they make. Some trainers feel that evaluations should be conducted by external professionals to

Training Today 11.1

Upper Management's Role in Training Evaluation

A few years ago, there was a rash of serious work accidents in a large transportation company. Some of these accidents were the direct or indirect result of operator errors due to the consumption of drugs and alcohol. As a result, the firm declared a zero-tolerance policy concerning the use of such substances. The policy required that no employee use substances that may impair effective and safe job performance, whether or not these substances are legal. The key element of the policy was that all supervisors were directly and personally responsible for enforcing the policy. Supervisors who failed to enforce the policy would themselves be subject to sanctions that could include dismissal.

The training department was directed to develop and administer a training program to all supervisory and managerial personnel in the company that was aimed at teaching the policy and its implementation. However, the CEO of the company also insisted that the training program be evaluated to ensure that it was effective. As

a result, the training department, which normally only administered "smile sheets" to evaluate their training programs, launched a much more sophisticated training evaluation program that included three measurement times and the collection of information on dozens of variables. Clearly, this effort was launched because the training program had attained high visibility and because top management demanded it. The training evaluation did uncover some problems with the training program and suggested a number of changes. However, none of these changes were ever implemented. This occurred because top management showed no interest in the results of the evaluation study, as these became available several months after the training program was administered.

The moral of the story is that high-level visibility can stimulate evaluation actions. However, maintaining that visibility is important to ensure that the evaluation results will prove of practical use.

avoid a perception of conflict of interest (how can the person doing the training also be the one responsible for evaluating its effectiveness?).

However, as long as training managers make use of the established methods of evaluation and document them, there is little ground for concern about conflict of interest. In some organizations, the effectiveness of the training department is sometimes measured by the number of courses provided or by the number of employees that have been trained.[6] In those cases, diverting training money to cover evaluation costs might very well reduce the number of training programs and participants that can be accommodated by the training and development function. It is a choice that, understandably, some training managers find difficult, even as the latest Conference Board of Canada survey reports, training departments devote 8 percent of their staff time to evaluation activities.

Types of Training Evaluation

Most training evaluations focus on the impact of a training program on trainees' perceptions and, to a much lesser degree, behaviours. Perceptions are assessed through questionnaire measures, while behavioural data may require a combination of techniques including self-reports, observation, and performance data. Evaluations may be distinguished from each other with respect to the data gathered and analyzed, and the fundamental purpose for which the evaluation is being conducted.

RPC 11.2

1. **The data collected:** Evaluations differ with respect to the type of information that is gathered and how that is accomplished.

   a. The most common training evaluations rely on *trainee perceptions at the conclusion of training* (did the participants like it?), while more sophisticated evaluations go further to analyze the extent of trainee learning and the post-training behaviour of trainees.

   b. More recently, there has been a growing emphasis on evaluation studies that also assess the *psychological forces* that operate during training programs and that impact outcome measures such as learning and behaviour change. Research in this area has helped to identify psychological states (affective, cognitive, and skills-based) that are important training outcomes because of the influence they have on learning as well as to improvements in job behaviours.[7]

   c. Finally, information about the *work environment* to which the trainee returns can be useful in evaluation.[8] For example, measures of training transfer climate and a learning culture have been developed.[9] Training programs provided by organizations that rank higher in terms of these dimensions tend to be more effective on a number of dimensions.[10] Specific organizational events and policies—such as on-the-job opportunities to practise new skills or trainee expectations about the type of support they will receive on the job—have been found to influence training success.[11] Other studies showed that (self-reported) transfer of training was higher for trainees who perceived a strong alignment between training and the firm's strategic vision, and training was more effective in firms that tie performance and rewards more tightly.[12]

2. **The purpose of the evaluation:** Evaluations also differ with respect to their purposes. Worthen and Sanders distinguished between *formative evaluation* and *summative evaluation.*[13]

a. **Formative evaluations** are designed to help evaluators assess the value of the training materials and processes with the key goal of identifying improvements to the instructional experience (the clarity, complexity, and relevance of the training contents, how they are presented, and the training context). Hence, formative evaluation provides data that are of special interest to training designers and instructors.

b. **Summative evaluations** are designed to provide data about a training program's worthiness or effectiveness: Has the training program resulted in payoffs for the organization? Cost-benefit analyses (see Chapter 12) are usually summative. Economic indices are often an integral and important part of these types of evaluations; consequently, organizational managers show great interest in these results.

A further distinction can be made between *descriptive* and *causal evaluations.* **Descriptive evaluations** provide information describing trainees once they have completed the program. What has the trainee learned in training? Is the trainee more confident about using the skill? Is it used on the job? Most evaluation designs have descriptive components. **Causal evaluations** are used to determine if the training caused the post-training behaviours. Causal evaluations require more sophisticated experimental and statistical procedures.

Models of Training Evaluation

Models of training evaluation specify the information (the variables) that needs to be measured in training evaluations and their interrelationships. The dominant training evaluation model is Donald Kirkpatrick's hierarchical model.[14] However, research and practical experience has indicated that Kirkpatrick's model can be improved. COMA and the Decision-Based Evaluation models are two recent efforts in that direction.[15]

Kirkpatrick's Hierarchical Model: The Four Levels of Training Evaluation

Donald Kirkpatrick's hierarchical model is the oldest, best known, and most frequently used training evaluation model. For example the Conference Board of Canada data summarized in Table 11.1 are organized using that model. The model identifies four levels of training evaluation criteria. According to this model, a training program is "effective" when:

L1. Trainees report positive reactions to a training program (Level 1 = reactions).

L2. Trainees learn the training material (Level 2 = learning).

L3. Trainees apply what they learn in training on the job (Level 3 = behaviours).

L4. Training has a positive effect on organizational outcomes (Level 4 = results).

TABLE 11.1

The Main Variables Measured in Training Evaluation

VARIABLE	DEFINITION	HOW MEASURED
Reactions	Trainee perceptions of the program and/or specific aspects of the course.	Questionnaires, focus groups, interviews.
Learning	Trainee acquisition of the program material. Declarative learning is knowing the information. Procedural knowledge is being able to translate that knowledge into a behavioural sequence.	Multiple choice or True-False tests (declarative); situational and mastery tests (procedural).
Behaviour	On-the-job behaviour display, objective performance measures.	Self-reports, supervisory reports, direct and indirect observations, production records.
Motivation	Trainee desire to learn and/or transfer skills.	Questionnaires.
Self-efficacy	Trainee confidence in learning and/or behaviour display on the job.	Questionnaires.
Perceived and/or anticipated support	The assistance trainees obtain and/or the assistance trainees expect.	Questionnaires.
Organizational perceptions	How trainees perceive the organization's culture and climate for learning and transfer.	Standardized questionnaires.
Organizational results	The impact of training on organizational outcomes.	Organizational records.

In more recent articulations of the Kirkpatrick model, the fourth level has been split: L4 = results, implying changes in job performance, and L5 = investment, which implies the degree to which changes in job performance are reflected in organizational success. However, for simplicity's sake we continue this description using the four-level version of the model.

The model states that the four levels are arranged in a hierarchy, such that each succeeding level provides more important information than the previous one. The model also assumes that all levels are positively related to one another and that each level has a causal effect on the next level. Hence, positive trainee reactions (L1) cause trainees to learn more (L2), which in turn leads to the behavioural display of the new skill at work (L3), which in turn impacts on organizational effectiveness (L4)—the ultimate reason for conducting training in organizations. Thus, a complete training evaluation would assess all four levels.

Critique of Kirkpatrick's Model

The contribution of Kirkpatrick's model to training evaluation cannot be underestimated. Organizations evaluate training more frequently now than in the past, largely because of the Kirkpatrick model. Organizations have adopted the model because it makes good sense to managers and trainers alike as it is a clear and simple systematic framework for assessing training. It has greatly demystified training evaluation and provided an impetus for research. As a result, we now know considerably more about the model than was the case when it was introduced, more than 40 years ago. Whereas there is general agreement that the four levels are indeed important outcomes to be assessed, other aspects of the model including its completeness have been questioned.

Research studies, especially those conducted by Elwood Holton (who concludes that Kirkpatrick's is *not* a model!) and by George Alliger and his colleagues have thrown doubt on the validity of the hierarchical aspect of the model.[16] The model would be valid if a positive correlation exists among the four levels. Hence, enjoyment (L1) would be correlated with learning (L2), and learning correlated with transfer (L3), and so on. In fact, that is not the case. The correlations between the levels are small or non-existent. Most students can easily explain this result: one may have learned little from an otherwise pleasant course or learned a great deal from a hated one (as exemplified by biochemistry for one of the authors!). As a further example, most people know that smoking is not healthy, yet many still do it—knowledge and behaviours are not synonymous. In short, the hierarchical aspect of the Kirkpatrick model lacks empirical support.

This flaw does not affect the effectiveness of the Kirkpatrick model for conducting summative evaluations, where global payoff is the main interest. The model remains helpful because no matter the relationships among the levels, there is intrinsic value in assessing whether the training program leads to learning (L2), results in a payoff to the organization (L4), or is boring (L1). However, relying on it can prove a handicap in formative evaluations where the goal is to use the results to improve training effectiveness. When "something goes wrong" with a training program (e.g., low transfer), the model does not indicate the specific nature of the problem or what to do about it. For example, as the relationship between learning and behaviour is small, improving L1 (reactions) or L2 (learning) is unlikely to improve transfer levels. As the model collects no other information (such as trainee motivation, self-efficacy, or conditions of the organization) it is unable to provide assistance in the formative evaluation process. For these applications, therefore, the Kirkpatrick model is insufficiently diagnostic.

The model has also been criticized for its lack of precision in the outcomes. For example, it fails to specify what is meant by "L2-learning" (declarative?

procedural? see Chapter 3) or by "L1-reactions." To demonstrate this last point, we used seven different terms to describe L1 in the preceding paragraphs (hated, enjoyment, like, pleasant, boring, detested, interesting). These are all reactions, but they do not describe equivalent realities. Similar arguments can be made for the other levels.

But perhaps the most important critique has been that Kirkpatrick requires *all* training evaluations to rely on the same variables and outcome measures. The current view is that the type of evaluation, as well as the measures and procedures, should be selected as a function of the organizational situation and the purposes of the evaluation. One model does not fit all in training evaluation situations. To that end, two improvements to Kirkpatrick's models have been proposed: COMA and DBE.

COMA Model

The **COMA** model has been proposed as a mechanism for enhancing the usefulness of training evaluation questionnaires by identifying and measuring those variables that research has shown to be important for the transfer of training.[17] Instead of relying exclusively on reaction and declarative learning measures, COMA suggests the measurement of variables that fall into four categories: cognitive, organizational environment, motivational, and attitudinal variables. These can all be measured by questionnaires administered before and immediately after the training session.

- **Cognitive** variables refer to the level of learning that the trainee has gained from a training program. Both declarative and procedural learning might be measured, but the latter is more important because it is more strongly related to transfer than the former.
- **Organizational** environment refers to a cluster of variables that are generated by the work environment and that impact transfer of training. This includes the learning culture, the opportunity to practise, and the degree of support that is provided to trainees once they return to the job.
- **Motivation** refers to the desire to learn and transfer on the job what was presented in training. As indicated in Chapter 10, motivation has been shown to be a powerful and persistent influence on the transfer of training. COMA suggests that training motivation (measured at the onset of the program) and motivation to transfer (measured immediately after) both be measured.
- **Attitudes** refer to individuals' feelings and thinking processes. Chief among these beliefs are self-efficacy, perceptions of control, and expectations about self and the environment.

According to the COMA model, training evaluation should assess the degree to which trainees have mastered the skills ("**C**"); accurately perceive that the organizational environment (including peers and supervisors) will support and help them apply the skills ("**O**"); are motivated to learn and to apply the skills on the job ("**M**"); and have developed attitudes and beliefs that allow them to feel capable of applying their newly acquired skills on-the-job ("**A**").

COMA

A training evaluation model that involves the measurement of Cognitive, Organizational, Motivational, and Attitudinal variables

COMA improves upon the Kirkpatrick model in three ways: it integrates in the reaction questionnaires a greater number of measures (the COMA variables); the measures added *are* causally related to training success (see Chapter 10, Transfer of Training); and it defines these new variables with greater precision. As the COMA model is still relatively new, it is too early to draw conclusions as to its value. Further, COMA's focus is limited to an analysis of the factors that impact on transfer only. Moreover, COMA does not specify how training evaluations should be conducted. Decision-Based Evaluation, the third evaluation model to be discussed, resolves some of these issues.

Decision-Based Evaluation Model

Decision-Based Evaluation (DBE)

A training evaluation model that specifies the target, focus, and methods of evaluation

Decision-Based Evaluation (DBE) is a model developed by Kurt Kraiger. As with the Kirkpatrick and COMA model, Decision-Based Evaluation specifies the variables to be measured. However, it goes further than either of the two preceding models in that DBE identifies the *target* of the evaluation (what do we wish to find out from the evaluation?); identifies its *focus* (what are the variables we will measure?); and suggests the *methods* that may be appropriate for conducting the evaluation.

The model specifies three potential "targets" for the evaluation: 1. Trainee change, 2. Organizational payoff, and 3. Program improvement. If trainee change is of consequence, the evaluator is directed to specify the "focus" of the change: Are we interested in assessing the level of trainee changes with respect to learning behaviours, or to the psychological states (such as motivation and self-efficacy)? Each evaluation study may include one or more foci. Once the focus or foci are selected, the model suggests the appropriate data collection method (e.g., surveys, job sample information, objective data, etc.).

Decision-Based Evaluation may well be a marked improvement, for different reasons, over both Kirkpatrick's model and the COMA model. Unlike Kirkpatrick's model, it identifies and ties the specific variables that should be measured in the evaluation (focus) depending on the chosen target. Unlike COMA, DBE is general to any evaluation goals (targets), not just transfer of training. Further, it is the only model that also specifies the types of methods that can be used for an evaluation. And, most importantly, DBE is a flexible model. It does not advocate a *one best way* for training evaluation nor does it compel the measurement of a single set of variables (as do Kirkpatrick and COMA) for all evaluations. DBE is the only training evaluation model that clearly specifies that evaluations must always be guided by a key question: What is the target of the evaluation? However, as with COMA, this model is recent and it remains to be tested more fully.

The Kirkpatrick, COMA, and DBE models of training evaluation all require that for each training course people with specialized skills develop the evaluation measures and questionnaires and analyze/interpret the data. This can limit the use of these evaluation models for only those organizations that do possess such resources. To help alleviate this constraint to training evaluation, Elwood Holton and his colleagues have proposed a more generic approach, described in Training Today 11.2, "The Learning Transfer System Inventory (LTSI)."[18]

The Learning Transfer System Inventory (LTSI)

The Holton-Bates approach is the Learning Transfer System Inventory (LTSI), which was described in Chapter 10. It is a questionnaire containing 89 questions that assess the 16 variables described in Chapter 10. These variables include all of the COMA dimensions plus additional ones such as learner readiness (e.g., "I knew what to expect from the training before it began"), resistance/openness to change (e.g., "People in my group are open to changing the way they do things"), and opportunity to use learning (e.g., "The resources I need to use what I learned will be available to me after training"). Trainees answer the 89 questions using a five-point scale (strongly agree to strongly disagree). The LTSI is available in both English and French (advantageous for use in organizations that operate in different cultural milieu). Importantly, the LTSI is also a research instrument that is being constantly refined with questions added or withdrawn depending on research results.

There are, however, some limitations with LTSI. It is a proprietary instrument, and organizations that wish to use it must obtain the authors' permission, must administer all 89 questions, and are required to provide the data collected to the authors. Organizations that do not wish to release their training evaluation data (e.g., for confidentiality or legal reasons), that believe the questionnaire taps dimensions of no relevance to their assessment, and/or that are unable to administer a lengthy questionnaire may judge this approach less applicable.

Source: Devos, C., Dumay, X., Bonami, M., Bates, R., & Holton, E. III. (2007). The Learning Transfer System Inventory (LTSI) translated into French: Internal structure and predictive validity. *International Journal of Training and Development 11*, 181–199.

Training Evaluation Variables

Training evaluation requires that data be collected on important aspects of training. Some of these variables have been identified in the training evaluation models. Table 11.1 provides a more complete list of the main variables that can be measured in training evaluation and how that is accomplished.

Training evaluation variables are relatively easy to develop. In this section, we will review some of the basic techniques and formats that may be used to develop them. Table 11.2 shows sample questions and formats for measuring each type of variable.

RPC 11.4

Reactions

Trainee opinions and attitudes about a training program are usually measured immediately following training. Typically, they are survey-type questions in which trainees indicate their answers on a rating scale. Reaction measures are easy to administer, collect, and analyze, and the questions may focus on the trainees' overall reactions to a training program (e.g., Overall, how satisfied were you with the training program?) and/or on specific elements of a program (e.g., To what extent were you satisfied with the instructor?).

In a major study involving thousands of responses to reaction questionnaires, Morgan and Casper identified six dimensions that underlie reaction measures: satisfaction with the instructor, the training process, the materials, the course structure, the assessment process, and the perceived usefulness (utility) of the training.[19]

TABLE 11.2

Examples of Questions and Formats Used in Training Evaluations

VARIABLE	EXAMPLE OF QUESTION	EXAMPLE OF ANSWER FORMAT
Reactions	"How much of the course content can be applied in your job?" (utility reaction measure)	1 = None, 2 = Little, 3 = Some, 4 = Much, 5 = All
	"How satisfied were you with the content of the program?" (affective reaction measure)	1 = Not at all satisfied, 2 = Not satisfied, 3 = Somewhat satisfied, 4 = Satisfied, 5 = Very satisfied
Declarative learning	Declarative: True or False: The earth is square.	Declarative True _____ False _____
	Multiple choice: What statement best describes the earth?	Multiple choice: round, square, triangular, flat
Procedural learning	Procedural Mastery: You need to write a letter using a computer. From the list below pick the four steps required to do so and list them in the order with which they should be performed.	Procedural Step Required Order Turn computer on Yes 1 Set the margins Yes 4 Select "new document" Yes 3 Open the word processor Yes 2 Test the hard drive No —
Behaviour	Self-report: How many "cold calls" have you made in the last week? Observation: By others including the supervisor and the analyst. May also include subordinates or customers.	Open-ended frequency scale (number of times) or rating scale: 1 = Always, 2 = Sometimes, 3 = Rarely, 4 = Never

Variable	Example of Question	Example of Answer Format
Motivation	How important is it to reduce accidents at work?	1 = Very important, 2 = Important, 3 = Neither important nor unimportant, 4 = Somewhat unimportant, 5 = Very unimportant
	The consequences to you of applying the behaviour at work?	Will make my job: 1 = much harder, 2 = somewhat harder, 3 = no effect, 4 = somewhat easier, 5 = much easier
	How likely is it that if you do apply the trained behaviours there will be fewer accidents?	1 = Extremely likely, 2 = Somewhat likely, 3 = Neither likely nor unlikely, 4 = Unlikely, 5 = Extremely unlikely
	The product of the three sets of questions produces the motivator scores.	
Self-efficacy	How confident are you that you can explain the new policy to your subordinates?	1 = Not at all confident, 2, 3, 4, to 5 = Very confident
Perceived and/or anticipated support	I expect that my supervisor will help and support me in my attempts to apply my new skills on the job.	1 = Completely disagree, 2, 3, 4, to 5 = Completely agree
Organizational perceptions	Supervisors give recognition and credit to those who apply new knowledge and skills to their work.	Standardized questionnaires
Organizational results	How much has quality improved as a result of the training program?	Number of units rejected per day; number of items returned per month; number of customer complaints per week

Reaction measures can be quite different, but two types have received the most attention: affective and utility reaction measures. **Affective reactions** assess trainees' *likes and dislikes* of a training program. **Utility reactions** refer to the perceived *usefulness* of a training program.

Whereas trainers are interested in the likes and dislikes of trainees (affective reactions), research has shown that affective reaction measures bear little relationship to other important training outcomes including learning and behaviour. On the other hand, *utility* reaction measures demonstrate some relationship to learning and behaviour.[20] Hence, collecting utility reactions is important because they tell us somewhat more about whether or not the trainee will transfer newly acquired skills to the job than do affective reactions.

Affective reactions

Reaction measures that assess trainees' *likes and dislikes* of a training program

Utility reactions

Reaction measures that assess the perceived *usefulness* of a training program

A recent study provides data that contest, to some degree, the previously thought advantage of utility measures over reaction ones: in this case there does not seem to be much proof that utility measures are superior to affective reactions in predicting learning outcomes.[21] But the most interesting result of the study is that the correlation between reactions and outcomes appears stronger for courses that utilize a high level of technology as opposed to those that rely on less technology. That result may serve as a warning for internet-delivered courses. It may be especially important that they not be boring—for, in that case, trainees may be very likely to abandon the course or, at the least, to pay scant attention to its contents.

Irrespective of the type of reaction measure used, they can be collected in a number of ways. The most common method is a questionnaire that is administered at the end of a training program. The questions are listed on one side of the page and a rating scale is placed next to each question (see Table 11.3 for an example). However, reactions can also be measured by open-ended discussions with trainees using focus groups or interviews, though such an approach might prove to be more expensive and time consuming and more subject to the biases of the interviewer, especially if the interviewer is also the course designer or leader.

The questions and the answers may be formatted in any number of different ways: 1. In the form of a statement (e.g., "The course materials captured my interest"), for which the trainee indicates his/her degree of agreement (from strongly agree to strongly disagree); or 2. In the form of direct questions (e.g., "How effective was the instructor?"), to which the trainee chooses a response from a linear rating scale (from very effective to very ineffective). Most rating scales have between four and seven response choices, though more or fewer points can be used.

No matter their relationship to other training outcomes, immediate post-training reaction measures remain somewhat useful because: 1. They are easy to collect and analyze and are easily understood by managers and employees alike; 2. They provide trainers with immediate feedback on their course; 3. Trainees who have had a chance to comment on a program and make suggestions for improvements might be more motivated to transfer their learning than others who leave a program without providing input; and 4. They are an easy and convenient mechanism for also measuring the dimensions of the LTSI and COMA model.

Learning

Declarative learning

Refers to the acquisition of facts and information and is by far the most frequently assessed learning measure

Although there are many types of learning outcomes that can be measured (Jonassen and Tessmer identify more than 10), most training evaluations measure "declarative" learning, which was described as a learning outcome in Chapter 3.[22] In rare cases, some evaluators also assess "procedural" learning. The contents of both the declarative and procedural learning measures are selected from the training content.

Declarative learning is by far the most frequently assessed learning measure. As described in Chapter 3, it refers to the acquisition of facts and information.

TABLE 11.3

Reactions Rating Form

Course or Session: _____

Instructor: _____

Content:

Please answer the following questions using the scale below:

1. strongly disagree 2. disagree 3. neither disagree nor agree 4. agree 5. strongly agree

_____ The material presented will be useful to me on the job.

_____ The level of information was too advanced for my work.

_____ The level of information presented was too elementary for me.

_____ The information was presented in manageable chunks.

_____ Theories and concepts were linked to work activities.

_____ The course material was up-to-date and reliable.

Instructor:

Please rate the instructor's performance along the following dimensions:

_____ Needs improvement.

_____ Just right, or competent, effective.

_____ Superior or very effective performance.

The instructor:

_____ Described the objectives of the session.

_____ Had a plan for the session.

_____ Followed the plan.

_____ Determined trainees' current knowledge.

_____ Explained new terms.

_____ Used work and applied examples.

_____ Provided opportunities for questions.

_____ Was enthusiastic about the topic.

_____ Presented material clearly.

_____ Effectively summarized the material.

_____ Varied the learning activities.

_____ Showed a personal interest in class progress.

_____ Demonstrated a desire for trainees to learn.

Perceived Impact:

_____ I gained significant new knowledge.

_____ I developed skills in the area.

_____ I was given tools for attacking problems.

_____ My on-the-job performance will improve.

Please indicate what you will do differently on the job as a result of this course.

Overall Rating:

Taking into account all aspects of the course, how would you rate it?

_____ Excellent _____ Very Good _____ Good _____ Fair _____ Poor

Would you take another course from this instructor? _____ Yes _____ No

Would you recommend this course to your colleagues? _____ Yes _____ No

Procedural learning

Refers to the organization of facts and information into a smooth behavioural sequence

Procedural learning involves the organization of facts and information into a smooth behavioural sequence. Research has shown that declarative learning has only a minor effect on behaviours. Procedural learning, however, is more strongly related to a number of training outcomes including transfer of training.

Declarative learning is usually assessed with multiple choice or true-false type questions. Students familiar with college or university exams know about these tests of learning. Table 11.4 presents an array of these options. The test items listed in Part A are termed "objectively scored" tests because there is only one correct answer possible. Part B gives some examples of "subjectively scored" test items. Test items that are considered subjective are essay questions, oral interviews, journals, and diaries. Here, several answers might be acceptable, and markers have some latitude in their interpretation of the correctness of the answer, which potentially exposes that judgment to "subjective" biases.

Procedural learning, however, is rarely measured because the development of such measures is much more complex. Desjardins developed a procedural learning measure for a "protecting a crime scene" course given to police officers where the police officers learned the do's and don'ts when called to a crime scene.[23] She interviewed task experts who demonstrated the proper actions and proper sequence of behaviours required and then summarized these steps, added some unnecessary and incorrect steps, and shuffled the order of the steps. Trainees had to distinguish between the required and erroneous steps and reposition them into the correct order. Completing this task successfully requires procedural understanding of the training content.

Cheri Ostroff used another approach to develop a measure of procedural learning.[24] Education managers were instructed on how to interact with parents more effectively in tense situations. Different anecdotes drawn from real experience were presented to trainees along with four different ways of handling each situation. The four options were carefully constructed. Trainees who had acquired a basic comprehension of the principles of conflict management would tend to select one option, while those with sophisticated comprehension levels would select another. The intermediate choices reflected comprehension levels between these extremes.

Procedural learning measures can also involve simulations conducted in realistic situations. For example, a pilot could be tested in a virtual-reality airplane. The skills of a drug counsellor could be tested using actors as drug addicts. A test could be conducted as a role play (for negotiation skills) or a practice session (for tennis certification). These tests are usually called performance tests or work sample tests.

Learning measures also vary in terms of when they are administered. For example, some researchers have divided learning measures into three subcategories: 1. Immediate post-training knowledge, which measures trainee learning immediately after a training program; 2. Knowledge retention, which measures trainee learning sometime after a training program; and 3. Behaviour or skill demonstration, which measures trainees' ability to perform the training task during the training program.

Learning measures are useful for a number of reasons besides determining if trainees have learned the training material. For example, a testing hurdle anticipated at the end of a course increases trainees' motivation to learn the material.[25]

TABLE 11.4

Declarative Learning Test Formats

True or False

1. A test is valid if a person receives approximately the same result or score at two different testing times. True _____ False _____

Multiple Choice

2. The affective domain of learning refers to

_____ skills

_____ attitudes

_____ knowledge

_____ all of the above

_____ 2 and 3

Matching

3. For each of the governments listed on the left, select the appropriate responsibility for training and place its letter next to the term.

_____ 1. federal   a. displaced workers

_____ 2. provincial   b. language training

_____ 3. municipal   c. student summer work

Short Answer

4. Kirkpatrick identified four levels of measurement. These are:

_____

_____

_____

_____

Essay

5. Describe the similarities between Kirkpatrick, COMA, and DBE.

Oral

6. The measurement of training has many potential benefits. Identify these benefits. Discuss the reasons why, given these advantages of measurement, most trainers do not evaluate training.

Observation Checklist

7. The customer-service representative:

_____ greeted the customer

_____ approached the customer

_____ offered to help

(continued)

TABLE 11.4 *(continued)*

Rating Scale

8. Indicate the degree to which you agree or disagree with the statements below:

   Scale: 1 = strongly disagree, 2 = disagree, 3 = agree, 4 = strongly agree

   During a selection interview, the interviewer:

   used behavioural-based questions   1 2 3 4

   looked for contrary evidence   1 2 3 4

   used probing questions   1 2 3 4

Diaries, Anecdotal Records, Journals

9. In your journal, write about your experiences working with someone from a different culture. Record the date, time, and reason for the interaction. Describe how you felt and what you learned.

For trainees at General Dynamics this was important because they were not allowed access to the manufacturing resource planning software until they had passed a competency test.

The information that learning tests provide to trainers is invaluable. In cases of accidents and litigation, the employer can prove that the employee was trained to the necessary levels. Furthermore, if trainees consistently score low on some aspect of the course, the trainer is alerted to the fact that this component needs to be revised. More information may be required or exercises might have to be added to ensure that learning does occur. At General Dynamics, trainers became extremely motivated because the trainees had to learn and could not be brushed off by hinting that they could "always learn misunderstood material back on the job." However, the trainer cannot assume that scoring well on tests necessarily means doing well on-the-job. It is on the job where the real measurement of the payoff of training begins.

Behaviour

MAKE THE
CONNECTION

Behaviour refers to the display of the newly learned skills or competencies on-the-job. This is also what we have referred to in Chapter 10 as "transfer of training" and is arguably the most important of all training effectiveness criteria.[26] The behaviours assessed should be those identified by the training objectives (see Chapter 5). Behaviours can be measured using three approaches:

a. *Self-reports*: The trainee indicates if and/or how often he/she has used the newly trained behaviours on the job.

b. *Observations*: Others observe and record whether and/or how often the trainee has used the newly trained behaviours on the job. Typically it is supervisors who provide these observations, but depending on the opportunity to observe, the trained person, trainers, subordinates, or even clients can provide it.

c. *Production indicators*: The trainee's objective output is assessed through productivity records, such as sales or absenteeism.

Self-reports remain the most frequently used measures of behaviour.[27] However, the accuracy of self-report measures can be problematic. How do we know that people are accurately remembering and reporting their own behaviours? It is generally agreed that self-reports tend to be *inaccurate*, although they might yet be *valid*. The distinction between accuracy and validity is important. Studies comparing self-reports of absenteeism with company records of absence show that, in general, people tend to report fewer absences than were actually taken (low accuracy). However, people who are more absent tend to self-report more absences than those who have fewer absences (validity). Hence, although self-reports are unable to measure transfer in absolute terms, they are able to reveal trends.

Observations by others (mainly supervisors) are sometimes used to measure behaviour. Typically, the observer rates whether or not the person has used the behaviour and/or how often that has occurred. As with self-reports, the issue of accuracy is of significance here. Moreover, the person's opportunity to observe the behaviour is very important. Observational data are more useful when there is strong evidence to suggest that the observer has extensive contact with the trainee thus enabling frequent observations.

For both self-report and observational data, it is important that the measure focus on specific behaviours (how many times in the last month has the trainee used the new machine) as opposed to general ones (has the trainee applied the skill on the job?). Measures of specific behaviours are more likely to be valid and accurate.

Performance indices (sometimes called "objective" measures) are a third type of behaviour data that might be gathered in an evaluation of behaviour. Performance indicators, such as sales performance, can often be obtained directly from company records. They are more frequently used when the evaluator is interested in measuring the impact of training on job performance.

In some cases, performance records can provide highly precise data on specific behaviours. For example, "the number of times that a trainee has accessed a database" can provide highly accurate behaviour data for evaluating a training program designed to train people in the use and application of a database. With the advent of computer technology, it is now increasingly easy to rely on this information to gauge training success. For example, in the Bell Canada opening case computerized records were used to accurately measure, for each trainee, his/her extent of use of each feature of the electronic telephone. However, performance indices are *not always* the best measure as they sometimes contaminate individual performance with other events that impact performance. For example, one "objective" measure of a telephone operator might be the number of calls he/she has taken in an hour. However, those data might not lead to accurate conclusions as the number of calls an operator takes is also affected by the number of calls that are received. Similarly, the performance of a salesperson is influenced by external factors such as sales territory and competition in addition to the salesperson's behaviour.

Xerox uses many methods to ascertain behaviour, including post-course observations of trainees performing their jobs, interviews with their managers, and a review of performance-appraisal forms.[28] TD Bank uses a very simple approach. Participants in training programs are asked to describe three or four examples of when they used the new knowledge or skill on the job.[29]

Whatever the approach used, behaviour data collection should take place only after the trainee has become comfortable with the newly acquired skills and has had opportunities to demonstrate them on-the-job. The time lag for the assessment of behaviour can range from a few weeks to two years or more in the case of managerial skills. It is recommended that the measurement of behaviour take place at several points following a training program in order to determine the long-term effects of a training program.

Motivation

Training evaluators consider two types of motivation in the training context: Training motivation, which we described in Chapter 3, and the motivation to transfer the skill on the job, which we discussed in Chapter 10. As described in Chapter 3, training motivation is a very important factor that influences training success. A number of scales have been designed to measure training motivation.[30]

Although there are no definitive and established methods to assess motivation to transfer, one important technique relies on expectancy theory (described in Chapter 3). Three sets of items are used to respectively measure the valence (the attractiveness of transfer outcomes), instrumentalities (the positive or negative consequences of transfer), and expectancies (the probability that transfer will result in successful performance). The principle is that trainees will be motivated to apply the training when they attach importance to the end result of training (valence), that the attainment of that end result leads to positive consequences or avoids negative ones (instrumentalities), and that applying the training is likely to lead to the desired end result (expectancies).

A study by Haccoun and Savard exemplifies the measurement of motivation to transfer.[31] Trainees (supervisors) were trained to apply a new organizational policy designed to reduce employee absenteeism (among other things). Motivation was measured through three sets of questions. 1. Valence: How important is it that absence be reduced in your work group? 2. Instrumentality: If you reduce absence what would be the consequences (positive or negative) for you? and 3. Expectancy: If you did apply the behaviours taught in training, how likely is it that absence levels would drop? Each question was rated on a five-point rating scale. The product of the three sets of answers (Valence × Instrumentality × Expectancy) produces the transfer motivation score.

Self-Efficacy

As described in Chapter 3, self-efficacy refers to the beliefs that trainees hold about their ability to perform the behaviours that were taught in a training program. Self-efficacy assesses a person's *confidence* in engaging in *specific* behaviours or achieving specific goals.

Self-efficacy is measured relative to a specific behavioural target. Measures of self-efficacy vary but most tend to focus on assessing trainees' level of confidence for performing specific tasks and behaviours. In one option people rate the likelihood of obtaining a certain result followed by ratings of the confidence they have in obtaining that result. For example, a measure of self-efficacy for an exam on training evaluation might read as follows: "Are you likely to obtain 50%; 60%; 70%; 80%; 90%; 100% on an exam on training evaluation?" (Yes/No response to each option). Next, the person rates how confident they are about obtaining the grade for each "Yes" response. The question might read: "How confident are you that you can obtain that grade?" (0 = Not confident at all, 10 = Totally confident). Another simple method lists the key behaviours demonstrating transfer and asks trainees to rate each on a confidence scale, such as: "How confident are you that you will obtain at least 70% on the training evaluation exam?" The response scales would range from totally confident to not at all confident. Although 10-point rating scales are common, scales employing a smaller number of points are also frequently used.

Perceived and/or Anticipated Support

As indicated in Chapter 10, the support provided to trainees as they return to work is a very important component of transfer and training effectiveness. Two important measures of support are perceived support and anticipated support. **Perceived support** refers to the degree to which the trainee reports receiving support in his or her attempts to transfer the learned skills. **Anticipated support** refers to the degree to which the trainee *expects* to be supported in his or her attempts to transfer the learned skills.

Perceived support

The degree to which the trainee reports receiving support in his or her attempts to transfer the learned skills

Anticipated support

The degree to which the trainee expects to be supported in his or her attempts to transfer the learned skills

The measurement of perceived and/or anticipated support can be easily constructed for any training program. Specific questions can be designed to include the source of the support (e.g., supervisor, co-workers, or the organization) and the support (perceived or anticipated) in applying the training content in general and/or in transferring specific aspects of the training program.

For example, in a study on the effects of a training program that trained nurses on a model of nursing, questions about anticipated support included: "If I am having difficulty writing a nursing care plan, I know I can obtain (very little—very much) help from my supervisor." An alternative phrasing could be, "Based on my previous experiences, I think I can count on (very little—very much) support from my co-workers in applying the training content to my job."

Notice that in the nursing study, the first formulation of the question refers to a specific component of the training program (i.e., nursing care plan) while the latter refers to the training program content in general. These two items also differ in terms of the source of support, with the former being one's supervisor and the latter being co-workers. The respondents use a rating scale to fill in the blank spaces (1 = Very little, 5 = Very much). Similar items can be constructed to refer to key parts of a training program and then administered before training to measure anticipated support and then again once trainees have completed training and returned to work to measure perceived support. In their study, Haccoun and Savard measured anticipated support (immediately after training) and both (perceived) actual support and transfer as assessed two years later. They show that the greater the discrepancy between anticipated and actual supports, the lower the transfer. Expecting help from organizational contexts that do not provide it depresses transfer.

Organizational Perceptions

Several researchers have designed scales to measure perceptions of the transfer climate and a learning culture, which were discussed in Chapters 4 on needs analysis and 10 on transfer of training. Transfer climate can be assessed via a questionnaire developed by Janice Rouiller and Irwin Goldstein.[32] The measure consists of a number of questions that identify eight sets of "cues" that can trigger trainee reactions that encourage or discourage the trainee to transfer the skill. The eight scales include: goal cues, social cues, task and structural cues, positive feedback, negative feedback, punishment, no feedback, and self-control. Trainees are asked questions about training-specific characteristics of the work environment, such as "In your organization, supervisors set goals for trainees to encourage them to apply their training on the job" (1 = Strongly disagree, 5 = Strongly agree).

In addition, J. Bruce Tracey, Scott Tannenbaum, and Michael Kavanagh proposed a scale to measure if an organization has a continuous-learning culture.[33] The questions measure trainees' perceptions, beliefs, expectations, and values with regard to individual, task, and organizational factors that support the acquisition and application of knowledge, skill, and behaviour. The Trainer's Notebook 4.1 in Chapter 4 presents some of the items from this scale.

Finally, the LTSI approach (described in Training Today 11.2 and in Chapter 10) is an example of yet another approach to assessing the role of the organization in fostering training transfer.

Organizational Results

Unlike all of the other variables we have discussed, results focus on the effects of training on the organization rather than on the trainee: How has the organization benefited from the training program? Results criteria are considered to be the "ultimate" criteria for training evaluation and may include such measures as turnover, productivity, quality, profitability, customer satisfaction, accidents, etc. However, some of these may be difficult to measure and, in any case, it is very difficult to clearly attribute changes in these variables specifically to the training program. Testing causality requires experimental designs that are generally difficult to implement in organizations (see "Data Collection Designs in Training Evaluation" section). In some instances, the objective is to cost the program and determine the net benefit. Chapter 12 is devoted to procedures for doing cost-benefit analysis.

Hard data

Results that are assessed objectively

Soft data

Results that are assessed through perceptions and judgments

Hard and soft data can be useful in assessing the results of training. **Hard data** are obtained when the information can be measured objectively, while **soft data** usually involve a judgment or observation. Phillips has produced a taxonomy of hard data and soft data that may be measured in training evaluations.[34] Hard data may include quantities (number of items sold or produced), quality (scrap rates and product returns), time (downtime or time to complete assignments), and costs (sales expenses, benchmarks). ACCO Brands Corporation, a manufacturer of school supplies ranging from paper clips to binders, uses hard data (quantity) to track the effect of training on new production hires. After training, new hires were able to produce vinyl binders at a 5 to 10 percent higher rate than tenured operators: a clear payoff to the organization.

In many cases, however, hard data are difficult to obtain or are simply not relevant to a training program. In these cases, trainers must use soft-data measures that are perceptions. Soft data are results of organizational value that are assessed through perceptions and judgments. Such measures include the perception of work climate, feelings and attitudes, and difficult-to-measure skills like decision making. Although these measures are not direct indicators of organizational outcomes, they are reasoned to be linked to concrete results. For example, communication skills are not bottom-line measures but they may ultimately have an impact on the organization's bottom line. However, it remains difficult to assign a dollar value to this, or to prove that changes in attitude do make a difference.

In some cases it is difficult or impossible to adequately assess the impact of training directly. An alternative is to calculate **return on expectations.** Those who are involved in training decide exactly what they expect from the training. These expectations form the goals for training, and some time after the course, managers decide if the performance results are in line with their expectations.

For example, an organization that was restructured into product-performance teams was unable to place a dollar value on the cross-functional training employees had received, but managers were able to articulate improvements they noticed after the training. The numbers are not absolute, but managers do not directly indicate that time is being managed better but that 95 percent of deadlines are being met. They feel that this anecdotal evidence does have an impact on the bottom line, and that profit improvements are noticeable.

According to the recent Conference Board of Canada survey (see Figure 11.1), a very small percentage of Canadian organizations measure results (similar findings have been reported for the United States by the ASTD). This is far from ideal, but there are good reasons for this. Not only is it more costly in terms of time (it may take months or years for a training program's effects to manifest themselves on the bottom-line results) and resources, it is very difficult to link training to organizational results. The fact that productivity increases after training may not be automatically attributed to training. Many other things unrelated to training, including other changes in the organization or its environment, may have caused the effect and improved productivity. This speaks to the issue of training evaluation designs, a topic to which we now turn.

| **Return on expectations** |
| The measurement of a training program's ability to meet managerial expectations |

Data Collection Designs in Training Evaluation

ⓇⓅⒸ 11.5

Training evaluation studies may be designed in many ways. The more sophisticated training evaluation data collection designs can detect the effect of training in precise ways. Other designs, though useful in some situations, produce more limited conclusions about the value of training. Data collection designs are a very important component of training evaluation as they determine the conclusions that can be validly drawn.

Data collection designs in training evaluation refer to the manner in which the data collection is organized and how the data will be analyzed. All data collection designs compare the trained person to something. They may compare 1. Trained people with untrained ones, 2. The same people before and after training, or 3. Each trained person to an absolute standard. When the comparison does not involve another group of (untrained) people, the

Data collection designs in training evaluation
The manner in which the data collection is organized and how the data will be analyzed

Non-experimental designs
When the comparison is *not* made to another group of (untrained) people

Experimental designs
When the trained group is compared to another group that does not receive the training and when the assignment of people to the training group and the untrained group is random

Quasi-experimental designs
When the trained group is compared to another group that does not receive the training but when the assignment of people to the training group and the untrained group is *not* random

designs are labelled **non-experimental**. When that comparison is to another group of people similar to those trained but that do not receive the training, the designs are called **experimental or quasi-experimental**. The main difference between an experimental design and a quasi-experimental design has to do with whether assignment-to-conditions is random or not random.

In experimental designs, the assignment of people to the trained group (labelled the "experimental" or "trained" group) and to the untrained group (labelled the "control" group) is done randomly. In quasi-experimental designs, we also compare trained to untrained employees but the assignment to the groups is not done randomly. In that case, instead of speaking about a "control" group we refer to it as a "comparison" group.

Figure 11.2 graphically represents several data collection designs. The uses and limitations of each data collection design are explained below, and Table 11.5 summarizes the main differences between the various methodologies. In general, non-experimental designs do not establish if trainee learning and behaviours were *caused* by the training program (with the exception of the IRS, design G below). On the other hand, they are easy to organize and practical for use in organizations. Quasi-experimental and experimental designs are more complex but they do provide evidence of causality. Compared with quasi-experimental designs, experimental designs provide even stronger evidence of causality, but they are more difficult to use in practice.

One of the reasons why experimental designs provide stronger evidence of causality is because one is able to have more confidence that any changes in trainees' learning and behaviour are due to the training and

FIGURE 11.2

Training Evaluation Data Collection Designs

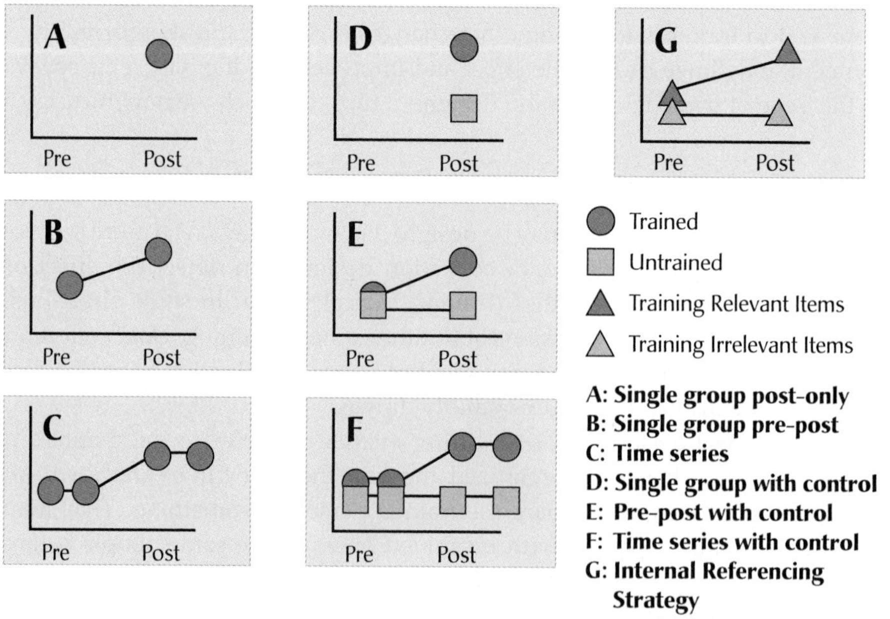
A
Pre
Post
D
Pre
Post
G
Pre
Post
B
Pre
Post
E
Pre
Post
C
Pre
Post
F
Pre
Post
Trained
Untrained
Training Relevant Items
Training Irrelevant Items
A: Single group post-only
B: Single group pre-post
C: Time series
D: Single group with control
E: Pre-post with control
F: Time series with control
G: Internal Referencing Strategy

TABLE 11.5

Uses and Limitations of Non-Experimental, Quasi-Experimental, and Experimental Training Evaluation Designs

Non-experimental designs cannot provide causal information (except for the Internal Referencing Strategy). Hence, such designs can't be used to infer the quality of the training program. However, they are most practical and can provide useful information when the evaluator has an external standard against which post-training performance can be compared and when demonstrating that training caused that proficiency does not matter.

Experimental designs estimate the degree to which a training program has caused trainee proficiency. They are used to establish if the training program should be eliminated or expanded to other parts of the organization. The downside is that experimental designs are more difficult to use in organizational settings.

Quasi-experimental designs provide indications of cause but the proof is not definitive. However, because they do not require random assignment they are generally more accessible to organizations. Hence, quasi-experimental designs may be appropriate when experimental designs cannot be used and when the training manager is willing to live with some risk.

not to something else. To learn more about some of the other factors that might explain a change in trainees' learning and behaviour, see The Trainer's Notebook 11.1, "Understanding Pre-Post Differences."

Non-Experimental, Experimental, and Quasi-Experimental Training Data Collection Designs for Training Evaluation

Training evaluation designs were developed from the principles of experimental scientific research, and there are many research designs within each of the three general types described in the previous section. Each data collection scheme graphically described in Figure 11.2 is now explained.

> **Training evaluation designs**
>
> The process by which evaluation information is gathered

Designs A, B, and C are non-experimental designs because the employees who are trained are not compared to untrained employees. Designs D, E, and F are causal models that compare trained and untrained people and, depending on trainee assignment, they may be experimental or quasi-experimental. Finally, design G—the Internal Referencing Strategy—is a hybrid design that permits some of the conclusions made by the causal designs (D, E, F) while collecting data exclusively from trainees.

In general, all training outcome measures may be used irrespective of the training evaluation design chosen: affective, cognitive, or skill-based as well as reactions and behaviours. *Hence, the choice of an evaluation design has less to do with the measures collected but much more to do with the inferences or decisions required about the training program relative to the original aims of the training program.*

Understanding Pre-Post Differences

Suppose we wish to evaluate this chapter's effectiveness in teaching training evaluation. We select a pre-post design in which knowledge is measured with a multiple choice test administered on the first day of class (pre-test) and again on the last day (post-test). The results show that the students greatly improved their test performance: the average score of the students on the post-test is significantly higher than the pre-test scores. Can it be concluded that reading this chapter caused this gain in knowledge? Before jumping to conclusions, you should consider four alternative explanations:

History or Time. Events in the environment that coincide with this course and that have nothing to do with it may, in fact, have caused pre-to-post changes. For example, the class may have done better because many students saw a PBS program on training evaluation that was aired the week before the final exam.

Maturation. People mature and change over time. As the students are taking this course they are also taking other courses. Even if none of the other courses deals explicitly with training evaluation, they may have helped the students develop higher levels of reasoning and critical thinking skills. This growing general competence may translate into better performance on the post-test.

Testing. Taking the pre-test may have made it easier for students to perform better on the post-test. Some students may have remembered some of the questions asked on the pre-test, while others may have gained a better "feel" for the kinds of questions that are asked. Hence, the post-test performance may be due, at least in part, with the mere experience of being pre-tested.

Mortality. Whereas most students who enroll in a course stay until the end, it is almost always the case that some students drop the course. Those who remain in the course and from whom post-test information will be available may be systematically different from those who dropped the course–they may be more interested in the subject matter, more motivated, more able than those who leave, and/or have more time to meet the course demands. These students may very well show large improvements in learning, shifting the average class performance on the post-test upward.

Source: Adapted from Cook, T. D., & Campbell, D. T. (1979). *Quasi-experimentation: Design and analysis issues for field settings.* Skokie, IL: Rand McNally.

In the remainder of this section we describe each of the seven designs represented in Figure 11.2. Design A is the most simple, while design F is the most complex, with the others falling in between these extremes. More complex designs allow clearer inferences about the effectiveness of the training program. However, these designs are more difficult to implement in practice. Designs A, B, and C are non-experimental because the trained group is not compared to another group. Designs D, E, and F are experimental when subjects are randomly assigned and quasi-experimental when subject assignment to trained and comparison groups is not random. Design G is a hybrid model.

Non-Experimental Designs

Design A: The Post-Only Design is the simplest and most common training evaluation data collection design. Data are gathered once after training and only from those who have completed training. Each trainee is compared to a pre-determined criterion of success and training is considered "effective" when the trainees meet that standard of proficiency. Three common examples of such programs include the exams in a college course on "organizational training," a course for new drivers, and the basic training program administered to new telephone operators. The basic strength (and popularity) of this design is its simplicity. The two drawbacks of the design are that it cannot indicate if the trainees changed (e.g., trainees may have been proficient before training) or if the achieved outcome is a result of training (their observed proficiency may have been "caused" by some other experience coincidental to training).

DESIGN B: THE SINGLE GROUP PRE-POST DESIGN is a non-experimental design because the comparison is not made to another group. Instead the comparison is made to the trainees themselves prior to training. This is the second most frequently used evaluation design. Training outcome data are gathered from trainees both before as well as after training. Used to assess *changes* in trainees, this design infers training effectiveness when the post-training data show statistically significant improvement from pre-training. There are a number of drawbacks of this design. When pre-post differences are noted it is not possible to know if the differences resulted from training, because events other than training may have caused the difference. Other drawbacks include history, testing, and maturation effects, which are described in The Trainer's Notebook 11.1.

DESIGN C: THE TIME-SERIES DESIGN is, in principle, an extension of the pre-post-only data collection technique. Because it requires several measurements, questionnaire data are infrequently used. Instead, the design principally relies on "objective" measures of job performance that can be collected without disturbing the employee. It requires several data collection points before and after training (the pre-post design requires only one pre- and one post-measure). Training is considered effective when there is a clear, evident, and stable difference between pre- and post-performance. The use of several pre- and post-measures, essential to this design, yields the decided advantage of this technique over the simple pre-post design. Objective performance measures tend to fluctuate (up or down) due to many circumstances that may have little to do with the employee. Multiplying the measurement moments will tend to cancel out these fluctuations. Further, the time-series design allows the evaluator to test if post-training improvements are persistent and stable over time. However, the quality of the conclusions depends on the number of times data are collected. The more data points the more valid the conclusion. For example, in a time-series design to assess a course on "selling earthquake insurance" the analyst would retrieve for each trainee the number of earthquake policies sold during each of the four quarters prior to training and each of the four quarters after training. Training is considered effective when the number of policies sold jumps after training and remains consistently higher. However, the statistical analyses required to assess the results are more complex than the ones needed with the simpler designs.

Experimental and Quasi-Experimental Designs

Data collection designs D, E, and F compare the trainees to another group of "equivalent" people who have not been trained. These designs can be either experimental or quasi-experimental depending on whether or not the assignment to the comparison and trained group is random.

DESIGN D: THE SINGLE-GROUP DESIGN WITH CONTROL/COMPARISON GROUP is the simplest quasi-experimental or experimental design. Post-training data are collected from both trainees as well as a group of people who were not trained. Effectiveness is inferred when those trained obtain higher scores on the training outcome than the untrained group. With this design, it is possible to state with considerable confidence that the training program caused the higher outcomes obtained by the trained group. We have greater confidence in this conclusion when the design is experimental (because random assignment ensures that both groups are initially equal). However, the statistical properties of randomness will equate the groups only when the number of people involved is large. This latter restriction is important because many training programs in organizations are administered to a limited number of people. When assignment to groups cannot be randomized (as is typical in organizational settings) the design becomes quasi-experimental and it cannot be categorically stated that the groups were initially equal. In that case the attribution of causality is more risky.

DESIGN E: THE PRE-POST DESIGN WITH CONTROL/COMPARISON GROUP with this design, data are gathered from trainees both before and after training. Simultaneously, data are also gathered from an untrained group. This is a more complete training evaluation design because it allows one to examine the two most important questions about training programs: "Did the trainees change?" and "To what degree was the training program responsible for that change?" Training effectiveness is inferred when pre-post changes are greater for the trained group. The main drawback of this model is practical: rare are the cases where random assignment and multiple measurements can be conducted. In Chapter 14, Training Today 14.4, "Are Corporate Universities Useful?" illustrates this design.

DESIGN F: THE TIME-SERIES DESIGN WITH CONTROL/COMPARISON GROUP is identical to the time-series design C except that data are simultaneously gathered from a comparison group. This additional group allows for stronger conclusions about changes as well as about the role that the training intervention played in creating that change. Take for example the course on "selling earthquake insurance" described above (see design C). Suppose that shortly after the course is offered, an earthquake does occur. Selling earthquake insurance is likely to become a lot easier and all salespeople, whether or not they had taken the training, would show a marked increase. Had we not had a comparison group, we would have falsely concluded that the training program was responsible for the pre-post changes.

A Hybrid Model

DESIGN G: THE INTERNAL REFERENCING STRATEGY. Design G is a hybrid model. It does not need a comparison group so it can't be considered an experimental design. However, it does generate some of the inferences produced by experimental or quasi-experimental data collection systems. The hybrid model was developed by Haccoun and Hamtiaux for use in those frequent cases where a causal inference is required but a control or comparison group is not available.[35] It assesses change from pre- to post-training and estimates if training caused the difference observed without the use of an external comparison group. With this design, it is the outcome measure itself that forms the basis of the comparison.

The heart of this technique is the careful construction of the pre-test and the post-test measures. Two types of test items—"relevant" and "irrelevant but germane"—are constructed. Relevant items are those that test the knowledge and behaviours that are covered in a training program. Irrelevant but germane items are those that could have been included in a training program but were not. For example, in testing the effectiveness of this chapter for teaching evaluation designs, one could ask questions about the time-series design. One could also ask questions about the interrupted time-series design. Questions testing your knowledge of time-series design would be "relevant" because the topic is covered in this chapter. Questions testing your knowledge of the interrupted time-series would be "irrelevant" because the chapter does not cover this design but "germane" because the interrupted time-series is a legitimate evaluation design that could have been included. Comparisons are then made between pre-post differences on the relevant and on the irrelevant but germane items. If the program was effective, the pre-post differences on the relevant items should be greater than the pre-post differences noted on the irrelevant but germane ones. This design is a practical and superior alternative to the pre-post design and it can be used for a variety of learning, behaviour, and job performance outcomes.[36]

Summary of Data Collection Designs

In summary, trainers have a variety of data collection designs to choose from when evaluating a training program. These designs differ in terms of the time involved, their cost, the level of expertise they require, and the kind of conclusions that one can derive from the evaluation. As stated at the beginning of this chapter, evaluation strategies and data collection designs always involve trade-offs (between the quality and the scope of the information gathered and their costs and practicality). A trainer will have to weigh the importance of each of these factors when deciding on an evaluation design. Ultimately, what is most important is the question that the trainer must answer and the information that management requires.

Summary

This chapter reviewed the main purposes for evaluating training programs as well as the barriers that prevent training evaluation. Models of training evaluation were presented, contrasted, and critiqued. Although Kirkpatrick's evaluation model is the most common and frequently used model, for formative evaluations at least, more recent models such as the COMA model and the DBE model might be required. We also described the variables required for an evaluation as well as some of the methods and techniques required to measure them. Whereas many of these are measured through questionnaires administered to trainees, their supervisors, or others, objective data can also be used. Advantages and disadvantages of each were discussed. The main types of data collection designs were also described along with their advantages and disadvantages. The choice of data collection design, as with most aspects of training, was seen as a trade-off between costs and practicalities and the information needs of management.

Key Terms

affective reactions p. 333	hard data p. 342
anticipated support p. 341	non-experimental designs p. 344
causal evaluations p. 326	perceived support p. 341
COMA p. 329	procedural learning p. 336
data collection designs in training evaluation p. 343	quasi-experimental designs p. 344
	return on expectations p. 343
Decision-Based Evaluation (DBE) p. 330	soft data p. 342
declarative learning p. 334	summative evaluations p. 326
descriptive evaluations p. 326	training evaluation p. 321
experimental designs p. 344	training evaluation designs p. 345
formative evaluations p. 326	utility reactions p. 333

Make the Connection

p. 334: declarative and procedural knowledge are discussed in Chapter 3 on page 68

p. 338: transfer of training is discussed in Chapter 10 on page 287 and p. 338: training objectives are discussed in Chapter 5 on page 137

p. 340: training motivation is discussed in Chapter 3 on page 83 and p. 340: motivation to transfer is discussed in Chapter 10 on page 291: expectancy theory is discussed in Chapter 3 on pages 79–81

p. 340: self-efficacy is discussed in Chapter 3 on page 74

p. 341: manager support for transfer of training is discussed in Chapter 10 on page 297

p. 342: training transfer climate and a continuous learning culture are discussed in Chapters 4 and 10 on pages 107 and 293

p. 342: the learning transfer system inventory (LTSI) is discussed in Chapter 10 on page 306

Web Links

ACCO Brands Corporation: www.acco.com

American Society for Training and Development (ASTD): www.astd.org

Bell Canada: www.bell.ca

Conference Board of Canada: www.conferenceboard.ca

General Dynamics: www.generaldynamics.com

TD Bank: www.td.com

Xerox: www.xerox.com

RPC Icons

RPC 11.1 Compiles, analyzes, and documents evaluation data based on feedback.

RPC 11.2 Documents participant feedback to evaluate effectiveness of program delivery.

RPC 11.3 Conducts an evaluation of the program.

RPC 11.4 Ensures participant and organizational feedback is documented and evaluated.

RPC 11.5 Interprets results of development programs in terms of contribution to organizational objectives, and does a post-development follow-up.

Discussion Questions

1. Discuss the similarities and the differences between the evaluation models discussed in the chapter. In your discussion be sure to include the practical implications of preferring one model over another.
2. You have two training programs: a) a course designed to teach the use of a PC and b) a course to improve supervisory feedback to employees. Which evaluation design would you use in each case? What if you wanted to determine if training caused the outcome? Which design would you use?
3. Many organizations do not evaluate their training programs. If you had to convince a manager to evaluate a training program, what would you tell him or her? Why should organizations evaluate their training programs and what should they evaluate?
4. What are the barriers to training evaluation? Discuss the main types of barriers and what a trainer might do to overcome them and evaluate a training program.
5. Discuss the different types of training evaluation and how they can be distinguished from each other.
6. What is the difference between formative and summative evaluation and between descriptive and causal evaluation?
7. Discuss the assumptions of Donald Kirkpatrick's hierarchical model of training evaluation. What are the implications for training evaluation if the assumptions are valid? What are the implications if the assumptions are not valid?
8. Explain each of the following and give an example: Hard data, soft data, and return on expectations. What are the advantages and disadvantages of each type of measure?
9. Explain each of the following and give an example: non-experimental designs, experimental designs, and quasi-experimental designs. What are the advantages and disadvantages of each type of evaluation design?

Using the Internet

1. To find out about the evaluation of executive training, visit the Treasury Board of Canada Secretariat at **www.tbs-sct.gc.ca/eval/pubs/eet-efcs/ eet-efcs_e.asp**. Read the article and answer the following questions:

   a. How has the public sector evaluated training in the past?
   b. How have executive development programs been evaluated in the Canadian federal government?
   c. What model of training evaluation is being advocated?
   d. Do you think that this model should be used to evaluate executive training programs?
   e. What other models would you consider to evaluate executive training programs and why?

The Great Training Debate

Conducting evaluation studies using full experimental designs and sophisticated data collection is almost impossible in real organizations. Some managers argue that training evaluations can provide meaningful conclusions only when conducted using these techniques. They therefore conclude that in most cases training evaluations are a waste of time and money.

Debate this conclusion: Is it the case that training evaluations should be conducted only when it is possible to use the more sophisticated procedures?

In preparation for this debate you should review the chapter's sections on barriers to training evaluation and models of training evaluation as well as data collection designs.

Exercises

In-Class

1. Training evaluation principles and variables can also be used to make important individual decisions. Following her graduation, your best friend Sally felt she lacked "work-life skills." To remedy her perceived problem, she enrolled in a private school that specializes in "enhancing the skills needed for a successful work life." Six months into her program you are meeting Sally, who is briefly visiting home before returning to the school to complete the year-long program. You are graduating at the end of the year and, for the same reasons, are thinking of enrolling in that program after graduation. But you are hesitating as the school fees are very high. You are willing to assume that burden, provided that the program is worthwhile. Assume that Sally is your only source of information about the

school's effectiveness. What are the changes in Sally that you will be looking for to help you decide if the school is worthwhile or not? Are there specific questions you would ask Sally? Refer to the models and variables of training evaluations to guide your thinking. Remember that Sally has not yet completed her course.

2. In most universities and colleges, students fill out an end-of-course questionnaire in which they evaluate the course. Describe how these evaluations are typically conducted in your university or college. What variables are measured, how is that done, and what type of data collection design is used? Keeping in mind each model and the variables in Table 11.1, what other variables do you think should be included as part of the evaluation process? Design an evaluation form that you would like to see used to evaluate your university/college's courses. For each variable you include, develop one sample question and/or a procedure for measuring it.

3. Suppose your university or college has decided to switch all computers from PC to Mac (or, if your university's current system uses Mac, to PC). Although some staff members already know both systems, the majority will need to learn and master the new system (Mac or PC). The university administration has therefore authorized Human Resources and the IT group to work together to develop and deliver a compulsory training program to all staff members. The top university administration has hired you to conduct an evaluation of the effectiveness of this program as it needs to know if the training program was worthwhile. a) Decide whether your client's request calls for a summative or formative evaluation and b) depending on that decision, develop the training evaluation plan. Keeping in mind the data collection designs (Figure 11.1) and the models and the variables of training evaluation, describe what will be measured, how, and when that will be done to meet the client's needs.

4. Suppose that in the same circumstances described in question 3, it is Human Resources and the IT group who are your clients. They are interested in identifying possible improvements to the course. Would the design you established in #3 be applicable? Would you change anything? If so what would you change and how? What would the plan look like if your clients were simultaneously both the administration and the HR/IT?

5. Consider a situation in which you are the director of training and development in an organization that is going to deliver a very expensive training program. It is very important to find out how effective the training program is, given the expense and the large number of employees who will be trained over the next several years. Your job is to develop a plan for the evaluation. Discuss what you will do in terms of the type of evaluation: What data should be gathered and analyzed? What is the purpose of the evaluation and should it be formative or summative? Should it be a descriptive or causal evaluation?

Now consider the different types of evaluation designs in Figure 11.1. What type of evaluation design do you think would be most appropriate? Consider the pros and cons of the various alternatives. Present your training evaluation strategy to the class.

In-the-Field

1. Identify the training manager of a local company, set up an appointment, and meet with him or her. During that interview identify

   - The types of training programs that are given in that company and the types of training evaluations (if any) that are conducted.
   - Is the same type of evaluation used across different programs or are different evaluations designs adopted for different ones?
   - How are the evaluation data used and by whom?
   - Finally, based on all of the information gathered, assess the quality of that company's evaluation efforts: What can the company conclude about training effectiveness given the types of evaluations it conducts, and what can it not conclude?

2. Identify a member of your family or a friend who is currently working and who has recently taken a training course and interview him or her. The purpose of the interview is for you to estimate the likelihood that the training program was "effective." Establish the interview guide (the questions you will ask) in advance of the interview. Your questions should focus on the dimensions to be measured using both the Kirkpatrick and the COMA models.

Case Incident

The Social Agency

A large governmental social agency, employing thousands of social workers and other specialized workers, trained all of its front-line professionals on a new service-delivery system. Simultaneously, it taught managers how to actively support and encourage their employees to implement the new system: that is, transferring their new skills. A consultant was asked to evaluate the effectiveness of the program directed to the managers and to offer suggestions for improvements.

Questions

1. What information should be collected and from whom should it be collected?
2. Discuss when and how the information should be collected.
3. What should the criteria for "effectiveness" be?

Case Study

The Alcohol/Drug Abuse Prevention Program (ADAPP)

The North American Transportation Company (NATC) is a very large organization that provides continent-wide facilities for the shipping of goods, from tonnes of wheat and iron ore to individual parcels. Headquartered in Canada, the company uses all forms of heavy equipment to load, transport, and deliver goods and materials for its clients.

In recent years, a number of accidents and near-accidents had occurred. In some cases the accidents caused injuries to people (mainly employees, though some injuries were sustained by bystanders). They also caused substantial material damage to property and/or the environment. In three cases in the last five years, people were killed.

Investigation of these accidents indicated that drug and/or alcohol abuse by company personnel was relatively common and that these may have been contributing factors to the accidents. This analysis also uncovered that absenteeism and job performance problems were also the result of drug/alcohol use by employees.

The CEO of the company asked the Human Resource department to solve the problem. In response, the department formulated a zero-tolerance policy toward workplace alcohol and drug abuse. The policy outlawed alcohol/drug use on the job and made the implementation and enforcement of the policy the direct responsibility of all supervisory personnel in the company. They further developed and implemented a training program to instruct all supervisors of the policy, the means to implement it, and the specific behaviours expected of them. This training program became known as the Alcohol/Drug Abuse Prevention Program (ADAPP).

The day-long training program explained that it was the responsibility of supervisors to be vigilant with respect to drug/alcohol use on the job and to act immediately when there is a problem.

The supervisors were required to do three major things: 1. Explain the policy to their employees as a group; 2. Observe their employees and note if employees show signs of being "under the influence." Were this to be the case, the supervisor was to individually meet the employee and direct him or her to the Employee Aid Program for further investigation and treatment; and 3. Immediately remove from the job any employee assigned to hazardous duties if the supervisor felt that the person was in no condition to do the work safely. Supervisors who failed to implement the procedure would face disciplinary actions including, in some cases, immediate dismissal.

The training program consisted of lectures and video presentations, followed by various role-playing exercises and discussions designed to help them learn the policy, to motivate supervisors into implementing it, and to enhance their confidence in their ability to do so.

Questions

1. Design a training evaluation for the ADAPP. The training evaluation must be both *summative* (has ADAPP led to an increase in the desired supervisory behaviours and has it led to a decrease in employee absence and workplace accidents and injuries?) and *formative* (what aspects of the training program, if any, should be improved?).
2. What model or models of training evaluation would seem appropriate in this case? Explain your answer.
3. What variables should be measured and how should this be done?
   a. Determine the main variables to measure.
   b. Determine the information to be collected to address program improvements.
4. What data collection design or designs would you consider most appropriate for the evaluation? Explain your reasoning.

References

1. Sackett, P. R., & Mullen, E. J. (1993). Beyond formal experimental design: Towards an expanded view of the training evaluation process. *Personnel Psychology, 46,* 613–627.
2. Twitchell, S., Holton, E. F. III, & Trott, J. R. Jr. (2001). Technical training evaluation practices in the United States. *Performance Improvement Quarterly, 13* (3) 84–109.
3. Sugrue, B., & Kim, K-H. (2004). *ASTD's annual review of trends in workplace learning and performance.* The American Society for Training and Development.
4. Hughes, P. D., & Grant, M. (2007). *Learning and development outlook 2007.* The Conference Board of Canada.
5. Grider, D. T. (1990). Training evaluation. *Business Magazine 17* (1), 20–24.
6. Laroche, R., & Haccoun, R. R. (2003). Buts complémentaires and contradictoires de la formation du personnel: Une typologie intégratrice. (Complementary and contradictory goals of employee training: An integrative typology) *Psychologie du travail et des organisations, 9,* 3–4, 147–166.
7. Kraiger, K., Ford, J. K., & Salas, E. (1993). Application of cognitive, skill based and affective theories of learning outcomes to new methods of training evaluation. *Journal of Applied Psychology, 78* (2) 311–328; Colquitt, J. A., Lepine, J. A., & Noe, R. A. (2000). Toward an integrative theory of training motivation: A meta-analytic path analysis of 20 years of research. *Journal of Applied Psychology, 85* (5), 678–707.
8. Pace, R. W., Smith, C. P., & Mills, G. E. (1991). *Human resource development: The field.* Englewood Cliffs, NJ: Prentice-Hall.
9. Roullier, J. Z., & Goldstein, I. L. (1993). The relationship between organizational transfer climate and positive transfer of training. *Human Resource Development Quarterly, 4* (4), 377–390; Tracey, J. B., Tannenbaum, S. I., & Kavanagh, M. J. (1995). Applying trained skills on the job: The importance of the work environment. *Journal of Applied Psychology, 80* (2), 239–252.
10. Tracey, J. B., Hinkin, T. R., Tannenbaum, S., & Mathieu, J. E. (2001). The influence of individual characteristics and the work environment on varying levels of training outcomes. *Human Resource Development Quarterly, 12,* 1, 5–23.
11. Quinones, M. A. (1995). Pretraining context effects: Training assignment as feedback. *Journal of Applied Psychology, 80,* 226–238.
12. Montesino, M. U. (2002). Strategic alignment of training, transfer-enhancing behaviors and training usage: A posttraining study. *Human Resource Development Quarterly, 13* (1), 89–108; Saks, A. M., Tagger, S., & Haccoun, R. R. (2002). Is training related to firm performance? *The HRM Research Quarterly, 6* (2).

13. Worthen, B. R., & Sanders, J. R. (1987). *Educational evaluations: Alternative approaches and practical guidelines.* White Plains, NY: Longman.

14. Kirkpatrick, D. L. (1976). Evaluation of training. In R. L. Craig (Ed.), *Training and development handbook: A guide to human resource development* (2nd ed). New York: McGraw-Hill.

15. Kraiger, K. (2002). Decision-based evaluation. In K. Kraiger (Ed.), *Creating, implementing, and managing effective training and development: State-of-the-art lessons for practice* (pp. 331–375). San Francisco: Jossey-Bass

16. Holton, E. F. III. (1996). The flawed four-level evaluation model. *Human Resource Development Quarterly, 7,* 5–21; Alliger, G. M., Tannenbaum, S. L., Bennett, W., Traver, H., & Shortland, A. (1997). A meta-analysis on the relations among training criteria. *Personnel Psychology, 50,* 341–342.

17. Jeanrie, C., & Saks, A. M. (1999). Concepts et pratiques contemporaines en évaluation de la formation: Vers un modèle diagnostic des impacts. In D. Bouthilier (Ed.) *Gérer pour la performance.* Montreal: Presses de HEC.

18. Holton, E. F., Bates, R. A., & Ruona, W. E. A. (2000). Development of a generalized learning transfer system inventory. *Human Resource Development Quarterly, 11* (4), 333–360.

19. Morgan, R. B., & Casper, W. (2000). Examining the factor structure of participant reactions to training: A multidimensional approach. *Human Resource Development Quarterly, 11,* 301–317.

20. Alliger, G. M., Tannenbaum, S. L., Bennett, W., Traver, H., & Shortland, A. (1997). Meta analysis of the relationship among training criteria. *Personnel Psychology, 50,* 341–357.

21. Sitman, T., Brown, K. G., Casper, W. J., Ely, K., & Zimmerman, R. D. (2008). A review and meta-analysis of the nomological network or trainee reactions. *Journal of Applied Psychology, 93* (2), 280–295.

22. Jonassen, D., & Tessmer, M. (1996–97). An outcomes-based taxonomy for instructional systems design, evaluation and research. *Training Research Journal, 2,* 11–46.

23. Desjardins, D. (1995). Impact de la présentation d'un organisateur avancé sur l'apprentissage et le transfert en formation du personnel. Unpublished Master's Thesis, Université de Montréal, Département de Psychologie.

24. Ostroff, C. (1991). Training effectiveness measures and scoring schemes: A comparison. *Personnel Psychology, 44,* 353–374.

25. Smith, J. E., & Merchant, S. (1990). Using competency exams for evaluating training. *Training and Development Journal, 44* (8), 65–71.

26. Flynn, G. (1998). The nuts and bolts of valuing training. *Workforce Management, 17* (11), 80–85; Kozlowski, S. W. J., & Salas, E. (1997). A multilevel organizational systems approach for the implementation and transfer of training. In J. K. Ford (Ed.) *Improving training effectiveness in work organizations* (pp. 247–287). Hillsdale, NJ: Erlbaum.

27. Salas, E., & Cannon-Bowers, J. A. (2001). The Science of training: A decade of progress. *Annual Review of Psychology, 52,* 471–499.

28. Olian, J. D., & Durham, C. C. (1998). Designing management training and development for competitive advantage: Lessons from the best. *Human Resource Planning, 21* (1), 20–31.

29. Larin, N. (April, 1998). Who understands return on investment better than a bank? *Canadian HR Reporter,* 2–8.

30. Noe, R. A., & Schmitt, N. (1986). The influence of trainee attitudes on training effectiveness: Test of a model. *Personnel Psychology, 39,* 497–523.

31. Haccoun, R. R., & Savard, P. (2003). Prédire le transfert des apprentissages à long terme role du soutien anticipé et perçu, de la motivation et de l'efficacité personnelle. (Predicting long term transfer of learning: The role of anticipated and actual support, motivation, and self efficacy). In G. Delobbe, C. Karnas, & C. Vandenberghe (Eds.), *Evaluation et développement des compétences au travail.* UCLs: Presses Universitaire de Louvain, pp. 507–516.

32. Roullier, J. Z., & Goldstein, I. L. (1993). The relationship between organizational transfer climate and positive transfer of training. *Human Resource Development Quarterly, 4* (4), 377–390; Tracey, J. B., Tannenbaum, S. I., & Kavanagh, M. J. (1995). Applying trained skills on the job: The importance of the work environment. *Journal of Applied Psychology, 80* (2), 239–252.

33. Roullier, J. Z., & Goldstein, I. L. (1993). The relationship between organizational transfer climate and positive transfer of training. *Human Resource Development Quarterly, 4* (4), 377–390; Tracey, J. B., Tannenbaum, S. I., & Kavanagh, M. J. (1995). Applying trained skills on the job: The importance of the work environment. *Journal of Applied Psychology, 80* (2), 239–252.
34. Phillips, J. (1996). How much is the training worth? *Training & Development,* 20–24.
35. Haccoun, R. R., & Hamtiaux, T. (1994). Optimizing knowledge tests for inferring learning acquisition levels in single group training evaluation designs: The internal referencing strategy. *Personnel Psychology, 47,* 593–604.
36. Frese, M., Beimel, S., & Schoenborn, S. (2003). Action training for charismatic leadership: Two evaluation studies of a commercial training module on inspirational communication of vision. *Personnel Psychology, 56,* 671–697.

CHAPTER 12

The Costs and Benefits of Training

Chapter Learning Outcomes

After reading this chapter, you should be able to:

- explain why trainers should calculate the costs and benefits of training programs
- describe the different approaches for costing training programs
- explain the difference between cost-effectiveness and cost-benefit evaluation
- describe how to calculate the benefits of training programs
- describe how to conduct a net benefit analysis, benefit–cost ratio, and return on investment
- define utility analysis and describe how to calculate the utility of training programs
- discuss the importance of credibility when estimating the benefits of training programs

ACCENTURE

Accenture is a global management consulting, technology services, and outsourcing company with more than 186,000 employees in 52 countries. A core value of the company is attracting and developing the best people and providing them with opportunities for personal and professional growth.

Accenture invests heavily in the training and development of its employees. Entry-level employees receive more than 750 hours of training during their first five years and during the next eight years they receive an additional 550 hours of training. More than 70 percent of Accenture's new hires say that training was an important factor in joining the firm.

However, several years ago in the midst of changes in the global economy, the company experienced a dramatic transformation. Among the many challenges facing the firm was a realization of the need to reinvent its learning programs in order to deal with the many changes facing the company.

A critical part of the reinvention was that it would no longer be acceptable to treat training as a cost centre. Rather, it would be necessary to demonstrate and prove the added value of learning programs to the company. With this in mind, the company conducted a major return on investment (ROI) study to determine the ROI of its training programs.

The study involved analyzing the ROI of training for all of the company's employees over the history of the company. They did this using a technique that begins with a comprehensive analysis of employee records and measures the impact of learning on recruiting, retention, chargeability, and performance. To isolate the training effect on a per-person margin, the analysis factors out the effects of inflation, market cycle, experience, and employee level.

The study indicated that the net benefit of training was $1.27 billion. To calculate the return on investment (ROI), they divided the net benefit by the total cost of training ($358 million). The result was that for every dollar invested in training, there was a return of $3.53 or an ROI of 353 percent. In other words, for every dollar invested in learning, the firm receives the dollar back plus an additional $3.53 to its bottom line.

The study also showed that employees who take more training (the top 50th percent) are more productive. They have 20 percent higher bill rates to clients, they are more "chargeable" to clients, and they stay with the company 14 percent longer compared to the bottom 50 percent.

The ROI study got the attention and respect of the company's most senior executives. It secured their ongoing support for the learning transformation and made it clear how important learning is for achieving business objectives and driving high performance.

Accenture's learning strategy is now aligned with its business strategy, and learning has had a positive impact on financial performance. Accenture has an evaluation system that collects data on all of its training programs, allowing the company to measure the ROI of each course. The company has won numerous awards for its ROI evaluation process, which is now featured in a book called *Return on Learning*.[1]

Organizations have become increasingly concerned about the costs and benefits of their training programs. As you can see from the Accenture story, it is possible to calculate the benefits of training programs in monetary terms and the return on training investments. Accenture's learning transformation shows that learning programs can be run like a business and that learning can have a financial impact on an organization's bottom line by maximizing the return on learning.

Information on the costs and benefits of training programs is an important part of the training evaluation process. In fact, some experts consider the calculation of return on investment (ROI) to be Level 5 in Kirkpatrick's evaluation model (see Chapter 11).[2]

This chapter describes different approaches for calculating the costs and benefits of training programs. In this chapter, you will learn how to calculate the costs, benefits, net benefit, benefit–cost ratio, return on investment (ROI), and utility of training programs. But first, let's discuss training and the bottom line.

Training and the Bottom Line

In Chapter 11, we described the process of training evaluation. This usually involves measuring trainees' reactions, learning, behaviour, and organization results. The intent is to show some improvement in employees' knowledge, on-the-job behaviour, and organizational outcomes. Typically, one hopes to see an improvement in employees' learning and on-the-job behaviour and a positive effect on organizational outcomes.

But what about the cost of a training program? What if a training program is very expensive? That is, what if the cost is greater than the benefit? Would improvements in employee behaviour and organizational outcomes still be significant? Would the training program be worth the cost?

Without information on the cost of training and the monetary value of training benefits, one cannot adequately answer these questions. Clearly, the effectiveness of a training program also depends on its costs and benefits. Management might be pleased to know that a training program has improved customer satisfaction, but managers will be even more interested to know the financial value of an improvement in customer satisfaction. Recall how the ROI study at Accenture got the attention and ongoing support of senior executives.

Costing is a complex and time-consuming process that many training specialists traditionally have avoided. Some managers are skeptical about the theoretical underpinnings of costing, while others suggest, rightly, that in business not everything is quantifiable. Indeed, many managers suggest that some quality and processes—job satisfaction, communication techniques—make people feel good about themselves and the company they work for, and you just cannot put a dollar value on them.

However, there is increasing pressure for human resource and training professionals to demonstrate the financial value of their programs. Organizations increasingly want to know the return on their training investments.[3] Therefore, trainers and human resource professionals must increasingly be able to calculate and demonstrate the costs and benefits of training and development programs. This not only demonstrates the value of training programs to management and the organization, but also justifies the training function's share of the budget and improves its credibility.

Furthermore, other members of an organization are more likely to see training and development as an investment rather than a cost and training budgets are less likely to be slashed during economic downturns. You might recall from Chapter 1 that most organizations in Canada view training and development as a necessary operating expense or cost that should be minimized rather than as an investment. Calculating the costs and benefits of training programs is necessary for viewing training as an investment. Financial information about the benefits of training programs also places human resource and training professionals on an equal footing with other functions in an organization.

Training and the Bottom Line in Canadian Organizations

According to the Conference Board of Canada, although most training programs in Canada are evaluated at Level 1 (trainee reactions), only 4 percent are evaluated at Level 5 or investment evaluation.[4] However, more organizations are beginning to conduct financial evaluations of their training programs.

For example, at CIBC financial advisers across Canada attended a workshop on how to advise clients on company pension plans. They completed detailed surveys of their knowledge before and after the workshop that were then compared to hard data on new pension-related sales in order to identify the percentage of new business that was due to the workshop. In 2007, CIBC integrated its internal mandatory training programs into the Corporate Mandatory Training and Testing Program. The training provides employees with information on how to recognize and demonstrate actions consistent with CIBC's core principles and practices. Most of CIBC's 42,000 employees have completed the training and the direct cost savings to CIBC are estimated to be over $2 million annually.[5]

At Firestone Canada, 15 supervisors attended a problem-solving workshop after a lack of skills was identified as the source of an internal problem. After the training the supervisors used their new skills to solve the problem. An assessment of the program's impact on the supervisors indicated that supervisors acquired new problem-solving skills, strengthened their analytical thinking, participated in more dynamic teamwork, and had better quality control. As for the bottom line, the company realized a cost savings of $10,000 per month.[6]

Of course, in order to calculate the effect of training on the bottom line, one has to first calculate the costs and benefits of training. In the next section, we describe how to calculate training costs and in subsequent sections we describe how to calculate the benefits of training.

Costing Training Programs

Costing is the process used to identify all the expenditures used in training. This is an important procedure in both the design and evaluation of a training program. In Chapter 9, we noted that the trainer must prepare a budget that includes the costs of all of the expenses incurred in the delivery of a training program.

The calculation of the cost of a training program usually involves the assignment of various costs to a number of meaningful cost categories. Over the years, a number of approaches have been developed. One approach categorizes the costs of training according to the stages of the training process. For example, one might calculate the cost of needs analysis, training design, delivery, and evaluation. These costs are usually listed on a costing worksheet. One can then calculate and compare the cost of each stage as well as the total cost of a training program.

An example of this kind of costing worksheet is presented in Table 12.1. Note that in addition to the cost of the needs analysis, program development, delivery, and evaluation, this worksheet also includes a category for fixed costs (e.g., overhead, equipment) as well as the costs of revisions.

Another approach to costing training programs is to categorize the costs according to the nature or kind of cost. An example of this approach uses the following five cost categories: direct costs, indirect costs, development costs, overhead costs, and trainee compensation costs.[7]

Direct Costs

Direct costs are costs that are directly linked to a particular training program. This would include the trainers' salary and benefits, equipment rental, course materials, instructional aids, food and refreshments, and the cost of travel to and from the training site. These costs are so directly linked to a particular training program that they would not be incurred if a training program were cancelled.

Indirect Costs

Indirect costs are costs that are not part of a particular training program per se but they are expenses required to support training activities. Indirect costs include clerical and administrative support, trainer preparation and planning,

Costing

The process of identifying all the expenditures used in training

Direct costs

Costs that are directly linked to a particular training program

Indirect costs

Costs that support training activities and are not directly linked to a particular training programs

TABLE 12.1

Costing Worksheet

1. Fixed-cost factors

    i. Overhead—AC/heat/light; space; rental/lease;
       communications; per input hour   _____

    ii. Supervisory allocation per input hour   _____

    iii. Equipment cost per input hour   _____

    iv. Administrative support cost per input hour   _____

    v. Training unit fringe benefits cost per input hour   _____

2. Total fixed costs per input hour   _____

    i. Professional hours _____ @ $____/hour = cost   _____

    ii. Support hours _____ @ $____/hour = cost   _____

    iii. Transportation expenses   _____

    iv. Material   _____

    v. Consulting fees   _____

    vi. Other costs   _____

    Total direct needs-analysis costs   _____

3. Program development

    i. Professional hours _____ @ $____/hour = cost   _____

    ii. Support hours _____ @ $____/hour = cost   _____

    iii. Material   _____

    iv. Consulting fees   _____

    v. Subject-matter expert/management and staff input
       _____ hours @ _____/hour = cost   _____

    vi. Other costs   _____

    Total direct program-development costs   _____

4. Program delivery

    i. Administration hours   _____
       @ $_____/hour = costs   _____

    ii. Administrative support hours   _____
        @ $_____/hour = costs   _____

    iii. Presentation/delivery hours   _____
         @ $_____/hour = cost   _____

    iv. Technical support hours   _____
        @ $_____/hour = cost   _____

    v. Trainee materials costs   _____

    vi. Transportation/accommodations/meals
        a. staff   _____
        b. trainees   _____

    vii. Facilities rental   _____

    viii. Equipment   _____

    Total direct program-delivery costs   _____

TABLE 12.1 (*continued*)

5. Evaluation

    i. @ $_____/hour = cost   _____

    ii. Support hours   _____

        @ $_____/hour = cost   _____

    iii. Management input hours   _____

        @ $_____/hour = cost   _____

    iv. Trainee input hours   _____

        @ $_____/hour = cost   _____

    v. Transportation costs   _____

    vi. Material costs   _____

    vii. Consulting fees   _____

    Total evaluation cost   _____

6. Revision costs

    i. Professional hours ___ @ $____/hour = cost   _____

    ii. Support hours ____ @ $____/hour = cost   _____

    iii. Management/staff collaboration hours ____ @

        $____/hour = cost   _____

    Total evaluation cost   _____

7. Total program cost

    1 + 2 + 3 + 4 + 5 + 6 = Total Cost   _____

training materials that have already been sent to trainees, and the cost of marketing training programs. These costs would still be incurred even if a training program were cancelled. In other words, unlike the direct costs, these costs cannot be recovered.

Developmental Costs

Developmental costs are costs that are incurred in the development of a training program. This would include the cost of doing a needs analysis, the cost of developing training methods such as videotapes, the design of training materials, and the cost of evaluating a training program.

Developmental costs

Costs that are incurred in the development of a training program

Overhead Costs

Overhead costs refer to costs incurred by the training department but not associated with any particular training program. Such costs are required for the general operation of the training function such as the cost of maintaining training facilities (e.g., heat and lighting) and equipment and the salaries of clerical and administrative support staff. A portion of these costs must be allocated to each training program.

Overhead costs

Costs incurred by the training department but not associated with any particular training program

Trainee Compensation Costs

Trainee compensation refers to the cost of the salaries and benefits paid to trainees while they are attending a training program. This might also include

Trainee compensation

The cost of the salaries and benefits paid to trainees while they are attending a training program the cost of replacing employees while they are in training. The logic behind this cost is simply that employees must be paid while they are not working and this is a cost of the training program.

Training Costs at Wood Panel Plant

Table 12.2 presents a training cost analysis using the five cost categories described above. The example is from a company that produces wood panels. The company had three problems that it wanted solved. First, it wanted to improve the quality of wood panels because they were experiencing a 2-percent rejection rate each day due to poor quality. Second, they wanted to lower the number of preventable accidents, which was higher than the industry average. Third, they wanted to improve the housekeeping of the production area, which was considered poor and a cause of some of the preventable accidents. Visual inspections that used a 20-item checklist indicated an average of 10 problems in housekeeping each week.[8]

The solution was to train supervisors in performance-management and interpersonal skills. Forty-eight supervisors as well as seven shift superintendents and a plant manager attended a three-day behavioural-modelling skill-building training program. The objectives of the program were to teach the supervisors how to discuss quality problems and poor work habits with employees; to recognize improvements in employee performance; to teach employees on the job; and to recognize employees for above-average performance.

The cost of the training program was calculated for each of the five cost categories. As shown in Table 12.2, the total cost of the training program was $32,564, or $582 per trainee. This was based on total direct costs of $6,507; indirect costs of $1,161; development costs of $6,756; overhead costs of $1,444; and compensation costs of $16,696.

It is important to recognize that the costing processes presented in Tables 12.1 and 12.2 are only examples. They represent two approaches for categorizing training costs and they might need to be modified to suit an organization's unique circumstances. The idea is to identify the main costs of a training program and not to worry too much about the labels assigned to them. The trainer should be most concerned about how to design a costing approach that has credibility within an organization and that will be accepted by management.

Once the costs of a training program have been calculated, they can be used for at least two purposes. First, they can be used to prepare a budget for a training program and to compare and contrast the costs of different programs. This is important when making decisions about whether to adopt a particular training program. Second, they can be used along with benefit information to calculate a training program's net benefit, benefit–cost ratio (BCR), and return on investment (ROI).

In the next section, we present examples of how to compare the costs of different training programs followed by a discussion of how to determine the benefits of training programs.

TABLE 12.2

Training Cost Analysis for Wood Panel Plant

Direct costs. The travel and per-diem cost was zero, because training took place adjacent to the plant. Classroom space and audiovisual equipment were rented from a local hotel; refreshments were purchased at the same hotel. Because different supervisors attended the morning and afternoon sessions, lunch was not provided.

Direct Costs	
Outside instructor	0
In-house instructor—12 days x $125 a day	$1,500
Fringe benefits—25 percent of salary	375
Travel and per-diem expenses	0
Materials—$60 x 56 participants	3,360
Classroom space and audiovisual equipment—12 days x $50 a day	600
Refreshments—$4 a day x 3 days x 56 participants	672
Total direct costs	**$6,507**

Indirect costs. Clerical and administrative costs reflect the amount of clerical time spent on making arrangements for the workshop facilities, sending out notices to all participants, and preparing class rosters and other miscellaneous materials.

Indirect Costs	
Training management	0
Clerical and administrative salaries	750
Fringe benefits—25 percent of clerical and administrative salaries	187
Postage, shipping, and telephone	0
Pre- and post-learning materials—$4 x 56 participants	224
Total indirect costs	**$1,161**

Development costs. These costs represent the purchase of the training program from a vendor. Included are instructional aids, an instructor manual, videotapes, and a licensing fee. The instructor-training costs are for a one-week workshop the instructor attended to prepare for facilitating the training. Front-end assessment costs were covered by the corporate training budget.

Development Costs	
Fee to purchase program	3,600
Instructor training	
Registration fee	1,400
Travel and lodging	975
Salary	625
Benefits (25 percent of salary)	156
Total development costs	**$6,756**

Overhead costs. These represent the services that the general organization provides to the training unit. Because figures were not available, we used 10 percent of the direct, indirect, and program-development costs.

Overhead Costs	
General organization support, 10 percent of direct, indirect, top management's time and development costs	....
Total overhead costs	**$1,444**

Compensation for participants. This figure represents the salaries and benefits paid to all participants while they attended the workshop.

Compensation for Participants	
Participants' salaries and benefits (time away from the job)	
Total compensation	**$16,696**
Total training costs	**$32,564**
Cost per participant	**$ 582**

Source: Robinson, D. G., & Robinson, J. (1989). Training for impact. Adapted from *Training & Development*, August, 34–42, American Society for Training & Development.

Comparing the Costs of Training Programs

While the costing of a training program is necessary for budgeting and reporting purposes, costing training programs is also necessary to determine the relative costs of different training alternatives. Consider the following comparison worksheet:

Program _____	Analyst _____	Date _____
Option	1. _____	2. _____
Performance Value	$ _____	$ _____
Minus Cost	_____	_____
Net Benefit	$ _____	$ _____

To complete the analysis, the program costs (see Table 12.3) are combined with an estimate of the value of the program (performance value) to the organization. To give you an example of how this type of cost-comparison works and how different organizations might require cost data at various levels of complexity and detail, consider the following situation.[9]

You are part of an organization that designs electronic systems. A recent reorganization has created a project-management division that places all lead engineers on projects in one group rather than being spread across several operations. The purpose of the reorganization was to allow the engineers to have less hands-on technical activity and focus more on theory development, design, and the management of others on projects. A manager from your firm with an outstanding record in project management now heads the management group. The group consists of 10 lead engineers. You have been experiencing an alarming rate of turnover in electronic engineers since this group was established. A needs analysis reveals that the engineer types who make up this management group are very unskilled in communicating directions, delegating, and handling people-crisis issues. Data from the exit interviews reveal that the inability of project managers to manage crises and the inability to transmit clear guidelines and directions have been the primary frustrations. Your needs analysis also confirms that the members of the organization and the management group itself feel that this reorganization was a good decision.

The crisis in the organization resulting from the high turnover rate is a financial one. Finding, hiring, and relocating an engineer with the appropriate credentials and experience costs the organization approximately $75,000. In the past nine months, your organization has replaced five engineers. At this rate you anticipate you will replace a total of six engineers before the year is complete. You have been asked to recommend a training program to address the management skills deficiencies in this group. The goal is to reduce the turnover rate to two engineers per year.

Your options are to send each project manager in the group to a management development institute identified by the president of the corporation, to

TABLE 12.3

Comparison Worksheet

Program _____   Analyst _____   Date _____

_____ Option name   1. _____   2. _____

Analysis:

Needs assessment _____   _____   _____

Work analysis _____   _____   _____

Proposal to management _____   _____   _____

Other _____   _____   _____

Other _____   _____   _____

Design:

General HRD program design _____   _____   _____

Specific HRD program design _____   _____   _____

Other _____   _____   _____

Other _____   _____   _____

Development:

Draft and prototype _____   _____   _____

Pilot test and revise _____   _____   _____

Production and duplication _____   _____   _____

Other _____   _____   _____

Other _____   _____   _____

Implementation:

Program management _____   _____   _____

Program delivery _____   _____   _____

Participant costs _____   _____   _____

Other _____   _____   _____

Other _____   _____   _____

Evaluation:

Program evaluation and report _____   _____   _____

Performance follow-up _____   _____   _____

Other _____   _____   _____

Other _____   _____   _____

Total training program costs $ _____ $ _____

(Option 1)   Option 2)

arrange for a vendor-delivered training program in-house, or to develop a coaching program to help these managers acquire the necessary skills.

Your director has suggested that the last option might take 9 to 12 months to achieve the desired results. The probabilities are low to none that the managers will develop the skills needed on their own on-the-job. Your organization will not consider salaries or other normal employee maintenance costs as training expenses.

A budget of $7,000 will be provided for materials and $17,000 for consulting fees to support a coaching approach to solving the problem. The following information is provided to help you make your decision:

MANAGEMENT DEVELOPMENT INSTITUTE:

80-hour program delivered off-site over a two-week period—$10,000 per trainee (this includes airfare, lodging, food, and materials).

VENDOR–SUPPLIED PROGRAM:

15 four-hour sessions delivered on site over a six-month period—$15,000 per trainee

MATERIALS BUDGET TO SUPPORT COACHING OPTION: $7,000

Needs Analysis	10%	
Work Analysis	5%	
Design	5%	
Development	15%	
Implementation	50%	
Evaluation	15%	
	100%	allocation

Table 12.4 shows the actual cost analysis worksheet used by the organization. This example demonstrates a number of important aspects of costing and comparing training program alternatives:

1. It shows how the original costing sheet (Table 12.1) can be modified to meet an organization's needs. The substitution of a "maintenance of behaviour" category for the nebulous term "performance follow-up," for example, makes this cost easier to sell. Also, there was no need to make a "proposal to management." The problem was well understood and immediate.
2. Management was not interested in a cost breakdown for either the institute or the in-house vendor program, hence the single cost entered in the "Delivery" column. In contrast, had this client been a government agency, a detailed breakdown of both bids might have been required.
3. As discussed previously, costs of salaries and benefits, overhead, and cost-productivity measures are not included. In this case, the problem had to be solved. Management was not interested in fine-tuning the costs.
4. Coaching, an on-the-job training method, is by far the cheapest option. Whether coaching will be the method chosen would require a benefit analysis. The important issue, however, is that a formal training program might not be the best investment. All appropriate training and development methods should be considered.

While this type of cost comparison analysis is useful for determining the costs of training programs and making sound choices and budgetary allocations, a decision should not be made without an estimate of the benefits likely

TABLE 12.4

	M.D. Institute	Outside Vendor	Coaching
Cost Analysis Worksheet for Project Manager Training Options			
Analysis:			
Needs Analysis	$ _____	$ _____	$ 10,700
Work Analysis	$ _____	$ _____	$ 4,350
Design:			
Program	$ _____	$ _____	$ 350
Instructional Aids	$ _____	$ _____	$ 0
Development:			
Pilot Testing	$ _____	$ _____	$ 0
Formative Evaluation			
(during the HRD activity)	$ _____	$ _____	$ 0
Instructional Aids	$ _____	$ _____	$ 1,050
Implementation:			
Delivery	$ 100,000	$ 150,000	$ 3,500
Management	$ _____	$ _____	$ 0
Evaluation:			
Summative Evaluation	$ _____	$ _____	$ 3,000
Training Revision	$	$	$ 0
Maintenance of Trainee			
Behaviour	$ _____	$ _____	$ 1,050
(A) Total	$ 100,000	$ 150,000	$ 24,000
(B) Trainees	$ 10	$ 10	$ 10
Cost Per Trainee (A)/(B) =	$ 10,000	$ 15,000	$ 2,400

to be received under each system. In the following sections, we describe how to calculate the benefits of training programs.

The Benefits of Training Programs

The benefits of a training program can be calculated in monetary or non-monetary terms. When the benefit is calculated in monetary terms, it is referred to as cost-effectiveness evaluation. **Cost-effectiveness evaluation** involves comparing the monetary cost of training to the benefit of training in monetary terms.

Sometimes, however, it is not possible to determine the monetary value of training benefits or to express them in financial terms. Further, in some cases there might be important benefits of a training program that are not monetary benefits. This kind of evaluation is called cost-benefit evaluation.

Cost-benefit evaluation compares the cost of training in monetary terms to the benefits of training in non-monetary terms. Non-monetary benefits are similar to what was described as results or Level-4 evaluation criteria in

 **12.2**

Cost-effectiveness evaluation

A comparison of the monetary cost of training to the benefit of training in monetary terms

Cost-benefit evaluation

A comparison of the cost of training in monetary terms to the benefits of training in non-monetary terms

Chapter 11 and include organization outcomes such as the rate of turnover, absenteeism, customer satisfaction, and so on. It is worth noting that such benefits might have a financial effect on the performance of an organization even though they might not be described in monetary terms.

For example, if a training program is expected to reduce the amount of scrap in the production of a product, then a cost-benefit evaluation would indicate how much the training program cost and the amount or percentage reduction in scrap. On the other hand, a cost-effectiveness evaluation would calculate the monetary value of the reduction in scrap.

How benefits are calculated depends on the training situation, management needs, and the data available. Because of these differences, we present several examples of the calculation of cost-benefit and cost-effectiveness evaluation.

Benefits of Project Manager Training Options

Recall from Table 12.4 that the coaching option has the lowest cost ($24,000) compared to the other two options ($100,000 for the institute and $150,000 for the outside vendor). However, when the Benefits Calculation Worksheet (Table 12.5) is completed, a different picture emerges.

First, we can do a cost-benefit evaluation by comparing the cost of each option to the non-monetary benefit of the estimated reduction in turnover. As shown in Table 12.5, the reduction in turnover for the Management Development Institute is estimated to be 4.8; for the outside vendor the estimated reduction is 3.0; and for the coaching option it is 1.0. Thus, the Management Development Institute is estimated to result in the greatest amount of turnover reduction followed by the outside vendor and then coaching. Also note that the Management Development Institute is the most expensive option followed by the outside vendor and coaching option. In this case, if one were simply interested in the greatest turnover reduction, then the Management Development Institute would be the preferred option.

It is also possible to conduct a cost-effectiveness evaluation. But first, we have to convert the benefit of a training program into monetary terms. Returning to the example in Table 12.4, recall that finding, hiring, and relocating an engineer with the appropriate credentials and experience costs the organization approximately $75,000. Therefore, the monetary benefit of each option is based on the reduction in turnover multiplied by $75,000 as follows: Management Development Institute is $363,000 (4.8 reduction × $75,000); the outside vendor is $225,000 (3.0 reduction × $75,000); and the coaching option is $75,000 (1 reduction × $75,000).

Once we know the cost of a training program as well as the benefit in monetary terms, it is possible to determine the net benefit of the program. The **net benefit** of a training program refers to the benefit minus the cost of the training program. Thus, to conduct a net benefit analysis one simply subtracts the cost of a training program from its financial benefit.

The net benefit of each of the three training options is simply the monetary benefit due to the reduction in turnover minus the cost of the program. These values are presented at the bottom of Table 12.5. The Management

Net benefit

The estimated value of the benefit minus the cost of the training program

TABLE 12.5

Benefits Calculation Worksheet for Training Options

	INSTITUTE OPTION 1	VENDOR OPTION 2	COACHING OPTION 3
A. Data Required for Calculations			
(a) What is the desired performance as a result of worker training?	4	4	4
(b) What unit(s) of measure will be used to describe the performance?	reductions per group	reductions per group	reductions per group
(c) What is the dollar value that will be assigned to each unit of measure?	$75,000	$75,000	$75,000
(d) What is the estimated training time to reach the goal?	.04 year	.5 year	1.0 year
(e) What is the current level of worker performance?	0 reduction	0 reduction	0 reduction
(f) How many workers will participate in the training?	10	10	10
B. Calculations to Determine Net Performance Value			
(g) What is the estimated performance level during training? Will trainee produce during training?	0	2	2
_____ No = 0			
_____ Yes = a + e / 2			
(h) What is the length of the period being evaluated (at a minimum this will be the longest "d" of all options under consideration)?	1.0 year	1.0 year	1.0 year
(i) What is the estimate of the total number of units (b) that will be achieved during training? [d × g]	0	1	2
(j) What is the estimate of the total individual performance (or the evaluation period [(h − d) × a] + 1)?	4.84 reduction	3.0 reduction	1.0 reduction
(k) What is the value for the total performance for the evaluation period? [c × j]	$363,000	$225,000	$75,000
(l) What is the net performance value gain? [k + (e × c × h)]	$363,000	$225,000	$75,000
(m) Do you want to calculate the total net performance value of all trainees?			
_____ Yes = l × f			
__X__ No = net performance value of 1 trainee	$363,000	$225,000	$75,000
Benefit	$363,000	$225,000	$75,000
Cost (from Cost-Analysis Worksheet)	$100,000	$150,000	$24,000
Net benefit	$263,000	$75,000	$51,000
Benefit–cost ratio	3.63	1.5	3.13
ROI	2.63	.5	2.13

Development Institute is the most attractive option with a net benefit of $263,000 ($363,000 − $100,000). The net benefit of the vendor-supplied program is $75,000 ($225,000 − $150,000), and for coaching it is $51,000 ($75,000 − $24,000).

Benefit–cost ratio (BCR)

The benefit divided by the cost of the training program

A related calculation is the **benefit–cost ratio (BCR),** which is derived by dividing the benefit by the cost. The benefit–cost ratio for the Management Development Institute is 3.63 ($363,000/$100,000); the outside vendor is 1.5 ($225,000/$150,000); and the coaching option is 3.13 ($75,000/$24,000).

Does this mean that the organization should choose the Management Development Institute program? The answer to this question depends on the criteria used to choose a training program. If one is simply interested in the net benefit or the benefit–cost ratio, then clearly the Management Development Institute is the best choice. If one is interested in the least expensive option, then coaching is the best choice.

Another way to determine the financial return of a training program is the calculation of the return on investment or ROI, which is described in the next section.

Return on Investment (ROI)

The most popular approach for determining the benefits or return of a training program is the return on investment. This is what Accenture did to demonstrate the value of its training programs to the company. You might recall that Accenture found that for every dollar invested in training, there was a return of $3.53—or an ROI of 353 percent.

Return on investment (ROI)

A comparison of the cost of a training program relative to its benefits that involves dividing the net benefit by the cost of the training program

Return on investment (ROI) involves comparing the cost of a training program relative to its benefits by dividing the net benefit by the cost of the training program. A survey of HR trends by *Workforce Management* magazine found that 86 percent of responding organizations formally or informally measure the ROI of training.[10]

For example, Cisco Systems calculates the ROI of e-learning by having employees complete a Web-based survey shortly after they have attended a training program. Employees are asked to select a percentage range that indicates the time savings or quality improvement in their performance since taking the course. The results are used to calculate the ROI of e-learning, which has been found to be 900 percent per course. In other words, every dollar the company spends on training results in a gain of $9 in productivity.[11]

However, many companies in Canada still do not calculate the ROI of their training programs. As indicated earlier, the Conference Board of Canada found that only 4 percent of training programs are evaluated at the investment level. This is partly due to the difficulty and complexity involved in the process. To help companies learn how to calculate the ROI of their training programs, a new program called Investing in People is providing Canadian organizations with methods and tools to assess the impact of their training investments. To learn more about this program, see Training Today 12.1, "Helping Canadian Organizations Assess the Impact of Training Investments."

Helping Canadian Organizations Assess the Impact of Training Investments

A new project called Investing in People is being funded by the federal government to evaluate the return on investment (ROI) of training programs in Canadian organizations and to provide evidence that training results in positive business outcomes and ROI. The program also aims to reverse the belief that training expenditures are a cost and that it is not possible to link learning investments to business outcomes.

Investing in People is a three-year project sponsored by Human Resources and Social Development Canada (HRSDC) as part of the Workplace Skills Initiative (WSI). The $1.3 million project was awarded to the Canadian Society of Training and Development (CSTD) and will be implemented by Learning Designs Online. Return-on-investment case studies will be carried out in 12 organizations where a chosen training program will be evaluated. The project will involve organizations from all geographic regions and include a wide variety of training programs across the country.

The aim of the program is to develop practical and innovative methods, tools, and instruments for Canadian organizations to use for assessing the impact of their training investments. The program will focus on small- and medium-sized companies in the manufacturing, services, and retail sectors. The main objective of the project is to provide evidence that training results in a positive return on investment (ROI) and is crucial to business success and economic growth. The program also aims to encourage Canadian organizations to invest more in training and to identify best training practices based on the most successful training programs. The results of the project along with the best practices and evaluation tools will be shared and made available to other Canadian organizations.

Business Development Bank of Canada (BDC) is one of the 12 workplaces that will be participating in the program. The Crown corporation has 1,700 employees and invests about 5 percent of its payroll in training. BDC will be evaluating a comprehensive sales management program for 200 managers.

Sources: Dobson, S. (2008, April 21). Project connects dots between T&D, profit. *Canadian HR Reporter, 21* (8), 3; Bailey, A. (2008, Fall). Meeting Canada's productivity challenge. *The Canadian Learning Journal, 12* (2), 25–27; www.cstd.ca.

The calculation of ROI involves dividing the net benefit (benefits – cost of the program) by the cost of a training program:

$$\text{Return on Investment} = \frac{\text{Benefits} - \text{Cost of the program}}{\text{Cost of the program}}$$

As an example, if a training program cost $100,000 and the financial benefit is $300,000, then the calculation of ROI is simply $300,000 – $100,000/$100,000 = 2. In other words, there is a return of $2 for every $1 spent on training (1:2). When the ROI is above 1 it indicates that the return of a training program is greater than the investment. A higher ratio of results to costs indicates a greater financial benefit to the organization. When the ROI ratio is less than 1 it indicates that the investment or cost is greater than the return. And when the ROI is 1, the return is equal to the investment and the training program breaks even.

The percentage return can also be calculated by simply multiplying the ratio by 100; so, in this case, the return is 200 percent. This can also be described as a 200-percent return on investment (the gain of $200,000 is 200 percent of the $100,000 investment).

ROI for Project Manager Training Options

If we return to the benefit and cost values presented in Table 12.5, we can calculate the ROI for each of the training options as follows: the Management Development Institute is 2.63 or 263 percent ($363,000 − $100,000/$100,000); the outside vendor is .5 or 50 percent ($225,000 − $150,000/$150,000); and the coaching option is 2.13 or 213 percent ($75,000 − $24,000/$24,000).

Thus, based on the ROI, the best option is the Management Development Institute. In other words, the organization receives the greatest return for each dollar spent ($2.63) on the Management Development Institute option. This is equivalent to a 263-percent return on investment, which is only slightly better than the return of the coaching option, which is 2.13 or 213 percent. However, if one is most interested in obtaining the highest return on the training investment, the choice would be the Management Development Institute option, which also resulted in the greatest net benefit and benefit–cost ratio.

Few managers, however, would make the final decision based on these criteria alone. As previously suggested, there are qualitative concerns that become part of the analysis—reputation of the training institute, past experience, trainee perceptions of the options, the degree to which the training can be customized, and the time factor all will be considered before a final decision is made. For example, if time is a factor then one might choose the Management Development Institute, since it has the lowest estimated training time to reach the goal while the coaching option has the longest estimated time. Thus, the preferred option will depend on the criteria used for selecting a training program.

ROI of Wood Panel Plant Supervisor Training Program

For another example of the calculation of ROI, let's return to the wood panel plant. Recall that a supervisor training program that cost $32,564 was designed to improve the quality of wood panels by lowering the daily rejection rate; to improve the housekeeping of the production area; and to reduce the number of preventable accidents.[12]

Table 12.6 shows how the benefits were measured in each of the three areas. The results in each area before and one year after training as well as the differences are shown. Before training, the rejection rate of wood panels was 2 percent per day or 1,440 panels. After training, this was reduced to 1.5 percent or 1,080 panels. The difference of .5 percent per day or 360 wood panels was calculated to be a saving of $720 per day or $172,800 per year. Housekeeping was measured in terms of a visual inspection using a 20-item checklist. Before the training there was an average of 10 defects per week while after training it was reduced to two defects. Thus, the training program resulted in a reduction of eight defects per week (this could not be calculated in monetary terms). The number of preventable accidents before training was 24 per year at a cost of $144,000. After training this was reduced to 16 per year or eight fewer accidents at a cost of $96,000 and a savings of $48,000.

TABLE 12.6

Benefits Calculation Worksheet for Wood Panel Plant

OPERATIONAL RESULTS AREA	HOW MEASURED	RESULTS BEFORE TRAINING	RESULTS AFTER TRAINING	DIFFERENCES (+ OR −)	EXPRESSED IN $
Quality of panels	percent rejected	2 percent rejected—1440 panels per day	1.5 percent . rejected—1080 panels per day	5 percent 360 panels	$720 per day $172,800 per year
Housekeeping	Visual inspection using 20-item checklist	10 defects (average)	2 defects (average)	8 defects	Not measurable in $
Preventable accidents	Number of accidents	24 per year	16 per year	8 per year	$48,000 per year
	Direct cost of each accident	$144,000 per year	$96,000 per year	$48,000	

Total savings: $220,800

Net Benefit = $220,800 - $32,564 = $188,236

Cost-Benefit ratio = $220,800/$32,564 = 6.8

$$ROI = \frac{\text{Benefits} - \text{Training Costs}}{\text{Training Costs}} = \frac{\$220,800 - \$32,564}{\$32,564} = 5.78 \times 100\% = 578\%$$

By comparing this information to the cost information in Table 12.2, we can calculate the net benefit, BCR, and the ROI of the training program. Recall that the total cost of the training program was $32,564. The net benefit of the training program in monetary terms can be determined by adding the savings from the reduction in rejected wood panels ($172,800) with the savings from the reduction in preventable accidents ($48,000) and then subtracting the cost of the training program ($32,564). Thus, the net benefit of the training program is: $220,800 − $32,564 = $188,236. The BCR is $220,800/$32,564 = 6.78.

To calculate the ROI, we simply divide the net benefit of the program ($188,236) by the cost of the training program ($32,564): $188,236/$32,564 = 5.78. Therefore, the ROI for one year after training is equal to 5.78 or 578 percent. It is worth noting that while this analysis is an example of cost-effectiveness evaluation, the results for housekeeping (i.e., a reduction of eight defects per week) is an example of cost-benefit evaluation.

In summary, this example as well as the project manager training options example are good illustrations of how the benefits of training programs can be measured in a manner that is consistent with the objectives of a training program (e.g., reduction in preventable accidents, reduction in turnover), and can then be translated into monetary terms and used to calculate a training program's net benefit, BCR, and ROI.

The Trainer's Notebook 12.1

Converting Benefits to Monetary Values

One of the most difficult aspects of calculating ROI is determining the monetary value of the benefits of training. Jack Phillips, one of the leading experts on the calculation of ROI, suggests the following five steps for converting benefits to monetary values.

Step 1: Focus on a single unit. Identify a particular unit of improvement in output (e.g., products, sales), quality (e.g., errors, product defects), time (to respond to a customer order or complete a project), or employee behaviour (e.g., one case of employee turnover).

Step 2: Determine a value for each unit. Place a value identified on the single unit identified in step 1. This will be easier for hard measures such as production, quality, and time because most organizations record the value of one unit of production or the cost of a product defect. It will be more difficult to do for softer measures such as the cost of one employee absence.

Step 3: Calculate the change in performance. Determine the change in performance following training after factoring out other potential influences. This change in units of performance should be directly attributable to the training.

Step 4: Obtain an annual amount. The industry standard for an annual performance change is equal to the total change in the performance data during one year.

Step 5: Determine the annual value. The annual value of improvement equals the annual performance change, multiplied by the unit value.

Source: Phillips. J. J. (1996, April). How much is the training worth? *Training & Development*, 20–24. Copyright © April 1996, *T+D*. Reprinted with permission of American Society for Training & Development.

To learn more about how to convert benefits data into monetary values, see The Trainer's Notebook 12.1, "Converting Benefits to Monetary Values."

Utility Analysis

As described in Chapter 11, in a typical training evaluation study the performance of a training group is compared to an untrained or control group that did not receive the training in order to determine how effective the training program was for learning, a change in behaviour, or job performance. While the results of this comparison might indicate that there is a significant difference between the two groups, it does not indicate the dollar value associated with the change or improvement in learning, behaviour, or job performance. Utility analysis, however, can do this and it is another approach for determining the costs and benefits of training programs.

Utility analysis is a method for forecasting the financial benefits that result from human resource programs such as training and development. Utility analysis involves procedures in which the effectiveness of a training program can be translated into dollars and cents.[13]

To calculate the utility of a training program, several factors must be considered. One of the most important is the effectiveness of the training program. In other words, what is the difference in job performance between employees who are trained and those who do not receive training? This is

Utility analysis

A method to forecast the financial benefits that result from human resource programs such as training and development sometimes referred to as the *effect size*. The larger the effect size, the more effective a training program will be and the greater the utility.

A second key factor is the *standard deviation of job performance* in dollars of untrained employees. This factor has to do with how much of a difference there is in the job performance of untrained employees and the monetary value of this difference. The standard deviation of job performance in dollar terms is an important factor because in jobs in which the contribution of individual employees is widely different, an effective training program will improve the performance of a greater number of employees and will, therefore, result in larger dollar gains. When individual contributions are relatively similar, an effective training program is less likely to result in large dollar gains. Therefore, it is necessary to estimate the standard deviation of job performance of untrained employees to make estimates of utility. There are several approaches for doing this, such as asking supervisors to provide an estimate of the dollar value of performance. The larger the standard deviation of job performance of the untrained group the greater the utility of a training program.

A third factor is the *number of employees trained*. The more employees who are trained the greater the utility. A fourth factor is the expected length of *time that the training benefits will last*. The longer the effects of training will last, the higher the utility of a training program.

Utility is equal to the multiplication of all of these factors minus the *cost of the training program* (cost per employee × number of employees trained). The following formula is used to estimate the utility of a training program:[14]

$$\Delta U = (T)(N)(d_t)(SDy) - (N)(C)$$

where

ΔU = utility, or the dollar value of the program
T = the number of years the training has a continued effect on performance
N = the number of people trained
d_t = the true difference in job performance between the average trained and untrained employee in standard deviation units (effect size)
SDy = the standard deviation of job performance in dollars of the untrained group
C = the cost of training each employee

Consider the following example. To increase the number of toys produced in a toy factory, a training program is implemented and 50 of the plant employees attend. Compared to a group of workers who do not attend the training program, the performance of the 50 trained employees is found to be twice as high (e.g., they produce 100 toys per day compared to 50 produced by untrained workers). We will assume that this equals an effect size of 2. We also assume that the standard deviation of job performance of the untrained employees is $100. The expected length of time that the training will last is estimated to be five years. The cost of the training program is $300 per employee. Using the utility equation above, we can calculate the utility of the training program as follows:

$$\Delta U = 5(50)(2)(\$100) - 50(\$300)$$
$$\Delta U = \$50,000 - \$15,000$$
$$\Delta U = \$35,000$$

Thus, the expected utility of the training program for the 50 employees trained is $35,000. This amount might be even greater if the training program lasts longer than five years or if the untrained employees learn how to improve their performance by working with and observing the trained employees. The BCR can also be calculated by dividing the utility by the total cost of the program ($35,000/ $15,000 = 2.33) and the ROI can be calculated by dividing the net benefit of the program by the total cost of the program ($35,000 – $15,000/$15,000 = 1.33).

Break-Even Analysis

Break-even analysis

Finding the value at which benefits equal costs and utility is equal to zero

An extension of the use of the utility formula is to conduct a **break-even analysis** or to find the value at which benefits equal costs and utility is equal to zero.[15] This can be done for any of the terms in the utility equation. However, it is most meaningful to conduct a break-even analysis for the effect size or the standard deviation. For example, what is the break-even effect size for the example presented above? This can be calculated by dividing the cost of the training program ($15,000) by the multiplicative function of the other factors: (N)(T)(SDy) or (50)(5)(100). The calculations are as follows:

$$d_t = 15,000/25,000$$
$$d_t = .6$$

Thus, a training program with an effect size of .6 will result in a utility of zero, and an effect size greater than .6 will result in a utility that is greater than zero. Therefore, a training program that is considerably less effective than the one in the example would still be likely to result in a financial gain as long as the effect size is greater than .6.

Break-even analysis can be very useful because it helps reduce the uncertainty associated with the estimates of the various parameters used to calculate utility. For example, to the extent that the break-even effect size is far below the actual effect size used to calculate utility, the greater the confidence one can have in the results.[16]

The Credibility of Benefit Estimates

We have been discussing the costs and benefits of training programs and how to calculate the ROI and utility of training programs. However, it is important to realize that this is not an exact science. Assumptions and judgments have to be made when estimating the monetary benefits of a training program. As a result, the process works only if managers and clients accept the assumptions.

Managing Performance Through Training and Development

The estimation of benefits is an inexact procedure and trainers should be concerned about professional credibility.

Credibility is a major issue in cost-effectiveness evaluation and the data must be accurate and the process believable.[17] Consider the example of a large bank that was experiencing a high rate of turnover. A training program was designed to counter the turnover problem. The cost of employee turnover needed to be estimated to calculate the ROI. However, the actual cost calculation was difficult because of the many interacting variables—administrative costs, interviewing, testing, relocation, orientation, increase in supervisory time, initial less-than-optimal performance, on-the-job training—all make up the cost of replacing one person. As the bank did not want to devote the considerable resources necessary to developing a precise calculation, turnover was classified as a soft cost and a combination of approaches was used to derive an acceptable figure.

Initially, a literature search was used to determine that another institution in the same industry had calculated a cost of $25,000 per turnover. This figure, derived by an internal-audit unit and verified by a consulting specialist in turnover reduction, was used as a starting point. The application of this statistic to another (even though quite similar) organization, however, was in question. The training staff then met with senior executives "to agree on a turnover cost value to use in gauging the success of the program. Management agreed on an estimate that was half the amount from the study, $12,500. This was considered very conservative because other turnover studies typically yield statistics of greater value. Management felt comfortable with the estimate, however, and it was used on the benefits side of program evaluation. Although not precise, this exercise yielded a figure that was never challenged" (p. 337).[18]

The term "never challenged" is significant. Trainers must perform cost-effectiveness evaluations from a position of strength. In this example, senior managers were brought on-side when they were used as experts. It mattered little that the turnover cost was set at $12,500 rather than $25,000, because the benefit estimation produced from these data was credible and accepted by those with the power to make investment decisions.

Thus, despite the appearance of quantitative rigour, virtually all but the simplest cost-effectiveness evaluations are dependent to a greater or lesser extent on some assumptions and expert opinion.[19] Trainers must ensure that their clients and management agree on the cost factors and the measurement and estimation of benefits. Management and clients must perceive benefit estimates as credible, believable, and acceptable. It is therefore critical that trainers find out what management deems to be most important in terms of the benefits and expected results, and whenever possible, obtain cost estimates (e.g., the cost of turnover) from management.

It also helps to use internal and external experts to assist in making benefit estimates. Because they are experts who are familiar with the situation, they are likely to be seen as credible by management. For example, if one wanted to estimate the cost of employee grievances, a good expert would be a manager of labour relations. Estimates might also be obtained from other sources that are close to the situation, such as trainees and their supervisors.[20]

For some guidelines on how to increase the credibility of the estimates of training benefits, see The Trainer's Notebook 12.2, "Increasing the Credibility of Benefit Estimates."

Summary

As organization investments in training and development increase, organizations want to know the financial benefits and ROI of their training programs. This chapter described the methods and approaches for calculating the costs and benefits of training programs. The differences between cost-effectiveness and cost-benefit analysis were described and examples of the calculation of the costs, benefits, net benefits, BCR, and ROI of training programs were provided. This information is important not only for budgeting purposes and for comparing the costs of training programs, but also for training evaluation. Utility analysis was also described as an alternative approach to calculate the financial benefits of training programs. The chapter concluded with a discussion of the importance of credibility when estimating the financial benefits of training and development programs.

Key Terms

benefit–cost ratio (BCR)   p. 374
break-even analysis   p. 380
cost-benefit evaluation   p. 371
cost-effectiveness evaluation   p. 371
costing   p. 363
developmental costs   p. 365
direct costs   p. 363

indirect costs   p. 363
net benefit   p. 372
overhead costs   p. 365
return on investment (ROI)   p. 374
trainee compensation   p. 365
utility analysis   p. 378

Make the Connection

p. 361: types of training evaluation is discussed in Chapter 11 on page 325

p. 362: training as an expense versus an investment is discussed in Chapter 1 on page 12

Page 378: training evaluation designs are discussed in Chapter 11 on pages 345–349

Web Links

Accenture: www.accenture.com

CIBC: www.cibc.ca

Cisco Systems: www.cisco.com

Firestone Canada: www.bridgestone-firestone.ca

RPC Icons

RPC 12.1 Assesses and reports on the costs and benefits of engaging internal and external suppliers of development programs, given the organizational constraints and objectives.

RPC 12.2 Conducts an evaluation of the program.

Discussion Questions

1. Discuss the pros and cons of calculating the ROI of training programs. Should trainers always do this as part of a training evaluation?
2. What can trainers do to increase the credibility of monetary estimates of the benefits of a training program?
3. What is the difference between cost-benefit evaluation and cost-effectiveness evaluation? What are some situations in which a trainer might want to calculate one or the other?
4. What is a utility analysis and how is it used to determine the cost and benefits of a training program? What is a break-even analysis and how can it help to understand the value of a training program?
5. Why should trainers be concerned about calculating the costs and benefits of training programs? What are the advantages and disadvantages of doing so?
6. What are the different approaches of categorizing the costs of training programs?
7. Why do so few Canadian organizations evaluate the financial benefits of training programs? Do you think that more organizations should do so? What needs to be done to increase the number of organizations that evaluate the financial benefits of training programs?

8. Explain how to calculate each of the following: net benefit, benefit–cost ratio (BCR), return on investment (ROI), and utility. What are the differences between each of these calculations?

The Great Training Debate

1. Debate the following: Calculating the monetary benefits and ROI of training and development is the most important way to evaluate training programs.
2. Debate the following: The calculation of a training program's ROI is more art than science and should be abandoned.

Using the Internet

1. To learn more about the Return on Training Investment (ROTI), go to: **www.futured.com/audited/ROTI.pdf** and answer the following questions: 1. What is ROTI? 2. What are the benefits of ROTI analysis? 3. What are the qualities of a good ROTI plan? 4. What is involved in setting the stage and getting ready for ROTI? 5. What are the cost and benefit categories on the sample ROTI worksheet for a business? How effective is the worksheet for calculating the ROTI?
2. To learn about one approach for calculating the ROI of training, go to **www.workplacebasicskills.com/frame/free_tools/roi/worksheet.htm** and find out about the Training ROI Worksheet. Make sure you find the link to access the worksheet at the bottom of the page. Think about the most recent training course you have taken in a current or previous job, and then calculate the ROI. Alternatively, ask a friend or family member about a recent training program they have attended and calculate the ROI. What is the ROI of the training program? Was the training program worth taking? What parameters would have to change in order to increase the program's ROI? How effective is the ROI Worksheet for calculating the ROI of a training program?
3. To find out how companies in Canada measure the success of training, visit Industry Canada at: **www.collectionscanada.gc.ca/ webarchives/20060205142457/http://strategis.ic.gc.ca/epic/internet/ incts-scf.nsf/en/sl00029e.html**.
   Answer the following questions:

   a. How do companies measure training success?
   b. What percentage of companies measure ROI?
   c. What types of training are the most frequently evaluated?

4. To learn about how some Canadian companies are calculating the ROTI (return on training investment) of their training programs, go to **www.collectionscanada.gc.ca/webarchives/20060205142459/http:// strategis.ic.gc.ca/epic/internet/incts-scf.nsf/en/sl00041e.html.**

Review the cases of companies that have calculated the return on training investment (ROTI) and write a brief summary with the following information:

a. How did each company calculate the ROTI?
b. What was the ROTI for each training program?
c. What were the training costs and benefits calculated for each training program?
d. Did the companies do a cost-benefit or cost-effectiveness evaluation?

Exercises

In-Class

1. In order to calculate the benefits of training programs, one has to develop measures that are consistent with a training program and its objectives. As well, some of these measures will need to be converted into monetary terms. For each of the following training programs, identify some of the benefits that can be measured for the purpose of cost-benefit evaluation and cost-effectiveness evaluation:

   a. Sales training
   b. Management development
   c. Customer-relations training
   d. Health and safety training
   e. Quality training
   f. Sexual harassment training

   To learn more about these training programs, refer to Chapters 13 and 14.

2. Consider a situation in which you, a trainer for an organization that manufactures sportswear, must present information on the costs and benefits of a training program to management, which is about to decide if the program will be implemented organization-wide. You have already designed the training program and delivered it to one group of employees and you want to begin offering it to the rest of the organization. How will you present the information to management? Will you present information on the net benefit, BCR, ROI, and/or utility analysis? Will you present cost-benefit information or cost-effectiveness information? What are the advantages and disadvantages of presenting information on each of these? Do you think that trainers should present financial information about the benefits of training to management? What are the advantages and disadvantages of doing so?

3. As the housing market began to heat up, the Renswartz Realty Company set high goals for increasing the number of listings and sales. In order to accomplish these goals, the company president believed they would have to do two things. First, they would have to better market the company's superior customer service. Second,

they would have to train their agents to improve their sales and customer-service skills. Choosing an advertising company turned out to be much easier than choosing a training program. Two consulting firms were contacted to provide a proposal to design and implement a training program that would be attended by all 200 of the company's sales agents.

The first consulting firm proposed a five-day program that would consist of lectures on "how to get more listings," "how to improve your service," and "making the sale," and would involve videos and behavioural modelling. According to the consulting firm, research has shown that the sales performance of those who have attended the training is significantly better than those who have not; the effect size of the program is .35. The training is expected to last for two years and will cost $1,500 per employee.

The second consulting firm proposed a similar program with the exception that it would be for only two days and would consist of sessions on "how to improve your sales," and "providing excellent service." Research on the training program has found it to be highly effective, with an effect size of .25. The effects have been found to last for one year at which time follow-up sessions are required. The cost of the training program is $450 per employee.

Based on the current sales performance of all 200 sales agents at Renswartz Realty, the standard deviation of sales is $15,000.

a. Calculate the utility of the training programs proposed by each of the consulting firms.
b. Calculate the break-even effect size for both training programs.
c. Calculate the BCR and ROI of each training program.
d. What are the advantages and disadvantages of each training program?
e. Which training program should the company purchase? Explain your answer.
f. What are the advantages and limitations of this approach for calculating the benefits of a training program?

4. Consider the costs and benefits of a university or college course such as the training and development course you are now taking. Using the five cost categories discussed in the chapter, identify the major costs of the course and try to estimate the costs of each category. Now consider the benefits. What benefits would you include if you were to conduct a cost-effectiveness analysis and a cost-benefit analysis? How would you determine the ROI and utility of your course? Consider the costs and benefits from the institution's perspective and the student's perspective.

5. Think about the last time you attended a training program. Based on what you know about the program, make a list of the costs in each of the following cost categories: direct costs, indirect costs, development costs, overhead costs, and compensation for participants. In addition,

make a list of the potential benefits of the program. What information would you need to determine the monetary value of these benefits? What additional information do you require to calculate the utility of the program?

In-the-Field

1. To find out about the evaluation of the costs and benefits of training in an organization, contact the human resource department of an organization and ask the following questions:

   - To what extent do they determine the cost of training programs, how do they do it, and who does it? What cost categories are used?
   - To what extent do they determine the benefits of training programs and how do they do it? Who is involved in calculating the monetary value of training?
   - To what extent do they conduct a cost-effectiveness evaluation and a cost-benefit evaluation and who does it?
   - To what extent do they determine the net benefit, benefit–cost ratio (BCR), and return on investment (ROI) of training programs and who is responsible for it?
   - What recommendations would you give the organization for improving its evaluation of the costs and benefits of training?

Based on your interview, how well do you think the organization evaluates the costs and benefits of training? What recommendations would you give the organization for improving its cost-benefit evaluation of training?

Case Incident

Measuring Results at CIBC

In an effort to measure the benefits of training, CIBC conducted a pilot project with 100 financial advisers across Canada. The participants took a quiz to diagnose their baseline knowledge of company pension plans, before taking a half-day workshop on how to advise clients on the subject. After the training the participants completed a survey that asks if they actually applied the knowledge and the business impact (e.g., did you build more business or generate more leads?).

Questions

1. Describe how to do a cost-effectiveness evaluation and a cost-benefit evaluation of this training program.
2. What information is required to calculate the net benefit, BCR, and ROI of the training program? What else has to be done to obtain all of the information required?

Source: Staples, S. (2003, November 9). Cult of accountability. *Canadian Business, 76* (21), 123–124.

Case Study

DATAIN

DATAIN is a company started by two students who saw an opportunity to make some money and help pay for their education. With an increasing number of organizations deciding to survey their customers and employees, they saw a need for data input and analyses. With a loan from their parents, they rented space, purchased 20 used computers, and set up shop. They hired other students to do data input and analyses and began advertising their services. Within a relatively short period of time they were having trouble keeping up with demand. In fact, business was so good they had to hire more students and purchase more computers.

After about six months, however, they began to notice some problems. The data files were often full of mistakes, and the data analysis was often incomplete and incorrect. As a result, almost 40 percent (20 jobs per month) of all jobs had to be completely redone. This turned out to be a rather costly problem. Each job took approximately 10 hours and cost the company $150 (students were paid $15 per hour). To make matters worse, they began to notice that their new hires were quitting after only a few months on the job. In the last six months, they lost an average of four employees a month. Every time an employee quit, they had to replace him/her and the cost of this was beginning to get very expensive. The cost of advertising, interviewing, and hiring a new employee was estimated to be about $5,000.

In order to cut down on these unanticipated costs, DATAIN decided to invest in a training program to reduce the mistakes and errors in data input and analyses and to improve employee retention. They hired a training consultant to conduct a needs analysis, develop and deliver a training program, and conduct the training evaluation.

Based on the figures provided by the consultant, DATAIN thought it would be a good idea to determine if the training program would be a worthwhile investment. The consultant estimated that the needs analysis and training evaluation would each take about 20 hours at a cost of $100 per hour. The fee to purchase the actual training program would be $5,000. The training program itself would be for one day (8 hours) at a cost of $200 per hour to the consultant.

In addition to the consultant fees, DATAIN would also have to give its 25 employees one full day (8 hours) of pay ($15 per hour); lunch that would cost $10 per employee; and coffee and snacks at a cost of $50 for the day. The training would take place at DATAIN so the only cost for classroom space would be a portion of the cost associated with room heating, lighting, and maintenance, which was estimated to be $100 for the day. As well, some administrative support work would be required to prepare and plan for the training, which would involve about two days (8 hours per day) of work on the part of DATAIN's secretary, who is paid $15 an hour.

According to the training consultant, DATAIN could anticipate an 80-percent drop in mistakes and errors and a 90-percent reduction in turnover.

In other words, instead of 20 jobs a month only 4 would have to be redone, and instead of four quits a month there would be on average fewer than one. This sounded like a great investment; however, DATAIN was concerned about the loss of a full day of work while employees attended the program. So they decided to get an estimate from another vendor that specializes in e-learning training programs.

The e-learning vendor told DATAIN that she could design an e-learning program for $25,000. The program would take four hours to complete and would include interactive exercises and opportunities for practice. Employees would be able to take the course on their own time and at their own pace. The anticipated benefits are a 90-percent reduction in mistakes and errors and a 60-percent reduction in turnover.

DATAIN wasn't sure how to calculate the potential financial benefits of the two training programs and so the company does not know which training program to purchase.

Questions

1. Calculate the costs of the consultant's training program in terms of the different categories for determining training costs. What is the cost of each category and the total cost of the training program?
2. Calculate the benefit, net benefit, benefit–cost ratio, and return on investment of the two training programs. Based on your calculations, are the training programs a good investment? Which one will you recommend and why?
3. What other factors should the company consider in deciding whether or not to purchase each of the proposed training programs?
4. If the company wanted to conduct a utility analysis, what additional information would it need? What would be required in order to obtain this information? In other words, what would DATAIN or the consultant and vendor have to do to obtain the necessary information?

References

1. Vanthournout, D., Olson, K., Ceisel, J., White, A., Waddington, T., Barfield, T., Desai, S., & Mindrum, C. (2008). *Return on learning: Training for high performance at Accenture.* Evanston, IL: Agate; Galvin, T., Johnson, G., & Barbian, J. (2003, March). The 2003 training top 100. *Training, 40* (3), 18–38; Galvin, T. (2002, March). The 2002 training top 100. *Training, 39* (3), 42–60.
2. Phillips. J. J. (1996, February). ROI: The search for best practices. *Training and Development,* 42–47.
3. Salas, E., & Cannon-Bowers, J. A. (2001). The science of training: A decade of progress. *Annual Review of Psychology, 52,* 471–499.
4. Hughes, P. D., & Grant, M. (2007). *Learning & development outlook 2007.* The Conference Board of Canada: Ottawa.
5. Staples, S. (2003, November 9). Cult of accountability: Does employee training pay off? Accounting techniques and science-inspired metrics evaluate return on investment. *Canadian*

Business, 76 (21), 123–124; The Canadian Society for Training and Development: 2008 Award Winners, CIBC Corporate Mandatory Training and Testing Internal eLearning Program (www.cstd.ca/awards/2008_award_winners.html).

6. Everson, B. (2007, November 5). Canadian companies lag foreign firms in training. *Canadian HR Reporter, 20* (19), 23.

7. Robinson, D. G., & Robinson, J. (1989, August). Training for impact. *Training & Development Journal, 43* (8), 34–42.

8. Robinson, D. G., & Robinson, J. (1989, August).

9. Prepared by Dr. Gary D. Geroy, Colorado State University at Fort Collins. Reproduced with permission from his client organization.

10. (2002, May). Companies continue to invest in training and evaluate ROI. Workforce Online: www.workforce.com.

11. Gale, S. F. (2002, August). Measuring the ROI of e-learning. *Workforce Management,* 74–77.

12. Robinson, D. G., & Robinson, J. (1989, August).

13. Cascio, W. F. (1991). *Costing human resources: The financial impact of behavior in organizations.* Boston, MA: Kent.

14. Schmidt, F. L., Hunter, J. E., & Pearlman, K. (1982). Assessing the economic impact of personnel programs on workforce productivity. *Personnel Psychology, 35,* 333–347.

15. Cascio, W. F. (1991).

16. Mathieu, J. E., & Leonard, R. L. Jr. (1987). Applying utility concepts to a training program in supervisory skills: A time-based approach. *Academy of Management Journal, 30,* 316–335.

17. Bedinham, K. (1998). Proving the effectiveness of training. *Education & Training 40* (4), 166–167; Phillips. J. J. (1996, April). How much is the training worth? *Training & Development,* 20–24.

18. Phillips, J. J. (1991, Autumn). Measuring the return on HRD. *Employment Relations Today, 18* (3), 329–342.

19. Geroy, G. D., & Wright, P. C. (1988). Evaluation research: A pragmatic program-focused research strategy for decision makers. *Performance Improvement Quarterly, 1* (3), 17–26; Wright, P. C. (1990). Validating hospitality curricula within associated-sponsored certification programs: A qualitative methodology and a case study. *Hospitality Research Journal, 14* (1), 117–132.

20. Phillips. J. J. (1996, April).

CHAPTER 13

Training Programs

Chapter Learning Outcomes

After reading this chapter, you should be able to:

- describe orientation training and essential skills training
- describe technical skills training and information technology training
- discuss WHMIS legislation and describe the type of information that should be included in health and safety training programs
- describe total quality training programs
- describe team training and the main skills required of team members
- describe sales training and the skills required to be effective in sales
- discuss customer-service training and the skills that employees require to interact effectively with customers
- define sexual harassment and describe sexual harassment training
- describe ethics training, diversity training, and cross-cultural training

ROYAL STAR FOODS LIMITED

Royal Star Foods Limited is a seafood processing plant in Tignish, Prince Edward Island, and a subsidiary of Tignish Fisheries Cooperative Association Ltd. With a workforce of 350–400, it is the largest single plant processor of lobster in P.E.I. and one of the most modern state-of-the art seafood processing plants in eastern Canada. In addition to processing lobster, Royal Star Foods also processes snow crab, rock crab, dogfish, scallops, mackerel, herring, mussels, and groundfish for international markets in Canada, Europe, Japan, and the United States.

Royal Star Foods' plant is a highly mechanized working environment from weighing product on the dock to using the computerized time clock. Employees' reactions to such "high-tech" gadgets have ranged from complete fear to "show me the button" to "teach me what I need to know." However, new processing equipment with new safety requirements, and the introduction of more sophisticated quality control procedures motivated managers to focus on employees' literacy requirements and the need to raise the literacy levels of employees.

A voluntary project team made up of employees, managers, and a Workplace Education PEI representative was put together to determine a "learning route" for both the company and its employees. An assessment was conducted to find out what learning programs were needed, who was interested in what, and how to go about implementing the learning initiatives.

A company-wide survey of employees indicated that many were interested in taking computer courses. In the winter of 1999, the first workplace literacy program began—a basic computer literacy program that the project team felt would pave the way to a "learning comfort zone" for the company.

Workplace literacy programs at the company are designed to enhance employees' reading and math skills using General Equivalency Degree (GED) materials that have been customized for the workplace. The curriculum has also been customized to the fish processing industry.

Royal Star Foods now has over 17 workplace literacy programs including computer training, General Equivalency Degree (GED) programs, and customized communication programs. The programs have increased the confidence level of employees and the entire company. This has resulted in a more productive and efficient workplace and a skilled workforce that is more willing to express their views and offer suggestions for improving the production process—ultimately helping the company's bottom line.[1]

By now you should be familiar with the training and development process. We have covered all of the major steps of the instructional systems design (ISD) model of the training and development process: needs analysis, training objectives, design, training methods, delivery, transfer of training, and the evaluation and costing of training programs. At this point, you might be asking yourself, "What type of training programs do organizations provide for their employees?"

Organizations offer many different types of training to their employees, like the workplace literacy programs at Royal Star Foods Limited. The purpose of this chapter is to describe the major types of training programs that are designed and delivered by organizations today.

Table 13.1 lists training types as a percentage of training expenditures in Canadian organizations. Notice that management and supervisory skills training, professional skills training, occupational health and safety training, information technology skills training, and technical processes and procedures training account for over half of the total training investment of Canadian organizations. On the other hand, basic skills training received the lowest percentage of training investment, with only 2 percent. Unfortunately, training programs like those offered by Royal Star Foods Limited are not very common in Canadian organizations.

In the remainder of this chapter, we will describe the major types of training programs provided by organizations.

TABLE 13.1

Training Types as a Percentage of Training Expenditures in Canadian Organizations

Management/supervisory skills training	15
Professional skills training	12
Occupational health and safety/government mandated	10
Technical processes and procedures training	9
Information technology skills training	9
Product knowledge training	7
New employee orientation training	7
Executive development	6
Interpersonal communication training	6
Customer relations training	6
Quality, competition, and business practices training	5
Sales and dealer training	4
Basic skills training	2
Other	2

Source: "Training Types as a Percentage of Training Expenditures in Canadian Organizations."
Hughes, P. D., & Grant, M. (2007). *Learning & development outlook 2007*. E/F Ottawa: The Conference Board of Canada.

Orientation Training

Orientation training refers to programs that introduce new employees to their job, the people they will be working with, and the organization.[2] Formal orientation and training programs have become the main method used by organizations to socialize new employees.[3]

Most organizations provide some type of orientation for new employees. For example, a study of 100 major British organizations found that an overwhelming majority provided new hires with formalized, off-the-job induction training within four weeks of entry. Most of the organizations provided standardized programs that were designed and conducted by in-house human resource practitioners. The content of induction training was general in nature and pertained mostly to health and safety, terms and conditions of employment, organizational history and structure, specific training provisions, and human resource management policies and procedures.[4]

Employees who attend orientation training have been found to be more socialized in terms of their knowledge and understanding of the organization's goals and values, history, and involvement with people. Furthermore, employees who attend orientation training also have higher organizational commitment as a result of their greater socialization.[5] Effective orientation programs can also shape corporate culture, increase new employees' speed-to-proficiency, and lower turnover.[6]

Essential Skills Training

Many working adults today have difficulty reading, writing, and understanding mathematics. They lack what are known as essential skills. **Essential skills** are the skills required for work, learning, and life. They are necessary and a foundation for learning other skills and being able to adapt to workplace change. The Government of Canada and other agencies have identified nine types of essential skills: reading text, document use, numeracy, writing, oral communication, working with others, continuous learning, thinking skills, and computer use. Essential skills are required for most occupations and in one's daily life.[7]

Many of the essential skills (e.g., reading text, document use, numeracy) are known as literacy skills. **Literacy** refers to the ability to understand and employ printed information in daily activities, at home, at work, and in the community—to achieve one's goals, and to develop one's knowledge and potential.[8] A report by the Conference Board of Canada found that 42 percent of all Canadians aged 16 to 65 score at the lowest literacy levels and are only semi-literate. About 4.7 million Canadians score in the upper Level 2 and low Level 3 range and their limited literacy skills pose a significant challenge to their workplace performance and success. It has also been reported that only 58 percent of Canadian adults can read well enough to meet most day-to-day requirements.[9]

It is becoming increasingly clear that organizations must provide their workforces with essential skills training if they are to compete and survive in a global and high-tech workplace. Evidence suggests that without first providing trainees with essential skills training, other programs and initiatives will not succeed.[10]

Essential skills training provides employees with the essential skills that are required to perform their job and adapt to workplace change. Organizations that have implemented essential skills training have not only experienced improvements in productivity, efficiency, and quality, but some also report a decrease in absenteeism and the number of workers' compensation claims made, and an improvement in cross-cultural communication and morale.

Essential skills training also has advantages for employees. Not only does the training improve their skills, self-esteem, and confidence, but it also improves their chances of remaining employed. The percentages of employees who receive essential skills training and remain employed or are promoted are higher than employees who do not receive training.[11]

Royal Star Foods Limited is an excellent example of an organization that has developed essential skills and literacy training programs and was recognized for excellence by the Conference Board of Canada in 2002. Unfortunately, Royal Star Foods Limited is the exception rather than the rule. As noted earlier, Canadian organizations spend very little on essential skills training, an under-investment that the Conference Board of Canada has described as "troubling" given that employees who improve their essential skills are more likely to learn new job-related skills more quickly and accurately, make fewer mistakes, work more efficiently, and be less resistant to change. Literacy is critical to productivity, which in turn is essential to Canadian competitiveness and prosperity.[12]

One group of workers that often requires training in essential skills as well as knowledge and skills to find employment is new immigrants. See Training Today 13.1, "CIBC Trains Newcomers for Work," to find out how one company provides training to prepare newcomers for a job in the financial services sector.

Essential skills training
Training programs that are designed to provide employees with the essential skills required to perform their job and adapt to workplace change

Training Today 13.1

CIBC Trains Newcomers for Work

Many newcomers to Canada have difficultly finding jobs even in areas where they have experience. To help new-comers acquire the skills they need to find a job and work in Canada, the CIBC and the YMCA of Greater Toronto now offer a new program to prepare newcomers for jobs in the Canadian financial services sector.

The CIBC Connection to Employment is a six-week job readiness program that is free for newcomers with a back-ground in financial services. Participants learn how to put together a resume, how to prepare for an interview, and how to conduct themselves during an interview. They also learn about the culture of the financial services industry and bank-specific information relevant to Canada. The program also includes soft skills training such as team-work, conflict resolution, and problem solving.

After the program, the participants can apply for jobs at CIBC and other financial institutions. In December of 2008, 24 newcomers graduated from the program to begin new careers. So far, CIBC has hired 15 of the par-ticipants for a wide variety of positions including com-mercial banking, retail banking, telephone banking, and operations.

Sources: Klie, S. (2009, January 26). CIBC trains newcomers for jobs in Canadian banks. *Canadian HR Reporter, 22* (3), 3; CIBC connection to employment, www.ymcatoronto.org/en/newcomers/cibc/connection_employment/index.html; 24 newcomers ready for employment, www.ymcatoronto.org/en/who-we-are/media_gallery/press_release/dec_10_08_cibc.

Technical Skills Training

Technical skills training

Training in specific job skills that all employees need to perform their jobs

Technical skills training is training in specific job skills that all employees need to perform their jobs. Among manufacturing firms, training for specific job skills is the most frequent type of training provided. This is not surprising given the changes in the workplace that have occurred over the past two decades. With increasing global competition, organizations have had to find new ways to stay competitive and to survive, often by adopting new technologies and the redesign of work arrangements and systems. As a result, employees have had to undergo a considerable amount of technical skills upgrading and training. Nowhere is this more apparent than in the manufacturing sector, where low-skilled employees have had to become highly skilled employees to keep their jobs and for their organizations to survive.[13]

Information Technology Training

Information technology training

Training programs that focus on the use of computers and computer systems

Information technology training refers to computers and computer systems training. Information systems training is a key factor in the successful implementation of information systems technology.[14] Research has shown that technological failures in the workplace are most often the result of training issues rather than the technology.[15]

Information technology training usually involves either introductory computer training programs in which trainees learn about computer hardware and software, or applications training in which trainees are instructed on specific software applications to be used within the organization.[16] Applications training is required whenever an organization upgrades its computer systems.

Computer software training

Training programs that focus on how to use a specific computer software application

One of the most common types of information technology training is computer software training. **Computer software training** refers to the planned, structured, and formal means of delivering information about how to use a specific computer software application.[17] Computer software training has been shown to increase trainees' ability to use the system and their motivation to use software.

Health and Safety Training

Workplace health and safety has become an increasing concern in Canadian organizations. The costs of work-related injuries and illnesses are on the rise and present a serious threat to employees and their organizations. Approximately 900 workers die each year in Canada as a result of workplace accidents, and more than 350,000 workers suffer an injury serious enough to warrant missing time from work or what is known as a lost-time injury. Workplace injuries are estimated to cost $12 billion a year.[18]

Safety training is one of the most important ways to deal with accidents before they occur by educating employees in safe work methods and techniques. Employees should also be trained to recognize the chemical and physical hazards in the workplace so that they are prepared and capable of taking corrective action in the event of an accident.

An important component of health and safety training involves the handling of hazardous materials and chemicals. The **Workplace Hazardous Materials Information System (WHMIS)** legislation is designed to ensure that workers across Canada are aware of the potential hazards of chemicals in the workplace and are familiar with emergency procedures for the clean-up and disposal of a spill.

An important component of WHMIS legislation is employee training. Training in WHMIS is designed so that employees can identify WHMIS hazard symbols, read WHMIS supplier and workplace labels, and read and apply the information on material safety data sheets (MSDS), which outline the hazardous ingredient(s) in a product and the procedures for the safe handling of that product.[19]

Workplace Hazardous Materials Information System (WHMIS)

Legislation to ensure that workers across Canada are aware of the potential hazards of chemicals in the workplace and are familiar with emergency procedures for the clean-up and disposal of a spill

Quality Training

To remain competitive, many organizations have implemented quality programs. One of the most popular examples is total quality management (TQM). **Total quality management** is a systematic process of continual improvement of the quality of products and services. In addition to an emphasis on quality and continual improvement, TQM also involves teamwork and a customer focus.[20]

TQM places the training function in a pivotal position, as the process often requires significant changes in employees' skills and the way employees work. Most TQM advocates emphasize the importance of training and development.[21] Training and development is the primary method of reinforcing employee commitment to the consistent delivery of high-quality products and services. TQM training involves team training as well as training in the use of statistical tools that are used for problem-solving and decision-making processes.[22]

Total quality management (TQM)

A systematic process of continual improvement of the quality of an organization's products and services

Team Training

Team training is designed to improve the functioning and effectiveness of teams in areas such as communication, coordination, compensatory behaviour, mutual performance monitoring, exchange of feedback, and adaptation to varying situational demands.[23]

According to Bottom and Baloff, team training is an "attempt to improve a group's process through the use of interventions targeted at specific aspects of the process such as effective communication" (p. 318).[24] Group processes are usually the focus of team training; however, because team members are often expected to perform a variety of the group's tasks, they often must also receive technical training to become multi-skilled.

Thus, team training focuses on two general types of skills: *task-work skills* refers to skills that are required to perform the team's tasks, and *teamwork skills* are skills that team members require in order to interact, communicate, and coordinate tasks effectively with other team members. Both types of skills need to be included in team training programs, and it is recommended that team members first master task-work and technical skills before they are trained on teamwork skills.[25]

Team training

Training programs that are designed to improve the functioning and effectiveness of teams in areas such as communication and coordination

Sales Training

Sales professionals must develop a different set of skills to be successful in today's competitive sales environment. They need to be more knowledgeable about their products and their business, as well as their customers' businesses. As a result, sales training has become more than simply sending the sales troops off to a motivational pep rally.[26]

Today, sales training programs are being designed to upgrade sales professionals' skills and help them deal with new competitive challenges. At the centre of these new training initiatives is an emphasis on "relationship-based" sales training. Sales professionals are being trained to develop more strategic and complex relationships with clients, and to create relationships across client functions. They are also being trained to become knowledgeable about their customers' business needs, and to develop customized sales strategies. Rather than just selling a commodity, integrated teams of people from sales, support, and service are learning to sell solutions that combine support and service agreements.

For example, TELUS had the entire sales force participate in a three-day realistic selling simulation that allowed them to experience first-hand a new selling environment. Sales teams had to compete against each other in order to win an account. This required understanding the client's needs and developing solutions. In addition to the simulation, the sales force also took part in classroom-based workshops and a comprehensive assessment process. The workshop focused on new approaches to client relationship building and selling skills and the assessment was used to develop performance goals and plans for the sales staff.[27]

Customer-Service Training

Organizations with a strong commitment to customer service invest heavily in training their employees. Customer-service training can be either informal or formal. Informal training might involve pairing new hires with the organization's best employees in terms of customer-service behaviour and philosophy. The kind of formal training required will depend on the type of service business that an organization is in and its service strategy. In other words, the training program must be tailored to an organization's strategy and characteristics as well as its customers.[28]

Service employees must have both the *ability* and *motivation* to perform effectively. Because you cannot always hire people with the required abilities or motivation, you must be able to train them. Many organizations that have reputations for superb customer service are successful because of their commitment to training. Organizations that provide the best service also provide the most training.

At Delta Hotels and Resorts, employees are trained and empowered to provide customers with excellent service such as settling a disputed mini-bar charge or offering a complimentary room if a guest has a reasonable complaint. As part of its training program, Delta has produced an award-winning training video and promises employees a certain amount of training every year.[29]

Sexual Harassment Training

Sexual harassment is defined as "unwelcome sexual advances, requests for sexual favours, and other verbal or physical conduct of a sexual nature . . . when submission to requests for sexual favours is made explicitly or implicitly a term or condition of employment; submission to or rejection of such requests is used as a basis for employment decisions; or such conduct unreasonably interferes with work performance or creates an intimidating, hostile, or offensive work environment" (p. 401).[30]

The most effective way for organizations to prevent sexual harassment is to develop sexual harassment policies and procedures for filing complaints and to provide training programs that educate employees about sexual harassment and the organization's policies and procedures.[31]

Training is especially important because the definition of what constitutes sexual harassment is not always clear or understood, and problems have occurred in situations in which employees and managers were unaware of an organization's sexual harassment policy or did not know how to report it and proceed with a complaint.

Sexual harassment
Unwelcome sexual advances, requests for sexual favours, and verbal or physical conduct of a sexual nature that is a condition of employment, interferes with work performance, or creates a hostile work environment

Ethics Training

While many companies provide ethics training to comply with legal mandates and to gain liability protection, ethics training is also important for creating an ethical culture and workplace, and for attracting and retaining the right type of employee. Ethics training programs teach employees about the organization's values and ethical policies. This usually involves opportunities for employees to practise applying company values and its code of ethics to hypothetical situations. As a result, employees learn to recognize ethical dilemmas and how to respond to them.[32]

To be most effective, ethical training programs must be mandatory for all employees and include a copy of the organization's code of ethics, a discussion of relevant compliance laws, an ethical decision-making model, resources for help, and role-playing scenarios. Organizations should first set standards for ethical behaviour and determine what the training should accomplish. Key elements of strong ethical programs are responsibility, respect, fairness, honesty, and compassion. Employees should be trained on the laws that apply to their jobs as well as decision-making models with questions they can ask themselves to help them make ethical decisions. Employees should also be taught how to report ethics violations and where they can go for assistance. Practical scenarios should be included in the training so employees can test their ethical knowledge. Ethical topics can include workplace romance, e-mail appropriateness, internet use, confidentiality, security, and harassment (physical, verbal, and emotional).[33]

Molson Coors Brewing Company has one of the most comprehensive ethics programs in North America. Its training program includes interactive online courses, ethics leadership training, a decision map, a detailed set of policies, and a help line that complements and supports a user-friendly and accessible code of conduct.[34]

Diversity Training

Diversity training programs are one of the most common and effective ways for organizations to manage diversity. **Diversity training** programs are designed to address the differences in values, attitudes, and behaviours of individuals with different backgrounds. The objectives are to increase awareness and understanding of cultural diversity, and to improve interaction and communication among employees with different backgrounds. Diversity training is reported to be one of the most widely used strategies for managing diversity in the workplace and there has been a dramatic rise in diversity training programs in the last decade.[35]

Diversity training has three main objectives: 1. Increase awareness about diversity issues, 2. Reduce biases and stereotypes, and 3. Change behaviours to those required to work effectively in a diverse workforce.[36] Some diversity training programs are designed to change people's attitudes by creating an awareness of diversity and an understanding of differences in values and behaviours. The expectation is that, by creating an awareness and understanding of these differences, people will change their behaviour and overcome any stereotypes they might hold. Another approach to diversity training is to change behaviour. This approach emphasizes learning new behaviours that might then lead to changes in attitudes.[37]

A recent study on diversity in the workplace found that diversity experts rated training and education programs as one of the best strategies for managing diversity. The study also suggested that diversity training should focus on increasing *awareness* of what diversity is and why it is important; providing *skills* required to work effectively in a diverse workforce; and providing *application* strategies to facilitate the use of diversity awareness and skills to improve work performance, interactions, and communication.[38]

In Canada, many organizations have implemented diversity programs. For example, BC Hydro has an "Aboriginal Cross-Cultural Awareness Program" that focuses on building relationships. Employees learn how diversity can affect their work in a particular community. Aboriginals serve as subject-matter experts for the training program, which includes face-to-face meetings. Training takes place in a traditional setting within a particular community and has included dancing and singing.[39]

L'Oréal Canada has an intergenerational training program that was designed to help different age groups communicate with each other. The program has become one of the company's most popular training programs.[40] The Winnipeg Division of Boeing Canada Technology provides diversity training that includes formal educational classes on respecting and honouring co-workers' origins, leanings, and affiliations in four target groups of people (women, Aboriginals, visible minorities, and people with disabilities).[41]

Diversity training
Training that focuses on differences in values, attitudes, and behaviours of individuals with different backgrounds

Cross-Cultural Training

Many companies send their employees on assignments in foreign countries. While these foreign assignments can be good for one's career, they can also be difficult if an individual is not familiar with the foreign culture. The purpose of **cross-cultural training** is to prepare employees for overseas assignments by developing the skills and attitudes necessary for successful interactions with persons from different backgrounds.[42]

A critical factor in the success of cross-cultural training is training rigour. According to Black, Gregersen, and Mendenhall, **training rigour** refers to "the degree of mental involvement and effort that must be expended by the trainer and the trainee in order for the trainee to learn the required concepts" (p. 97).[43] Training rigour also refers to the length of time spent on training.

Table 13.2 lists some of the major types of cross-cultural training. Cross-cultural training programs that are considered to have a high degree of rigour include interactive language training, cross-cultural simulations, and field trips. Programs with a moderate degree of training rigour include role plays, cases, and survival-level language. Cross-cultural training programs that are considered to be the lowest in terms of training rigour include lectures, films, books, and area briefings. More rigorous cross-cultural training programs require trainees to be much more active and involved in practising cross-cultural skills.[44]

The degree of cross-cultural training rigour required by an expatriate for a particular foreign assignment depends on three dimensions: cultural toughness, communication toughness, and job toughness. *Cultural toughness* refers to how difficult it is to adjust to a new culture. Generally speaking, cultural toughness will increase the greater the difference or distance between one's own culture and the foreign culture.

Communication toughness is a function of the extent to which the expatriate will have to interact with the locals of the host country. When an expatriate

Cross-cultural training

Training that prepares employees for working and living in different cultures and for interactions with persons from different backgrounds

Training rigour

The degree of mental involvement and effort that must be expended by the trainer and the trainee in order for the trainee to learn the required concepts

TABLE 13.2

Types of Cross-Cultural Training Programs

- Environmental briefings about a country's geography, climate, housing, and schools.
- Cultural orientation to familiarize expatriates with cultural institutions and the value systems of the host country.
- Cultural assimilators that use programmed learning approaches to expose persons of one culture to the concepts, attitudes, role perceptions, and customs of another culture.
- Language training.
- Sensitivity training to develop attitudinal flexibility.
- Field experience such as visiting the country where one will be assigned to see what it is like to work and live with people in a different culture.

Source: Tung, R. L. (1982). Selection and training procedures of U.S., European, and Japanese multinationals. *California Management Review, 25* (1), 57–71.

will be required to have frequent interactions with host nationals that will involve face-to-face, two-way, and informal communication, the level of communication toughness will be high, and more rigorous communication training will be required.

Job toughness refers to how difficult the tasks will be for the expatriate compared to what he/she is used to doing. If the expatriate will be working in a new area and the demands of the job will be different and require new responsibilities and challenges, then the degree of job toughness will be greater. As a result, the expatriate will require more rigorous job-specific training.[45]

As the levels of these three dimensions increase, the type of cross-cultural training required will need to be more rigorous. In addition to pre-departure training, it is also important that the expatriates and their families also receive follow-up or in-country cross-cultural training in the host country.[46]

Research on the effectiveness of cross-cultural training has found that it is effective for enhancing one's success on overseas assignments and is related to adjustment and performance. However, the effectiveness of cross-cultural training depends on a number of factors such as the timing of the training and the cultural differences between one's own country and the assignment country.[47]

For guidelines on how to design a cross-cultural training program, see the Trainer's Notebook 13.1, "How to Design an Effective Cross-Cultural Training Program."

The Trainer's Notebook 13.1

How to Design an Effective Cross-Cultural Training Program

Here are some recommendations for the successful design and implementation of a cross-cultural training program:

1. Cross-cultural training should be considered a mandatory process.
2. The location of training should be established in accordance with the needs of the family as part of the preparation process and corporations need to accept that training can be done at home or in the host country.
3. The depth of training is of utmost importance. If corporations are going to provide cross-cultural training, it needs to be done properly with depth and with care.
4. Families must be incorporated into the training process. Training for expatriates alone is only sufficient if the expatriate is on an individualized assignment.
5. Language training should be incorporated into cross-cultural training wherever possible and should be encouraged as an ongoing aspect of the assignment.
6. Education and expectations of training must be laid out by training companies for international human resource professionals and in turn be easily translated for the preparation of each individual expatriate. This can be through appropriate written information being prepared for the expatriate and reinforced by the service provider reiterating the goals and expectations prior to the training.

Source: Bross, A., Churchill, A., & Zifkin, J. (2000, June 5). Cross-cultural training: Issues to consider during implementation. *Canadian HR Reporter, 13* (11), 10, 12. Reprinted by permission of Carswell, a division of Thomson Canada Ltd.

Summary

This chapter has provided an overview of the different types of training programs in organizations today. You should now be familiar with orientation training, essential skills training, technical skills training, information technology training, health and safety training, quality training, team training, sales training, customer-service training, sexual harassment training, ethics training, diversity training, and cross-cultural training. These training programs are a result of the many challenges facing organizations in today's rapidly changing and competitive environment. Many of these training programs have become key components of an organization's corporate strategy and are major factors in their efforts to remain competitive.

Key Terms

computer software training   p. 396
cross-cultural training   p. 401
diversity training   p. 400
essential skills   p. 394
essential skills training   p. 395
information technology training   p. 396
literacy   p. 394
orientation training   p. 394

sexual harassment   p. 399
team training   p. 397
technical skills training   p. 396
total quality management (TQM)   p. 397
training rigour   p. 401
Workplace Hazardous Materials Information System (WHMIS)   p. 397

Web Links

BC Hydro: www.bchydro.com

Royal Star Foods: www.royalstarfoods.com

TELUS: www.telus.ca

WHMIS: www.hc-sc.gc.ca/hecs-sesc/whmis/

Discussion Questions

1. Diversity training programs have been criticized for doing more harm than good. In fact, there is some evidence that they may be ineffective at best and harmful at worst. Why do you think this is the case? Do you think this is true and should organizations abandon diversity training or embrace it?

2. Why do you think Canadian organizations invest so little in essential skills training (see Table 13.1, basic-skills training)? What are the implications of this for employees, organizations, and society? Should Canadian organizations spend more on essential skills training? What are the advantages and disadvantages?

3. What would be your reaction if your employer wanted to send you on an overseas assignment? What would be your reaction if the assignment was in: 1. England, 2. France, 3. China, or 4. Egypt? Would you accept the assignment and if so, what training would you require? Describe the training you would need in terms of the content and methods.
4. What aspects of a cross-cultural training program affect its degree of training rigour? Discuss the factors that need to be considered to determine the degree of cross-cultural training rigour required by an expatriate for a particular foreign assignment. If you were sent on a foreign assignment to France to manage a new restaurant, what degree of cross-cultural training rigour would you require?
5. What is the Workplace Hazardous Materials Information System (WHMIS) and what are its implications for safety training? What should be covered in a health and safety training program?
6. Why is team training important for organizations that want to implement teams? What skills should be the focus of team training programs?
7. Why should an organization provide orientation training? If you were going to design an orientation program, what material would you include and how would your program be delivered?

The Great Training Debate

1. Debate the following: Diversity programs result in more harm than good and organizations should abandon them.
2. Debate the following: Essential skills and literacy training are the responsibility of government, not organizations.

Using the Internet

1. To learn more about workplace literacy and basic skills in Canada, go to **www.conferenceboard.ca/workplaceliteracy** and find out about the challenges that employers face and the solutions. Prepare a brief report in which you summarize the challenges, solutions, and best practices for small, medium, and large businesses.
2. To learn more about the types of safety training programs available, visit the Canadian Centre for Occupational Health and Safety at **www.ccohs.ca/education/**. What kinds of training programs are available? Choose one of the programs and find out what the program is about, the topics covered, the program objectives, target audience, and delivery options.
3. To find out about WHMIS education and training go to **www.ccohs. ca/oshanswers/legisl/whmis_education.html**.

Answer the following questions:

    a. What is WHMIS education and training?
    b. Who should be educated and trained in WHMIS?
    c. What is the purpose of WHMIS training?
    d. What, in general, is the content of a WHMIS training program?
    e. Can people in the same plant receive different training?
    f. What are the criteria of a successful program?

Exercises

In-Class

1. The extent to which organizations provide certain types of training programs is often driven by external and internal factors. In other words, social, political, and economic changes in the work environment, as well as internal changes to organizational systems and work arrangements, have a substantial influence on training activities. Choose several of the following training programs and discuss the role of external and internal factors and how these factors might influence the need and importance of each type of training:

    a. Orientation training
    b. Essential skills training
    c. Technical skills training
    d. Information technology training
    e. Health and safety training
    f. Quality training
    g. Team training
    h. Sales training
    i. Customer-service training
    j. Sexual harassment training
    k. Ethics training
    l. Diversity training
    m. Cross-cultural training

2. Assume you are a training director for a large retail organization. To increase your training budget for next year, you have to make a persuasive argument to convince other members of the organization of your need for an increase in resources. An important part of your argument will involve proving the need for and importance of several training programs. For some of the training programs listed in Exercise 1 above, describe how you will argue that it is important, the impact it will have on employee attitudes and behaviour, the benefits it will have for employees and the organization, and how it can help the organization gain a competitive advantage.

3. Design a training program for one of the types of training discussed in this chapter. In designing your program, specify each of the following:

   a. The training objectives
   b. The training content
   c. The trainer
   d. The trainees who should attend the program
   e. The training methods to be used
   f. The required training materials and equipment
   g. The training site
   h. The schedule for the training program
   i. The lesson plan
   j. The criteria you will use to evaluate the program

4. Describe the orientation training you received in the most recent job that you held. Some of the things to consider are:

   a. How long was the orientation training?
   b. What content was included?
   c. What methods were used?
   d. What did you learn from it?
   e. Were you satisfied with the program and did it help you perform your job?
   f. What did you like about it and what did you not like?
   g. How would you change the orientation training you received to make it more effective?

5. Choose one of the types of training programs described in this chapter that you have attended in a current or previous job. Describe the content and methods used and how effective the training was for your learning and on-the-job behaviour. Based on the material in the chapter and your experience, how effective was the program? How would you change it, improve it, and make it more effective?

6. Imagine your employer has just informed you that you are going on a foreign assignment for three years to a country that you have never been to and know nothing about. Furthermore, the culture is very different from your own. Your employer has informed you that you will be receiving some written information about the country and its culture as well as a videotape to help you prepare for your assignment. Prepare a memo to your employer in which you evaluate the training they are offering you and describe the type of cross-cultural training that you require if you are going to accept the assignment.

7. Students often have to work in groups on course projects without any knowledge of how groups function and what it takes for them to be effective. Some students experience difficulties when working in groups and some groups fall apart and the work is not completed. Therefore, it might be helpful if students receive team training. Your task is to design a training program for students to prepare them for group work. Describe the nature of your training program including the objectives, content, and methods.

In-the-Field

1. To learn more about the training programs discussed in this chapter, contact a training professional or a human resource professional to arrange an interview about the types of training provided in their organization. Choose a few of the types of training programs described in this chapter and ask them the following questions:

   - Does your organization provide this type of training?
   - What are some of the reasons why you do or do not provide this type of training?
   - What are the objectives of this type of training program?
   - What is the content of this type of training?
   - How is this training program designed (e.g., what methods, techniques, etc.) and who is the trainer?
   - What effect does this type of training have on employees' attitudes and behaviours?
   - What effect does this type of training have on the organization?

   Based on your interview, what is your evaluation of the training programs provided by the organization? Do you think they could be improved and if so what would you recommend and why?

2. Contact several employees you know who work in different organizations, and ask them the following questions about some of the types of training programs discussed in the chapter:

   - Have you ever received this type of training?
   - If yes, what was the reason why you attended the training program?
   - What were the objectives of the training program?
   - What was the content of the training program?
   - How was the training program designed (e.g., methods, techniques, etc.) and who was the trainer?
   - What was your reaction to the training program and what did you learn? What effect did the training have on your behaviour and job performance?
   - What effect did the training have on the organization?

   Based on your interview, do you think the training program was effective? What changes do you recommend to make it more effective?

Case Incident

Saving Theatre Calgary

Theatre Calgary is one of the largest professional theatres in Western Canada, with a 40-year history. However, lagging ticket sales and competing claims on the philanthropy dollar brought Theatre Calgary to near bankruptcy in 1996.

A decision was made to overhaul the company's marketing approach that would raise the standard of performance expected from employees, especially those in the areas of sales and customer service.

To support the new approach, the company invested in training for aggressive marketing and up-selling. Employees attended seminars on a range of techniques from how to cross-sell to how to analyze demographics for marketing opportunities and how to create a customer profile from the client database. Employees also had to improve their customer contact skills, from telephone manner to up-selling to meet-and-greet. They spent time developing scripts and rehearsing how to deal with people and how to deal with people with problems.

Questions

1. How important is training for saving the company from bankruptcy and what type of training is most important?
2. What do you think about the training programs provided to employees at Theatre Calgary? What would you recommend for improving them?

Source: Garcia, C. (2004, May 17). CloseUp: Training and development. *Canadian HR Reporter,* 17 (10), 7–10.

Case Study

Police Sensitivity Training

On September 14, 2000, several police officers raided a special event known as the Pussy Palace, a lesbian bathhouse in Toronto in which 355 scantily clad women were gathered. Two undercover female officers entered the bathhouse to check for possible liquor violations. They then called in five male officers, who raided the palace and spent 90 minutes walking around on what was described as a routine liquor licence inspection.

The officers allegedly opened doors, entered private rooms, questioned the women, and lingered in areas where the patrons' nudity was most evident in rooms such as "the sling room" and "the photo room." Complainants alleged that their feelings of violation and intimidation were akin to being strip-searched. Police charged two organizers with six liquor violations and three counts of permitting disorderly conduct. The raid outraged the gay community.

Justice Peter Hryn of the Ontario Court threw out the liquor licence infractions and ruled that the defendants' privacy rights had been seriously violated in a situation that did not require urgent police action. He compared the officers' entry into the club to a strip-search, calling it outrageous, flagrant, deliberate, unjustified, and a violation of the women's Charter rights.

During the defamation trial that followed, Justice Janet McFarland of the Ontario Superior Court described the raid as a violation of the Charter of

Rights of the women present and declared, "It is no part of a police officer's job to breach the Charter of Rights of any citizen. To do so is misconduct of the most serious kind."

The Toronto Women's Bathhouse Committee launched a human rights complaint, and several of its members also initiated a $1.5-million class-action lawsuit alleging harassment and discrimination. In December 2004, a settlement between the Toronto Police Services Board and seven complainants was announced and approved by the Ontario Human Rights Commission.

The settlement requires all current and future Toronto police officers to attend gay and lesbian sensitivity training. The Toronto Police Service also had to pay $350,000 to the complainants, that went toward charities and to cover legal fees. In addition, the five male officers who raided the bathhouse provided a signed apology to the women who were attending the event stating that they did not intend to breach their rights or privacy. As a result of the settlement, the $1.5-million class-action suit and the complaint to the Ontario Human Rights Commission were dropped.

According to the settlement, everyone on the 7,260-member force—from rookie constables to the chief of police—will be required to take training on gay and lesbian sensitivity. The training will pay particular attention to searches involving the gay, lesbian, and transgendered communities as well as inspections of gay and lesbian venues, businesses, and bathhouses. The program will be designed in consultation with the Ontario Human Rights Commission and members of the gay community.

Then-Police Chief Julian Fantino responded to the settlement by stating that the Toronto Police are already bogged down in training programs and scarcely need the added burden of enforced gay and lesbian sensitivity training which he called an unnecessary overreaction. He told a local newspaper that, "it's being forced on us," and "we are conscientious about diversity and sensitivity issues and all those kinds of things. Is it necessary? I think that in many respects this is a duplication of much of the work we already do." He went on to say that the force shouldn't have to "bow to all kinds of pressures," and "we have made extraordinary efforts to reach out and work with all entities in the community." Toronto Mayor David Miller called the sensitivity training "a very positive step" and "a very good part" of the settlement.

Sources: Makin, K. (2004, December 17). Toronto police to face gay-sensitivity training. *The Globe and Mail*, A1, A15; Porter, C. (2004, December 18). Fantino attacks deal; Sensitivity training "being forced" on police force, chief says: Agreement ends lawsuit over 2000 raid on lesbian bathhouse. *Toronto Star*, A1; Makin, K., & Gray, J. (2004, December 18) . . . . but calls sensitivity training a burden. *The Globe and Mail*, A17; Reinhart, A. (December 18, 2004). Fantino has proved he can exemplify tolerance . . . *The Globe and Mail*, A17; Brown, D. (2005, January 31). Toronto cops grudgingly accept sensitivity training. *Canadian HR Reporter, 18* (2), 1, 3.

Questions

1. Do you agree that all current and future Toronto police officers should be required to attend gay and lesbian sensitivity training? What do you think the effect of this will be on the police and the gay and lesbian community?

2. If you were to design a training program for the Toronto Police, how would you design it in terms of content and methods? Develop a lesson plan for your training program.
3. Consider the relevance of diversity training for the sensitivity training program. What aspects of diversity training are relevant and might be used in the design of the sensitivity training program? Are there are other types of training programs that are relevant and might be part of the sensitivity training program?
4. Do you think the sensitivity training will be effective? What else might be required in order for it to result in a significant change in police attitudes and behaviour?
5. How would you evaluate the sensitivity training program?

References

1. Excerpt from Watt, D. (2002, September). Excellence in Workplace Literacy, Medium Business Winner, 2002: Royal Star Foods Limited. *The Conference Board of Canada*: Ottawa.
2. Klein, H. J., & Weaver, N. A. (2000). The effectiveness of an organizational-level orientation training program in the socialization of new hires. *Personnel Psychology, 53*, 47–66.
3. Feldman, D. C. (1989). Socialization, resocialization, and training: Reframing the research agenda. In I. L. Goldstein (Ed.), *Training and development in organizations* (pp. 376–416). San Francisco: Jossey-Bass.
4. Anderson, N. R., Cunningham-Snell, N. A., & Haigh, J. (1996). Induction training as socialization: Current practice and attitudes to evaluation in British organizations. *International Journal of Selection and Assessment, 4*, 169–183.
5. Klein & Weaver (2000).
6. Ostroff, C., & Kozlowski, S. W. J. (1992). Organizational socialization as a learning process: The role of information acquisition. *Personnel Psychology, 45*, 849–874; Schettler, J. (2002, August). Welcome to ACME Inc. *Training, 39* (8), 36–43.
7. Understanding essential skills. Human Resources and Skills Development Canada. www.hrsdc.gc.ca/eng/workplaceskills/essential_skills/general/understanding_es.shtml.
8. Campbell, A. (2005, December). *Profiting from literacy: Creating a sustainable workplace literacy program.* The Conference Board of Canada: Ottawa.
9. Campbell, A. (2005).
10. Kuri, F. (1996, September). Basic-skills training boosts productivity. *HRMagazine 41* (9), 73–79.
11. Kuri, F. (1996, September).
12. Harris-Lalonde, S. (2001). *Training and development outlook.* The Conference Board of Canada: Ottawa; Campbell, A. (2005).
13. Baker, S., & Armstrong, L. (1996, September 30). The new factory worker, *BusinessWeek*, 59–68.
14. Harp, C. G., Taylor, S. C., & Satzinger, J. W. (1998). Computer training and individual differences: When method matters. *Human Resource Development Quarterly, 9*, 271–283.
15. Martocchio, J. J. (1992). Microcomputer usage as an opportunity: The influence of context in employee training. *Personnel Psychology, 45*, 529–552.
16. DeSimone, R. L., & Harris, D. M. (1998). *Human resource development* (2nd ed.). Fort Worth, TX: Dryden Press.
17. Harp, C. G., Taylor, S. C., & Satzinger, J. W. (1998).
18. Kelloway, E. K., Francis, L., & Montgomery, J. (2006). *Management of occupational health and safety* (3rd ed.). Toronto: Nelson Canada.

19. Kelloway, E. K., Francis, L., & Montgomery, J. (2006).

20. Dean, J. W. Jr., & Bowen, D. E. (1994). Management theory and total quality: Improving research and practice through theory development. *Academy of Management Review, 19,* 392–418.

21. Oakland, J. S. (1989). *Total quality management.* Oxford: Butterworth-Heinemann Ltd; Schonberger, R. J. (1992). Total quality management cuts a broad swath—through manufacturing and beyond. *Organizational Dynamics, 20* (4), 16–28; Tenner, A. R., & DeToro, I. J. (1992). *Total quality management, three steps to continuous improvement.* Reading, MA: Addison-Wesley.

22. Harper, L. F., & Rifkind, L. J. (1994). A training program for TQM in the diverse workplace. *Human Resource Development Quarterly, 5,* 277–279.

23. Tannenbaum, S. I., & Yukl, G. (1992). Training and development in work organizations. *Annual Review of Psychology, 43,* 399–441.

24. Bottom, W. P., & Baloff, N. (1994). A diagnostic model for team building with an illustrative application. *Human Resource Development Quarterly, 5,* 317–336.

25. Salas, E., Burke, C. S., & Cannon-Bowers, J. A. (2002). What we know about designing and delivering team training: Tips and guidelines. In K. Kraiger (Ed.), *Creating, implementing, and managing effective training and development: State-of-the-art lessons for practice* (pp. 234–259). San Francisco, CA: Jossey-Bass.

26. Stamps, D. (1997). Training for a new sales game. *Training, 34* (7), 46–52.

27. Connal, D., & Baskin, C. (2002, November). Transforming a sales organization through simulation-based learning: A TELUS Communications case study. *Training Report,* 4–5.

28. Schneider, B., & Bowen, D. E. (1995). *Winning the service game.* Boston, MA: Harvard Business School Press.

29. Anonymous. (1999, May 31). Delta promotes empowerment. *The Globe and Mail,* C5.

30. Schneider, K. T., Swan, S., & Fitzgerald, L. F. (1997). Job-related and psychological effects of sexual harassment in the workplace: Empirical evidence from two organizations. *Journal of Applied Psychology, 82,* 401–415.

31. Ganzel, R. (1998); Peirce, E., Smolinski, C. A., & Rosen, B. (1998).

32. Tyler, K. (2005, February). Do the right thing: Ethics training programs help employees deal with ethical dilemmas. *HR Magazine, 50* (2), 99–102.

33. Tyler, K. (2005, February).

34. Greengard, S. (2005, March). Golden values. *Workforce Management, 84* (3), 52–53.

35. Chrobot-Mason, & Quinones, M. A. (2002). Training for a diverse workplace. In K. Kraiger (Ed.), *Creating, implementing, and managing effective training and development: State-of-the-art lessons for practice* (pp. 117–159). San Francisco, CA: Jossey-Bass; Wentling, R. M., & Palma-Rivas, N. (1998).

36. Hanover, J. M. B., & Cellar, D. F. (1998). Environmental factors and the effectiveness of workforce diversity training. *Human Resource Development Quarterly, 9,* 105–124.

37. Noe, R. A., & Ford, J. K. (1992). Emerging issues and new directions for training research. *Research in Personnel and Human Resources Management, 10,* 345–384.

38. Wentling, R. M., & Palma-Rivas, N. (1998). Current status and future trends of diversity initiatives in the workplace: Diversity experts' perspective. *Human Resource Development Quarterly, 9,* 235–253.

39. Allerton, H. E. (2001, May). Building bridges in Vancouver. *Training & Development,* 84–97.

40. Klie, S. (2007, October 22). L'Oréal a pretty picture of diversity, training. *Canadian HR Reporter, 20* (18), 11.

41. Shaw, A. (2008, May 5). Boeing puts diversity to work—silently. *Canadian HR Reporter, 21* (9), 18.

42. Noe, R. A., & Ford, J. K. (1992).

43. Black, J. S., Gregersen, H. B., & Mendenhall, M. E. (1992). *Global assignments.* San Francisco, CA: Jossey-Bass.

44. Black, J. S., Gregersen, H. B., & Mendenhall, M. E. (1992).

45. Black, J. S., Gregersen, H. B., & Mendenhall, M. E. (1992).

46. Black, J. S., Gregersen, H. B., & Mendenhall, M. E. (1992).

47. Aguinis, H., & Kraiger, K. (2009). Benefits of training and development for individuals and teams, organizations, and society. *Annual Review of Psychology, 60,* 451–474.

CHAPTER 14

Management Development

Chapter Learning Outcomes

After reading this chapter you should be able to:

- define management and management development and explain how it is different from employee training
- describe the main roles, functions, and critical skills of managers
- discuss emotional intelligence and its relevance for management
- describe the models of management skill development
- describe the use of error-management training for management development
- describe the content of management skills development programs
- discuss the different types of management development programs
- describe outdoor wilderness training programs and their effectiveness for management development
- define job rotation and coaching and discuss the characteristics of great coaches, the five conditions that are necessary to ensure the development of managers, and the challenges of coaching
- discuss the research on the effectiveness of management development programs

As an industry leader in training and development, IBM spends more than $1 billion a year on training. IBM is a world leader when it comes to the development of sophisticated training programs. Perhaps, then, it is no surprise that the company launched a new two-year company-wide program to transform the role of the manager.

The program is called Role of the Manager@IBM and is the largest management development initiative in the company's history. It involves 32,000 IBM executives and managers and is designed to transform the role of the manager and to create a new model of 21st-century leadership.

Manager@IBM uses cutting-edge technology to provide managers with a new kind of learning experience that includes a blended program for leadership teams, performance support, and an online "e-coach" to guide managers in creating personal management development plans.

The program allows employees to manage their training using three "tracks," thanks to a sophisticated system called Edvisor. In track one, employees can access more than 150 online best practice management-support modules. In track two, managers' learning activities are assessed as they prepare for a two-day, face-to-face workshop focused on improving organizational climate and coaching skills. Edvisor helps managers to master specific Web-based program modules that prepare them for the face-to-face learning.

In the third track, an "intelligent agent" analyzes a manager's 360-degree leadership survey feedback and online responses. Edvisor then provides leadership advice and assists managers in building a personalized management development plan that includes access to a customized list of management development programs.

More than 22,000 managers have participated in the program and the financial impact of manager action plans has been substantial. More than $280 million in new revenue has been generated resulting in a net gain of $200 million over the $80-million cost of the program. Managers credit the program with enabling them to achieve these results. In addition, survey results indicate that business units with greater participation in Role of the Manager@IBM have greater improvements in employee satisfaction, clarity, and leadership ratings than units with less or no participation. In 2002, *Training* magazine ranked IBM fourth on its list of the Training Top 100, thanks to its Manager@IBM program.

Another successful program at IBM is called Basic Blue for Managers, which is a blended learning program for new first-line supervisors. The program combines four tiers of training. Three technology-delivered labs and one week-long classroom learning lab teach first-line managers to become better people managers. This year-long program immerses managers in a combination of online self-study, simulations, competency assessments, management coaching, and classroom experiences. In 2003, Basic Blue for Managers was highlighted by *Training* magazine as a best practice.[1]

The management of our global economy is no simple matter, challenging companies, even smaller ones, to excellence. Evidence indicates that the single characteristic that best distinguishes a successful organization, large or small, from others is the calibre of the management team.[2] As exemplified in the chapter-opening vignette, the development of the skills required of successful managers is a very serious business. This is because, like many companies, IBM understands the impact that managers have on the company's performance. It will be no surprise to learn that *Training* magazine has consistently ranked IBM's training program among the very best in North America (first in 2004–5 and second in 2006).

This chapter is placed near the end of the book, but this is not because the training of managers is unimportant. On the contrary, developing managers is among the most important, complex, and difficult of the challenges that trainers face today. It is also one of the major issues now facing organizations, as the Baby Boomer generation has reached retirement age. Organizations must recruit and develop those high-potential men and women—referred to as "bench strength"—who will soon take over the leadership of organizations. It is increasingly recognized that a major shift in the leadership of organizations is upon us (for more, see Training Today 14.1, "Bench Strength").[3] To meet this challenge, management development experts make use of the full slate of principles and techniques described in the earlier chapters.

As you have learned in previous chapters, successful training and development involves three key aspects: 1. The identification of training needs, which requires an understanding of the jobs and an identification of the skills required of people who do them (see Chapter 4); 2. The choice of training design and delivery techniques (see Chapters 5–9); and 3. An integration, within the training experience, of elements that contribute not only to learning, but also to other psychological forces like motivation and self-efficacy (see Chapter 3). These enhance the odds for successful transfer (see Chapter 10). In this chapter, we describe managers' roles and functions (what managers do) and their competencies (the critical skills they need). We describe the techniques and guiding principles that create the training experience (management training design and delivery) and conclude by describing several types of management development programs and their content. But first, we briefly explain what management is.

What Is Management?

"**Management** refers to the process of getting things done, efficiently and effectively, through and with other people" (p. 7).[4] The work of managers is to orchestrate the work of others. Although managers and management jobs

Management
The process of getting things done, efficiently and effectively, through and with other people

Bench Strength

Every two years or so, Executive Development Associates (EDA) conducts a major survey of managerial and leadership development practices and priorities by sampling 100 of the largest companies in the USA. Although the survey is concerned with many aspects of managerial development, the most striking result is the importance currently attached to the development of future managers (known as the development of "bench strength"). Clearly, as the Baby Boomer generation retires the replenishment of the leadership pipeline is an increasingly urgent priority. Interestingly, although companies still make use of the full gamut of development activities including formal courses and informal learning, they are increasingly turning to three mechanisms for creating that bench strength: leader-led development, action learning, and executive coaching.

Leader-led development refers to having top executives share their experiences and insights with future leaders. Action learning refers to job rotations and special assignments specifically designed to enhance certain specific competencies. Executive coaching remains a very important development activity, the use of which is increasing.

The Conference Board of Canada's 2007 survey shows similar results for Canada, where mentoring and coaching are increasingly favoured. This trend is also evident in Quebec. Daoud and Gosselin, researchers from the École des Hautes Études Commerciales in Montreal,

report a qualitative study conducted with Quebec-based pharmaceutical and insurance companies. In-depth interviews held with managers from these companies reveal that whereas both are assigning increasing importance to managerial development, insurance companies are motivated to do so, as with the USA study, because of the demographic concerns (i.e., retirement of the Baby Boomers). Pharmaceutical companies in Quebec are smaller and more recently created than are insurance companies, and as such are likely to have a younger work force. Yet both emphasize the same techniques for growing their future managers.

The broader USA and Canadian studies, as well as the narrower Quebec study, report the same fundamental issue: All see the development of managers as a critical priority and, within this, the development of soft skills—such as human interaction skills—as much more important than the development of hard skills—such as technical ones. Clearly, these results are telling us that new managers should be better at handling people.

Sources: Bolt, J. F. (2007). Mapping the future of leadership development. *The 2007 Pfeiffer Annual: Leadership development.* John Wiley & Sons; Daoud, M., & Gosselin, A. (2007). Évolution récente du développement des gestionnaires dans les secteurs pharmaceutique et de l'assurance au Québec. Paper presented at the Annual meeting of Administrative Sciences Association of Canada.

are all different, they share common aspects that help us grasp their essential natures. Figure 14.1 groups these commonalities by describing what managers do: their roles (interpersonal, informational, decisional), and the functions these roles serve (controlling, organizing, planning, and leading work organizations). As an example, whereas controlling budgets or organizing a task may have very different meanings for the National Ballet of Canada or Petro-Canada managers, accomplishing these tasks requires them to have conceptual, technical, and interpersonal skills as grouped in Figure 14.1.

It is axiomatic to management development that managerial skills and competencies are learnable and that they can and should be nurtured and developed through training and related experiences. These development experiences (indicated in Figure 14.1) occur on and/or off the job with instructional systems that are informational and experiential.

FIGURE 14.1

Managerial Roles, Functions, Skills, and Development Approaches

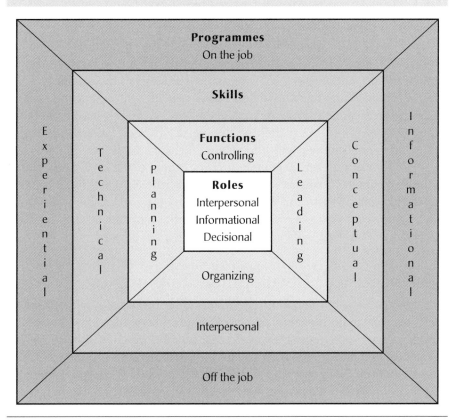

Management Development versus Employee Training

The topic of management development is separated from employee training for a number of reasons. First, managers are effective when those they manage are effective. That is, managers work mainly through other people. Whereas some management development programs are strictly technical (project planning or budget preparation, for example), most are focused on the development of people and interpersonal skills, a training task of considerable difficulty. Second, and as a result of this different focus and its inherent difficulties, the training design techniques tend to be different (training for managers tends to be experiential and informational). Third, and related to the previous point, the work of management is more influenced by individual managerial preferences and personalities and training must take into account these important individual differences. Fourth, management development is a longitudinal and gradual *process* by which the complex skills and competencies required of managers are built—that is, developed—over time, with training and with experience. Fifth and most important, incompetent managers can have a catastrophic effect on an entire organization's ability to survive: Management development is different than employee training because it has unique strategic significance.

What Is Management Development?

Management development refers to the "complex processes by which individuals learn to perform effectively in managerial roles" (p. 270).[5] Management jobs are not easy. Managers are responsible for delivering tangible results while tending to unforeseen problems and obstacles of all types: supply problems, machinery breakdowns, personnel issues, etc., all within the current organizational context characterized by change. A diverse and sometimes international work force, frequent technological changes, increased competition, shorter time frames, and a focus on efficiency are all serving to make the job of managing ever more complex. For example, the 2009 global financial crisis compelled managers to deal with totally unexpected circumstances. Successful adaptation to this difficult reality requires extensive managerial skills. These skills require strengthening and updating to retain their currency and effectiveness. That is the mission of management development.

Is Management Development Important?

Management development, a multi-billion-dollar business, is without doubt one of the most important applications of training in organizations.[6] In Canada as well as many other countries, per capita training expenditures are greater for managers than for any other category of employees: more managers are trained and more is spent on each of them. Corporate expenditures on management education and training are estimated to be $45 billion annually, with approximately $12 billion spent on executive education, and one-fourth spent on university business schools. The average cost of executive education for an organization today is reported to be about $2 million annually.[7] This high level of concern about the development of managers is true in North America as well as in many other areas of the world, including the United Kingdom, Lithuania, Spain, and Iran.[8] Why is that? It is because the development of managers is a prudent business investment.

To a very large degree, managers define the organization and it is they who are most responsible for its financial and psychological health. They are responsible for ensuring that the organization functions effectively and efficiently. Organizations are systems composed of people, technologies, procedures, and communications designed to achieve specific valued objectives. It is management's purpose to define these objectives (products and services) and to ensure that they are achieved. In effect, organizations invest more heavily in managers and in their development because theirs is *the* pivotal role in organizations.

Management Development and Leadership

As you will see, the fundamental roles that managers play in organizations are interpersonal, informational, and decisional ones. These three roles are core for the main functions of managers: controlling, organizing, and planning (which makes the convenient acronym COP). However, the last 20 years have seen a growing recognition of the exercise of leadership as a fundamental function of managers. **Leadership** refers to the individual qualities and behaviours that define and shape the direction of the organization and that inspire others to pursue that direction in the face of obstacles and constraints.

In the past, this "leadership" function was thought to belong more exclusively to the apex of the organizational pyramid: the senior managers.[9] However, in line with current thinking (e.g., Kotter,[10] or Whetten and Cameron[11]), we subscribe to the view that the exercise of leadership is a function of *all* management. Hence, the functions of managers are now thought to be controlling, organizing, planning, and leading (which makes COPL, though some prefer the less literal but more colourful acronym CLOP).

Adapting to the global economy and its competitive pressures requires ever-increasing levels of resiliency and flexibility in organizations. This flexibility requires that people at all levels of the organization, from the top to the bottom, adapt their job behaviours in response to the changing requirements of their jobs and the contexts in which they are to be performed. As Kotter explains, managers are the motors that propel this process of adaptation to change. From first-line supervisors to CEOs, from production to R&D, managers need to possess the knowledge, skills, attitudes, and behaviours that enable them to foster in the people they manage the attitudes and behaviours that are conducive to the attainment of the individual and organizational goals. The current economic realities compel managers to assume this challenge. They need to lead.

The starting point for a discussion of management development is the identification of training needs. To define these needs, as discussed in Chapter 4, a thorough understanding of the managerial job is required. We therefore begin by reviewing research results that describe what managers do in order to identify the skills they require.

Leadership

The qualities and behaviours that shape the direction of the organization and which inspire others to pursue that direction in the face of obstacles and constraints

Core Managerial Roles

Henry Mintzberg analyzed management from the perspective of the manager's day-to-day activities.[12] Derived from the formal authority and status that a manager has, Mintzberg broke these activities into three roles: interpersonal, informational, and decisional. This research is important because it helps define, with greater precision, the skills required of managers and hence the focus of training and development efforts.

Interpersonal Roles

Interpersonal roles refer to the relationships that managers develop with other people because these can provide significant help (or obstacles) to the attainment of group goals. As such, the manager is the organizational person who provides *leadership* (motivates others), and who *liaises* with others both within and outside the unit with the goal of securing information that is of use to the attainment of goals. For example, the training manager who serves on the board of the local community college is better able to gauge the match between the skills taught in the college and those required by his/her organization. The manager also plays a *figurehead* or representational role wherein he or she participates in routine, social, and legal contexts as a representative of the group managed. For example, the Prime Minister, as the manager of Canada, has the duty to meet with his foreign counterparts at annual G8 meetings. Successful achievement of this role requires people skills.

Informational Role

Managers must *monitor* the environment (both internal and external) to accumulate information pertinent to the attainment of organizational goals. He or she reciprocates by assuming the role of *disseminator* of information by informing others about the unit and informing the unit about relevant developments occurring outside the unit. For example, the dean of research in a university might set up systems to provide professors with information about government or private programs that fund research. The manager also acts as a *spokesperson* informing others and "selling" them on the plans, values, or goals of the unit. The manager of an oil company, for example, may be called upon to describe to the community the steps that the organization is taking to curtail greenhouse gas emissions. Hence managers require communication skills.

Decisional Role

Managers must make decisions about people and about goals and the means to attain them. As an initiator of change, the manager is an *entrepreneur* moving the unit in directions that take advantage of opportunities or shifting the activities of the group to reduce threats. For example, to respond to the growing threat from Apple, which had developed a more user-friendly operating system for its computers, Bill Gates moved Microsoft away from the classic DOS system to the Windows operating environment. The manager *allocates resources,* choosing from competing proposals and projects those that will receive additional funding and personnel and those to be curtailed or discontinued. Downsizing or staff expansions are such resource-allocation decisions.

The manager is also called upon to act as a *negotiator,* bargaining with others in the environment to acquire the resources required to meet the planned goals. This negotiation role may involve interactions with the external environment (e.g., by negotiating with government regulatory agencies, suppliers, or unions), or it may be focused internally (e.g., securing additional resources for the work group). In addition, the manager is also a *trouble-shooter* reacting to unanticipated and unplanned environmental events that can severely disrupt the unit. An extreme example of the trouble-shooting and negotiation roles occurred in late 2008, when the financial meltdown compelled most organizations in the world to modify their business development plans and projects and in many cases to solicit and negotiate help from governments. Hence managers require problem-solving skills.

Clearly, managers play a complex role requiring sophisticated skills. Although most managers will have to accomplish each of the roles, the relative emphasis placed on them will depend on the specifics of the hierarchical position, the organizational and social-cultural context, the overarching organizational strategies, and the technologies and structures in which they operate and exercise their functions. For example, although interpersonal, informational, and decisional skills are all important, the display of interpersonal roles may be particularly significant for the manager of a classical ballet company, while the decisional role may be even more critical for the management of a production department.

Managerial Functions

The **functions of management** are controlling, organizing, planning, and leading (COPL). That is, managers are responsible for ensuring that things get done. They monitor the work processes and progress toward goal attainment (controlling); they allocate resources and tasks (organizing); they establish what should be done and how (planning); and they maintain the motivation and zeal of those who do the work (leading). In completing these functions, they play one or more of the interpersonal, informational, or decisional roles and rely on the skills that each implies.

Functions of management
Controlling, organizing, planning, and leading

Controlling

Controlling, as its name suggests, refers to the process by which the activities of the organization and its members are monitored to ensure that they contribute positively to the attainment of organization goals and objectives. It involves establishing mechanisms to monitor and resolve performance gaps and address any constraints and problems that hinder the attainment of performance goals.

- For example, the manager of an automobile engine assembly plant is required to monitor quality control indicators to ensure that the engines built meet the quality specifications required, that they start, run smoothly, and function with the fuel efficiency standards specified. Deficiencies from required standards must be identified, diagnosed, and corrected in a timely and efficient manner. In such cases, management would review the quality indicators and institute corrective actions as needed.

Organizing

The accomplishment of most contemporary organizational goals requires the efforts of a diversity of units, each composed of many individuals. Major activities are identified and components of these major tasks assigned to units and individuals. The manager's job is to establish systems that ensure these efforts are efficiently and effectively coordinated and organized.

- Automobile manufacturing provides a clear example of organizing. One plant may build engines, while another plant builds chassis. Yet another one may place the engines in the chassis. Within each plant (engine, chassis, and final assembly) managers must organize the activities as well. Hence, the engine plant would be organized such that separate units produce the valves, pistons, and fuel injection systems. And each of these sub-systems of the manufacturing process is in turn organized to produce the valves, pistons, and injection systems efficiently and effectively and in such a way that they all fit together, in a timely manner, to produce the final engine.

Planning

Planning, in the context of management, means defining the direction toward which the efforts of individuals are to be directed. It involves defining objectives and developing goals to be met by the organization and the departments or the units for which the manager is responsible. The scope of the goals and objectives depends on the level of management, and the specifics of the planning tasks depend on the nature of managerial responsibility. As one moves from the lowest to the highest levels of the organization, the objectives and goals become broader and more strategic.

- For example, the highest levels of the automobile industry may choose as a fundamental strategy the production of "high quality" cars and trucks. At lower levels of the organization, meeting this strategic goal requires plans that are more local and more specific. Hence mid-level managers may focus their planning efforts on "ensuring that 99 percent of automobile parts meet the established quality standards" while even lower-level managers may plan to "establish a system by which assembly line workers meet once a week to discuss ways of improving the quality of the work that is done" or to ensure "that all employees who provide suggestions for improvements be provided feedback within one week of their making the suggestion."

Leading

Leading is a critical people-oriented function of management. It means influencing the actions of others such that these actions are coordinated to produce the desired outcomes. Managers mainly operate through others. Hence, managers require people skills. Management is responsible for obtaining and keeping employees committed to their goals. This is facilitated when employees believe that the attainment of the goal is important, when they believe that attaining the goal will result in positive outcomes, and when they also believe that their individual efforts make a difference in goal attainment. A leader, according to Kouzes and Posner, is successful by being a role model (i.e., preaching by example), by inspiring a shared vision, by challenging the status quo and encouraging others to do the same (asking why), and by recognizing the contributions of others (through verbal feedback and tangible outcomes).[13]

- In the automobile industry example, building quality cars involves ensuring that people care about quality and view their own work with an emphasis on quality. To inspire all levels, leaders would "sell quality" through their actions and their words. Quality would

Taking Management Development Seriously: The PricewaterhouseCoopers Story

PricewaterhouseCoopers (PwC) is one of the largest professional services organizations in the world. PwC takes the development of its people seriously. It has instituted widespread coaching and mentoring programs for managers, but it has gone one step further.

As part of the performance management program, all managers must indicate the steps they have taken to develop their own subordinates. The performance assessment—and the rewards and bonuses paid out to managers based on it—is determined, in part, by the degree to which they have helped their employees achieve higher levels of competencies, both managerial and technical.

Moreover, all partners in the firm are offered a series of workshops delivered by leading professionals to help them gain a deeper understanding of the help that they can provide to their employees and the importance of that function for the organization.

Why would a prestigious organization like PwC attach importance to this policy? Because it is good for their employees and good for business! Such policies help the company retain its valued employees and help them service their clients even better. Developing and growing the competencies of employees also increases their employability, both on client projects with PwC and even if they should leave the organization.

In the end, the value of these practices is that they seamlessly and simultaneously provide benefits both to the organization and to employees. It's a win-win scenario.

be one of the important criteria against which all decisions would be weighed.

Although managers are still viewed as those responsible for "getting things done" through the functions of controlling, organizing, planning, and leading, increasingly managers must provide support to their employees, assist them in the development of new skills, and act as coaches and facilitators for employee task accomplishment.[14] Leading organizations have formalized these functions by integrating them into the performance management system for managers. To learn more about this, see Training Today 14.2, "Taking Management Development Seriously: The PricewaterhouseCoopers Story."

Management Skills

In the previous sections, we identified and described the various roles and functions of managers as this process is essential to pinpoint the ensemble of skills and knowledge that are required of managers and that may be developed through training.

Skills may be defined as sets of actions that individuals perform and that lead to certain outcomes.[15] The literature is replete with descriptions of the types of skills that are needed to accomplish the managerial roles and functions. Two types of approaches have been used to identify the skills required of managers. Some authors rely on their extensive experience with management to infer the skills needed for effective management (or leadership). They then propose mechanisms by which these can be developed.

Skills

Sets of actions that individuals perform and that lead to certain outcomes

Others have tended to place a higher emphasis on empirical research to guide their prescriptions. The classic empirical technique for identifying these skills has been to conduct surveys of managers—sometimes within a single firm and sometimes across several firms. Managers rate the importance of many potential skills and statistical analyses are conducted to identify those skills and competencies that distinguish successful managers from their less successful counterparts.

One such study involved observations of 52 successful managers and compared them to less successful ones in three organizations. Successful managers appeared more skillful in a number of ways. They were better than their less successful counterparts in building power and influence, communicating (with insiders as well as outsiders), managing conflict, decision making, developing others, processing paperwork, planning, and goal setting.[16]

Confirmation of these attributes was obtained in a more recent study where, instead of focusing on successful managers, as is usually the case, the authors looked at the problem from the opposite pole. They conducted 166 group interviews (focus groups) with 830 U.S. managers who were identified as *less* successful. These managers tended to be poorer in a number of dimensions that closely mirror those identified by other studies. They tended to display ineffective communication and interpersonal skills, they failed to clarify expectations, they were poorer in delegating and empowering subordinates, they tended to be more distrustful of others, they were less able to organize and encourage teamwork, and they had more trouble motivating others. Furthermore, these less effective managers were poorer at planning, monitoring performance, and providing feedback and they tended to be less effective in identifying and removing obstacles to effective performance that their employees had experienced.[17]

Taking a somewhat different approach, Cameron and Tschirhart asked a large sample of managers working in 150 organizations to identify the most important skills and competencies required of managers.[18] The results showed that the managerial skills fall into four basic clusters. One cluster focuses on human relations skills and includes skills such as providing supportive communication and team building. Another focused on competitiveness and control. A third cluster focused on behaviours that foster individual entrepreneurship and innovativeness, and the fourth focused on order and rationality. Hence, effective managers support and encourage the work of their employees (cluster 1) while focused on achievement and results (cluster 2). They allow employees to display innovation and creativity (cluster 3), while maintaining control and rationality (cluster 4).

As Cameron and Tschirhart note, the skills required of successful managers are "paradoxical," requiring them to possess a number of skills that may appear contradictory (e.g., cluster 3 versus cluster 4). But Whetten and Cameron showed that successful managers did resolve this paradox: Even as they were controlled, stable, and rational, they were still able to be creative and flexible.

As result of these extensive and varied approaches to understanding managerial roles and functions, a number of critical managerial skills have

TABLE 14.1

The Most Frequently Cited Skills of Effective Managers

Verbal communication (including listening)

Managing time and stress

Managing individual decisions

Recognizing, defining, and solving problems

Motivating and influencing others

Delegating

Setting goals and articulating a vision

Self-awareness

Team building

Managing conflict

Source: Whetten, D. A., & Cameron, K. S. (2002). *Developing management skills* (5th ed.) Upper Saddle River, NJ: Prentice Hall.

been identified. Table 14.1 presents a summary of the most frequently mentioned skills of effective managers. As you will see, many of these involve "people skills" (communicating, motivating others, delegating, goal setting, self-awareness, team building, and conflict management). The "people" side of management and its subsequent salience for management development cannot be underestimated. As an example, the Stanford Graduate School of Business produces a large number of briefings videos delivered by corporate and academic stars and intended for the development of managers. They cover a very wide range of topics (such as mergers and acquisitions, preparing financial statements, supply chain strategies, etc.), but the single most frequent topic, about a third of all videos, focuses on dealing with people (such as coaching and providing feedback).

A manager controls, organizes, plans, and leads people. In practice, this means that one of the most important aspects of management involves interacting, communicating, and dealing with other people: their peers, subordinates, and superiors, as well as customers and, in many cases, members of the general public. You will not be surprised to learn that some managers are better at it than others. Research has shown that those who have superior people skills possess, in addition to other talents, higher levels of a specific type of intelligence called "emotional intelligence," a topic to which we now turn.

Emotional Intelligence

Most human interactions have an emotional component and the success of these interactions often depends on how well emotions are managed. Moreover, because of the heavy responsibilities of the management role and the sheer number of tasks that managers perform, they must often deal with their own emotional issues and pressures. Thus, they have to cope with conflict, performance pressures, and uncertainty. Because much of this involves emotions, managers must develop skills in managing their own emotions and in understanding those of others. The skills that people have in managing emotions—their own and those of others—have been labelled *emotional intelligence* (EI).[19]

As with coordinating, planning, etc., the training needs of managers now additionally include developing in them greater people skills, and underlying those people skills lie the various aspects of emotional intelligence. It is for this reason that we devote a specific section on this topic. To obtain an appreciation for the prominence of this concept, search "emotional intelligence" or "emotional quotient" (EQ) on the internet. You will find thousands of entries!

Emotional intelligence

The ability to manage your own and others' emotions and your relationships with others

Emotional intelligence has to do with the ability to manage and cope with emotions—one's own emotions as well as those of others. This involves five sets of skills that foster better understanding of oneself and effective interactions with others:

1. *Self-awareness:* Being aware of, and understanding, oneself and one's emotions when interacting with others.
2. *Self-control:* Managing and regulating one's emotions (both positive and negative) that arise from encounters and events.
3. *Motivation or drive:* Channelling emotions and energies in support of one's goals.
4. *Empathy:* "Reading" and recognizing the emotions of others and responding to them appropriately.
5. *Interpersonal skills:* The ability to manage interactions with others in an appropriate and effective manner, through an understanding, integration, and management of emotions—yours and theirs.

Notice that the components of EI (e.g., self-awareness, interpersonal skills, etc.) are listed as skills. That is, they are believed to be controllable and learnable behaviours rather than "fixed" character-like traits. Unlike intellectual intelligence (IQ), which is a relatively stable and enduring characteristic of people's cognitive abilities, EI is believed to be a learnable and changeable factor. In other words, through appropriate management development and training, emotional intelligence can be modified and improved. However, unlike project planning or other "hard skills" associated with management, emotional intelligence involves people-oriented skills that often are labelled as "soft skills". As you read in Training Today 14.1, soft skills are considered to be even more important today.

EI, as with other "soft skills," tends to be developed indirectly, through enhanced skills in dealing with others. As people learn to receive and deliver feedback, to manage stress, or to defuse conflicts, for example, they also simultaneously enhance their own levels of emotional intelligence.[20] Training in emotional intelligence involves group and individual activities that include role plays, assessments, and practical exercises all intended to enhance self-management and empathy.

The fact that emotional intelligence can be developed is extremely important because empirical research has shown that managers with higher levels of emotional intelligence are more effective and successful than managers with lower levels of EI. They are more likely to be promoted and to rise to the highest levels of management in their organizations. Furthermore, emotional intelligence has been found to be much more important than IQ or cognitive ability in predicting a manager's success, and to also predict organizational success. Not surprisingly, research indicates that organizations prefer to hire for management positions people with higher levels of the skills associated with emotional intelligence.[21]

In summary, emotional intelligence involves the ability to manage one's own and others' emotions and relationships with others. Given that managers spend most of their time interacting and communicating with others and that the main functions and roles of management involve people, emotional intelligence is a critical factor in management development and effectiveness. Therefore, in addition to training experiences that are directly focused on its development, those programs that include activities and experiences that encourage self-awareness and self-control, motivation, empathy, and interpersonal skills serve to enhance emotional intelligence.

Clearly, managers require myriad skills. Whereas some fortunate managers excel in all, most managers have strengths and weaknesses, some of which require development. What are the principles that underlie how we are to go about doing that? It is to that end that models of management skill development have been proposed.

Models of Management Skill Development

A model of management skills development is a basic blueprint that identifies the components or steps to be included in the development of programs. Many skill development models exist in the management literature, some specifying a greater number of steps than others (e.g., Whetten and Cameron list five steps, while Hunsaker lists 10—see The Trainer's Notebook 14.1, "The TIMS (Training in Management Skills) Procedure").[22]

However, most models of management skill development that are commonly practised in organizations share four basic commonalities. That is, management development programs that have better chances for success will minimally include these four sequenced steps: 1. Initial skills assessment (identifying where people are), 2. Skill acquisition (learning and understanding the basic principles associated with the specific skill of interest), 3. Skill practice (developing procedural learning by integrating the principles into smooth behavioural actions), and 4. Skill application on the job (applying the learned principles in job situations that require the skills).

Table 14.2 summarizes these four basic components of management development programs and identifies the outcome each is expected to influence.

a. *Skill assessment.* This process identifies the skill level of the manager before development. Initial skill assessment is used to identify the strengths and weaknesses that managers hold relative to the specific skills to be trained and most importantly to help managers become aware of them. Skill assessment is a key component of IBM's

RPC 14.1

The TIMS (Training in Management Skills) Procedure

Phillip Hunsaker provides the following 10-step process to management development that he refers to as TIMS or Training in Management Skills.

1. Self-assessment.
2. Learn skill concepts.
3. Check concept learning.
4. Identify behaviours that define the skill.
5. Model the skill (i.e., observe others performing the skill).
6. Practice the skill during training (to build self-efficacy and to contribute to procedural learning).
7. Re-assess skills (to test for progress and to intervene when skill changes are insufficient).
8. Questions to assist in skill application (questioning trainees to ensure that they have a clear understanding of the situations in which the application of the trained skill is warranted and to identify constraints and coping strategies for overcoming these constraints).
9. Exercises to reinforce skill application (as well as self-efficacy and procedural learning).
10. Planning for future development (as a specific preparation for transfer).

The TIMS model (and most other models) helps training developers and management trainers focus their efforts by providing a template of the activities required to increase the odds that managerial skill levels do improve as a result of training. Although the TIMS model is somewhat more detailed than some other models, it reflects the key dimensions common to most management development models: skill-assessment (steps 1 and 7), learning (steps 2 though 5), and practice and preparation for application on the job (steps 6, and 8 through 10).

Source: Hunsaker, P. L. (2001). *Training in management skills.* Upper Saddle River, NJ: Prentice Hall.

TABLE 14.2

The Basic Components of Management Development and Their Expected Impact on Trainees

	MOTIVATION	SELF-EFFICACY	LEARNING	BEHAVIOUR CHANGE (TRANSFER)
initial skills assessment	X			
skill acquisition			X	
skill practice	X	X	X	
skill application on the job	X	X	X	X

Managing@IBM program and it is developed in close symmetry with the learning objectives set for the training program (see Chapter 5). Skill assessment contributes to and builds self-awareness. This is critical because people must recognize a need for development before development can take hold. That is, skill assessment affects and contributes to training motivation. Initial skill assessment also serves to identify the learning and the basic behavioural styles that managers hold. There is general recognition that the purpose of management development is not to change individual personalities or styles, but rather to help managers translate these personal preferences into practices and behaviours that are appropriate to their work context and that are effective in meeting the goals of the organization.

Initial skill assessment is usually established through self-administered (and often self-scored) standardized validated questionnaires given to training participants at the onset of training. For this reason these questionnaires are relatively short, easily administered, and easily scored under themes that directly reflect the training content. For example, the initial questionnaire for a stress-coping program would ask trainees to describe the degree to which they engage in behaviours that are known to be associated with stress reactions. Typically trainees retain their answers, and after training answer the questionnaires again to note changes.

Although initial skill assessment is of importance to all training programs, it is especially critical for management development because "development" is a gradual process where *improvement* in skills is the main objective. Managers will need to practice and rehearse the skill before mastery can be achieved. Keeping managers motivated and confident in the development of the specific skills requires reinforcement. Skill assessment before and after the development experience can be reinforcing as this helps managers perceive the degree of growth in their level of skills mastery. Helping managers perceive improvements helps to build motivation, thus encouraging managers to continue to exert the efforts that lead to mastery. Hence, skill assessment and growth is immediately useful to the trainer (to know how things are going), but it makes an indirect contribution to the motivation of the learner.

b. *Skill learning.* Learning the required principles and behaviours that form the core of the intervention is central and all training programs focus on it. However, as contrasted with most technical training where the trainee is taught specific procedures and steps required to accomplish a task, the managerial role is more diffuse, requiring that managers learn how to recognize the need for the skill in a diverse number of circumstances. Hence, management development programs will almost invariably include group discussions where managers help each other discover the opportunities for application that may exist on the job, the obstacles that may inhibit skill use, and the strategies and tactics that may be used to circumvent these obstacles.

In management development, the purpose is to help managers learn managerial principles and processes that can be integrated with their personal styles and applied to the conditions they are likely to meet on the job. Hence, most management development programs will include substantial lectures or presentations that outline the reasons for the training and the principles that will guide their future actions. For example, performance planning and reviews (PP&R) tend to be more constructive when subordinate and managerial anxiety and defensiveness are minimized. To achieve this, most PP&R training programs emphasize the importance for the manager to clearly explain the evaluation process to the subordinate ahead of time. There are many ways of explaining the same thing, and no specific manner, or set of words, will be appropriate for all managers and/or with all subordinates. Therefore, the effectively trained manager will have understood the principle (reducing subordinate defensiveness) but will "choose" his or her own specific words and approaches depending on the specifics of the person under review and the specifics of the situation. The ultimate objective of these development programs is to help managers attain procedural learning (see Chapter 3). Attaining that goal generally requires *practice,* the third major component of management development programs.

MAKE THE CONNECTION

c. *Skill practice.* As described in Chapter 5, practice is the key to learning how to do most things well. The practice of learned skills serves three fundamental purposes. First and most obvious, practice reinforces learning and, more formally, helps shift the learning from the declarative to the procedural learning stage (see Chapter 3). This is essential if the manager is to integrate the learned skill with his or her own style. A second use of practice is to enhance the manager's beliefs in his or her ability to perform the skill. That is, practice contributes to the development of self-efficacy and, as you have read in both Chapters 3 and 11, the development of self-efficacy is one of the keys to successful training. Managers who feel more confident in their capacity to learn and display the skill on the job are more likely to learn and transfer that skill. Third, skill practice can take a variety of forms including role plays, simulations, and videotaped behaviour with feedback. These activities are inherently more active, maintaining trainee interest, attention, and motivation on the learning task. However, as training time is invariably limited in the North American context, it is not realistic to expect that the amount of time devoted to practice during training will be sufficient to automatically produce high levels of transfer on the job. As rehearsal and practice on the job is essential, all development models include as a final component "skill application on the job."

MAKE THE CONNECTION

d. *Skill application on the job (transfer).* This final step in management development has to do with the transfer process (see Chapter 10). Managers establish, during the training session, specific plans for the application of the learning on the job. Once on the job, however, organizational support in the form of follow-ups, additional coaching, and reinforcement is frequently required to ensure that managers transfer their newly learned skills. The reason for this is that in light of the very numerous tasks that managers perform, usually under pressure, it is very easy and tempting for them to relapse into their traditional, well-honed pre-training behaviours. Specific immediate post-training interventions such as relapse prevention (see Chapter 10) can also be integrated at this point to augment the odds of successful transfer.

In summary, models of management skill development focus on a number of important steps or stages in the development process. This usually begins with self-assessment and then proceeds to skill learning, practice, and application. These steps favour the development of the motivational, self-efficacy, learning, and/or transfer outcomes that define successful training.

Error Training for Management Development

Traditional models such as TIMS regard errors as undesirable and detrimental to learning. Trainee skills are assessed, then skills are taught, then they are practised and applied. This sequential approach is designed to focus the training content and processes to reduce errors until, at the application stage, they are mostly eliminated. However, errors are inevitable when mastering new content or a new task, and that can be very discouraging. As most students know, it is very difficult to exercise continued effort in the face of failure.

In Chapter 5 we discussed error-management training (EMT), which involves allowing and encouraging trainees to make errors. Let's consider how EMT can be used for management development. Recall that EMT has been found to be more effective when the trainee has to generalize learning to new tasks. Thus, if the training transfer task is to reproduce—more or less mechanically—a learned skill, EMT programs do not offer much advantage over traditional ones, designed using TIMS approaches. However, for jobs that require problem-solving skills, where reproduction of learned behaviours is not sufficient, EMT may prove superior.

This latter result is of special relevance for management jobs, where constant adaptation to an ever-changing environment is the norm. Trained managers must be able to use new skills flexibly in a variety of contexts. In Chapter 5 this was called adaptive expertise. As EMT appears pointedly more effective in producing adaptive expertise, and since that type of transfer is required for management jobs, organizations might consider EMT when developing managers.

The Content of Management Development Programs

Based on our earlier discussion, management skills can be clustered around three general categories: conceptual, technical, and interpersonal skills. These three clusters of skills are not completely independent. For example, the mastery of technical skills (planning a project) often requires conceptual skills (such as linear programming). Conversely, some interpersonal skills (e.g., convincing R&D scientists of the importance of respecting deadlines) often require specific technical skills (understanding the complexities of research).

Nevertheless, this categorization provides a useful way to organize management development programs.

In this section, we describe the content of programs used to develop some of these managerial skills. More complete descriptions of management development programs may be found in texts specialized in management development (e.g., Whetten and Cameron or Hunsaker) and by consulting the Web links identified at the end of the chapter.

Conceptual Skills

To accomplish the control, organizing, and planning functions of management, managers require various conceptual skills. We will limit the discussion to three especially important conceptual skills—problem solving and decision making, planning, and performance management.

a. *Problem-solving and decision-making skills.* Because managers are required to make myriad decisions—small and large—it is essential that they have the skills to do so. Many years ago, James March and Herbert Simon, in one of the most influential studies of managerial decision making, showed that most people are uncomfortable making decisions, and that they tend to adopt solutions to problems that are not optimal but "adequate."[23] Typically, the first solution that minimally solves the problem is selected.

Contemporary decision-making programs are designed to specifically avoid this tendency. As a result, most programs are organized around four basic steps: 1. Definition of the problem, 2. Generation of alternative solutions, 3. Evaluation and selection of a solution and 4. Implementation of the solution and follow-up. The actual training programs include introductory lectures where the basic steps required for effective decision making are explained and defended. Videotapes, role plays, and structured individual exercises are used to reinforce each learning point, and to provide some of the all-important skills practice.

b. *Planning skills.* Planning is an essential requirement of management. Planning involves first the clarification and specification of the goals the manager wishes to achieve. Next, the manager is taught to scan the environment to ensure that the plans are relevant and have a high probability of being successfully implemented. This second step is referred to as a "SWOT" analysis. That is, the manager is taught how to identify the strengths (S) and weaknesses (W) of the unit managed (i.e., its capabilities and weaknesses) relative to the opportunities (O) and threats (T) that exist in the environment. Based on this analysis, the manager is taught to translate these strengths and weaknesses, opportunities, and possible threats into specific actions in order to establish the strategies and tactics required for implementation. Finally, managers learn the processes by which the success (or lack thereof) of the plan is evaluated.

c. *Performance management and goal-setting skills.* Almost all organizations in North America require managers to review, assess, and manage the performance of their units and the people in them. Performance appraisal involves two distinct steps: assessing the performance of people (to provide feedback on past performance and to ensure that rewards and sanctions are applied fairly), and establishing goals and directions for future performance (to encourage improved future performance). Whereas these two steps are usually associated with a yearly formal review session, it is now widely acknowledged that managers need to review the performance of others on an ongoing basis. Motivating employees to improve performance is one of the key skills that successful managers possess.

Goal setting is an integral part of this process. As discussed in Chapter 3, goals have strong motivational effects and are one of the most important mechanisms for managing one's own performance as well as the performance of others.[24] Goals focus and direct one's efforts and can be self-reinforcing by providing specific feedback information that allows people to evaluate their progress.

However, in order for goals to be motivational, they must be SMART goals. That is, they must be Specific, Measurable, Achievable, Relevant, and specified in Time. Managers need to know how to structure such SMART goals. Moreover, goals are motivating and effective only when they are perceived to be challenging yet achievable, and when there is commitment to goal attainment. Most goal-setting training programs are structured to teach managers how to obtain the employees' commitment to the set goals and to provide feedback relevant to goal attainment.

Goal setting is now an integral part of performance management, and many managers are trained in this area in order to enable them to conduct performance appraisals and to help their employees improve their performance. Many Canadian organizations including PricewaterhouseCoopers, the National Research Council of Canada, and Bell Canada have provided their managers with performance management and assessment training courses that include goal setting as one of the key dimensions of the program.

Performance management training programs emphasize, through lectures and discussions, the key advantages of performance reviews and the fundamental difficulties of the process. Such programs include many experiential components such as role plays and simulations.

Technical Skills

Managers of marketing departments know something about marketing, and research directors know something about research. Such knowledge and skills are generally acquired through university programs that may be general (such as a general MBA) or more specialized (such as a university program in human resource management, marketing, statistics, or accounting). Additionally, technical skills can be further developed through targeted training courses and workshops and/or readings. For example, controlling budgets requires expertise in computer spreadsheet programs such as Excel, and the informational role requires presentation skills, which in turn often requires knowledge of how to use presentation programs such as PowerPoint.

As additional examples, university professors tend to build technical skills by reading scientific journals and by attending conferences, and medical doctors and pharmacists in Canada are required to attend a certain number of conferences and workshops that instruct them on new research, treatments, or diagnostic procedures in their areas of practice. Accountants and lawyers are also required to attend periodic specialized information sessions, such as when there are changes to auditing standards or tax regulations or when new laws are enacted.

Interpersonal Skills

Interpersonal skills refer to the manager's ability to interact with others in a constructive manner. This includes skills in communication, in coaching (see "Coaching" later in the chapter), and in managing conflict and stress. Although we limit our discussion in this chapter to these skills, it is important to note that other skills are also important. For example, there is a growing recognition of the importance for managers to develop "political" skills designed to help them gain power and influence. Moreover, as organizations move toward knowledge-based systems, they require that their members increasingly self-manage their behaviour and show initiative in their own development, including innovative ways of integrating Web-based learning, as with Kraiger's "third-generation" models of learning.[25] Although that particular approach is somewhat controversial, it remains that managers need to learn how to function in this new environment by learning how to empower and motivate their employees and to build effective teams.[26]

   a. *Communication.* Communication skills are central to most management positions because much of a manager's time involves gathering and disseminating information from the environment to the people in the unit and from the people in the unit to the environment. Often managers must communicate expectations to employees and provide feedback—not all of which is positive—to employees. In communicating effectively, managers are taught to recognize their own *biases and styles* in "hearing" and in "speaking" with others. Hence, managers need to understand their *frame of reference* (knowing "where they are coming from"), how their interpretations of what they hear and communicate are affected by their *values,* and their *trusts* or distrusts of others. These in turn affect *selective listening* (hearing what we want to hear) and *filtering* (telling only that which others want to hear). In addition to alerting managers to these tendencies that obscure communication, most communication training programs teach managers the principles and the practice of effective communication. This involves *congruency* (ensuring that the message sent is in line with their own actions), *clarity* (using language that is appropriate for the listener), and most importantly to ensure *comprehension* by actively soliciting feedback from the listener. Again,

Managing Performance Through Training and Development

in addition to learning the principles of sound communication, trainees are provided with many opportunities to practise these skills during training by analyzing cases and engaging in role plays with other training participants.

b. *Managing conflict.* Managing conflict is an essential skill for managers because they are invariably competing for resources with other managers and because they may be involved in managing the competition and conflict between employees.

Conflict can be described as being of one of two types—conflict that is *interpersonal* (co-workers who may dislike one another) or *issue-based* (people who may have conflicting views on a problem or its solution).[27] Conflict is not an inherently "bad" thing, because issue-based disagreements often can serve to enhance the quality of the final decision.[28] However, when conflict is not properly managed it can quickly create organizational problems.

There are five ways of managing conflict: *avoidance* (ignoring it), *accommodation* (giving in), *forcing* (getting your way), *compromise* (providing each party with some of the things they want), and *collaboration* (finding a solution together that gives the parties what they both want).

Collaboration is the ultimate conflict resolution outcome but it is not always possible or appropriate. Which style is appropriate depends on the situation faced by the manager. Forcing, for example, may be appropriate when the resolution requires an unpopular decision and when gaining the commitment of people to that decision is not important. Hence managers are taught to recognize and choose the conflict management response that is appropriate to the circumstances they face. This, above all, requires of managers that they pay attention to the emotional aspects of the conflict. To do so requires that the manager 1. Treats the parties with respect, 2. Listens to the other party and ensures that they know they have been heard and understood, and 3. Shares his/her needs and feelings.

c. *Managing stress.* Considering the scope, time pressures (managers spend about nine minutes on each problem!), difficulties, responsibilities, and ambiguities of managerial life, it is no surprise that managerial jobs tend to be very stressful. A stress reaction is a person's emotional and physical response to a perceived threat. Stress reactions, like pain, are useful warning mechanisms that inform people that "something is wrong" and that they should do something about it. However, how a person deals with stress may or may not be particularly functional. Reacting to someone cutting you off on the highway by tearing after them with vengeance on your mind is unlikely to lead to an enjoyable or safe driving experience!

Stress reactions in the context of work are responses to events that may find their source in the work itself and in the organization. For example, two well-known work-related stressors are role conflict and role ambiguity. *Role conflict* is associated with having contradictory task demands (e.g., jobs that require experimentation and innovation in organizations that do not tolerate errors); *role ambiguity* refers to not knowing what is expected. Stressors that impact work behaviours might also find their source in non-work events (a family or health problem, for example). Managers need to recognize stress reactions both in themselves as well as in those they manage, because some stress reactions can be quite dysfunctional, damaging one's health and/or work performance.

There are two basic ways to deal with stress. First, one can change the environment by removing the stressors. Second, one can learn to cope with and manage stressors more effectively. As individuals are generally better able to learn how to react to stressful situations than they are able to change organizational environments, the second approach is more likely to be successful.

However, most people experience stress and are unaware of it. In learning how to cope with stress, the first and most important step, then, is to recognize the signs of stress: to know when one is in fact experiencing it. As a result, the initial "skills assessment" phase of such training is critical and these programs spend considerable time helping managers become aware of their own reactions to stress. The manager can then learn proactive behavioural and cognitive tactics and strategies (learning how to perceive these situations differently) that will reduce the harmful effects of a stress reaction.

Stress-related training programs rely on the typical informational (reviewing basic principles related to stress and its management) and experiential (principally simulations and role plays) techniques. Usually, these programs offer techniques that can be beneficial to managers' ability to deal with stress not only in the context of work, but also in their non-work lives.

In summary, management development programs are often designed to focus on the development of conceptual, technical, and interpersonal skills. There are of course many different approaches and methods for developing these skills, some "on the job" and others "off the job," a topic to which we now turn.

ⓇⓅⒸ 14.2   Methods of Management Development

Whereas virtually all of the on-the-job and off-the-job training methods described in Chapters 6 and 7 can and have been used by some management development programs, management training methods tend to rely on highly informational and highly experiential procedures.

Management training programs are strongly informational and focused on the principles and the applications of the skill or technique being taught. That is, they teach principles relevant to specifics in the core roles and functions of management. You may have noticed that in the sections describing management training programs (conflict management, decision making, etc.), emotional intelligence, or coaching (see below), we emphasized their principles. Lectures, readings, informative videos, and group discussions structured around these principles and their concrete applications constitute major elements in management training programs. This informational, principles-based approach is of great importance in management development because managers operate in fluid and varied environments and each manager needs to develop his/her own idiosyncratic ways of comfortably applying the principles learned in training. Management development cannot consist of memorizing and applying a set of prescriptions. If, for example, all computer operators can be drilled in exactly the same behaviours for loading a hard drive, all managers cannot be equivalently drilled into using the same words to communicate with all employees effectively. It is only by understanding and integrating the principles taught that different managers can correctly apply them in a manner that is appropriate to themselves and to the work group situation.

Helping managers adapt principles and techniques in conformity with their personal styles, given the context in which they work, requires effort on the part of the learner and that effort requires motivation. Managers who do not believe in the usefulness of a training program are unlikely to exert the efforts required to learn and apply its content. Focusing on the principles (and their application) contributes motivationally to successful management training: It sells it!

Because of the importance of motivation, management training programs tend to be experiential. **Experiential learning** refers to learning experiences that include skill practice exercises that actively engage and involve the learner: activities likely to be more intrinsically motivating. Hence role plays with feedback, active exercises, and simulations are important components of the programs. Experiential approaches provide, in addition to motivational benefits, two other important ones. First, extensive hands-on practice builds procedural knowledge (see Chapters 3 and 11). That is, direct experience helps managers integrate the newly learned skills. Second, experiential learning is favoured because it contributes to managerial self-efficacy, which is an important precursor for transfer of training (see Chapter 10). As you will recall from the COMA model (see Chapter 11), motivation, self-efficacy, and procedural knowledge all have important effects on training success and transfer.

Experiential learning

Learning experiences that include skill practice exercises that actively engage and involve the learner

Although informational and experiential components are present in most programs, the balance between the two is not always identical. Many short-term programs (such as the Stanford Graduate School of Business DVDs) are essentially informational. Some development programs are more fully experiential, providing few if any formal informational components. One such example is outdoor wilderness training. The interesting origins of this popular technique are described in Training Today 14.3, "The Origins of Outdoor Wilderness Training," and its effectiveness as a training strategy is discussed later in this chapter.

There are three general approaches or techniques to management development: management education programs, management training programs, and on-the-job management development.

The Origins of Outdoor Wilderness Training

During World War II, the allied navies played a major role conveying and protecting ships supplying England. German U-boats opposed these convoys, taking a heavy toll on men and ships. Hundreds of ships were torpedoed, forcing thousands to confront the rigours of survival in rafts and lifeboats. Many successfully escaped their burning ships only to perish awaiting a rescue that did not come.

Paradoxically, casualty reports revealed that older, less physically able shipwrecked men had better survival rates than younger, fit sailors. Discussions held with survivors indicated that younger sailors adopted unsuccessful life strategies such as panic, while the older sailors, those with greater life experience, remained calmer and hence better able to meet the demands of their extreme situation.

Years after the war ended, this experience spawned "outdoor wilderness training," an experiential team and management development technique. For several days trainees are tasked with arduous and/or hazardous duties that are intentionally stressful, such as winter wilderness camping.

These stressful situations bring out the best and the worst in ourselves and others allowing us to gain direct experience with what we and others are capable of doing. With its exposure to extreme conditions, outdoor wilderness training is intended to build "life experience" which, in turn, is supposed to contribute to the development of coping skills.

Management Education Programs

Management education

The acquisition of a broad range of managerial knowledge and general conceptual abilities

The development of managers has typically involved management education. **Management education** refers to the types of activities that are typically conducted by colleges and universities and that develop a broad range of knowledge, principles, and general conceptual abilities relevant to the managerial role.[29] These education programs target the development of the principles and techniques required to effectively control, organize, plan, and lead. Examples and case studies drawn from specific organizations are often used to exemplify the general principles and techniques of management that are presented through lectures and discussions. Three examples of such content areas are accounting, organizational behaviour, and business statistics.

The ever-popular MBA that most business schools offer provides the classic example of a management education program. Executive MBA programs are especially desirable for individuals who are already in managerial roles and want to advance in their organization. These programs provide individuals with a general education in management and are highly informational although they usually include much experiential learning as well. Students not only learn about management concepts and theory, but also are expected to develop managerial skills. In fact, many MBA programs have managerial skills courses that focus on the kinds of skills listed in Table 14.1.

MAKE THE CONNECTION

Management education programs make use of a number of instructional methods such as role plays, games, simulations, and behaviour modelling that were described in Chapter 6. The case study method, however, is the most often used method to teach management skills in most MBA programs.

A second, complementary approach to management education has been the development of corporate universities. To learn more, see Training Today 14.4, "Are Corporate Universities Useful?"

Training Today 14.4

Are Corporate Universities Useful?

A corporate university (CU) is a function or department, independent of the human resource department, that offers an integrated set of learning and development experiences that are strategic for that specific organization or industrial sector. The main objective of a CU is to develop individual competencies that are of relevance to the organization. They do not replace training departments. Rather, they operate in parallel to them, developing in managers and employees competencies and attitudes (including attitudes toward learning itself) that will be beneficial to their actual and future performance in the company.

Although they are owned by the companies, corporate universities are sometimes affiliated with universities that provide some of the teaching. The Eaton School of Retailing, developed with Ryerson University in Toronto, is one such partnership. In some cases, CU participation can contribute credits toward formal degrees and diplomas. Other examples of corporate universities include BMO's Institute for Learning (Canada); the Federal Express Leadership Institute (USA); and the Lufthansa School of Business (Europe).

Organizations accept the large investment required by corporate universities because, in part, it is thought that they will contribute to improved individual job performance. However, this remained an untested hypothesis until Morin and Renaud conducted an evaluation of a Canadian financial institution's corporate university.

Over a two-year period, annual individual job performance data, demographics, and other variables were gathered from more than a thousand employees, some of whom had enrolled in one or more courses provided in the CU (the "experimental" group), while others had not enrolled in any (the "comparison" group). The results showed that CU participation had a very small, though statistically significant, effect on job performance. At first glance, the corporate university's impact on individual job performance appears to be marginal at best.

Whereas advocates of corporate universities may be disappointed that participation in it had such a small impact on overall job performance, they may take solace in that the data also showed a statistically significant interaction between pre-training performance and participation in the CU: those employees who demonstrated the most improvement following participation in the CU were those who had poorer pre-training job performance. This suggests that CU participation may provide its greatest benefit to those organizational members who need it most. The implication of that finding is obvious. Rather than dismissing sub-performing managers and employees, organizations that have CUs may be able to recuperate them through their enhanced job performance.

In addition to providing insight into corporate universities, this study demonstrates the advantage of the pre-post with comparison design over both the post-only and the simple pre-post designs as described in Chapter 11. Had either of these other designs been used, we would have been compelled to conclude that corporate universities have little impact on job performance. However, through the inclusion of "before-after" measurements and the comparison group, it was possible to detect the all-important interaction between CU participation and improvement in job performance. That interaction, more than any other result of the study, may well indicate the true importance and value of corporate universities to organizations.

Source: Morin, L., & Renaud, S. (2004). Participation in corporate university training: Its effect on individual job performance. *Canadian Journal of Administrative Sciences, 21* (4), 295–306. Reprinted with the permission of the authors and the Canadian Journal of Administrative Sciences (CJAS).

Management Training Programs

Management training

Programs and activities designed to develop specific managerial skills

Management training refers to training programs that involve activities and experiences designed to develop specific immediately applicable managerial skills (e.g., communication, decision making) in a particular organizational setting. Many of the specific training programs described in the technical, conceptual, and interpersonal skills development efforts discussed in this chapter's section on the content of management development programs fall in this category.

Management training programs usually focus on specific topics or particular skills. Some management training programs take place in classrooms and consist of specialized workshops and seminars. Management training programs can also take place outside of the classroom in any number of settings. Outdoor wilderness training is one management development activity that takes place off-the-job.

Outdoor wilderness training

Highly experiential programs designed to help managers develop greater levels of "life experience" by participating in physically and psychologically demanding tasks and activities

Outdoor wilderness training programs are typically organized around a series of outdoor tasks that expose individuals to physically and psychologically demanding activities in which the trainees have had little or no prior experience, such as rock climbing, white-water rafting, or even winter camping. Though outfitters are careful to provide instructors who are safety conscious, it remains that many of the activities are inherently dangerous. Generally, the successful and safe accomplishment of these tasks requires self-reliance as well as teamwork, strong communication skills, and the development of trust in others. This in turn is expected not only to help enhance the individual skills of trainees—such as leadership skills—but also to improve the individual's ability to function collaboratively with others (teamwork).

A key question, however, is just how effective is wilderness training? Research on Outward Bound Australia trainees indicates that an overwhelming proportion of participants retain highly positive reactions to their training experience.[30] Moreover, the research indicates that such training appears to have effects on a very wide set of variables from leadership ability and mood to social skills and well-being, and that this effect may be very durable and long-lasting. In addition, these programs appear to have their largest impact in increasing the participants' self-efficacy and their ability to manage time. However, the research also shows that there is considerable variation between programs, some being more successful than others in creating these changes. Beyond some mild indications that shorter programs (one to three days) are less successful than longer ones, we do not know with much clarity what makes one program more successful than another. Hence, whereas it is possible that such programs do lead to improvements in managerial job performance, the research data—being principally based on self-reports—remain insufficient to draw a firm conclusion.

Some management training programs are developed in-house by the training group with or without external consultants, while others are purchased from specialized firms (such as Xerox). These training programs are usually of short duration (one-half to three days is typical) and can be delivered by internal staff or by specialized external resources. Moreover, an increasing number of management development programs are being made available through electronic media (see Chapter 8). IPM, for example, offers an integrated package of 12 CD-based training modules that covers key management skills including staffing, performance management, team building, and employee relations (more details are available from www.workplace.ca).

On-the-Job Management Development

On-the-job management development programs are designed to provide individuals with managerial learning experiences on-the-job. Two of the most common examples are job rotation and coaching.

Job Rotation

Recall from Chapter 7 that **job rotation** involves exposing an individual to different areas and experiences throughout the organization. As briefly described in Training Today 14.1, this technique continues to enjoy high levels of popularity. With job rotation, the individual not only acquires new skills from working on different projects and interacting with people throughout an organization, but also learns about the organization itself. Job rotation as a development technique is particularly useful for the development of managers when the match between the skills the managers possesses and those required in the new job is well thought out: jobs that require the manager's skills and provide opportunity for building others are best. As indicated in the TIMS model, accurate initial skills assessment is especially important when job rotation is contemplated as a development technique for managers.

Coaching

In Chapter 7 it was noted that coaching and mentoring are common methods of on-the-job training. Mentoring and coaching are often used to develop managerial competency. In both cases they are one-on-one sessions held between the manager and another person. They both share the same distal goal of helping managers be more effective. Mentors help less experienced managers to understand and to gain perspective on the general managerial problems and difficulties with which they are confronted. Mentors contribute to the strategic development of managers. Coaching is more goal-oriented. It is a one-on-one individualized learning experience in which a more experienced and knowledgeable person is formally called upon to help another person develop the insights and techniques pertinent to the accomplishment of their job.

In the last 15 years or so, coaching has grown both as an on-the-job method to develop managers and a function that managers are expected to use with their own subordinates. Indeed, the 2007 Conference Board of Canada "Learning and Development Outlook" has documented the growth in this approach to management and leadership development in Canada.[31] It reports that more than one-third of Canadian organizations maintain coaching and/ or mentoring programs, and 55 percent of these consider them effective tools for the development of their people.

Coaching involves one-on-one individualized learning experience in which a more experienced and knowledgeable person is formally called upon

On-the-job management development

Programs designed to provide individuals with managerial learning experiences on the job

Job rotation

Exposing an individual to different areas and experiences throughout the organization

 14.3

Coaching

One-on-one individualized learning experience in which a more experienced and knowledgeable person is formally called upon to help another person develop the insights and techniques pertinent to the accomplishment of their job

to help another person develop the insights and techniques pertinent to the accomplishment of their job. The coach interacts with and provides feedback to the manager with the intent of developing his or her insight, skills, attitudes, and motivation.

Coaches may be external or internal to the company depending on budgets, coaching goals, and the organizational contexts. For example, the CEO who is struggling with a downsizing decision may well prefer to be coached by an external person. However, the manager who needs to hone her political skills might benefit more from a trusted internal coach. If coaching is to be provided to all employees on an ongoing basis, relying on internal coaches may be more economically realistic.

Many coaches are specialized in specific sectors such as pharmaceuticals or manufacturing, or in specialized contents as the following illustrates.

A marketing manager was promoted to head a different group: the organizational learning group in the Canadian operations of a multinational pharmaceutical organization. Her boss, the vice president of human resources, asked her to develop and present to upper management six weeks hence a training plan for the marketing division. Although experienced in marketing, the new manager lacked direct experience and knowledge of "organizational learning." She therefore signed a six-week contract with an external coach who was an expert in training and development with extensive experience in the pharmaceutical industry. The coach's role was *not* to produce the training plan, but rather to help the manager develop hers. During the weekly two-hour coaching sessions they discussed best practices, what other companies did, the advantages and disadvantages of various options, the obstacles likely to be encountered and how best to prepare for them, and how to present the plan, including setting up the actual slides for the presentation to her bosses. This coaching episode ended when the manager presented (successfully as it turns out) her training plan.

In this very typical case, the coach was an external consultant hired to help a manager complete one major task within an established six-week deadline. However, many organizations require that managers serve as coaches to subordinate employees and managers on an ongoing basis. In that case the mandate may be much broader (the issues to be coached are not specified in advance) and/or more open-ended (without a specific end date). The coaching system in place in the Canadian branch of PricewaterhouseCoopers (as described earlier in Training Today 14.2) provides one such example. However, this approach requires that the managers be trained in the science of coaching.

David Peterson lists several characteristics of great coaches, of which three stand out: Great coaches are goal-oriented, challengers, and person-focused.[32]

1. *Goal orientation.* Great coaches are great listeners who empathize with the learner and who are honestly interested in helping people achieve their goals.
2. *Challengers.* Great coaches are able to "feel" the mood state of the learner and know when to listen and when to challenge the beliefs and thinking of the learner.

3. *Person-focused.* Great coaches focus their efforts and attention on the learner. They do not try to impose their views on the learner by insisting that there is "one best way" to do things. Rather, they focus on helping the learner use his/her own previous knowledge and experience to develop his/her own perspective, understanding, and styles in dealing with the problems to be solved.

The coach who is goal-oriented, challenging, and person-focused is more likely to develop the manager. This is because these are the skills that will help the person coached to develop insight, motivation, capabilities, real-work practice, and accountability, the five conditions of successfully accomplished coaching. These five form what Peterson labels the "development pipeline." Coaches are maximally helpful when they structure their efforts to help managers develop:

- *Insight.* Recognizing and understanding their own strengths and weaknesses.
- *Motivation.* Understanding and caring about changing the ways in which they operate.
- *Capabilities.* Identifying resources and best practices for dealing with complex decisions and situations and by exploring alternative ways of dealing with them.
- *Real-world practices.* Identifying opportunities to implement, on a day-to-day basis, the little changes that should be made and to develop the critical perspective needed to assess what works, what does not, and why.
- *Accountability.* Encouraging the manager to demonstrate the new skills and knowledge through commitment to specific actions.

To achieve these objectives, coaches face a number of important challenges. First and foremost, coaches must act to gain the trust of the "coachee." Confidentiality, discretion, and honesty are three of the key behaviours coaches must demonstrate. With this developing trust it becomes easier for the coach to provide feedback that is more likely to prove constructive to the manager. For example, the suggestion from a trusted coach that a manager enroll in a specific seminar or read a particular book is likely to be well received.

Applying new skills is difficult and attempts to do so are often subject to obstacles and hurdles that can discourage the use of the new skills. Coaches have a special responsibility to be attentive to these situations and to help managerial persistence. Building self-efficacy, helping managers construe obstacles as "problems" rather than "failures," and providing emotional support are three techniques successful coaches use. Finally, coaches who are in a position to do so sometimes intervene elsewhere in the organization to remove obstacles. That is, successful coaches are sometimes proactive as opposed to strictly passive in their interventions. Compared to external ones, internal coaches are often in a better position to help in this way.

A number of research studies have shown that coaching does help managers become more successful and more effective in accomplishing their tasks. Coached executives showed progress in a number of dimensions including the management of people, relationships with others, communication skills, goal setting, engagement, and productivity.[33] This study also showed that the effects are greater when the coaches are committed to change and when the organizational environment actively supports them in their attempts to change. Yet another study—this one relying on a very large sample of executives using a quasi-experimental research design—showed similar results, although here the changes were significant but somewhat modest.[34] Finally, other research has shown that managers who received coaching experiences as part of their executive education program in a university also reported higher levels of self-efficacy and improved skills in developing others.

While this evidence speaks highly of coaching, it is important to note that most of the research has relied on self-report measures and/or on the perception of others (mainly supervisors and/or subordinates) to assess the effectiveness of coaching as a management development technique. Although this is true of most training evaluation of management development programs (see the following section, "Is Management Development Effective?"), the reliance on questionnaire responses as a criterion of success must be viewed with caution. Perceptions may not be accurate substitutes for objective criteria as measures of effectiveness.

Is Management Development Effective?

Clearly, management development is important; most organizations provide training for their managers either in-house or through the use of specialized firms and programs. Yet the question remains: Are these efforts effective? The latest Conference Board of Canada report concludes that only one-quarter (26 percent) of organizations are pleased with the results of their leadership development practices. This result is highly consistent with those shown by multiple studies demonstrating that the effectiveness of these development efforts is highly dependent on careful planning and on environmental support.

The Conference Board results are derived from perceptions rather than from hard facts, and they represent the results of one specific survey conducted at one specific moment. More general results have been obtained from meta-analysis. Meta-analysis is a powerful statistical technique that allows researchers to summarize, in quantitative terms, the results obtained from many evaluation studies that have focused, in this case, on the effectiveness of management training.

In 1986, Burke and Day analyzed all studies conducted prior to the early 1980s and concluded that management training was, at best, "modestly" effective.[35] However, because few studies actually collected objective data and even fewer measured level 3 or 4 outcomes (see the discussion of the Kirkpatrick model in Chapter 11), the results of that meta-analysis have been considered tentative by all—including its authors. Twenty years later, Collins and Holton returned to the literature and reported a meta-analysis of all pertinent studies (K=103) published since Burke and Day's.[36] Here, the focus was on investigating the degree to which managerial leadership development efforts produced positive results with regard to learning, expertise, and organizational outcomes. Both perceptual and objective data were considered in this study, as were many different types of training evaluation studies both with and without control or comparison groups (see Chapter 11).

The results indicate that training programs are highly effective in increasing learning levels. However, they are moderately effective in building expertise, though that result varies depending on the specific training evaluation design used. As for system outcomes—such as impact on firm effectiveness or profits—the results are less complete, as few studies actually assessed such outcomes. Fewer still were able to isolate the effect of management training from all other potential impacts on these outcomes. Nevertheless, the data indicate that, on average, leadership development programs do seem to contribute to the organization's effectiveness. Hence, to date we can be reasonably certain that leadership training has a major impact on learning, and to a lesser degree on expertise and organizational outcomes. Perhaps more important is the finding that there remains much variation in results across development efforts: while many training programs are effective, others remain ineffective.

Unfortunately, the data available from the Collins and Holton study do not permit us to clearly identify the characteristics of training programs that are effective versus those that fail. For example, we do not clearly understand the conditions under which coaching or mentoring programs are effective. This is an important area for future research because mentoring and coaching programs are gaining in popularity for the development of managers. In Canada, more than one-third of companies sampled maintain systematic coaching and mentoring programs, and the majority of those consider these programs effective. Whether this optimism is empirically justified remains an open question.

Summary

This chapter described the roles, functions, and critical skills of managers and how they are developed. Managers engage in a number of interpersonal, informational, and decisional activities in order to accomplish their organizational goals of controlling, organizing, planning, and leading the work of others. This requires them to master and display conceptual, technical, and interpersonal skills, and to have emotional intelligence. Management development programs are designed to develop these skills. Models of management development involve skill assessment, skill acquisition, skill practice, and skill application. The content of management development programs was described in terms of conceptual, technical, and interpersonal skills. Management development programs involve both informational and experiential learning and include management education, management training, and on-the-job management development. Management education programs such as an MBA provide individuals with a general management education. A popular example of a highly experiential management training program is outdoor wilderness training. Examples of on-the-job development include job rotation and coaching. The chapter concluded with an assessment of the effectiveness of managerial development programs for improving organizational performance and it closes with a discussion of the research findings as to the effectiveness of management development efforts.

Key Terms

coaching   p. 441
emotional intelligence   p. 426
experiential learning   p. 437
functions of management   p. 421
job rotation   p. 441
leadership   p. 419
management   p. 415

management development   p. 418
management education   p. 438
management training   p. 440
on-the-job management development   p. 441
outdoor wilderness training   p. 440
skills   p. 423

Make the Connection

p. 430: practice and active practice are discussed in Chapter 5 on page 145

p. 430: the stages of learning are discussed in Chapter 3 on page 68

p. 430: self-efficacy is discussed in Chapter 3 on page 74

p. 430: the transfer process and transfer interventions are discussed in Chapter 10 on page 289 and pages 303–305

p. 431: error-management training is discussed in Chapter 5 on page 153

p. 433: goal setting is discussed in Chapter 3 on page 81

p. 437: procedural knowledge is discussed in Chapter 3 on page 68

p. 437: the COMA model is discussed in Chapter 11 on page 329

p. 438: off-the-job instructional training methods are discussed in Chapter 6 on page 167

p. 441: job rotation is discussed in Chapter 7 on pages 204-206

p. 441: coaching and mentoring are discussed in Chapter 7 on pages 208–213

Web Links

Bell Canada: www.bell.ca

IBM Canada: www.ibm.com/ca

Links to Managerial and Professional Training Programs: www.trainingreference.co.uk/directory

Microsoft: www.microsoft.com

National Research Council of Canada: www.nrc-cnrc.gc.ca

PricewaterhouseCoopers: www.pwc.com

RPC Icons

RPC 14.1 Provides the appropriate assessment tools for determining career development options for employees.

RPC 14.2 Facilitates the implementation of cross-functional development work experiences for employees.

RPC 14.3 Facilitates coaching and post-training support activities to ensure transfer of learning to the workplace.

Discussion Questions

1. What are some of the differences between management development and employee training?
2. Why is management development important?
3. Imagine the CEO of a company who has read this chapter and the section on coaching. She decides that coaching is a good idea and sends a memo to all managers telling them to formally take on the role of coach for each of their subordinates. Is this a good idea? How likely is it to improve performance? Had the CEO consulted you prior to announcing her decision, what would you have suggested she do?
4. Compare and contrast management education, management training, and on-the-job development. What are the advantages and disadvantages of each of these approaches for management development? How effective do you think each approach is for teaching the skills listed in Table 14.1?
5. What is emotional intelligence and what does it have to do with management and managerial skills? Can managers be trained to improve their emotional intelligence? If yes, how can this be done?
6. What is outdoor wilderness training and how effective is it for developing managers? What would be your advice to an organization that was considering sending its managers to an outdoor wilderness program?
7. What is the difference between informational learning and experiential learning and when should they be used for management development?
8. Describe the four basic commonalities of models of management skill development.
9. What is the difference between the traditional models of skill development and error-management training?

The Great Training Debate

1. Debate the following: Some people have argued that management development is a waste of time and money because great managers are born, not made. Is it the case that managers cannot be developed?

Using the Internet

1. Many internet sources describe the types of management training programs that exist for different levels of management. Do a Web search for "management training programs," and visit **www.crmlearning.com** or **www.cmctraining.org**.

a. Once you have visited some of these sites, identify the types of programs that are most frequently proposed.

b. How do these "popular" and frequently offered courses relate to the management roles, functions, and skills discussed in the chapter?

2. Coaching is one of the more important one-on-one management development techniques in today's business environment. Go to **http://teragram.ca/coach_preassess_corp.html** and answer the following questions:

   a. Suppose you had to implement a coaching program for junior executives and a coaching program for senior managers. Would the content of a coaching training program be the same or different for these two groups?

   b. If they did differ, how would they differ and why?

3. Among the many sources available to find out about wilderness training in Canada are Outward Bound at **www.outwardbound.ca** and the Banff Centre at **www.banffcentre.ca/departments/leadership**. Prepare a brief report about the kinds of programs offered at each site and the skills they focus on.

4. Management education provided by universities is one of the three basic approaches to management development described in this chapter. You have read that the basic functions of management are control, leadership, organization, and planning (CLOP). As such, we should expect that universities offer courses that teach each of these. Let's find out if this is really the case.

   Choose two universities and, using the internet, examine the courses in their General MBA programs. Using the course titles and the brief descriptions available on the Web, categorize each course under a CLOP dimension. Do the same for the Executive MBA programs offered by these universities.

   a. Do MBA and Executive MBA programs cover all of the CLOP dimensions?

   b. Do they give equal emphasis to each?

   c. How do the two universities you have chosen differ in the courses they offer?

   d. What conclusions do you draw from your analysis?

5. In the last several years critical questions have been raised, as to the validity of the approaches that business schools have taken to the development of their students. In particular the 'case study' approach has been singled out for comment. On the internet go to the Financial Times and key in 'The Future of Business Schools'. After reading these comments and others (Henry Mintzberg's, a Professor at McGill University, has been very vocal about this) list and analyse the pros and cons of the current philosophy of teaching in Business Schools. What is your conclusion? Should this approach be retained, modified or abandonned? Defend your point of view.

Exercises

In-Class

1. In an article called "The smart-talk trap," Jeffrey Pfeffer and Robert Sutton (1999) described a phenomenon in organizations that they call the "knowing-doing gap." According to the authors, many managers are knowledgeable and very good at talking but not very good at doing or acting. In other words, talk substitutes for action. An especially dangerous form of talk is "smart talk," where the speaker is particularly good at sounding confident, articulate, and eloquent. Unfortunately, smart talk tends to focus on the negative and is often unnecessarily complicated. It tends to result in inaction or what the authors call the "smart-talk trap." Problems are discussed and plans for action might be formulated, but in the end nothing is done. This can have serious negative consequences for organizations. The authors suggest that one of the main reasons for the knowing-doing gap and the smart-talk trap is that managers have been trained to talk.

   a. What do you think about the knowing-doing gap and the smart-talk trap? Do you think that this is a serious problem in organizations?
   b. The authors argue that one of the reasons for the existence of the knowing-doing gap and the smart-talk trap is the training that managers receive. Do you agree with this assertion? How can management training result in so much knowing and talking and so little doing?
   c. Discuss the knowing-doing gap and the smart-talk trap with somebody you know in a managerial position. Find out what they have to say about the prevalence of it in their organization, why it might or might not be a problem, and what can be done to avoid it.
   d. What advice would you give organizations about how to develop managers in order to avoid the knowing-doing gap and the smart-talk trap?

2. This task will help you integrate much of the material in this book. Starting with the TIMS model, construct a table, similar to Table 14.2, in which you indicate for each of the 10 steps of the model the probable impact on trainees for each step.

3. Think of your manager from a current or previous job. Keeping in mind his/her behaviour and performance, how effective do you think he/she was in his/her performance of the core functions and roles of management? What skills do you think he/she needs to improve? What would you recommend your manager do to improve his/her performance and managerial skills?

4. If you were hired in a managerial position and you were told to design your own plan for development, what would you do? Refer to the section on models of management skill development, and for each step in the process develop a plan for your own management development. Be sure to indicate what you will do in each step.

In-the-Field

1. To find out more about management development, contact a human resource professional and ask about management development in his/her organization. To guide your discussion, consider the following issues:

   - Describe the main skills that are the focus of management development programs. What are these skills and why are they the focus of management development?
   - Describe the process of management development. What are the main steps involved in the process?
   - Describe the content of management development programs.
   - What types of management development programs are used and why? Does the organization use experiential learning approaches, and if so, what are they? Does the organization use management education programs, management training programs, job rotation, and/or coaching and how effective are they?
   - How effective is management development for improving managerial and organizational effectiveness?

2. Contact several people who work full-time for an organization. In each case, focus the interview on their perceptions of their own immediate supervisor/manager/boss. Focus on the skills of managers as described in the chapter. Do they perceive the manager as competent or not and what are the skills they think the manager should most urgently improve? Summarize your results in a report in which you discuss the extent and nature of management skills that subordinates feel should be improved.

Case Incident

Middle Manager Burnout

In a recent article in *Harvard Business Review*, Morison, Erikson, and Dychtwald surveyed more than 7,000 mid-career employees between the ages of 35 and 55. The authors report that many middle managers are burned out, dissatisfied, feel that they are in dead-end jobs, and most are no longer energized by their work. Feeling neglected, many are actively searching for new jobs. As a result, many organizations face a stark choice: risk losing some of their best people or continue to work with a host of unhappy managers.

Your consulting advice is requested by the company president. She is asking you to provide suggestions for combating this growing managerial apathy in her organization.

Questions

1. What do you think are some of the causes of this growing problem?
2. In order to improve the situation, what, if anything, should be done with the middle managers, the bosses of the middle managers, and the subordinates of the middle managers, by top management?

Case Study

Market Research Inc.

Market Research Inc. is a Vancouver-based firm that specializes in conducting surveys and interviews with members of the general public. The company has a number of different teams that work on many different projects for its many corporate clients. It is usually the case that several projects are conducted at the same time.

The company is composed of three departments: production, technical, and marketing. The marketing group is responsible for selling the company's services to corporate clients. The technical department is mainly composed of research personnel who are responsible for developing and analyzing the results of the surveys, focus groups, and interviewing studies for the clients. The production department is composed of several teams of interviewers. It is that department's job to conduct the data collection. They are responsible for identifying the customers who will be interviewed or surveyed, for enlisting their cooperation, and for interviewing them either personally, by phone or mail, depending on the project.

Thomas Waterfall (Tom) is the manager of the production department. The department is responsible for ensuring that all of the data-collection projects are conducted in a professional and timely manner. More specifically, Tom is responsible for ensuring that there is always enough staff on hand to conduct each study (never too many nor too few), for hiring (or letting go) the interviewers, for training them on the specific project requirements, and for ensuring and controlling the quality of the work done by the production department. He must keep himself informed of the activities of the marketing and technical departments to ensure that his department meets the demands of these other groups. Finally, the production department is a high-pressure environment where tensions among interviewers and between interviewers and the technical staff can sometimes flare up, threatening the efficient and effective production of the studies. The production manager must often act as an arbiter of disputes and act to soothe people when they get upset, a skill for which Tom is famous.

Mary Milend has been working for the last five years in the production department of Market Research Inc., where she is an interviewer. She has been doing a remarkable job conducting her interviews with professionalism and competence. She always meets her deadlines, and has never been the object of a complaint, either by consumers or by her co-workers. She has always shown great cooperation, often volunteering to help other interviewers with their tasks when they were submerged. Finally, in the tense atmosphere of conducting the data collection under tight deadlines, she has always maintained extremely good relationships with the technical staff with whom the production department interacts routinely.

Tom, the manager of the production department, has announced that he will be retiring next year. Because of her superb record as an employee and her extensive hands-on knowledge of the production department, the vice president has offered to promote Mary to the job of production manager when Tom retires.

Mary is quite interested in the job, as this would mean a much higher salary, better benefits, vacations, and greater influence in the company. However, as Mary is a very honest person, she told the VP, when he offered her the promotion, that although she was keenly interested in the job, she was not sure that she was the best choice. She explained that she had never acted in a managerial role before and that she felt uncertain that she had the skills to do the job well. Impressed by Mary's honesty, the VP indicated to her that he would be willing to provide her with all of the training she requires to acquire the managerial skills that she will need to perform her new job.

Questions

1. What are the main skills that Mary will need to develop if she accepts the promotion?
2. What are some of the training experiences that might benefit Mary?
3. Should Tom be invited to play a role in Mary's development? If so, what could that role be?
4. How effective do you think each of the following programs would be for Mary's development: management education programs, management training programs (i.e., outdoor wilderness training), and on-the-job development (i.e., job rotation and coaching). What are the advantages and disadvantages of each, and which one(s) do you recommend and why?

References

1. Schettler, J. (2002, March). Training top 100: IBM. *Training, 39* (3), 48–49; Schettler, J. (2003, March). Training top 100: Best practices. *Training, 40* (3), 58–59; Johnson, G., Johnson, H., Dolezalek, H., Galvin, T., & Zemke, R. (2004, March). Top five profile and ranking. *Training, 41* (3), 42–58.
2. McCallum, J. (1993). The manager's job is still to manage. *Business Quarterly, 57* (4), 61–67; Brown, T. L. (1995). Leadership is everyone's business. *Apparel Industry Magazine 56* (9), 14; Tannenbaum, S. I., & Yukl, G. (1992). Training and development in work organizations. *Annual Review of Psychology, 43,* 399–441.
3. Bolt, J. F. (2007). Mapping the future of leadership development. *The 2007 Pfeiffer Annual: Leadership development.* John Wiley & Sons.
4. Robbins, S. P., De Cenzo, D. A., Condie, J. L., & Kondo, L. (2001). *Supervision in Canada today* (3rd ed.). Toronto: Prentice-Hall.
5. Whetten, D. A., & Cameron, K. S. (2002). *Developing management skills* (5th ed.). Upper Saddle River, NJ: Prentice Hall.
6. Baldwin T. T., & Patgett, M. Y. (1994). Management development: A review and commentary. In C. L. Cooper & I. T. Robertson (Eds.), *Key reviews in managerial psychology.* New York: Wiley.
7. Fulmer, R. M. (1997, Summer). The evolving paradigm of leadership development. *Organizational Dynamics,* 59–72.
8. Marquardt, M. J., Nissley, N., Ozag, R., & Taylor, T. L. (2000). International briefing 6. Training and development in the United States. *International Journal of Training and Development, 4* (2), 138–149; Mabey, C., & Thomson, A. (2000). Management development in the UK: A provider and participant perspective. *International Journal of Training and Development, 4* (4), 272–286; Cornuel, E., & Kletz, P. (2001). An empirical analysis of priority sectors for managers' training. *Journal of Management Development, 20,* 5, 402–413; Agut, S., & Grau, R. (2002).

Managerial competency needs and training requests: The case of the Spanish tourist industry. *Human Resource Development Quarterly, 13* (1), 31–51; Analoui, F., & Hosseini, M. H. (2001). Management education and increased managerial effectiveness. The case of business managers in Iran. *Journal of Management Development, 20* (9), 785–794.

9. London, M. (2002). *Leadership development*: Mahwah, NJ: Lawrence Erlbaum Associates; Tichy, N. M., & Cardwell, N. (2002). *The cycle of leadership: How great leaders teach their companies to win* (3rd ed.). New York: HarperCollins Publishers; Ketz de Vries, M. (2001). *The leadership mystique*. London: Prentice-Hall.

10. Kotter, J. P. (1996). *Leading change*. Boston, MA: Harvard Business School Press.

11. Whetten, D. A., & Cameron, K. S. (2002).

12. Mintzberg, H. (1973). *The nature of managerial work*. New York: Harper & Row; Mintzberg, H. (1975). The manager's job: Folklore and fact. *Harvard Business Review, 53* (4), 49–61.

13. Kouzes, J. M., & Posner, B. Z. (2002). *Leadership challenge* (3rd ed.). San Francisco, CA: Jossey-Bass.

14. Orth, C. D., Wilkinson, H. E., & Benfari, R. C. (1987, Spring). The manager's role as coach and mentor. *Organizational Dynamics*, 67–74.

15. Whetten, D. A., & Cameron, K. S. (2002).

16. Luthans, F., Rosenkrantz, S. A., & Hennesy, H. W. (1985). What do successful managers really do? An observation study of managerial activities. *Journal of Applied Behavioral Science, 21*, 255–270.

17. Camp, R., Vielhaber, M., & Simonetti, J. L. (2001). *Strategic interviewing: How to hire good people*. San Francisco, CA: Jossey-Bass.

18. Cameron, K., & Tschirhart, M. (1988). Managerial competencies and organizational effectiveness. Working Paper, School of Business Administration, University of Michigan.

19. Goleman, D. (1998). *Working with emotional intelligence*. New York: Bantam.

20. Ryan, A. M., Brutus, S., Greguras, G. J., & Hakel, M. D. (2000). Receptivity to assessment-based feedback for management development. *Journal of Management Development, 19* (4), 252–276.

21. Pfeffer, J. (1998). *The human equation: Building profits by putting people first*. Boston, MA: Harvard Business School Press.

22. Hunsaker, P. L. (2001). *Training in management skills*. Upper Saddle River, NJ: Prentice Hall.

23. March, J. G., & Simon, H. A. (1958). *Organizations*. New York: Blackwell.

24. Locke, E. A., & Latham, G. P. (1990). *A theory of goal setting and task performance*. Englewood Cliffs, NJ: Prentice-Hall.

25. Kraiger, K. (2008). Transforming our models of learning and development: Web-based instruction as enabler of third-generation instruction. *Industrial and Organizational Perspectives: Perspectives on Science and Practice, 1*, 454–467.

26. Saks, A. M., & Haccoun, R. R. (2008). Is the "Third-generation model" new and is it the holy grail of adaptive learning? *Industrial and Organizational Perspectives: Perspectives on Science and Practice, 1*, 480–483.

27. Eisenhardt, K. M., Kahwajy, J. L., & Bourgeois, L. J. III (1997, July-August). How management teams can have a good fight. *Harvard Business Review*, 77–85.

28. Haccoun, R. R., & Klimoski, R. J. (1975). Negotiator status and accountability source: A study of negotiator behavior. *Organizational Behavior and Human Performance, 14*, 342–359.

29. Wexley, K. N., & Baldwin, T. T. (1986). Management development. *Journal of Management, 12*, 277–294.

30. Hattie, J., Marsh, H. W., Neill, J. T., & Richards, G. E. (1997). Adventure education and Outward Bound: Out-of-class experiences that have a lasting effect. *Review of Educational Research, 67*, 43–87.

31. Hughes, P. D., & Grant, M. (2007). *Learning and development outlook 2007*. The Conference Board of Canada.

32. Peterson, D. B. (2002). Management development: Coaching and mentoring programs. In K. Kraiger (Ed.), *Creating, implementing, and managing effective training and development: State-of-the-art lessons for practice* (pp. 160–191). San Francisco, CA: Jossey-Bass.

33. Kombarakaran, F., Yang, J., Baker, M., & Fernandes, P. (2008). Executive coaching: It works! *Consulting Psychology Journal: Practice and Research, 60* (1), 78–90.

34. Smither, J. W., London, M., Flautt, R., Vargas, Y., & Kucine, I. (2003). Can working with an executive coach improve multisource feedback ratings over time? A quasi-experimental field study, *Personnel Psychology, 56,* 23–44.

35. Burke, M. J., & Day, R. R. (1986). A cumulative study of the effectiveness of managerial training. *Journal of Applied Psychology, 71,* 232–246.

36. Collins, D. B., & Holton, F. E. III. (2004). The effectiveness of managerial leadership development programs: A meta analysis of studies from 1982 to 2001. *Human Resource Development Quarterly, 15* (2), 217–248.

CHAPTER 15

Training Trends and Best Practices

Chapter Learning Outcomes

After reading this chapter, you should be able to:

- describe the changing role of training professionals
- discuss the outsourcing of training and development
- explain the role of ethics in training and development
- discuss just-in-time learning, rapid e-learning, and learning management systems (LMS)
- define lifelong learning and describe the four pillars of lifelong learning
- describe the main reasons why training programs fail and describe training design factors that facilitate learning and transfer

PRICEWATERHOUSECOOPERS

PricewaterhouseCoopers (PwC) is a global accounting firm with more than 155,000 employees in 150 countries. PwC is known for is its extensive training and development programs and a continuous learning culture. PwC invests over $130 million in training and development through formal and informal learning programs.

The learning function sponsors traditional and virtual classroom courses, self-studies, team-based learning activities, action learning projects, coaching/mentoring frameworks, and large-scale conferences. Employees at PwC have access to a user-friendly learning system called MyDevelopment to manage all their learning activities.

For the last seven years, PwC's learning function has served more than 150,000 discrete users annually with 6,763 courses, 12,120 classroom-based sessions, and 19,701 Web sessions.

In 2008, PwC restructured its Learning & Education (L&E) team. According to PwC's chief learning officer Tom Evans, one of the goals was to better link L&E with PwC's business goals and objectives. "We looked at how we can enhance the linkage between learning and knowledge in the course of work. We looked at the methods of education appropriate for our culture and the 21st century. As an output of that, we reorganized the group."

The new L&E structure highlights the importance of key educational skills, including design, assessment/evaluation, instructor development, and team-based learning; streamlines development and implementation through dedicated program management specialists who pull resources together and drive projects to completion; and ensures ongoing innovation through a global network of e-learning practitioners who evaluate emerging technologies in the learning space and commission pilot projects using those technologies.

According to Evans, overall investments in training have gone up. "The new investment is easier to get because of the relevance of the learning to the firm's goals and objectives. We're getting learning closer to achieving business goals and helping to differentiate the firm in the marketplace—both from our clients' and our people's perspective. In that vein, we avoid using the word 'training.' Instead, we look at learning and development. We embrace the notion of stretch and accelerated development. We're not asking about the gap we're trying to close. Instead, we're bringing learning and education to the forefront."

In addition to determining how to best use technology, another challenge is driving a more holistic and lifelong approach to education. Two L&E programs that take a more holistic, experiential approach are Next STEP, which is geared toward senior associates, and Forward

Thinking, which is a senior partner-level experience. Both programs were designed with business objectives in mind.

In 2009, PwC was ranked number one on Training's Top 125 list of the best companies for training and development. The company was also ranked number 1 in 2008 and number two in 2007.[1]

Training and development at PwC is an excellent example of best training practices and trends, the focus of this chapter. In this chapter, we discuss the changing role of trainers, the outsourcing of training and development, and ethical issues associated with training and development. We also describe several training trends including just-in-time learning, rapid e-learning, learning management systems (LMS), and lifelong learning. The chapter concludes with a review of best training practices.

The Role of Training Professionals

In recent years, the trainer's traditional status as a staff employee of HR has been changing. Trainers have begun to move out of the training department to work with management to solve organizational problems and create learning opportunities that support the organization's strategy. This reflects a movement and evolution of the trainer from a staff employee to a strategic business partner.

Thus, while many training professionals still spend most of their time designing and delivering training programs, they are increasingly becoming more involved in strategic functions such as facilitating organizational change, managing organizational knowledge, career planning, and talent management.[2] Recall that one of the goals of the restructured L&D function at PwC was to better link L&E with PwC's business goals and objectives.

A recent study conducted by the American Society for Training and Development (ASTD) on the areas of expertise and competencies expected of training and development professionals identified four key roles for training professionals: learning strategist, business partner, project manager, and professional specialist.[3] These four roles are part of the ASTD competency model for learning and performance and the foundation for its professional certification program. Figure 15.1 shows the ASTD competency model. The certification program covers the nine areas of expertise found in the middle tier of the model.

The training and development function is also expected to transform into a learning and performance strategic function. It will focus more on results rather than activities and it will be integrated into the business of the organization at a strategic level; learning will be embedded into the jobs that individuals perform.[4] In addition, training functions will become performance consulting centres and training professionals will become performance consultants. As a **performance consultant,** the role of the trainer is not just to provide training and development, but to provide solutions to performance problems.

Finally, given the increasing importance of lifelong learning and the learning organization, the role of the trainer is increasingly shifting from training to learning. Thus, the role of the trainer is to facilitate and create

Performance consultant

Responsible for providing solutions to performance problems

FIGURE 15.1

ASTD Competency Model

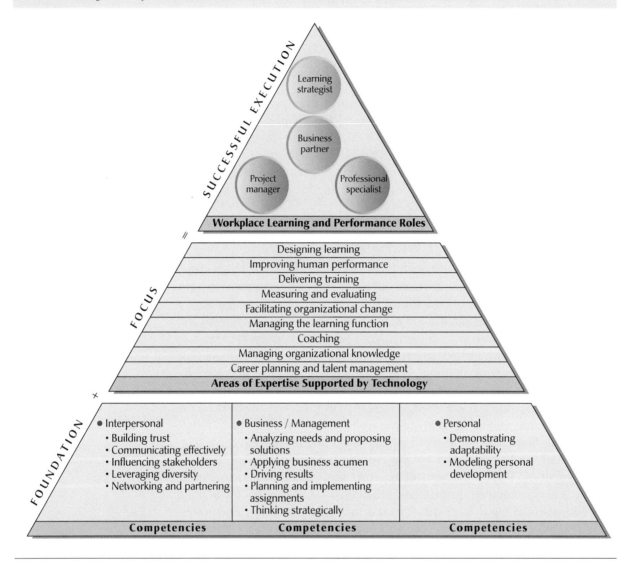

learning opportunities throughout the organization, and to help organizations manage the transition to a learning organization.

Outsourcing

The use of an external supplier to provide training and development programs and services

Outsourcing Training and Development

Outsourcing involves the use of an external supplier to provide training and development programs and services. This follows from the discussion in Chapter 5 on purchasing training programs and services. Outsourcing involves the purchase of training services and products from external suppliers rather than using in-house services.

A recent survey found that 57 percent of HR and training professionals outsource all or portions of their training and development programs.[5] In Canada, it has been reported that 52 percent of direct learning expenditures go directly to outside trainers or indirectly to outside trainers through tuition reimbursement, and this is expected to increase in the coming years.[6]

There are a number of reasons for outsourcing training and development. For example, outsourcing provides organizations with access to specialists who have expertise in a particular training area. In addition, external vendors can provide a greater variety of training programs more efficiently and less expensively than in-house training departments.[7] This is especially true for small companies that do not have in-house expertise or enough staff to train to justify the expense of in-house training design and delivery. In addition, the use of external vendors can often result in trainees being trained and back on the job much faster than designing a new training program in-house. One study found that the top reasons for outsourcing included cost savings, time savings, and improvements in compliance and accuracy.[8]

Outsourcing training and development has been found to result in increased performance and improvements in the design and delivery of training, and training professionals report a high level of overall satisfaction with their training suppliers. However, outsourcing does have certain risks such as a loss of control, situations where the vendor does not understand the organization's culture, loss of in-house expertise, and increased vulnerability that can result in harmful consequences for an organization.[9]

Thus, a trusting relationship between the organization and its external vendor is important for a successful outsourcing relationship. Furthermore, the positive outcomes associated with outsourcing have been found to be higher when there is frequent vendor–client interaction, when contractual agreements are explicit, when there is greater trust in the vendor, and when the organization's primary motivation for outsourcing is quality improvement.[10]

The Ethics of Training and Development

Ethics involves systematic thinking about the moral consequences of one's actions and decisions on various stakeholders. Stakeholders refer to people inside or outside of the organization who might be affected by one's actions and decisions. For training professionals, ethics involves following a set of standards and principles in the design, delivery, and evaluation of training and development programs. Training professionals must adhere to a set of ethical principles that guide their behaviour and they must serve as role models of proper ethical conduct to the rest of the organization.

One ethical issue of particular concern is the refusal of employees from attending a training program, which can result in workplace discrimination and human rights complaints. In fact, there have been a number of cases in recent years in which an employee was denied training and then filed a complaint of discrimination. The Canadian Human Rights Act at the federal level, as well each of the provincial human rights codes, governs human rights issues that can be invoked when an employee is denied training.[11]

Ethics

Systematic thinking about the moral consequences of one's actions and decisions on various stakeholders

Ethical codes and standards are often set by organizations and associations. For example, the Canadian Society for Training and Development (CSTD) has a member code of ethics that sets standards of practice and professionalism for its members. To learn more about the kinds of ethical issues that are important for training professionals, see The Trainer's Notebook 15.1, "Ethical Guidelines for Training Professionals."

Trends in Training and Development

In this section, we discuss several trends in training and developing including just-in-time learning, rapid e-learning, and learning management systems (LMS).

Just-in-Time Learning

Given the rapid pace of change in organizations today, trainers often do not have very much time to design and deliver training programs. Employees increasingly need to obtain new knowledge and skills immediately. Thus, trainers must find ways of providing learning opportunities when they are needed, or what is known as "just-in-time learning."

Just-in-time (JIT) learning

The capability to provide learning and training opportunities when they are needed and where they are needed

Just-in-time (JIT) learning refers to the capability to provide learning and training opportunities when they are needed and where they are needed. To meet this need, trainers have to find new and innovative ways to design and deliver training. Some of the new technologies described in Chapter 8 will become increasingly useful for JIT learning.

In addition to being able to provide training on-demand when it is needed, trainers also need to find innovative ways to accelerate learning. To learn about one such approach, see Training Today 15.1, "Scenario-Based Learning."

The Trainer's Notebook 15.1

Ethical Guidelines for Training Professionals

Trainers must conduct themselves according to a set of ethical guidelines and standards as follows:

1. **Voluntary consent:** Trainers should not implicitly coerce unwilling or skeptical participants into self-revealing or physical activities.

2. **Discrimination:** Age, sex, race, or handicaps should not be used as barriers to determine who receives training.

3. **Cost effectiveness:** Training activities should be based on demonstrated utility, should show a demonstrated benefit vis-à-vis costs, and should not be undertaken simply to spend a training budget.

4. **Accurate portrayal:** Claims for the benefits of training need to be accurate; training should be consistent across time and trainers; training materials should be appropriately depicted.

5. **Competency in training:** Teaching methods that do not work, such as talking down to audiences, should be avoided.

6. **Values:** Trainers should believe in the value of what they teach.

Source: Lowman, R. L. (1991). Ethical human resource practice in organizational settings. In D. W. Bray (Ed.), *Working with organizations.* New York: Guilford. Reprinted with permission from The Guilford Press, New York, NY.

How can trainers accelerate learning? One approach is known as scenario-based learning (SBL). SBL is an instructional method in which trainees solve carefully constructed, authentic job tasks or problems that are derived from experts. While solving the problems, they are carefully guided to learn the associated concepts, procedures, and heuristics of expert performers.

A program at PricewaterhouseCoopers for employees who have reached the level of manager or partner, called "Managing Complex Relationships," has seasoned employees describe scenarios in which they had to deal with difficult relationships. Participants discuss how they would handle the situation in small groups and then find out how the senior employee handled the situation. Participants learn about complex relationships and how to handle them before they experience them.

SBL works best for training on non-routine tasks that involve judgment and decision making and for trainees who have some relevant job experience. In one study of Air Force technicians, 25 hours of scenario-based e-learning that simulated multiple electrical equipment failures raised the expertise of two-year technicians to the same level as 10-year veterans. A study on medical students found that learning was better among those who received online scenarios compared to students who received traditional training.

Thus, when trainers need to compress years of experience into a few hours of training, SBL is one approach to consider. SBL can be successfully implemented in face-to-face or e-learning environments.

Sources: Clark, R. (2009, January). Accelerating expertise with scenario-based learning. *T&D, 63* (1), 84–85; Weinstein, M. (2007, March). Balancing act. *Training, 44* (2), 22–28.

Rapid e-Learning

In addition to providing training on-demand and accelerating the pace of learning, trainers are facing demands to shorten the length of training programs. Managers are often concerned about employees taking too much time off-the-job for training and are requesting that courses be condensed. At some companies full-day training courses are being conducted in two hours.[12] For example, Sierra Systems, a Vancouver-based information technology consulting firm, recently converted a two-day managing-people course into a series of one-hour webinars.[13]

Thus, trainers increasingly must redesign training programs and find creative ways to make up for the reduction in content by assigning more pre-course readings, using more job aids following training, creating more on-the-job training opportunities, and using technology to deliver part or all of some training programs.

One approach is to transform traditional classroom programs into e-learning programs. However, this can be a time-consuming and expensive process. **Rapid e-learning** refers to developmental software that allows organizations to develop e-learning more quickly and easily and at a lower price than conventional e-learning development tools. The software uses a template approach to develop courses and easy-to-use interfaces that guide trainers through the course development process.[14]

Rapid e-learning

Software that allows organizations to develop e-learning more quickly and easily and at a lower price than conventional e-learning development tools

Learning Management Systems (LMS)

Many organizations today use software to manage and track training activities, or what is known as a **learning management system (LMS).** These are sophisticated systems that track and report administrative activities of training such as enrollment and completion of programs as well as training results. A LMS allows organizations to integrate and organize all of their training data and programs. LMSs are also used by employees to access Web-based training programs and materials in their organization. At PwC, employees have access to a learning system that enables them to find course information, register for courses, book travel arrangements, and track their learning activities.

The most sophisticated LMSs have many features such as assessments, course catalogues, communication tools, and individual learning plans.[15] One of the main benefits of an LMS is the increased efficiency of tracking, reporting, and delivery of e-learning.[16] Given the increasing use of technology for training, LMSs are likely to become an increasingly important part of the training function for employees and organizations.

Lifelong Learning

Although the focus of this text has been on learning at work and in organizations, it is important to understand that training and development is part of a larger approach to learning that is known as lifelong learning.

Lifelong learning is an approach to learning that recognizes that learning takes place throughout a person's life and involves all aspects of one's life including the workplace, personal development, the community, and physical well-being. The Canadian Council on Learning has developed a measure called the Composite Learning Index (CLI) to measure Canada's progress in lifelong learning. The CLI measures the following four pillars of lifelong learning:[17]

- *Learning to know* refers to the development of skills and knowledge needed to function in the world (e.g., literacy, numeracy, critical thinking, and general knowledge).
- *Learning to do* refers to applied skills that are often required for occupational success (e.g., computer training).
- *Learning to live together* refers to developing values of respect and concern for others, social and interpersonal skills, and an appreciation of the diversity of Canadians.
- *Learning to be* refers to learning that contributes to the development of a person's body, mind, and spirit (e.g., personal discovery and creativity).

The CLI recognizes that lifelong learning is critical to the success of an individual, the community, and the country. Individuals benefit from better jobs and higher wages and Canada benefits from higher productivity and a stronger economy.[18] Training and development is an important contributor to lifelong learning and many organizations today, like PwC, are taking a more holistic and lifelong approach to continuous education and learning.

Training and Development Best Practices

Much of what you have read in this text represents best practices for training and development. As a final review of effective training programs, we conclude the chapter with the main reasons why training programs fail (see Table 15.1) and training design factors that facilitate learning and transfer (see The Trainer's Notebook 15.2, "Training Design Factors that Facilitate Learning and Transfer"). This information should be helpful for designing and delivering effective training programs.

TABLE 15.1

Main Reasons Training Programs Fail

1. **Lack of Alignment with Business Needs**. Training programs often fail because they are not linked to business and organizational needs.
2. **Failure to Recognize Nontraining Solutions**. Training is often implemented with the intention of improving a performance problem even though it is not always the best solution.
3. **Lack of Objectives to Provide Direction and Focus**. Training programs sometimes fail because they lack clear objectives.
4. **The Solution Is Too Expensive**. Although a training program's ROI is an important measure of effectiveness, a negative ROI does not mean that a training program has failed. There are often many intangible benefits of training programs that add value to an organization.
5. **Regarding Training as an Event**. When training is treated as a separate or isolated event, it is likely to fail.
6. **Participants Are Not Held Accountable for Results**. When employees are only expected to attend a training program without any responsibility for what they learn or do after training, they are not likely to show any change in behaviour or improvement in job performance.
7. **Failure to Prepare the Job Environment for Transfer**. Barriers in the job environment can undermine the success of an otherwise effective training program.
8. **Lack of Management Reinforcement and Support**. If management does not support, encourage, and reinforce the use of new knowledge and skills on the job, training programs will not be effective.
9. **Failure to Isolate the Effects of Training**. It is difficult to demonstrate that changes or effects in employees and the organization are due to a particular training program and not something else. Failure to isolate the effects of training might leave some wondering about the need and value of training and development.
10. **Lack of Commitment and Involvement from Executives**. Training and development programs are doomed to fail without the commitment and involvement of senior executives.
11. **Failure to Provide Feedback and Use Information about Results**. Training programs cannot be improved and are not likely to reach their expectations if the various stakeholders do not receive feedback and information about the results of training.

Source: Phillips, J. J., & Phillips, P. P. (2002, September). 11 reasons why training and development fail . . . and what you can do about it. *Training, 39* (9), 78–85. © ROI Institute, www.roiinstitute.net. Used with permission.

The Trainer's Notebook 15.2

Training Design Factors that Facilitate Learning and Transfer

For training to be effective, trainees must meet four criteria. They must be ready to learn and be motivated, they must learn the content of the training program, and they must transfer the training on the job. The following training design factors have long been recognized as important for enhancing learning and transfer.

1. Trainees must understand the objectives of the training program. The purpose and outcomes expected should be explained and understood.
2. Training content should be meaningful. Examples, exercises, assignments, concepts, and terms used in training should be relevant to trainees.
3. Trainees should be given cues that help them learn and recall training content. This can be done using diagrams, models, key behaviours, and advanced organizers.
4. Trainees should have opportunities to practice. Many of the instructional methods described in the text can be used (e.g., role play, games, simulations).
5. Trainees should receive feedback on their learning. This can come from trainers, observers, video, or the task itself.
6. Trainees should have the opportunity to observe and interact with other trainees.
7. The training program should be properly coordinated and arranged.

Source: Noe, R. A., & Colquitt, J. A. (2002). Planning for training impact: Principles of training effectiveness. *Creating, implementing, and maintaining effective training and development: State-of-the-art lessons for practice* (pp. 53–79) by Kraiger, K. © 2002 Jossey-Bass Inc. Reprinted with permission of John Wiley & Sons, Inc.

Summary

This chapter began with a discussion of the changing role of the trainer and the outsourcing of training and development. We then discussed ethical issues in training and development. Some important training trends were also described including just-in-time learning, rapid e-learning, and learning management systems (LMS). We then described how training and development is part of the larger process of lifelong learning. The chapter concluded with a review of the major reasons why training programs fail and training design features that facilitate learning and transfer.

Conclusion

It should now be clear to you that training and development is an important part of the management of performance in organizations. Training and development plays a critical role in helping organizations meet the challenges of an increasingly complex and competitive environment. Unfortunately, training programs often fail to achieve their objectives and, as a result, hinder an organization's ability to remain competitive. The good news is that the science of training, as described in this text, contains practical information on how to design, deliver, and evaluate effective training and development programs. By applying the theories, concepts, and principles described in this text, it is possible to design and deliver training programs that will benefit individuals, organizations, and society.

You now know the science of training; it is up to you to translate training science into practice.

Key Terms

ethics   p. 459
just-in-time (JIT) learning   p. 460
learning management system (LMS)   p. 462
lifelong learning   p. 462

outsourcing   p. 458
performance consultant   p. 457
rapid e-learning   p. 461

Make the Connection

p. 458: the decision to purchase or design a training program is discussed in Chapter 5 on page 140

Web Links

Canadian Society for Training and Development: www.cstd.ca

PricewaterhouseCoopers: www.pwc.com/ca

Sierra Systems: www.sierrasystems.com

Discussion Questions

1. What are some of the ethical issues for training professionals?
2. How has the role of the trainer changed and what are the new and emerging competencies and roles of trainers?
3. Why do organizations outsource training and development and what are the advantages and disadvantages of outsourcing? Do you think that organizations should outsource training and development?
4. What is just-in-time learning and what are the implications for training and development?
5. Why do training programs sometimes fail and how can they be designed to be more effective?
6. What is lifelong learning and how is it related to training and development? What is the role of organizations in lifelong learning?

The Great Training Debate

1. Debate the following: Organizations should outsource all of their training and development.

Using the Internet

1. To learn about ethical standards of practice for training professionals, visit the website of the Canadian Society for Training and Development (CSTD) at **www.cstd.ca** and click on "About Us" and then "Member Code of Ethics." Review the ethical standards and describe how they apply to the different stages of the training and development process and to training research, practice, and consulting.
2. To find out about lifelong learning and the Composite Learning Index (CLI), visit the Canadian Council on Learning at **www.ccl-cca.ca/CCL/ Reports/CLI/AboutCLI.htm**.
   Answer the following questions:

   a. What is the Composite Learning Index (CLI) and how does it work?
   b. What is lifelong learning?
   c. What are the effects of lifelong learning?
   d. What are the most recent CLI scores for your city or town and how do they compare to the average CLI score in Canada?

Exercises

In-Class

1. If an organization wanted to hire a training professional today, what should it look for? Find several job advertisements for a training manager or director in your local newspaper. Bring the advertisements to class and summarize the main competencies and responsibilities of the position. Describe how the job matches the traditional role of a trainer as well as more current roles and expectations described in the chapter.
2. Consider the ethics of the most recent training experience you have had either in a current job or in a previous job. Review the six ethical guidelines listed in The Trainer's Notebook 15.1, "Ethical Guidelines for Training Professionals," and determine how well they stand up against your most recent training experience. Based on your analysis, was the trainer and the training program ethical? Be prepared to explain and defend your answer.
3. If you were responsible for training in your organization and management decided that it wanted to outsource most of the company's training and development programs, what would you do? Prepare a brief presentation in which you must present your case to management. What will be your position and what will you present to management in order to defend it?
4. Think about your knowledge and skills and the extent to which you are prepared for the new competencies and roles expected of training professionals today. Conduct a self-assessment using the material

presented in this chapter, with particular attention to the ASTD competency model. What competencies do you have and which ones do you still need to develop? Prepare an action plan that describes some of the things you can do to develop the competencies that you need to develop and improve.

In-the-Field

1. Contact the training manager in an organization to find out how his/her role has changed and how it will change in the future. What was his/her role five years ago? What is his/her role today? What will be his/her role in five years? What skills and experiences do trainers need in order to perform their current and future roles, and how has this changed over the last five to 10 years?
2. Review Table 15.1, "Main Reasons Training Programs Fail," and then contact a manager or director of training in an organization and ask him/her about the success and failure of training and development programs in his/her organization. Make up a question for each of the 11 reasons for failure to find out how the organization deals with them (e.g., Are training programs in your organization based on a needs analysis and linked to business needs?), and if best practices are used in the design and delivery of training and development programs. What recommendations can you provide for the organization to make their training and development programs more effective?

Case Incident

Outsourcing at Nestlé Canada and Hudson's Bay Company

Nestlé Canada has been outsourcing parts of HR services to external providers for years in areas such as payroll, pension administration, and benefits administration. Although the company is using external providers more often for training and development, there are no plans to outsource all of it. If they are planning to develop a course in a particular area, they look for a provider who has experience in that area and then partner with them to develop something specific for the company. For example, the company partnered with an external organizational psychologist to develop a new leadership development program.

Hudson's Bay Company keeps most of its human resources in-house. The company believes it is best served when HR support is delivered by those who most understand the organization—its own employees. In the case of training and development, it is important to have employees who started out working in stores deliver customer-service training. They have an understanding of the customer and the way the stores operate.

Questions

1. Comment on the two companies' approaches to outsourcing training and development. What are the advantages and disadvantages of each approach?
2. What advice would you give each company about its current and future outsourcing of training and development?

Source: Cook, T., Household, J., Cormier, B., & Kolida, B. (2003, September 8). HR leaders talk: The constant pressure to add value and control costs combined with the growing desire to play a strategic business role has caused many HR leaders to at least consider outsourcing some part of their operations—if they haven't done so already. *Canadian HR Reporter, 16* (15), 13.

Integrative Case Study

Training Security Guards

In 1999, Patrick Shand was wrestled to the ground by security guards at a grocery store in Toronto. He was handcuffed and kept face-down on the ground where he died of asphyxiation after being accused of shoplifting baby formula.

In February of 2004, a coroner's inquest into Shand's death ruled that his death was accidental and that he died of restraint asphyxia with complications from chronic and acute cocaine use. One of the findings of the inquest was that Shand might not have died if the guards who apprehended him had been trained in the use of force and life-saving.

The inquiry made 22 recommendations to reform Ontario's security industry. For example, it recommended that all in-house security guards and bouncers in Ontario be licensed and receive mandatory training in areas such as first aid, CPR, and use of force training that identifies the hazards of restraint asphyxia and excited delirium as well as appropriate training in the use of handcuffs and expandable batons. The inquest concluded that "It is important that the government act quickly, responsibly and diligently."

The Ontario government responded to the inquest's 22 recommendations with the Private Security and Investigative Services Act in 2005. This was the first time the act had been updated since it was passed in 1966. The act went into effect in August 2007, with a deadline of August 2008 for 22,000 previously unlicensed security guards and bouncers to get licensed.

In addition to mandatory licensing for all security personnel and standards for uniforms, equipment, and vehicles used by security personnel, the act also includes mandatory training standards. The basic training standard would be developed to include knowledge of relevant legislation (the new Private Security and Investigative Services Act, Trespass to Property Act); power of arrest; use of force; communications and public relations skills; first aid and cardiopulmonary resuscitation; on-the-job skills (report writing, note taking, and diversity sensitivity); and the use of equipment (batons, handcuffs).

Security guards and bouncers in Ontario now must pay $80 to meet the new requirements. However, the Ministry of Community Safety and

Correctional Services has not yet implemented the training program that is part of the licensing. Those in the industry are now left questioning the law.

Thus, despite a proposed curriculum and government plans for a 40-hour mandatory training program, the current licence requirements only require in-house security guards and bouncers to submit an application to the ministry, pay a fee, and pass a criminal record check. There is no use-of-force training and no first-aid training is required. As a result, security guards continue to work at local stores and nightclubs without the basic training needed to safeguard lives.

In May of 2008, the ministry announced that it was pushing back plans to implement the training program from November 2008 to an undetermined later date because the curriculum for training had only recently been finalized. However, according to the director and registrar of the ministry's private security and investigative services branch that is responsible for the new licensing procedures, "The onus of responsibility is at this state on the employer to make sure that their staff are adequately trained." As for the province's slow pace in implementing the training, he said that it takes time to implement such a wide range of changes in an industry that has never had to be licensed or trained.

However, other provinces already have similar training programs in place. British Columbia has a 40-hour course for security guards that is taught by the same people who train the police.

Unfortunately, the problem has not gone away. In 2008, a 20-year-old man died in Hamilton after being pinned to the ground by a security guard and store employees who suspected him of stealing a $15 radiator hose from a Canadian Tire store. In June of 2008, bouncers found a woman unconscious and frothing from the mouth in the back of an after-hours club. The bouncers did not have first-aid training and did not know how to help the woman, who later died. In February of 2009, two security guards at St. Michael's Hospital in Toronto were dismissed following the alleged beating of a man who had broken ribs and a punctured lung. The hospital said that it will assess and review its use-of-force policy and procedures and intends to provide additional diversity training to its security officers.

Sources: Popplewell, B. (2008, July 14). Training lag angers guards. *Toronto Star*, A1, A9; Editorial (2007, August 23). Security industry cleanup overdue. *Toronto Star*, AA6; Black, D. (2004, April 24). Tough rules on security demanded: "This is Patrick's legacy," Shand's mother says of coroner's jury findings. *Toronto Star*, B1; (2004, December 9). McGuinty government introduces new legislation to make Ontarians safer. Ministry of Community Safety and Correctional Services. Government of Ontario. www.ogov.newswire.ca/ontario. Retrieved on March 16, 2009; Henry, M. (2009, February 19). Man says ribs broken by hospital guards. *Toronto Star*, A2; Henry, M. (2009, February 27), Hospital CEO apologizes to beaten man. *Toronto Star*, GT4.

Questions

Chapter 1

1. Explain how a mandatory training program for security guards is an example of performance management. What effect will it have on security guards and their organizations?

2. Describe the role of the environmental context for mandatory security guard training. How will the organizational context and the human resource system in organizations influence the training and the effect it has on organizations and society?

3. Explain how the instructional systems design (ISD) model can be used in the development, delivery, and evaluation of a security guard training program.

Chapter 2

4. Explain the use and potential effects of formal and informal training for security guards. Are both necessary, or is formal training sufficient?

Chapter 3

5. What are the learning outcomes of security guard training?

6. Explain the relevance of learning styles for a security guard training program. How could the four learning modes be used to train security guards?

7. What are the implications of conditioning theory and social cognitive theory for the security guard training program? How can principles from each theory be used in the training of security guards?

8. What are the implications of adult learning theory for the security guard training program? Explain how adult learning theory principles might be included in the training.

9. How important is training motivation for the training of security guards? Explain how motivation theories can be used to ensure that security guards are high on training motivation.

Chapter 4

10. Refer to the needs-analysis process in Figure 4.1 and explain its use and relevance for the mandatory security guard training program.

11. Explain the relevance and use of an organizational, task, and person analysis for the security guard training program. What information would be obtained from each level of needs analysis and how it would it be useful in the design of the training program?

12. Is training the best solution to the security guard problem? Run the situation through Mager and Pipe's Performance Analysis Flowchart to determine solutions to the problem indicated in the case. Is training the best solution and are there other possible solutions? Explain your answer.

Chapter 5

13. Write some training objectives for the security guard training program.

14. Describe the content of the program and some potential training methods that should be considered.

15. Explain how active practice can be used for the security guard training program. How can the conditions of practice before and

during training be used? Explain the use and relevance of each condition of practice.
16. Is active learning and adaptive expertise relevant for the security guard training program? Explain how active learning elements might be included in the training.
17. Is error management training (EMT) relevant for the security guard training program? Explain how you might use EMT in the training and its potential effects.

Chapter 6

18. What off-the-job training methods should be used for the security guard training program? Consider each of the instructional methods described in Chapter 6. Which ones would you recommend and which ones would you not use? Explain your answer.

Chapter 7

19. Consider each of the on-the-job training methods described in Chapter 7 for the security guard training program. Which ones would you recommend and which ones would you not use? Explain your answer.

Chapter 8

20. Can technology-based training methods be used for the security guard training program? How might technology-based methods be used and do you think they would be effective? What are the advantages and disadvantages? Explain your answer.

Chapter 9

21. Develop a lesson plan for the security guard training program. Be sure to indicate the training objective, classroom requirements, training materials and equipment, supplies, and handouts. Be sure to indicate the sequence of activities and events that will occur during the training program as well the timing of them.
22. Who should be the trainer for the security guard training program? Explain your answer.
23. Explain how you would use Gagné's nine of events of instruction for the security guard training program. Be sure to give specific examples.
24. What are some training delivery problems that might occur in the security guard training program? What can a trainer do to avoid them or manage them during training?

Chapter 10

25. What are some barriers that might inhibit the transfer of the security guard training program? Who is responsible for these barriers?

26. How can the security guard training program be designed to facilitate the transfer of training?
27. What are some activities that can be used before, during, and after training to facilitate the transfer of training? Be sure to also indicate activities for the trainer, trainees, and management.

Chapter 11

28. How should the security guard training program be evaluated? Be sure to indicate the type of data to be collected, the purpose of the evaluation, and whether it should be a descriptive and/or causal evaluation.
29. Explain the application of Kirkpatrick's Model, the COMA model, and the Decision-Based Evaluation Model for evaluating the security guard training program. What model would you recommend and why?
30. What variables would you include in the evaluation of the security guard training program and how would you measure them?
31. What data collection design would you use to evaluate the security guard training program? Explain the advantages and disadvantages of non-experimental, experimental, and quasi-experimental designs. What would make the most sense to use and why?

Chapter 12

32. What are the main costs of the security guard training program? Be sure to indicate the main cost categories.
33. What are the main benefits of the security guard training program? Explain how you would conduct a cost-effectiveness and a cost-benefit evaluation.
34. How would you estimate the net benefit, benefit-cost ratio, return on investment, and utility of the security guard training program? Be sure to indicate what you would include in the estimation of each (e.g., what costs and what benefits).

References

1. Based on Freifeld, L. (2009, February). PWC does it again. *Training, 46* (2), 24–28; www.pwc.com (About us; Learning; Formal learning).
2. Vu, U. (2004, July 12). Trainers mature into business partners. *Canadian HR Reporter, 17* (13), 1, 2.
3. Vu, U. (2004, July 12).
4. Robinson, D. G., & Robinson, J. C. (2005, Anniversary issue). A heightened focus on learning and performance. *HR Magazine, 50* (13), 65–67.
5. Johnson, G. (2004, August). To outsource or not to outsource . . . that is the question. *Training, 41* (8), 26–29.
6. Hughes, P. D., & Grant, M. (2007). *Learning & development outlook 2007.* The Conference Board of Canada: Ottawa.

7. Kraiger, K. (2003). Perspectives on training and development. In W. C. Borman, D. R. Ilgen, & R. J. Klimoski (Eds.), *Handbook of psychology: Industrial and organizational psychology* (pp. 171–192). Hoboken, NJ: John Wiley & Sons, Inc.

8. Johnson, G. (2004, August).

9. Gainey, T. W., & Klaas, B. S. (2002). Outsourcing the training function: Results from the field. *Human Resource Planning, 25,* 16–22.

10. Gainey, T. W., & Klaas, B. S. (2002).

11. Macdonald, N. C. (2004, November 22). Workplace discrimination prohibited—and that includes training. *Canadian HR Reporter, 17* (2), G3, G11.

12. Zielinski, D. (2006, January). Wanted: Training manager. *Training, 43* (1), 36–39.

13. Harder, D. (2009, February 9). Sierra systems earns top marks for training. *Canadian HR Reporter, 22* (3), 19.

14. Boehle, S. (2005, July). Rapid e-learning. *Training, 42* (7), 12–17.

15. Woodill, G. (2007, April 23). The evolution of learning management systems. *Canadian HR Reporter, 20* (8), 14.

16. Bersin, J. (2006, December). What you still need to know about LMSes. *Training, 43* (12), 17.

17. Canadian Council on Learning. About the CLI. www.ccl-cca.ca/CCL.

18. Canadian Council on Learning. About the CLI. www.ccl-cca.ca/CCL.

Index

A

L

Labatt Breweries of Canada, 13, 129
Lave, Jean, 47
Leadership, 418–419
Learner control, 236
Learning. *See also* Motivation
  Adaptive Character of Thought
    (ACT) theory, 67–69
  adult learning theory, 76–77
  Canadian Cancer Society, 64–65
  culture, 107, 293
  cycle, 70–71
  defined, 65
  general principles of, 174
  outcomes, 66–67
  people, types of, 70
  personalization, 71
  stages, 67–69
  styles, 69–71
Learning management systems (LMS),
    460, 462
Learning organization
  Canada, 38–39
  defined, 36, 43
  disciplines, 36–37
  organizational effectiveness, 40
  principles, 37
  training, 53
Learning style, defined, 69
Learning theories
  adult learning theory, 76–77
  conditioning theory, 72–73
  social cognitive theory, 73–75
Learning Transfer System Inventory
    (LTSI), 306–308, 331
Lecture, 167
Lesson plan, 255–258
Liaises, 419–420
Lifelong learning, 462
Literacy, 394
LMS. *See* Learning management
    systems (LMS)
Locus of control, 83–84
L'Oréal Canada, 166, 400
LTSI. *See* Learning Transfer System
    Inventory (LTSI)
Lufthansa School of Business
    (Europe), 439

M

Maintenance, 287
Management, 415–417
Management development
  "bench strength", 415, 416
  controlling, organizing, and planning
    (COP), 418–419
  controlling, organizing, planning, and
    leading (COPL or CLOP), 419
  core managerial roles, 419–420
  defined, 418
  emotional intelligence (EI), 425–427
  employee training, versus, 417–418
  error training for, 431
  error-management training (EMT), 431
  Executive Development Associates
    (EDA), 416
  executive education, cost of, 418
  hard skills, 426
  IBM, 414–415
  importance of, 418
  intellectual intelligence (IQ), 426
  leadership, 419
  methods, overview, 436–438
  on-the-job, 441–444
  skills, 423, 426, 427–431
Management development programs
  (content)
  goal setting, 433
  overview, 431–432
  skills, 432–436
  SMART goals, 433
  SWOT analysis, 432
Management education, 438
  programs, 438–439
Management skills, 423–425
Management training
  defined, 440
  programs, 440–446
Managerial functions, 421–423
Managing@IBM program, 430
Maslow, Abraham, 78
Massed versus distributed practice,
    149–150, 266
Mastery goals, 82, 83
Material safety data sheets (MSDS), 397
MBA, 438
McDonald's, 46
McDonald's Canada, 198
McFarland, Janet, 408–409
Mental models, 48–49
Mentoring, 211–214, 218, 444
Meta-analysis, 444–445
Metacognition, 147
Metacognitive activity, 148
Metacognitive strategies, 147
Microsoft, 420
Miller, David, 409
Ministry of Community Safety and
    Correctional Services, 468–469
Mintzberg, Henry, 419
Mobile learning, 242
Modality principle, 236
Models, training effectiveness, 84–86
  cognitive ability, 85
  locus of control, 86
  self-efficacy, 85
  training design, 155
  transfer of training, 309–310

Molson Coors Brewing Company,
    19, 399–400
Motivation
  defined, 77
  extrinsic, 77
  goal-setting theory, 81–82
  intrinsic, 77
  model of training effectiveness,
    84–86
  need theories, 78–79
  theories, 79–81
Motivation to transfer, 291
Motorola Inc., 46, 238
Mr. Lube, 234
MSDS. *See* Material safety data sheets
    (MSDS)
Multimedia principle, 236

N

NATC. *See* North American
    Transportation Company (NATC)
National Ballet of Canada, 416
National Research Council
    of Canada, 433
Near transfer, 288
Needs analysis
  defined, 100
  just-in-time, 124
  methods, 119–123
  obstacles, 124
  organizational analysis, 104–108
  outcomes, 103–104
  performance problems, 114–119
  person analysis, 113–114
  process, 100–103
  sources, 123
  task analysis, 108–111
  team task analysis, 112–113
Negative feedback, 151, 153, 342
Negative reinforcement, 72
Negotiator, 420
Net benefit, 372–373
Nike, 247–248
Non-experimental designs, 344
Non-monetary benefits, 371–372
North American Transportation
    Company (NATC), 355
Nycomed Canada, 170

O

Observation, 74
Off-the-job training methods
  action learning, 181–182
  advantages, 214
  audio-visual methods, 170–171